ELENI

Nicholas Gage was born in Greece and emigrated to the United States ten years later. He was an investigative reporter and foreign correspondent for the *New York Times* when he wrote *Eleni*, working as their bureau chief in Athens. The book was published in 1983 and went on to win the Royal Society for Literature's Heinemann Award for the best book of the year in 1984. *Eleni* became a bestseller all over the world and was made into a feature film.

ALSO BY NICHOLAS GAGE

The Bourlotas Fortune

Hellas: A Portrait of Greece

A Place for Us

Greece: Land of Light

*Greek Fire: The Story of Maria Callas and
Aristotle Onassis*

NICHOLAS GAGE

Eleni

VINTAGE BOOKS
London

Published by Vintage 2006

10

Copyright © Nicholas Gage 1983

First published in Great Britain in 1983 by The Harvill Press

Vintage
Random House, 20 Vauxhall Bridge Road,
London SW1V 2SA

www.vintage-books.co.uk

Addresses for companies within The Random House Group Limited
can be found at: www.randomhouse.co.uk/offices.htm

The Random House Group Limited Reg. No. 954009

A CIP catalogue record for this book
is available from the British Library

ISBN 9781860463464

The Random House Group Limited supports The Forest Stewardship
Council (FSC®), the leading international forest certification organisation.
Our books carrying the FSC label are printed on FSC® certified paper.
FSC is the only forest certification scheme endorsed by the leading
environmental organisations, including Greenpeace. Our
paper procurement policy can be found at
www.randomhouse.co.uk/environment

Printed and bound in Great Britain by Clays Ltd, St Ives PLC

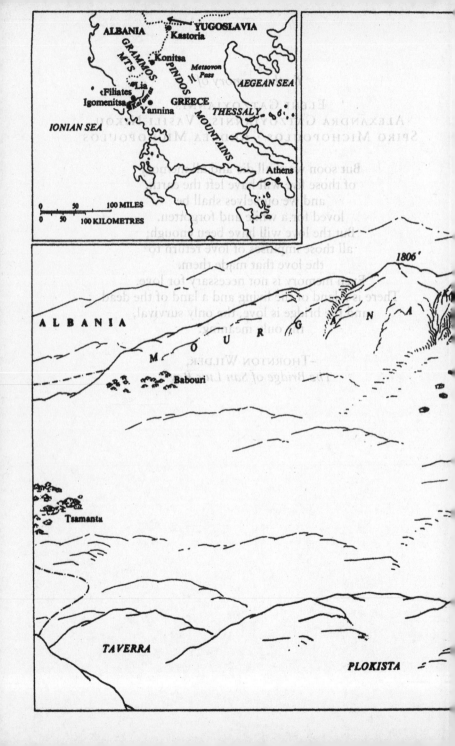

The Village of Lia

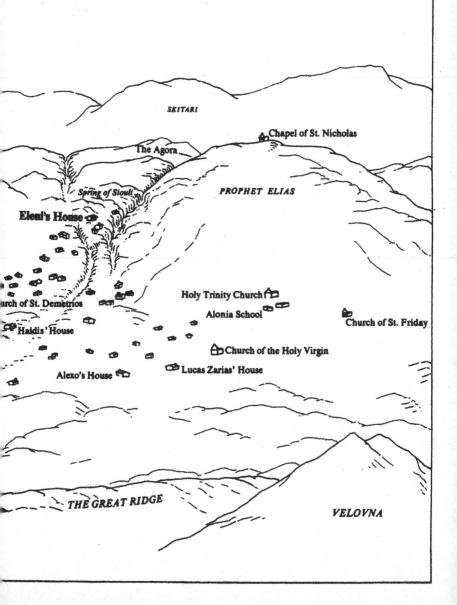

SKITARI

Chapel of St. Nicholas

The Agora

Spring of Siouli

PROPHET ELIAS

Eleni's House

Holy Trinity Church

Alonia School

Church of St. Friday

...rch of St. Demetrios

Haidis' House

Church of the Holy Virgin

Alexo's House

Lucas Zarias' House

THE GREAT RIDGE

VELOVNA

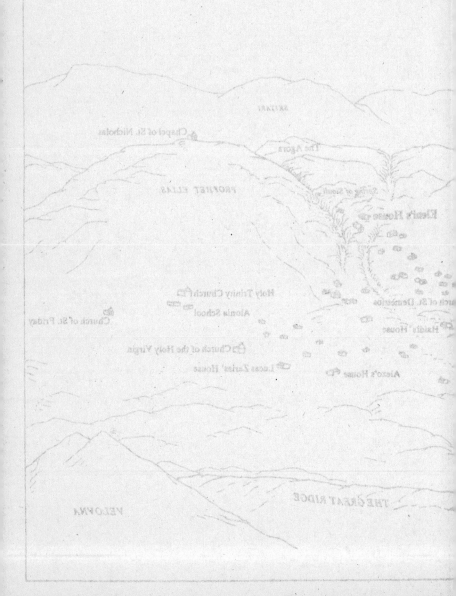

Part One

Pursuit

On the road to vengeance . . .
one discovers life.

– ANDRÉ MALRAUX,
Man's Fate

THE PATH TO THE RAVINE

ON AUGUST 28, 1948, at about twelve-thirty on a hot, windless day, some peasant women with firewood on their backs were descending a steep path above the Greek village of Lia, a cluster of gray stone houses on a mountainside just below the Albanian border. As the women came into view of the village below them, they encountered a grim procession.

At the front and rear, carrying rifles, were several of the Communist guerrillas who had occupied their village for the past nine months of the Greek civil war. They were guarding thirteen prisoners, who were walking barefoot to their execution on legs black and swollen from the torture called *falanga*. One man, too beaten to walk or even sit up, was tied onto a mule.

Among the prisoners were five people from Lia: three men and two women. The older woman stumbled along with a fixed stare of madness. She was my aunt, Alexo Gatzoyiannis, fifty-six. The younger woman, with light-chestnut hair, blue eyes and a torn blue dress, caught the gaze of the villagers and shook her head. She was my mother, Eleni Gatzoyiannis, forty-one years old.

One of the peasant women began to cry, seeing her brother among the condemned. A thirteen-year-old boy who had stopped to drink at a spring watched the prisoners climb the mountain; soon they disappeared over the horizon. A few minutes later there was a burst of rifle fire, then scattered shots as each victim was finished off with a bullet to the head. When the guerrillas passed again on the way down, they were

3

alone. The executed had been left in the ravine where they fell, their bodies covered by rocks.

Sixteen days later, when it was clear that the guerrillas were losing the war to the Greek nationalist forces, they rounded up every civilian left in the village and herded them at gunpoint over the border into Albania. Lia became a ghost town, the crows descending on the corpses left behind. A village that had been inhabited for more than twenty-five centuries ceased to exist.

I learned of my mother's execution twenty-three days later at a refugee camp on the Ionian coast where three of my sisters and I had found shelter after managing to flee our village. Although our mother planned the escape, she was forced to stay behind with my fourth sister at the last moment. Six months after the news reached us, we boarded a ship bound for the United States to join our father, who had been cut off from Greece by World War II and the insurrection that followed it. I was nine when I saw him for the first time.

My mother was one of 600,000 Greeks who were killed during the years of war that ravaged the country from 1940 to 1949. Like many of the victims, she died because her home lay in the path of the opposing armies, but she would have survived if she hadn't defied the invaders of her village to save her children.

I had been her favorite child and the focus of her life, loved with the intensity a Greek peasant woman reserves for an only son. I knew that I was the primary reason she made the choices she did. No one doubted that she died so I could live.

As a boy growing up in the city of Worcester, Massachusetts, living with my sisters and the stranger who was my father, I couldn't talk about my mother and her death the way the rest of my family did, although it was with me waking and sleeping. Every Sunday, in the church full of Greek immigrants, I heard the priest recite a *trisagion* to her memory. My older sisters spoke of her constantly, often reporting dreams in which our mother appeared to them with some message or warning from the land of the dead. In *my* dreams, she was always alive, engaged in familiar scenes from the past, baking

4

bread, harvesting the fruit of our mulberry tree, laughing at my pranks. My sisters had accepted her death, but each time I awoke it came as a new shock.

As a nine-year-old boy struggling with the English language, I felt helpless against the fact of my mother's death. It was not something that I could talk about to anyone. There seemed to be nothing I could do to make up for her sacrifice except to hope that my sisters were right, that God would ultimately punish those who had betrayed, tortured and murdered her.

Then, in the seventh grade, a teacher assigned me to write about my life in Greece. It was one of the first days of spring. I looked out the school window, remembering our mountainside blazing with purple Judas trees, the Easter kid roasting on a spit outside each house, my mother boiling the eggs in a vat of blood-red dye.

I wrote how, in the spring of my eighth year, I overheard two guerrillas say they were going to take the village children away from their parents and send them behind the Iron Curtain. I ran to tell my mother what I had heard and she began to plan our escape, setting in motion the events that would end in her execution four months later.

The essay won a certificate of merit, and I realized that I was not as helpless as I had thought. I would learn to write and eventually describe what was done in that ravine in 1948 and by whom. I didn't speak of these ambitions to my father and sisters, who were working in factories and diners to keep us alive.

By the time I finished college I had saved enough money from part-time work on local newspapers to make a return visit to the village which I had left as a refugee fourteen years before. I intended to begin my search for the details of my mother's death.

When I walked out of that village as a boy, I knew every tree and rock of my circumscribed world, but as I followed the new dirt road back up our mountain in 1963, I mistook two villages in the distance for my own before I reached Lia. Clearly, my memory was not as accurate as I had believed. When I finally reached it, the village was no longer deserted;

5

many of the civilians who had been taken into Albania and then dispersed throughout Eastern Europe by the retreating Communists had drifted back since 1954. The guerrillas and their collaborators, however, were still not permitted by the Greek government to return.

I was met by my eighty-three-year-old grandfather, the only male relative I had known as a boy. I remembered him as an aloof, menacing tyrant. He was the one who returned to the empty village to unearth the bodies of my mother and my aunt, then brought the news of their deaths to us children. When he saw me, now twenty-three, my grandfather was the first of many villagers to exclaim over my physical resemblance to my mother. My face seemed to incite the neighbors to pour out details of her torture and suffering. As soon as they began, I discovered that I could not bear to listen. When one man tried to tell me how her feet and legs were swollen to grotesque proportions by beatings, I got up and left the room.

On that first afternoon, when my grandparents were taking their siesta, I left their house and climbed the path up to our old property, now deserted and shunned by the villagers because it had been used by the guerrillas as a military police station, jail, killing ground and cemetery. I knew that my mother had spent the last days of her life being tortured there, imprisoned in the filthy cellar where we once kept our sheep and goats. I forced myself to enter the front door and look into the room which had served as a kitchen, where my mother, sisters and I used to sleep on the floor around the hearth. The room seemed to have shrunk over the years. There was nothing inside, no sign that I belonged here. I tried to recall happy times, feast days, but all I could think of were the condemned prisoners in the cellar, my mother among them. I didn't approach the cellar door but left the house, knowing I would not come back.

That fall, when I returned to America to begin graduate school, I made a tentative assault on the book but barely got past the first few pages. I started by trying to describe the oppressively hot afternoon when my grandfather came to tell us that our mother had been murdered. Just the memory of my sisters' screams stopped me and I put the pages aside, channeling my energies for the next few years into completing graduate school and finding a job as a reporter. As a boy, I naively thought that I could write the story of my mother's death from my own memories. Now I knew that those memories were flawed and incomplete. I knew also that I did not have the strength to face the details of her suffering.

My sisters had neither the desire nor the money to return to Greece until 1969, when two of them resolved to go back to the village and hold a memorial service for our mother. I decided to go with them, although I knew it would be a painful journey. When we reached Lia, I followed them up the path as far as our land, but when my sisters entered the house, I refused to go with them and waited outside until they emerged, in tears.

The next day the whole village gathered in our neighborhood Church of St. Demetrios for the memorial service. The church was used only on special saints' days, but the village priest agreed to open it and conduct the liturgy. In a small ossuary, divided from the sanctuary by a wall, lay the bones of my mother and my aunt in a small wooden box, mixed together as they had been when my grandfather disinterred the bodies from the mass grave.

Sun slanted through the dusty windows of the crowded church as the priest began to chant and the altar boys swung the censers, the heavy perfume mingling with the odor of decay. Unexpectedly, the schoolteacher stood up to speak. He was the only educated man in the village and he wanted to deliver a eulogy. As soon as he said our mother's name, my sisters began to wail: keening, ululating cries, the Greek expression of sorrow for the dead.

'This woman's death was not an ordinary one,' the schoolteacher continued over the commotion. 'She was executed alone, with her husband far away, because she tried to save her children. She was a victim of her fellow Greeks. This is not an ordinary memorial service for the dead; she was murdered!'

As I stood there, trying to wish myself anywhere else, the air pressed in on me and I was aware of my mother's bones only yards away. Nearly every day of my childhood I had watched her light a candle before this altar. The shrieks of my

7

sisters stripped away the veneer of control I had built up, layer by layer. Even when I was a boy, on the day my mother said goodbye, and again, when I learned she was dead, I had held my grief inside. Now it erupted. Sobs welled up from where they had been hidden for so many years and shook my body like a convulsion. The rush of emotion blurred my vision and then my knees buckled. Two men nearby grabbed my arms and supported me out of the church, setting me on the ground, my back against the trunk of one of the towering cypress trees surrounding the graveyard.

That outburst was the first and last time I lost control and abandoned myself to my grief, but when it passed, I discovered a new strength within me. At last I was ready to learn what the villagers had to tell me and to look directly at the details of my mother's death.

When I began asking questions, I found that many parts of the story were still beyond my reach. The villagers who had betrayed her, who testified against her to curry favor with the guerrillas, were still in exile behind the Iron Curtain. And the witnesses to her last days who were living in Lia gave me contradictory testimony about many incidents, obviously withholding details that might compromise them or their relatives. Those who were willing to talk about the war years openly remembered the guerrillas only by the pseudonyms they had assumed to mask their identities. I spent all the summer of 1969 in Lia, but when I left in the fall to return to America, it was clear that despite my emotional readiness to hear my mother's story, I did not have access to key people involved or the skills to get the truth out of them.

On my return to New York I submerged myself in the business of life. I married a girl I had known since graduate school and in rapid succession we had three children, first a son named Christos for my father, then two daughters, the elder one baptized Eleni after my mother.

I began a job for the *New York Times* as an investigative reporter, a brand of newspaperman who is as much a detective as a journalist. I learned how to ferret out facts that others wanted hidden and to make witnesses trip themselves up, trapping themselves with their own words. I shadowed

8

subjects and followed up anonymous tips and took care to verify and recheck every scrap of information, spending weeks going through dusty files and government papers. I wrote about corrupt politicians, crooked judges, narcotics traffickers and Mafia chieftains. On occasion I was subpoenaed, once by Vice President Spiro Agnew, but my evidence was always too well documented for anyone to sue me. The seven years that passed after the memorial service for my mother were hectic and distracting ones. Only later did I realize that I was unconsciously honing my skills and training myself for the task I had chosen as a boy: to find out what happened to my mother and who was responsible for her death. My circuitous path was leading inexorably back to the ravine where she was executed.

In July of 1974 the collapse of the dictatorial right-wing military junta ruling Greece opened the gates for Communist guerrillas living in exile to return to the country. Many of those I wanted to question about my mother's trial and death would now be accessible to me. In 1977 I persuaded my editors to send me to Athens as the *New York Times*' foreign correspondent in the eastern Mediterranean. The conditions necessary for me to begin the search for my mother's story were all coming together.

The arrival in Greece in 1977 was a shock to someone who remembered the civil war years. I discovered that the fall of the junta and the establishment of a new civilian government, which legalized the Communist Party in an effort to ensure acceptance of Greece in the Common Market, had created a renaissance of Communist power in the country. Posters, movies, books, popular songs and the youth organizations in the universities were united in celebrating the guerrillas of the civil war as heroes. It seemed that the best talents of Greece were busy rewriting the history of the war, while everywhere, Communist leaders were denying that such things as the execution of civilians and the abduction of large groups of children from the mountain villages had ever happened.

As soon as I settled in Athens with my family I hoped to spend every spare moment tracking down and questioning those who had been my mother's interrogators, jailers, torturers and the judges at her trial, as well as relatives and neighbors who had witnessed her last days. But the volatile political climate in the area left me time for little else but my job. I spent most of my first years in Greece traveling outside the country, covering terrorism in Turkey, battles in the Middle East, a revolution in Iran, and civil war in Afghanistan.

By 1980 it was clear that I had to give myself up entirely to the investigation of my mother's story at once or never do it. I learned that some of the guerrilla leaders responsible for her trial and execution had died in exile. Others were likely to die of old age before I could track them down. Furthermore, Greece has a thirty-year statute of limitation on all crimes – including murder. Anyone who had committed any atrocity during the war years could now return to the country without fear of punishment, and the former leaders of the guerrillas were flooding back in.

In 1980 I was forty-one years old, the same age that my mother had been when she was killed. My son was nine, as I was on the day I learned she was dead. My older daughter, growing out of babyhood, resembled my mother more every day. Seeing my children grow had taught me a lesson that made my mother's story easier to confront.

When I was young I was convinced that her existence was one of unrelieved misery because for the last decade of her life she struggled every day to keep us five children alive, despite war and famine, with no help from anyone. But as I watched my own children I realized that there must have been joy and laughter to reward her while she lived. Knowing that made it easier to face what I would learn.

Finally, clues about the identities of some of her killers began to filter to me in Athens and I knew I couldn't hesitate any longer. I decided to leave my job with the newspaper to devote all my energy to the search for my mother's story.

The first clue came from a childhood friend who told me about a visit back to Lia on a summer feast day when he fell into conversation with another villager, named Antoni Makos. Makos said that he was the thirteen-year-old boy drinking at the spring on the day my mother passed by to her

10

execution. He told of a strange coincidence: twenty years later, in 1968, he happened to enter a bar in the northern Greek city of Yannina and recognized the owner of the place as one of the armed guerrillas who led the condemned to their deaths.

I found Makos at the shop in a suburb of Athens where he bakes pastries for cafés. Wearing a floury apron over his ample stomach, he led me into the back room and agreed to talk. We were both nervous: I was afraid of what I was going to hear and he was reluctant to open old wounds.

The years had built scar tissue over the fact of my mother's death, but there were questions gnawing at me that I had always been afraid to ask. I heard whispers that she was so badly tortured before her execution that she had to be carried up the mountain on horseback. I took a deep breath and asked Makos. When he told me that she had walked past him – barefoot, yes, on legs swollen from torture, but walking and apparently in her right mind – I felt a great weight lifted. One of the nightmarish scenes that had haunted me dissolved.

Seeing that I wouldn't become emotional, Makos relaxed and told me proudly about the day when he recognized the guerrilla in a soldiers' bar in Yannina. He struck up a conversation with him and learned that he had been stationed in Lia. His name, said Makos, was Taki Cotees. If I went to Yannina, he said, to the bar just opposite the back of the military post, I'd probably find him still sitting at the same table.

It takes only forty-five minutes to fly from Athens to Yannina, a provincial capital of crumbling minarets and peasant women in village costume. I arrived on a rainy winter day. With a distant cousin, an army major stationed there, I began combing the bars that cater to soldiers. When we reached the one Taki owned, we found that it had been closed.

Discouraged, we went into another bar close-by where my cousin knew the bartender, a talkative fellow who said he knew Taki Cotees, who pimped for the prostitutes employed in his bar until it was closed down. Although the bartender didn't know his present address, he volunteered that Taki was a frequent visitor to the political office of a local member of Parliament because he was trying to wheedle permission for a sister still exiled in Russia to be allowed back into Greece.

Political patronage and reciprocal favors are the lubricants that turn every wheel in Greece. As it happened, I knew that politician from my days as a correspondent and convinced him to look up the former guerrilla's file for me. Luckily, Taki was one of the few guerrillas who hadn't hidden behind a *nom de guerre* during the war. The deputy called Taki into his office and introduced me as a friend from the United States, a writer who 'wants some information you can give him. Please help him all you can.'

My stomach was knotted with tension as I looked at the face of a man who, when he was twenty years old, had watched my mother die, perhaps even fired one of the shots. Taki bore no resemblance to my image of him. He was a small, frail, gnomelike man, untidy wisps of gray hair spiking out around his bald pate, his lower face caved in around an overbite. He had the sly, shriveled look of a doll made from a dried apple. The only thing still young about him was his eyes, which were a startling gold color and darted about nervously.

Taki listened obsequiously to what the deputy said, and nodded. He promised to do whatever he could. I steered the former guerrilla to my rented car, and once he was inside, began to drive aimlessly, leaving the city behind, meanwhile asking about where he spent the war. He was posted in the Mourgana village of Lia, Taki said.

Weren't there five people from that village executed? I asked.

Taki frowned. Yes, he had been at the execution himself, he said, as one of the guards. No, not on the firing squad; that was made up of guerrillas stationed higher up the mountain who came down to the killing ground. Those executions were a very bad thing, he opined, shaking his head. One of those killed was an eighteen-year-old boy, one of their own guerrillas, who was charged with treason. After the execution, Taki said, he had personally filed a complaint with his commander about the boy's murder.

Did he remember two women? I asked.

12

He thought for a moment. One was a woman with light-brown hair who had a home near the church at the western edge of the village, he recalled, a house with a mulberry tree nearby. That house had been used as the jail and he had been posted there as a guard. Taki was getting visibly uneasy, watching the deserted countryside flash by. 'Was that woman related to you?' he asked.

I told him who she was. Taki became more agitated and suggested that we stop somewhere for coffee. He knew that in my car, on these lonely roads, he was in a vulnerable position. But once we stopped and he found himself in the security of a well-lit roadside café, he relaxed a little and described what he remembered of the executions. He was still trying to appear helpful. Clearly, he thought that I could use my influence with the deputy to bring his exiled sister back from Tashkent. He even promised to travel with me to Lia to the execution site, where he would try to remember more details. It was a promise that he would repeat several times but never keep. Every time I tried to get him to fix a date to go to the village he'd find some excuse to cancel it at the last moment, no doubt for fear of what might happen if we found ourselves alone in the isolated ravine where my mother died.

During several subsequent meetings with Taki in Yannina, I pumped him for the names of his guerrilla superiors and the men who served as judges at my mother's trial. His memory was blurred and he could only give me the pseudonym of one of the judges – Yiorgos Economou – but, he added, it was another judge who was head of the court.

Taki was a repulsive little man who combined shallow cunning and false amiability, but I believed his account of the execution, as much as he remembered it; he was convincingly angry about the murders because they hurt the cause of Communism in the village and claimed one of his fellow guerrillas. In our last meeting, which took place in the nearly empty bar section of the lobby of Yannina's largest hotel, I pressed Taki to remember details of the tortures that the prisoners had been subjected to during the twenty days he stood guard duty outside the jail in Lia. He admitted he had seen one of the woman prisoners being interrogated in the garden. It was the woman with the light-chestnut hair, the owner of the house that was the jail, he said. While other guerrillas hit her, one of them held her shoulders and pressed his knee against her back.

I stared at him uncomprehendingly and asked him to repeat it. He went over it several times but I still looked blank. I didn't understand how the guerrilla could hold her shoulders and put his knee on her back at the same time.

Taki and I were sitting side by side on a couch with a marble coffee table in front of us. Finally he stood up with a shrug and motioned for me to stand. After looking around to be sure no one was watching, with an apologetic smile he went behind me and seized my shoulders. Taki was several inches shorter than I was, a frail man of fifty-two whom I could easily overpower in a fight. From behind he grasped my arms just below the shoulders, then lifted his knee and placed it in the small of my back. Then he twisted my arms back at an angle that threatened to dislocate them from the sockets and pushed with his knee against the curve of my spine. He didn't apply much pressure; it was only a friendly demonstration.

I felt myself in a position that left me totally helpless. The inability to move, coupled with the pressure on the fragile vertebrae of the spine, was the surprising thing. I pictured my backbone snapping like that of a fish on a plate. A startling pain, considering the lack of force, shot up across my shoulders into the base of my skull.

With a nervous chuckle Taki released me and sat down again. He continued talking, but I didn't hear anything he said. I was perspiring and there was a roaring inside my head. That one flash of pain had left me weak as a child, not because of the pain itself, but because I had suddenly imagined it magnified many times over, heightened by fear and being done to my mother. For an instant I had felt a tiny fraction of the suffering she experienced, day after day, increasing in viciousness until she was killed.

The reality of the pain washed my mind clear of illusion. In that split second, in the hotel lobby in Yannina, I realized what I hadn't yet admitted to myself: it wasn't enough to find out the details of her torments. The only way I could live with that knowledge and find some sort of relief was to exact payment in kind for the agony she had gone through. That day was the first time I understood that my search for my mother's killers would not end when I wrote her story. I had to go a step further and make them suffer the way they hurt her.

Face to face for the first time with the need for revenge which possessed me, I had a quick image of smashing Taki's smiling face open on the marble table before us, but I sat there, forcing myself not to move as he talked on. Taki was not the proper object of my rage; he was a nonentity, only a bit player in my mother's murder. Besides, a fistfight in a hotel lobby would spoil any hope I had of finding the rightful target, the person whose hands were stained with her blood.

I didn't meet with Taki again. The sight of him turned my stomach, and he had told me everything he knew about the judges. I would have to uncover the rest by other means. So before I left Yannina I stopped at the small apartment of a woman named Dina Venetis. She is one of the few prisoners held captive in the cellar jail in Lia who survived to tell what went on there. Dina had been on trial with my mother but she was exonerated and set free. I wanted to find out what she remembered of the judges.

Dina is now an unremarkable matron with grizzled short hair, and a kindly smile revealing three gold teeth, but once she was a beauty. Photographs taken before the war show a dark, sultry-looking young woman in a black kerchief, with a full mouth, high cheekbones and black-fringed eyes staring solemnly at the camera. When the guerrillas arrested her, leaving her three small children unprotected in the house, her husband was somewhere in the south, fighting on the side of the Greek government forces.

Dina welcomed me hospitably into her stuffy apartment, crowded with memorabilia of her children, including the small son taken from her by the guerrillas and sent to a camp in Russia for seven years. She shook her head when I asked her about the judge called Yiorgos Economou; the only judge who had made an impression on her at the trial was the man who conducted it, a man with a voice so deep and terrifying that 'when he spoke you thought you were hearing Death himself.' He was the man the villagers knew as Katis.

The name 'Katis' struck me like a blow, although I had heard it many times before. *Katis* is simply an Albanian word that means 'judge,' but it was the pseudonym of a man whom many villagers had described to me. He worked for the judicial branch of the guerrillas and assembled evidence against defendants at trials. He conducted interrogations and orchestrated the tortures. He was universally remembered as the chief judge at my mother's trial. I had often heard the name 'Katis' from my sister Glykeria, the only one of us who was left behind when the rest escaped the village. On the last day of my mother's life, my fourteen-year-old sister was allowed to see her while Katis stood by watching. Glykeria said that my mother took him aside and whispered to him, pleading that the girl be spared. If I were to find my mother's killers, I had to find Katis, but first I had to learn his real name.

Dina was vague on the details of the trial, saying that she was too frightened to remember, but she vividly recalled her imprisonment in the cellar and was perfectly willing to describe it to me, sometimes smiling and shaking her head over an anecdote as if unconscious of the tears that she kept wiping away.

The prisoners, covered with lice, their hands tied behind their backs, were so crowded into our cellar that they had to sleep in a sitting position, she said. For some reason my aunt Alexo was left untied, perhaps because of her age, and she moved among the others, massaging their hands and rocking their bodies to keep them from going numb.

I was disturbed when Dina said that my mother was not kept with the others in the basement while she was there. 'There were other rooms in your house where they might have kept her,' she suggested. I wondered why my mother was singled out for special treatment, kept isolated from the rest.

Dina told me many details about the prison that were painful to hear, but one story that made a deep impression on me was that of a tall woman with curly black hair from the

16

village of Mavronoron, whose name was Despo – that's all she knew of her – a nervous girl who cried all the time for her two children. 'Despo couldn't stand the beatings,' Dina said. 'One night she found a large nail stuck in one of the beams, pulled it out and plunged it into her stomach, trying to kill herself. Drove it deep, poor thing, but she couldn't die. Afterward she begged constantly for something to help the pain, but they wouldn't give her anything.'

She told how Despo was taken upstairs one night, a signal that she was about to be executed. 'You're going to kill me! I know it!' the other prisoners heard her screaming. Then they heard Katis reply in his sonorous voice, 'How can you think that? Would we kill Despo, our pampered one, our favorite?' After that the prisoners never saw Despo again.

I left Yannina discouraged, knowing scarcely more than when I had arrived. All I had was the pseudonyms of two judges – Economou and Katis. But back in Athens, by hounding sources in the Ministry of Public Order, I managed to uncover one solid lead: the real name of Yiorgos Economou was Yiorgos Anagnostakis, a lawyer who had returned from exile in Tashkent in 1975 and was now living not far from me in Athens. As for Katis, there was nothing in the files. 'You'll have to get his real name,' I was told.

Before my search was over I would encounter several coincidences so unlikely as to seem invented. The first one happened on a February afternoon when I arrived outside the modern apartment building where the former judge Anagnostakis lived, to see a black, glass-enclosed 1950's Cadillac hearse parked at the door. I asked an old man outside the entrance, perhaps the concierge, if the lawyer Yiorgos Anagnostakis lived inside. He raised his eyebrows and protruded his lower lip in the gesture Greeks use to indicate the fickleness of fate. 'His body is inside, yes,' he replied, 'but his soul has flown.' On the day I went looking for him, the judge Anagnostakis had died of a heart attack.

I left the building in despair. A malevolent fate had snatched one of my mother's judges out of my grasp and I was now at a dead end, with my only clue the useless nickname Katis.

Eventually I tracked down several former guerrillas who claimed to have heard of Katis, the judge, but most of them told me they thought he had died in exile. The closest thing I could get to a lead was the comment of one ex-guerrilla that a certain retired lawyer living in northern Greece might have known Katis during the war because the man had served in a similar position as a judge at guerrilla headquarters in the Grammos mountains. The lawyer's name was Demitris Gastis, and he was currently recuperating from a heart attack in his native village of Dilofo just north of Yannina.

With little optimism I flew to Yannina again and drove to the village of Dilofo, hidden among the foothills of the Zagoria mountains. The inquisitive woman who sat outside her doorway at the entrance to the village was happy to lead me to the imposing stone mansion of the lawyer Gastis and rouse the ancient crone in the servants' quarters who woke him from his siesta.

I knew that Demitris Gastis, as judge for the Eleventh Division of the guerrilla army in the Grammos mountains, had sentenced many to the firing squad, but if I expected him to look like a killer, I found instead a debonair figure of gracefully aging urbanity with a neatly trimmed mustache, square horn-rimmed glasses and wavy salt-and-pepper hair. Dressed in slippers and a fashionable Italian jersey and slacks, he ushered me into the cool depths of his house, where pillowed banquettes lined the hand-decorated walls. Coffee and a box of chocolates appeared in honor of the visitor.

While I explained that I was a Greek-American journalist researching a book about the civil war, the former judge listened intently, then smiled and became expansive. He prided himself on his erudition and suggested a long list of reference books that I should consult, but I assured him that I had read them all. Convinced that I had an adequate background knowledge, he began to describe the workings of the military trials he had conducted. 'We let a prisoner speak in his own defense for as long as he wanted,' he said, 'and permitted anyone who wished to stand up and speak for him, something that even the civil courts today don't do.'

In response to my questions Gastis calmly stated that he

18

had sent only two men to their deaths; then, later, he contra-dicted himself and mentioned a third – a guerrilla executed for raping a girl – whose dead body was sent on horseback through the occupied villages to dramatize that the Communists didn't tolerate mistreatment of women. I did not bother to dispute Gastis' body count because I was eager to get him on the subject of trials in my own area, the Mourgana mountains.

Did he recall the chief judge in the Epiros Command? I asked.

Yes, a man named Anagnostakis, he replied, who had unfortunately just died.

There was another judge whom the people remembered as Katis, I prompted, but it seemed that he had died in exile.

'Oh no, he isn't dead,' Gastis said casually. Katis was alive somewhere in Athens, he thought. Of course, Katis wasn't his real name, he continued, but a corruption of the word for 'judge.'

I hoped my excitement didn't show as Gastis sat smiling, jiggling one slippered foot, pleased at the breadth of his knowledge. When I got control of my voice I asked if he happened to recall the real name of Katis.

'Lykas,' he replied promptly. 'Achilleas Lykas.'

The man who had prosecuted and sentenced my mother to death and supervised her torture was suddenly resurrected and put within my reach. While I considered this unexpected stroke of luck, Gastis went on talking, saying that I really should speak to Lykas as part of my research; he had presided at an important trial in Tsamanta when a number of captured officers of the nationalist forces were condemned to the firing squad.

As a rumble of thunder rolled over the house, presaging a rainstorm, I stood up and thanked Gastis for his time. He was delighted to have been of some help, he said, extending his hand. He had a last piece of advice for me: if I wanted to learn details of the military operations in the Mourgana during the war, I should stop on my way back through Yannina and interview the then chief of staff of the entire Epiros Command, Major General Yiorgos Kalianesis. I'd have no trouble finding him, Gastis said, because the former guerrilla general now worked as a night clerk in a small tourist hotel, Hotel Alexios. He was on duty there every night.

I wrote down the address and hurried out into a pelting rain, still stunned by the news that the judge who sentenced my mother was alive. As soon as I was out of sight of the village I pulled off the road. My hands were shaking and I couldn't see where I was going. I turned off the ignition and sat there for a long time, wondering whether I would finally meet the man called Katis, and if I did, what I would do to him.

When I reached Yannina I took Gastis' advice and walked toward the Hotel Alexios. Once, as a boy, I had glimpsed Kalianesis, the military commander of the Epiros guerrilla army, in the midst of a critical battle in 1948, and the impression he made was still strong. The government soldiers were approaching, threatening to wrest our village from the Communists, and the guerrilla commanders decided to move their headquarters higher up the mountain for safety, above the house where I lived. Kalianesis passed right by our gate. As I stood there with my mother, searching the commander's face for a clue to the outcome of the battle below, I was dazzled by the imposing, bulldoglike figure of Kalianesis, his fine horse, his gleaming pistols and accoutrements and the deference of the retinue of guerrillas around him. At the age of eight I thought he was the epitome of power and success.

When I entered the dingy hotel lobby and found Kalianesis stationed behind the desk, he was still a powerful figure despite his bald pate fringed with gray hair, his rolled shirtsleeves and wrinkled slacks. His small brown eyes were buried in a heavily jowled face over a thick neck, which disappeared into a massive torso. His receding forehead bore depressions like thumbprints – the scars of shrapnel wounds. He reminded me of an aging gangland enforcer, still capable of breaking a man in two with his hands.

But Kalianesis showed none of the suspicious reticence of other guerrillas I interviewed. As soon as I mentioned that Gastis had sent me, his eyes brightened. He eagerly launched into a recitation of his military triumphs in the Mourgana.

The former major general now commanded nothing more than the rows of room keys hanging behind him and he was delighted to relive his past glory for an interested stranger.

Kalianesis was a living textbook on the military campaigns of the guerrilla army in my section of Greece during the civil war. That night, and in subsequent conversations, he provided me with invaluable information about the conduct of battles and the squabbles and ambitions of the Communist Party leaders who directed the war. Kalianesis resented bitterly that, as one of the few Communist generals with a real military education, he was reduced to listening to the complaints of scruffy tourists all night long in a third-rate hotel while the men who were his classmates at the Greek equivalent of West Point and became generals for the other side now enjoyed retirement on large pensions.

I was disappointed to learn that Kalianesis had been transferred from our area two months before my mother's execution, so he couldn't provide any firsthand details of her trial. He made it clear that such civilian trials were not within his purview; he directed the military side, while the administration of guerrilla justice was the responsibility of the political commissar in Epiros, Kostas Kalianesis, who had died in exile in 1979. But there was a judge still living who presided over many such trials, he said, 'a man named Lykas, although everyone called him Katis.'

I tried to maintain an expression of scholarly interest as I said I would very much like to talk to this Lykas, if only I knew where to find him. I had heard he lived in Athens. Kalianesis' jowls arranged themselves into a grin; he was delighted to be of service. 'He's not in Athens, he lives right here in Yannina,' he said. 'I see him walking around sometimes. In fact, Lykas lives only a few blocks away. I don't know the exact address, but he has an apartment on Napoleon Zervas Street.'

I could hardly absorb this new revelation. The hunt that was at a standstill only two days before had climaxed so suddenly that I wasn't prepared. I thanked Kalianesis and hurried out into the fragrant summer night. Walking over toward the busy thoroughfare Kalianesis had mentioned, I considered the irony of Katis' address: he lived on a street named for the greatest enemy of the guerrillas during the occupation: Napoleon Zervas.

I began going from door to door, reading the names posted beside the bells at each apartment house, looking for the one I wanted. Finally I found it in a modern six-story building. Lykas lived on the fourth floor of 46 Napoleon Zervas Street.

I retreated to the edge of the pavement and stared up at his apartment, where a lamp was burning behind curtained windows. I imagined Katis sitting there in the security of his living room, sleek and complacent like the other judge I had just interviewed, confident that his war crimes were buried in the past. I wanted to knock on his door, push my way inside and show him that someone still remembered what he had done in Lia.

My rational side reminded me that I had no idea who lived up there with him. I could hardly burst in, without even a weapon, and attack him. Everything I had learned so far suggested that Katis was the one person still alive who held the greatest guilt for my mother's murder, but as an investigative reporter I had to learn the exact degree of Katis' culpability. Was he the initiator of her torture and execution or an involuntary agent of others? I had to decide what punishment would be commensurate with his crimes and at the same time sufficient to appease my own need for revenge. I needed to gather more evidence and form a plan of attack. That's why I stood on the sidewalk and watched the window until it went dark; then I turned away and walked off through Yannina to take a hotel room, where I sat up most of the night, trying to decide what to do.

By morning only one thing was clear: I was going back to my village. I had to return to the places where my mother lived and died, to think things through. Heading out of Yannina, I came to a fork in the highway and impulsively turned north. The road on the left led toward my village, but I remembered that the right-hand one led to the village of Mavronoron, the home of the young woman, Despo, who tried to kill herself in the cellar prison by driving a nail into her abdomen. I felt a compulsion to learn if anyone remem-

22

bered Despo and could tell me at least her full name.

Past ever smaller villages, where storks nested on chimneys and telephone poles, I continued north on a dirt road until I reached a jumble of houses and a large church. I asked a group of women in the churchyard if they knew the name of someone called Despo who disappeared from the village during the war. They clucked and sighed as if it had been yesterday. Her name was Despina Tassis, they said. She left two little motherless boys – grown-up now and living in Athens – but Despo's husband was still around. I could find him outside the coffeehouse playing cards with the other men.

When I spoke to some of the men gathered around the card tables, the tall, unsmiling figure of Stephanos Tassis rose and followed me out of earshot of the others. I told him about my interest in the war and my mother's fate, and said that I had recently talked to a woman who was in prison with his wife.

He showed little interest in my statement, although he told me this was the first concrete news of his wife since her disappearance thirty-two years before. He told me that their two sons had been four and two years old when everyone fled the village of Mavronoron in the wake of the invading guerrillas. But after a while the family, living as refugees in Yannina, had nothing to eat. Despo sneaked back to their village to get some corn she had hidden in their house, and was never seen again. Seven years after Despo's disappearance, Stephanos Tassis managed with much difficulty to find a priest willing to marry him to another village woman, even though there was no proof of his first wife's death.

It wasn't easy wringing answers from the taciturn man in front of me. Clearly, he had no interest in learning about Despo's last days, so I didn't elaborate. I could see that he didn't want the ghost of his first wife intruding on the life he had built for himself since the war. His eyes strayed back to the card game.

If ever he or his sons wanted to learn more, I said, I could put them in touch with the woman who shared Despo's imprisonment. I wrote down my address and telephone number on a piece of paper. Stephanos Tassis scarcely glanced

23

at it as he put it in his pocket and pointedly wished me goodbye.

I felt angry, almost personally injured, by the indifference of Despo's husband. In my uncertainty over what to do about my mother's death, I had sought out someone who was similarly bereaved, only to learn that not only did he intend to do nothing about his wife's murder, he didn't even want to be reminded of it.

Later I would find many more victims of the guerrillas like him. In the course of hunting down the identities of my mother's killers, I uncovered the names and addresses of guerrillas who had killed other civilians and I confronted many of their survivors with details about the murderers. In each case I was met with apathy and rationalization. 'Don't tell me where he is, because I might feel compelled to do something to him,' said a postman whose father was shot dead by a guerrilla intelligence officer as he stood in his own field and refused to inform on his neighbors. 'Let God punish the guilty,' said a man who, as an eight-year-old boy, had watched his mother condemned to death for refusing to give up her children to be sent to the Iron Curtain countries. 'The government should bring them to justice,' muttered a third, who saw his parents executed in the churchyard of his village while the guerrillas warned him that he would die too if he made a sound.

These excuses kindled in me a growing disgust, rage and despair. Thousands of innocent people like my mother had been killed during the war and now their murderers were living in Greece, their sleep untroubled by fear of reprisals. Just one act of vengeance against the men who now bragged of their war exploits would have made all of them feel a little of the anguish they had inflicted on their victims. But not one father, husband or son had found the will to do it.

My dark mood evoked by the apathy of Despo's husband lifted a little as I drove toward my own village. Whenever I crossed the narrow bridge over the Kalamas River, which isolates the Mourgana mountains, I felt a comforting sense of returning to my childhood, of coming home.

From the river the road leads up, past waterfalls, ruined

mills and white chapels perched on sheer cliffs, around
hairpin turns and through tiny villages scattered like pebbles,
until the asphalt ends in a bone-rattling path leading ever
higher, through the hiding places of mountain goats and wild
boar, to the edge of the timberline where the gray slate roofs
of Lia become visible nestled among the scrub pine and holm
oak of my village.

Bare light bulbs now hang inside the stone huts, testament
to the power lines that reached Lia in 1965, but from the road
– another recent incursion of civilization – the village still
looks as primitive as the day I walked out of it thirty-three
years ago.

As I drove past the Church of Aghia Paraskevi (St. Friday)
on the easternmost boundary of the village, the grizzled
shepherds surrounded by their goats and the black-clad
grandmothers bent under loads of kindling shouted greetings
to me.

The pleasure of these familiar sights dissolved when I
noticed the stooped, white-haired figure of Christos Skevis at
work in his yard. In 1948, when my mother and the others
were killed, Skevis was one of the villagers who methodically
went around to the houses of the victims and stole the last
remaining pieces of food from the survivors, among them my
fourteen-year-old sister.

In those climactic days of the war, close relatives and
neighbors turned against us. The handful of villagers who had
the courage to speak up for my mother at her trial and who
tried to console my sister after her execution were not the ones
we had always considered our friends. In some cases her
defenders were well-known Communists, but they trans-
cended political beliefs and fear for their own safety because
they refused to speak against innocent people. But for the
most part, our neighbors avoided or betrayed my mother in
hope of improving their own chance of survival.

As I drove toward the central square, I kept hearing over
the sound of the car's engine a phrase that my sister and my
father had repeated a hundred times: '*Tin fagane i horiani*' –
'It was the villagers who devoured her.' To my family, the
Communist guerrillas like Katis were an impersonal act of

25

God, unleashed on our village by war, like a plague. It was our neighbors whom they held responsible for my mother's death; the villagers who whispered secrets to the security police and testified against her at the trial.

This was something I had to resolve: perhaps the villagers really were more culpable for her death than the men who passed the sentence and fired the bullets. I wondered if something about my mother incited the people of Lia to offer her up like a sacrificial lamb. Or perhaps the villagers had only been manipulated by the guerrillas, who exploited their moral weaknesses, petty jealousies and fears, because the guerrillas wanted my mother killed for some political purpose. What was the real reason that she was executed?

The beauty of the village all around me, the familiar tang of wood smoke and the music of goats' bells in the air, seemed to refute my suspicions. I passed through the square and stopped near the western boundary of Lia. I left the car at the foot of the path that led up the mountain toward our old neighborhood and the Church of St. Demetrios.

It was August 6, the feast day of the Transfiguration, one of the three times a year when the church was used for a service. As I climbed, I saw elderly worshipers approaching from all directions.

The sun was high, but inside, the church was dark and filled with shadowy figures in somber clothing. The gnarled faces and the gold of the ancient carved altar screen shone in the candlelight. I stood for a while outside the church door beneath the cypress trees, listening to the priest's chanting and the indistinct voice of an old woman who was seated cross-legged next to a recent grave, carrying on a conversation with the dead.

The door to the ossuary stood open, but I didn't go in. I knew that none of the answers I needed would be found inside the wooden box that held my mother's bones. She was frozen in my memory as I had known her from the perspective of a child; a source of unfailing strength, security and love. But in delving into the events of her last years, I had begun to glimpse a more complex and ambiguous person, a troubled peasant woman who tried to live by the rules of the primitive

26

mountain culture that constituted her world, and when they failed her, defied them.

My mother had scarcely gone to school; she put on the kerchief at the age of eleven like every other village girl, and from that moment never dared to speak to a man until the day she was handed over as a bride to a husband she didn't know. The politics that shattered her universe during the last decade of her life made no sense to her. She never traveled farther than the provincial capital. Her husband lived half a world away in a country that she longed to see but knew nothing about, although she was branded, because of her marriage, with the name 'the Amerikana' and all the prejudices that came with it.

My mother's world was ruled by magic, superstition, ghosts and devils to be invoked or appeased by holy oil and charms, but these were not enough to save her and her children from the war that swept into their mountains. When she saw that living by the strict village canons was not enough, when it became a choice between losing her children or her life, she discovered a strength that I now know is given to few.

Before my search was over I had to find my mother, to see her with the eyes of an adult, and to uncover her secret feelings about the world that caged her. I had to do this in order to learn how she wanted me to deal with her murderers. I had to communicate with her across the chasm of death to discover if, as she climbed toward that ravine to her execution, she was Antigone, meeting death with resignation because she had purposely defied a human command to honor a higher law of the heart, or if she was Hecuba, crying out for vengeance. What did she want me to do?

Interrupting my reflections, over the priest's singsong and the chanter's responses, rose a mechanical roar that I had never heard as a boy. It came from above, in the direction of my house. I started up the path leading from the churchyard.

I found the house a complete ruin, overgrown with ivy, deserted except for lizards; the roof and floor collapsing into the cellar. I discovered the source of the noise: it was a bulldozer at work, extending a horizontal path for a road across the lower boundary of what had been our garden. The low stone wall around the property had disappeared and the remaining walls of the house stared with empty eye sockets at the monster shaving away another great swath of red soil, perilously close to the lone mulberry tree that had been our landmark.

Although the house was a grim monument to the killings that had taken place there, I realized that I wanted that mulberry tree to survive. I motioned to the bulldozer operator to stop and then went over and asked him to cut around the tree, that piece of my childhood.

As the machine set to work again, I walked over to the house, looking down for the first time into the exposed cellar where my mother and so many others had spent their last hours.

The mulberry tree and all the pleasant memories clinging to its branches made me understand that my search would give me as much joy as sorrow. This was the house where Eleni Gatzoyiannis suffered and died, but it was also the house where she was brought as a nineteen-year-old bride, where my sisters and I were born, where we played and fought. The terrace was still there, where my mother would bring her hand-turned sewing machine outside on warm evenings to take advantage of the breeze and look up occasionally from her work to gaze at the valley stretching away below her. We were hungry there but we were happy, too, and our memories would outlast the house. 'We have eaten bread and salt together,' the Greeks say, meaning that we have shared the most elemental foods, suffered the same hardships, known the same joys, and that nothing can ever break that bond that ties us together, not even death.

I would have to rebuild this house, stone by stone, in my imagination, before I could face Katis and the others. I would have to re-create her lost village – a mysterious world as faded now as a tapestry from the Middle Ages, with only a face visible here, an arm there. When I had re-made it, weaving it from the memories of scores of different witnesses, then I would have reached the end of my search for my mother. I would understand what it was that she wanted me to know as she left our gate for the last time to climb to the ravine.

The witnesses to my mother's fate were a generation of leaves scattered by winds of war all over the world – Canada, the United States, England, Hungary, Poland, Czechoslovakia and every corner of Greece. I had to track them down and use all my professional skill to get the truth from them.

In the course of the journey I would find not only my mother but myself. By re-creating the last decade of her life, I would learn how much I had been formed by that now-dead world. Whatever I decided I must do to my mother's killers, was I capable of it? Others in my place were unable to find the will to claim vengeance. Did I have that will?

When I had uncovered the answer, which lay buried somewhere in the ruins of my house and my childhood, then I would be ready to confront Katis and the rest. But my search had to begin with the discovery of a dead woman and the child who walked out of this mountain over three decades ago. I had to find the story not only of my mother's death, but of her life as well. And to do that I had to go back to the autumn of 1940.

PART TWO

WAR

When buffalo battle in the marsh,
it's the frogs that pay.

— GREEK PROVERB

CHAPTER ONE

In Rome, Benito Mussolini was sulking. The dictator complained to his son-in-law, who was also his foreign minister, that Hitler was humiliating him by the conquests he was making in... standing him. It was not until a few days after the seizure of Romania that Hitler got around to writing him. "Let about it" Italy keeps occupying me with Greece no more ... Mussolini said. His son-in-law. "This time I shall pay him back in his own coin. By small times finds he news spaper that I have occupied Greece"

As the social elite of Athens moved among tables.

In the mountain villages of northern Greece, life moves to the slow rhythm of the seasons, punctuated now and then by the feast days of the saints. October culminates in the feast of St. Demetrios, which marks the end of summer, when the fattened goats and sheep are brought down from the mountain pastures and shut up in the basements under the stone houses for the winter.

But sometimes the saint comes clothed in a brief reprise of fine weather, the 'little summer of St. Demetrios': a last blaze of gold before winter locks the villagers into their huts. October of 1940 brought such a respite to the hamlets of the Mourgana mountain range, along the northwestern border of Greece, and the villagers took advantage of it to store the autumn harvest: children gathered walnuts, men sorted over the amber and amethyst grapes for the wine making, women strung garlands of dried beans, peppers, onions and garlic to hang from the rafters. The sunshine splashed the mountainside with butter-yellow autumn crocuses, gilded beech trees rustled with ghosts, and everywhere, pomegranates, squashes and pumpkins glowed like miniature suns.

In Athens the social season was in full swing and the Italian ambassador there, Count Emilio Grazzi, was planning an elegant midnight reception at the legation after a special performance of *Madame Butterfly* to honor the visiting son of Giacomo Puccini. The Greek royal family and the prime minister, Ioannis Metaxas, were expected to attend the opera.

In Rome, Benito Mussolini was sulking. The dictator complained to his son-in-law, who was also his foreign minister, that Hitler was humiliating him by the conquests he was making in Europe without even consulting him. It was not until three days after the seizure of Rumania that Hitler got around to writing his ally about it. 'Hitler keeps confronting me with *faits accomplis*,' Mussolini ranted to his son-in-law. 'This time I shall pay him back in his own coin; he shall learn from the newspapers that I have occupied Greece!'

As the social elite of Athens moved among tables decorated with intertwined Greek and Italian flags and banners reading 'Long Live Greece,' a coded telegram from Rome began to arrive at the legation. The Italian staff members deciphering it stopped now and then, their faces pale, to mingle with the Greek guests so that nothing would seem amiss. The message was an ultimatum which the horrified Grazzi was to deliver to Metaxas, demanding that Italian troops be allowed to occupy his country.

At three o'clock on the morning of October 28 Grazzi woke up Metaxas, who received him in dressing gown and slippers, and handed him the ultimatum. Mussolini had given the Greek prime minister three hours to reply. The two men spoke in French. Metaxas' hands trembled as he looked up from the paper and rejected the ultimatum with the words '*Alors, c'est la guerre!*'

Popular legend has condensed Metaxas' refusal into the single word '*Ochi!*' ('No!'), which has become a Greek battle cry that blooms defiantly every October 28 on walls throughout Greece. It is permanently emblazoned in ten-foot-high letters of white stone on a peak of the Mourgana range above a small village called Lia in the northwestern corner of Greece, just below the Albanian border.

But Mussolini didn't wait for Metaxas' reply. Before the ultimatum had expired, five heavily armed divisions of Italian soldiers began moving from Albania over the border into Greece.

34

'THE AMERIKANA'

IT WAS DURING the little summer of St. Demetrios in 1940 that Eleni Gatzoyiannis attended the disinterment of the bones of her mother-in-law, Fotini Gatzoyiannis, in the village of Lia.

Eleni had lived with Fotini for almost ten years, from the day she was brought to the woman's home as a nineteen-year-old bride by Fotini's fifth son, Christos. She had held her mother-in-law's hand when she died, worn out by eighty-four years of life and the birth of nine children. Five years had passed since Fotini's death and it would not be easy to watch the bones taken from the earth, washed and stored in the church ossuary, but in Greece, even in a mountain village of 787 people, grave plots were few and could be occupied only temporarily.

When Eleni led her children to the burial ground behind the Church of St. Demetrios, in the shade of the giant cypress trees, the professional mourners were already there, clucking sociably like a flock of crows. Soon they would be ripping the bosoms of their dresses, throwing dirt on their heads and weaving the story-songs of Fotini's life into dirges that could raise the hair on a heathen's scalp.

Father Zisis, in his black robes and flat-topped hat, joined the mourners, making the sign of the cross. Eleni picked up a shovel, for it was the duty of the closest relatives to dig up the corpse. Her brother-in-law Foto Gatzoyiannis did the same. He was the only one of Fotini's children who was not dead or too far away to return.

Eleni handed the baby boy, Nikola, to her eldest daughter, Olga, twelve, who balanced him on one hip, clearly bored

35

with the ceremony. Alexandra, eight, called by the village nickname 'Kanta,' had refused to come at all. Kanta was a nervous, superstitious child who hid in the outhouse, hands pressed over her ears, at the first death knell of the church bells. The sight of a corpse would leave her screaming in her sleep for weeks.

Fat, flaxen-haired Glykeria, six, was the opposite, pushing to the front, eager for the first glimpse of her grandmother's skeleton. Whether it was a wedding, a funeral, a traveling shadow-puppet show or the mating of the family ram to a neighbor's ewe, Glykeria, with her impish eyes and angel hair, was always in the front row. In her excitement, Glykeria had forgotten to look after her little sister, Fotini, two, who now sat deserted on a grave nearby where she was screwing up her face for a wail of misery.

The survivors began to dig and the mourners lifted their keening voices, inspiring one another to ever greater displays of poetry and grief:

> Where are you, *Kyria* Fotini,
>   where did the worms lead you?
> Leaving your sons and their brides
>   to weep black tears of sorrow.
> The silver has lost its shine,
>   the flute has forgotten its melody.

Eleni took her turn at the shovel and soon the black shroud wrapped around Fotini's body became visible. They cleared away the last of the dirt with their hands.

The mourners held their breath. Sometimes the corpse would not be fully decomposed, which meant that the soul was not at peace, but rather a wandering vampire, a *vrykolakas*. This would require an exorcism by the priest while the remains were carried three times around the church and then reburied for another few years.

But all was well with Fotini. There was a pungent, mossy odor of decay as the black shroud was lifted off. As so often happened, the collapsed features lay exposed, complete as in life for one last instant before they crumbled into dust. The priest's voice rose in the *trisagion* – the thrice-holy hymn: 'Holy God, Holy Almighty, Holy Immortal, have mercy on us.' The skeleton lay face up, its arms crossed over the icon, the gold cross lying on the breastbone, the coins to pay the journey to Hades long ago fallen into the eye sockets. Then the women lifted the bones into a copper ewer, where they were washed and sprinkled with red wine, in preparation for reinterment in the small wooden box less than two feet square with crude lettering on the side: 'Fotini Nik. Gatzoyiannis, 1851–1935.'

After the bones were washed clean of dirt and bits of clinging flesh, then piled into the box, the skull was turned upside down like a chalice and red wine poured into the cranium. This cup was passed from hand to hand so that whoever wished could drink from it to erase any curse that Fotini might have spoken against him in life.

Foto, fiercely mustached and bold as always, held his mother's skull for a moment, then drank deeply. He had been her sorrow, jailed for murder, a poor provider for his ten children, a notorious adventurer and braggart, and he had good reason to drink, for fear that she might have died with some uncanceled curse against him. Alexo, Foto's tall, open-faced second wife, dutifully took a swallow after him. The skull passed farther around the circle, and the wails of the mourners rose in pitch.

Eleni scarcely heard them. She was thinking of the round, smile-creased face of her mother-in-law, an illiterate, wide-hipped village woman who never complained despite the gall life had served her: four of her nine children dead before adulthood, plundering and burnings by the Turks, nagging hunger and deaths that came swiftly as a summer storm. The evil eye had carried away her beautiful daughter Vasiliki when she was sixteen. Her fourth son, Constantine, was a deaf-mute. Her tinker husband Nikola was felled by an attack of pneumonia and left her a widow, pregnant with a little girl who died before they could baptize her.

But Fotini had managed to rear five sons who helped support the family after her husband's death. Her favorite, Christos, walked out of the village at seventeen, wearing the fez of the Turkish occupiers, to find the golden land of

America. He returned fourteen years later, a bald, prosperous foreigner in a straw hat and pin-striped suit, so changed that Fotini didn't recognize him until she bent down his head and found the scar from the time he fell out of the walnut tree.

The arrival of such a bachelor – thirty-one years old, magnificently dressed, the owner of a flourishing business in America – set the local matchmakers atwitter. Christos' family pressed him to choose a wife from among the village girls before he returned to the other side. The one most often recommended by his relatives was Eleni Haidis, seventeen, the second daughter of Lia's most prosperous miller. She was described as being of irreproachable character, with the cleverness of her wily father but the gentle nature of her mother. And she was so beautiful, Christos' elder brother Foto told him, that as she walked down to her father's mill, the villagers, looking at her, whispered, 'God give me two more eyes!'

Christos took the path to church that passed by the miller's property, and there he saw Eleni working in the garden. He recalls how the sun seemed to shine from her golden brown hair and poppy-red cheeks, but he insists that it was the modesty of her demeanor and her downcast eyes that attracted him.

Kitso Haidis was not one to confide in his daughter, but when Foto Gatzoyiannis came to call, the girl suspected what was in the air. She had seen Christos Gatzoyiannis going to church in his fine foreign clothes. He was not handsome and he was fourteen years older than she, but unlike her tyrannical father, whose house she could leave only as a bride, this man with the soft white hands and fine manners was rumored to be kind and generous.

Naturally, her father did not consult her on what qualities she would like to see in a husband, nor did Eleni exchange a single word with Christos, but she was not unhappy when he arrived at the house one evening and her father directed her to bring the customary coffee. She didn't even look at the stranger's face as he took the cup and in its place on the tray put an American $20 bill, saying, 'This is for you.' She knew her future had been decided.

After the engagement was sealed with food, wine and a fusillade of bullets fired at the heavens to notify the neighbors, Eleni was allowed to converse with her fiancé on the occasions when she walked with her parents to church. Christos strutted at her side in his straw boater, his starched white shirtfront radiant in the sun, and told her that when he returned to Lia in a year or so, he would pay for the finest wedding the village had ever seen. He would bring cloth from America and hire the best dressmaker in the region to make the wedding costumes. Eleni spoke little; she didn't know what to say to such a sophisticated man, but she loved listening to his stories of the wonders of the world beyond the mountains. He seemed so different from the rough, sun-blackened village youths. After Christos left the village, as she put the finishing touches on her dowry, Eleni reflected that she had been incredibly fortunate in her father's choice of a husband.

True to his word, Christos returned in November of 1926, and on the last permissible day before the Christmas Lent, their wedding crowns were exchanged in the Church of St. Demetrios.

In a tearful conversation before the wedding Eleni told Christos that she would not be able to go to America with him. Her mother, whom she had always tried to protect from her father's temper, insisted she would commit suicide on the day Eleni left the village. Christos was disappointed, but he was not angry or surprised. He knew that ties of blood superseded all others in village society. A woman was judged by her sense of duty to her aged parents almost as much as her dedication to her children. Eleni's parents had no male heirs, and her elder sister, Nitsa, had not only married into a poor family but seemed unable to provide any grandchildren. After Eleni's brilliant marriage, her parents' welfare would be her responsibility.

Christos decided to spend at least a year in the village, setting up his bride in his mother's household before returning to America. It was hardly unusual in the mountain villages for a husband and wife to spend much of their lives apart. The majority of men in Lia were itinerant tinkers and coopers who traveled far from their homes for most of the year, leaving their wives to farm the fields, rear the children, care for their parents and look after things until their husbands returned for a well-deserved period of idleness, which they spent exchanging stories in the *cafenions,* the village coffeehouses. The Greek emigrants who settled in foreign lands and supported their families by regularly mailed checks had only extended the traditional periods of absence. Christos was glad that Eleni would be there to look after his mother as well as her own parents.

He installed his bride in Fotini's two-room house and brought workmen from Konitsa, a day's walk to the northeast, to add on two more rooms, making it the largest dwelling in Lia. Before Christos left for America in 1928, Eleni gave birth to a girl. Two extended visits home over the next ten years produced four more children.

Now, with her mother-in-law dead, Eleni lived alone with the children, dependent on the checks her husband sent every month. She knew if that life line was cut and her husband disappeared into the golden land, forgetting his Greek family, as sometimes happened, their four young daughters would become beggars, with no chance of dowries, and her son, Nikola, would never see his father's face.

At the thought of Nikola, Eleni's eyes filled. She and Fotini had prayed so often for a boy. They lit daily candles, hid garlic under the pillow during Christos' visits from America, bought malewort from the witches and brewed it into bitter tea. But each visit produced another girl. Though villagers began to mock Eleni, her mother-in-law never reproached her. She took each tiny girl in her hands and crooned songs of wedding veils, dowry chests and golden rings. The villagers whispered that Eleni could make only girls, but Fotini comforted her that it was God's compensation for her own three girls who had died. These granddaughters, Olga, Kanta and Glykeria, would be her solace, Fotini said. She sat up with Eleni through their bouts of croup and whooping cough, rubbing their gums with home-distilled *tsipouro* when they fussed with teething pains. The old woman and the young bride had been bound together by their shared struggles, and Eleni grieved that

Fotini hadn't lived to see the fourth girl, who bore her name, or the boy, who had finally answered their prayers.

The skull was passed to Eleni with the dregs of wine inside. Tonight it would rest at the left of the altar of St. Demetrios, and tomorrow it would be placed in the ossuary below the church, where more than two centuries of villagers' bones lined the walls.

Eleni passed the Church of St. Demetrios every day and usually stopped to light a candle. Many times she had seen the basement cavern, where the wall of bones, the old ones stacked like kindling, glowed with a pale-yellow phosphorescence in the darkness. They did not frighten her; it was the natural epilogue. She felt comfortable surrounded by the hundreds of skulls, empty now of all love, sorrow, foolishness or wisdom, anonymously awaiting Judgment Day.

Eleni held the skull in her hands for a moment, feeling the firmness, the lightness of it, and decided not to drink. She had no fear that Fotini had left a curse against her. The woman had bequeathed her nothing but blessings; most of all the example of her own life.

Three days after the ceremony, the spurious summer of St. Demetrios was gone and a gray rain drummed on the slate roof of Eleni's house in the highest part of Lia, Perivoli – the orchard.

The Perivoli was near the top of a triangle of green vegetation that spilled down the cleft between two naked granite peaks of the Mourgana mountain range, bisected by a deep ravine. Lia's 150 crude stone huts clung precariously to each side of the ravine. The neighborhood of the Perivoli covered the western bank, and the houses to the east, surrounding the village square with its giant plane tree, Holy Trinity Church and the schoolhouse, made up the middle village. As the land sloped more gently toward the foothills, scattered houses flanked the ancient Church of the Virgin to form the lower village. Below, the fertile triangle of holm oak, scrub pine and underbrush spread down into soft ripples of foothills, then rose ten miles in the distance to splash up against the other rim of the bowl of mountains that circumscribed the

41

villagers' universe; vast and complete, jagged mountain peaks piercing whipped-cream castles of cumulus clouds to the south, mists smoking up from the valley floor far below.

It was an isolated and magnificent world that every villager saw from his window; a constant reminder of the overwhelming power of nature and the insignificance of man. To his back, high above him, loomed the Mourgana range, its summit forming the border with Albania and closing the northern edge of his horizon. Lia stood at the center of the range, huddled below two heights like sentinels: the Prophet Elias, named for the tiny stone chapel on its tip, and a truncated peak called Kastro because it bore a crumbling acropolis, the fortress of the Hellenistic community that lived there three hundred years before Christ. To the east and west, tucked into folds of the mountain and out of sight of Lia, were ten more villages strung along the timberline, without even a road to connect them to the rest of the world. To the south, across the bowl of foothills, rose the gray bulks of mountains in the distance, like sounding whales: the double peak of Velouna on the east, named for its resemblance to an archer's bow, flowed into the dark spine of the Great Ridge, which terminated in the smooth, scrub-covered hump of Plokista and the arched back of Taverra. Closing the rim to the west were smaller mountains, where the sun disappeared into the distant depths of Albania.

The landscape in which the villagers of Lia spun out their lives like spiders clinging to a wall affected them in ways that could never be understood by those who walk on flat land. Mankind seemed an afterthought of the gods who created such mountains. The relentless cycles of the seasons, rain and snow, sunlight and darkness, ruled the daily lives of the peasants who worked with one goal: to wrest food out of the stony mountain slopes, digging terraced steps on which to plant their crops.

Cut off from the rest of the world and driven together by the need to survive, the peasants of the Mourgana villages had no privacy. Every house looked into the one below. Voices traveled for miles through the thin air, and wherever they walked on the mountain paths, they felt eyes watching them from above or below or from a neighboring cliff. Despite the vastness of their universe under the sky, the villagers knew that everything they did was observed and overheard.

These mountains have always bred stern, ascetic people, cut off from the wealth of the seas and the temperate climate of the flatlands, so isolated that for centuries no strangers had diluted their Dorian blood or adulterated their fair complexion and classical features. The isolation and cruelty of the landscape, especially in winter, made the peasants short-tempered and sometimes drove them mad, but those who managed to escape from these mountains would never find any other place as beautiful.

On October 28, 1940, the relentless rain had driven most of the inhabitants of Lia indoors. In the Gatzoyiannis kitchen, close to the fire, eight-year-old Kanta combed Glykeria's maize-yellow hair for lice and plaited it into two long braids. Olga was bent over a shift she was embroidering for her dowry and two-year-old Fotini was being coaxed out of a fit of whining with a doll that Eleni was weaving from the leaves of the Judas tree. Nikola was asleep in his carved wooden cradle.

Over the sound of the rain tumbled a great roll of thunder that stopped Glykeria's complaining in mid-sentence and made everyone look up. Eleni stepped out on the flagstone veranda, which commanded a view straight down the mountain. To the south, in the direction of Povla, four miles away, she saw red flashes of light on the horizon.

Suddenly there was a shriek from the house of Lambrini Fafouti below. Her daughter had just married, only to have the groom drafted into the army amid rumors of war with Italy. Now Lambrini ran through the rain, her black shawl flapping, her kerchief askew, screeching, 'My brave little Tsavo! Those are his cannons! He's shooting at the Italians! It's war!'

Eleni turned at the threshold and looked at her silent children. 'She's right!' she told them. 'It's not thunder; it's artillery! The war has begun!'

Eleni had never seen war, but from earliest childhood she had been told of the glorious deeds of the War of

Independence against the Turks in 1821: white-skirted *palikaria* with sweeping mustaches embracing danger with defiant songs and flashing eyes under the banner of 'Freedom or Death.' Only fifty miles to the south, the women of Souli had hurled their children over the cliff at Zalongo and then, hands clasped as at a wedding feast, danced off the precipice, choosing death on the rocks below rather than dishonor at the hands of the Turks. Now war had come to Eleni's doorstep, heralded by the screeching of Lambrini Fafouti.

Kanta wasn't sure what 'artillery' meant, but the way her mother said it made her sit down suddenly, dropping the braid she was plaiting. Glykeria hopped with excitement. Eleni saw fear on the face of her eldest daughter, Olga, and understood what she was thinking. It may have been over a hundred years since the Souliote women died, but in a Greek village in 1940, it was still incumbent on a woman to choose death before dishonor.

The grumbling of the guns rose, and Eleni turned to look at the photograph of Christos, in its ornate brass frame on the mantelpiece, wondering what he would tell her to do: stay and protect the house or take the children and flee. But he only gazed back from behind his gold-rimmed glasses with a complacent smile, his bow tie rakish beneath his double chin; the image of a man of substance who lived in a sane and logical world. There was no way he could advise her. Though Eleni couldn't know how accurate her premonition was, she sensed that this war had just cut her last link to her husband.

Eleni was trying to calm the girls when her sister, Nitsa, puffed through the gate like a squat black tugboat, her pair of goats and her thin, worried-looking husband struggling in her wake.

The hand-turned bell on the gate jangled again and Eleni opened it to find her gaunt, hawk-faced mother, who was called Megali ('the Old One') as a sign of respect, her black kerchief covered by a hooded oil cloth. Behind her was Eleni's father, the white-haired miller Kitso Haidis, holding their sleeping rugs.

Everyone shouted and argued about what to do, stopping now and then to listen to the sounds of the distant battle.

44

Finally the ten of them arranged themselves to sleep on the floor around the kitchen fireplace, Nitsa and Megali closest to the warmth, as the guns coughed fitfully through the night.

Three days of indecision ended when a shepherd boy arrived at Eleni's house with the news that the Italians were advancing. The villagers were going to have to flee.

As Megali and Nitsa loaded the donkey with bread and cheese, Eleni walked through the four rooms of her house, touching the luxuries that Christos had brought her over the years, the wonders of the village. The Singer sewing machine and the gramophone with its trumpet speaker were too big to hide. They'd be the first things the Italians would take. But smaller objects could be concealed in the hollow oak tree out back. She gathered the golden pitcher from Constantinople, etched with minarets and gardens, and the iridescent Turkish pillow. From her wooden dowry chest Eleni took the silver jewelry; the huge belt buckle and breast ornaments. Last of all she picked up Christos' brass-framed photograph and the sandal-wood box that held his letters.

Outside her gate the narrow mountain path toward the caves above was already a flood of jostling, shouting families with their goats and lambs and the donkeys carrying great pots of food and the rainbow-colored tufted sleeping rugs called *velenzes*. The brown-limbed children laughed, enjoying the outing, while the adults cursed the others' slowness and pleaded with donkeys and grandparents to hurry up. Gunfire reverberated through the mountainside.

Nitsa's husband Andreas took two-year-old Fotini on his back like a monkey. Nitsa lashed the baby Nikola into his round-bottomed wooden cradle and tied it onto Eleni's back, throwing a rope across her throat, around the cradle and then fastening the rope to the first loop on her chest.

Eleni didn't look back at her house as she plunged into the exodus leading up the mountain. At the spring above the house, where she went daily to fill the water barrels, another stream of refugees, coming from the village center, joined the torrent. It was hard not to get elbowed off the path and over the cliff as they pushed up past the mill of Tassi Mitros.

45

The tide of humanity surged toward the series of small caves hidden in the rock above the Perivoli, near the top of the ravine: the women moving like giant black land snails, their backs bent under cradles, bundles of pots and sleeping rugs. The mountain dwellers had taken refuge from invaders in these caves since the dawn of time: Dorians, Illyrians, Romans, Goths, Franks, Bulgars, Slavs, Turks, all had swept over the Mourgana spine, looting and killing. With an atavistic sense of self-preservation, the children of those who had survived now returned to the same spot.

Weary from the weight of the cradle, Eleni led her brood into one of the overcrowded caves, full of the smell of bodies; people wedged too close together to lie down, their backs against the sweating stone walls. The daylight slowly faded and the cavern became claustrophobic with the breath of the fugitives.

Eleni looked at the dim faces of the women around her, incongruous away from their neat stone houses, well-swept dirt floors and whitewashed walls, frightened at being plucked from their carefully regulated existence and driven here like leaves in a storm.

From the moment a female was born in the village, her life was prescribed and ordered by centuries of custom, so deeply etched that no one stopped to question, for a woman was as innocent of self-determination as a member of a beehive. If she survived the first forty days of her life, a girl child was taken to the church to be blessed. But she was carried by the priest no farther than the narthex, while an infant boy was shown to God before the Holy Gates leading to the altar.

'May you have male children and female goats' the villagers always toasted one another, raising glasses of *tsipouro*. A female child was a liability, burdening her parents with the need to guard her virtue and accumulate a dowry until she was taken as a bride to live out her life working for her husband's family.

A girl had to put on the kerchief at age eleven so that no wayward curl could invite the lust of a stranger, nor could she utter even a 'Good morning' to a male outside the family. Only twice a year was an unmarried girl seen in public, sitting among the women at the Christmas and Easter liturgies. The rest of the time, walls of stone and the vigilance of father and brother surrounded her as she learned a woman's duties: tending the animals and the fields, cutting firewood, cooking and cleaning, sewing, spinning and embroidering for her dowry. Virtue and beauty counted little if the dowry was too small. If a match was successfully concluded by the go-betweens, after many secret midnight meetings, the bride was carried off to the household of a man she had never spoken to, whose face she might never have seen, to spend the wedding night sleeping not beside the groom, but with his mother, to symbolize her subjugation. Her sexual initiation would be terrifying, sometimes accomplished by force under the gaze of the animals in the basement stable – with four generations in a two-room house, there was little chance for privacy.

Some unfortunate brides were sent home before the wedding guests had left when proof of their virginity had not been convincing. And for a tainted village girl there was no alternative but life as a spinster, going from door to door doing chores in exchange for food.

A woman named Vasilo from the neighboring village of Babouri had been seduced by her mother's brother while the family slept, all crowded together on their pallets under shared sleeping rugs. Only fourteen, as ignorant of sex as any village girl, she didn't realize what had happened until her belly started to swell under the shapeless black homespun. The baby was born by the side of the road and left there as the mother, bleeding and hysterical, ran screaming into the woods where she was finally found. The uncle was never seen again. The villagers composed a humorous song about her, suggesting that she throw herself off a cliff, but she was now huddled in the cave, her face still a child's, one of the shadow women who had broken the village code.

Even an unblemished bride might find herself deserted. There were many temptations for the tinkers and coopers, who traveled for six months at a time. The traditional journeys were becoming more extended, some men going to Egypt and South Africa; some, like Christos, as far as America, returning now and then to father a child. Some never came back. Anastasia Yakou, Eleni's neighbor in the Perivoli, had lost her husband to the flesh-pots of Kalambaka when her two girls were babies. Eleni often hired Anastasia to help with housekeeping and planting chores, and the sight of the ragged Yakou girls was a constant reminder of what would happen if Christos forgot them.

But no matter how far the men went and for how long, it was the responsibility of the women, their roots deep in the earth, to protect the family name and the village traditions. Anastasia Lollis had married in 1911 and lived with her husband only a year before he sailed off to America, where, returnees said, he had acquired a wife and family in Chicago. But Anastasia still waited for his return and would continue to wait for more than seventy years.

Women went into labor and gave birth alone, or tried to abort themselves with herbs, wooden stakes and heavy rocks if a pregnancy occurred during a husband's long absence. Even if the seducer was a bride's father-in-law, the ruler of her household, she would get no mercy. Many women died in labor despite the best efforts of the village midwife. Eudoxia Kolokithi had labored for five days, exhausting eighteen neighborhood women who took turns holding her upright in their embrace while the midwife worked, but in the end they took the baby out of her in pieces as with a calf-bound cow.

Eleni's sister-in-law Chryso, first wife of Foto Gatzoyiannis, captured the eye of a Turkish peddler with her beauty in 1909. When Foto heard of the Turk's offer of a gold sovereign for a night with his wife, he shot the peddler dead. But Foto lost his young wife early, when she died trying to give birth to twins, who were buried in the same shroud as their mother. Unlucky in death as in life, Chryso was found turned when they dug her up, convincing the villagers that she had awakened in the grave. Foto was not one to mourn, though. He had already married Alexo, who would give him nine more children.

Chryso's death, Anastasia's abandonment, Vasilo's disgrace were all threads in the tapestry of village life, but for Eleni it was her mother-in-law, Fotini, who wove the threads

48

into a pattern so that she could understand the proper behavior for a woman who was *taxidimeni* – the property of an absent husband.

A village wife was constantly reminded that she was her husband's property. From her wedding day the villagers addressed her by the feminine form of her husband's name: 'Nikolina' (Nikola's woman), 'Tassina' (Tasso's woman), 'Papadia' (the priest's woman), so that everyone nearly forgot their real first names. Eleni's friends sometimes called her 'Kitchina' (Christos' woman), but the village had given her another name, which would follow her to her death: 'the Amerikana' – the American's woman.

Because she was *taxidimeni*, Fotini made Eleni understand, she must wear clothes of somber colors and be more formal in her dealings with men than other village women. Eleni was an intelligent pupil, and she understood the perils of flouting the village code. She chose her friends among women much older than herself, dressed her daughters in the most conservative way, watched their behavior with unfailing vigilance and took Olga out of school even before the traditional age of eleven.

In a world as closed as Lia, tradition was the scaffolding that supported the village. One betrayal of the moral code and the entire structure could come tumbling down on everyone's head. Thanks to the example of her mother-in-law, Eleni had become one of the most admired women in Lia, despite the dangers posed by an absent husband and her own fine-boned beauty. But since Fotini's death, the village had begun to tighten around her like a prison. There was no man to advise her or share the burdens, no mother-in-law to protect her from the constant scrutiny of the villagers, eager to find a flaw in the behavior of the prosperous 'Amerikana.'

When the cave had been in darkness for hours, the rain became heavier, and the dampness seeped into the fugitives' marrow. After midnight Nikola began to cry and Eleni put him to her breast, but he refused to nurse and turned his head away, wailing louder. A dozen voices shushed him and threatened his mother with expulsion from the cave. Eleni dug a box of matches from her apron. She lit one to look at the

49

baby's face. Instantly he stopped crying, the flame reflected in his chestnut eyes, but when it sputtered out, he began again.

'He wants light!' Eleni exclaimed, and begged the invisible women around her, if they had candles, to help. A few inched forward, holding tapers, and the boy began to nurse as grotesque shadows flickered over the cavern's walls. Eleni looked around at familiar faces, distorted by their anger at the baby's crying, made monstrous by the eerie light.

She felt her separateness like an ache. From birth she had been one of them, but now, more than ever, she sensed the otherness signified by the name 'Amerikana.' Since Fotini's death she had thought of escaping. The desire began at the same time as her illness. She had tried to explain it to Christos, but he hadn't understood.

The burning started in her lower abdomen, flaring up whenever she ate, making her vomit, so that she couldn't stand the sight of food. 'My navel has unraveled,' she would say in the village phrase, as the women worked over her.

It was Eleni's sister who finally called Christos back from America in the winter of 1937. Nitsa secretly made nine-year-old Olga write the letter because like most village women, she was illiterate. They had done everything they could, Nitsa told him: the ceremony of tying up the navel, exorcisms, leeches, *venduses* – the glasses upturned on the belly with a candle burning inside to draw out the evil humors. They had even sent to Povla and Lista for doctors. But nothing helped. Eleni was becoming thinner every day and couldn't eat or stand up. 'You can always find America again,' Nitsa dictated to the little girl. 'But if you lose your wife, you're not going to find her again. And what are you going to do with your daughters?'

The daughters – that was the burden that no one wanted if Eleni should die.

The villagers knew perfectly well what was wrong with the Amerikana. It was the evil eye, which was attracted by envy. No woman in the village was more envied than Eleni Gatzoyiannis.

Eleni herself knew the risk of jealousy, and always tried to be more generous and discreet than any woman in Lia. She had been envied even when she was simply the second daughter of Kitso Haidis, the millwright. 'Such red cheeks, such blue eyes!' the older women would say as she passed, spitting at the evil eye.

After Eleni was selected as a bride by Christos and moved into the four-room house, complete with a brass-ornamented arched gate, a separate entrance for the animals, a hand-turned food grinder and an outdoor shower made of barrels, then there was too much temptation for the evil eye. No wonder each of Christos' visits had produced only girls, the villagers whispered, and no wonder the fine Amerikana now lay dying, her cheeks the color of Good Friday candles.

When Christos received Nitsa's letter, he had just taken on a new partner in his produce business, a native of the village next to Lia, and it worried him to leave the truck in the hands of the profligate Nassios Economou, who pursued young girls with the passion Christos reserved for fine clothes. But when he learned of Eleni's illness, Christos set out at once for Greece. He was a responsible man, devoted to his young wife, and he couldn't allow her to die. He prepared himself for the mission with characteristic thoroughness and efficiency. They were killing her with village superstition and he would save her with American know-how.

Christos prided himself on being a real American. From the third-class deck of the liner *Themistocles* steaming out of Corfu in 1910, he had thrown his red fez and white baggy breeches into the waves and begun to study the English dictionary in his pocket. He quickly assimilated the American virtues of cleanliness, honesty and industry. He worked two jobs, in a factory by day and a bowling alley at night, making $9 or $10 a week, until he had enough to buy a half-interest in a vegetable wagon.

Christos would go hungry to buy the finest suits available in Worcester, Massachusetts. On his rounds as a tinker's apprentice in Greece, it was the sight of two stylishly dressed Greek-Americans that had first put America in his mind. Although he was short and portly, Christos always dressed so well that people took him for a professional man rather than a vegetable peddler.

On one of the first warm days of June 1937, the villagers of Lia were drawn from their houses by the sound of bells: not the deep knell of the church's *cabana* or the clanging of the lead goats, but the special sound of the mule train belonging to the Turk, Mourtos Gajelis, who brought people from the outside world after the end of the road deposited them in Filiates. The few Greeks of the Mourgana who had made their fortune abroad and returned for a visit had dubbed his five mules 'the American Express.'

Throughout the northern province of Epiros, there were still large communities of Moslems like Mourtos, remnants of the Turks who had ruled until 1913 and of the Greeks who had been converted to Islam, who were called 'Chams,' after the region they came from, Chamouria. Although they were transformed overnight from rich landowning rulers to a tolerated minority, for the most part the Moslems hid their resentment behind a smile. Christos always tipped Mourtos generously and threw in a silk tie or a pair of American socks. He was sure that Mourtos, baptized or not, was his friend.

Christos rode into Lia seated on the lead mule, the sun reflecting from his white short-sleeved shirt, his glasses and bald pate, for he had removed his straw boater and the seersucker suit coat. He nodded to the excited crowd but never let his pashalike dignity lapse.

Kanta, then four, and Glykeria, three, didn't recognize the apparition at their gate. Glykeria, taking in his well-fed appearance and soft gentleman's hands, insisted it was another doctor for their mother, despite the neighbors' claims that it was her father.

Christos stalked into the good chamber, and shooed out the women crowded around the invalid. Eleni tried to cover her waxy cheeks with her hands and said she should have had enough warning to prepare properly for his arrival. He came and sat next to her.

'I didn't tell them to send for you,' she said apologetically.

'I know.' He took her hand. 'I'm going to make you well.'

The tears spilled over. 'It hurts so much,' Eleni said and turned her face away.

While the crowd of villagers in the yard gaped, Christos set about with American efficiency, launching his plan to cure his wife. He had brought everything he needed. First he unrolled a great coil of wire screening and nailed it up at all the open windows. Then he produced a Flit spray gun and annihilated the clouds of flies inside the house. Finally he unpacked some choice beef that he had bought in Filiates and began to cook a meal with his own hands.

The onlookers buzzed. Did American men cook for women? they wondered. Hearing them, Eleni was embarrassed, but she vowed to eat whatever he brought her, and she did, already calmed by his presence.

Christos had arranged for the mule driver to take them the next day on the eight-hour journey to the old port of Saghiada, where they would hire a boat that would take them to Corfu. There, European-trained doctors would examine Eleni. She was sure the long journey would kill her, but she would not disobey her husband. Also, the thought of Corfu seized her imagination. Although everyone called her 'the Amerikana,' Eleni had never been farther from the village than the provincial capital of Yannina, forty miles southeast of Lia.

The next morning Eleni put on her best costume, with a gold-embroidered vest, necklaces of Turkish piastres, a large silver belt buckle and the burgundy flowered kerchief she had worn on her wedding day. She had become so thin that the skirt hung loose.

The immensity of the sea was terrifying to the two mountain women and the small caïque seemed to toss helplessly toward the abyss. When the boat passed safely between the two forts guarding the entrance to the port of Corfu, Eleni's strength left her and she couldn't stand. Christos picked her up and carried her off the boat and across the short distance to the Hotel Nea Yorki, owned by a man from a village near Lia who welcomed them like kin and gave them a room overlooking the harbor.

Eleni was scarcely conscious when Christos placed her on one of the scarlet-covered beds in their hotel room. When she came to, she saw Christos bursting through the doorway carrying a pair of European leather shoes for her and a bottle of the native kumquat liqueur that he made her taste.

The next morning Christos brought two doctors to the room. They examined Eleni, then consulted in the musical accents Corfiots had acquired under years of Venetian rule. They asked about the prescriptions of the provincial doctors, shook their heads, and finally announced that Eleni had something called enterocolitis. Having a name for it made her feel better.

'There's nothing seriously wrong with her,' said the taller of the two doctors. 'High-protein diet. Let her eat and drink what she wants. Give her some chicken to start.' He wrote out some prescriptions, pocketed several of Christos' traveler's checks and concluded, 'She'll get well.'

Flushed with triumph, Christos rushed out and returned with a waiter bearing three whole cooked chickens. Eleni did her best to eat, and before the day was over, she had managed to walk from the bed to a chair on the balcony, where she watched as all of Corfu seemed to pass below. Unmarried youths and maidens eyed one another, and carriages rattled by, drawn by horses in flowered straw hats. Gypsies entertained the crowd with monkeys and dancing bears. Peddlers of pistachio nuts, Turkish delight and multicolored syrups chanted their wares. At the edge of the water, a molten sheet of copper in the setting sun, fishermen mended their nets.

Corfu began to glow in Eleni's eyes with the supernatural brilliance visible to someone recovering from a long illness. Christos and Eleni sat every day in the great Esplanade, only steps from their hotel, eating colored ices and listening to musicians in starched uniforms singing Italian *cantatas* on the bandstand. When she was stronger, Christos led her through the maze of streets to the great, echoing Church of St. Spyridon, where she stood before the jeweled silver casket with the saint's mummified body. Every year St. Spyridon's corpse was said to wear out a pair of slippers performing miracles. Half the boys in Corfu were named for him. Eleni lit a candle and prayed for a boy.

Christos bought her first European-style dress and when the

blood returned to her cheeks, they hired a carriage and took an outing to the seashore. Once outside the town, rolling between the turquoise sea and the silver-green olive groves, Eleni drew strength from the air, heavy with the scents of heather, gorse, lavender and thyme. There were orange and lemon trees, wild orchids, sea gulls and flocks of turtledoves wherever she looked. The stucco houses of the villages were washed in vibrating pastels: pink, orange, mauve, turquoise and yellow. They visited the famous beach of Paleocastritsa and the thirteenth-century monastery on the cliffs above, and ate squid and lobster next to the sea.

On the way back, the heat of the sun and the wine they had drunk made Eleni feel dizzy. The driver stopped in one of the tiny villages before a hut washed in a brilliant robin's-egg blue and overgrown with purple bougainvillaea. A young woman came out in a white kerchief and offered the strangers glasses of cold water and apricots warm from the tree.

It was during those sun-drenched, fragrant days in Corfu that Eleni understood what had made her ill. It hadn't been the evil eye. She needed to break free of Lia, where everything – the people, the mud, the mountains – was etched in grays, blacks and browns. Corfu showed her the rainbow that lay beyond her own mountains. She regretted giving in to her mother's demand that she stay behind, and longed to see the colors of America. Free of the prison of the village, with her husband beside her, she would never be ill again.

Christos was gratified with his success in curing his wife. He felt like a newlywed walking at her side, and if she so much as slowed her pace to admire something in a shop window, he bought it. Christos carried his American money in his breast pocket in a big roll, secured with a rubber band, and he liked watching the shopowners' eyes bulge when he began peeling off the bills. Anyone could tell by his clothes and his manner that he was not a Greek but an American, he knew – and a big shot, at that.

They nearly argued when Christos decided to buy Eleni a gleaming brass bed. Eleni raised her chin. No one in the village slept in a bed and she was too old to begin after sleeping on the floor for thirty years.

Christos explained to her, as to a child. Sleeping on the floor was a filthy village custom. Every 'high class' person slept in a bed. Seeing how much it meant to him, Eleni bowed her head, and the gleaming monstrosity, to the delight of the Armenian shopkeeper, was paid for and disassembled to be loaded on the caique.

Eleni's two eldest daughters still remember how shocked they were, summoned out of the house by the bells of Mourtos' mules, to find their mother, who had left an invalid, coming up the path, riding side by side with their father, both singing at the top of their voices, like two drunken gypsies at a wedding. They had never heard their mother sing before.

Eleni's cheeks became round again as she gathered wood, baked bread, planted the crops and carried water from the spring in the summer of 1937. Christos spent every day hunting or sitting in the coffeehouses. Within weeks of their return Eleni knew that she was pregnant, but she hugged the secret to herself for a while, certain that the child conceived in Corfu would be a boy.

On March 17, 1938, Eleni sent for the midwife. Christos sat in the good chamber next to the kitchen, nervously clicking his worry beads and letting the girls turn out his pockets for the candies they knew were there.

When the midwife caught the baby in her apron, there was an anguished cry from Megali, who was crouched in the corner of the room. Another girl! Eleni began to sob. A son would have made her husband so grateful that he couldn't refuse to take them all to America. Christos composed his face, took the child from the midwife and announced that the baby was beautiful and that he would name her Fotini for his dead mother.

Fotini's birth was the first ripple in the happiness of that year. A worse shock was the arrival, two months later, of Christos' partner, Nassios Economou, who had been left in charge of the business in Worcester, Massachusetts.

The Irish maids and Swedish cooks who worked in the silk-stocking suburbs of Worcester, in mansions built by tycoons of the industrial revolution, had always liked dealing with Christos because of his old-fashioned courtesy and the

56

consistently high quality of his fruits and vegetables. But after Christos agreed to take Nassios on, at the pleading of a relative, the dissolute young man set the kitchens abuzz. Christos was ashamed to tell his wife how often Nassios would return from collecting outstanding bills empty-handed, with a grin like a tomcat, saying he had collected in other currency. When Nassios occasionally brought a couple of women home to the Spartan flat the two men shared at 1 Ledge Street, near the produce market, Christos would succumb to temptation and then despise himself afterward. 'Nothing but whores in America!' he ranted. 'It's no place to bring decent women!'

One morning at the coffeehouse in Lia a breathless urchin arrived and told Christos that Nassios Economou was in Babouri waiting for him to call. Christos was stunned. He found Nassios in Babouri, dressed like Al Capone, luxuriating in the attentions of his wife and son. Christos shouted questions, the words garbled in his anxiety. What had Nassios done with their gleaming blue GM Reo truck, the cornerstone of their business?

Nassios replied as if he had nothing on his conscience. He was tired of getting up at 5 a.m. to go to the market, he said. He had heard that the Armenian proprietor of the greasy spoon near the railroad station, the 'Terminal Lunch,' was ruined in a poker game. So Nassios had sold the vegetable truck to a Syrian for $1,200 and bought the diner for $200 cash.

'Running a restaurant is a proper job for a man,' Nassios said as he handed Christos $600 – his half share of the business he had spent twenty-four years building. 'When the war comes – and it's coming for sure – the railroad station will be mobbed and that diner will make a fortune! I'll pay you fifty dollars a week to cook for me now, and when the money starts coming in, I'll make you a partner. Meanwhile, I thought I'd come over and share your vacation.'

Christos tasted the ashes of his life's work and his head was spinning. He thought about killing his smirking ex-partner in front of his wife's eyes, but knew deep down that he couldn't slaughter a goat, much less a man. After a few glasses of

57

Nassios' whiskey, Christos' unfailing optimism asserted itself. Perhaps Nassios was right, and the day of fruit peddler was over. It wouldn't be bad to be a partner in a restaurant. In any case, it would liven things up in the village to have Nassios around.

For the remainder of the summer Christos and Nassios reigned over the coffeehouses of Lia and Babouri like a pair of sultans. The weather-beaten, manure-stained shepherds couldn't get enough of Nassios' lurid tales of American women or of the free drinks and appetizers that the two 'Amerikani' vied in ordering. The villagers had already learned Christos' stories by heart, how he had arrived in America with $27 in his pocket, and how by dint of hard work and Spartan living he had risen to owning a produce business 'that brings in – how much do you think?'

They'd all wait, looking expectant.

'Ninety, ninety-five dollars a week!' he would shout triumphantly. 'God bless America!'

'God bless America!' was the refrain that concluded every anecdote my father ever told me about his life. Not until I became an adult did I understand his complicated feelings for his adopted country and the reasons why he didn't bring us there to join him. As a child it had seemed to me natural that my father lived in America and we lived in Lia. When, at the age of nine, I finally met him for the first time, I had come to the conclusion that he had abandoned us. Only later did I realize that given the times and his nature, it was the only thing he could do.

To every immigrant America was the promised land, where hard work was rewarded with gold. As my father labored sixteen hours a day at two jobs, however, he quickly learned that America was also filled with traps for the innocent and the unwary. He saw fellow Greek immigrants, released from the bonds of village morality and poverty, quickly ruined by women, alcohol and gambling, among them the two younger brothers he brought over as soon as he could raise their fares. By nature a Puritan, my father quickly sent his brothers back to Greece to save them.

58

When he married and had children, he decided that the United States was far too treacherous a place to raise a family, especially four daughters. Working long hours, he could not supervise them properly and his wife would be cut off from the support system of relatives and neighbors she had in Lia. In the village, wives and daughters knew exactly how to conduct themselves; the strict ethos permitted no lapses, but America was full of fallen women. Furthermore, his modest income allowed him to make his family the wealthiest in Lia, at the pinnacle of the social ladder, but if we ever came to Massachusetts, we would find ourselves children of a struggling vegetable peddler. Worse, we would see him treated with the scorn that rich Yankees displayed toward the immigrants who served them. Instead, when my father returned to Lia on his periodical sabbaticals, his wife and children considered him a sophisticated and successful American tycoon.

He loved passing long days of luxurious idleness in the *cafenions*, basking in the adulation of family and friends, but he also had become accustomed to the conveniences of America: fine clothes, weekly baths – and no relatives to answer to. That was the other side of the coin: my father had been seduced by American comforts and the bachelor life he created among other immigrant men in Worcester.

While he never became perfectly American, my father absorbed the country's optimism and naïveté. Greek peasants at home were the opposite, profoundly suspicious of their neighbors, proud of their wiliness. They have a disparaging term for people like my father: *Amerikanaki* – 'little American' – implying a wide-eyed innocent, eager to be duped. My father had come to America at seventeen and stayed away from the village too long. With time and distance, Greece began to take on a nostalgic aura of security and safety in his mind. He saw danger to his family among the industrial smokestacks and noisy streets of Worcester, but he couldn't imagine that his wife and children were in greater danger in the simple mountain village where he was born.

As the harvest season passed and the winter rains began, the roll of bills in the rubber band became alarmingly thin. Christos and Nassios knew it was time to give up their pleasant idleness and return to America. One morning in late October, Christos took out his suitcases and began to pack.

Nursing Fotini, Eleni watched him, realizing that she should have spoken before. She had been waiting for the right moment and now he was about to leave them behind again! She tried to prepare her speech, to convince him of the logic of her reasoning, and then, stammering in her eagerness, she blurted it all out. He had to take them back with him. It was too difficult to raise the girls alone! They needed their father. Hadn't he always said that America was the finest country in the world? 'I don't want them to grow up here! I want them to have something better!' she concluded, her voice sounding shrill in her ears.

Christos looked at her as if he had never seen her before. 'What's the matter with your life?' he demanded. 'Don't you have the best life of any woman in this village?'

Eleni opened and shut her mouth, determined to stand her ground. 'I don't want us to be separated anymore!' she said. 'I'm tired of raising the girls alone, not knowing if you're alive or dead! I'll get sick again!'

Her words hit home and made him strike out at her in anger because with his produce truck and his money gone, he knew there was no way he could give her what she wanted. 'Don't you know there's a depression on in America!' he shouted. 'People are starving! In America you pay for electricity, food, clothes! Here you live off the land. Haven't I just bought you another field to farm? You need money in the bank before they let you bring a family into America! And it's not a fit place for children, especially if the children are girls!'

He might as well have slapped her as reminded her of her failure. The shock of his words suddenly brought Christos clearly into focus for Eleni. For the first time she understood that he enjoyed having his family far away in Greece. He didn't want to be burdened with the responsibility of their presence. He preferred returning now and then, hands full of gifts, to be admired by everyone.

60

As if he could see her disenchantment, Christos turned defensive. 'I came because you were sick! I've spent everything on this trip. Look what's left!'

He pulled out the much-handled roll of bills, now limp and pitifully small. Eleni stared in astonishment. 'If that's all you have, why were you spending like a pasha, keeping every good-for-nothing in these two villages in food and drink?'

At a loss, he replied, 'They expect it of me! I'm an American!'

Eleni did not mention America again. The weight settled back on her shoulders. But she could not forget that she had seen, in a flash of insight, Christos' vanity and his reluctance to take on responsibility. Like every village girl, she had married a stranger. But like every wife, she had finally seen through to her husband's core.

As the leaves of the beech trees turned yellow, Christos and Nassios planned their departure. They would meet Mourtos the mule driver at the monastery of St. Athanassios, which lay halfway down the mountain between Lia and Babouri.

After midnight on November 17, 1938, Christos, Eleni and Olga set out for the monastery on foot, climbing quietly over the garden wall so that no one would hear them go. Nitsa had warned Christos that if he was seen, jealous villagers could throw black magic in his path and he would never return.

When Mourtos arrived with the mules, Christos threw an arm around his shoulders and whispered in his ear. Eleni overheard the words 'Just enough for the ferry to Italy.' She noticed the fleeting look of contempt on the Turk's face and the exaggerated friendliness in her husband's manner.

Christos kissed her on both cheeks and said she must have courage; soon he would either send for her or come back to stay. She answered with a hint of defiance, 'When we meet again, I want it to be on American soil.'

Christos ignored the remark, and contented himself with giving her some final words of moral advice. The girls' reputations were her responsibility, he reminded her. The house and all their land were in her hands. He quoted once

61

more his favorite maxim: 'Honor is beyond price or measure. A woman has no greater treasure.'

Eleni listened silently to his advice, her fear growing at the thought that she was about to be left alone again with all the responsibility for the children in a world overshadowed by the threat of war. Then he kissed her again and was gone, mounting the lead mule with an agility surprising in a man of his bulk.

She was lonely and irrationally afraid, like a child who senses something terrible lurking in the darkness. She didn't cry. She only waved at the departing figure of her husband.

As the mule approached the first bend in the road, Christos turned around in the saddle to look back. All he could see of Eleni were two white spots made by her apron and her face. It was the last time he would ever see her.

The exodus to the caves took place almost two years after the day Christos left Eleni, neither of them suspecting that there was a new life growing in Eleni's womb. During that time the impending war that Nassios thought would be good for business had grown into a tidal wave which had already inundated Poland, Denmark, Norway, Holland, Belgium and France. Now it had spilled over the tops of the Mourgana mountains into Greece.

After two days of being crowded into the caves, the villagers grew short-tempered and food supplies ran out. Some women ventured down to their homes to make fresh bread, then returned with the news that the Italians had advanced no closer than the distant ridges of Plokista and the village of Povla, and seemed uninterested in crossing the foothills to scale the mountains.

Apprehensively, the villagers returned to their homes. Life settled into a tense normalcy, although Eleni left her treasures hidden in the oak tree, and the old men of the village who were not away on their annual working journeys or fighting in the army cleaned their hunting rifles.

A few days later a small patrol of Italian soldiers arrived in Lia, guided by local Chams, including Mourtos the mule driver. The Italians were polite to the terrified villagers as they

62

searched their houses for weapons.

When the patrol was leaving the gate of the Gatzoyiannis house, Eleni pulled Mourtos aside and asked him for news of the war. The young Turk whom Christos called his friend turned on her with a look of triumphant hatred. 'The Italians have promised to make all of Epiros, as far as Preveza, part of Albania, as Allah willed it,' he said. 'Moslems will rule here as before. The Italians will be in Preveza tonight, and in Athens by the end of the month!'

Both Mourtos and Mussolini were disappointed in their expectations of an easy victory. Fourteen miles inside the Greek border, the Italians were stopped for days by a ragged army of soldiers in mismatched uniforms and shepherds' cloaks. Outnumbered two to one, the Greeks astonished the Italian generals with their courage and the accuracy of their artillery, although they had only six mortars for each division against the invaders' sixty.

An early and bitter winter fought on the Greek side. Freezing rains flooded the Kalamas River, which cuts off the northwestern corner of Greece, turning it into an impassable yellow torrent, clogged by dead animals and the rubble of blown-up bridges. In the pass above Metsovo called Katara ('the Curse') Italy's proud Alpinists of the Julia Division became victims of the white death, which turned their legs and feet black and swollen like potatoes.

They rubbed mud on their shiny black-plumed helmets, which seemed to draw the Greek mortar shells. They slept in the yellow mud, their once white puttees sodden and heavy. They urinated on their frozen fingers and learned to crack open the skulls of the donkeys dying of exhaustion and use the steaming brains for warmth. In the end, 12,368 Italians returned home mutilated by frostbite, 13,755 were buried in the mud of Greece, and another 25,067 were missing.

Within a month of the invasion, the Greeks drove the Italians back into Albania and kept on going. On the morning of November 21, the villagers of Lia saw the denouement of the Italian campaign taking place in the hills below them.

Greek troops attacked and routed the Italians at Plokista to the south. The Liotes, looking down from their vantage point near the top of the natural amphitheater, watched as the fleeing Italian troops left their animals, supplies and guns and took to their heels, scrambling up the side of the bowl created by the Mourgana like an army of ants in disarray, retreating on bloody, frostbitten feet right through their village toward Albania, leaving many dead and wounded: gray-green forms that stiffened in the mud. When the last of the Italians had gone, with the Greek soldiers at their heels, some of the villagers began to climb down to the battlefield to strip the corpses of anything useful.

Among the scavengers was Foto Gatzoyiannis, who returned to his house triumphantly carrying a pair of fine leather boots and two dismembered fingers, sliced from an Italian corpse, still encircled by gold rings. His wife Alexo, horrified, begged him to take the plunder back. Belongings stolen from the dead brought *harami* ('bitterness') to their taker, and she feared God would make their children pay for his sacrilege. Foto was unconcerned. 'I'll handle God!' he roared at her. 'You clean the boots!'

The villagers had finished with the Italian corpses by the time the carrion birds began to circle. The Greek peasants were disappointed to discover that contrary to the popular rumor, not one of the dead Italians was wearing silk underwear.

The Greek forces pursued the fleeing Italians all the way into Albania, and by December of 1940 they had even taken the port of Aghies Sarantes, which had been renamed Edda by the Italians in honor of Mussolini's daughter. The entire Western world took hope from the incredible Greek victory, the first defeat of the Axis powers. The Greeks went mad with pride and patriotism; church bells rang, flags blossomed everywhere and pedestrians shouted 'On to Rome!' In Nashelis' coffeehouse in Lia the drinks were free and the walls fluttered with tacked-up newspaper clippings about the triumph.

But the rejoicing was short-lived. Hitler had to enter the fray, not to save Mussolini's face but to secure his own southern flank for the invasion of Russia. He threw at the

Greeks four panzer divisions, eleven motorized divisions, the Luftwaffe, and his elite corps of parachutists. The German war machine mowed over the Bulgarian border into Greece on April 6, 1941. There was no hope of resistance. Within days, every Greek airplane had been destroyed.

As the king's brother was knocking at the door of the mansion of Prime Minister Alexander Koryzis, who had taken over after Metaxas' death from cancer, he heard a gunshot inside. The prime minister had just blown his brains out. King George II and his government escaped to Crete, and then to Cairo, where he remained in exile for the duration. On April 26, as the last British tank rolled past the old flower market in Omonia Square, leaving Athens just ahead of the Germans, the abandoned shopowners threw blossoms in its path, then closed their stalls and went home to wait.

On April 27, 1941, the streets were empty and all windows were shuttered as the Germans marched into Athens and raised the swastika on the flag pole high atop the Acropolis.

The arrival of the Germans isolated Greece from the rest of the world, cutting off vital imports to a land that could grow only 40 percent of its food. As the Greeks braced themselves for the occupation, Eleni Gatzoyiannis saw her worst fears becoming a reality. Her life line to Christos had been broken. There would be no more money. There was not even the chance to ask him how to save herself and the children. She had always relied on tradition or a man to tell her what to do. But war washed away all laws except the fundamental one of survival.

She missed her mother-in-law more than ever. Fotini had been her closest friend and adviser. But even when her husband died, leaving her destitute, Fotini had brothers and grown sons to help her fend off starvation. Eleni was more alone than her mother-in-law had ever been, for she had only five small children, all dependent on her for their lives. For the first time she realized that there would be no one else to share her burden, and not even the example set by her mother-in-law could help her through the ordeal ahead.

65

CHAPTER TWO

During the first winter of the occupation, 1941–42, the blockaded cities and the mountain villages, cut off from the plains which had supplied them with grain, salt and oil, suffered the most. Athens became a nightmare landscape of skeletal figures with bellies swollen, shuffling hopelessly in search of food, falling dead and lying unburied in the streets. The children and the elderly died first.

In the first two months of winter, 300,000 people starved to death in the capital. In order to keep the deceased's ration cards, families did not report deaths but threw the corpses surreptitiously over the walls of cemeteries. Every morning trucks patrolled the streets, picking up the bodies of those who had died in the night. There were rats and the smell of sewage everywhere.

The ration cards were nearly worthless, since bread was nonexistent, the food shops closed and shuttered. The smallest purchase required sacks of paper money, and cemeteries were ravaged by graverobbers looking for gold teeth and rings. If a baker happened to find enough flour to bake and sell a loaf of bread, he set the price in British gold sovereigns.

Everyone who could walk spent the entire day until curfew searching for food. The poor stripped the countryside of greens for miles outside of Athens. Trees in the avenues and parks were cut down for firewood. Servants of the wealthy were sent to outlying villages and islands with family treasures in search of a loaf of bread or a chicken.

Babies were born without fingernails, and nine out of ten

of them died within a month. There were epidemics of cholera, diphtheria, whooping cough, scurvy, enteric fever, and everywhere, typhus spread by lice.

Stewed cat passed for rabbit, barley would have to do for coffee. The only dinner party in Athens featuring real meat and wine was given by Greece's most successful undertaker for eight of his gourmet friends, whom he sent home through the German patrols after curfew hidden in the back of one of his hearses.

Nighttime brought mass executions of Greek prisoners accused of sabotage. By day the streets around the palace of Archbishop Damaskinos were black with crowds of gaunt women and children begging for news of their imprisoned men.

The towering, white-bearded archbishop moved between the Greeks and the Germans, pleading for food for the starving, and news of the prisoners. Shortly after Christmas Day he defied German orders by digging up the graves of fourteen newly killed men so that the bodies could be blessed and identified.

When two hundred prisoners were secretly shot in a mass execution, Damaskinos obtained their clothes, which had been stripped from the bodies, and hung them on lines strung across the great hall of his palace. Then he opened the doors to the women who, with their children, moved between the ranks of bloodstained clothes – stylish suits and muddy peasants' rags – fearfully searching for those of a husband or son. A bride of a month found the clothes her husband had worn at their wedding; a mother identified the clothes of both her sons. The archbishop's staff watched in horror as one woman after another fell to the floor shrieking, clutching a bloodstained jacket, while others, numb with dread, tore through the pockets of a familiar-looking coat, searching for some certain identification in bits of paper, cigarette butts and combs.

During the winter of 1941 in Athens, packs of stray dogs howled on the hills below the Acropolis, mass graves were dug in the gardens of the royal palace, and death waited on every street corner.

BOBOTA AND SHILIRA

THE FIRST FOODSTUFF to disappear from Lia in the springtime of the German occupation was coffee, Eleni Gazoyiannis' special passion. It was replaced by a weak brew of ground, toasted barley or chickpeas. Soon rice was gone too, and like the other women in Lia, Eleni used the little wheat that remained instead, grinding it between stones into a coarse rice substitute called *kofto*. Because wheat was too precious to use for flour, white bread was supplanted with rough corn bread, called *bobota*, which would become the staple diet of the villages throughout the occupation.

In the summer of 1941 the villagers anxiously planted every square foot of soil they owned. The only tillable land in Lia had to be cut straight out of the mountainside, terraced and shored up with stones. The families who owned not even a handkerchief-sized plot faced the winter with growing dread.

There had been no word from Christos since before the Italian invasion and Eleni's money was gone. She managed to hire Tassi Mitros and his oxen by paying him in corn to plow the family fields, but she couldn't pay Anastasia Yakou and her two daughters any longer to sow the crops, nor could she afford to have the half-witted shepherdess, Vasilo Barka, take the animals up to the pastures. So Eleni decided to sow the wheat and corn in the high fields herself and take one of her daughters with her to help. But the problem was which girl should be sent up to watch the sheep and goats. There were men hidden in those gullies and ravines: shepherds and brigands whose numbers were growing now that hunger was turning the poor to thievery. At thirteen, Olga was maturing rapidly. Just to be seen going up with the flocks could ruin her reputation. Eleni knew that Olga was flighty and naive; not wary enough for her own good. She finally settled on Kanta as the one to take the flocks. Only eight, Kanta was thin and wiry, and not likely to inspire lust. She was also shrewder than Olga; in fact, one of the best students in the village school. Kanta resembled her mother not only in her lean, chiseled features, but in her love of learning as well.

Eleni was one of the few village women of her generation who was literate. She had attended only two years of school, but after she was put in charge of her parents' flocks she amused herself scratching letters on rocks with a piece of charcoal. She also bribed a cousin who lived next door to teach her what he had learned in school every day.

Eleni decided that Glykeria, who was now seven, would accompany Kanta to the pastures, even though her chubby legs would tire quickly trying to match Kanta's long strides. Glykeria could guard the back of the flock while Kanta walked at the head, on the alert for wolves, snakes, robbers and straying animals. Meanwhile Eleni would take Olga with her to plant the fields, and the two of them could keep an eye on Fotini, three, and Nikola, who was now nearly two.

Kanta balked when she was told of her new responsibility. She despised the filthy animals, she wailed, but Eleni was adamant. She said that Kanta was to go along with Crazy Vasilo for several days to learn how to care for the flocks.

On a warm spring morning in June, Eleni and Kanta set out down the mountain toward the central square, where they would take the path to Vasilo's house. On the way they passed some of the tinkers of the village straggling toward the *cafenions*. Since the occupation began, the far-flung cobblers, coopers and tinkers of Lia had begun drifting home. No one had money anymore to buy new shoes, barrels or pots, and the men, forced into idleness, now passed the time tilling their fields or just sitting listlessly in the coffeehouse near the village square at bare tables.

Most of the men of Lia were tinkers, the traditional occupation of the Greek villages north of the Kalamas River in the province of Epiros. They called themselves *kalantzides*, a word derived from the solder, or *kalai*, which was the staple of their trade. Christos Gatzoyiannis had learned the tinker's trade from his father and traveled as an apprentice from the age of eight, earning one English pound a month, scouring pots with hydrochloric acid and sand, sometimes applying it to flat-bottomed casseroles with an expert shuffling of his bare feet on the leather rags.

The *kalantzides* ordinarily left the village in mid-February, before the beginning of the Great Lent, fanning out to Macedonia, Thessaly, Roumeli, Euboea, Attica, and even north to Albania. Those who went as far as Crete and Rhodes would not see their families again for two or three years. They traveled with their tools and pots on their backs or loaded on a donkey.

Before the occupation, a housewife was happy to pay a few drachmas to have a pot cleaned, patched, resoldered and polished to a new-penny shine while the tinker brought her up to date on births, deaths and kidnappings of brides from the villages he had passed through. The tinkers of the Mourgana had developed their own language, *alifiatika*, for talking together without being understood by the customers. Tinkers were generally regarded as rascals and thieves who mixed their solder with lead and who beat and starved their boy apprentices, but many tinkers of Lia prided themselves on their skill and integrity.

Sometimes the men returned home coughing with tuberculosis contracted from sleeping on the ground in abandoned shacks between the blazing fire of the forge and the wet damp of the night. But if he avoided card games, prostitutes and brigands, a *kalantzis* before the war could return with close to 20,000 drachmas a year.

Now all sources of *kalai* and copper, both imported, were dried up. Some tinkers tried to scrounge bits of solder by burning the tin cans thrown away by the Italian soldiers on the banks of the Kalamas, then sifting the ashes. But most simply gave up. Among them was the cobbler Andreas Kyrkas, the husband of Eleni's sister, a quiet, worried man with basset-hound eyes and his black hair combed up over his bald pate in an upside-down question mark. Andreas nursed his last bottle of *tsipouro* and reflected aloud, 'By winter we'll be eating the shoe leather.'

The *cafenions* of Lia were not real coffeehouses like those in the cities, but *pantopoleons* – general stores of the same gray stone as the houses, filled with exotic odors and a jumble of everything the villagers could not grow themselves. Before the war there had been open sacks of aromatic coffee beans, rice, sugar and salt, boxes of salty smoked herring and sheets of dried cod, barrels of pungent feta cheese and olives in brine, kegs of wine and the local moonshine, *tsipouro*, distilled from the crushed grapes, huge blocks of soap and chocolate from which pieces were cut to order, school notebooks, hoe, pick and ax heads, needles, ribbons, handkerchiefs, boxes of Turkish delight in drifts of powdered sugar, and bottles of jewel-colored syrups for cool summer drinks.

Inside these crowded emporia, surrounded by the piles of riches, women used to count out their coins and gossip with the proprietors while their children eyed the jars of hard candies, hoping for a free sample. Outside was the kingdom of the men, where affairs of state were settled while the owner and his family scurried back and forth, bringing drinks, coffee, backgammon boards, playing cards, and tidbits of cheese and olives. Now there was nothing left to order and no money to pay with, but the men still sat like broken clocks gathered around the half-dozen metal folding tables outside each coffeehouse, playing backgammon and *kseri* and watching the passing parade, hoping that a traveler would bring news of the war from beyond the Kalamas.

The returning tinkers reported that the Germans had taken over the largest cities, ports and major islands, allowed the Bulgarians to occupy the easternmost provinces and left the less desirable interior regions, including the Mourgana villages, under the administration of the Italians. Because they had no appetite for living on mountain peaks, the Italians settled in the large towns – Filiates was the closest to Lia, twenty-eight miles away. They sent a dozen *carabinieri* to Keramitsa, six miles southeast, to oversee the region. Travel from one town to another was difficult, the tinkers reported, because passes had to be obtained from the local Italian and German authorities in every town.

The Italians showed little interest in Lia apart from sending occasional patrols of *carabinieri* and Chams to search for hidden weapons, and dispatching four Greek constables to man the village police station, which had been empty since the former gendarmes left to join the war. The new men, members of the Greek rural police recalled to duty by the collaborationist government, settled in nervously.

As Eleni and Kanta traversed the main square, passing the coffeehouse of Kosta Poulos, they saw a spot of color in the drab crowd. Like peacocks in a flock of crows, three young men sat at one table, dressed in white high-collared shirts and European suits, idly clicking strings of onyx worry beads in clean hands embellished by a long pointed nail on the little finger – the hallmark of an educated Greek gentleman who does not do manual labor. The young men, schoolteachers all, were holding court.

The rank of schoolteacher was at the very apex of the social ladder in Lia, inspiring almost religious awe in the souls of the villagers. In all of Lia's history, only a handful of local children had gone beyond high school, and it seemed to the Liotes a near-miracle that these three had become schoolteachers.

No one was surprised that Minas Stratis, thirty-two, had reached such eminence, for he was the son of one of the prosperous clans of the village. The Stratis family owned a thriving shop in Albania where copper pots were made and sold, and they could well afford to educate one of their own. But the two Skevis brothers, Prokopi and Spiro, were sons of a poor farmer who scraped a living from a few small plots of land below the village. Although his nails were permanently rimmed with dirt, Sioli Skevis burned with the ambition to educate his boys somehow.

He had sold one of his precious fields to send them to school in Filiates, and then, determined to find a place in the academy at Vela – a combination high school, teachers institute and seminary twenty miles east of Lia – Sioli took his dark-eyed, solemn son Prokopi to court Bishop Spyridon of Yannina.

72

Sioli and the boy camped outside the Bishop's palace, accosting him every day as he passed, dogging his footsteps until he relented and agreed to find room at Vela for Prokopi, even though it was a school created for impoverished Greek children from Albania. Sioli felt triumphant, but Prokopi never forgot how his father and he had been forced to beg for a place that should have been his by merit.

Two years later Sioli tried to enroll his youngest son in Vela as well, but months of beseeching the bishop in Yannina did no good and he finally dragged the boy off to Corfu, where he threatened to place Spiro in a Catholic seminary to serve the Pope. The bluff succeeded where entreaties had failed. Finally Bishop Spyridon relented and agreed to let Spiro, too, into Vela.

Sioli felt he had done well. No other farmer's sons in Lia would have such an opportunity. But he was a simple man who didn't suspect that his boys would come home with more than a knowledge of history and mathematics.

They had grown to scorn their father for the toadying he did on their behalf and to despise the system that forced them to grovel. They were fertile ground for the ideology that had infiltrated the school at Vela.

It happened that nearby, in the town of Kalpaki, the Greek army had set up a military camp where suspected Communists in the ranks were sent to a disciplinary company to complete their military service under rigorous control.

Among the penalized soldiers at Kalpaki were many who would emerge as major Communist figures during the war. They succeeded in spreading Communist ideas within the school at Vela, instilling in impressionable boys like the Skevis brothers the determination to build a future Greece free of privilege and favor.

The seeds planted at Vela would soon bear deadly fruit, but in the summer of 1941 the three unemployed teachers sat in the village square of Lia discussing the war, and no one thought of the Skevis brothers as Communists, nor did Minas Stratis suspect what a gulf already separated him from his two colleagues.

Minas, as befitted the most prominent of the three, always

73

sported a carefully knotted foulard at his throat, and a heavy watch chain draped across his thin chest and attached to a gold watch which he consulted so frequently that one might think his life was filled with important engagements.

The two Skevis brothers spent the days in his company, even though they resented Minas' superior status in the village and the fact that before the war he had won the plum that all three wanted: assignment to the school in Lia, where he could live in the Stratis compound of houses with his wife. Prokopi Skevis had been exiled to a remote school in a poor Moslem village outside Filiates. Spiro, after a long wait for an assignment while he substituted occasionally for Minas, had finally been assigned to Riniasa, a village near the southern tip of Epiros.

The two Skevis brothers burned with the same revolutionary fervor, but they were opposites in appearance and temperament. Prokopi, twenty-nine, was short and swarthy enough to pass for a gypsy. He was a man who thought before he acted, and his eloquence inspired trust and loyalty. Spiro, who was two years younger, was taller and fairer than his brother and so thin that if a fly should alight on one of his matchstick legs, his friends joked, it would snap under the weight. Spiro's flesh seemed consumed by the intensity of his soul; his temper could boil up into raging anger and, ultimately, drive him to murder.

But as Eleni and Kanta approached them, the three young schoolteachers were chatting amiably, trying to fill the empty afternoon with talk. Eleni greeted them, speaking first to Minas Stratis, who was her second cousin as well as Kanta's schoolmaster. With formal courtesy and the elaborate vocabulary that he affected, Minas replied to her greeting and asked where they were bound. When Eleni explained about taking Kanta to learn from the shepherdess, Spiro Skevis broke in angrily. 'It's a waste!' he snapped. 'The village girls go simple-minded up there with the flocks, and Kanta's the most promising of the lot!'

Eleni replied coolly that she would try not to neglect Kanta's education, but that in times such as these, everyone had to make sacrifices. Mother and daughter continued on

74

their way, leaving the schoolmasters to the tedium of the hot afternoon.

The three could feel the worried eyes of the villagers upon them, waiting for a word or a sign. In Greece's history, rebellion had always been ignited by educated men. The peasants of Lia, full of admiration for their schoolteachers, expected them to do something about their plight.

Inevitably, the three men spoke together about forming a resistance movement, which would take root in the secret places of the mountains, like the freedom fighters of the War of Independence. They always spoke theoretically. 'Tell me your thoughts, Minas – who would you want in a resistance group if you happened to form one?' Prokopi asked politely.

Minas paused to consider the question from all angles, as he always did, before he spoke. 'Men like Foto Gatzoyiannis, the miller Yiorgi Mitros, Nashelis, I suppose,' he replied finally. 'Men who know the mountains and are good marksmen.'

Prokopi listened with a show of respect and suggested that Minas make a list of likely candidates. But after Minas had left the table, the two Skevis brothers laughed together at the other teacher's naïveté. They knew that men with flocks and families weren't likely to desert them and take to the mountains. It was the young, hungry and poor who would die for an idea. Those were the men they wanted and the ones whom the Skevis brothers secretly began to organize in the summer of 1941. They did not tell Minas what they were doing.

The swallows abandoned their mud nests and the autumn rains sent walnuts rattling down onto the roofs like bony fingers tapping, as the people of Lia harvested and stored every bean and ear of corn. In November, when the skies became heavy with the threat of snow, the collaborationist government ordered the schools to reopen, and the three schoolteachers returned to their posts. But the villagers wondered aloud how they could send children to school when there was no money for bread, much less shoes.

Spiro Skevis was sent back to Riniasa, near Preveza, and

used his position as a cover while helping to organize a resistance group under the very noses of the Germans. Prokopi Skevis returned to the school in the Moslem village of Solopia, near Filiates. Now and again he would be recognized, traveling from village to village in the company of itinerant peddlers, stopping to speak to men who had fought the Italians.

Minas Stratis had long ago prepared his lessons and he rejoiced when the government decided that the schools should open at last. His students considered him cold and distant, but Minas believed wholeheartedly in improving the future of Lia's children by teaching them to read and write and to wonder about the world beyond their mountains.

The authorities warned Minas to leave history, politics and 'opinions' out of his lessons. When school opened, on a frosty day late in November, he surveyed the sixty ragged, foul-smelling children who stumbled into the classroom on feet that were bare or bound with rags, and wondered how anyone could expect him to sow defiance on such unpromising soil.

By the time school opened, the Gatzoyiannis family and everyone else in Lia were living on a diet which, along with *bobota*, consisted almost exclusively of *shitira* – a porridge made by thickening goat's milk with some yogurt and yeast and allowing it to sit for a day. It was enough to keep them alive, but Eleni, like all village women, tried ingenious ways to supplement it. Kanta and Olga combed the woods and fields for wild onions and dandelion greens, which Eleni boiled and thickened with corn flour. On wet mornings the children swarmed up the mountain gathering fat snails, which were cooked with garlic and tomatoes. Anastasia Yakou, two houses below Eleni's, could no longer find chores for herself and her daughters to do in exchange for scraps. One day Kanta saw the eldest Yakou girl, Stavroula, bearing homeward a large wood tortoise. She watched, horrified, as Stavroula stood poised over the mottled gray-green shell, two forks at the ready, until the head ventured far enough out to be skewered.

Olga and Kanta complained the loudest about the inevitable

bobota and *shilira* while Glykeria finished off their uneaten portions. Olga was certain her beauty was fading, while Kanta, who had always been finicky about food, grew even thinner and wept at the memory of rich spinach-and-cheese pies and stews of goat in gravy with onions and potatoes.

As the snows began, the number of students in Minas' classes dwindled daily, and those who appeared learned nothing, but huddled close to the wood-burning stove and fell asleep. Minas shouted and rapped them on the head with his ruler, but he knew that no one could bewitch children into learning the alphabet when they were starving.

The unseasonable cold added to the miseries of the first winter of the occupation. From November on it snowed every day. As the drifts became deeper, the number of students shrank to those who lived a stone's throw from the school. Children often fainted in class. Minas doggedly continued to chant his lessons, determined to carry on until there were no students left to listen. But when Father Zisis began draping the white satin Christmas banners on the altar of the Church of the Holy Trinity next door, there were only six students still attending school. Among those who had disappeared were Kanta and Glykeria Gatzoyiannis.

In the kitchen of the Gatzoyiannis house the girls contemplated their portions of the white, viscous *shilira,* Kanta complaining that the very sight of it made her sick. Eleni told them sharply to eat it; they wouldn't see any more for the next two weeks. Their suddenly hopeful faces fell as she reminded them that the Christmas fast was beginning. From now on, milk, eggs, cheese – anything that came from an animal with blood – was prohibited until the feast day.

Clutching her belly histrionically, Glykeria wailed that God couldn't be cruel enough to expect them to fast when they were already starving. In the unhappy silence that followed, she began to console herself aloud with fantasies of the roast kid they would have on Christmas Day, garnished with potatoes, savory with oregano and garlic, dripping with juices. Eleni couldn't bring herself to tell them there would be no meat for Christmas; they couldn't afford to slaughter one of their half-dozen remaining goats for a single meal when it could be traded for two weeks' worth of corn flour. Her children were still too young and spoiled to imagine that one of the two great feast days of the year could pass without a taste of meat. Her voice hard, Eleni lectured the girls that they would survive the fasting days well enough eating potatoes, boiled greens and *bobota;* they should be grateful they had that.

Olga was sulking. Her mind was concerned not with food but with the other privilege that came with Christmas. The joyful mass on Christmas Day was one of the two occasions in the year when the eligible men in the village had an opportunity to appraise the charms of prospective brides.

'Why should I fast when I couldn't possibly take communion?' Olga burst out. 'You can't expect me to show myself to the village like this.' She had on her only dress, black wool, shiny with age and patched at the elbows. Eleni sighed and didn't answer. Olga, nearly fourteen, was a headstrong girl who believed that life was not worth living without a bright velvet dress, trimmed with the three black stripes of braid on bodice and skirt to indicate a family of high status.

A few nights later, after a sullen meal of *bobota* and greens boiled with onions, Eleni examined the stores in the small room behind the good chamber. The wooden chests full of dried cod and the canned goods that Christos had laid in on his last visit were depleted long ago, and now even the dried figs and the olive oil were nearly gone. Garlands of onions, garlic and mountain tea whispered as she passed. There was a slice of moon hanging outside the window, surrounded by the haze that promises snow.

Back in the kitchen, Eleni sat down on the floor next to the wooden cradle. Nikola was chewing his fist in his sleep, his eyes sunken, his thin face looking like a worried old man's. His features – small, finely chiseled mouth, wide forehead, high cheekbones and deep-set eyes – were copies of her own, but his fair hair was lighter than her chestnut braids.

Eleni always regarded her son with wonder. Afraid that the intensity of her love for him would attract the evil eye, she tucked paper images of saints into his clothing for protection.

He was her pride and her obsession, and the greatest happiness she had ever known was the day of his birth, July 23, 1939.

It had happened on the third day of the annual festival in honor of the village's patron saint, the Prophet Elias. The saint's pagan predecessor had been Helios, the sun god, and on every July 20th, in a ritual that was thousands of years old, the inhabitants of this mountain climbed to the highest peak as dawn broke, lit bonfires, sacrificed a rooster and prayed for a year of fine weather. After the prayers at dawn, the Liotes descended to the Vrisi, the triangle of flatland just below the peak where the itinerant dark-skinned *yifti* musicians were ready with clarinet, fiddle and tambourine to begin the dancing and feasting.

Eleni had stayed behind in the Perivoli, knowing her time was near. On the third day she sent Olga up to the dancing field to bring the midwife, Vasilena Kyrkou, and Eleni's sister-in-law Alexo Gatzoyiannis, who had agreed to assist at the birth.

The two arrived shortly after noon, giddy with the dancing and wine, and found Eleni lying curled up, her body focused on the pains. The midwife put on a clean apron and began boiling a narcotic tea from the flowers of the village's only lime tree while Alexo massaged Eleni's belly.

The girls huddled on the other side of the closed kitchen door, frightened by their mother's groans. As the hours passed, Eleni's mother crept into the kitchen and crouched in the corner, waiting like a thin, sharp-beaked black bird. The good-natured midwife whispered to Eleni that her father, Kitso, was puttering in the garden outside, staying within earshot while pretending to take no interest in what was happening. Although he would never show his feelings, the miller was undoubtedly reflecting that he had fathered six daughters, four of them dead, one sterile and the last a mother of four girls. If he was ever to see a male descendant to his line, this was his last chance.

As the sun set, the shadows of the cypresses around St. Demetrios were reaching up the mountainside when the midwife announced that the baby was ready to come. Alexo helped Eleni stand. Vasilena threw a sash over one of the ceiling beams, and while Alexo clutched her in a bear hug, holding her up, Eleni pulled on the sash with all the strength she had left. The rhythmic contractions, faster now, with no respite, carried Eleni off on a tide of pain, her only anchor the strong grip of her sister-in-law. She moaned with each wave, pulling on the sash, the muscles of her belly like iron bands. There was a pain worse than all the others, a rush of blood, and the baby was expelled into the midwife's waiting hands as Eleni lost consciousness and Alexo gently lowered her to the floor.

Quickly Vasilena wrapped the child, glancing mischievously in the direction of Megali, and sighing, 'Oh dear, another girl!' The old woman threw her apron over her head and began to keen, but the midwife's next words silenced her. Calling Olga from the hall, Vasilena said, 'Go out into the garden, child, and get me your grandfather's hat!'

The word 'hat' set everyone screaming. Olga, Alexo, Megali, Kanta and Glykeria rushed to see what the midwife held. They all knew why she wanted Kitso's hat: the bearer of great news, *shariki,* must snatch the hat off the head of the lucky recipient until it is ransomed with money. Vasilena had news for Kitso Haidis that was worth a sovereign at least. But she never got his hat. The moment Olga asked for it, the white-haired miller seized the girl with a cry and swung her around – the first time anyone had ever seen him embrace one of his granddaughters.

There was a babble of female voices around Eleni's pallet and then one deep one, her father's, shouting, 'If you're torturing me with a joke, midwife, I'll kill you! Let me see the boy!'

The word 'boy' seemed to echo and re-echo. Eleni opened her eyes to see the midwife grinning, holding in her white apron a red thing, surely too tiny to be human, flexing and unflexing and mewling angrily. Eleni reached out to take him. Her body felt the first raw pain of separation and of loving too much. She lay back against the pillow. At last she had fulfilled her purpose as a woman.

80

In the twenty-nine months that passed, the tiny creature grew to fill the empty places in her life: the absence of her husband, the void caused by her mother-in-law's death. But in December of 1941 when Eleni looked at the boy, she saw how thin the little arms had become and she was seized by a fear greater than any that had gone before: Nikola was starving to death.

The only quarter she could turn to for help was her father. Kitso had always been cold and silent to his children, and Eleni had longed to marry to escape his tyranny. But beneath the hard words and silences that passed between father and daughter, she knew there was love as well as anger. Her father surely could not refuse to save his only grandson. So Eleni wrapped her cape around her, closed the door on the sleeping children and set out down the mountain to her father's house.

As a child I found my grandfather a terrifying, fascinating, mysterious figure, the one model I had to teach me what it meant to be a man. I remember always being afraid in his presence, of his distant coldness and the sudden flashes of violent temper.

Kitso Haidis was a legend in the village for his cunning and for his reputation as a womanizer. In his youth he had been as handsome as the languid mountain war lords in a nineteenth-century engraving, with high cheekbones, luxuriant black hair and heavy brows above startlingly blue eyes. As he aged, his features never softened, while his hair and mustache turned entirely white. His cleverness won him respect throughout Lia and he was elected president of the village twice. He and his two brothers' families took turns operating the southernmost mill for two years at a time, and when it was my grandfather's turn, business improved noticeably. When he wasn't working the family mill, he was in demand to travel to other villages, building and repairing mills and running them, for a percentage of the profits, until they were flourishing.

My grandfather's reputation as a Lothario only added luster to his name. In a society as rigid and devoid of privacy as the mountain villages, adultery was almost impossible

81

and it could mean death for both parties, but everyone whispered that Kitso Haidis did more than grind flour for his women customers, and was smart enough never to get caught in the act.

Although he was the most lavish host in Lia on the occasions of his name day or the feast of his house, he was a miser and tyrant to his own family. My mother often told us how our grandmother would post her daughters as lookouts when she made herself the forbidden luxury of a cup of coffee. If Kitso suddenly appeared at the gate, Megali would toss the coffee into the fire and have the cup wiped clean before he got in the door. Kitso had taken her as a bride when she was fourteen, and for the next seventy-one years she suffered his adulteries and his brutal temper with the patience of a saint.

Although he never struck me, his only grandson, I feared and avoided him as a child. It was with great trepidation that I returned to the village in 1963 to the house of the eighty-three-year-old grandfather I hadn't seen for fourteen years. He was exactly as I remembered him, with the same vigor and mesmerizing presence, but he seemed astonished to find me an adult, with features that mirrored his own. He was never a man who could bare his feelings, but he tried in his own way to build a bond between us, to win my admiration. I recall one afternoon when we were sitting in the village *cafenion* and several men began arguing about what was the most important quality for having success with women. 'Good looks,' said one. 'Money,' suggested another. 'A way with words,' argued a third. Then my grandfather leaned forward with an air that silenced the room. 'The one key to success with women,' he said, glancing in my direction, 'is the ability to recognize those who want it.' Clearly, his reputation was well earned.

On the last night of my visit, as my grandfather and I sat in the darkness near his hearth, his face in shadow, he began to talk, and I sensed that he wanted to say something that was difficult for him. He told me that in the summer of 1916, when he was renting and operating a mill outside the village of Yeromeri, he killed a man. It was a Turkish brigand who came to him and threatened to burn his mill or worse unless he paid protection money every month, a common form of exploitation in those days. My grandfather agreed, plied the Turk with *tsipouro*. and then, when his guard was down, killed him with an ax. Working quickly, he redirected the millstream escaping from the chutes into a half-circular ditch which was there in case the machinery needed repair, pulled up the stones lining the channel and buried the Turk's body in the red clay, where it probably still lies today, deep below the ice-cold water that turns the millstones.

My grandfather never told anyone about the murder, unlike my uncle Foto, who often bragged about killing the Turk who insulted his wife. I understood that he was telling me the story as a kind of peace offering. There had been only one other person who knew his secret, he said. My mother, a nine-year-old girl at the time, had been visiting him at the rented mill, sleeping in the loft, and saw the killing. 'She never told anyone,' my grandfather said quietly in the darkness, 'but I could always see it in her eyes.'

We sat in silence as I considered his revelation. I knew how difficult it was for him to expose himself to me even this much. Before he died four years later, at the age of eighty-seven, he never apologized for his treatment of my mother and his grandchildren, or spoke of his feelings about her execution. Although he would never admit it, I knew that even an affirmed cynic like my grandfather subscribed to the universally held village belief that God often visits the sins of the father on the children.

With his confession, he had also given me the key to understanding the thorny relationship he and my mother shared throughout their lives. Every time he looked into his daughter's eyes he read there not only fear but also an unspoken accusation. She understood him better than any other person on earth, and he could not forget it. Her knowledge and her silence must have been a constant rebuke to him.

*

83

When Eleni entered her father's door on that snowy evening in 1941 and saw him waiting hostilely to learn what had brought her, she tried to sound calm and businesslike. 'We have the milk from the goats,' she told him, 'but the corn will last only another month. The six goats are all we have left. I know Uncle Yiorgi has the mill now, but perhaps if you spoke to him, he'd lend us some flour, enough to stay alive until the mails open and Christos can pay him back.'

Kitso listened in silence, frowning. He could see it hurt her to beg, and sympathy, mixed with knowledge that he could do nothing, boiled up into anger. 'Yiorgi has five children plus Mitros' orphans to support!' he shouted. 'Fourteen Haidis mouths to feed off the mill, and business down to nothing! Once you married into the Gatzoyiannis clan it became their responsibility to keep you alive, not mine! If your husband can't help you, let his brother Foto feed you!'

Eleni bowed her head, knowing she was defeated. Her father was right and she had no hope of assistance from Foto. Only a week before, her brother-in-law had passed their gate carrying a sack full of quail; when she asked for one to make soup for the baby he refused her. Her husband had sent money to support Foto and his large family ever since 1910 when Foto was in jail for killing the Turk, and now he denied her a bird the size of a sparrow.

Eleni would not let her father see her desperation. She sat silent for a moment, thinking. There was one option left if her strength didn't fail her. 'I'll take the things Christos gave me and sell them in Albania!' she said defiantly.

While Greece was starving, Albania was still well supplied with goods, because Mussolini had made it an Italian protectorate. On the other side of the mountains, the Albanians had plenty of corn which they were willing to trade to the Greeks in exchange for valuables. The most destitute women in Lia had been cheating starvation by walking two days to the sea at Igoumenitsa to gather salt, then bringing back as much as they could carry on their backs, and climbing over the snow-covered mountains to the landlocked Albanians, who would exchange an equal weight of corn for salt. But only the most desperate and strongest women took this expedient because the mountains were death traps of brigands, wolves and snowdrifts that had been growing since November.

Only the week before, Eleni had seen the frozen body of her neighbor Sotirena Papachristo dragged past her gate, the head thumping on the stones, mouth frozen open, eyes staring sightlessly at the sky. Sotirena and her twenty-two-year-old son George had set out for Albania, each carrying fifty pounds of salt, and on the way back, loaded down with corn, they became lost in a snowstorm and huddled together all night under a stand of pine trees. In the morning the boy awoke to find his mother stiff and blue. His cries roused the villagers, who rushed up the mountain, wrapped her in a blanket and dragged her down the path to her house. Eleni followed the procession into the woman's good chamber, bare except for a rough wooden table, on which they laid her while her three youngest children shrank from the sight of their mother. When the women turned Sotirena to close her eyes, a gargling moan broke from her throat, and her son fainted. The women rushed to massage Sotirena's hands and feet, but as soon as they touched her they knew she was now dead beyond question. The sound had been her soul leaving her body, they agreed. Three days later the villagers saw crows circling over the spot where Sotirena had dropped her bags of corn. They gathered the kernels and dried them in the stone oven so her children could have the food she died bringing them.

Eleni thought of Sotirena's face in death and shuddered, but her father's angry refusal to help had resolved her to follow the dead woman's path over the Albanian border.

Kitso stared in shock at her words, then began to mock his daughter. Three years ago she was too ill to walk, and now she was planning to climb through the snow to Albania. Wouldn't it be quicker to jump into the ravine and have done with it? No one had told her to have five children!

The more he taunted her, the more determined Eleni became. If it was the only way to feed her children, then she would find the physical strength somehow to climb the mountain as soon as the Christmas holidays were over. She stood up and put on her cape, then stormed out the door, her eyes as hard as her father's.

'Yes, get yourself killed!' Kitso shouted after her. 'Leave five orphans! Then who will be stuck with putting food into their mouths?'

In the good chamber of her house, the room reserved for special occasions, where the family's wealth was displayed, Eleni sorted out the possessions that she might be able to trade for corn.

The Gatzoyiannis' good chamber was more splendid than any other in Lia, dominated by the great brass bed, which was used only when Christos was in residence. In the eastern corner, in the glass-and-wood family iconostasis, a garnet-colored lamp burned before the figure of the Virgin frozen in a presentiment of sorrow, holding her Child in dark, narrow hands, the ruby glass and her silver ornamentation scattering stars of light on the whitewashed walls.

Eleni picked up the engraved golden pitcher from Constantinople. On a wooden table nearby were the sewing machine and her beloved gramophone, which each would bring two hundred pounds of corn if she could carry them.

From her dowry chest Eleni removed the filigreed silver belt buckle and necklaces of coins from her wedding costume. They were folded between linen sheets and thick American blankets, the only ones in the village. She took out a warm peacock-blue blanket and looked at it thoughtfully, struck by an idea. Then she reached for her scissors.

Two days before Christmas, Eleni told the children that there would be no roast kid for the feast. Yiorgi Mitros, who owned the mill above their house, had agreed to buy the twin baby goats in exchange for corn flour. The news was greeted with a general outburst of misery. Fotini wailed the loudest, because the kids had been her pets, but Eleni grimly tied a rope around their necks, and ignoring the bedlam, led them up the mountain. When she returned from the mill with two heavy bags of corn flour, no one spoke to her.

The day before Christmas was haunted by memories. On Christmas Eve in the past, Eleni would set the table for the

86

next day, which was also her husband's name day, when half the village would come to eat and pay their compliments. There would be the sweet Christ's bread, which took nearly a full day to make and decorate, a laurel leaf finishing each arm of the cross. The bread was set in the place of honor, surrounded by honey, fruit, walnuts, wine and a minimum of nine cooked dishes for good luck. But this Christmas Eve, no one mentioned the Christ's bread or the holiday ahead.

Only one ragged trio of urchins had come by to sing the *kalanda* in the doorway, to the accompaniment of their metal triangles. 'In the blessed hour, Christ is born, as the new moon,' their shrill voices caroled in the softly falling snow, and because she had nothing else to give them, Eleni put the last of the walnuts into their hands. Her children fell asleep early, huddled together under their *velenzes,* wearing, as always, the same clothes they had worn all day long.

On Christmas morning Olga awoke to find a brilliant blue dress hanging on her wall hook, made from the American blanket, complete with three black stripes pieced out of one of Eleni's old aprons. Eleni had even made Olga and Kanta new kerchiefs, cut from the linen sheets, fringed and dyed burgundy with the root of the alizarin tree.

Olga tore off her black dress and buttoned up the new one over her shift. It wasn't velvet, but it fit snugly over her budding bosom and flared out at the skirt, making her waist look even smaller. She tied the wine-colored kerchief over her long braids and knotted it at the nape of the neck, letting a daring inch of auburn hair show at the temples.

The other girls marveled as Olga twisted this way and that, trying to see the total effect in the small hand mirror.

'I'm beautiful!' she announced, pirouetting in the center of the room. 'Every single person in church will be staring at me!'

'At your feet, probably!' retorted Kanta.

Olga looked down. Her toes were visible through the holes in her flat leather shoes – the last pair Eleni had bought before the war.

'I don't see why you won't be sensible and put on the new *patikia* your uncle made you!' Eleni complained.

At her mother's reprimand, Olga raised her chin and clicked her tongue 'no.' 'I'm not going to church on Christmas Day wearing rubber sandals!' she said. 'These shoes may be full of holes, but at least they're real shoes!'

Eleni sighed and said nothing. Olga was becoming far too spirited for a well-brought-up young girl.

The bells of the Church of the Holy Trinity called the faithful out into a heavy snowstorm. Eleni carried Nikola wrapped in her shawl, followed by the girls. Despite the angry scene with her father, she stopped by to congratulate him on his name day, because it was his festival as well as Christos', but when they reached her parents' house, Megali said that Kitso had left on a mysterious errand two days before, revealing only that he was going to Lista, a village three miles to the southeast.

The path to the church was treacherous, flooded in several spots by swollen streams, but as they approached the square, the windows of Holy Trinity glowed invitingly through the fallen snow. Inside, the air was heavy with incense and the warmth of many bodies. The men and boys stood toward the front, the old and infirm leaning on their elbows against the arms of the seatless miserere stalls that lined the sides of the nave. The women and small children stood at the back, watching as each new arrival lit a candle and kissed the icon of the Nativity.

Father Zisis chanted the ancient verses of St. Basil, but few members of the congregation paid strict attention. They were whispering together, catching up on neighbors they hadn't seen since the first snows, and eying the finery that the others had managed to assemble on this bitterest of Christmases.

Olga had been right; she was the center of attention. Men in the front of the church turned around to stare at the flushed cheeks and downcast eyes under the burgundy kerchief, her white skin set off by a dress as blue as the Virgin's robes. Father Zisis frowned at the distraction and chanted louder, the altar boys swinging their censers faster in accompaniment.

Olga crossed herself as frequently as the most pious woman in the church, and only occasionally stole a glance at the congregation to measure the impression she was making. But her moment of glory was soon eclipsed by the arrival of a family who were strangers to most of the assemblage. As they entered the narthex, even the priest turned around to look. A buzz arose like the sound of a thousand bees.

At the head of the group was a middle-aged woman in black leaning on the arm of a thin young man with a face the color of parchment. It was the two girls behind them, though, who made the congregation stare. They wore printed dresses of a clinging fabric, visible under light cloth coats. It was their hair that attracted all eyes. Outside of the big cities no one in the village had ever seen women with uncovered bobbed hair, but the curls of these two swung shamelessly above their shoulders, bare beneath the eyes of Christ the All-Powerful, who glowered down from the vault of the central dome.

The younger of the two young women was pretty and blond, and she returned the disapproving stares of the congregation defiantly. The Gatzoyiannis children sucked in their breath and stared with a mixture of fascination and horror at the girl. Eleni saw that the newcomers wore no shoes, only sodden knee-high knitted stockings. Olga noticed only that all the men were no longer looking at her.

Before the church service was over, everyone knew that the strangers were the widow Alexandra Botsaris and three of her five children. The woman's husband, the tinker Vasilis Botsaris, had taken his family from Lia to Athens eight years before but had died almost immediately. The boy, Yiorgos, now twenty-two, had contracted tuberculosis fighting in the Italian campaign and was evicted from the hospital when the food ran out. The widow Botsaris had brought her children back to escape from the famine in Athens, but there was nothing left for them in the village; even their deserted house had been turned into a stable.

After church Eleni took her family over to speak to her old friend. Yiorgos was coughing badly, and the two girls, Demetroula, twenty, and Angeliki, eighteen, were shivering in their thin city clothes.

The two families walked home together. On the way Eleni and the children stopped at the Botsaris house. They were appalled to see that not a pane of glass was intact; the corners of the hovel were heaped with dirty hay. Snow drifted through the holes in the walls. The only furnishings were sleeping *velenzes*. Alexandra told Eleni how they had left everything – clothing, pots, pieces of furniture – in Yannina when they could no longer hitch a ride and were forced to set out on foot over the two-day journey from the provincial capital, sleeping in hay sheds, their feet so swollen they couldn't force them into their shoes anymore.

She described the horrors of the famine in Athens, the anonymous children lying dead at their doorstep, her daughters walking ten miles out of town to steal greens from other people's fields at night. There was not an olive, not so much as a raisin left on the vines for miles beyond the city, she said. When the children were given a loaf of bread by a sympathetic baker in Yannina, their stomachs were so unused to food that they rolled on the floor with stomach cramps.

'But you have nothing here, Alexandra!' Eleni exclaimed. 'The house is a ruin, you have no crops, no wood, no food – how will you survive?'

'I'd rather my children died in Lia than in Athens,' the widow replied. 'I've heard that women here are selling salt to the Albanians for corn. When I'm stronger, I'll walk to the sea.'

Eleni saw hope in the sunken face. She took her friend's hand. 'Then we can climb the mountain together,' she said.

When they crossed their own threshold, a tantalizing aroma from the kitchen greeted the Gatzoyiannis family. Eleni remembered the surprise and went to the fireplace, where she brushed away the glowing coals heaped over the *gastra*, a flat, covered copper pan. She lifted the lid, and the scent of meat rose like incense. Glykeria began squealing with excitement and the others ran to see. The pan was full of steaming *briami* – a mixture of boiled ricelike *kofto* and mountain herbs, studded with thick chunks of liver.

'Christ and the Virgin Mary!' exulted Glykeria. 'Meat! Where did you get it?'

Eleni smiled. 'I told Yiorgi Mitros, when he slaughtered the kids, to save me the liver and pay me that much less corn.'

The children ate with their hands, sitting cross-legged

around the low table, stuffing bits of the savory stew into their mouths. When they were finished, Eleni's plate was nearly untouched.

'I'll eat that if you don't want it!' Glykeria and Kanta said in unison.

Eleni shook her head. 'Today is the day when every house prepares a plate for the stranger who is the Christ child in disguise,' she said. 'This is His portion, and I'm going to send it to the Botsaris family.'

A chorus of protests drowned out her voice. The first meat they'd seen all year! Giving it away to strangers!

Eleni silenced them with a look. 'Olga's going to take it to them now,' she declared, in a tone that permitted no argument. She watched Olga flush an angry red, then added, 'As soon as you've put on your new *patikia*.'

New Year's Eve passed without the usual fortunetelling rituals because no one had the heart to ask about the future. Shortly after, on January 6, came the annual celebration of the Epiphany, the blessing of the waters. Father Zisis made his rounds of the village, sanctifying each house by sprinkling the corners with a sprig of sweet basil dipped in holy water.

After the priest's blessing, Eleni set out to make name day calls, for Epiphany – *ta fota* – is the feast of every Fotios and Fotini, and Eleni intended to visit Foto Gatzoyiannis and her young second cousin, Fotis Haidis, who lived in the other half of her parents' divided house. Megali was there already, looking worried. Kitso had sent a message, she said, demanding that Eleni come at once to meet him in Lista.

Leaving the children with their grandmother, Eleni immediately set out on the two-hour walk over the mountain paths. She found her father sitting in the main coffeehouse in Lista with a grizzled old man whom he introduced as the miller Yiori Stolis. Somewhat flushed with plum *raki*, Kitso informed Eleni that she could give up her plan of walking to Albania. Stolis had agreed to rent Kitso his mill on the Kefalovriso River in exchange for fifty okas of flour a month.

Light-headed with relief, Eleni sat down in a chair in that exclusively male bastion and began to thank the old man for

91

his kindness, but he waved away her gratitude. 'No, it's your father who's done *me* a favor!' he said. 'The mill has been idle since the Germans came. The whole region is crawling with bandits! I was afraid for my life.'

Eleni turned to look at Kitso, who got up abruptly and ordered her to follow him. He would take her to Kefalovriso and give her a sack of corn flour to take home, he said. She should come back with the mule every month to get more.

On the way, struggling to keep up with her father's stride, Eleni worried aloud that he was risking his life. 'You'll be robbed and we'll find you dead one morning!' she said.

Kitso shrugged. 'You know well enough that I can protect myself against thugs!'

It was the closest he had ever come to acknowledging the secret they shared. Eleni had never spoken of the murder of the Turkish brigand, and now that he referred to it obliquely, she fell silent. As they neared the turnoff to Kefalovriso, she awkwardly began to thank him for finding a way to feed her children.

'I don't give charity and I don't take charity,' Kitso replied curtly. 'I'll keep your family alive until the war is over, and in exchange, your husband will support me and your mother in our old age.'

Eleni protested that she would do that anyway, but he cut her off. 'I don't want any favors. This is a business arrangement!'

As the pair approached the mill, walking along the well-traveled road that led to the Kalamas and on toward Yannina, they encountered a large gray mule, plodding head down in the opposite direction, loaded with two huge baskets full of oranges. Eleni reached for its reins, but her father pulled her back.

'It must have gotten away from someone!' she protested.

'Don't touch it!' snapped her father. He saw her questioning look and continued reluctantly, 'It's Griva, the mule of the tinker Nikola Koukas. It knows the way back to Lia.'

Eleni was afraid that something had happened to Koukas. Perhaps he had been set upon by brigands.

92

Her father knew better. He had seen the traffic along this road during the days he was working at the new mill. 'Leave it alone. There's something in those baskets besides oranges,' he advised her. 'That's why Koukas is letting the mule go on ahead of him through the Italian checkpoints. If they search the baskets and find things that shouldn't be there, they can't connect it with him.'

'What things?' Eleni asked, mystified.

'Guns. Messages. Who knows?'

Eleni insisted that he tell her what he was hinting at.

'Better to be ignorant,' he snorted, but finally he gave in. 'Prokopi Skevis is sneaking around, talking to fools like Koukas, filling them with ideas about armed resistance and open revolution,' he said. 'It's an epidemic! Costa, my own brother's son, is one of them. They hold meetings in our mill! Idiots from all over the Mourgana. Prokopi calls them and they come.'

That was the first Eleni had heard of it and her reaction was to worry that the young men would get themselves killed, leaving their wives and mothers a bitter cup to drink. As they walked farther, she spied two tiny figures climbing the ribbon of road that curved below them. They were Nikola Koukas and Prokopi Skevis following far behind the mule.

'What did I tell you?' Kitso exploded. He warned Eleni that they should leave the road and take an overland path to the mill rather than encounter them. Before turning away, he extended his palm toward them, fingers spread, in the familiar imprecatory gesture. 'May they go to the devil!' he muttered. 'They're going to bring the Germans down on us like the ten plagues of Egypt. Any fool can throw a stone into the sea, but once he does, a hundred wise men can't pull it out.'

CHAPTER THREE

One June morning in 1942, the peasants of the small village of Domnitsa, 185 miles northwest of Athens, were startled to see a detachment of fifteen heavily armed men marching into their main square behind a bugler and the Greek flag, the sun reflecting on the bandoliers across their chests and the damascened daggers thrust into their belts. Their leader, a short, husky man with a fierce black beard and the eyes of a hunter, stepped forward to address the astonished villagers: 'Patriots! I am Aris Velouchiotis, colonel of artillery. Starting today, I am raising the banner of revolt against the forces occupying our beloved country! The handful of men you see before you will soon become an army of thousands.'

He was not telling the truth about his name or military rank, but his prediction about his little band was accurate. It would grow into a vast resistance force, the Greek Popular Liberation Army, known by its Greek initials, ELAS. And 'Kapetan Aris,' its thirty-six-year-old leader, would become a legend throughout Greece, electrifying the peasants with his daring, annoying his Communist Party bosses by his tendency to make independent decisions.

Aris was really Athanasios Klaras, a lawyer's son and agronomy student. An active Communist by the time he was drafted, he was sent in 1925 to the disciplinary company at Kalpaki, Epiros. Nearby was the school at Vela, where the Skevis brothers from Lia had won places through the machinations of their father, and where they were indoctrinated by Communist soldiers from the camp. Aris spent most of the next fourteen years in prison or island exile but was released in 1939 after signing a 'declaration of repentance,' for which the hard-line Communists would never quite forgive him.

As Aris was to become the hero of the left, his opposite number, the resistance hero of the right, was a portly fifty-one-year-old retired army colonel named Napoleon Zervas who had a weakness for gambling, drink and good food that hardly fitted the Spartan ideal of a guerrilla leader. On July 23, 1942, a month after Aris' debut in Domnitsa, Zervas left Athens to form his own resistance army in the mountains of his native Epiros. He soon had grown a beard as thick as Aris' and collected a small but tough force that persisted throughout the occupation, while other non-Communist resistance groups were crushed by Aris' leftist ELAS. Zervas called his rightist army EDES, the initials of the National Democratic Greek League.

The Allies showed little interest in either ELAS or EDES until the fall of 1942 when they realized they needed Greek help to blow up the railway link between Germany and Piraeus, the life line of General Rommel's forces in North Africa. The most vulnerable point was the viaduct over the Gorgopotamos, the 'rapid river' at the foot of Mount Parnassos. On October 1, a small group of British commandos was dropped into Greece by parachute. They approached ELAS bands in the area to engage the large force of Italians guarding the bridge while they set off the explosives to blow it up. Aris, however, avoided meeting the British altogether on orders from the Communist Party, so the deputy leader of the British mission marched a hundred miles over mountain passes to find Zervas, who agreed to help and hurried to the Gorgopotamos with sixty men. Suspecting that Zervas' EDES would get all the credit for this important mission, Aris decided to ignore the orders of his Communist superiors and joined in with over a hundred fighters. On the night of November 25, as ELAS and EDES guerrillas battled the eighty Italians guarding both sides of the bridge, twelve British saboteurs blew a seventy-foot span into the gorge far below, interrupting the main German supply route to North Africa for three critical months.

This triumph was the first and last time the two resistance groups ever fought together against the enemy. For the next three years they concentrated on annihilating each other, each group determined to take control of Greece when the war was over.

REBELLION ON THE THRESHING
FLOOR

WHILE RESISTANCE GROUPS of guerrillas were organizing in the mountain villages of Greece, Eleni Gatzoyiannis and her children were surviving the famine thanks to the bags of flour that her father sent regularly from Kefalovriso. Others in Lia were not so fortunate, and the death knell of Holy Trinity became a familiar sound.

The widow Botsaris and her children managed to stay alive through the first winter by begging and borrowing food and trading copper pots for corn in Albania. By the autumn of 1942, the two Botsaris girls had found work picking olives near the Albanian port of Chimara. Their brother, Yiorgos, still suffering from tuberculosis, walked over the mountains to visit them and died in the arms of Angeliki on September 26, 1942.

Eleni wept with the widow Botsaris over the loss of her son. Nikola, now three and a half, was strong enough to run about in his white little gown, but she knew that without her father's help he might be dead. On Candlemas, February 2, 1943, the 'Millers' Holiday,' she decided to thank God for the family's deliverance by sending Olga with a full tin of olive oil to light the lamps of the Church of the Virgin.

Olive oil was almost nonexistent in the village, and Olga clutched the tin carefully to her breast as she set off down the mountain, feeling the sun on her hair and life rising in her like sap in the trees. She had not been out of the house since the Christmas liturgy, and to her fifteen-year-old eyes, everything seemed new.

The centuries-old Church of the Virgin lay below the village

97

at the end of a long path that wound past her grandparents' house and through a deep ravine where a spring bubbled below the ancient plane tree, the sentinel of the village. It was said that the local saint, Kosmas, had rested in the shade of this tree before continuing on to Albania and martyrdom in 1778.

Olga had only begun her walk when she was forced to stop by two men coming out of the gate of the Bollis house. The older one was Mitsi Bollis, a thin, sallow tinker whose shirt was open to reveal a tuft of gray hair rooted in fleshless skin.

Of all the people in the village, Mitsi was the last person Olga wanted to encounter, even though he was married to her mother's cousin. He was a braggart, a petty sadist and malicious practical joker. Just two weeks before, the Gatzoyiannis family had been awakened by a terrible squawking in their henhouse. When they ventured out into the darkness, they found that someone had removed the stones under the door, letting in a fox that had already killed three hens. As they were cleaning up the mess, Olga saw a figure moving in the field below theirs in the moonlight. It was Mitsi Bollis.

Now, as she tried to walk around the tinker without acknowledging him, Olga recognized the fair-haired young man at his side, Vangeli Poulos, the son of the coffeehouse owner. He had gone to Athens to be a peddler of cheap jewelry, knives, fabrics, pins and needles, but returned to Lia, defeated by his shyness, to help in his father's store. His eyes stared at her with a new aggressiveness over his bristling reddish mustache.

Olga bowed her head and hurried her steps, but Mitsi Bollis would not let her pass. 'Where are you going, girl, with a whole can of oil?' he demanded.

She drew herself up to her full four feet, ten inches, and tried to look haughty. 'To light the lamps of the Virgin.'

Mitsi winked at his companion. 'There's no Madonna!' he said. 'There's no St. Athanassios or St. Demitrios either! For that matter, there's no God, only hungry people . . . So give me the oil to feed my children!'

He reached out and Olga shrank back, automatically

crossing herself at the blasphemy. Then she found her voice. 'My mother told me to light the Virgin's lamps and I'm going to do it! This oil doesn't belong to you!' She looked toward the Poulos boy for help, but Mitsi teasingly stepped in front of her and said, 'It belongs to everybody.'

Bored with the game, Poulos said, 'Let the girl alone, Mitsi! How do you expect her to understand? That's all she knows. And we're late. They're waiting for us.'

Olga scurried off, trembling and feeling somehow mortified. And by a piece of goat's dung like Mitsi Bollis! When she returned from her pilgrimage she complained to her mother, 'You should go yell at Eugenia about Mitsi! Trying to steal our oil! And spitting in God's eye at the same time!'

Eleni sighed and shook her head. 'You don't see how men like Mitsi have changed in the last year because you haven't been out of the house,' she told her daughter. 'The Skevis brothers are giving them guns and big words that puff them up like frogs. Next time, get out of Mitsi's way before he sees you, just as you would with a rabid dog.'

Olga remembered the blond peddler and how his eyes had disturbed her. 'Vangeli Poulos was with him.'

'He used to be a polite, shy boy,' Eleni said. 'Blushing every time someone spoke to him. Now he's like a wild man!'

When Olga encountered Mitsi Bollis and young Poulos, they were on their way to the village square, where a tragicomic farce was unfolding in the coffee shop of the boy's father. The star of the drama was Vangeli Kontoris, a red-faced, mud-stained field warden from the nearby village of Raveni who had been interned for his role in helping the Italians and was then released by the Germans.

Kontoris had arrived in Lia three days earlier from Filiates, settled himself at a table in Poulos' coffeehouse and put three objects on the table in front of him: a piece of paper, a pencil and a hand grenade, which had been painted red. Then he began drinking plum *raki*.

As his complexion took on a ruddier hue from the moonshine, Kontoris began to rant at the men sitting around him. Lia had fine wire fences, he said. The Italians needed wire. He was going to note down the names of those who had wire fences for the war effort. And if anyone tried to stop him, he would blow them straight to Charon. Then he picked up the bizarre red grenade and brandished it until nearly everyone fled to the coffee shop across the way, except for the men who secretly belonged to the Skevis group of partisans. They sat and watched Kontoris and waited.

With eyes as patient as a lizard's, Prokopi Skevis sat at a nearby table beside the tinker Nikola Koukas, the owner of the mule laden with oranges that Eleni had encountered on the road near the Kalamas. When Mitsi Bollis and young Poulos arrived at the *cafenion*, they sat down at a table near the now raucous field warden. Kontoris was serenading the patrons with a ribald sailor's song when Prokopi called the Poulos boy to him with a lift of his eyebrows.

Prokopi, Nikola Koukas and Vangeli Poulos moved to a table farther away, and Prokopi told his two disciples that the time had come to act. He had information that Kontoris was carrying a letter to the Italians in Keramitsa, a list of the names of their comrades in the resistance group. 'Tonight he's leaving to visit his whore,' Prokopi said. 'I want you two to make sure she sleeps alone.' Koukas looked grim, but Vangeli Poulos sat up straighter, flushed with the honor of being chosen for the first execution.

The sun was setting when Kontoris left Lia, and Koukas and Vangeli Poulos were already hiding in a field overlooking the road he would take. So intent were they on their mission that they didn't see Vasilo Economou, the widowed daughter of Father Zisis, working in a neighboring field. But she was a witness to what took place that evening.

The two guerrillas heard Kontoris before they saw him, singing Italian *cantatas* in anticipation of the romance ahead. Koukas' Mannlicher rifle was aimed at the spot, but when the lurching figure appeared, the barrel of the gun began to quiver and Koukas froze. Fighting the Italians in the battlefield was one thing, but ambushing a man was something he had never done before.

Seeing his failure of nerve, Vangeli Poulos eagerly wrenched the rifle out of Koukas' grasp and squeezed the trigger, sending a bullet into Kontoris' stomach which knocked him off the road and into a nearby field. When they got to him, he was trying to hold his intestines in place and crawl at the same time.

When he finally lay still, they searched his body but found no list, only a handful of Italian coins and a bloodstained picture of Mussolini. The red grenade turned out to be a harmless war souvenir that had been fashioned into a cigarette box.

When the corpse was discovered, no one in Lia was sorry, least of all those who had wire fences. Soon everyone knew who had killed Kontoris, and Vangeli Poulos was offered many free drinks at the coffeehouses. He drank more than he could handle and was often heard spouting propaganda about 'the cause,' but the villagers smiled indulgently. The warriors of the glorious War of Independence had been the same: hard-drinking and fearless.

The next day the arrival of a stranger at Prokopi Skevis' table in the coffeehouse set the Liotes to speculating that something else was going to happen. The man was a pock-marked young teacher from the village of Kokina named Evangelos Doupis. He was Prokopi Skevis' protégé and had been secretly organizing resistance groups in the lower Mourgana villages. But now Prokopi had summoned him.

On a moonless night in early March, as the village slept, twenty men moved about in the darkness of their houses, dressing in pieces of unmatched uniforms and loading old guns and muskets. They cast no shadows as they crept down the ravine toward the ancient plane tree. When they were all gathered, they climbed noiselessly up the other side and came out just beyond the village square at the two-room police station.

As his men surrounded the building, Prokopi shouted. Lamps flickered on inside and within seconds the four constables came out, one with his hands raised, one still buttoning his pants. Their sergeant was in uniform and his face showed no emotion. While the other three constables shivered in the cold, Prokopi took the sergeant aside. After some argument, the two men appeared to reach an agreement. The constable slowly walked back into the police station, then emerged holding four rifles which he handed to Prokopi.

The next morning as Olga was milking the she-goat, Kanta scattering crumbs to the chickens and Eleni stirring a pot of corn-meal porridge for breakfast, there was a great clanging of the bells of Holy Trinity. Everyone froze and listened, wondering if the Germans had come at last. The wind brought them a shout: 'People of Lia! Everyone to the Alonia at once!'

The Alonia, which was what Liotes called the village square, literally means 'threshing floor,' and the spot once served that purpose, but because it was the only flat piece of land within Lia, shaded on one side by a giant plane tree, it had become the hub of village life, where dances and important meetings were held and gossip exchanged.

Eleni herded the children into the house and warned Olga not to open the gate to anyone. With a shawl over her head and shoulders, she joined the frightened crowd hurrying to the square.

What she and the other villagers saw as they gathered on the threshing floor in front of the Church of the Holy Trinity was neither Germans nor Italians nor Chams but, to their relief, a line of twenty familiar faces – local boys of Skevis' band all decked out in a motley assortment of military uniforms. Prokopi Skevis and Nikola Koukas had on the faded gray uniforms they had worn in the Italian campaign, but Vangeli Poulos was wearing an oversized green fatigue jacket that had clearly come from an Italian corpse, and Mitsi Bollis had a black Italian beret perched at a rakish angle. Eleni noticed that only her cousin Costa Haidis made no attempt at a uniform.

Half the men held weapons, some nearly antiques, but the center of all eyes was the flag proudly held by Vangeli Poulos. It was the familiar white cross on a blue field, but someone had stitched the mysterious letters, ELAS, across the middle.

Many of the Liotes, relieved to see that the enemy had not come, smiled at the sight of the grim-faced band, but no one scoffed aloud, for all the village knew what they had done to the collaborator Kontoris. Besides, the four constables of the village were standing among the ragged group of rebels.

When Prokopi was satisfied that most of the villagers were

present, he climbed up on a chair and scanned the weather-beaten faces before him. 'People of Lia!' he shouted. 'Today the brave young men of our village have taken up arms against the invaders. We will not lay down our guns until they are driven out of our land and we are free!'

At first the crowd stared at him skeptically. The ragtag band before them hardly looked capable of taking on the Germans. But relatives of the twenty men began to punctuate Prokopi's rhetoric with shouts of 'Long Live Greece!' and clapping their callused hands.

Prokopi described the Greek Popular Liberation Army and talked of a democratic new order, based on justice and equality for all workingmen. He explained that ELAS now ruled Lia, that every able-bodied man in the village would be part of its reserve forces, that even the constables appointed by the traitorous collaboration government had crossed the line to fight for freedom.

Prokopi scanned the crowd and saw doubt still lingering on many faces. 'As you know, I'm a teacher,' he shouted, challenging them. 'After the war is over, I'll be a civil servant with an assured salary month after month and a pension in my old age. I'm not a tinker like you, wandering from one town to another for crusts of bread, scrubbing pots until your hands bleed, sleeping in shacks and alleys. It's not for me, but for you that we all embark on this struggle! To put shoes on your feet, food in your children's mouths! We are fighting to change your life, to raise you up from poverty and humiliation, to make you men!'

There was a moment of silence, then a thunderclap of cheers. Prokopi studied the faces he knew so well. Some eyes were wet. He could see they all were with him now. He had conquered his own village with his words, and the rest of Greece would follow.

He raised his hands for silence. 'Be warned!' he glowered at them with the look he used on unruly students. 'We will not tolerate opposition! The movement is prepared to take harsh steps against all those who betray it! You will hear of others who call themselves resistance fighters, but they are collaborators and traitors!'

Behind him, his men began stamping their feet and shouting 'Down with traitors!' Although they didn't understand that he was referring to Zervas' guerrilla army, the crowd took up the chant, warmed by their shared longing for freedom and their loathing for those who had stripped them of their livelihood, their food, their self-respect. Prokopi let them chant and stamp until they were ready to kill anyone he named as a traitor. Then he gestured once more for silence. 'Now that the army of ELAS has liberated Lia, you will be governed by a committee of your own people, and it seems appropriate to me that the honor of heading it should go to my colleague and your schoolmaster, Minas Stratis.'

He climbed down from the chair and pushed through the crowd to throw his arm around the shoulders of Minas, who was shaking his head, disconcerted by suddenly finding himself in the spotlight.

Minas had answered the call of the church bells in such haste that he had forgotten his cravat and his watch chain, and his hair was standing up in tufts. He whispered urgently to Prokopi that he wanted to take up arms and fight, not stay home and chair a committee, but Prokopi refused his protestations. 'You're needed here,' he said with finality. It was only later that Minas realized Prokopi knew it was inevitable that as committee chairman, adjudicating every disagreement, he would become one of the most unpopular men in the village.

The emergence of the ELAS guerrillas, called *andartes* in Greek, and their takeover of the village gave the people of Lia a new purpose and hope in the dark hours of the occupation. Villagers who could not even read or write found themselves with important jobs: collecting cheese to sell for money to buy black-market guns, conscripting mules for the guerrillas' use, levying taxes on each farmer's harvest. There were committees for administration, security, justice, supplies and recruitment, and many who had never thought of joining the resistance were flattered to be put in charge of them. The teenagers were organized into a youth league to assist the guerrillas, and even the children were drafted into the 'Little Eagles' and carried messages from one village to another.

Just as Prokopi had promised, collaborators and traitors were dealt with swiftly and severely. Kontoris had been the first, but other bullet-riddled bodies were soon found in gullies throughout the mountains. For the first time in centuries, brigands stopped plundering the Mourgana mountain villages and peasants could travel between them without fear, holding papers issued by the ELAS committee in each village.

Although no direct attacks were made on the Italian outposts by the Skevis group *of andartes,* they helped another ELAS group just on the other side of the Kalamas River drive off a company of Italians and Chams. This victory, coupled with the murders of collaborators and brigands, so unnerved the Italians that they retreated from their positions at Keramitsa and Aghies Pantes ('All Saints'), back to regional headquarters in Filiates. The Mourgana villagers found themselves out of the shadow of the invaders, if not yet free, and gave the credit to ELAS.

In the spring of 1943, just as the village began to hum with new hope and purpose and the first almond and Judas trees burst into bloom, the families of the Perivoli were saddened by the return of Angeliki and Constantina Botsaris, carrying between them the emaciated figure of their sister on a wooden stretcher. Demetroula had fallen ill working in the Albanian olive fields, and the girls carried her back on foot. As Demetroula lay in the family's decrepit house, she recognized no one and clutched each visitor with a hand of transparent thinness, begging for water. Within twenty-four hours of her arrival in the village, the bells of St. Demetrios tolled her death.

The atmosphere in the Botsaris house after the funeral was as bitter as the barley coffee the mourners sipped while they asked repose for Demetroula's soul. Angeliki's indomitable spirit seemed eclipsed, like her bobbed golden hair under the black kerchief, and her mother didn't reply to the condolences tendered to her. Everyone left as soon as they decently could.

Eleni Gatzoyiannis set off up the mountain in the company of her destitute neighbor Anastasia Yakou and her twenty-

105

year-old daughter, Stavroula. Although Stavroula had grown into one of the tallest and handsomest girls in the village, the desertion of her father, who still lived among the brothels of Kalambaka, and her family's poverty left her small hope of finding a husband.

Mitsi Bollis and his wife caught up with the three women, all headed in the same direction. Mitsi remarked with a sigh that it was a shame Demetroula didn't live long enough to reap the fruits of the revolution. 'It's the poor, like the Botsaris family, who will benefit most from our struggle,' he opined.

'What benefits?' scoffed Anastasia Yakou, who shared Eleni's estimation of Mitsi. 'I'm as hungry as ever! Hungrier, in fact! You've requisitioned two days of our goat's milk to make cheese for the guerrillas, but you haven't given me or my girls a bean yet.'

'Everyone has to sacrifice to build a new order!' Mitsi exclaimed. 'Think of something besides your stomach! Look at what we've already accomplished!'

He recited the list of brigands and collaborators eliminated by the ELAS guerrillas and added that ELAS was freeing the young men of the Mourgana from the vices of drinking, card playing and fornication. ELAS had already shot some of its own soldiers for dishonoring women. The guerrillas were constantly warned that to build the new order they must keep themselves pure. Inspired by his theme, Mitsi said, 'You remember that collaborator Demetri Koulioutas, who was executed in Yeromeri? He wasn't just a traitor. The thing he was charged with and convicted for was raping his own sister!'

The women's faces showed their disgust. Only Eleni looked skeptical. 'His own sister?' she asked. 'How could someone from these mountains do such a thing? Did his sister testify against him at the trial?'

'Of course not!' Bollis said with a shrug. 'He was her brother, after all, no matter what he had done.'

'Did he confess?' Eleni persisted.

'The questions you ask, woman!' Bollis laughed. 'Who would confess to such a crime? But everyone in his village

106

knew it. "Wipe this stench from us!" they begged us. His judges were a priest, an army officer and the schoolteacher Doupis. Do you think men like that would make a mistake?'

Stavroula Yakou nodded. 'It must have been true,' she said. 'Otherwise the guerrillas wouldn't have killed him.'

Her mother was less impressed. 'You'd better pray that kind of justice doesn't come to Lia, Mitsi!' she laughed. 'If your fate hung on what everyone in the village said about you, you'd be dead a long time ago!'

Offended, Mitsi hurried his pace and left the women behind, as his wife raced to keep up. After the Bollis couple had turned off toward their own gate, Eleni reflected to Anastasia Yakou, 'It's true, they've rid the mountains of brigands, and the Italians have withdrawn from the Mourgana, but so many killings so quickly! With every execution it becomes easier.'

Anastasia agreed, but her daughter said nothing and stored Eleni's remark away in her mind, as a squirrel hoards a nut against the winter ahead.

On Holy Saturday there were few families who could afford to slaughter a kid for Easter and hang the skinned carcass from the rafters, but Eleni paid her neighbor Tassos Bartzokis in corn flour for a share of the goat he and his wife would be roasting. The whole family gathered around to watch Tassos prepare it for the spit while the women cleaned the intestines for the spicy kebabs called *kokoretsi*. While they were working, there was a commotion on the road below. Everyone hurried toward the sound and found twenty-seven neatly stepping soldiers entering the village from the direction of Babouri. After the first shock they recognized the invaders as their own men, led by Prokopi Skevis, but splendidly transformed since the day they seized the police station.

Now, instead of motley pieces of clothing, they all wore new gray uniforms set off with gleaming bandoliers criss-crossed over their chests. On their heads, tilted to the right, were soft two-pointed hats, embellished with a small brass badge reading ELAS. Each guerrilla carried a new Mannlicher or Mauser rifle, except for Vangeli Poulos, ruddy with pride, who had a Hotchkiss machine gun strapped across his shoulders. The village children ran to fall in behind the splendid *andartes*. It was the finest parade they had ever seen.

That night every person in the village, even the unmarried maidens like Olga Gatzoyiannis, crowded into the Church of the Holy Trinity, hushed with expectation. The stentorian voice of Father Zisis, aided by the clear tenor of Minas Stratis chanting the responses, poured out through the open windows over the heads of the latecomers who had to stand in the churchyard. The bier of Christ had been covered with flowers, which the village urchins crawled under for good luck, and everyone held a new candle, ready to receive the holy flame from the priest at the moment of the Resurrection.

It was an ancient drama, but it stirred the passions no less every Easter. Out of the tomblike silence of the darkened church the priest, at the stroke of midnight, would emerge from the Royal Doors, splendid in his white vestments, incense curling around him, a single lit candle in his hand. 'Come and receive the light!' he would call to the congregation as the bells pealed out the news that Christ had risen. The village boys were ready to set off firecrackers in the courtyard as the flame traveled from candle to candle, and each worshiper would wend his way home, sheltering the flame from the wind so that he could inscribe a new cross on the ceiling of his house with the candle's smoke, to mark yet another triumphant return from the dead.

But shortly before midnight, as the crowd waited tensely on Holy Saturday of 1943, there was a commotion in the churchyard that soon spread into the nave itself, and the congregation parted to let the band of *andartes* push through. One of the guerrillas stepped forward. He wore a gleaming Beretta rifle over his shoulder and a chestnut mustache embellished his thin mouth.

There was a communal gasp as the guerrilla climbed the two steps to the bishop's throne, a canopied wooden chair with a miter carved on top, which was off-limits to any ordinary mortal, even Father Zisis. It was kept faithfully dusted and polished in the hope that one day the mighty Bishop Spyridon of Yannina might pay a visit to his flock in Lia.

108

With one movement, everyone looked at Father Zisis to see his reaction to the desecration of the bishop's throne on this holiest of days, but the priest watched with resignation as the uniformed guerrilla cleared his throat and began to address the congregation. He only spoke for a moment, in the resonant voice of a professor. On this high holy day, he said, he wished to invoke the dedication of the people of Lia to their most holy cause – the liberation of Greece from the tyrant. 'If you are wholeheartedly with us, ready to spill your blood for our sacred liberty, then we cannot be defeated!' he concluded. The congregation stirred and looked again at their priest, not certain whether it was proper to applaud in church. Like many of the other women, Eleni crossed herself and whispered a prayer.

The next day, Easter Sunday, the village drew together in an outburst of thanksgiving at having survived another year of hunger and war. Even the poorest managed to collect a few eggs and dye them red. In the afternoon the Liotes again flooded into the church for the service of the second resurrection, celebrating the rebirth every Christian will experience because of Christ's sacrifice. It was an ancient service of love and ended with everyone embracing his neighbor, exchanging the glad news: 'Christ is risen!' 'He is risen indeed!'

As the greetings faded away, the moment of brotherhood was shattered by a guttural scream, a male bellow of pain coming from the schoolhouse next door. Eleni reached out to pull her children close to her, but Glykeria was already at the head of the crowd racing across the churchyard toward the sound.

The door to the school was blocked by two armed *andartes*. From inside, the hoarse cries formed words: 'Please, no more! I didn't do anything! I don't even own a rifle! God help me!'

In answer to the shouted questions of the crowd, one of the guards said that a boy named Antonis Kollios was being 'disciplined' for owning a weapon he had not reported to the people's army. At once, everyone understood what had happened, and they all began trying to explain to the guards that it was a terrible mistake.

Antonis Kollios was a boy of eighteen, given to pranks but

not a troublemaker. His family owned fields next to those of Stavros Daflakis, an elderly farmer whose sight was growing dim with glaucoma. The Daflakis and Kollios families were forever feuding over the exact placement of their mutual boundary lines.

In a world where status and survival depend on land-ownership, battles over boundaries are common. Daflakis often stormed into the Kollios fields, complaining that their cabbages were trespassing into his garden, and Antonis liked to frighten him off by brandishing a stick that resembled a rifle. The old man was too blind to know the difference. No doubt he had taken his grievance to the *andartes*, who were now beating the boy because they wanted his 'weapon.'

As Antonis' cries weakened, the villagers' protests became more frantic. The two guards raised their guns. Suddenly the screaming stopped. The crowd stepped back when the door opened, and half a dozen guerrillas, including Mitsi Bollis, appeared, surprised at seeing so many people. The villagers fell back to let the uniformed men pass, then surged into the school, where they found Antonis Kollios lying unconscious on the floor of Minas Stratis' classroom, his clothes striped with blood where the flexible switches from the cornel tree had cut through his skin. The villagers picked him up and carried him away, wondering how the stirring words of Prokopi Skevis and his followers could be reconciled with this senseless beating.

Before the procession reached Antonis' house, the Skevis band of guerrillas was marching out of Lia in the direction of Babouri. On the way Prokopi Skevis confided to his protégé, the pockmarked schoolteacher Doupis, that he was worried about the effect the incident would have on the village's opinion of the *andartes*. 'Yesterday, in church, they were solidly behind us,' he told Doupis. 'Now they'll be saying we've beaten an innocent boy!'

Later that afternoon two guerrillas returned to Lia and ordered Father Zisis to summon the people by ringing the church bells. When they had gathered, one of the partisans took a small bag from his pocket and emptied it into his palm. 'This money was to buy our food for tomorrow,' he told the

110

villagers, 'but we've learned that the Kollios boy was innocent. ELAS does not spill innocent blood. Therefore, we've agreed to go without eating all day tomorrow and, instead, to give this money to Antonis Kollios in reparation for our mistake.' Putting the bills back in the bag, he handed it to the priest. 'You will take it to him.'

Several villagers remarked that the *andartes* had shown they were just, after all, but when Father Zisis went to see the boy, Antonis snatched the open bag from him and threw it on the floor! His mother quickly gathered up the bills and begged the priest not to report her son's thoughtless action to the guerrillas.

Except for the unfortunate incident with the Kollios boy, the villagers welcomed the presence of the guerrillas, not only for the new purpose and importance it gave to their lives, but also for the diversions it added to the dull daily routine. On many afternoons, around the hour of five, the church bells would announce a *synkendrosi* – a compulsory gathering – in the Alonia, and the villagers would hurry to the square to be entertained. Even the small children went, and Olga and Kanta begged, unsuccessfully, to be permitted to hide out of sight and peek at the festivities, the way certain less carefully supervised maidens did.

Sometimes the *synkendrosi* would be Prokopi Skevis speaking to the villagers about goals of the struggle. On other afternoons the guerrillas would educate the villagers in the aims of their movement with dancing, singing and skits.

These ELAS convocations loom large in my earliest memories of life in the village. To a small boy they seemed marvelously exciting and entertaining. Although I don't remember a word of the speeches, I remember the serpentine line of uniformed men, led by Prokopi himself, dancing the slow steps of the *tsamiko* or performing acrobatic leaps and somersaults to the lively rhythm of the dance of the eagles. When the guerrillas raised their voices in the songs of ELAS, even the smallest children like myself would join in, and I'd hear the sweet sopranos of unseen village girls, peering from behind shutters, as they sang the stirring verses:

111

If our comrades ask you any questions about me
Don't say I stopped a bullet, don't say I was unlucky
Just tell them I've got married . . .
With a big flat stone for a mother-in-law,
New pebble brothers, and the black earth for my bride.

Even more than the singing and the dancing, we children loved the skits. I joined in loudly cheering the heroes and hissing the villains as Mitsi Bollis, with a pillow under his belt and a huge false black beard, played the swaggering EDES leader, Zervas. Taking pratfalls, he would run to collect sovereigns from Churchill, kiss the boots of the Glücksburg puppet king and then, with a Nazi salute, scamper over to Hitler and whisper military secrets in his ear. When the ELAS warriors tied 'Zervas' up and dumped a sack of goat dung on his head I laughed until my sides hurt. It was even more wonderful than the rare traveling shadow puppet shows, and it drew the villagers together in a warm feeling of shared emotion and dedication to the cause of our local resistance fighters. If some of the adults, like my mother, did not join as loudly in the laughter or cheers, if they silently perceived a danger in the propaganda exercises, I was too young to understand.

One day in late May the songs, dances and speeches gave way to a drama of real bullets and blood. Eleni had left the house early in the morning and taken Olga and Kanta up to the high fields near the eighteenth-century Chapel of St. Nicholas to start on the spring planting, leaving Glykeria in charge of Nikola and Fotini, so she didn't hear the pealing of the church bells calling everyone to the square. It was early in the day for a *synkendrosi*, but the Liotes hurried to the Alonia, expecting to be entertained. As soon as they arrived, however, they realized that something was wrong. Vangeli Poulos was striding up and down, his face flushed with *raki*. Prokopi Skevis stood with a frown like a thundercloud while the uniformed guerrillas whispered together. When the square was full, Prokopi took his bull horn and shouted to the assembled villagers that the time had come to act, to lay their

112

lives on the line. The fascist EDES troops of Zervas had crossed the Kalamas River. They were only ten miles away. Today the *andartes* would take up their scythes and mow down the traitors who blocked the way to the glorious tomorrow they were building.

A babel of excitement arose, but Prokopi shouted it down. This was a moment for action, not words, he said. All the men of the village were to prepare themselves for battle. He would select twelve reservists to take up the dozen extra guns and join his guerrilla band in the front lines, but as soon as more weapons were captured, the rest of the men would be sent for.

Since the day they seized the police station, Prokopi's small band had grown to more than a hundred men, drawn from the various Mourgana villages. Not all of them shared the Skevis brothers' vision of a Communist future for the country, but many had thrown in their lot because they believed that the resistance movement was the best hope of saving Greece from the Germans. Among the non-Communists who wore the ELAS uniform that day were career army officers, the constables from Lia's police station, teachers, lawyers, and even two priests. In Lia, nearly every able-bodied man, regardless of political sympathies, had signed on as a reservist – 150 in all.

Prokopi's grim announcement triggered weeping among the women, and as he chose the twelve reservists who would go with them, mothers and wives embraced their men and begged God to bring them through the battle alive. The soldiers lined up, trying to look brave, shouldered their rifles and set off down the mountain toward the southeast.

Glykeria was under strict instructions from her mother not to let Fotini and Nikola leave the yard, so she ignored the summons of the church bells, and, annoyed at missing the *synkendrosi,* set out the midday meal for the two smaller children. It was a warm, humid afternoon, and after lunch Nikola climbed to the flat ledge of stone over the gate to the yard, his favorite place to be alone. He was only four years old and because his stomach was full, he soon fell asleep.

Glykeria, feeling very important at being left in charge, sat down on the front step, where she could keep an eye on

113

Nikola, and called Fotini, who was five and liked playing at being grown-up. Glykeria ordered Fotini to comb out and delice her silky, yellow hair because she liked the sensuous feeling.

While Fotini was struggling with Glykeria's hair, Nikola rolled over on the cement slab and suddenly plunged from the top of the gate and fell the eight feet to the stone walk below, landing on the back of his head. He was stunned for a moment, then emitted a terrific wail. Glykeria rushed over to find blood from a gash in the back of his skull trickling down his neck. Nikola cried louder, but the neighborhood was deserted and there was no adult to help. Glykeria felt acutely that she was only ten years old and didn't know what to do.

'You're all right. I'll give you a fig if you don't cry!' she pleaded and led him into the house, where she grabbed a white pillowcase out of her mother's dowry chest and bound it around the wound as best she could.

Sucking on the dried fig, Nikola finally stopped crying, and as soon as his sobs diminished, Glykeria regained her poise; imitating her mother, she told him to lie down and go back to sleep. He was nodding already, worn out by his ordeal, and Glykeria left him on the sleeping pallet, went back outside and told Fotini to resume combing her hair.

The battle in Keramitsa began shortly after noon. Prokopi's band fought bravely, even though vastly outnumbered by Zervas's EDES guerrillas and their superior weapons, but the ELAS forces were relentlessly pushed back. When Prokopi finally issued the order to retreat, everyone moved quickly, except for Vangeli Poulos, who had been manning their only machine gun with the assistance of another village boy. Vangeli was drunk with *raki* and courage. He refused to retreat.

The other boy did not share young Poulos' thirst for martyrdom. They were seen by their comrades arguing fiercely as Vangeli peppered the approaching EDES troops with the last of the ammunition. At twilight, the same hour that he had killed the collaborator, Kontoris, young Vangelis Poulos became the first ELAS martyr from the village of Lia, and the first villager to die in the war. The other boy survived him by a few minutes.

In the fields of St. Nicholas, high above the village, Eleni, Olga and Kanta were near the end of an exhausting day of preparing the newly plowed earth for the spring planting. Eleni was startled by the sound of gunfire, mortars and machine guns bursting out from the southwest. She could see smoke but nothing else. It was the first time she had left Glykeria with the little ones and her mind suddenly filled with scenes of carnage and death, her children in the midst of it all. Terrified, she led the two older girls helter-skelter down the mountain.

She arrived out of breath at the gate to find Glykeria and Fotini happily eating some apricots which they had stolen from Tassos Bartzokis' tree across the path. 'Thank God!' Eleni gasped. 'I heard guns! The neighborhood is empty. Where's Nikola?'

Glykeria stopped eating and frowned. 'He's inside lying down,' she said. 'He bumped his head a little, but he's fine now.'

Eleni's momentary relief vanished and all her premonitions of disaster returned. She rushed into the kitchen to find Nikola lying with a blood-soaked pillowcase around his head like a turban. At the sight her fears burst out in a terrible scream. When the toddler opened his eyes, she saw that he was still alive, and she managed to control her trembling hands long enough to find scissors, cut off the hair around the wound and clean it with *tsipouro,* all the while crooning to Nikola. She cursed herself for leaving her son, the cornerstone of her life, alone and unprotected.

As soon as the wound was dressed and she got her breath back, Eleni went after Glykeria, who was hovering on the edge of the yard. 'You – you black devil, is this the way you look after your brother?' Eleni screamed, reaching down for stones to throw at the girl. Glykeria was already running as fast as her chubby legs could take her, and all the while she was shouting dramatically, 'Go ahead! Kill me! I don't care! I'm ready to die! Come down, St. Demetrios, and take me! My mother is murdering me!'

None of the stones found their mark and Eleni was tripped up in her pursuit by Fotini's small hands grabbing at her skirt. 'Glykeria didn't do it!' Fotini pleaded. 'Nikola fell off by himself! I was doing Glykeria's hair, just like a big lady!'

'You too?' Eleni shouted, looking at the serious face and trembling lips. 'Nikola's littler than you, and you should have been looking after him!' But she sank down on the ground, her fury draining from her. Ever since Nikola's birth Fotini had been a weepy child, who felt cheated of the attention she craved. For that reason Eleni could never bring herself to spank her, although the girl's whining often drove her to distraction. Nor could she whip Glykeria properly, for the shameless girl, who was now disappearing down the path toward the Bartzokis house, was still shouting to all the saints in heaven to carry her away to her death. The doleful sound of her voice made Eleni laugh in spite of herself. She went back into the house to take her son in her lap, rocking him in the security of her arms. Glykeria was still missing when Olga Venetis came up the path with the news that Prokopi's band had been pushed back from Keramitsa and was retreating north to Kastaniani, passing right through the village. She told Eleni the news of the two boys' deaths, which had already reached their families. Eleni looked down at Nikola, asleep in her lap, his bandage like a lopsided cap. The misgivings raised in her breast by the guerrillas' actions had been well founded. Sons of her neighbors were being sacrificed under the banner of revolution. She would never give her son up to any cause. She turned to her neighbor. 'It's a blessing that Vangeli's mother is not alive to suffer this!' she said harshly. 'God grant that I die rather than see one of my children taken before me.'

When the news reached Lia that Zervas' forces were on their way in pursuit of ELAS, everyone, including the Gatzoyiannis family, prepared to flee to the caves, terrified of falling into the hands of the dreaded right-wing EDES guerrillas. But Zervas' *andartes* never advanced closer than Keramitsa, intimidated by the ferocity of Prokopi's fighters and unwilling to follow

116

them into their own mountains. When it was clear that Lia would not be occupied by EDES, Prokopi's men returned to the village, and an uneasy waiting period began.

Although they had been defeated at Keramitsa, Prokopi was proud of the way his men had comported themselves in battle when faced with EDES' superior strength. He had turned his army of tinkers and shepherds into a disciplined fighting unit. But the regional leaders of the Greek Communist Party, which controlled ELAS, could not forgive the defeat. They were convinced that Prokopi's ELAS group had a fatal weakness: he allowed the Mourgana unit to be directed by a local committee rather than men hand-picked by the party leaders in Yannina. They felt he was giving his group an autonomy that undermined party discipline and weakened its military strength. The party decided to tighten the reins on the Mourgana guerrillas.

The man sent to bring the group into line was a thin, swarthy, balding Macedonian Slav who used the name 'Inoes.' The villagers were surprised to see their local hero cower before this stranger. Inoes accused Prokopi of weakness because he had allowed men into his organization who were not true believers.

Prokopi was outraged at the criticism. The village was solidly behind him, he protested. 'If we eliminate the local committee and put it all in the hands of the party, we'll lose some of our best men, who aren't Communists!' Inoes was not persuaded. The Mourgana group was taken out of Prokopi's hands and merged into the 15th ELAS Regiment, which was under tight party control. Within a week, as Prokopi feared, a dozen of the unit's most experienced fighters, including former army officers and the head constable, Kaloyeropoulos, took their boots in their hands and crept out of Lia; they surfaced in Keramitsa, where they joined Zervas' rival EDES forces.

Prokopi's humiliations were not over. Using the defections as an excuse, the party removed him from the group he had created and nurtured for two years, and exiled him to a job in a small village in the Yannina valley.

The person in Lia who benefited most from this purge was

Costa Haidis, Eleni Gatzoyiannis' cousin, who, as the local Communist Party commissar, became the most powerful man in the area. Spiro Skevis returned from Preveza, where as an ELAS lieutenant he had fought more successfully than his brother. Because he supported the party's decisions, he was given command of a company in the 15th Regiment made up mostly of men from Lia.

Surprised by the takeover of the local ELAS group, the Mourgana villagers began to understand that the movement begun locally by the Skevis brothers was being controlled by mysterious forces and extended far beyond their own local horizons. Every day new *andartes* passed through the village, sometimes staying overnight in the schoolhouse or demanding lodgings in village homes. Many wore unfamiliar uniforms and spoke in strange regional accents.

Near the end of the summer of 1943, Prokopi Skevis reappeared in Lia, thoroughly chastened by his exile in the Yannina valley. Eleni noticed that he seemed hardened, more distant from the local people and that he rarely spoke anymore about the common struggle of the Allies and *andartes* against the Germans. Instead, in his speeches he concentrated on denouncing 'monarcho-fascists,' which meant Zervas; imperialists, which meant admirers of the king, like her father; and bloodsucking exploiters of the masses. As a reward for his new ideological orthodoxy, Prokopi was named secretary of the Communist Party committee for the entire prefecture of Thesprotia. Most of the Liotes were glad to see the local resistance founder back and took pride in the promotion of their native son in ELAS' ranks.

The endless warring of ELAS and EDES guerrillas had hamstrung the whole resistance effort so much that in July, under prodding from the British Military Mission, an agreement was negotiated between the guerrilla groups to cease hostilities against one another and put themselves under the orders of a joint general headquarters based in Pertouli, Thessaly, made up of representatives from each resistance band and the British commandos.

In the Mourgana area, EDES was well dug in at Keramitsa,

and ELAS had a firm hold on the upper villages: Lia, Babouri and Tsamanta.

Hoping to keep the two sides from erupting into battle with each other and to make them concentrate on the real enemy – the Germans – the British Military Mission to Greece decided to send representatives to the Mourgana mountains, which were assuming increasing strategic importance. In case of an Allied invasion on the Greek west coast, opposite Corfu, a strong resistance army in the Mourgana could block the route of German reinforcements to the landing site both from Albania in the north and Yannina in the east. The region also contained one of the two evacuation routes the Germans could take out of Greece – through Albania to the Adriatic Sea. The Germans preferred this route because it avoided going through Tito's strong partisan army in Yugoslavia, and the Allies wanted it closed.

The British Empire arrived in Lia in the unlikely person of a tall, nervous, fair-haired Scot of about thirty-five named Lieutenant John Anderson. The villagers soon came to call him 'Captain Ian.' He was accompanied by another subject of His Majesty, Corporal Kenneth Smith, a large, lusty, dark-haired Geordie from the north of England with a wireless radio on his back. Most extraordinary of all was their interpreter, a shy, coffee-colored man named Peter Saramantis, who had a Greek sailor for a father and a black South African for a mother. He told the villagers that the British were setting up an Allied mission right in Lia and that they had rented the two-room Fafoutis house in back of the police station for the purpose.

Nearly everyone in the village felt proud and a little more secure with the arrival of British commandos in their midst. There was no way to foresee that the British presence would heighten the tensions between ELAS and EDES and bring civil war right to their doorsteps.

CHAPTER FOUR

On September 9, 1943, Italy capitulated to the Allies. Its surrender destroyed the tenuous equilibrium which the British had been trying so hard to maintain between the Greek resistance groups.

The 100,000 Italian soldiers in Greece were suddenly faced with the dilemma of giving themselves up to the Germans or to the *andartes*. Their morale broken, most surrendered to whichever side reached them first. On the island of Rhodes, 40,000 Italian soldiers surrendered to only 5,000 Germans.

When the Nazis in other parts of Greece encountered resistance from their former allies, they were merciless. In Cephalonia some Italian soldiers tried to defend themselves and the German commandant told his men, 'Hunters! The next twenty-four are yours!' Overnight, 4,000 Italians were shot.

The Germans and the guerrilla resistance groups throughout Greece raced one another to capture the precious Italian weapons. The plum was the Italian Pinerolo Division in central Thessaly, led by General Alberto Infante, which controlled about 12,000 men and all their arms. ELAS was the predominant guerrilla group in that area. Knowing that the *andartes* were nearly as dangerous as the Germans, Infante contacted the British and asked them to oversee his surrender to the guerrilla leaders. At the same moment the Germans were rushing a convoy of armored units and an SS regiment toward the spot to prevent such a prize from falling into ELAS hands.

The chief of the British mission knew that Infante's thousands of weapons would give ELAS such an advantage that it would threaten the fragile truce with the other resistance groups, but there was nothing he could do. He nervously initialed the treaty signed by Infante and *Kapetan* Aris of ELAS. As soon as they surrendered, the Italians joined the ELAS guerrillas in fighting off the German onslaught.

To render the Italians powerless, ELAS divided them into small detachments, sent them to separate localities, then disarmed and dispatched them to work camps in the mountains, where about 1,000 died that winter.

The sudden windfall of Italian weapons – 10,000 rifles, 20 pieces of artillery, 2 armored cars, 100 trucks and more than 50 smaller vehicles – made ELAS so superior to EDES in firepower that it began to seem inevitable they would attack EDES, setting off a civil war.

General Infante and his staff were taken for their protection to the headquarters of the British commandos that had been established at Pertouli, Thessaly, where British officers began making plans to spirit them out of Greece. Infante would be evacuated overland to Albania and the sea, where a submarine would carry him to Italy. The evacuation of Infante was assigned to a new Allied commando post which had just been set up by the British near the Albanian border in the village of Lia.

THE BOVINGTON MISSION

JUST AS THE ELAS skits had enlivened the tedium of life in Lia, the establishment of a British commando post there provided an exciting diversion for the villagers.

No foreigner had ever lived among them, and the peasants studied these three Englishmen as if they were rare and fascinating zoological specimens. It was hard to believe that the mighty British Empire, which the Greeks had long held in awe, would manifest itself in the persons of the tall, nervous Scottish captain, the husky, loud-voiced radio operator and the mulatto interpreter. They had many peccadilloes. For one thing, they wore short pants like children. They also ran up and down the mountain paths for exercise. The first time that happened, all the villagers who saw them took to their heels running in the same direction, certain that the Germans were in hot pursuit. They were astonished to learn that the English were running for recreation. The villagers associated the mountainsides with toil and fatigue and would no more walk or run about for amusement than fishermen would relax by swimming in the sea.

Nevertheless, however strange the habits of the English, the Liotes considered it an honor to have them there and shouted 'Long live England!' when they passed the officers and pressed gifts of fruit and vegetables into their hands. Dimitri Stratis, a second cousin of Eleni Gatzoyiannis, told her that by their patronage, the British had saved his *cafenion* near their headquarters. He had been about to close down for lack of goods to sell when the Scot offered to pay him gold sovereigns to get Italian beer on the Albanian black market, along with such luxuries as marmalade and candles. Captain Ian, confided Dimitri, drank a prodigious amount of beer.

From another distant cousin – Nikola Paroussis in Babouri – a young guerrilla who happened to be in charge of the makeshift landing field on the night of September 17, Eleni learned how the last member of the mission, a dashing young captain named Philip Nind, was dropped from an airplane near the monastery of St. Athanassios along with twenty-four parachutes bearing boxes of supplies. Paroussis had tracked down four boxes that got lost in the bushes and carried them up to the British headquarters, hoping to be rewarded with a new pair of boots at least. 'But as you can see, I'm still wearing sandals,' he told Eleni ruefully. His only reward was a strange English phrase: 'Thank you.'

The villagers watched with interest as the British set up housekeeping. The officers hired a cook from the village of Faneromeri, nicknamed him 'Henry' and installed him in the separate shack which served as a kitchen. They used one room of the Fafoutis house for a bedroom and the other for the wireless radio. They bought a mule and christened it 'Edda,' for Mussolini's daughter. It was even rumored that they pinned pictures of naked women to the walls of their bedroom.

Father Zisis was as eager as everyone else to welcome the English and offered his services, but he was stumped by the assignment they gave him: to find two village women to be their housekeepers. No respectable village women would work in the British mission, the priest knew. Women did not go into the living quarters of nonrelatives without tarnishing their reputation beyond repair, but it was impossible to make the British understand this. After all, they were offering to pay the housekeepers each a British gold sovereign a month, plus their meals during working hours. Finally Father Zisis thought of the two surviving daughters of the widow Botsaris, with their bobbed hair and Athenian manners. They brazenly greeted village men whom they passed on the road. They desperately needed money for food, and their mother was too distracted by grief over her dead children to interfere.

That was how Angeliki Botsaris and her sister Constantina

became housekeepers for the English mission in Lia, which had been grandly named the Bovington Mission by Allied Headquarters in Cairo. Because Angeliki was a neighbor of the Gatzoyiannis family, she would often drop by Eleni's house for a visit and relate the mysterious activities going on there. She described the English officers' strange eating habits; instead of fresh food they preferred powdered eggs, canned meat and something called cocoa, and refused to put olive oil on their salad, saying it was only fit for fueling lamps. But they were almost excessively clean and disconcertingly polite to their housekeepers despite the language barrier.

Angeliki described with awe how the radio crackled day and night, bringing messages from distant countries for Ken, the radio operator, to transcribe. She whispered that she often saw the two commanding officers, Ian and Philip, arguing with each other over these messages. The mulatto interpreter explained to her that the two men came from different classes of society in England. Philip was well-educated and rich. Although he was a dozen years younger than Ian, Philip had been made a captain first; then Ian was promoted for this mission. Ian was a dour, suspicious man, Angeliki reported, who resented his fellow officer, but she found the radio operator good-natured, easygoing and funny, even though she couldn't understand a word he said. The Gatzoyiannis family listened enthralled to her gossip, imagining that they were learning inside secrets of great significance to the Allied war effort instead of a housekeeper's view of an isolated outpost of lonely men.

I remember my first close view of the English one afternoon when I accompanied my mother and sisters to the village square, where the foreigners sat, looking strange and comical in their short pants, receiving the homage of the villagers. They appeared exceptionally tall, cleaner and blonder than the men of our village, and as they sat with their interpreter at a table drinking beer, the Liotes bowed to them as if they were kings. Like all the children, I was a bit afraid of the dusky interpreter, but I listened as he translated their polite words of greeting. It was clear that these were men of great power, and in my mind I associated them with my father, who also lived in a distant land, wore extraordinary clothes and bathed often. I wanted to ask the strangers if they knew my father, but my mother refused to let me bother them with my questions. Looking back on the memory, I couldn't help wondering what they made of our isolated village and their role there.

Thirty-eight years later I learned their impressions when I tracked down one of the two captains, Philip Nind, by then the director of a foundation and the holder of the Order of the British Empire. He allowed me to read the journal he made of his first commando mission. Nind, who was twenty-five when he landed in Lia, the son of a British civil servant stationed in India, spoke fluent French and had graduated from Oxford University, where he excelled at athletics and became enamored of the political philosophy of Karl Marx. An explosives expert, he trained saboteurs outside London before being accepted as a commando and sent to Egypt. When he was air-lifted from Allied Headquarters in Cairo to the Mourgana mountains, Nind, like many well-born young Englishmen of his generation, viewed Greece in a romantic mist distilled from the poetry of Byron and Keats, the tragedies of Aeschylus and Sophocles. He was quickly disappointed. 'The area is a very poor one,' Nind wrote in his journal. 'The mountains are particularly barren and the villages mean and dirty. But at this time it was strategically important and could have been the base for useful operations against the Germans . . . Our immediate task was therefore to weld the units of the two organizations, EDES and ELAS, into some kind of fighting force.'

With the two sides now under a truce, that seemed a simple enough task for an English officer with Philip Nind's education and training, but his youthful ideals would soon be put to a hard test, and as he told me ruefully while we sat in his gentlemen's club in London in 1981, more disillusionment was quick to follow.

As she studied the English officers in the village square, Elini contemplated them with admiration and hope. They were representatives of one of the world's great powers and were there to protect the villagers from the Germans. She hoped they would also be able to prevent further unnecessary bloodshed between the rival guerrilla groups like the deaths of the two local boys in the battle against Zervas' forces in Keramitsa. Like her son, she was reminded of her husband, with his naïveté and optimism.

The British received the homage of the villagers, apparently unaware of Prokopi and Spiro Skevis sitting nearby, their faces dark with anger. After the foreigners finished their beer and left the square, Prokopi Skevis stood and spoke to the crowd of peasants. He warned them not to believe everything the English said. 'Remember, it's the British sovereigns that are paying for the EDES mercenaries of the traitor Zervas,' he said heatedly. 'Be polite to the English; they have the money, guns and supplies we need. But the ally who will win the war for us is Russia, not England.'

Chastened, the villagers nodded and resolved to curtail their enthusiasm for the British in the future.

The local ELAS guerrillas milling around the village square found more than ideological reasons to resent the Englishmen, as they watched the two Botsaris girls arrive every morning at the British mission, dressed in their clinging, pastel-colored Athenian dresses, their frayed cloth coats clutched around them. As she passed the guerrillas, who had been assigned to spy on the activities at the British headquarters, Angeliki always greeted them with a dimpling smile and a toss of her honey-colored hair. They stared after her with the eyes of a pack of starving dogs contemplating a slaughtered lamb on a butcher's hook. Most of the ELAS guerrillas were young village men who had never had a woman. There was no opportunity in a place like Lia for sexual adventures. The only unions possible were in the conjugal bed with partners who had been chosen by one's parents with much thought for dowries and little concern for compatibility. The married men among the ELAS group watched the way the thin fabric of Angeliki's bright dresses clung to her ample hips as she walked. Her skin was soft and smooth as a ripe apricot, and she smelled of lemon blossoms. It was impossible not to compare her with their rough-skinned, sinewy wives who wore homespun and smelled of the stable even in bed.

Despite the atheism of their political movement, the ELAS guerrillas were subjected to sexual repression as strict as that of any monastery. 'Your rod is only to piss with!' *Kapetan* Aris often lectured his troops. To lay a hand on a woman was to risk immediate execution by a firing squad. The Skevis men posted outside the British headquarters watched with feverish eyes as Angeliki and her sister Constantina smiled invitingly and moved in and out of the commandos' quarters. They fantasized what went on between the shameless Botsaris girls and the British officers inside those walls, and the thoughts filled them with envy and hatred.

Within a week of Philip Nind's arrival, the British commandos were galvanized by the kind of message from headquarters that they had been hoping for. Ken stood up from the table, where he had been decoding the latest orders, and held out a paper with shaking hands. The Allies were going to land on Corfu in about seven days, it said, and Philip and Ian's assignment was to gather local guerrillas and use them to dynamite the Yannina-Igoumenitsa road so that German reinforcements from the interior could not reach the island.

While Ian prepared the explosive charges, Philip begged first the Skevis ELAS group and then the nearest EDES guerrilla headquarters for men to go with him to the target spot, which lay inside territory held by the Moslem collaborators of the Germans. Both groups refused to give him any more than one man each to act as guides, and those two guerrillas slipped away as soon as they approached Cham territory. With only forty-eight hours left until the expected invasion, the frantic British officers found themselves without a single guerrilla to help in blowing up the road. They were saved by a last-minute message from Cairo canceling the whole operation. Much later they learned that the 'Allied landing' had been a red herring, a smoke screen to distract

127

Hitler and keep the Germans away from other fronts.

Ian and Philip had been taught a lesson: the local guerrillas could not be counted on in a crisis. They decided to ask for men from both guerrilla groups whom they would personally train for future missions. While the Skevis brothers refused them outright, the EDES forces based in Keramitsa agreed to let them have fifteen *andartes*.

A thunderous, window-rattling explosion made Eleni drop the plate of beans she was holding. It seemed to come from the eastern edge of the village and her first thought was of Nikola, who was playing outside. She found him in the nearby yard of Foto Bollis, with Foto's small son Sotiris. Like his cousin Mitsi, Foto Bollis was a devout Communist. He came out and smiled at Eleni's alarmed expression as she gathered her four-year-old son in her arms. The repeated boom of dynamite in the distance had set all the village dogs to howling. 'It's only the British, teaching a few EDES guerrillas how to blow holes in the mountainside,' said Bollis. 'They think they can turn the fascist bootlickers into commandos.'

Eleni listened in astonishment. 'There are EDES *andartes* in the village?' she exclaimed. 'What does Spiro Skevis think about that?'

Foto Bollis shrugged and said sarcastically, 'What does it matter to Spiro? Haven't you heard, ELAS and EDES, we're all friends now, under the kindly wing of the British.'

Shaken by the explosions, Eleni shooed Nikola home as she wondered what was beneath the mocking tone in Foto's voice. She decided to visit her friend Alexandra Botsaris that evening to see if she could learn any more from her daughter Angeliki.

As Eleni was drinking mountain tea with the widow, she was startled to see Angeliki and Constantina escorted to their doorstep by the burly English radio operator, with two fierce-looking dogs on chains and a rifle over his shoulder. The Englishman didn't come in the door but disappeared into the darkness once the girls were inside.

Eleni looked at them curiously. First the explosions, then the news that EDES guerrillas were being trained by the

British, she thought, and now the Botsaris girls coming home with a bodyguard. She asked Angeliki what was going on. The young woman sat down with a sigh and said, 'If you ask me, the English have made a mistake bringing EDES guerrillas here, but they're determined to train a group in explosives and Skevis wouldn't give them any of his men. The English are too trusting; they shouldn't take Skevis' word that he'll leave them alone.'

Angeliki told Eleni that from the first, Skevis had posted spies outside the British mission around the clock, and every night the ELAS guerrillas intercepted her and her sister on the way home to question them about what they had seen and heard inside. 'I just smiled and told them I couldn't understand a word of what went on,' said Angeliki, 'which was the truth. We spend most of the time in the kitchen, anyway. But then they started searching us to see if we were carrying messages and money to EDES from the British. That's when I complained to Captain Philip and he assigned Ken to escort us to and from work every day.'

Angeliki tossed her blond hair, and her cheeks reddened slightly. 'I know what they think of us – they think we're the Englishmen's whores,' she said. 'I hear the words they whisper as we pass by. The rest of the village is no better – everyone calls us "girls from the sweet water" because we go into the British headquarters. They can call us what they like. All I know is that the British saved our lives and my mother's too. Without the money they're paying us, we'd never have survived the year. If they'd come earlier, my sister and brother might still be alive too. But I'm afraid for the English; they don't realize that Skevis is planning trouble.'

Angeliki's premonition proved to be correct. On the evening of October 12, only seven days after the British officers had begun training the commando unit, the borrowed EDES guerrillas and the mulatto interpreter, Peter, got cheerfully drunk, celebrating a new shipment of plum wine from Povla at Dimitri Stratis' coffeehouse where their meals were paid for by the British. At about eleven-thirty they headed for the schoolhouse, where they were quartered, singing klephtic songs.

In the headquarters the British officers were startled by a burst of machine-gun fire and ran out the door to see their interpreter and their commando unit being pushed down the road, hands above their heads, while Spiro Skevis' ELAS *andartes* prodded them with their guns. Captain Philip pulled the interpreter out of the line and with his help launched into a loud protest: hadn't Skevis agreed to leave the commandos alone? Skevis coolly insisted that the men were his prisoners, although he would let the interpreter go. 'I'm only acting on orders from headquarters,' he said levelly. 'All EDES men are to be arrested.'

Captain Philip, with the interpreter in tow, steamed off on the three-mile walk to ELAS headquarters at Kouremadhi to demand an explanation, but as soon as he approached the town he heard the sound of gunfire and realized that Skevis' actions weren't an isolated incident. ELAS and EDES, defying the truce they had signed at the urging of the British, were engaged in an all-out civil war. Philip learned from the commanding officer at Kouremadhi that the ELAS leader, Aris, was moving to attack Zervas' EDES forces near Arta. As for the British commandos, he was told, ELAS no longer recognized their authority.

Philip Nind returned to Lia in despair. A civil war between the two resistance groups was precisely what he and the other British commandos had been sent to the Mourgana to prevent. He sent a message to Cairo detailing the night's events and within twenty-four hours received an answer advising all British liaison officers in Greece to 'sit on the fence, grin cheerfully, and swallow insults' for the time being. In the morning the British sent their cook and the Botsaris girls out to round up supplies and withdrew into their small house to await the outcome of the battles on the hills below.

The British officers learned that ELAS had broken the truce because of a sudden movement by the Germans northward which made the leftist guerrilla army mistakenly think the Nazis were about to evacuate the country and that the time had come to annihilate the rightist guerrilla forces so that ELAS could remain in complete control of Greece after the Germans left. The attacking ELAS guerrillas were so victorious throughout northern Greece that EDES leader Napoleon Zervas ordered his men to run, saving themselves as best they could, melting into the crags and ravines of the mountains and returning to their villages to regroup six weeks later. The only spot where Zervas' troops were victorious was in a small pocket at Keramitsa, six miles southeast of Lia. The EDES forces there were so cut off that they never got the orders to retreat and disband. Instead, they repelled the attacking ELAS forces, even though nearly all their officers died or were wounded in the effort.

The freak EDES victory so close to Lia decided Spiro Skevis to take his guerrillas out of the village for a while in case the rightist EDES forces moved from Keramitsa into the Mourgana mountains. As the local *andartes* pulled out, the villagers barricaded themselves into their houses. They had heard enough of Prokopi Skevis' propaganda speeches to be convinced that the EDES guerrillas of Zervas were ruthless, bloodthirsty savages. Eleni Gatzoyiannis was as frightened as the rest, even though her father scoffed at Prokopi's tirades.

On the day the EDES guerrillas marched up the mountain and arrived in Lia, the only inhabitant who was not locked indoors was the schoolteacher Minas Stratis, who, despite the frantic warnings of his family, publicly welcomed their commander, Major Theodoras Sarantis, to the village. Sarantis took up headquarters in Lia's schoolhouse along with his bodyguards and sent the rest of his men on to Babouri to find quarters.

Once the villagers of Lia discovered that the EDES guerrillas did not burn, rape and pillage, despite the Skevis brothers' predictions, they emerged from their houses. Most of the Liotes kept their distance from the EDES guerrillas to show their sympathy for ELAS, but a few inhabitants began to enjoy their presence.

The men of Skevis' leftist guerrilla band had been forbidden to drink or play cards, prohibitions which Zervas' rightists did not share; and the British officers as well as the schoolteacher Minas Stratis enjoyed convivial evenings with the urbane, bilingual Major Sarantis. Kitso Haidis, who had returned from the mill he rented in Kefalovriso to take over his turn at running the family mill in Lia, also enjoyed socializing with Sarantis, who shared his royalist views. When the EDES officers held a memorial service on November 7 in the main church of Babouri to honor their comrades who had fallen in the recent battle, Kitso and Minas Stratis made the twenty-minute walk to the neighboring village to attend.

On her way home from church that morning, Eleni Gatzoyiannis encountered her cousin Eugenia, the wife of the ELAS guerrilla Mitsi Bollis, who had set the fox on the Gatzoyiannis chicken coop. Eugenia warned Eleni sternly that her father was going to get himself and the whole Gatzoyiannis family in trouble by attending the EDES memorial service. Eleni smiled and shrugged. 'Everyone knows father likes to do the opposite of whatever the majority do,' she said.

'It may be an old man's foolishness,' Eugenia replied, 'but some people don't see it in such an innocent light.'

Spiro Skevis' forces were collecting in Pogoni, sixteen miles to the northeast, and joined by other ELAS guerrillas, they planned an attack to retake the Mourgana. They conscripted women from Pogoni to carry heavy guns over snow-choked mountain paths that were too steep even for mules, and one of the women fell dead under the weight of the mortar she carried.

At midnight on November 14, Major Sarantis, the EDES commander, was awakened in the schoolhouse of Lia by a messenger warning that ELAS was about to attack. He ran to warn Minas Stratis and the British officers. After a heated debate, the British commandos decided not to flee with Sarantis, for that would ruin their claim of being neutral in the guerrilla war. As the machine guns of ELAS began to strafe the village, Major Sarantis and his men disappeared in the direction of Keramitsa. Minas went with them, but in the rainy night he was separated from the EDES officer and lost his way.

The next morning the Gatzoyiannis family and the rest of Lia awoke to discover that ELAS had reoccupied the village, the Skevis company being reinforced by several hundred more ELAS fighters whom they had never seen. There was an outburst of joy that the local guerrillas were back, but it quickly turned to apprehension as word spread that the guerrillas were rounding up all persons suspected of sympathizing with EDES.

The first one arrested was eighteen-year-old Vasili Stratis, the younger brother of the schoolteacher Minas. His mother wept as the second son she had lost in the past twenty-four hours was taken from her house.

Kitso Haidis was setting out for his mill when two unfamiliar ELAS *andartes* arrived on his front step. When they seized him, he shouted that it was a mistake: they must want someone else. 'I've done nothing and my nephew is Costa Haidis, the commissar here!' he ranted. But when they marched him out before Megali's frightened eyes, Kitso silently cursed himself for attending the EDES memorial service in Babouri.

The village square was a sea of guerrillas, some in unfamiliar uniforms, all wearing the two-pointed caps and carrying guns. Kitso looked in vain for a familiar face as he was dragged toward the schoolhouse.

Inside were two classrooms and two small offices, painted a muddy gray-green. Kitso was shoved into one of the small cubicles, which was crowded with two dozen prisoners. There were three other men from Lia: Vasili Stratis, the cooper Vasili Nikou, and Yiorgos Boukouvalas, an owlish old man who walked with two canes because he was born with malformed feet. Like Kitso, they were all considered royalists. He also recognized at least a dozen men from Babouri who had been at the memorial service, and as the afternoon wore on, more prisoners brought from Tsamanta, three miles to the west, were thrown into the room, filling it until they could scarcely find a place to stand, much less sit.

As soon as Kitso was arrested, Megali ran up the mountainside to tell Eleni. The sight of her mother's distraught face forced Eleni to remain calm. She knew there was no one else in the family with enough presence of mind to help her father except herself. While she assured her mother it must be a mistake she tried to think what to do. Her only hope was her cousin Costa Haidis. Despite what Eleni thought of the

133

political commissar, he could hardly allow his uncle to be imprisoned, or worse, by ELAS.

Telling Megali to go home and wait, Eleni hurried off to the village square, where Costa had requisitioned one of the houses as his office. She was prepared to humble herself and to plead, but when she gave a guard outside the door the message that she wanted to speak with her cousin, he returned to say that Comrade Haidis was much too busy to see *Kyria* Eleni. She felt angry blood rising to her face, but she said nothing. She walked over to the schoolhouse at the southern edge of the square, where a crowd of weeping women and children had gathered, pleading for news of the prisoners inside.

The sound of their lamentations unsettled Eleni more than she admitted. She tried to reason with herself: the guerrillas were local people, after all, not Germans. They were only trying to frighten the village by making an example of those who had been friendly to EDES. To escape the frantic crowd, Eleni began to walk around the school building, searching for a clue to what was going on inside. At the eastern wall, where the slope dropped abruptly, she paused under one of the high windows where she saw a shadow. Then she made out a familiar shock of white hair. *'Patera!'* she called softly.

His face appeared at the window. She could see at once that he was terrified. Her father had always been such a formidable presence to Eleni that she never imagined him looking so old and so vulnerable. She cupped her hands around her mouth and hissed, 'Don't be afraid! We'll get you out.'

Kitso regarded her in silence. Perhaps he, too, was aware that for the first time he was helpless and dependent on one of his daughters to save him. Suddenly he disappeared from the window, then something white fluttered to Eleni's feet. She bent over and picked it up. It was a handkerchief with a knot tied in the corner. She loosened it and found a pair of gold hoop earrings. She looked up at her father in confusion.

'I was going to give them to Olga when she married,' Kitso said in a hoarse whisper. 'See that she gets them.' Then he was gone. Eleni stood holding the two golden circles in her hand

134

and realized that her cheeks were wet. She closed her fingers over the earrings and turned away.

The prisoners in the tiny room sat silent as the guards called them out, one at a time. They could hear the screams from where they were, a rising and falling wail like a death song, punctuated by the dull sound of wood striking flesh. Every time a prisoner was taken from the room, the remaining captives drew closer into themselves, avoiding the eyes of the others.

Eleni ran straight through the ravine down to the house of her uncle Yiorgos Haidis, father of Commissar Costa. She found him feeding his chickens. When she told him that the ELAS guerrillas had arrested her father, the old man spat in the mud. 'Damn Costa!' he exclaimed. 'He talks about a new Greece, but I warned him it would come to this. "You will dig with pick for water," I said, "and blood will gush forth!"'

Together, Eleni and her uncle hurried back up the mountain toward the village square.

The sun was slanting through the fly-specked windows of the school office when the guards came in and motioned to Vasili Stratis. Every other man in the room breathed an involuntary sigh of relief. Vasili discovered that his legs wouldn't support him.

They dragged him through a dark hall to the tiny office at the western end. The guards pushed the door open. The first thing the boy saw was the cripple Boukouvalas lying in a fetal position on the floor. His clublike feet were bare, but Vasili could see they were unscarred; the stumps were too twisted to provide a grip for *falanga*, and in frustration the guerrillas had beaten every inch of the old man's body. Now he was curled on his side, moaning wordlessly.

The odor of blood and shit hit Vasili's nostrils. This was his brother's office, where Minas tended to his duties as secretary of the village and helped illiterate Liotes fill out official papers. The pencil-marked desk and filing cabinets were familiar, but the two guerrilla officers who stood silhouetted

135

against the dirty windows were not. There was a pile of clubs and switches in one corner.

Vasili squinted into the light and the features of the two ELAS officers came into focus. The short one was paunchy, with the intelligent face of a fox. Vasili recognized him with surprise as a teacher from Zitsa named Polychronis Vayis, who had gone to the teachers academy with Minas Stratis and later became notorious fighting for ELAS under the name of *Kapetan* Petritis. A veneer of civilized erudition masked his brutal nature. Later the Gatzoyiannis family would come to know Petritis well.

Vasili Stratis was careful not to indicate that he recognized the officer, for he knew it could cost him his life. Petritis began by asking questions in a conversational tone, his smile revealing a gold tooth. He asked for the names of EDES sympathizers and especially the whereabouts of Vasili's brother Minas, never referring to and totally ignoring the moaning body of Boukouvalas on the floor. When Vasili mumbled that he had no idea where Minas was hiding, Petritis motioned to the other man, who stepped forward. They grabbed his hair and bent him over, beating him on the back and flanks with a piece of wood as thick as his wrist. Vasili instinctively put his hand behind him and the club opened a three-inch gash, which began to drip blood onto the floor. The blows fell in a relentless rhythm as Vasili felt his bones snap.

After the clubbing it was time for *falanga*. Two armed guards came in to hold his feet flexed between the strap and barrel of a rifle as the officers smashed their clubs against his soles. When Vasili squirmed on the floor, Petritis stepped on his face, filling his mouth with dirt, teeth and blood.

The boy was still conscious when the officers told him that they would give him another chance to remember where his brother was hiding and kicked him into a corner next to Boukouvalas. He saw the door open, revealing Kitso Haidis standing there, held firmly by two guards. Petritis let Kitso get a good look, then motioned to the guards to drag out the two inert bodies.

They were slung into one of the large classrooms and as

they fell among others who had been beaten, Vasili saw next to him a young man named Dimitrios Kyratsis whose father owned the general store in Tsamanta. His face was gray and blood was trickling from his nostrils. Vasili could see a puncture wound, as if made by a nail, over his left eyebrow. That night the body of young Kyratsis disappeared from the schoolhouse and his family never learned what became of it.

Eleni and Yiorgos Haidis pushed their way through the crowd outside Costa Haidis' office. Yiorgos insisted so loudly on seeing his son that the guards finally let him pass, but they forced Eleni to wait outside. When he came back out the old man was leaning heavily on his cane, his head bowed. 'I talked to Costa,' he said harshly. 'I told him that if anything happens to my brother, I will no longer recognize him as my son. He wouldn't look me in the eye. He said he would do what he could, but the matter wasn't within his authority.'

Seeing Eleni's face, he put his arm around her and told her she had to at least act hopeful so that her mother and children wouldn't despair.

In the inquisition room Kitso Haidis stood facing the two officers. He blocked out the smell and the way Boukouvalas and Vasili Stratis had looked, trying to think clearly. His cleverness had always saved him until now. He stared around the room and gazed upward at the smoky patches over the hanging kerosene lamps. Then, walking past the uniformed officers, Kitso casually pulled out the only chair and sat down, crossing his legs comfortably and gazing raptly at a fly that was treading its way across the ceiling. Petritis and the other man watched him in surprise.

Petritis glanced at a piece of paper and spoke sternly. 'You are the miller Kitso Haidis,' he said. 'Your fascist sympathies are well known. You have been seen repeatedly fraternizing with the EDES mercenaries and with the traitor Sarantis. The only way to save yourself is to tell us where he's hiding.'

Kitso began to giggle as the officers looked at each other in alarm. The miller pointed at the ceiling. 'He's right up there,' Kitso chortled, 'watching everything you're doing!'

There was a moment of startled silence, then Petritis

reached for a club. 'Maybe we can pound your brains back into place,' he said. They were interrupted by a knock at the door. A man in civilian clothes passed a folded note to Petritis.

The next morning a heavy fog lay on the mountainside when Minas Stratis' wife opened her door to find her husband standing there. 'What are you doing?' she gasped, pulling him inside. 'They've already taken Vasili! Do you want to see our house shuttered in mourning?'

Under cover of the fog, Minas had come home because there was no place else to go. He had been cut off at the Great Ridge by the battle between ELAS and EDES and had spent two nights in a haystack.

Even though she was distracted with worry for her younger son, Minas' mother managed to convince a trusted neighbor to hide the schoolteacher in the tiny storage space under his kitchen floor. 'I'm putting my son's life in your hands and the hands of God,' she told him. Minas huddled in the tiny space for the next forty days and often heard the sound of his own two children playing overhead, never suspecting where their father had gone.

As the sun burned off the mist, a crowd of villagers began to gather outside the schoolhouse. By noontime nearly everyone in Lia was assembled. Their numbers and their silence unnerved the armed *andartes* standing in front of the door. The villagers and the guerrillas returned one another's stares, their breath rising like smoke in the frigid air, until suddenly an appalling chorus of pain burst from the western classroom of the school where the officers had waded into the group of prisoners and were clubbing them, flailing at the writhing mass of heads, arms and legs like threshers harvesting wheat. A shudder passed through the crowd outside.

As the great cry rose from the schoolhouse, the armed *andartes* outside began to sing at a signal from their leader. At first their voices were tuneless and uncertain, but with the defiant words they gained conviction until they were shouting out the verses and stamping their feet to the rhythm.

138

With my rifle on my shoulder
In town, on mountainside and field
I'm clearing a path for liberty
Strewing palms for her advancing feet.
Forward, ELAS, for Greece!
Justice and Liberty!

The villagers watched as one guerrilla began to dance, slow emphatic steps, his arms outstretched, now and then slapping his palm against the side of his shoe. The voices became louder as the song began again, brave words that the peasants had heard many times before at the propaganda gatherings. Until today, their own voices had joined in, united with the guerrillas in their longing for freedom and hatred of the enemy. Now there was a new undertone to the words. The wails of the prisoners created a terrible cacophony. The silent peasants stared at the guerrillas with disbelief, wondering how the fine speeches of Prokopi Skevis had given birth to this ghastly chorus.

Among the frightened faces turned toward the guerrillas, who were grinning now as they shouted out the words, was that of Eleni Gatzoyiannis. She felt her skin crawl as she heard the wails, a hellish antiphon to the martial music. The cries from within the schoolhouse ceased abruptly and the guerrillas' song trailed off. Everyone held his breath. The door opened slowly and the guards stepped aside. The four prisoners from Lia stood there, blinking in the light. There was a groan as the villagers saw what had been done to them.

Vasili Stratis was first, holding his shoes in his hand because his feet were swollen to twice their normal size. He staggered, then fell down the four steps to the ground. No one moved to catch him. The only sound was the thud of his body hitting each step. As he lay there, the crowd drew back in horror. Then two boys, former classmates of Vasili's, pushed forward and carried him home. At the sight of him, his mother slaughtered one of the goats and wrapped the boy inside the raw hide to draw the black blood from his bruises. She could see that he would never walk upright again. She did not tell

Vasili where Minas was hiding, nor did she tell Minas what the *andartes* had done to his younger brother.

Kitso Haidis came out the door next, walking by himself, apparently unhurt. Eleni covered her mouth with her hand, as if to stifle a cry, then she pushed forward and embraced her father, but he pulled away, refusing to be helped. She led him out of the crowd as her children trailed behind, staring at their grandfather curiously.

'Did they beat you?' she whispered.

Kitso winked at her and tapped his temple with his index finger. 'They didn't touch me,' he said. 'I outfoxed them. I convinced them I was crazy!'

Eleni said nothing, but wondered if Costa Haidis had intervened on behalf of his uncle. She later put the question to her cousin directly, but he changed the subject and refused to answer. When her father repeated and embellished the story of how he had fooled the guerrillas, Eleni never contradicted him.

Only the four prisoners from Lia were released. Another twenty-one men from nearby villages were held in the school for a week longer, then led off on an eight-day march to a town in western Macedonia where they were put in prison camps. Two of them, a Greek army officer who had been fighting for EDES, and a schoolteacher from Yeromeri, were held back and shot just outside of Lia.

The dream of revolution and freedom painted by the Skevis brothers had turned into a nightmare, and fear settled over the village. The British commandos felt it as much as the Greeks. Eleni learned from Angeliki that the officers, barricaded inside their house and informed of the beatings and executions by their domestic staff, were beginning to crumble under Spiro Skevis' psychological warfare against them. Skevis was convinced that the British were supplying food, sovereigns and arms to Zervas' EDES forces. He came to the mission nearly every day demanding the same compensation for his own men. Each time, the officers told him that none of the guerrilla groups would receive British aid until they stopped fighting among themselves.

Angeliki described the claustrophobic atmosphere of the headquarters. Skevis' men prowled the edges of the house day and night, making noises to intimidate those inside. The cold December weather and heavy rains increased the gloom. Captain Ian contracted influenza and a high fever, and Angeliki was sent to bring a Greek doctor, who bled him with leeches.

The Skevis guerrillas stepped up their harassment of the mission, and wouldn't let Angeliki and her sister go as far as the spring to draw water. No one wanted to venture to the outhouse. The interpreter had told her that one night Captain Philip took advantage of an open window to relieve himself and was rewarded with a string of Greek oaths and the sight of a drenched Mitsi Bollis scrambling into the bushes.

Captain Ian was 'coming a bit unglued,' Angeliki whispered to Eleni. He imagined enemies everywhere and even accused her and the others of trying to poison him by putting olive oil on the salad greens. Eleni shook her head, wondering what protection there would be for the villagers themselves if the British commandos could be so intimidated by the local Skevis guerrillas.

On Christmas Day of 1943, the Liotes were alarmed to see the ELAS *andartes* gathering in the square in battle formation. They soon learned that Zervas' EDES army had crossed the barrier of the Kalamas River and was moving toward Pogoni, where ELAS was going to try to stop them. Skevis ordered all the reservists to prepare for battle. Before the day was over, the guerrillas and the reserves marched off, leaving Lia nearly empty of men. Within twenty-four hours a small detachment of EDES guerrillas arrived in the village, and to everyone's astonishment Minas Stratis emerged from below his neighbor's kitchen floor, nearly unrecognizable with a forty-days' growth of beard.

A few days later Lia received the most illustrious visitor it had ever seen: the dapper little Italian General Alberto Infante, commander of the ill-fated Pinerolo Division, which had been disarmed by ELAS two months before. He was brought to the Bovington Mission so that the British could evacuate him and the several Italian officers with him north over the mountains to Albania where they would escape by sea to Italy. On January 2, 1944, Captain Philip set out to lead the Italians to safety. In the nine days he was gone, the seesaw of power in the village changed once again. Zervas was being driven southward, and the EDES forces pulled out of Lia, taking Minas Stratis with them. A decisive ELAS victory on the night of January 4 left most of the Mourgana mountains, including Lia, in ELAS hands, where it would remain for the rest of the war.

With Captain Philip away, Ian was alone in charge of the British post when Spiro Skevis returned with his men and resumed hounding him. Ian's predicament worsened with the addition of a new responsibility – two downed air crews, one British and one American, who arrived in Lia to be evacuated to safety. Of the seventeen fliers, more than half were suffering from malaria. Even though Angeliki and her sister worked far into the night cooking for the new arrivals, there was not enough food, medicine or bedding to go around. Even the outhouse was inadequate for the crowd, so trenches had to be dug on the hill above the headquarters, and they overflowed with the first heavy rain.

The news that a crew of American pilots was in the village filled Eleni with the hope that one of them might be from Massachusetts and have some news of her husband. She had not received a letter from Christos for three and a half years, since the Italian invasion cut off communications. She hurried to the village square, where the fliers who were not ill passed the time in snowball fights with the village children. Eleni resolutely approached the interpreter and handed him a piece of paper with Christos' address in Worcester written on it. She knew it was unrealistic to expect that one of the young soldiers might have heard of her husband, but she was determined to find out. She watched with falling spirits as the paper was passed from hand to hand and the strangers shouted the words 'Worcester, Massachusetts' to one another and shook their heads. Finally the interpreter passed the paper back to her and explained kindly that even if one of them had been from Worcester, American cities were larger than she thought, larger even than Yannina, and the chances of any one American soldier knowing her husband were infinitesimal.

Trying to hide her disappointment from the foreigners, Eleni decided to visit Nitsa, who lived just above the British headquarters nearby. She found Nitsa and Andreas entertaining 'Henry' the cook from the mission, a round, garrulous man named Andreas Tsifoutis. He loved to gossip, and with much shaking of his head and expressive gestures, he described how Captain Ian had become unstrung to the point where even the Greek-speaking staff could tell he was having a nervous breakdown. The cook hoped that the other captain would return before something tragic happened. He told how Spiro Skevis had arrived one night, loudly demanding money and arms, and Ian became so frantic that he pulled out a hand grenade and threatened to blow up the entire house if Skevis didn't leave. The next day Ian called the staff together and told them that the doors and windows of the headquarters were being wired and booby-trapped with explosives because he feared an attack by the Skevis guerrillas. 'In the morning, if you don't see the door open,' Ian advised the Botsaris girls through the interpreter, 'don't come in. Don't touch anything, because if you do, you'll blow yourselves to bits and us with you.'

Nitsa rocked back and forth, her hands over her ears, and exclaimed that if the Fafoutis house exploded it would take her house with it. To distract her, the cook launched into a comical recitation of Ian's behavior when he was drunk, which now was most of the time. Ian slept every night with a pail of Albanian beer at his bedside as well as an empty bucket to use as a chamber pot, and sometimes in the night he'd be so groggy he'd confuse the two.

The hostility between the British and the ELAS guerrillas reached a climax soon after Captain Philip returned, when Spiro and Prokopi Skevis organized a massive demonstration in the village to pressure the British into giving them supplies and money. ELAS supporters flooded in from all over the Mourgana villages and beyond. The central square was not large enough to contain the thousands of demonstrators, who arrived shouting, 'Give us food! Give us arms! Give us medicine! We are fighting for you and you have forgotten us!' It was the largest gathering in the history of the village, and the Liotes marveled at the number and strength of the supporters rallied by the Skevis brothers.

Eleni could see that the mood of the demonstrators was ugly and she forbade her children to leave the house, worrying that someone might be hurt. She followed her neighbors to the square and watched apprehensively as the two British officers and their interpreter walked, grim and pale, from their headquarters to the square through the gauntlet of shouting Greeks. They were clearly frightened, and she wondered if Ian's fragile mental balance would survive the demonstration.

Four decades later Philip Nind remembered his apprehensions. 'I was more afraid of Spiro Skevis than of the Germans,' he said, and in his journal made at the time he described the Skevis brothers: 'The elder [Prokopi] was a politician . . . filled with book-read Marxism which used to pour out from his mouth in rather amusing contexts and clichés. The younger [Spiro] was the most dangerous man I met in Greece. He commanded a battalion and commanded it well. Energetic and shrewd, his fanaticism had warped his mind in the most disagreeable manner. He was a sadist with, to my knowledge, many cold-blooded murders to his name; and all the complaints of ELAS torturing in that area were laid at his door.'

The knot of British officers tried to keep their feet in the shouting throng until Prokopi Skevis silenced the people with a gesture and climbed up on a table to address them. He spoke stirringly, demanding that the British honor ELAS requests for money and aid so that they could defeat the traitor Zervas. The crowd cheered every word.

When the applause died down, Eleni saw Captain Ian climb shakily onto the table with the interpreter beside him. She was surprised to hear him speak simply and effectively. 'We are soldiers under orders, who do what we are told, just as you do!' he shouted. 'You ask for arms. You complain that the dropping of supplies has stopped. It will start again when you end your civil war and return to fighting the enemy!'

144

He blinked as an angry voice from the crowd interrupted him. 'One question, Captain!' someone shouted. 'When you fight traitors, is that called a civil war?'

When the question was translated, Ian paused, thinking hard. Then he answered with an analogy that clearly struck home to the family-oriented Greek peasants. 'My father has four sons,' he said. 'When we fought with each other, he would never take the side of one or the other, no matter what the circumstances. He had to try to restore peace in the family so that it could work toward the good of all of us. We needed the strength that comes from unity.'

Spiro Skevis was too angry to let him go on. 'Answer the question, Englishman!' he called out. 'Zervas is a traitor! Down with Zervas! Death to Zervas!'

The crowd had wavered for a moment, but now they joined in. 'Down with Zervas!' they shouted. 'Death!' Eleni was reminded of the guerrillas singing outside the schoolhouse while their prisoners were being beaten inside. Her neighbors' faces were transformed with hate as they began stamping and shouting for blood. To Eleni, Ian's parable had seemed sensible and apt. She was reminded of how, when she assigned Glykeria and Kanta each to sweep half of the front steps and terrace, they would wrangle over who had the dirtier, harder part, arguing until nothing was accomplished, and in disgust, Eleni ended by cleaning the steps herself. In the same way, ELAS and EDES were depending on the Allies to sweep the Germans out until not only the steps but the whole house was clean. Then they planned to battle for control of the house, and if they continued wrangling like children, they could end by destroying it and bringing the roof down on their heads.

The crowd was in no mood to listen to parables or explanations, and Eleni watched as the British officers hastily pushed their way back toward the safety of their headquarters before the demonstrators decided to turn their anger on them.

In early February, Eleni walked down the path to the Botsaris house and found Angeliki in tears. The girl told her that the British were preparing to leave. The last straw had been the attempt of the Skevis guerrillas to lead the English and the downed airplane crews into a German ambush.

145

Captain Philip intended to lead the American and English fliers into Albania, she explained, as he had successfully evacuated General Infante. As always, he notified the guerrilla commanders in the areas he would cross of the route he would take. ELAS gave him a go-ahead, but once they left Lia and crossed the mountains, the British stumbled directly into the path of a German drive which had been in progress for four days. Obviously the ELAS commanders had known the Germans' position when they okayed the route. The British and the fliers managed to save themselves by hiding out for several days, some of them in a cramped underground baking oven. Angry and demoralized, they retraced their steps to Lia. Years later Philip Nind said, 'Clearly, ELAS was hoping that the Germans would kill us, because we were an embarrassment to their efforts to persuade the villagers that the English and American allies were not really fighting the Germans effectively compared to the Russians.'

The attempted sabotage by ELAS drove Captain Ian over the edge, Angeliki said. She described how he called the staff of the mission together, ranted at them in his foreign tongue until his voice broke, and then burst into tears. Suddenly he fainted, falling over 'like a cedar tree,' she said. From that moment he was entirely out of control, weeping and raging, and throwing things at his fellow officers.

Angeliki was desolate at the news that the British were leaving. Not only would she lose the income that had kept her alive, she said, she would be left unprotected from the Skevis guerrillas, who considered her a traitor and worse. She didn't know how her family would survive without the commandos, and despite their eccentricities, she had become truly fond of them.

In the last week of February the two downed air crews set out for the Ionian coast to the southwest, where they were to be evacuated. Captain Ian went with them after a tearful farewell to his fellow commandos. Philip Nind would never see him again, but he later learned that Ian was evacuated to Cairo, hospitalized in a psychiatric ward and after his recovery was killed in action in Italy.

On the cold, misty morning of February 26, 1944, a large

146

crowd of villagers gathered to wish Captain Philip and the radio operator, Ken, farewell. Eleni was among them. She was nearly as saddened as Angeliki to see them go. She had hoped that the British might curb the brutality and internecine fighting of the guerrillas, and now she feared their departure would mean that more Greeks would die at Greek hands.

The British commandos were as downcast as the villagers. Decades later Philip Nind remarked that the few months he spent in Lia changed him radically. 'I came with very clear ideas of right and wrong,' he said. 'The Greek mountains were totally different from anything I had known and I soon realized that politics there had nothing to do with the undergraduate politics I had known at Oxford, gentlemen's politics. In Lia it was politics tooth and claw, and the blood ran literally. It was the first time I saw dead bodies – not dead Germans or dead British, as I had expected – but Greeks killed by Greeks, and worse, some of the bodies were obviously mutilated. During the whole time I was in Lia, I was never given the men to organize a single operation against the Germans, and the ELAS guerrillas constantly tried to indoctrinate the villagers against us. I was almost a Marxist myself until I saw Communism put into practice by the *andartes* in Greece. I left Lia a very disillusioned young man.'

The villagers Nind left behind were more than disillusioned. The commandos were scarcely out of sight when the rumor swept Lia that the British had abandoned them to their fate because the Germans were approaching.

CHAPTER FIVE

When the Germans suspected a village of harboring guerrillas, the punishment was swift and all-embracing. Throughout Greece more than 150 villages were burned.

In Kalavryta, near Patras, the Germans entered the town in early December and told the 2,500 inhabitants there was nothing to fear. But at six o'clock on the morning of December 8, 1943, the church bells called the people to the town square. They were divided into two groups: women and children under twelve years old, and men and boys over twelve. There was chaos as mothers tried to convince the Germans their sons were too young to go with the men.

The women and children were locked in the schoolhouse and the 800 men and boys led to a wheat field on a hill behind the cemetery, where, after watching their village burn, they were cut down with machine guns.

As the school was set ablaze, the women began throwing their children out the windows. One German soldier took pity on them and opened a door, setting them free moments before the burning roof collapsed. When they found the corpses of their husbands, the homeless women had no shovels and buried the men with their bare hands. Every night wild animals dug up the shallow graves.

By the early months of 1944 the Germans knew they were losing the war and their reprisals became more vicious. All 228 inhabitants of Distomo, near Delphi, were murdered and mutilated, including twenty children under the age of five. The young women were mutilated and cut open from the genitals to the breasts, and the children were disemboweled, their entrails wound around their necks.

Before Easter of 1944 the German commandant in Epiros, Lieutenant General Hubert Lanz, began to plan an assault on the villages of the Mourgana along the Albanian border to flush out the *andartes* hiding in the mountains and clear a route for a possible evacuation. But first it was necessary to attend to the Jews in Yannina.

Since the ninth century there had been Jewish communities in the large Greek cities, and in March of 1943, 46,000 Jews in Salonika were rounded up and shipped to German concentration camps. But the 1,950 Jews living in the provincial capital, including seventy prosperous merchant families, did not flee. They knew the German troops stationed in their city depended on the Jewish community for food and supplies, and they were reassured when General Lanz promised them they would be safe. The general severely reprimanded the mayor of Yannina for ordering all Jews in the city to sign in at the city hall each morning.

ELAS distributed leaflets to Yannina's Jews urging them to flee the city and join the *andartes,* but they became suspicious when they read the leaflets, which said: 'Take your money and come to the mountains of ELAS to be saved.' Only forty-two Jews answered the call. The rest stayed in their homes hoping that the German commandant was a man of his word.

WAITING FOR THE BARBARIANS

MARCH BROUGHT THE return of the swallows and the weaning of the lambs. When the Germans did not appear in Lia on the heels of the departing British, the villagers relaxed and began to prepare for Easter.

On March 26, the day after the Feast of the Annunciation, Eleni Gatzoyiannis and her sister sat on the steps of their mother's house, enjoying the warm sun, while four-year-old Nikola played nearby. Nitsa called the boy over and began to undo a bracelet of twisted red and white threads tied to his arm. 'Now that Annunciation's come and gone we can take off your March thread and hang it on the tree for the swallows,' she said. 'And you won't have to worry about sunburn or insects all summer!'

Solemnly Nikola watched his aunt drape the grimy threads over the walnut tree near the door. Eleni looked on with a mixture of amusement and vexation. 'Why do you fill the child's head with all that nonsense?' she asked. 'A red thread won't protect him from sunburn any more than garlic and a nail in your pocket will keep you safe from wolves!'

'Maybe you can read and I can't,' Nitsa replied, 'but it's one thing to learn and another to be wise. You like to laugh at my amulets, but if it weren't for me, you wouldn't have a son today but another daughter!'

Eleni turned to her in amazement and Megali gave her elder daughter a warning glance, but Nitsa was already swept away by the drama of her sacrifice. 'Ach, what I went through for you to have a son!' she exclaimed, lifting her hands and gazing heavenward for sympathy. 'If it wasn't for that piece of umbilical cord I fed you, you'd be looking at another daughter right now!'

Eleni stared. 'I ate *what*?'

Nitsa nodded, full of self-importance. 'I had to walk all the way to Kostana to buy a piece of umbilical cord from the midwife there. Of course, it had to be taken from a firstborn son, born in the forty days after Fotini's birth. Remember that nice cheese pie I made you, full of fresh eggs and butter? You said it was the best one I ever made!'

Eleni didn't know whether to laugh or be sick, but Nitsa was only beginning the saga of her spells. She had saved a bit of Fotini's umbilical cord after it fell off and on New Year's Day baked it in a loaf of bread which was fed to the rooster, she said. 'That's how your luck was turned around and Nikolaki came out a boy! For myself, I can't grow a boy *or* a girl,' she concluded sadly. 'But for you I did everything, and it worked!'

Megali was waiting for Eleni to show the quick temper that she had inherited from her father, but instead she threw back her head and laughed until the tears came, scaring Nikola so that he ran over and tugged at her skirt. Nitsa's smug expression turned to annoyance until Eleni hugged her and gasped, 'After all you've done for me, sister, perhaps God will relent and give you a child!'

Solemnly Nitsa crossed herself.

The drowsy quiet of the morning was suddenly broken by shouts coming from the direction of the Petsis house. Nitsa sniffed the air like a pointer and they all got up to see why Lambros Petsis' girl was so excited.

Petsis owned a small tinker's shop and a house in Yannina, dividing his time between the provincial capital and the village. He had a son scarcely older than Nikola, but his dark, almond-eyed daughter, Milia, just turned eighteen, was his favorite.

Petsis was visible, just rounding the last curve in the road leading three heavily laden mules. As he came closer, the growing knot of onlookers could make out what he was carrying: bolts of velvet, satin and wool; shiny leather shoes dangling from the saddles; fine linen sheets; lacy woven coverlets; and men's suits. After four years of turning worn hems and sewing on patches, they stared in wonder at the sight of Lambros Petsis carrying enough finery to ransom a king.

When he reached his front gate, Petsis climbed off his mule and embraced his daughter, who was squirming with excitement. 'Where did you get all this, *Patera*!' she squealed. 'How could you afford it?'

'It's all free, my sultana,' he grinned. 'There's enough here for two dowries with plenty left over for our neighbors!'

Everybody began shouting questions.

'It's from the Jews,' Petsis explained. 'Yesterday at dawn, the Germans rounded them all up and herded them down to the lake where they locked them into trucks and drove them off. What a noise they made! Women crying for their children, husbands and wives separated. It would have made an icon weep! They took the family that lived over my store too.' He cleared his throat. 'But you know what they say about an ill wind. They left the Jewish houses and stores with the doors wide open. Better us than the Germans, everybody said. The Jews won't be back! So we took what we could carry. Good thing I moved fast. By nightfall the Germans had locked everything and strung up two boys for looting.'

Petsis, a generous man, began handing out gifts to the women crowding around: an apron, an initialed pillowcase, a little-girl's dress, dotted with pink rosebuds. When his eyes met Eleni's, they faltered. Then he said, 'I've got a fine piece of green velvet here, and when I saw it, I said, "That would make a handsome dress for *Kyria* Eleni's eldest daughter, Olga."'

'Thank you, Lambros,' Eleni replied, 'but I can't take it.'

'Then a cap for your only son,' he said quickly, holding up a gray wool one. 'I've never seen a cap on his head.'

'No, thank you,' said Eleni. 'They've gone so many years now without a cap, without a new dress, they can wait until the war is over and America opens up.' She saw he was hurt. 'I can't take clothes that belong to people who are being led away to their deaths,' she explained.

Aware that she had punctured his joy at his good fortune,

152

Eleni took her son's hand and turned away. As she climbed the path she could hear some of the women insisting that Lambros take the gifts back. God punishes those who steal from the dead, they said. Other women scolded them for talking foolishness. It's not as if Lambros had done anything to the Jews!

By the evening of the next day two tailors and a seamstress from neighboring villages had taken up residence in the good chamber of the Petsis house and set to work on Milia's dowry, making long sleeveless tunics, short black velvet vests, satin aprons and twenty dresses in a rainbow of colors. The seamstress embroidered everything with threads of real gold and silver.

The dowry was nearly finished when Milia fell to the floor one morning as if dead. She awoke with her face twisted into a grimace that would remain for the rest of her life. Everyone told the heartbroken father that he must not blame himself.

Milia couldn't say a word; she lay on her pallet making signs to her parents that she wanted to die. After some months she learned to utter garbled words which only her family could understand. But by then the tailors had returned to their villages, and the prospective groom had fled to Athens.

Milia's tragedy occurred just before Easter, which fell on April 16 in 1944. War or no war, the Liotes were determined to celebrate Christ's resurrection and their survival through another year.

At Saturday midnight the bells of Holy Trinity caroled the triumphant news: 'Christ is risen!' From mountain to mountain other church bells answered: 'He is risen indeed!'

Easter Sunday dawned fresh and bright, even though there was still snow in the shadows of the peaks. Eleni awakened early to help her next-door neighbor Tassos Bartzokis prepare the Easter kid, which their families would share. Tassos' wife was eight months pregnant and not well enough to do the heavy cooking, so Eleni made the big pot of hot, lemony, dill-fragrant soup from the goat's entrails to break the long fast. Fotini and Glykeria had been busy since Thursday burnishing the crimson eggs with olive oil.

153

The next morning the pot of soup was still warm on the hearth when an ELAS *andarte* raced into the village square, and the bells began to toll with the news everyone had feared for so long: a battalion of Germans was on its way to the Mourgana from the direction of the Great Ridge. The scraps of the Easter feast were left on the tables as everyone piled blankets, pots, food and cradles on the mules and set off up the mountain.

The threat of the Italian invasion over three years before had sent the villagers only as far as the caves, but their fear of the Germans was so much greater that they now fled over their own mountains to the last level clearing before the Albanian border.

It was up the cornucopia of green vegetation between the peaks of Kastro and the Prophet Elias that the Liotes hurried, rushing toward the high plateau beyond them which concealed a sheltered triangular patch of flat land the villagers still call the Agora, the ancient word for marketplace, although it had been empty for twenty-three centuries. In this hidden spot the Liotes hoped they could camp, safe from the invading Germans.

The old and crippled were carried on stretchers or lashed onto mules. Tassina Bartzokis, heavy with the weight of the unborn baby, struggled behind her donkey, which was so burdened with her invalid father and pots of food that it lost its footing and nearly rolled down the cliff. Eleni pulled Nikola by the hand up the steep path and caught up with Megali, who was driving the goats and worrying aloud about her stubborn sister-in-law, Anastasia Haidis. Anastasia was one of the two old women who had refused to leave the village. If the Germans wanted her old bones, she insisted despite her family's protests, they were welcome to them. 'I've eaten my bread, I've burned my oil.'

As Anastasia watched the tide of humanity surge up the mountainside, leaving her behind, she saw a movement on the hill above her and realized she was not entirely alone. The blind woman, Sophia Karapanou, was puttering around in her garden. There was no one to lead her to the Agora, and the ancient crone could no more leave the village than could

154

the huge plane tree. Anastasia decided that she would take a plate of the stew she was making up to poor Sophia.

The streams of escaping villagers from different neighborhoods of Lia converged at the narrow pass between the two peaks of Kastro and Prophet Elias. As they hurried, jostling each other, through the gap that led to the sanctuary of the Agora, the Gatzoyiannis family looked up to their right and saw, ascending the slope toward the summit of Prophet Elias, a single file of ELAS *andartes*, their rifles silhouetted against the sun. The last one in line was Mitsi Bollis.

No longer venting his malice in petty tricks like letting the fox into the Gatzoyiannis' chicken house, Mitsi had gained renown as one of ELAS' most zealous and sadistic 'interrogators.' He had even been immortalized in a popular bit of doggerel: 'Better to be hit by rifle volleys / Than by the club of Mitsi Bollis.'

As the simian figure of Bollis followed the line of guerrillas up the mountain, the villagers hurried through the cleft below, gazing fearfully at the armed men. But the cobbler, Andreas Kyrkas, emboldened by the fact that Bollis was a relative, shouted up at him, 'Comrade Mitsi! Don't tell me you're planning to take on the Germans with a handful of *andartes?*'

'We'll shit on their fathers!' crowed Bollis, brandishing his rifle.

'And they'll chop the whole village into their salad,' Andreas answered dryly. 'It's better to melt in the sunlight and strike by the moon.'

Bollis eyed him. 'I'll report your advice to the *kapetanios*,' he said and turned back up the mountain.

'Well done, husband!' Nitsa moaned when Bollis was out of earshot. 'Now you've fixed us all! He'll have your name written on their slate for certain!'

'If they're crazy enough to fire on the Germans, none of us will live to worry about the club of Mitsi Bollis,' muttered Kitso Haidis, who was behind her. 'In Kefalovriso the Germans roasted twenty-one men, including a priest, because the *andartes* there fired on their patrol.'

Carrying Nikola astride her back and holding Fotini by the

hand, Eleni led her family into the Agora, only to find that all the sheltered spots had already been taken by goats, cradles, pots and old women. As darkness fell, all fires had to be extinguished for fear of betraying their hiding place.

Tuesday passed with cold food and foreboding. Occasionally someone would walk as far as Prophet Elias and report back that there was no sign of life in the village, but that on the peak the *andartes* had dug themselves into a foxhole with their machine gun.

Eleni and her children were already asleep on Tuesday night, huddled together for warmth, when a shadowy figure rushed into the clearing and shouted that the monastery of St. Athanassios was in flames. For seven hundred years, the monastery had been a white landmark against the green foothills, three kilometers southwest of the village. It was there that the British airplanes had dropped supplies, and Christos Gatzoyiannis had said goodbye to his wife for the last time.

The news of the burning sparked furious disagreements among the refugees. If the Germans were at St. Athanassios, the majority insisted, they must be heading westward toward Tsamanta. That meant they would move through the pass above Tsamanta into Albania, circle around the opposite side of the Mourgana and sweep back down the mountain into Lia, flushing out *andartes* on the way and passing right over the spot where they were all now hiding. No one had anticipated that the Germans might come from the north.

The cobbler, Andreas, felt his courage snap. He was not a coward, but during the Anatolian wars in 1921, somewhere outside of Ankara, he had been shot and left for dead in a muddy ditch for four days. Nightmares of that ditch began to wake him after he saw beaten villagers stagger out of the schoolhouse, bleeding from the blows of the ELAS inquisitors. Now the approach of the Germans had shattered his nerves altogether. 'We've got to get out of here,' he begged. 'They'll catch us like sparrows in quicklime!'

Kitso Haidis began to pace. 'But if they veer east at Kamitsani and we head down, we'll run right into them,' he worried. Eleni looked from her father to her brother-in-law, praying that they would stop arguing and make the right decision before the Germans arrived.

The argument raged all night. Should they stay or leave, and where could they go? Tasso Bartzokis watched his wife sleeping, a vein pulsing in her neck, her belly swollen like a ripe pomegranate. Her lips were blue. He was sure the cold would kill the baby. He thought of his dead parents' house near the village of Kostana in the foothills, where his sister-in-law now lived. The other side of the house was empty. They could hide there, out of the cold. He turned to Eleni and asked if she wanted to bring her family and hide with them at Kostana. His wife's baby might come early and it would make her feel safer to have her close friend and neighbor along. Eleni was tempted. Her children were suffering from exposure on the cold mountainside. In a house she could heat them some food. She looked at her father, who shook his head and said, 'It's too dangerous!' Then, for the first time, Eleni decided to take the decision for her family's fate into her own hands. 'You can stay here,' she told Kitso, 'but I'm taking the children and going to Kostana.'

By morning Eleni's choice had prevailed and Kitso and Megali as well as Nitsa and Andreas had all elected to go with her. As soon as it was light they put Tassina on the mule and set off while the rest of the villagers on the plateau warned them they were walking straight to their deaths.

At the same moment, the inhabitants of Babouri were also wondering how to save themselves. The smoke of the monastery meant that the Germans would be in their village soon. All the young men had fled the previous day, but before they left, Fotis Economou, one of the EDES sympathizers who had been beaten in Lia's schoolhouse, made a pact with one of the ELAS leaders, both men setting aside their mutual hatred to save the village. Fotis advised the women and old men staying behind to welcome the Germans and offer them refreshments, and the ELAS captain there commanded his guerrillas hiding in the foothills below not to fire on the enemy for the sake of the village.

'The drowning man grasps his own hair,' the peasants often

157

remarked, and in their terror the people of Babouri grasped at the one hope in their midst, Katina Tatsis. She was no different in appearance from any other black-clad, middle-aged peasant woman, but in her youth she had been a schoolteacher in Kavala and she could speak six languages, including German.

The villagers asked her to interpret for them. As everyone made ready for the enemy's arrival, Katina was the only person in the Mourgana mountains who was thinking of Cavafy's poem: 'The barbarians will arrive today/And they're bored by eloquence and public speeches.' Now the fate of her community depended on Katina's eloquence in a tongue she scarcely remembered.

I hung on my mother's hand during the three-hour walk to the outskirts of Kostana, trying not to listen to my uncle's nervous whispers and my grandfather's curses. Descending the mountain in the chill morning air, we saw no sign of the Germans, but by the time we reached the Bartzokis house and found the key to the empty half, Tassina was so weak she had to be lifted from the mule. While she was carried into her sister-in-law's quarters, Fotini and I explored the other side. There was a fireplace, large stuffed floor pillows, a low table and even a kneading trough.

My uncle Andreas followed us in and stationed himself at the northern window, where he muttered, 'They're coming closer, I can feel it.' To escape his forebodings, I wandered into the other side of the house, where Tassina was resting. It startled me to find her crying. Her husband was explaining that he was leaving to camp atop the hill called Lykou, four miles to the east, where he could see the Germans from a distance, whether they came from the north or the south. If they were coming down from the mountains, he said, he'd run back and warn us. If they came from the south – well, he said, stroking her hair, they weren't likely to harm a house full of children and a pregnant woman. Tassina didn't answer, but just kept crying and turned her face to the wall.

Everywhere I turned I was met with the sight of the adults

158

in our party, including the men who had always seemed so decisive, falling apart before the threat of the Germans' arrival. I tried to imagine the Germans and could think only of a fierce wind, churning its way inexorably toward us, uprooting huge trees in its path and tossing them aside.

The general hysteria was beginning to affect me, and I returned to the other side of the house. I found my mother and grandmother making corn bread, aprons tied around their waists, kneading the yellow dough in the bread trough, while delicious, yeasty smells filled the room. The homely sight of my mother doing these familiar chores reassured me and made me feel less vulnerable to the faceless dangers outside.

'After three days in the mountains the children need to get some warm food in their stomachs and sleep under a roof for one night,' my mother said, straightening up from her work and rubbing one floury arm across her forehead.

'They'll see the smoke from the chimney,' Andreas protested, his voice rising. 'Our best chance is out there where we can run and hide.'

My mother said in an even voice that held an unfamiliar firmness, 'We'll go tomorrow. Tonight we'll sleep here.'

My uncle shrugged and capitulated, resuming his vigil at the window as he, muttered to no one in particular. 'And if tomorrow is too late?'

Despite his doubts, the calm resolution of my mother's face, her cheeks wanned by the cooking fire, comforted me, and I curled up near the hearth, waiting for the corn bread to be ready.

The next morning before dawn, the Gatzoyiannis family, under the prodding of Kitso and Andreas, left Tassina in the care of her sister-in-law, and, driving the goats ahead of them, crept through the shuttered village toward a ridge crowned by a small chapel to St. Marina. On the far side, in a dried-up river bed that ran through a field, they made camp.

The same dawn found the women and old men of Babouri gathering at the churchyard on the western boundary of their village with Katina Tatsis at their head. The young women and children had hidden themselves behind closed shutters. Sometime after midday the old people watched in horrified fascination as a battalion of two hundred Germans and about sixty black-shirted Chams led by four mounted officers approached from the direction of the monastery of St. Athanassios.

The red earth shook under their boots as they stamped to a halt before the villagers, and their commandant dismounted. At a nod from Katina Tatsis, a dozen village grandmothers in their best black churchgoing dresses stepped forward holding large trays of walnuts, Turkish delight, white goat cheese and thimble-sized glasses of fiery moonshine. Katina began the speech she had been rehearsing all night.

'You and your men are welcome in Babouri, *Herr Kommandant*,' she said. 'Our small village is at your disposal. Please to have some little refreshment.'

The man with the eagle patch above his breast pocket smiled and asked how she knew German. Katina told him she was a schoolteacher, a student of Goethe and Schiller, and uttered the second part of her prepared speech. 'There are no *andartes* in Babouri. We beg of you not to judge our village by what other Greeks have done!'

If there were no *andartes* here, where were the young men? he asked. Katina replied that they were all itinerant peddlers or shepherds now in the high pastures with the animals.

The German soldiers passed a pleasant two hours lounging in the churchyard under a plane tree. They smacked their lips over the *tsipouro* and toasted the hospitality of the Babouriotes. 'Good health!' they shouted to the assembled old people. 'Heil Hitler!'

'Heil Hitler!' the villagers responded, and Katina could feel sweat trickling between her breasts.

The commandant was a large, florid man who showed Katina photographs of his children and complimented her on the local cheese.

It was late afternoon when the Germans made ready to leave. The commandant thanked Katina for the village's hospitality and added, 'You see, if we are not provoked, it is not necessary to fear us.'

160

Then the battalion marched through the village moving toward Lia while hidden eyes followed them from behind every shuttered window. When they were gone the villagers crowded around the exhausted Katina to congratulate her. They had escaped Armageddon thanks to some *tsipouro* and a middle-aged schoolmistress who knew a little German.

Half an hour later the euphoria dissolved with the news that the Germans were not quite gone. They had camped for the night halfway between Babouri and Lia, only ten minutes outside of the village.

That night a fine rain fell on the Germans in their tents outside Lia and on the Gatzoyiannis family huddled in the field by St. Marina. Eleni held Nikola and Fotini in her lap with an oilcloth draped over the three of them. The rainwater ran down her arms and the children's bare legs.

The sun rose on mountains washed as clean as on the day of creation. The Germans awoke damp and irritable, looking down on foothills still hidden in morning mist. The commandant ordered an early start. He knew from his intelligence reports that just ahead was the home of the Skevis brothers, in a village so strongly sympathetic to ELAS that it was called 'Little Moscow.' He was expecting trouble.

As the battalion rounded the last bend in the path to Lia, they saw the gray slate roofs of the village spread before them, touched by the first fingers of light. The heathery green of the mountainside was punctuated with puffs of golden broom and mauve Judas trees. Over it all glowered a sky heavy with rainclouds. It was the same supernatural light once painted by a man from Crete called El Greco, but the Germans were not admiring the view.

Near the western edge of the village Anastasia Haidis had risen early and left the house to take a covered copper pot of stew up the mountain to the blind woman, Sophia Karapanou.

The German battalion marched into the village, past the deserted Petsis house, and was just abreast of the double Haidis house when the morning hush was punctuated by the sound of machine-gun fire spattering from the heights of

Prophet Elias, too far away to do any damage, sending puffs of smoke drifting up into the sky.

The German commandant shouted orders in a voice full of excitement. Perhaps the guerrillas were trying to lure them into the crags and hollows in order to have the advantage, but they would soon learn the price of their arrogance. Within moments, the Germans assembled half a dozen machine guns and an equal number of mortars, all trained toward Prophet Elias. Suddenly the whole side of the mountain below the chapel began to erupt as the Germans strafed it from bottom to top. Soon the slope was black and smoking.

The commandant ordered the firing to stop. Any *andartes* still on the mountainside must have been hit or driven off. Now it was time to punish the people who had sheltered them.

'Burn the village,' he ordered.

The moment the German fusillade ceased, Anastasia Haidis ran out of the blind woman's house. She looked down and saw a thin wisp of smoke rising above the screen of cypress trees. 'They're burning my house!' she gasped. 'My God, the goats are in the cellar!'

Sophia reached out sightlessly to hold her back, but Anastasia was already stumbling down the path, her hands waving at the unseen enemy. A knot of German soldiers watched her descending upon them like a shrieking raven. 'Have mercy on my house, spare my goats!' she screamed, making the Chams smile. She threw herself against the door to the cellar, where the three goats could be heard bleating. One of the Chams came forward to pull her back. 'Get away, old woman, or we'll let you roast along with your goats!' he said.

As she watched the flames devour the house where she had lived since she was a bride of fourteen, Anastasia crumpled and they let her fall. Then, suddenly, she was on her feet, flying toward the door once more. As they dragged her back again, Anastasia's screams rose over the roar of the fire and could be heard by Tassina Bartzokis all the way down to Kostana. The air carried the cries like disembodied spirits:

162

'Children, where are you? Save me!' Above in the Perivoli, Sophia sat waiting in her own house, listening with the preternatural hearing of the blind to every moan that Anastasia uttered.

Drawn by the commotion, the commandant approached. He had just completed a tour of the village and was pleased with the progress. The school building and most of the houses were in flames. He looked down with satisfaction at the lower village and its centerpiece, the Church of the Virgin.

If the *cafenion* is the heart of a Greek village, the largest church is its soul. For seven centuries the Church of the Virgin had nourished the souls of the Liotes. Its interior was their pride and their Bible. No one needed to be literate to know the Holy Scriptures, for they were all illustrated here in the frescoes painted by the hand of monks long vanished into anonymity. In the soaring vault of the cupola, Christ the All-Powerful, thirty times the size of a mortal man, scrutinized the congregation below, his Gospel clasped in his hand. In the spaces between the windows, the prophets and apostles, painted full-length with bristling beards and mournful eyes, made their eternal parade toward the altar.

The villagers of Lia never tired of staring at the wonders of the Church of the Virgin: the walls glowed with every saint and martyr, the twelve feast days, the Last Supper, the life of the Virgin, and as a final warning, on the wall near the door, the Last Judgment, where bizarre dragons and devils punished every sort of evil, with the priests in the front rank of the sinners.

The jewel of the church was the magnificent golden carved iconostasis, the shimmering screen which hid the mysteries of the sanctuary until the priest emerged from the Royal Doors carrying the blood and body of Christ. The iconostasis held four tiers of icons, splendid with gold leaf and jewels, and between the sacred pictures the native wood-carvers had allowed their imagination to create a fantasy of twining vines and mythical birds and beasts perched in the lacy fretwork.

The most sacred object in the church was the silken *antimin* on the altar table, with the death of Christ embroidered on it and the bone of a saint sewn into its lining. It was this cloth which the Chams set alight. Thanks to the kerosene they spilled, the flames climbed swiftly to the top tier of the iconostasis, making the sinuous vines and animals come alive. The flickering light was reflected in the saints' eyes and on the face of the Pantocrator, but the only living witness to the magnificent final spectacle was the German commandant.

Convinced that the church would burn nicely, he set out toward the starting point of his promenade, where he found a number of his men gathered around an old woman in black who was struggling in the grasp of two Chams.

The commandant had decided not to send his men into the upper village for fear partisans were still hiding there and he had satisfied himself that all of the middle and lower village was burning. But he felt disappointed that no prisoner had been taken from this serpents' nest of rebels whom he could use as an example.

The two Chams were getting tired of holding Anastasia as she flapped and screeched. For the onlookers the joke had lost its interest. The Chams glanced at the commandant and he gave a small nod. They picked up the old woman like a doll and tossed her through one of the now empty windows. The floor was gone and she fell directly into the flames of the cellar as a long wordless scream came from her mouth that raised the hairs on the arms of the listeners in Kostana. Tassina heard it and felt an answering pain start at her sides and travel toward the center of her abdomen. She realized that her time had come early, and felt warm liquid flowing down her legs.

The commandant ordered his men to assemble. There was nothing more to be accomplished here. They marched through the village and left, heading southeast toward the rise of St. Marina, where the Gatzoyiannis family was hiding.

On the far side of the ridge dedicated to Marina, the martyred saint of the grape harvest, the Gatzoyiannis family watched their sheep and goats graze while Fotini and Nikola played in the dry riverbed. They were too far away to hear Anastasia Haidis' screams, but the barrage of German gunfire shocked them into a fearful silence. They sat, scarcely daring to move, waiting.

After a few minutes there was an exclamation from Nitsa, and everyone looked into the sky where a delicate finger of smoke was rising. 'They're burning the village!' Megali blurted out. She began to cry and Eleni put her arms around her.

'I'm going to the top of St. Marina to see what's happening,' said Kitso Haidis.

'I'm going with you, Father,' Eleni said quickly. At once Glykeria and Kanta begged to go too.

Reluctantly Eleni said that Kanta could come if she stayed behind her, ready to run. To ten-year-old Glykeria she said, 'You know you're as slow as a tortoise! You'd get us all caught.'

Andreas, afraid to stay, afraid to go, finally decided they needed his military expertise to assess the situation properly. After warning Megali, Nitsa and Olga to stay close to the little ones and keep the animals quiet, Eleni, Kitso, Andreas and Kanta climbed out of the sandy riverbed up the rise toward St. Marina.

On the other side the German battalion approached from the direction of Lia. Scouts were running ahead, searching every gully for signs of partisans. Just as the main body was coming down out of the mountains near a spot called the Little Springs, an advance patrol surprised two young men from Lia. They were part of a group who had concealed themselves in the foothills, but these two men, Gregori Lollis and Vasili Stoungas, were caught as they were leading nearly forty sheep and goats up a hill to graze. The advance patrol brought them at gunpoint to the commandant. At almost the same moment another patrol arrived, dragging a middle-aged tinker, Yiorgi Billis, who had walked right into them. He was indignantly waving a pass stamped by the German authority in Yannina. The Chams translated his protests, but the German officer listened without interest.

The three men couldn't keep their eyes off the sight high above them of their village in flames. The commandant told them through an interpreter that he was going to ask them one question; their survival would depend on how they answered it. Were there any partisans hiding in the foothills around them? The captives looked at one another, then in

165

unison began making vigorous gestures of denial. 'All the partisans are up in the mountains,' said Gregori Lollis.

The Germans let the man with the pass go, but the commandant decided to take Lollis and Stoungas as far as the next village, Kostana, to check their identities. Their hands were tied behind them and they were pushed along the road at the head of the batallion, their flocks left behind.

Yiorgi Billis, the tinker with the pass from Yannina, was still in sight, walking quickly away, when a sound came from the foothills that froze everyone in mid-step – the pop of two faraway rifle shots. The Germans took cover on either side of the road. The commandant snapped an order and several Chams ran after Yiorgi Billis, who was standing in a daze, looking from the Germans behind him to the spot where he had seen puffs of smoke. By the time he started to run, they were on top of him.

Two ELAS guerrillas from the Skevis group had impetuously fired the shots that would cost the lives of three of their fellow villagers. At the first shot a shepherd who was hiding below them and could see what they could not, shouted, 'Hold your fire, boys! They have hostages!' But it was too late.

The tinker, Yiorgi Billis, was dragged back to where the other two captives stood. He screamed that he was innocent, he had been away for six months; how could he know there were partisans in the foothills? He didn't stop screaming until the German commandant slapped him.

Out of rifle range of the hidden partisans, the Germans continued on their way, pushing the captives ahead of them. The commandant had three more Liotes to make an example of, and he intended to execute them in the churchyard at Kostana with every person in the village watching.

Eleni, Kitso, Andreas and Kanta, who were halfway up the other side of the ridge, stopped and looked at one another when they heard the *andartes'* two rifle shots.

'Why are they shooting?' asked Kitso. 'They sound far away.'

Andreas was visibly trembling. 'It's a bad sign,' he said. 'They're withdrawing this way. We've got to go back!'

'Let's just go high enough to see what's on fire in the village,' said Eleni.

Andreas' legs wouldn't move and his shirt was drenched with sweat. He felt just as he had in 1921 in Turkey when the Greek soldiers threw down their guns and fled into the swamps.

'You do what you want,' he shouted at the others. 'I'm going back!' He turned and stalked down the incline toward the camp, trying not to run.

Eleni took Kanta's hand and continued slowly up the ridge to the point where the mountainside, with Lia huddled in the large cleft, came slowly into view. She stopped, horrified. The whole lower half of the village was obscured by smoke, and the Church of the Virgin was a torch.

Her father came abreast of her, squinting into the distance; then his eyes picked out the gaping hole that had been his house, and with a cry he fell to his knees. Great, painful sobs exploded from him and like some rabid animal he dug in the dirt with his hands. Kanta was more frightened by her grandfather's behavior than the sight of the burning village. His loss of control terrified her, and she ran up the hill to get away from the sound of his grief. When she arrived at the top of the ridge, the girl looked down and suddenly clapped her hands over her mouth. Eleni hurried to her side.

Below them were more Germans than Kanta thought the world contained; their helmets and gun barrels reflecting the sunlight so that her eyes watered, a river of marching men flowing straight toward her. She stared, paralyzed, until her mother wrenched her by the shoulder and pulled her flat on the ground.

At the sight of the German army Kitso turned and waved frantically at Andreas, who stood watching from the bottom of the ridge. The old man began to run down so fast that his feet slipped out from under him and he rolled to the bottom of the hill. Andreas needed only a glimpse of Kitso's frantic retreat to know that his worst fears had come true – the Germans were upon them. He took off like a mountain goat, shouting, as he crashed through the group in the riverbed, 'The Germans are behind me!' Hardly slowing his pace, he

167

scooped Nikola up from his sand castles and continued running.

Olga dropped the spoon she was using to stir the rice pudding and pulled Fotini in the same direction. Glykeria ran after Andreas too. Megali and Nitsa had become so frantic they were going in circles, gathering up blankets and then dropping them.

Everyone followed Andreas toward a wooded area, not realizing it took them closer to Kostana. He finally stopped among the trees near a large boulder and the girls collapsed beside him. As Megali puffed up, holding her blankets, Olga found her voice: 'What did you see, Uncle? Where are the rest?'

'The Germans were close enough to bite us!' he panted. 'Your mother and grandfather deserve what happens to them for going up that rise.'

The girls and Nikola started to cry, and the sound attracted the missing members of the family, who were searching for them. The food and the animals had been left behind at the dry riverbed, but the family huddled together under the boulder like hens hiding from the shadow of the hawk.

Kanta described the huge army of Germans over and over again, as if she still couldn't quite believe it. When she stopped, Eleni said quietly to her father, 'Did you see that they had captured three men? I recognized Gregori Lollis and the Stoungas boy.' Kitso bit his lower lip and shook his head in a gesture that meant there was no hope for them. Eleni thought of Gregori's pregnant wife and wondered if she knew her husband had been taken by the Germans.

No one spoke of the burned village, but Megali wept all night, a nasal drone. Kitso didn't even bother to make her stop. He seemed far away in his thoughts. The children cried too because they were cold and hungry, but they huddled together for warmth and eventually slept.

Sometime in the night I awoke, feeling the warmth of my mother's side against my cheek. It was the beginning of an earthquake that had roused me, a rhythmic trembling of the earth. It formed itself into the sound of marching feet. The Germans were passing so close to us that if I opened my eyelids a crack I could see the shapes of their boots. There were guttural shouts in a language I couldn't understand. Although I didn't know it then, they were on their way from Kostana, heading southeast toward Igoumenitsa, having finished with the executions of their hostages.

I felt my mother's hand tight over my mouth, but it wasn't necessary; I didn't have the strength to move or make a sound. I could feel the shuddering of her body and the thud of her heartbeat, as quick as my own. Automatically, to make the fear go away and to protect us, I silently began to repeat the evening prayer that she had taught me, the four-line poem that every Greek child says before going to sleep: 'I kneel and cross myself / Arms for battle at my side / God's servant, they call me / And I fear nothing.'

It didn't work. I was so afraid I could taste it; a steely bitterness on my tongue. The thing that frightened me most was not the Germans, passing yards from where we were hidden, but the convulsive trembling of my mother. In the house at Kostana, she had laid my fears to rest with her calm decision to go about ordinary tasks as if things were indeed normal. But that night when the German army passed by, I discovered that there were things so powerful and so evil that even my mother couldn't make them go away. She was as terrified as I was and there was nowhere to turn for protection. That night remains the most vivid memory of my early childhood.

The next morning while everyone was still marveling at their hair's-breadth escape from the Germans, Kitso Haidis could think of nothing but getting back to Lia. He was obsessed with seeing the ruins of his house. Eleni, Andreas and Kanta, the better walkers of the group, decided to go ahead with him, leaving the rest to gather the animals and herd them up the mountains.

By the time the four reached the outskirts of Lia, it was already afternoon. They were among the first to return to the burned-out village. The hallucinatory feeling of seeing something so familiar completely changed increased as they walked on. A few old women scratched about in the smoking ashes of what had been their homes, occasionally digging up a usable object and putting it aside. The Haidis house was almost the last on the western edge of Lia, and they approached it with dread. Because the path wound around the mountain at a point several yards above the roof level of Kitso's house, they could see from a distance that only the wall which divided his half from that of Anastasia Haidis was still standing. Eleni started to cry as soon as she saw the burned-out shell, but Kitso, ashamed of his previous weakness, steeled himself to look at it without emotion. On the day the house was completed in 1895 and the cornerstone put in place, Kitso was fifteen years old. His father had built it as a monument to the Haidis family just as a church is a tribute in stone to the saint whose name it bears.

Kitso and his two brothers had loaded the gray-pink granite for the walls from high on the mountain onto the mules and carried the dark gray sheets of slate for the roof from the lowland riverbanks on their own backs. The women of the family whitewashed the inner walls with lime and the most skilled stone carver was hired to cut the two-headed eagles, the cypresses and rosettes on the four faces of the fireplaces. The hyacinths on the wooden *rosetta* in the center of the ceiling and the acantha leaves on the cornices were done by wood-carvers from Metsovo. A veranda draped with grape vines stretched around three sides of the house and in its shade Kitso had watched nearly every sunset of his life.

When he became its master after his father's death, Kitso always celebrated the house's nameday – St. Athanassios – with even more splendor than his own. He brought his bride to its door, and in its good chamber he put four infant daughters in their coffins. Kitso took more pride in that house than in any mill he ever built, and now it was gone. Every room had been fragrant with memories, just as the holy water and sweet basil scattered by the priest scented each corner on the day it was consecrated.

Kitso knew, as he looked at the ashes of his father's dream, that eventually he would build another house, but he promised himself never to build one that could leave such a wound on his heart.

170

Eleni wiped her tears away with her apron and tied the mule at the gate to the courtyard. She told Kanta to sit at the threshold of the gate and not to come any closer, while the others examined the wreckage.

Kanta was tired from the long walk but much less upset than the adults at the loss of her grandfather's house and belongings. After all, their own house was intact – they had seen that from the ridge of St. Marina. As she sat and watched the shadows lengthen, Kanta heard what sounded like Anastasia Haidis' voice, raised in the shrill ululating village cry, calling the name of her small grandson from somewhere down the hill: 'Ooohhh, Fotooouu!' After a while Eleni returned to where Kanta was sitting and said that no one could find Anastasia, only the bullet-riddled carcass of one of her goats halfway up the ravine, the solitary victim of the ELAS guerrillas' ill-advised fire on the Germans.

'She's down there somewhere,' said Kanta, pointing. 'I heard her calling Fotis.'

Andreas went down the ravine to hunt for the old woman. Eleni looked to see if she was at the Petsis house next door, but found it, too, in ashes. Kanta stayed where she was, feeling uneasy as the light faded. She heard the tapping of a cane and slow, shuffling steps coming down the hill just in front of her. Soon the bent figure of the blind woman, Sophia Karapanou, came into view.

'Over here, *Yiayia*!' called Kanta, and the woman turned chalky blue eyes, clouded with cataracts, in her direction. She tottered over and put her hand on Kama's head, then carefully sat down on the stone beside her.

'Everybody's looking for *Yiayia* Anastasia,' said Kanta. 'I heard her calling from down in the ravine.'

'She's not in the ravine, she's in the house,' replied the old woman.

'But the house is gone,' Kanta explained patiently to the blind woman. 'The Germans burned it, and half the village, and the school and the Church of the Virgin too!'

'I know,' Sophia replied. 'They burned Anastasia too. They threw her into the house. Name of God, how she screamed!'

Kanta felt sick. 'But I heard her just now! I heard her voice.'

171

'You may well have heard her, but that was her soul calling,' the old woman went on. 'She's not at peace, the way she died. She's a vampire wandering. You need to get her a priest.'

Kanta did not budge, but when her mother and grandfather returned, she told them what the blind woman had said. They turned toward the ruins of the house, but it was still smoking and darkness was setting in.

In the twilight the rest of their group arrived with the animals. Megali nearly fell off the donkey when she saw what was left of her house. They had to carry her, weeping and invoking the saints, up the hill to Eleni's house.

It seemed incredible to find their own house unchanged after all that had happened. Eleni went immediately to the hollow oak in the backyard and found her treasures still inside. The goats bleated with joy at seeing their usual quarters. Megali was laid gently on a pile of *velenzes* near the fireplace and eventually fell asleep, but Kitso refused to come in. No one knew where he spent the night.

The next morning the boy Fotis Haidis returned from the Agora with his mother and joined in the search for his grandmother. It was Fotis who spied a gold signet ring shining from beneath a pile of fallen rocks in the still-smoking cellar. In the ring was a bone.

They lifted the rocks, blistering their hands, and found more bones and the silver cross she had always worn. Some of her hair still clung to the back of her skull. Someone found a piece of cloth and they gathered the bits of bone and teeth in it. As they worked, the women began to wail the death songs, and the keening sound brought neighbors, who joined in, pouring out their grief for their burned houses along with the lament for old Anastasia, who was not allowed to die as befitted her years.

The funeral procession began to wind up the path toward the Church of St. Demetrios. They passed Sophia, who stood at her gate with a look of contentment on her blind face and made the sign of the cross as they passed. Soon her friend would be at peace.

Outside St. Demetrios the mourners encountered a handful

172

of *andartes,* including Spiro Skevis and Mitsi Bollis, descending from the mountaintops. The guerrillas stopped at the sight of the funeral procession, but the mourners stopped too, facing them. None of the villagers spoke, but their eyes eloquently laid the blame for the death of four innocents at their feet.

'Well, we scared them away, didn't we?' blurted Mitsi Bollis in the tense silence.

No one answered.

Eight days later Tassina returned to Lia on a mule, carrying her new son, who would be christened Haralambos. His birth had begun with Anastasia's death cry. Eleni learned how he was born in the little room near Kostana without even clean rags to swaddle him, but the child was healthy and would live. Eleni believed that his birth on the day the village burned must be a sign from God that a new beginning would rise from the ashes.

The Germans had come, and despite the tragedies, her family had survived. Every scrap of news from the outside world said that Hitler's troops were being defeated. The rumors were that he would soon pull his divisions out of Greece.

Eleni longed for the war to end so that they could start rebuilding their lives. But the *andartes* who had become as omnipresent as swallows in the village were also talking about a new beginning. The way they whispered about a 'second round' made her fear that they were preparing not for peace but for more war.

173

CHAPTER SIX

By the autumn of 1944, the end was clear. The Germans
had lost Italy and Rumania as allies, and when even Turkey
severed its ties with the Third Reich, Hitler's forces in
Greece began to withdraw. The last disheartened Germans
limped out of Athens on October 12, the same day British
forces landed in Piraeus, expecting to find Athens a scorched
shell. Instead they found the city intact, the population
emaciated but exultant. 'For three days and nights,' said an
observer, 'hungry, sick people spitting blood marched
without sleeping, kept going by a collective delirium, the joy
of new-found freedom.'

The withdrawal of the Germans left the Communist-
controlled ELAS the most powerful military force in the
country. In late September its chief *kapetanios,* the black-
bearded Aris Velouchiotis, was sent to secure the
Peloponnesian peninsula by wiping out the last remnants of
the Security Battalions appointed by the collaborationist
government. With his hand-picked personal guard (the
'Black Bonnets,' in their black sheepskin caps), Aris
launched unprecedented massacres throughout Peloponnesos
to terrorize the population into total submission to ELAS.
On September 12 they executed 1,450 men, women and
children in the town of Meligalas and threw them all in a
well.

The British arrived to find ELAS in control of all Greece
except for a corner of Epiros held by EDES under Napoleon
Zervas. With almost the entire country in their grip, the
ELAS fighters were furious that the previous spring their

174

leaders had signed an agreement in Lebanon with the ministers of the exiled King George II, giving ELAS only four seats in the Parliament that would now rule Greece.

Convinced that they had been cheated of their rightful victory, ELAS troops decided to stage a coup. On the night of December 3, 1944, they attacked British and Greek troops in Athens, following a demonstration in which ELAS supporters were fired on by police, and according to various accounts, seven to twenty-eight were killed. At the height of the battle, ELAS had its enemies pinned into a few pockets near the city center. Throughout Athens the Communist Party's secret police, OPLA, fanned out, knocking on doors, executing thousands of real and imaginary enemies of the party. By Christmas Day, OPLA had executed 13,500 Greeks, in three weeks eliminating twice as many of their own countrymen as the number of Germans killed in Greece during three years of occupation.

The ELAS leaders made an even more serious blunder than the Lebanon agreement when they decided to send their best divisions not to join the battle of Athens but to launch a simultaneous attack on the army of Napoleon Zervas in Epiros. While they succeeded in driving Zervas off the mainland to the island of Corfu, the British, sent to Athens to prevent a Communist takeover of the country, inspired by a surprise Christmas Day visit by Winston Churchill, beat back ELAS and won control of the city.

Humbled, the defeated Communist Party signed an agreement in Varkiza, a suburb of Athens, on February 12, 1945, that would disarm ELAS in exchange for being allowed to remain a legal political entity in Greece.

In the four months of bloody civil war, 25,000 Greeks perished, joining the half million who had died during the occupation. But the deaths counted for nothing. Four months earlier, during a meeting in Moscow on October 9, 1944, between Winston Churchill and Joseph Stalin, the two men had already divided up the Balkans. 'How would it do for you to have 90 percent predominance in Rumania, for us to have 90 percent of the say in Greece, and go 50–50 about Yugoslavia?' Churchill asked Stalin, pushing the paper on which he had written the figures toward the Soviet leader. Stalin 'took his blue pencil and made a large tick upon it,' Churchill wrote later, 'and the post-war fate of millions was sealed.'

GHOSTS AND DREAMS

AT THE BEGINNING of 1945 when the Communist-dominated ELAS guerrillas drove the EDES forces of Napoleon Zervas into the sea, the rising sun of ELAS seemed to have finally dawned on the new tomorrow that Prokopi Skevis had promised so often. But the Varkiza agreement of February 12 burst that sun like a helium balloon and sent the ELAS guerrillas limping home to their villages, stripped of their weapons, which they were required to surrender.

If the Varkiza agreement meant defeat and betrayal to the ELAS fighters, to the villagers like Eleni Gatzoyiannis and her family it meant the end of war and the beginning of a period of hope. For the first time in four years they could pick up the pieces of their lives, plant the fields and wait for letters from the outside world.

With Athens no longer embroiled in civil war, Eleni knew the mails would soon begin functioning, bringing envelopes from America filled with news of Christos, money to buy much-needed seed for the spring planting, and perhaps before long, the precious papers that would allow them to emigrate to America. Although their stomachs were still empty, they could feed on dreams.

'All the people are fat in America,' Eleni would say in her storytelling voice. 'Everyone has shoes. Every time you buy something, they give you a free paper bag to carry it home in. There are machines to do everything, even machines to eat up the dirt in the house. Hot and cold water comes out of a pipe instead of carrying it from a spring. There are toilets right inside the house, washed clean by running water like a

177

waterfall. People can take a bath every day if they want to.'
The children would hang on her words, making her tell every
detail over and over.

Olga was now seventeen, and Eleni saw how the village
women had begun paying visits to the house, measuring the
girl with appraising eyes as a potential daughter-in-law. As
soon as the mails opened up, there would be enough money
to buy Olga a dowry as grand as the daydreams she was
always spinning.

Every day Eleni found an excuse to walk to the Alonia, to
ask the coffeehouse owner Spiro Michopoulos if by chance
the postman had left a letter for her from America. The whole
village was suffused with a new energy as they prepared for
the first planting in four years that they could harvest without
fear of the Germans confiscating their crops and burning their
homes.

Only in the houses of the half-dozen ELAS stalwarts was
the prospect of spring a bitter one. Prokopi Skevis was
inconsolable. 'If we'd concentrated all our strength in Athens
instead of wasting three divisions on Zervas, the British
couldn't have held out and today we'd be running the country
instead of the puppets who spent the war sunbathing in
Cairo!' he mourned. The Skevis brothers both agreed,
however, that the important thing was for the Communist
Party to survive despite its mistakes, even if it meant
destroying ELAS to do it. Although unarmed, they still had an
important role in the struggle. When the ELAS regiments were
dispersed, their officers ordered them to go back to their
villages and maintain a tight grip on the loyalty of the
inhabitants.

To that end, Spiro Skevis organized all the adolescent boys
and young men of Lia into a theatrical troupe. They performed an instructive skit entitled 'Homes in Ruins,' a
dramatic melodrama about a brave ELAS *andarte* who
returns after the war to find his house burned and his starving
sister preyed upon by an evil-minded black marketeer. Most
of the food and supplies available in Greece after the war had
found their way into the thriving black market, to be sold at
exorbitant prices, and the sneering, capitalist black

178

marketeer, played by Christos Bartozokis with a penciled-on mustache, was a natural villain.

The unfortunate girl was played by Yianni Kepas, an ideal choice, Spiro thought. Of course, no respectable maiden would be allowed to act in a public skit or even sit in the audience, so Yianni, who was a handsome, fair-haired young fellow, floured his face for the play to hide his stubble, tied a scarf around his head and wore a dress with an embroidered apron. In all, there were seventeen men and boys in the cast. They rehearsed for a month, built a small raised stage in the village square, and brought benches out of the half-burned schoolhouse to make a horseshoe of seats for the audience.

The drama, performed on a Sunday afternoon before a crowd that overflowed the square, lasted for two hours, climaxing in the bloody killing of the black marketeer by the wronged maiden. The audience sat spellbound until the part where the villain placed his hands on the breasts of the weeping girl and demanded that she pay for food in a coin dearer than gold. In the hush, a voice could be heard from the back of the crowd, saying in a stage whisper, 'Kepas looks so pretty in a dress, he'd better watch out they don't send him off to Aris!'

The audience froze, and the 'leading lady' forgot his lines at this outrage. EDES forces had widely circulated rumors that Aris, the revered ELAS hero, was a pederast. All eyes, including those of the actors, moved to the Skevis brothers in the front row. Spiro, the author of the play, turned to survey the men at the back, who returned his stare innocently. When the silence became oppressive, Spiro turned back to the stage and nodded to the performers. Kepas managed to recall his next line and the end of the play was greeted with a thunderous applause.

After it died away, Spiro got up and elaborated on the moral. 'Under our brave leaders, including *Kapetan* Aris,' he began with pointed emphasis, 'we drove the German invaders out of our beloved country. Now some false friends are trying to bring back the capitalist bloodsuckers and the cowardly Glücksburg king. As this play shows us, these forces will exploit, torment and humiliate all of us and' – he paused and

179

scanned the crowd – 'they have lackeys even in this village! But if we stand united behind the Communist Party of Greece, the party of the poor and oppressed, we will triumph!'

Someone in the audience interrupted. He sounded more respectful than the heckler who had mentioned Aris. 'Everyone has heard of the courage your men showed, Comrade Spiro,' Kitso Haidis said. 'When the Germans came here, you challenged their whole battalion with only six men and one machine gun from atop the Prophet Elias. But I have one question: When you provoked the Germans enough to burn down half our village, couldn't you at least have hit a German ass instead of poor old Anastasia's goat?'

There were several involuntary snorts of laughter and the crowd turned back to Spiro, whose face was the color of his shirt. Before his brother could react, Prokopi stepped up from the front row. 'You were lucky one time, old man!' Prokopi snapped. 'Don't think you're going to be lucky next time!'

On the way home the villagers whispered among themselves about the remarkable events of the afternoon. Two rightists had been rash enough to jeer at the ELAS propaganda (of course, you could expect something like that from Kitso Haidis!) but more astonishing, none of the *andartes* had raised a hand against the hecklers. The British must really have cut off their balls.

The ELAS guerrillas had been sent home from the battlefield with the warning that government 'security forces' might come on a witch hunt looking for them. Even though the Varkiza agreement provided amnesty for all political crimes, and, in Athens, required warrants for arrest, it did not pardon violent crimes such as murder. Former ELAS *andartes* soon discovered that in the countryside the many local rightist-dominated security forces used this loophole to avenge old grudges, arresting leftists for killings they had allegedly committed while serving in the resistance. As they swooped down, often without warning, the jails quickly filled to overflowing. Less than a month after the propaganda skit, a company of Greek army soldiers passed through the village, and the news of their approach sent the local ELAS guerrillas

180

running for cover into the mountains, where they camped in the gullies and crevices, moving every day.

While the *andartes* were worrying about the security forces, Eleni was brooding over the silence from her husband. The international mails had resumed and many villagers in Lia had already heard from relatives in the United States, but there was not a word from Christos. The only explanation she could think of was that something had happened to him during the four years they were cut off from each other. The fear that he was dead grew in her and the old pain began to gnaw at her bowels as she tried to stretch the little food they had left. It had been hard enough to see the children becoming ragged and thin during the war, but now it was unbearable.

One day in late spring, as Eleni was picking lettuce in the small garden and thinking dully that there was nothing else for the evening meal, a fit of uncontrollable weeping seized her. From inside, Kanta heard her mother crying. She looked out the window to see Eleni ripping lettuce leaves out of the ground, tearing them to pieces like a madwoman, all the while screaming, 'He's dead! He's dead! Aiiee! He's died and left us here!'

During the first months of the peace, the people of Greece still moved about the landscape like survivors of a holocaust; ragged, barefoot and close to starvation. The country was devastated by the years of occupation and the months of civil war; more than 100,000 homes had been destroyed, 500,000 Greeks had died of starvation or murder and the economy was bankrupt. The first promise of help appeared in the form of the United Nations Relief and Rehabilitation Administration (UNRRA) with shipments of charity food and clothing.

To administer the aid, UNRRA relied on regional government officials, who in turn appointed village committees composed of men they knew were anti-Communists. In Lia there were few rightists to choose from, but five were found, including three who had been imprisoned in the schoolhouse by ELAS: the cooper Vasili Nikou, the cripple Boukouvalas, and Kitso Haidis.

Every month a shipment of relief supplies was unloaded at Igoumenitsa, then carried overland to Filiates. The committee members from Lia would go there to sort the village's allotment and then distribute it to their list of families. It was a hard eight-hour walk from Lia to collect the handouts, but the villagers would have walked any distance to receive the lifesaving monthly ration of 8 pounds of flour per person, a half pound of sugar, 6 ounces of rice, 6 ounces of lentils, two cans of evaporated milk per child, some powdered milk and eggs, and with luck, some canned goods. On rare but unforgettable occasions, there were even chocolates, cookies, tea and Camel cigarettes.

At first it seemed an honor to be chosen as a member of the UNRRA committee distributing the largess, and Kitso couldn't help thinking that he might squirrel away an extra can or two of food for himself, but he quickly discovered that the problems of his new office far exceeded the honor. Within weeks of their appointment, the men on the committee became the most hated people in the village. Every person who came for their family's ration confronted Kitso with sick children and ailing parents, and accusations that he had favored other villagers.

He always replied righteously, 'Every person gets the same amount!' But no one believed him, and the hatred grew like a vine. As it increased, the whole village became convinced that Kitso's basement must be a treasure house of filched UNRRA supplies, hidden away for himself and his daughters and grandchildren. The suspicions twined themselves around the families of all five UNRRA committee members and would eventually burst into deadly flower.

At the time of the first UNRRA distribution, in May of 1945, Kitso warned Eleni not to travel to Filiates with him nor to arrive too early for fear that he would be accused of giving her preference. She decided to make the long trek in the company of her sister-in-law, Foto Gatzoyiannis' wife Alexo, and gave in to Kanta's pleading to come along too.

With six children still in the house and her husband a

182

haphazard provider at best, Alexo needed the UNRRA food even more desperately than Eleni did. Her unflagging good humor had endeared Alexo to Eleni long before she assisted at the birth of Nikola. They had laughed and cried in each other's arms when they saw it was a boy, and by now Alexo seemed more like a sister to Eleni than a sister-in-law.

The two women set out down the mountain, traveling southwest through the ravines, quickly reaching the rolling foothills, which were heavy with the smell of spring. They each held a branch as a walking stick and moved with long, steady mountain strides. Thirteen-year-old Kanta meandered back and forth in their wake, picking dandelion puffs and blowing them to the winds. A cuckoo called and listened to its own echo, and the spice of the flowering quince trees filled the air.

Eleni's mood was the opposite of the day. She dreaded their arrival in Filiates when she would have to stand in line to receive charity from strangers. Once she had been the giver of charity to poor families in her neighborhood.

She turned around to check on Kanta, who was walking barefoot on feet as hard as leather, wearing a brown dress of shiny wool cut from one of Eleni's own. The patches on the elbows had worn through, and the scratchy fabric was thick with dandelion fuzz. Christos, always the dandy, would have been embarrassed to walk next to her, Eleni mused, but then, Christos was probably dead and would never know how low his family had sunk in the village.

The sunshine felt like a physical weight on Eleni's shoulders as they hiked on, straggling into Filiates by midafternoon and finding their way to the distribution center, a former Turkish inn.

As the two women joined the long line outside the building, Kanta wandered about, staring at such marvels as the Turkish mosque in the central square and the great outdoor market. She joined a crowd around a couple dressed in the khaki UNRRA uniforms with the blue United Nations insignia on their shoulders. The woman was slim and blond with white eyelashes and reminded Kanta of pictures in the American magazines she had once dreamed over.

The couple distributed several boxes full of secondhand

183

clothing to the clamoring crowd. Kanta edged closer, fascinated. The woman's eyes lighted on her and she motioned Kanta to come forward. Then she reached into a carton of wadded-up clothes and searched until she pulled out a little-girl's dress of bright blue with puffed red short sleeves. The woman folded the dress and thrust it into her hands with a little pat to show it was really hers.

Afraid she might have to give it back, the girl fled, running until she found a tiny shed half filled with hay. There she tore off her scratchy brown dress and put on the blue and red one. She ran her hands over her flat chest, feeling the fabric, then flung the old dress into the hay and ran to the town square to find her mother.

Eleni's mouth dropped open at the sight of the new finery. Kanta stood straight, then turned right and left. 'Do you like it?' she exclaimed. 'A nice lady from UNRRA gave it to me. Free! To keep!'

Eleni looked at her daughter, wearing a charity dress that some other little girl had worn, probably in America, and then discarded. She flushed. 'Where's your own dress?' she snapped. 'You can't go back to the village like that! What will people think, a thirteen-year-old girl going around letting the world look at her bare arms?'

All morning and into the afternoon, the doors of the distribution office did not open, and the line did not move as Eleni, Alexo and Kanta sat in the hot sun. Kanta had put her brown dress back on, but the blue and red one was folded up small and hidden under her clothes. Eleni was leaning against her sister-in-law's shoulder when she heard a man's voice shouting her name.

She looked up to see her cousin, the same Costa Haidis who had refused to see her when she was trying to get her father released from the school-house jail. Costa's thin face was red with exertion, and there were large perspiration stains under the arms of his wrinkled suit. He stood panting in front of her. The proud commissar was gone and in his place was a man with a fugitive's eyes and a false smile.

'Hello, Costa! I thought you'd gone to the mountains to hide with the Skevis men,' Eleni said.

184

'No one authorized them to hide!' he snapped. 'The party's policy is to go and face the police, break their terror by confronting them. That's what I did. They can't jail all of us.'

'And they let you go?'

'The bastards slapped me around some, asked me questions, but finally they released me. The police can do whatever they want out here, but in Athens they have to be careful because other countries are watching. That's why I'm going there.' He put his smile back in place. 'Of course, I was planning to call on you in the village before I left. I thought you might have an old suit that Christos doesn't need anymore.'

The sound of her husband's name reminded Eleni of her fear. 'I've lost him, Costa!' she cried. 'Not a word since the mails opened. I'm certain he's dead and nobody will tell me!'

Costa fumbled inside his coat, beaming. 'But, cousin, that's why I've been chasing you! I have such good news that your grandchildren will put flowers on my grave!'

He thrust toward her a packet of letters and postcards, a dozen at least, covered in the precise, old-fashioned script that Eleni knew so well. She looked from the extended hand to her cousin's face, searching for an explanation, then whispered, 'But why do *you* have them?'

He grinned. 'When I got here, I told the postmaster to hold any letters for you so that I could take them back personally, to see your joy. But I just found out you'd come here instead.'

It took a moment for his words to register, then anger engulfed her and she leaped to her feet, snatching the packet out of his hands. She spat on his wing-tipped shoes. 'You thought you could collect a reward!' she shouted. 'Do you know how many years you've taken off my life?' Then she broke down, and Costa, embarrassed, scurried off as gap-toothed women stared after him.

There were fifteen letters in the packet, each bearing a strange return address. Christos wrote:

My beloved Eleni:

I send you greetings and pray to God that you and my sweet children are well and were not hurt by the terrible

185

things we are reading – famine and killings. I know that my brother must have been a help to you as I have always helped him.

Christos was now living on an island called Staten, he told her, very near to New York City, cooking in a diner owned by the son-in-law of a Greek priest from Povla.

They are nice people here and treat me good, not like that snake Nassios who kept promising to make me a partner in the Terminal lunch but never did, even when he started pulling in big money from all the soldiers. So I heard about this job and left him. I make $90 a week and live in a room near the restaurant. I am enclosing an envelope with my address written on the front. As soon as I hear from you I will send money in care of the bank in Yannina. How is our son? Does he ask for his daddy? I kiss your eyes and those of my angel children. I, your loving husband, write this.

He had also sent a postcard, a dramatic black and white view of the Empire State Building, rising like the tallest taper in the church candelabra. Christos had inked in an arrow pointing to the observation terrace of the skyscraper and on the back of the card he had scrawled:

I am writing this from the top of the tallest building in the world. It has 102 floors. On one side I can see the Atlantic Ocean and the statue of the woman called St. Freedom, which is so big you can climb up and stand in one of her fingers. This is how America looks.

As she tore open his letters, Eleni became so agitated she couldn't make sense of the dancing words and had to ask Kanta to read them to her. When she heard every line, she went to a nearby kiosk and bought a leaf of writing paper and a pencil. 'Dear husband,' she began, sitting on the pavement, frowning in concentration.

186

I thank God that you are well! My heart was shattered thinking that you were dead. If only the mountains would bow down and the trees could stretch across the sea so that I could tell you face to face what miseries we have suffered in the past five years! Foto did not help us at all, but my father found us enough corn flour to stay alive. The Germans burned the lower half of the village, including my parents' house. Our children are as ragged as the poorest family in the village, but with God's help we have all survived and now that I know you are well, I will take a white candle to St. Demetrios.

She told him how badly they needed the money and any clothing he could send, and then, writing in a firmer hand, she told him to begin at once to arrange the papers for their immigration:

You have never seen your son. The war has taught me how wrong it is for us to be apart. In America, houses are not burned and people do not starve to death. I beg you, arrange for our passage at once. I ask you with my whole heart.

Eleni

When Eleni and Kanta returned to Lia, the children fought to hold the photograph of the immense tower. Their father was alive and, they thought, living in this great spire. Nikola, nearly six, studied the photo, frowning and squinting, trying to make out the face of the father he had never seen in the pinhole windows next to the arrow. Olga fretted that he would certainly fall to his death into the black canyons of the street. Kanta, the logical one, asked how people could gather enough wood in New York to heat all the skyscrapers when not one tree was visible in the photograph.

'Everything is easier in America,' Eleni explained. 'Trucks bring black rocks – coal – and pour them into a great oven, like the one we use for the bread, in the basement of the towers, and pipes carry the fire's steam up to every room and heat it.'

187

'Burning rocks!' Glykeria marveled. 'I wouldn't have to gather firewood! What an easy life!'

Nikola thought the America stories were better than fairy tales about warriors and princes and wolves. The one that impressed him most was the story of the swimming-pool rooms. 'When it gets too hot or they feel dirty and want to go swimming,' Eleni said, 'people jump into a pool as big as the whole room. Like the little irrigation dam up at the spring but thirty times bigger.'

'With their clothes on, *Mana*?' asked Fotini.

'With special swimming clothes, like underwear,' she replied, embarrassed. 'Both men and women go into the same pool. Of course, good women don't.'

Nikola fell asleep thinking about swimming-pool rooms, and when he awoke to the kind of early morning heat that promises a rainstorm, he followed his mother around, asking questions. 'If they have rooms full of water, *Mana*, how come the water doesn't pour out when they open the door?'

'Because it's a hole in the ground,' she replied absently. 'Now go outside and stop getting under my feet!'

Nikola went out and climbed up on the wide slab over the arched gateway and lay down. It was the same spot from which he had fallen when he was three years old, but this was still where he did his best thinking.

Glykeria and Kanta were sent early in the morning to take the goats and sheep up to the family's field in the Agora, behind the Chapel of St. Nicholas. The wheat had recently been cut and now pale-green shoots, grass and weeds were poking up through the stubble. Until the spot was plowed and replanted, it was the one time of the year when the girls could allow the animals to graze on flat ground while they sat under a tree watching from afar, not having to worry that a stray kid would fall down a ravine, get picked off by a wolf, or attack another villager's crops.

Glykeria was lying under a holm oak, recovering from the long climb and eying the bulging pockets of Kanta's apron. 'Walking so far makes me hungry!' she complained.

'I warned you not to eat your bread and onions before we

even got up here!' Kanta scolded. 'You can't have mine, so don't ask.'

Far below them they noticed Vasilo Barka, the simple-minded shepherdess, climbing up toward the same fields with the large flock of animals she was paid to look after. She stopped to water them at a spring, and Glykeria and Kanta saw a young boy named Yianni pass by and start talking to her. He playfully tried to grab her, and they heard her squeals of anger. Vasilo began throwing rocks at him to drive him away, and he laughed and ran out of sight.

Vasilo and her flock climbed higher and the girls soon could hear her ranting angrily to her goats, as if they were human, 'Filthy men, they're all after one thing! Trying to get into poor Vasilo's drawers. Trying to ruin poor Vasilo.'

When she arrived at the pasture, Glykeria called to her teasingly, 'You were talking to Yianni, Vasilo! What did he want?'

'He was begging me. He was pleading!' she answered.

'But for what, Vasilo, for what?' both girls chorused.

Vasilo only blushed and turned away, ignoring them. Glykeria composed a song for the occasion:

> Vasilo, my sweet rose
> Who walks where the spring flows
> Why do you throw stones
> To hit your sweetheart on the nose?

Vasilo came after them with her shepherd's crook, and the girls scrambled, laughing, toward the small white Chapel of St. Nicholas on the western end of the pasture. They ducked into the shadows behind the rounded projection of the apse. They huddled there, making themselves as small as possible, their bodies pressed against the cool wall, listening to their hearts beating. They soon became aware of another sound, muffled but unmistakable. From inside the Holy of Holies, where only a priest could enter, there came the hollow rhythm of slow, dragging footsteps. Back and forth the walker paced. The sound came closer. The girls stared at each other; despite the heat, there were goose bumps on their arms.

Kanta felt a scream welling up inside her and flinched when Glykeria grabbed her arm and whispered hoarsely, 'It's the ghost of Soterina. This is where she froze to death!' With that, they hurled themselves out of the shadows, as if they could already feel Soterina's icicle fingers clutching at their necks. They nearly trampled Vasilo, who came puffing toward them.

'Run, Vasilo!' Kanta screamed. 'There's a ghost in the church!'

Vasilo seemed unconcerned. 'You girls are sillier than I am! I see ghosts all the time up here, and I always tell them a nice "Good day."'

Despite Vasilo's aplomb, Kanta and Glykeria huddled at the edge of the Agora farthest from the chapel for the rest of the afternoon.

While Eleni was busy in the house, Nikola perfected his plan. After lunch, when everyone settled down for the siesta, he began. The earth in the garden just below the house was soft from recent rains, but even so, it wasn't easy for a six-year-old to break it up with the hoe. Next he took a spade and began to dig. An hour later he stopped, and proudly examined the results. He had created a rectangular hole, as long as he was tall, nearly as wide, and a foot deep – the largest he'd ever made.

Eager to finish before his mother woke up, Nikola found a pail and hurried the dozen yards up the path to the spot where the millstream broadened into a shallow pond. It was hard dragging the filled pail back down to the hole, but he struggled manfully and finally tipped it in, only to see the water disappear into the earth.

By five o'clock, after two hours of lugging water, he had achieved two inches of liquid mud in the bottom. It didn't look like the swimming pools of his fantasies, but he was hot and tired, and his palms were blistered. It was time to take his enjoyment for all the hours of hard labor. He slipped off the straps of the striped knee pants his mother had made him and undid the button in the front. The only other garment was his short-sleeved knitted white shirt, which also served as a

190

nightgown. Now it would be a swimming costume as well. With a shout like an attacking warrior, he threw himself face down into the swimming pool.

Tsavena, the ancient mother of Marina Kolliou, who lived in the house above the Gatzoyiannias family, woke up with an urgent need to go to the outhouse. From the small veranda she heard a strange noise and looked down at the Gatzoyiannis garden. The top half of a chocolate brown figure was projecting out of the dirt. She thought at once of the evil *daoutis*, half goat, half child, who frightens the sheep and goats to death during Advent.

'Ooooohhh, Eleni!' Tsavena screamed in a voice that brought everyone in the neighborhood awake with a start. 'Run, Eleni!'

As the neighborhood assembled around his swimming pool, Nikola was doing his best at what he thought must be the backstroke. He looked at the circle of faces peering down at him. Every mouth was stretched wide in laughter. His mother was laughing hardest of all. Nikola felt that his efforts were not being properly appreciated. 'I only wanted us to have a swimming pool, like in America,' he said reproachfully, blinking back the tears.

The episode of the swimming pool ended with the excited return of Glykeria and Kanta, while Eleni and Olga were still scraping mud off the boy in the basin used for boiling clothes. Eleni paid no more attention to the girls' encounter with a ghost than she did to Nikola's plans for improving his swimming pool. But a week later, as she went up to oversee Tassi Mitros' plowing of their fields for the second planting, Eleni encountered the ghost herself.

She stopped at the chapel to light a candle to her son's name giver, and as she stood in front of the altar she saw a movement behind the iconostasis. She peered forward into the Holy of Holies and found the white-haired miller Yiorgi Mitros crouched in a corner. 'What are you doing here, *effendi*?' she asked in amazement.

'Hiding from the coming storm, Eleni!' he answered. 'Have you seen anyone looking for me?'

'Two men in uniform came around asking for you,' she

innocently replied. 'But why should you be afraid? You've done nothing.'

Yiorgi Mitros' ruddy cheeks paled and he flung his open hand toward his face, cursing himself. 'Damn the day I stood up to speak for ELAS!' he moaned. 'Now they're hunting me down like a hare. And for nothing! I'm heading for Albania right now, Eleni. And for God's sake, don't tell anyone you saw me.'

Eleni returned home, wondering sadly at the old man's plight. She found her brother-in-law Andreas in her house.

'You didn't happen to catch sight of Yiorgi Mitros up in the fields, did you?' he asked.

'Why? What's he done?'

'Nothing,' Andreas answered, explaining that Minas Stratis, who was now working for army intelligence in Yannina, had recommended the miller Mitros for mayor of Lia. 'But no one's been able to find him for weeks.'

And that was how Yiorgi Mitros sentenced himself to fifteen years of homeless wandering in Albania and Yugoslavia, while the post of mayor fell to the cripple Boukouvalas, who had recovered enough from his beating in the schoolhouse to take the helm of the village.

For everyone who had aligned himself with ELAS, it was a time of fear and flight. There were rumors of night raids and brutal reprisals in the larger towns to the south. One evening at the hour of dusk, Eleni heard a faint knock on the back door and opened it to find her cousin Antonova Paroussis from Babouri standing in the shadows, her scarf tied close around her face. Antonova begged Eleni to hide her cousin Nikola Paroussis (the young ELAS guerrilla who had welcomed Philip Nind) and his comrade Kosta Tzouras. Nikola's mother was terrified that they'd be arrested and perhaps killed for their wartime activities. 'None of the ELAS houses are safe,' Antonova said to Eleni, 'but they'd never think to search here because your husband's in America and your father is a rightist. Please, Eleni, just for a few days until we see whether it's safe for them to turn themselves in or if they have to flee the country! Do this thing for his mother and me and someday it will be returned to your own son.'

At first Eleni hesitated. She couldn't compromise Olga's reputation by hiding single young men under the same roof, but after all, Nikola Paroussis was her husband's relative, and the other was the brother of Christos' close friend in America. Her husband would expect her to help them.

'I'll send Olga to my sister's house, and keep Costa and Nikola here,' Eleni finally agreed. 'They've always been good, God-fearing boys.'

She put the two *andartes* in the dirt-floored pantry behind the kitchen, and although they spent the daylight hours in the storage space under the floor, in the evenings the young men would tell the children stories and teach Nikola and Fotini how to play jacks with pebbles.

Two weeks later their hiding came to an end with news that appalled every ELAS supporter. The picaresque Aris Velouchiotis, hero of ELAS, who refused to recognize the Varkiza agreement and still rode the secret mountain passes with his band of savage 'Black Bonnets,' was denounced as 'an adventurist and suspect person' by the chief of the Communist Party himself on June 12, 1945. Aris did not learn of his excommunication until six days later when, trying to escape from an ambush near a village in the Pindos mountains, he ran into two shepherds, one of whom showed him a six-day-old newspaper.

Aris sat down on a rock with the newspaper, told his second in command to stay with him and sent the rest of his men on ahead. A few minutes later, a grenade exploded. No one would ever know if Aris and his aide committed suicide or were killed. Government soldiers cut off their heads and suspended them from a double gibbet in the main square of Trikala by ropes strung through their ears.

Aris' repudiation by the Communist Party and his grisly death left no doubt in the minds of ELAS *andartes* still at large. No matter what the party said about confronting the authorities, they streamed over the border into Albania and Yugoslavia to save themselves. The two fugitives hidden in Eleni's house joined the exodus, crossing over to Albania along with Mitsi Bollis and the Skevis brothers. They stayed in a village just over the border, occasionally creeping back

193

after dark; shadowy figures now and then glimpsed by the children who took them for ghosts. In the fall they left Albania for the base of Greek communists in Bulkes, Yugoslavia.

The first letter that Eleni had written to Christos brought a quick reply, overflowing with relief at the news of their survival. He said that four large trunks full of clothing and gifts were already on their way. Unfortunately, an emergency appendectomy and the cost of all the things he was sending had depleted his bank account, but as soon as he had enough to fulfill the legal requirement for bringing the family into the country, he said, he would send Eleni immigration papers.

Christos' main concern was his daughters' virtue once they were exposed to the hedonism of his adopted land. 'You have no idea how free the girls are here, running with strangers from an early age, without even a brother along to protect them!' he wrote. 'It would be best if you make a match now for Olga with a man of good name in the village and marry her there. Then she'll be safely settled and after the rest of you come to the States, she can follow with her husband.'

Another responsibility, Eleni thought. Christos didn't understand how hard it would be to find someone with the right family name and reputation who would satisfy Olga as well. But she had to admit she saw the logic in his plan.

The whole family waited anxiously for the trunks to arrive while they threshed the summer wheat, dug the potatoes and celebrated the three-day festival of the Prophet Elias. Finally word came from Yannina that the trunks had arrived. Eleni and Andreas went to bring them back by mule. By the time they entered the Gatzoyiannis gate, the yard was full of neighbors. Everyone stood around the trunks exclaiming. Even the rope that bound them was wonderful! It was American rope, strong and thick as a snake, and they carefully untied it so that lengths of it could be given as gifts – not only practical but full of the glamour of the golden land. There were clothes for everyone, even Kitso and Megali, although Foto Gatzoyiannis' family did not fare as well as before the war. There were bright dresses and lengths of fabric, exotic

194

shoes, scarfs and silk stockings. All of the wealth of America flowed out of those trunks and some of the mystery too. There was a shiny round pink box with a puff on top and powder inside that smelled nice and made you sneeze. There was a large glass bottle full of bright-colored large round tablets. 'Sweets,' said some. 'Medicine,' said others.

'Let me test it,' said Kitso Haidis, 'before you children poison yourselves!'

As everyone watched in suspense, he bit into one. Under the bright shell was chocolate and a peanut. 'Better taste another to be sure,' he said. He kept on tasting until the bottle was empty.

If Kitso got the candy, the girls got the expensive ties that Christos had meant for him. They thought the bright lengths of silk must be fashionable new belts, and wound them around their waists while their girl friends gritted their teeth in envy.

For the three oldest girls there were fine crocodile shoes with funny-looking high heels. They were as tricky as stilts, and Olga broke hers the first time she wore them up the mountain to the brook where the women beat the laundry.

The greatest mystery of all was a large colorful bunch of feathers at the end of a stick. No one knew what it was, but it glowed with tawny hues of orange and red. Eleni found a glass vase and put the thing in the center of the table in the good chamber.

People began to arrive from as far away as Babouri. They were led into the room where the feather duster reigned, upside down in the vase. Like a bouquet of flowers, but it never dies, they said. They think of everything in America.

Eleni found something to fill every visitor's hands – a pair of stockings, a handkerchief, a length of fabric, or some of the precious aspirins. For days, people came to admire. 'What wonderful things, *Kyria* Eleni!' they all marveled. 'You are the luckiest family in the village!' And they would go away clutching a bit of the riches.

Some weeks later, on a day so hot that the dust did not move and the cicadas screamed, Eleni put Nikola on the mule, Merjo, and headed into the center of town to buy some

195

supplies with the money Christos had sent. When she got there, Spiro Michopoulos called out to her from his *cafenion*. The postman had left a letter for her from America.

Eleni's sense of good fortune evaporated when she read Christos' letter, bitter with anger and accusations. Her father, Kitso, had written him demanding five hundred British sovereigns as payment for feeding the family during the occupation, he told her. 'I was prepared to take care of your parents for the rest of their lives,' Christos wrote, 'which you told me was the agreement you had with your father. I sent them all those clothes and gifts in gratitude, and now he's demanding a fortune in gold! What kind of trick is this? Why did you get me knitted into such a problem? If I pay him, I'll be broke and can't afford to bring you and the children over.'

Eleni's mind spun. How could her father have written such a letter without telling her? Shopping was forgotten as she led the mule with Nikola upon it toward her father's mill, where he was living until he got his house rebuilt.

Kitso was unmoved by her rage. Yes, he'd written the letter, he said and shrugged. Rebuilding the house was eating up everything he had. He was an old man – too old to keep working the mill. He wanted to open his own business, a store in the Alonia, and that's why he needed the sovereigns. 'Your husband owes me for what I did for you,' he concluded.

Eleni accused him of exploiting his own daughter and grandchildren to get rich.

'I kept you alive!' he answered brusquely. 'Can you deny that?'

She ached to slap him the way he had so often hit her. Choking back tears, she accused him of being a greedy, selfish old man who cared for no one but himself.

Nikola saw how his mother stormed out of his grandfather's house and swatted Merjo sharply with the switch, a hard, distant look on her face. The animal lurched slowly into a walk. The great white mule, big as a horse, was nearly blind with age; his legs were stiff and scabby and he was always reluctant when the path lay up the mountain.

Eleni did not speak as they passed the ruins of the Haidis

house and continued up. She felt caught like a hare in a hunter's trap between her father and her husband, the metal teeth puncturing her skin, grinding toward the bone. All she had wanted was to keep her children alive, any way she could, and now the two men who should have protected her were both angry at her.

Just below the Church of St. Demetrios, where the narrow path cut between two large boulders, Merjo came to a complete stop. Eleni struck him on the flanks, but he seemed to go into a trance, standing like the rocks on either side, saliva dripping from his lips, his rheumy eyes glazed.

She shouted fiercely at Nikola to slide off, then began beating the stick on the mule's flanks with all her strength, shrieking curses at him as if he could understand her. The stick splintered, but Merjo's only movement was to lay back his ears with an expression of malicious stupidity.

Something snapped in Eleni's mind and suddenly she was sobbing and hurling stones against the immobile white flanks until a trickle of blood appeared. She scrabbled for more stones and threw them blindly.

I backed away, terrified by the sight of my mother suddenly turned into a madwoman, screaming and hurling stones at the old mule who stood there, immobile as a mountain. The sight of this raging anger coming from the one person who had always given me security and love was more frightening than an unexpected attack from anyone else. I was sure the mule had done something terrible when I wasn't looking that set her off like this, and I was even more afraid that I would inadvertently anger her too and have that murderous rage directed at me. Too frightened to cry, I ran up and threw my arms around her, begging, 'Please stop it, *Mana*! Merjo didn't mean it!'

She looked at me in surprise, as if she had forgotten about my existence. When she saw how frightened I was, the anger seemed to drain from her. She collapsed on the ground, burying her face in her arms and sobbing. I could see that the fury was gone and hugged her, trying to console her, but she wept uncontrollably. I began to understand that it was not the mule who had driven her into this frenzy, but something that concerned my grandfather.

Neither my mother nor I ever told my sisters about the moment when she lost control and attacked the mule. Later, guilty about her outburst, she blamed herself unreasonably for Merjo's fate. When I was old enough to understand the pressures tormenting my mother at that moment, I was surprised that her frustrations didn't explode more often. Looking back, I was glad that once, during that brief respite between the wars, she allowed herself the indulgence of collapsing.

She was brought up to be dependent on others and was so sensitive that in 1937 she became ill from her unhappiness. But when the world war broke out and her personal problems were overshadowed by the necessity to keep us alive, my mother never allowed herself to break down. And when, after that brief two-year period of tranquillity, civil war erupted, bringing with it torments that drove many others to despair or madness, she would never permit herself to take refuge in weakness again.

A week or so later the family found Merjo on his knees in the stable, unable to get up under the weight of his twenty-two years. His eyes were clouded and he made no sound. They burned straw under his nostrils but he didn't move. They pried open his great bloodless lips and poured in camomile tea but he wouldn't swallow. As the sun rose higher, his head sank to the floor. At the end a terrible ague seized him until, like an oak falling, he rolled over dead. Eleni started to cry, and Nikola and Fotini, seeing her tears, began to wail. Olga watched with amusement. 'He's only a mule – an old mule!' she shouted. 'What are you all carrying on about?'

'He was like one of the family!' Eleni said, trying to explain her grief. 'When you were babies, he carried you. He went through the war with us.'

Olga pointed out that the carcass would stiffen quickly, and they'd never fit it through the door of the stable. Eleni sent Fotini for Andreas and began tying a rope under the animal's forelegs. When her brother-in-law came, they managed to drag the corpse out the door, the legs bumping awkwardly against the doorjamb, but once they reached the rocky path, they couldn't budge it any further.

Still shaking with sobs, Eleni tied another rope around Merjo's hind legs and directed Olga and Kanta, who had been found hiding in the outhouse, to start pulling. The mule's body jackknifed, and with much yanking and angry shouting, they managed to force him through the gate. By now most of the neighborhood had come out to see the reason for the uproar and began shouting encouragement.

It was only about three hundred yards up and over to a great cliff on the western edge of the village, but it took an hour to inch the great white carcass that far. Olga and Andreas were laughing while the others wept. The neighbors followed behind like a real funeral procession.

As they dragged the mule to the edge, Fotini's playmate, seven-year-old Alexandra Bollis, came down the path and took in the lugubrious scene. She had been taught by her mother what to say in such situations. She came up to the family, who were drenched with sweat and breathing hard. 'May his death bring you life and may he prepare the way to Paradise ahead of you,' she chirped solemnly, extending her hand to Eleni. The onlookers burst out laughing and Eleni threw back her head and laughed with them, tears still wet on her face.

They all crouched down facing the ravine, put their hands on Merjo's back, and with one last 'Heave!' pushed him over the edge. At first it seemed he wouldn't go, then slowly, as a shower of stones preceded him into the great emptiness, the mule rolled majestically off the cliff and revolved in the air, legs extended like twigs. Over and over he turned, diminishing in size until, with the dull sound of a wine skin, he settled into the underbrush far below, and a cloud of dust and startled birds flew up in his wake. There he lay, until the vultures and crows picked his bones clean.

In July, Eleni was distracted from the gloom caused by Merjo's death and the estrangement with her father by the news of Stavroula Yakou's engagement.

Stavroula was the tallest and handsomest maiden in the village, but no one expected her to marry, for her family was at the bottom of the social ladder, and she had no hope of a decent dowry. When Stavroula was only seven, her father, Panayiotis, a tinker, had gone on a working trip to Kalambaka at the foot of the great Meteora crags and discovered that there were women there with perfumed hair and oiled bodies who would give him sex for money. That's when Panayiotis decided not to return to Lia and his rough-skinned wife Anastasia.

Anastasia had barely managed to keep herself and the two little girls alive doing housekeeping and farming chores for others. The sight of her knocking on doors and begging for work had always filled Eleni with a sympathetic terror, imagining herself in the same position. Before the war cut off her money, she regularly hired Anastasia to help with the chores and never passed her house without dropping off a gift of oil or sugar.

Because of her poverty and her father's scandalous behavior, Stavroula seemed destined to become an old maid, but besides being a beauty, Stavroula was a woman of spirit, and if there was any escape from her plight, she meant to find it.

Salvation presented itself in the person of Dimitri Dangas, who had grown up in a house only five hundred yards from Stavroula's but now worked in a bakery in Khalkis on the Euboean Straits, fifty miles north of Athens. Dimitri, a tall, polite, personable lad, was younger than Stavroula, and one of the few in the village even taller than she was. He had curly black hair and high cheekbones, and his father, who had a tinker's shop in Khalkis, had managed to find him the fine job in the bakery, a guarantee of security – for who had ever heard of a baker starving?

Dimitri had come home for a visit during the annual festival of the Prophet Elias and happened to pass by the millstream where on Saturday mornings the women of the Perivoli gathered to boil, beat and wash their laundry while they caught up on the latest gossip.

His eyes were drawn to the figure of Stavroula, beating

200

some homespun dresses on the ferny bank. Her sleeves were rolled up, and the sun, filtering through the overhanging plane trees, touched the golden fuzz on her round arms as she raised and lowered the flat paddle. Her kerchief had slipped back, and wisps of her hair clung moistly to her cheeks. Gold against white, Dimitri thought, like the gilded crusty loaves he made from the finest white flour. He stepped on a dry stick, and Stavroula turned around, leveling on him the full force of her azure eyes. He was as hopelessly bewitched as if she had fed him a love potion made of the combined milk taken from a mother and daughter who were both nursing at the same time.

Dimitri waited by Stavroula's gate for her to pass with the freshly laundered clothes. She did not snub his greeting, despite her mother's admonitions, for she sensed an opportunity.

Soon Stavroula was finding frequent need to visit her girl friends or go to the outhouse at night, and during moments snatched from these outings, she and Dimitri would meet. Because she knew that his parents would oppose the match, Stavroula advised Dimitri to come personally to ask her mother for her hand instead of sending a go-between. He went, and despite the unorthodoxy of having a groom speak for himself, poor Anastasia was only too glad to promise her twenty-two-year-old daughter to this handsome man who did not mention a dowry.

When presented with the fact of her son's engagement, Dimitri's mother, Alexandra Dangas, wept, pleaded and threatened. She wrote his father in Khalkis, who wrote back: 'Of all the respectable doors that there are in Lia, couldn't you have found one to knock on?'

But Dimitri could see no farther than the blue depths of Stavroula's eyes. He threatened to take his love with him and go away forever if his parents didn't agree to the marriage. His mother rapidly gave ground at this threat. To never see Dimitri again would be death itself! She forced herself to look on the bright side of things: Stavroula was a big, strong girl. She would make fine grandchildren and be useful around the house. It was time for her to reap the rewards due a mother-in-law after all those decades of slavery.

The mother-in-law was the cross that every Greek village bride had to bear, taking comfort in the knowledge that, God willing, someday she would be a mother-in-law herself. It was customary in Lia for the bride to spend her wedding night sleeping not with her new husband, but with his mother, to dramatize whose property she was.

'My mother-in-law's speaking of me,' a Greek wife says as she chops onions and tears run down her face. Mothers-in-law were notoriously cruel to the brides brought home by their sons. One of Eleni Gatzoyiannis' cousins, Tassia, was a daughter-in-law of the most infamous mother-in-law in the village, Kostena Makos, whose sons had brought three brides to her house, all of whom went about the village permanently marked with bruises from their mother-in-law's poker.

The first person Anastasia Yakou told of her daughter's miraculous engagement was Eleni Gatzoyiannis. The two old friends embraced and Anastasia's joy overflowed in a tear or two. 'We both know what it is to bring up girls without a husband to guide and protect them,' Anastasia said. 'You've always helped us, Eleni. Stavroula wants to have your Nikola to be the boy who sits on the dowry chest and Olga as the "fortunate girl" to decorate the wedding breads.'

Eleni was moved that her children had been selected for these important roles, and volunteered to make the bride's wedding dress herself from a piece of fine wool that Christos had sent them.

The cooking began a week before the wedding, and on Wednesday the women of the neighborhood prepared the dough for the six huge wedding breads. On Thursday the breads were brought to the Gatzoyiannis house, fat and round as millstones, and Olga, using two spoons, 'embroidered' the tops of each one with crosses and lovers' knots, wild roses and doves, studding the patterns with Jordan almonds for fertility.

On Saturday the married women gathered at the groom's house to sing and make bawdy jokes as they prepared the nuptial bed, turning each sleeping rug in the four directions of the cross before laying it in place. Finally the bed was sprinkled with rice and sweet-smelling flowers, and Nikola was placed in the middle – terrified at being the center of so much hilarious fun – while the women threw silver coins, or copper coins if they could afford no other, onto the mattress. Nitsa tucked some cloves of garlic among the blankets and whispered to Nikola that if Stavroula had a baby boy first, it would be thanks to the magic he was making.

The wedding day dawned bright and mild as the bride's family and friends began to dress Stavroula in the full-skirted dress of a brilliant mulberry color. Eleni had included a secret inner pocket to hold the three magic objects: the scissors, the padlock and the comb, which would protect the bride against the evil eye. The great spiral belt buckle of silver filigree that her mother had worn was fastened about Stavroula's trim waist, and over the dress went the black satin apron, embroidered in gold. Stavroula's wheat-colored hair had been plaited down her back by an old woman of many fruitful years; her burgundy flowered wedding kerchief, with a few Turkish florins sewed to its corners, was tied over her head and behind her ears so that the blond hair made an aureole around her face. Last of all they helped her into the long black sleeveless tunic, which reached to the hem of her dress and bore a vertical red stripe. Everyone was astonished at Stavroula's composure and remarked that she was the first bride they'd ever seen who did not weep on this, the most significant and terrifying day of her life.

The members of the groom's party were stoking their spirits with moonshine in preparation for the ritual kidnapping of the bride. Finally the best man, satisfied with Dimitri's appearance, dusted off his suit, stuck a sprig of sweet basil behind his ear, and announced, 'The eagle flies to take the partridge!'

With a shout, the groom's party launched the siege; at their head was the banner of war – a Greek flag with a crosspiece at the top bearing three oranges for fruitfulness and an olive branch tied with a white handkerchief for harmony. The crowd intoned stanzas of the melancholy klephtic wedding songs in a slow and long-drawn roar, ending with a mournful rising wail, sounding more like a dirge than an epithalamion.

Hearing the clamor of the approaching groom's party, the

women in the bride's house seized Nikola, dressed in his new suit and uncomfortable American shoes, and set him on top of the wooden chest to protect the bride's trousseau from the invading groom until it was properly ransomed. The boy was frowning with the magnitude of his responsibility while everyone else was laughing with excitement – even the bride. Within minutes the groom's army was in the Yakou courtyard wailing:

> We've come to take our bride
> And if you don't give us our prize
> We'll take her by force!

Inside, Anastasia seized Eleni's hand, overcome by nerves, as the bride's party trumpeted:

> My mother's marrying me
> I'm not coming by force!

Anastasia controlled her trembling and formally invited the groom to come in and claim his bride.

Stavroula stood to greet him, glowing like an icon. The older women crossed themselves as they saw her smile at her husband-to-be. Stavroula was leaving her mother's house and her childhood behind, and this was a time for weeping, not smiles.

Nikola sat fiercely, arms folded, on top of the chest as the groom approached. Dimitri, splendid in his dark suit, formally handed three coins to the boy, and Nikola allowed himself to be lifted down while the groom's men carried the wedding chest and the linens out to the flower-wreathed mule waiting at the door.

The bride's party followed the groom's to the church, keening alternate stanzas of sad wedding songs. At the crossroads between her family's house and the groom's, Stavroula stopped and turned, throwing the first wedding bread, aiming it at Olga, who caught it amid much joking and congratulations.

In the church Stavroula knelt, head bowed, as the best man

placed the ribbon-linked orange-blossom crowns on the couple's heads. Even her future mother-in-law had to admit she had never seen a bride so beautiful. But when the moment came for the priest to lead the couple in the dance of Isaiah, and for the groom to stamp on the bride's toes to underscore his dominance, Stavroula slyly pulled back her foot. Dimitri's shoe came down loudly on the floor, wringing a gasp from the shocked crowd.

At the feast, held in the groom's courtyard, the whole village riotously celebrated not just the wedding of poor Stavroula, but the end of hunger, want and war. Glasses clanked joyfully, miraculously filling as soon as they were drained. There was the crunch of hewn bones as the roasted kids were carved, the eyes saved for the groom to give him strength. Eleni watched the acrobatics of the younger men as they took the handkerchief to lead the dances, clearly trying to impress Olga, who sat demurely next to her mother.

Later many of those who attended Stavroula's wedding said that they felt at the time a sense of foreboding, for such an outpouring of happiness could only augur approaching tragedy. But they were just expressing the national sense of fatality that all Greeks feel when they are happiest; the reason they spit when confronted with good fortune, and cover the mirrors and seal the doors when heaven gives them a son. They know that the fates have some evil up their sleeves to counterbalance such blessings. This cynicism is so universally Greek that it even has a name: *baskania*.

As the revelers sang the fierce and melancholy wedding songs, their heads flung backward, eyes half closed, veins throbbing in temples and throats, the bride and groom took their places at the head of the line, followed in turn by their best man and parents. After Anastasia Yakou made her round, she went over and pulled Eleni up to lead a slow, graceful *syrto*. When she sat down again, her cousin, Eugenia Bollis, Mitsi's wife, remarked acidly, 'Enjoy yourself now, Eleni. When the third round comes, others will lead the dance.'

Eleni took no offense but looked at her cousin blankly. 'What third round?' she asked. But Eugenia didn't answer.

CHAPTER SEVEN

The thousands of ELAS partisans who fled Greece after the Varkiza agreement, seeking sanctuary in the Communist countries to the north, were collecting by the fall of 1945 in the town of Bulkes, Yugoslavia, north of Belgrade. There, Moscow-trained Greeks were building a model community of the purest Stalinist orthodoxy.

The exiles in Bulkes were organized into five-man cells of Kafkaesque paranoia for the purpose of informing on one another. The ELAS military heroes who had won glory and popular followings during the occupation were treated especially harshly by the hard-liners who ran the camps, for fear that their popularity would make them feel they could defy the party leaders. The slightest questioning of camp discipline was considered treason, and there were frequent purges of those who wavered, who were labeled 'earthworms.' Twenty such suspects were made to walk a gauntlet of spitting men before being sent back to Greece and certain capture.

For the mistrusted, not even a trip to the outhouse in Bulkes could take place without the whole five-man cell present, the two most 'secure' members walking on the outside with the most suspect man in the middle. When civil war broke out again in early 1946, the exiles, unlike Communists who had stayed behind in Greek cities, leaped at the chance to go back to Greece and demonstrate their zeal, fighting in the mountains.

The reprise of the civil war began with a change in policy by the Greek Communist Party. Although legal under the

Varkiza agreement, the party was finding it hard to gain strength by political action within the rightist governments in Athens. At the UN Security Council on January 21, 1946, Russia condemned persecutions of leftists in Greece – 1,219 of them had been killed and 18,767 arrested since the Varkiza agreement – and the Greek Communists took this as proof that Russia would throw its support behind a new armed rebellion in the country.

The leader of the Greek communists was Nikos Zachariadis, a doctrinaire Communist who had been born in Asia Minor in 1902. Trained in Moscow in his youth, he became Greek Communist Party leader in 1934, survived imprisonment in the Dachau concentration camp and returned to Greece in 1945 to retake command of the party.

Against the advice of other European Communists, Zachariadis, a strong-willed man with a thick bush of black curly hair and a determined jaw, decided to go ahead with the rebellion after party leaders met with Yugoslav and Bulgarian representatives in December of 1945 and were promised material aid for an armed insurrection in Greece.

He ordered a boycott of the first postwar Greek elections, scheduled for March 31, 1946, and sent a message to the party organization in Macedonia to plan an armed attack on a target of its choice on the eve of the elections. Markos Vafiadis, a leader of the Macedonian committee and later commander of guerrilla forces, chose the town of Litochoron, where three ELAS officials had been disemboweled, as their target.

An armed group of thirty-three men, all but four of them natives of the town, entered Litochoron on March 30 and opened fire on its defenders – an army platoon, which quickly surrendered, and a detachment of rural police, which held out until their barracks were set on fire and twelve of their men were killed. The guerrillas retreated without a scratch when British troops approached.

The attack on Litochoron was the spark that set off the third and bloodiest round of the Greek civil war, and as news of the assault spread, ELAS *andartes* throughout Greece dug up their weapons and began to head for the mountains.

CLOSING DOORS

IN LIA, THE news of the outbreak of the third round and the attacks on Macedonian villages by the reforged army of *andartes* were discussed like reports of a local team's victories in a distant country. Although the villagers rooted for the guerrillas, Macedonia was far away, and they were weary of war.

More compelling, in the spring of 1946, was the day-to-day news of births, deaths, weddings, land feuds, and the battles between Stavroula Yakou and her mother-in-law.

The prophets of doom at Stavroula's wedding nodded sagely. The bride had no more than entered her mother-in-law's threshold, stepping carefully with the right foot on the lucky coin placed there, than the trouble began.

From the start Alexandra Dangas could see that Stavroula was not the kind of bride any mother-in-law could tolerate. She muttered and stomped as she got up in the morning to light the fire, poured the olive oil with a heavy hand despite constant warnings to economize, and took advantage of the fact that she quickly became pregnant to avoid doing the heavy gardening and beating of laundry.

Dimitri bent first toward his wife and then toward his mother, blown like a reed in a hurricane, and finally he withdrew from the battlefield altogether, returning to the bakery in Khalkis. Local skirmishes then intensified into frequent stormy scenes that culminated with Stavroula rushing home to pour out her grief to her mother, who would nervously send her right back. While Stavroula's girl friends took her side – after all, she was pregnant, poor thing! – most of the married women clucked and agreed that this is what comes of young people choosing their own mates.

Eleni noticed that Olga consistently sided with Stavroula and decided it was time to lecture her on proper behavior for a bride, for her oldest daughter already showed distressing signs of willfulness.

'When you get married,' Eleni told her, 'I want your in-laws to congratulate me for bringing up such a bride. Whatever your husband or mother-in-law tells you to do is law. No grumbling! You must never tell secrets that you hear in your mother-in-law's house, not even to me. I don't want the kind of shame Stavroula is heaping on poor Anastasia.'

Olga listened dutifully and promised to add luster to the Gatzoyiannis name through her conduct, but Eleni knew that her first child was a bit spoiled and tried to warn her of the traps ahead.

'Your mother-in-law will test your honesty by dropping a coin on the floor to see what happens when you're sweeping and find it, so be sure to give it to her at once instead of putting it in your pocket,' she admonished.

Christos owned a large piece of forest land below the village which was to be divided among the girls as part of their dowries, and Eleni always warned them, as they went to collect firewood there, 'Go in deep and cut the wood from the difficult places now, so that when you're married and pregnant like Stavroula and your mother-in-law sends you for wood, then you can cut from the easy places.'

In the village it was believed that the less an innocent girl knew about sex, the better, but Eleni ventured to broach the subject with Olga, for she knew the damage a harsh sexual initiation could do. There was a girl from the nearby village of Kostana who had become the subject of a bawdy popular song on such an occasion. The girl, named Milia, had been taken by her mother on a trip to the village of Lista, where, to her complete surprise, her mother wed her to a middle-aged widower named Stefo.

On the wedding night the bride's mother slept on the first floor below the newlyweds' room before returning to Kostana. Shortly after everyone retired, terrible screams issued from the bridal chamber. 'Mother, Mother, come and save me!' screamed Milia piteously. 'This man is a devil! He's got a big red intestine between his legs and he's trying to stab me with it!'

Louder and louder she implored her mother to help her and at each outburst the embarrassed woman would bellow from downstairs, 'Hit her in the mouth, Stefo!' The uproar so entertained the neighbors that they composed a song called 'The Big Red Intestine,' with a rousing chorus of 'Hit her in the mouth, Stefo!' and the tale of the unhappy wedding night quickly spread throughout the Mourgana villages.

Eleni had come to her own wedding night nearly as innocent as the unfortunate Milia, and the next morning she arose from the nuptial bed, and without a word to anyone, set out to return to her parents' home. She was convinced she could never endure such an ordeal a second time.

But as Eleni grimly walked from her new husband's neighborhood toward the Haidis house, she ran into her cousin Tassia Makos, one of the three ill-starred daughters-in-law of the infamous Kostena Makos. When Tassia asked where she was going, and Eleni replied that she was leaving her husband of less than twenty-four hours, the older girl smiled sadly, her face marked by her mother-in-law's blows. 'You might as well turn around and go right back, Eleni,' she said. 'Everyone would laugh at you if you came home now, and your father would skin you alive!'

Later, when Eleni was the mother of five children and told the story of her momentary rebellion to her neighbor Olga Venetis, her friend chuckled, as married village women always do at such confessions, and said that it took her own husband eight days of siege before he could conquer her unwilling virginity.

Thinking of all the unhappy sexual initiations, Eleni sat Olga down one afternoon when the other children were out of the house. Taking a deep breath and searching for the right words, she warned her that after she was married, her husband would expect her to do things with him in bed that might frighten her. She told Olga about her own qualms on

210

the morning after her wedding and added consolingly, 'In time you'll get used to it and even begin to enjoy it.'

Olga wasted no time worrying about the mysteries of the marriage bed, however. As far as she was concerned, being married meant buying beautiful things for her dowry, receiving the wedding crown in her flattering red bridal dress, leading the village in the wedding dances, and settling down with a husband so wealthy and respected that all her friends from the washing pond would be consumed with jealousy. Olga had decided that she would settle for nothing less than a teacher, doctor or lawyer as a husband.

She didn't waver in her resolution, despite Eleni's constant reminders that the only teacher living in Lia was already married, and there was not a doctor or lawyer within miles of the village. Her mother wearily pleaded with her to consider one of the better families of tinkers, merchants or millers in Lia, but Olga raised her chin, clicked her tongue and said she would never compromise.

Olga was besieged by many swains, but she gave them all short shrift. Poor Sotiris Botsaris, a good-looking lad but only a tinker, mooned around the Gatzoyiannis gate, hiding notes under stones where everyone could find them ('I love you, when can we meet?') until Eleni became so angry that she waylaid him on the path and threatened to dump a pail of goat's dung on his head the next time he tried to leave compromising notes on her daughter's doorstep.

So many eager go-betweens arrived at Eleni's door, hymning the virtues of this potential husband or that one, that she became heartily sick of the whole subject of Olga's engagement. At each name that was suggested, Olga turned up her nose, while thirteen-year-old Kanta eagerly piped up, 'Then I'll take him!' Eleni would dramatically throw open the door and tell Olga to take herself off to the convent of Yeromeri. 'Black one!' she raged. 'If you don't get married, I'll marry Kanta and let you be an old maid!'

While Eleni grappled with Olga's stubbornness, the villagers of Lia and all of Greece faced the referendum on the monarchy on September 1. Partly as a result of pressure from the security forces, 68.7 percent of the electorate voted in favor of King George. The return of the monarch on September 27 increased the number and ferocity of attacks by the guerrillas on villages in Macedonia. In each case the local police would be attacked and killed, their commander mutilated, and rightists executed.

The number of guerrillas fighting under General Markos Vafiadis reached 13,000 by the fall of 1946, partly due to forced conscription of villagers, and by December the general had organized his army into regional commands, including one for Epiros. These forces were renamed the Democratic Army of Greece, or its acronym, the DAG.

The Liotes learned that Spiro Skevis and his followers were among those fighting, but the former ELAS sympathizers who had remained in the village were, for the most part, involved in their peacetime lives and reluctant to go to the mountains again to join him. As one former Skevis guerrilla put it: 'The gun is heavy.'

In March of 1947 President Harry Truman announced that the United States was granting Greece $300 million to fight the Communist insurrection supported by its Communist neighbors. The Truman Doctrine stirred up anti-American feelings in Lia, which overflowed onto 'the Amerikana' in their midst.

The hostility toward Americans aroused by the Truman Doctrine did not diminish the stream of suitors for Olga's hand, however; and Olga's refusal to consider any of them was driving Eleni to distraction. If only she would say yes, everything could be set in motion: the dowry purchased, the wedding arranged, and Olga settled in a house in Athens or Lia. Then the rest of the family would be free to emigrate. Olga would no doubt come to America a year or so later, bringing her husband and perhaps a tiny grandchild. Eleni castigated herself for letting Olga veto the choice of a groom, but she was too soft-hearted to force her eldest child to marry a man she didn't want, and Christos was not around to knock sense into the girl's head.

Unable to stand the uncertainty, Eleni decided to do

something that nearly every woman in Lia had done at some point in her life – usually when agonizing over a question of romance or marriage. Eleni resolved to visit the woman named Konstantina Ballou, who lived in a hovel almost two hours' walk away. The fat, stooped old hag was known to everyone in the Mourgana villages as 'Flijanou' for her uncanny ability to read one's fortune in the dried grounds left in the coffee cup, the *flijani*.

Every Greek village was full of old women who claimed to be able to read the future in coffee grounds, but none could equal the clairvoyance of Flijanou. When going to consult her, the village women always pretended they were only setting off to cut shrubbery for the animals. Eleni, too, told no one except her family of her quest, but she agreed to let Kanta make the long walk with her while Olga stayed behind with the younger children.

On the morning they set out, Eleni folded enough finely ground coffee in a piece of paper to make two cups, one for the Flijanou and one for herself, and put it in her apron pocket. By noontime she was seated in the shabby one-room shack crowded with offerings of walnuts, corn and tomatoes left by clients who had no money to pay for readings.

Deftly the old woman filled the long-handled copper coffee pot with coffee, sugar and water and then held it over the fire until the brew foamed up and filled the room with a rich aroma. She poured cups for Eleni and herself, and as the two women sipped, they chatted of inconsequential matters, Eleni being careful to give away no personal details.

When Eleni had drunk her coffee down to the layer of thick muddy grounds, the Flijanou took it and sloshed the residue around a bit to make sure it was evenly distributed. Then she nodded at her client, who turned the cup upside down into the saucer, letting the liquid coat the insides. Quickly the Flijanou inscribed the cross three times on top of the overturned cup with her bony fingers. They chatted for several minutes more until the grounds were certain to have dried and marked the cup with arabesques and designs like frost etchings on a winter window.

Eleni always felt a stab of worry when someone held her

cup up to the light to read it, although, she told herself, she didn't really believe in fortunetelling. The old woman frowned as she turned the cup between her gnarled, dirt-stained hands. She pursed her lips and softly muttered, 'Po! Po! Po!' Then she set down the cup and looked at Eleni.

'It's not a good cup, my dear, I'm sorry to say.'

'What do you see there, old woman?' Eleni snapped. 'It's my daughter I want to know about.'

The old woman picked up the cup again and held it close to her eyes. 'I see you have four daughters,' she said. 'Here is the oldest one.' She pointed, but to Eleni it looked like nothing but coffee grounds. 'You want to know whom she'll marry. But the cup shows that the man is not someone she knows now and he does not yet know her. He'll swoop down and take her like an eagle takes a hen.'

'Why is it a bad cup?' Eleni asked.

The Medusa-haired old woman shook her head and peered into it again. 'I'm sorry, my sweet, but I see your house empty and everyone gone within a year's time.'

Eleni's heart leaped. 'But that must mean my husband will take us to America!' she exclaimed.

The old woman shook her head again. 'No, I see bad things here. The head of the household is gone. The house is empty. I see death . . . within a year's time.'

Eleni felt her skin prickle and thought, Christos will die, and we'll be left destitute!

The next instant she was furious with herself for listening to the old hag's nonsense. 'I ask you whom my daughter will marry, and you give me enigmas and lies!' she shouted.

'I'm sorry, dear,' protested the Flijanou. 'I never like to see a bad cup, but I don't tell you just what you want to hear, as other women do. Perhaps if we try again in three months' time, we'll see a better cup.'

She held out her hand.

Angrily, Eleni put a few coins in it and hurried out of the gate to where Kanta was waiting, tossing pebbles into the great drop below. The girl asked what the Flijanou had said, and Eleni told her, adding that the woman was a charlatan. But Kanta could see that her mother was upset, for all the way home she alternated between worrying aloud that Christos would die and speculating on the unknown eagle who would carry Olga away.

Soon after the visit to the Flijanou, the postman, Sotiris Venetis, brought a brown envelope for Eleni which he did not leave at Michopoulos' *cafenion* but carried up the mountain path to her door. He required her signature before turning it over to her, and it bore the embossed eagle stamp of the United States Embassy in Athens. Eleni opened the thick packet and stared at the pages of words, printed in both Greek and foreign letters that writhed like serpents. She imagined she could feel a current flowing from the papers through her fingers, for they held the power to transport her family from Lia to the golden land.

The attached letter informed her that a petition had been filed for herself and her children to immigrate, and that she must have the enclosed papers filled out, notarized and submitted to the embassy along with documents proving birth and relationship of each individual to the American citizen. Eleni trembled, remembering that all the official papers of the village had been burned when the Germans set fire to the schoolhouse. But when she went to see the new president of Lia, the cripple Yiorgos Boukouvalas, he assured her that he could issue her substitutes. When these were ready, she set out on the long trip to Filiates to have the papers filled in and stamped by the town's notary.

Wearing the European-style dress Christos had bought her ten years before in Corfu, Eleni entered the office of the notary in Filiates, whose name, in gold letters on the door, was Christos Konstantopoulos. He was a balding, middle-aged man in a shiny suit, wearing gold-rimmed glasses and a small drooping mustache. He cultivated the clawlike long nail of a gentleman on each little finger; the shelves of leather-bound law books behind his desk intimidated the visitor by their very weight.

He picked up Eleni's packet of papers and put them down again as if they smelled bad. 'I see you have no proper birth certificates,' he said.

'They were burned by the Germans,' Eleni replied. 'The village president has issued us papers explaining this.'

'I see,' he said wearily. 'How long has your husband been living in America?'

Eleni was frightened at a direct question. If she gave the wrong answer, would it spoil their chances of emigrating? 'He first went there in 1910,' she replied uncertainly.

'I see,' he said again. After a pause, during which he hefted the papers as if to guess their weight, he cleared his throat and announced in the manner of a judge, 'This will cost twenty-five hundred drachmas.'

Eleni couldn't suppress a gasp of amazement. She calculated rapidly. The year before, new money had been issued to counter the wildfire inflation, and the exchange value was artificially set very low at 12 drachmas to a dollar, which would make his fee over $200. All she had was the $300 Christos had sent to buy Olga's dowry.

'I can't afford that much,' she quavered. 'That's far too high!'

'That's the price,' he said and turned away as if he couldn't be bothered to give the matter any more of his attention. 'It's up to you if you want to go to America or not.'

Eleni felt her face flush with anger, but she clamped her mouth shut and pondered her alternatives. The first priority was to get Olga married. Somehow, Christos could send the money for filling out the papers later. With as much dignity as she could muster, Eleni stood up and removed the precious envelope from the desk. 'I'll come back in the fall, when I have enough,' she said, embarrassed by the contrast between her village accent and his acquired Athenian lisp.

'As you wish,' he replied absently and turned completely around in his swivel chair, presenting her with his back.

Outside, as she stumbled blindly through the cobblestone streets toward the town square, Eleni heard someone call out her name and turned to see Minas Stratis, splendid in a new tweed suit, his familiar gold watch chain across his chest.

'What good hour brings you to Filiates?' Eleni said, genuinely glad to see a friendly face after the debacle in the notary's office. 'You look like you've been elected to Parliament!'

'Not quite,' he replied, preening a bit. 'I'm working for the army on intelligence matters, as you may have heard, besides teaching in Yannina, and they sent me here on an inquiry. What brings *you* here?'

She poured out what had happened to her dreams of emigrating to America, and Minas insisted on buying her a coffee at a nearby café. When she seemed calmer, he leaned forward and spoke quietly so as not to be overheard. 'If you're not emigrating, Eleni, I want you to take my advice and get yourself and the children out of Lia. The guerrillas have been moving closer to the Mourgana. It's just a matter of time. And if you're there when they come, it won't go well with you. They're killing police and rightists all over northern Greece.'

'We're a household of women and children,' she protested. 'Why should they bother us? We've done nothing against them!' She didn't mention that she had even hidden two ELAS *andartes* in her home.

Minas raised a warning finger to his lips. 'Sell your part of the store in Yannina that Christos and my father own together. Use the money to move your family to Yannina until the papers come through for America. My father's been talking about selling anyway, so I know he wouldn't object.'

Eleni shook her head. 'If I went to Yannina, a woman with four unmarried daughters and no husband, everybody would call us whores! We'll put through our papers in the fall, and before then I'll get Olga engaged to a boy from a good village family.'

But Minas' words had disturbed her, and when she got home, Eleni wrote an anxious letter to Christos, telling him to send more money for the notary as soon as he could, adding: 'I ran into Minas Stratis in Filiates and he warned me that the Communists might come back to Lia. He said that we should get out before that happens, that I should take the family to Yannina, but I'm worried what people would say. What do you want me to do?'

A month later, in June of 1947, she received Christos' reply, a letter that became widely quoted in their neighborhood of the Perivoli. 'You have no business going anywhere,' he

217

wrote. 'If they're lighting at the spring right above the house, you stay in your home with your children. After all, who are these *andartes*? They're Greeks, fellow villagers some of them, fighting for their rights. I have worked for my living all my life and never bothered anyone. Why should they bother my family?'

In late June of 1947 my mother informed me that we were going to Babouri to say goodbye to my godmother, Eugenia Economou, who had finally obtained the immigration papers for herself and her son Stavros to join her husband Nassios in Worcester, Massachusetts. I could tell by the set of my mother's jaw as we walked toward Babouri that the visit was going to be difficult for her. I wasn't looking forward to it either.

Nearly eight years old, I had become increasingly sensitive about being the son of an American. Since the passage of the Truman Doctrine several months before, the older boys of Lia had started taunting me for being the son of one of the foreign capitalists whose money was paying for guns that were being used against the brave partisans of ELAS. I was developing secret resentments against my father and wished that he would either bring us to America, like Stavros' father, or come to live in Greece so that I wouldn't have to put up with the scorn of the other boys.

I had always been a little afraid of Stavros Economou, a strong, husky boy four years older than myself. Because he was the only son of Nassios Economou to survive infancy, Stavros was brought up by his doting mother to consider himself the crown prince of Babouri. None of the children in his village would dare to tease him about his American father. Furthermore, Stavros was lionized by the other children because he owned the only toys we had ever seen – wonderful American toys: a truck and an airplane that sped about the floor when you turned their keys, and a rainbow-colored spinning top. My father never sent anything as frivolous as toys, just practical things like clothes and shoes. I resented that too.

When we arrived in Babouri, my godmother received us

218

wearing a white wool European-style dress which was the talk of the village for its daring color and design. She dimpled and preened as she served us sweets and chattered about the house and furniture awaiting them in America. My mother's polite good wishes sounded strained to me. I knew that it was agonizing to her that Eugenia was setting out on the journey to America while we were left behind in the increasingly hostile atmosphere of Lia.

I found Stavros holding court outside his house. With princely *noblesse oblige* he had bequeathed the three famous toys to the daughter of the postmaster. They were old and boring, he said, all right for babies, but he had dozens of better toys waiting for him in America, including an electric-train set. He was wearing new American long trousers, like a man, not short pants like me. I hung back as I watched the children of Babouri dancing attendance on him.

When the time came to leave, my mother called me inside to kiss my godmother goodbye. Eugenia put a white lace handkerchief in my hand – she had made it especially as a last gift to her godson, she said. I took it sullenly, wondering why she imagined I would want a handkerchief. Then she embraced my mother and they both began to cry, realizing they might never see each other again. My mother took hold of both Eugenia's hands and said in an unsteady voice, 'When you see Christos in America, tell him to hurry. Tell him that coming to join him is all we want in the world.'

She abruptly seized my hand to lead me away, not wanting Eugenia to see how much her good fortune stung. When we were at the first bend in the road, we turned around and waved back at my godmother and Stavros. Then, when we were out of sight, my mother let herself cry openly. I felt like crying too. I had wanted Stavros at least to give me that airplane.

In the heat of July, Eleni's discontent grew apace with the fields of corn, and the end of the month brought a new and more serious quarrel with her father.

One day a daughter of Foto Gatzoyiannis came by to see

Eleni. She was married to Dimitri Stratis, proprietor of one of the coffeehouses, and brother of Minas and Vasili Stratis. She told Eleni that her father-in-law, who owned the store on a busy shopping street in Yannina in partnership with Christos, had sold his half to the tenant, who was paying only a tiny rent because of strict postwar rent-control laws. Eleni realized the sale made Christos' share of the store nearly worthless because there would be no possibility of raising the rent with the tenant as co-owner, and no one else would want to buy into it either.

Eleni suddenly remembered that Christos had left her father the power of attorney to look after his business interests. It had never occurred to her that Kitso might use the papers against them. She hurried to her father's house, which he had rebuilt on the foundations of the burned one. He was breaking up slates with a sledgehammer to fix a leak on the roof, while the sweat drenched his shirt.

Eleni blurted out what she had just heard – that Stratis had sold his share of Christos' store to the tenant. Kitso continued swinging the hammer with vicious accuracy. 'And what do you want me to do about it?' he asked. 'Am I going to spend all my life handling your concerns?'

Eleni felt sick at the unfairness of it all. Christos had left him in charge, she shouted. He should have looked after their interests. Now the store was worthless. Kitso stopped and wiped his face. 'I looked after his wife and family through the whole war, and what did I get for it?' he asked. 'Nothing. I don't owe him a fucking thing! I told Stratis to go ahead and do what he wanted.'

He turned back to splitting the stones and Eleni was reminded of the way he drove the hatchet into the skull of the Turkish brigand when she was a child.

'I stayed behind after I was married because of you and Mother!' she nearly screamed, the words coming out in a rush. 'I've raised my children here so you wouldn't be alone. But I'm going to take them to America, where they belong, with their father. I'll see that you get every sovereign of what you say we owe you. But one day you'll wish you could see just the hem of my dress, and you'll die alone with your gold!'

Kitso continued smashing the slates with grim ferocity, not looking up as she turned and ran away.

This last and worst battle with her father shook Eleni's equilibrium to its foundations. She forbade the children to visit their grandfather anymore, although Megali dropped by their house almost daily. Often at night the girls and Nikola would hear their mother crying.

By the end of summer, Olga's trunk in the good chamber was filled to overflowing with dresses, embroidered shifts and stockings turned out by the sewing machine along with the flashing needles of herself and her mother. When in early August the day finally arrived for them to travel to Yannina and buy the rest of the dowry, Eleni asked her brother-in-law Andreas to go with them for protection and propriety, because she was no longer speaking to her father. Olga, tipsy with excitement, had never been to a big city. She dressed carefully for the excursion in a blue dress with two black stripes around the border, topped by the traditional long black sleeveless tunic. On her head was a black kerchief with red and pink roses, and she carried her good shoes in her hand.

They took the mule as far as Vrosina, where the road began, and found a truckdriver to take them the rest of the way to Yannina. Olga had never ridden in a vehicle before and rode the whole way to Yannina with her eyes closed tight.

As they approached the city, Eleni made her look. Rising from the velvety green fields, dotted with popcorn sheep, were the houses and minarets of Yannina, and in the middle the lake, smooth as a mirror. They rattled over the cobblestone streets, and Olga stared open-mouthed at the storks in their chimney-top nests, the gypsies with their dancing bears and monkeys, the old women selling lottery tickets, the little boys hawking mastic gum.

Eleni took a firm hold of Olga's hand and led her across Averoff Street, through the busy traffic of horses, mules, trucks and carts, and up Venizelos Street, toward the inn called Vrosgou's Hani, where Liotes usually stayed on their forays into the city. Like all the buildings it was Turkish in

221

style with a courtyard in the back, turning a blind face to the street except for latticed harem windows projecting from the second floor, where women could watch the bustle below without being seen.

While Andreas carried their belongings up to the rooms, Eleni and Olga sat in the triangular courtyard of the Yiali Kafene across the street. It was raised several feet above pavement level, affording a perfect view of the passing crowd and the splendid neoclassical buildings on the right and left, fantasies of wrought-iron balconies, curlicues and gargoyles. As they ordered a meal Eleni was mentally girding herself for the shopping expedition ahead. The $300, knotted into a handkerchief, felt heavy on her bosom.

They had come to Yannina to buy the 'outside' dowry, the sleeping rugs, blankets, pillows, mattress and coverlets, which were to be piled on top of the dowry chest, for the 'inside' dowry – enough clothes for a year – was already collected. Other villagers had given Eleni the names of Vlach women who wove the shaggy, bright-colored sleeping rugs, the *velenzes,* in their homes.

They set out for the neighborhood of the Vlachs, a mysterious, taciturn nomadic race of shepherds who still spoke Latin as well as Greek. Vlachs were proverbially wily, but they also wove the best *velenzes.* As they pushed past the tiny caves of shops with the proprietors soliciting them from their rush-seated chairs outside each door, Olga stared. When they reached the neighborhood of the rug weavers, black-dressed crones and young boys called to them from their thresholds, 'Come in, take a look! The finest *velenzes* in Epiros!'

In each house, in the room nearly filled by the great loom and piled high with rainbow stacks of *velenzes,* Eleni expertly felt the weight of the rugs, stroked the pile, examined the underside for flaws and asked questions about the dyes. Each woman would give a price – so many drachmas per kilo – and when Eleni and Olga left the house, they would run after them, offering to lower the price by a few drachmas a kilo. But this was only the first day; too soon to buy.

On the second morning, mother and daughter returned to

the home of a woman whose rugs, Eleni had decided, were of the best workmanship. Cups of coffee appeared from nowhere. 'Feel the pile, *Kyria*,' the woman crooned. 'Only the flower of the wool. Not an ounce from the underbelly or legs. The dyes will still be as bright when this beautiful bride has grandchildren.'

The prize of her collection was a bridal *velenza* – the rug which goes over the saddle of the mule carrying the dowry – woven in multicolored, elaborate geometries 'with a silver flywheel.' Olga fell in love with it, but Eleni managed to appear unimpressed.

After they got up to leave twice, and twice were physically dragged back into the house, Eleni and the Vlach woman settled on a compromise price which was fair enough to convince both parties they had outwitted the other. There were other things to buy: a large striped mattress, a bright flowered quilt for winter nights, a pair of pillows, and some geometrically patterned bed covers. The night of the second day in Yannina, Olga and Eleni slept the sleep of victorious warriors.

Before hiring a truck to carry their treasures back to Vrosina, Eleni, Olga and Andreas stopped for a last meal at the Yiali Kafene. As they were halfway through a plate of trout and crayfish fresh from the lake, there was a commotion. From their table they could see a crowd of peasants in village dress excitedly waiting for something. When two open army trucks rolled down Venizelos Street and came to a stop, the crowd erupted into wails and screams.

The trucks were jammed with young women, no older than Olga, who were also weeping, their faces scratched, their hair snarled and untidy and uncovered by kerchiefs. Eleni got up to see what was happening, but Olga was more interested in her first taste of fish and stayed behind with Andreas. After some time Eleni returned to their table, her face drawn.

'It's a group of girls from villages in the Pogoni area,' she said, referring to a region fifty miles northwest of Yannina. 'Two months ago they were taken by force by the guerrillas and made to put on uniforms and fight. Those outside are some of the girls that managed to flee to the national army.' She looked at Olga. Like her daughter, the *andartinas* were only children, but they had eyes like old women. 'You should see how the parents cried when they saw them,' she said. 'The worst was the parents of daughters who didn't come back.'

Olga took little interest in the fate of the unwilling girl soldiers, except to notice with fascination that some of them wore khaki trousers, which shocked her more than the fact that they had been kidnapped from their villages. Olga was lost in anticipation of her triumphant return to Lia with the new dowry, but Eleni couldn't get the girls' faces out of her mind. The pitiful reunion with their parents was proof that Minas Stratis had been right in his predictions. And even he had not told her the *andartes* would conscript girls. What if they tried to take her own daughters? But Christos had given strict orders not to leave the house. In the back of the truck all the way to Vrosina, where they had left the donkey, Eleni turned over this new threat in her mind. For Olga, the aftermath of the trip to Yannina was like an endless name-day celebration. Every female in Lia dropped by to examine the new dowry piled on top of the trunk, to feel the pile of the *velenzes,* exclaim over the workmanship, sip tiny glasses of ouzo or coffee, and offer good wishes for her future engagement.

Stavroula Yakou came and the Gatzoyiannis girls were especially solicitous of her, for her little son had been born dead some months before. Stavroula no longer moved with the same careless grace, and there were dark circles under her eyes. Like everyone else, she exclaimed over the magnificent dowry and uttered the conventional wish, 'May the marriage be well rooted,' but as she spoke, Olga felt an involuntary shudder. Stavroula was looking at her as a caged canary watches a passing swallow.

In later years, every time Olga thought of her dowry, she'd sigh and say, 'I only had three months to enjoy it.' For by the end of November the tide of war would carry the guerrilla force back to Lia, and celebrations of the ordinary ceremonies of life would be ended forever.

While Olga was buying her dowry in Yannina, the DAG of Markos Vafiadis was concentrating its strength in the Zagoria

224

villages to the north of Yannina. After an unsuccessful late-October attack on Metsovo, the town thirty-five miles north-east of Yannina that was the gateway to the only route over the Pindos mountains, the *andartes* withdrew to sanctuaries on the Pindos massif. It seemed likely that the men in the Epiros Command of the DAG would spend the winter on the Pindos range, launching occasional raids to the south and east. But in late November, under cover of thick fog, six battalions unexpectedly left the Pindos chain and moved westward with the objective of cutting Epiros in half along an east-west axis.

This force of 1,500 guerrillas intended to base themselves in the rugged Mourgana mountain range that extends along the Greek-Albanian border where Lia was located. They could hold this natural fortress easily with a small force and would have access to Albania, to bring in supplies and evacuate the wounded. From the Mourgana the guerrillas hoped to expand south into Epiros, capture a major town there and set up a provisional government as their first step toward recapturing control of Greece.

On November 27, 1947, the six constables stationed in Lia received word from their headquarters in Filiates that the guerrilla forces were approaching. They were ordered to take all the weapons and important papers they could carry, hide the rest and evacuate to Filiates at once. The constables moved fast – they had heard about the mutilated bodies of gendarmes in other invaded villages. While two of them dug a hole in the corner of a field behind the police station, screened by a hedge and a shed, the others ran to warn the few men in the village who belonged to MAY – the auxiliary security unit of villagers who helped the police. In Lia there were not many rightists willing to work with the gendarmes against the guerrillas; Andreas Kyrkas was one of them. On that Thursday, the constables woke him from his siesta, telling him to come help them pack the police files and then to get himself to Filiates before he was caught and executed.

As two constables hurriedly buried a cache of weapons behind the police station, they looked up to see the thin, sunburned, sardonic face of seventeen-year-old Andreas

Michopoulos, hovering over them from atop the wall that separated the police station from the house that had been the British commando headquarters. Andreas Michopoulos was the bad egg among the boys of Lia, the one always suspected if someone's apricot tree had been stripped or a flock stampeded by a well-aimed rock. 'He's a devil!' Andreas' mother often said, crossing herself. 'I can break the broomstick beating him one day and the next he'll get in worse trouble.'

The constables were not happy to find Andreas watching them bury the guns. The young troublemaker could be counted on to reveal the hiding place to the guerrillas just for spite.

'You'd better come along with us to Filiates, Andreas!' called the sergeant, motioning to the boy to come out from behind the wall. 'You're just the right age for the guerrillas to conscript you the minute they lay eyes on you.'

'I'll take my chances,' Andreas replied casually.

'Better come with us,' the sergeant repeated more firmly. 'Otherwise we'd have to report in Filiates that you insisted on staying behind to help the guerrillas.'

Andreas wasn't willing to risk going to jail, so he shrugged, and with obvious reluctance, set out with the constables toward the west.

The activity at the police station had spread to the whole village, electrified by the news that the guerrillas were practically in town. Some Liotes were delighted that they were returning, but many former ELAS supporters prepared to flee alongside the terrified rightists because they didn't want to be conscripted.

In the town square Spiro Michopoulos, the thin, pale bachelor who ran the *cafenion,* was surprised to see his rebellious nephew Andreas, who shared his own admiration for the *andartes,* leaving town in the company of the constables. Spiro went over to investigate and realized that Andreas was not leaving entirely by choice. 'You should come along too, Spiro,' the sergeant told the shopowner. 'The guerrillas are conscripting anything that moves.'

Spiro grinned. 'They're not so hard up they'll take me,' he

said, joking about his near-fatal brush with tuberculosis, which had left him a semi-invalid. 'Besides, I don't dare leave the store. It's full of goods, and they'll clean it out if I'm not here to keep an eye on everything. They'll be gone in a few days, anyway.'

When Tassina Bartzokis came running into her house with the news of the approaching guerrillas, Eleni thought immediately of the weeping *andartinas* she had seen in Yannina. For herself, there was no choice; her husband had ordered her not to leave the house no matter what happened, but she wondered frantically if there was some way to save the children. She knew that Olga, now nineteen, and Kanta, who was fifteen, might be taken by force. Instinctively she headed down the mountain toward her father's house. She was so used to turning to a man for advice in a crisis that now, in her fear, she had forgotten the last bitter exchange between them.

When Eleni reached her parents' house, she found Megali alone, crouched in a corner, starting at every sound. 'He's gone, Eleni,' she whimpered. 'He left with Foto Gatzoyiannis and a crowd of other men for Filiates. He told me to stay here, that the *andartes* won't hurt women, but I'm afraid!'

She could hardly believe that her father had left without a goodbye, even though Christos had charged him with her family's safety. Kitso had turned his back on her as emphatically as she had threatened to do to him. He had left her helpless and her children in danger.

Eleni felt she was in a dark room; a room with many doors, and behind each door was a crack of light. Her father had shut one door on her, but, she thought quickly, there was still her brother-in-law Andreas. She hurried toward his house and found him outside the police station, loading a mule with boxes of files. 'Take Olga and Kanta with you when you leave,' she begged him. 'I'm afraid of what the *andartes* will do to them!' She paused. 'I want you to take Nikola too,' she added. 'It won't be safe for him if they start fighting here. I'll keep Glykeria and Fotini so they won't think I've sent all my children away.'

Andreas looked at her nervously, then went back to tying

227

bags full of police files onto the mule's back. 'I'll take all of you or nobody!' he said. 'It's no good having half the family down there in Filiates, worrying about you and the rest up here.'

'But Christos told me not to leave the house!' Eleni cried. 'If we all flee, they'll burn it, but they wouldn't hurt a woman and two little girls!'

Andreas nodded, relieved at finding an excuse not to be burdened with the children. 'You're right. Keep all the children inside while they're here and they won't bother you. But if I don't leave now, I'm a dead man.' He slapped the mule's flank, and as Eleni watched her brother-in-law head off through the village square, the second door closed.

She took a shortcut up the mountain and over toward the Perivoli. On the way she caught up with Tassos Bartzokis, who was just returning from a trip to Yannina. Learning that the guerrillas were almost on top of them, he was rushing home to pick up some changes of clothes and join the exodus of men for Filiates. Tassos, like Eleni, knew that young girls had been conscripted by force in other villages. He feared that his sister-in-law Rano was a likely victim as well as her friends, the two elder daughters of Eleni Gatzoyiannis. 'Get Olga and Kanta ready,' Tassos said as soon as he saw her on the path. 'I'm leaving right now and I'll take Rano and your two girls too.'

A door swung unexpectedly open and flooded Eleni with light. When the Germans came, Tassos had looked after her along with his own family. He had brought them sweets from Albania in the worst of the famine, and now he was offering her salvation once again. 'That's something my own father didn't say to me,' she told him with emotion.

'Go home and get them,' said Tassos urgently. 'I'm going to the house to get Rano, and I'll meet you there.'

Eleni ran ahead, but the closer she got to the house, the more she remembered what Christos had written her: 'You have no business going anywhere . . . stay in your home with your children . . .'

She slowed down to a walk. What would Christos, not to mention all the villagers, say if they learned she had sent the

228

eldest girls away with a man who was not a relative? Olga and Kanta shouldn't even speak to Tassos, much less travel all night alone with him. By the time she reached the house, Eleni knew she couldn't send them, no matter how good a friend Tassos was. She turned off to the Bartzokis house, where she found Tassos throwing things into a sack.

'I'll always be grateful that you offered to take the girls, Tassos,' she said, 'but I've decided not to send them away. I'll hide them around here somewhere until the guerrillas leave.'

Hearing this, Rano decided she'd stay too. Olga Gatzoyiannis was her best friend; they could hide out together, she said. Besides, she didn't want to leave her sister alone, because she was pregnant again. Tassos did not waste time arguing with their decision. He set off at once, almost running to catch up with the village men who had gone before. Eleni had closed the third door herself because of her fear of what people would say.

Nearly two hours had passed since word first arrived that the guerrillas were coming, and in that time all but a handful of men, most too old to be conscripted, had left the village.

Eleni went back to her own house and sat on the small veranda at the top of the steps. In the yard below, Nikola and Fotini played with pebbles, and Kanta and Glykeria squabbled over their chores. Olga sat in the shade, snapping the ends off string beans, humming as she worked. None of the children seemed worried about the approach of the guerrillas, but Eleni couldn't shake off a sense of oppressive dread. Her mind searched for a way to get the children out before it was too late. Suddenly she thought of one last possibility: the tinker Antonis Paroussis, who lived in Babouri, was Christos' first cousin. It was his wife, Antonova, who had pleaded with Eleni to take in and hide the two ELAS *andartes*. Now they owed her a favor, and they were family. Eleni knew that both husband and wife were pro-ELAS but that Antonis, a frail, shy man, was not eager to be conscripted into the guerrilla army. He would probably be fleeing just as the men of Lia had done.

'Quick, leave the beans and put some clothes in a sack!'

Eleni shouted at Olga. 'You're going to take Kanta and Nikola to Babouri to your uncle Antoni Paroussis. Tell him I want you to go with him to Filiates until the guerrillas have passed through. Quick, girl! For once, don't dawdle or you'll be too late!'

Eleni was in such a rush to get them under way to Babouri that it wasn't until they were far down the road, their figures shrinking into punctuation marks among the ilex and scrub pine, that she felt a terrible panic of loss. Nikola left carrying his shoes in one hand, the other clutching Olga's, turning now and then to look back at his mother.

Eleni had hardly returned to the two younger girls when she heard Tassina Bartzokis pounding at the gate, shouting that the guerrillas were already in the Perivoli. They had come down the mountain from the north. She said that an advance party of three men were at Yiorgi Mitros' mill, and the women of the neighborhood were going to meet them. 'We've got to welcome them, to put a good face on things,' Tassina panted, one hand on her swollen belly. 'It worked in Babouri when the Germans came. Maybe it will save us too.'

Eleni picked up a jug of moonshine from the storeroom and a sack of shelled walnuts. She warned Glykeria to watch Fotini carefully and not to open the gate whatever happened. With Tassina she climbed the several hundred yards up past the washing pond, to where three bearded strangers in threadbare uniforms were sitting with their backs against the wall of the mill, smoking cigarettes while a crowd of neighborhood women looked on. Eleni offered them her walnuts and *tsipouro*, but one of the men refused, saying, 'Now that we're here, we'll have plenty of time to eat, drink and learn about all of you. But first I need some answers.'

He took out a pencil and a notebook. 'Are there any constables in the village?'

'No, we heard they've left,' said one of the women.

'How many men in the village?' the guerrilla asked.

'A few, we don't know exactly,' said Tassina. 'You know that men from Lia are always on the road working, so there are never very many here.'

The guerrilla wrote on his pad for a while, then he looked

230

up. 'I want one of you to take this letter to Comrade Skevis, who's camped with his men in the field behind the chapel.'

All the women looked at Eleni, but no one said anything.

The guerrilla followed their eyes. 'You take it,' he said, holding the letter out to her.

'But I've left small children at home alone!' she protested.

'Olga's there to watch them, isn't she?' said Anastasia Yakou.

Eleni hesitated. She couldn't reveal that she'd sent Olga and Kanta to escape. She looked around at the faces of the women, all of them as familiar as her own. There was a coldness in their eyes that she'd never noticed before: none of them wanted to make the dangerous journey to find the *andartes,* and with one accord, they all had turned on her.

'I'm afraid to go alone!' Eleni exclaimed. 'At least let me have someone go with me.' She looked from one hard face to the next, then turned to the one in the group who seemed to show a glimmer of sympathy – her distant relative Tsavena Makou. 'Go with me, *zonia,*' Eleni pleaded, using a village word meaning 'kinswoman.' Tsavena nodded and came to stand next to her.

The *andarte* with the letter told them that his battalion, led by Spiro Skevis, was camped up the mountain to the north 'behind the little chapel on the other side.' Eleni assumed he meant behind the Chapel of St. Nicholas, but when she and Tsavena climbed up there, they found no sign of an army.

Perhaps he meant another chapel. They walked on, eastward along the spine of the mountain range, searching desperately for the guerrillas, their leg muscles cramping and their breath coming fast in the thin air. Two hours after they set out, Eleni and Tsavena finally saw smoke from the fires of a large encampment at the base of the hill called Tserovetsi.

When they reached the camp, where circles of shadowy figures crouched around campfires, Eleni stared in astonishment at the hundreds of men huddled together under ragged blankets shivering in the November frost. The last time she had seen the ELAS guerrillas in Lia they wore clean gray uniforms and carried new weapons taken from the Italians. Now they all were in rags, their beards matted, some

231

barefoot, and others wearing shoes held together with twine. They sat like stones, watching the women with terrible eyes. None of them got up to greet her.

There was a stir and Eleni heard hands clapping, as if summoning a waiter in a restaurant. She turned toward the sound and saw a gaunt, bearded, fair-haired man in a heavy coat. By his eyes she recognized Spiro Skevis, completely transformed from the days when he held court in the square with the other schoolteachers. Now he was even thinner, if possible, and the cold fire in his eyes was the only thing that animated his face. The men around her looked possessed, Eleni said later, like the swine into which Christ cast the devils.

Spiro motioned her to come to him, and she handed over the note. 'Welcome back to the Mourgana, Comrade Spiro,' she said, forcing her voice not to tremble. 'Everyone in Lia is waiting for you.'

He said nothing but unfolded the piece of paper she had given him. Slowly a smile spread over his face, not reaching his eyes. He stood up and shouted to the shivering guerrillas around him, 'Come on, men, pack up! Saddle the animals! We're moving out now!' He paused, and cupped his hands to his mouth, then shouted even louder. 'Tonight we'll be in my village, and we're going to squeeze water out of it!'

With curses, laughter and groans, the men heaved themselves up off the frigid ground and began to saddle the few bony mules and horses. Eleni watched, not daring to ask Tsavena what Spiro could have meant.

The guerrilla army followed the two women back to Lia, and when they reached the crest of the Prophet Elias, Spiro led the men down toward the village center while Eleni and Tsavena continued on to their homes in the Perivoli.

Eleni entered her own gate, limping with exhaustion. She shouted through the door, and when it opened, her mouth fell open at the sight of Olga. Behind Olga, Nikola and Kanta were playing happily with the two other girls. All the way home Eleni had been consoling herself that they at least would escape the fate that she had glimpsed in Spiro Skevis' eyes, and now here they were, closed in the trap with her.

232

'What are you doing back?' she cried to Olga. 'Didn't you find Antoni?'

Olga was tired and cross after all the fruitless walking. 'We got to the Paroussis house, and he had already left,' she said. 'Antonova said if we hurried we could catch him, but it was already getting dark, and I was afraid I wouldn't be able to find him. Antonova said the guerrillas wouldn't harm us. They're on our side, she said. So I came back.'

Eleni was overcome with despair and weariness. 'You should have gone on alone,' she murmured. But she had already gathered Nikola into her arms and she couldn't let go of him.

As she sat, watching the fire burn down, her cheek resting on the boy's hair, Eleni began to feel sick with anger. Her father had left them all behind without a word, saving himself and leaving his wife, daughter and grandchildren unprotected. Andreas, her brother-in-law, didn't want the responsibility of looking after her children. She had foolishly turned down Tasso Bartzokis' offer of help because of her automatic concern for maintaining propriety. Her daughters would be compromised if they left the village with Tassos, but far worse things could happen to them here. And she herself had automatically discarded any thought of taking her whole family and fleeing because Christos had ordered her to stay and protect the house. He wrote her that the *andartes* were 'Greeks, fellow villagers . . . fighting for their rights . . . Why should they bother my family?' But he had never looked into their eyes as she had today. He had been gone for ten years and lived five thousand miles away, yet like an archbishop he issued edicts about what she should do. She had always shown him the obedience required of a wife, but she wondered, when it was a question of her children's safety, if she shouldn't have defied him and the edicts of village propriety which had always ruled her life.

When it was very dark, Tassina and Rano came. There was another soft knock at the gate; Gregory Tsavos, the sixty-five-year-old field warden who lived in the house just above. He, too, wanted to hear what Eleni had learned from her encounter with the guerrillas.

'I've just come from the Alonia,' Tsavos told the group of women, shaking his gray head, 'and I saw evil omens everywhere. Just as the *andartes* came down the mountain, Andreas Michopoulos turned up, saying he gave the constables the slip outside of Povla. "Give me a uniform and a gun and I'll show you where everything's hidden," he was shouting. And he said he'd tell them all the spots to post guards, so that no one could sneak in or out of the village.'

'We should leave now, before the guards are posted!' Tassina exclaimed.

'How can you walk seven hours to Filiates at night in your condition?' retorted her sister, Rano.

Eleni was staring at the embers of the fire. 'It's too late,' she said dully. 'Spiro Skevis knows every corner of this village. We're already in the lion's mouth.'

She had seen the last door close, and there would be no more chances. They were alone in the dark.

PART THREE

REVOLUTIONS

Therefore is the anger of the Lord
kindled agaist his people, and he
hath stretched forth his hand against
them, and hath smitten them: and
the hills did tremble, and their
carcases were torn in the midst of
the streets.

– ISAIAH 5:25

CHAPTER EIGHT

When Spiro Skevis' *andartes* entered Lia on the evening of November 27, 1947, they were one of six batallions invading the Mourgana mountains, part of a guerrilla army of 25,000 fighters spread through the mountains of western Macedonia and Epiros along the Yugoslav and Albanian borders.

Although the Democratic Army of Greece contained many former ELAS fighters, it was now solely under the control of the Greek Communist Party, and unlike ELAS, it tolerated no divergence in its ranks from the hard party line.

The appearance of the insurgents in the Mourgana mountains was part of a radically new strategy. At the third plenum of the Greek Communist Party in mid-September, its doctrinaire secretary general, Nikos Zachariadis, insisted that the DAG should be changed from a guerrilla force, launching hit-and-run operations, into a traditional army fighting a positional war, holding the mountains it had previously been using as staging areas for operations and spreading out to capture major towns below.

The aim of the new policy was to 'liberate' a large area in northern Greece where a provisional government could be established. This, according to Zachariadis, would convince Soviet leader Joseph Stalin that the insurgents could win and therefore deserved the full support of the Communist bloc.

The man who stood up to oppose Zachariadis, insisting that the proposed strategy spelled disaster, was Markos Vafiadis, commander in chief of the DAG, a thin, fair, hawk-faced man who would soon become, like Aris, a popular

237

hero, the subject of folk songs and legends. Like Zachariadis, 'General Markos' had been a refugee set adrift from Asia Minor following the disastrous defeat of Greek forces by the Turks in 1923, when he was only seventeen, and managed to reach Salonika, where he worked in the tobacco factories and joined the Communist Party in 1928. Then he began the inevitable seesaw between militant action and imprisonment. Escaping from Gavdos island prison in the Aegean at the outbreak of World War II, he made his way back to the Macedonian mountains to join ELAS as a *kapetanios*.

A soft-spoken, paternal yet tough commander who urged his forces to win 'by fire and ax,' General Markos chose his words carefully. He argued with Zachariadis that consolidating the army for a positional war would make it vulnerable to the government forces equipped by the Americans and now numbering 170,000 men – six times the size of the DAG.

'This is defeatism! Treason!' shouted Zachariadis. Markos realized that if he didn't want to end up with his head hanging from a lamppost like Aris', he would be wise to back down.

The new policy was launched. The party moved its headquarters from Athens to the mountains, put together a cabinet for a provisional government, which it intended to announce on Christmas Eve, and began to plan a Christmas Day attack on the town it had chosen for the seat of the new government. The target was Konitsa, fifty miles from Lia and lying in a pass only twelve miles from the Albanian border between Mount Grammos, base for the bulk of the DAG, and the Mourgana range, which the six battalions of guerrillas had just taken. When guerrillas occupied the Mourgana villages, the women and children who had been left behind by their fleeing husbands and fathers expected that the insurgents would soon move on, as they had in other villages in northern Greece. The villagers didn't yet realize that the DAG was operating under a new strategy, and that the guerrillas had come to stay.

238

ONWARD TO THE STRUGGLE

ON THE NIGHT the guerrillas arrived in Lia, they began prowling in packs, pounding at the gates of the houses, demanding firewood, bread and shelter from the frightened villagers. While the intruders stood in the good chamber of the Gatzoyiannis house, warming themselves at the hearth and waiting for Eleni to produce the food they had demanded, Fotini and Nikola peeked at them from the hallway, staring at their ragged uniforms, unkempt beards and their wild eyes, glowing in the firelight.

The next morning more guerrillas came, bringing flour to each house in the Perivoli with orders to bake bread for the troops. 'Don't get any idea about keeping some flour for yourselves,' they warned Eleni. 'We're going to weigh the loaves when you're finished.'

A few hours later, as Eleni and Olga were kneading dough at the wooden trough, two more *andartes* came and ordered them, when the bread was baked, to cut it up and dry it into rusks, which the guerrillas could take with them without fear of it going moldy. 'Hurry it up,' ordered one of the two, a thin, blond man with a tangled, nicotine-stained beard. 'A lot of men are moving on to the front.'

He tried to avoid Eleni's eyes as she studied him. 'Why, Nikola!' she exclaimed. 'Is that you behind that beard?'

She had recognized Nikola Paroussis, the soft-spoken young kinsman she had hidden in her storeroom, the same polite boy who had taught Nikola and Fotini to play jacks two years before. But now he looked a decade older, his face haggard, weathered by the sun. 'Yes, it's me,' he said with a shrug.

'But, Nikola, child, I never would have known you!' Eleni said. 'You look so much older than the boy who stayed here for two weeks, eating with us, playing with the children.'

Nikola was uncomfortable at being reminded of his debt to her. 'These are different times, Amerikana,' he said. 'We have the fascists on the run now, and we need bread for our boys – quickly!' With that he was gone, leaving Eleni wondering at the change in him.

Within a few days of their arrival, Spiro Skevis set the bells of Holy Trinity ringing to announce a compulsory gathering in the village square. He was brief, with little of the flowery rhetoric of his brother. The DAG was engaged in a battle for the country's independence and for the people's rights, he told the assembled villagers. 'You will all have the privilege of taking part in this great struggle.' He looked at the worried faces – nearly all women and children. 'Our friends who throw in their lot with us have nothing to fear,' he went on. 'But our enemies, who have gone off to collaborate with the monarcho-fascists will not escape our punishment, no matter how far they run.'

If the villagers wondered how they would have a part in the great struggle, they were not long in finding out. Everyone was given a job. Spiro's first action was to reward the few men who had stayed behind by putting several on the local council to administer the village. At the head of the committee he put Spiro Michopoulos.

Michopoulos was one of the few Liotes who had contracted and survived the most dreaded disease in the mountain villages – tuberculosis. He had contracted it while in his twenties, when he and his brother traveled as itinerant coopers. The treatment for tuberculosis was drastic. The victim was locked in a room, deprived of all company and given his food pushed through a window until he died, whereupon his clothes, bed and possessions were burned and his house decontaminated with smoky fires. Or he was sent up to the highest pastures to live with the animals, sleeping on the ground, drinking milk straight from the ewe, eating fresh meat until the exposure to the elements either killed or cured him.

Spiro had survived by the second method, coming out of it with prematurely gray hair and a lingering weakness that made him unable to continue as a cooper. His brother helped him set up a small store and coffeehouse in the village square, and after Spiro stopped coughing, the Liotes gained enough confidence in his cure to patronize his *cafenion*. During the five years of being treated like a leper, Spiro acquired the deferential manner of one who is not sure his presence is welcome. Without being obtrusive, he was always trying to be helpful in small ways so that he would not be snubbed. To be appointed the head of the whole village was for Spiro Michopoulos an undreamed-of honor.

As Spiro Skevis had promised, all the villagers were given a part: every house billeted guerrillas, every woman cooked for the troops and every child gathered wood for them. Whenever a work force was needed, the slow-witted tinker Petro Papanikolas, who had been the church chanter and was now the town crier, would climb to the hillside above the ravine and shout in his high-pitched voice a verse that he was proud to have composed himself:

> Attention! Attention!
> Grab a rope and sack.
> Put a loaf in your pack
> And to Venetis' house make track!

The house of Eleni's friend Olga Venetis, just down the path from hers, had been taken over as a commissary, and the one next door was made into a slaughterhouse, while the families who owned them were evicted.

One of the first orders of the guerrillas was that every family should contribute fifty pounds of corn to the troops. As the women carried their quotas to the new commissary, they were shocked to find that the cattle confiscated by the guerrillas were being stabled inside the Church of St. Demetrios, where the women went almost daily to light candles and pray. Now lowing cows were milling around among the sacred frescoes and icons, the brass candle stands and the gilded wooden iconostasis.

Eleni felt fortunate compared to most of her neighbors because the family of Elias Gagas, a schoolteacher from the nearby town of Vishini, was assigned to her as boarders. When Gagas arrived in civilian clothes, accompanied by his wife, two teenaged daughters and a young son, Eleni moved her own family's possessions into the two rooms comprising the old part of the house – the kitchen and the dirt-floor pantry behind it. This gave the boarders the good chamber and the room next to it, which was used as an auxiliary storeroom and sometimes a bedroom.

The newcomers seemed to be polite, well-spoken people. The two daughters, about the same ages as Olga and Kanta, were well-dressed and sophisticated. The little boy, Demitris, who was only a year older than Nikola, was often homesick. Eleni would boil him eggs as a treat, and taking him on her lap, told him fairy stories until his tears dried. When the three Gagas children lined up every night to brush their teeth, Fotini and Nikola stared in fascination at this strange ritual.

Elias Gagas organized the village children under the age of ten into a one-room school, which he conducted in a house on the square, since the schoolhouse remained gutted. There were no desks, books or blackboards, but Gagas could make lessons interesting with only pencils and scraps of paper. Nikola liked learning the Communist songs and hearing stories about their Russian brothers. He stood proudly every morning before the framed pictures of Stalin, Marx, Zachariadis and Markos, to sing:

Take up your weapons, take up your arms!
Onward to the struggle
For our precious freedom!

While the children were receiving a Communist education, their mothers were being summoned nearly every day to the commissary, headed by a former butcher, Dimitris Bolofis, who was called 'Hanjaras' for the huge meat cleaver, or *hanjari*, which he wielded.

One day, shortly after the *andartes*' arrival, Petro Papanikolas summoned the women of Lia, one from every

242

house, to set out on a march to Kerasovo, a prosperous village twelve miles to the northeast, to load donkeys with any food, clothing and supplies that they found in the deserted town for the guerrillas. They would be allowed to keep for themselves any additional spoils they carried on their backs.

When they reached Kerasovo, Eleni and her friend Olga Venetis were surprised to find a ghost town of imposing two-storied stone houses with iron balconies and neat hay sheds and barns. 'What idiots we were,' Olga Venetis exclaimed, 'staying in Lia to protect our miserable huts when people with houses like these left everything behind to save themselves!'

The women of Lia loaded the mules and their own backs until long after midnight, and then, without stopping for food or rest, they set off toward home. Staggering under their burdens, they arrived at the commissary as dawn was breaking, their muscles cramped with fatigue. Hanjaras was there to greet them. He seemed pleased. 'Unload everything right here,' he told them.

'But we were told we'd get to keep what we brought on our backs,' said Rano, her voice loud in the morning hush. 'We've carried it all night through the mountains.'

Hanjaras' smile didn't waver. 'That statement has been rescinded,' he said. 'We need it all for our fighters.'

From that day the women of Lia mistrusted Hanjaras, but as the dispenser of food to the troops, he was one of the most powerful men in the village. They soon learned to take advantage of the fact that Hanjaras had a soft spot in his heart for children.

All the goods confiscated from stores in invaded towns and villages were sent on to Hanjaras. Among them would be such trifles as chewing gum, sweets, barrettes and charms, hair ribbons and small plastic toys, which he enjoyed handing out to the children of Lia. Nikola and Fotini were among those who hung around the commissary in hopes of a treat from the husky butcher. Fotini carefully collected the small treasures he gave her, keeping them tied in a handkerchief in a secret place.

Whenever the guerrillas slaughtered animals, they threw away the lungs, stomach and intestines, which the village women eyed longingly, for they would have made nourishing soup or sausages. But Hanjaras refused to let them have the scraps. 'The Democratic Army does not feed its people offal!' he thundered, tossing it all to the dogs. The women learned that if they sent their children to beg, they would often return triumphantly with a dripping lung or a lamb's head for the dinner pot.

The wheat which the women had collected in Kerasovo was ground to flour and distributed to each house in the village to bake into loaves of bread. Eleni had Olga to lend a hand, but she knew that her mother would be hard put to it to do so much baking, so she sent Kanta down to the Haidis house to help Megali.

Kanta carefully tied her black kerchief over her head and lower face before she set out. Ever since the arrival of the *andartes*, Eleni had insisted that Olga and Kanta wrap their kerchiefs over the lower part of their faces, before tying them in back, so that only the nose and eyes showed. It was the way Greek women had always hidden their beauty from invaders, especially from the Turks, who often descended upon the villages, collecting pretty girls for the harems and young men for the sultan's Janissary guards.

Kanta was naturally pale, but Olga had apple-red cheeks, so Eleni taught her to rub ashes on her face to dull the color. With the black kerchief and her heavy homespun clothes, Olga might have been a stocky grandmother instead of a nubile girl of nineteen. 'If anyone asks you why you wear your kerchief that way,' Eleni advised her, 'tell them it's to hide the tumor on your neck.' The tumor wasn't an invention. Olga, like many in Lia, suffered from goiter due to lack of iodine in the water, and when she was tired, there was a noticeable swelling under one side of her jaw.

Kanta arrived at her grandmother's house with her kerchief over her face like a Greek nun. Soon she and Megali finished kneading the dough for the *andartes* and set out the loaves to rise under a clean cloth. There was a banging at the door. When Megali opened it she was pushed aside by two *andartes*.

Rumors of the UNRRA supplies which everyone said Kitso had hidden away had reached the ears of the guerrilla officers, and the two men were sent to find and confiscate them. They began by pulling all the foodstuffs out of the small room that was the pantry. Everything that was edible was carried away as Megali and Kanta watched. Then they went below and emptied the handmade barrels and wooden chests of everything Kitso had stored for the winter. They began digging in the dirt floor of the cellar, trying to find his secret cache.

When they turned up nothing, the *andartes* came back upstairs and began ripping apart the sleeping pallets, tearing linings out of clothing and carting off even the kerosene used to start the fire. Megali crouched in a corner, but when one of the men pocketed a half-eaten piece of bread she shrilled, 'Aren't you going to leave me as much as a crust?' The taller of the two slapped her so hard that she fell sideways, her head thudding against the wall. Megali's cheek showed the imprint of the guerrilla's fingers, and blood was trickling from her mouth where her teeth had split the inside of her lip.

Kanta stood up and let the kerchief fall from her face. 'Aren't you ashamed of yourself, hitting an old lady?' she shouted.

The guerrilla started toward Kanta, warning 'Get out of here and shut up, or I'll give you the same!' Kanta pulled her weeping grandmother out the door and led her up to the Gatzoyiannis house.

When Eleni saw her mother's face she began to cry. It was decided that Megali should move in with Eleni's family. Kanta and Glykeria were sent down to bring up the unbaked loaves of bread. When the girls returned, Eleni came out to meet them and was startled to see a column of smoke rising from a house in the lower part of the Perivoli that belonged to Father Theodoras Karapanos, the priest who took over when Father Zisis died in an ELAS prison during the occupation. The new priest was the son of the blind woman, Sophia Karapanou. When Father Theodoras and the other men of Lia fled the village, old Sophia once again stayed behind. Her daughter-in-law, Eleftheria, remained to look after her, confident that they wouldn't be harmed because her own brother was one of the approaching *andartes*.

But Spiro Skevis was launching the fulfillment of the second part of his prophecy – that the enemies of the Democratic Army would be punished no matter how far they ran. In every village they captured, the guerrillas began by taking vengeance on the important citizens who chose to flee instead of staying behind to welcome them. In hamlets like Lia, the leading citizens were always the priest, the village president and the schoolteacher. Father Theodoras' house was the first to be put to the torch, but Eleftheria was given a few minutes' advance warning because her brother was one of the guerrillas.

The young woman began to rush about, grabbing a photograph, a *velenza*, snatching clothes off the hooks and tugging at a wooden chest full of corn, which she couldn't budge. Hearing the commotion, the blind woman reached out, trying to catch her hysterical daughter-in-law. 'Who is it, child?' Sophia quavered. 'Who's there?'

'We have to leave, Mother!' Eleftheria replied. 'They're going to burn the house!'

'Oh my God, the Germans have come back!' Sophia cried.

'No, it's not the Germans!'

Sophia crouched by the fireplace and put her apron over her head, rocking back and forth as people hurried by in excitement.

Finally someone stopped and picked Sophia up like a child, carrying her out the door as the guerrillas began pouring kerosene everywhere. Her savior was Angeliki Botsaris, the girl who had worked for the British commandos. She was now Angeliki Daikos, having married an itinerant peddler two years younger than herself. Although she was three months pregnant with her second child, Angeliki carried the blind woman in her arms to her own house and tried to comfort her.

Watching the priest's house in flames, Eleni shivered, wondering which of the villagers would suffer the guerrillas' vengeance next. She didn't have long to wonder. Soon a second finger of smoke rose toward the sky. It was the house of the schoolteacher Demos Bessias.

Spiro Skevis was personally on hand when they set the torch to the house of Minas Stratis. Minas had removed his wife and children from the village long before the guerrillas approached, knowing that Skevis would go to any lengths to punish him for evading them the last time. But Minas' mother, Christina, insisted on staying behind, hoping to protect the family property.

Before they set the Stratis house afire, Spiro Skevis walked through it, looking with a satisfied smile at the possessions of the man who had always been his rival. Minas had amassed the only library the village had ever seen; a whole wall of books. 'So many books; too many for a schoolteacher,' the villagers used to whisper, suspiciously. 'Too many even for a professor! Who knows what he really does with all these books?'

Spiro was eager to see Minas' fine library in flames, but first there was something else he was looking for. He knew that for years Minas had bred rabbits. With scholarly thoroughness he kept notes on their markings, coats and progeny. In the cellar Skevis found Minas' prize pair of angora rabbits, bought in Yannina to cross-breed with the village strain.

Spiro picked up the quivering balls of fur, their pink eyes rolling back in their heads, and carried them outside. He took a length of leather thong and tied them by the feet, then hung them, kicking and squeaking shrilly, over the saddle of the horse his equerry was holding outside.

These rabbits would be the banner of Minas' defeat. Spiro mounted his horse, the rabbits dangling in front of him, and signaled to the guerrillas who were waiting for his instructions, torches in their hands. 'Burn it!' he shouted, and turned the horse around for his triumphal parade through the village.

As Eleni and her children were watching the smoke of the burning houses, Nitsa arrived, puffing breathlessly up the hill. 'Boukouvalas' house is burning!' she shouted. 'Minas' house has fallen into the cellar. Christina's just standing there, watching it burn!'

'Poor Christina! Wherever will she live now?' said Eleni, full of pity for her cousin who had already suffered so much.

'She can live in the cooking shed, they haven't burned that,' Nitsa retorted. 'Don't worry about Christina, she'll survive. Let me tell you what Skevis did to me.'

After setting fire to the houses of the four village elders, the guerrillas began seeking out the members of MAY, the civilian security force, who included Nitsa's husband. Spiro Skevis arrived at Nitsa's house, where she was sitting on her front step. He told her, in a conversational tone, that he had nearly killed her husband one day, when as a member of a MAY posse, Andreas was hunting in the mountains for ELAS fugitives and stopped just in front of a boulder where Spiro was hiding. 'If Andreas had turned around and seen me, you'd be a widow now,' Spiro said with amusement. Nitsa trembled until he got up to leave, certain that he meant it as a warning. As soon as he was out of sight she packed her things and set out for the Perivoli to move in with Eleni.

Now they were a household of three women and five children crowded into two rooms: the kitchen and the small storeroom behind it. The kitchen was only 12 feet square. They had to sleep in heaps like cords of wood. On one side of the fireplace, under one *velenza*, slept Megali and Eleni with Nikola between them. On the other side slept Nitsa, who appropriated the spot next to the fire, as well as Fotini, Olga, Glykeria and Kanta.

Within weeks of the guerrillas' arrival, life in Lia took on a feverish activity. In order to have their western flank secured before the planned Christmas Day attack on Konitsa, the guerrillas' orders were 'complete and quick preparation.' According to the account of one of the *andartes*, Dimitri Hadjis, who later became a well-known novelist in Greece, 'Here in the Mourgana this meant telephone lines passed over deep ravines and passable roads opened in untrodden heights of the mountains. It also meant steps chiseled into the sides of the rock, machine-gun nests built with beams carried for many hours without the help of machines or even tools – everything by hand.' The women of the village worked alongside the guerrillas, building pillboxes in strategic spots throughout the village with the stones they gathered.

Although everyone suffered under the occupation of the guerrillas, by the second week of December, Eleni began to suspect that she had been singled out for special attention.

There was a freezing rain falling when a young *andarte* knocked at her gate and asked if he could come in to dry himself at the fire. She took him into the kitchen and offered him a boiled egg. As he stood near the fireplace, he noticed the photograph of Christos in its shiny brass frame. He asked where her husband was and she explained that he lived in America.

'Look at the gold frames on those glasses!' the young guerrilla said, picking up the photograph. 'Do you know how long it would take a workingman to earn enough for such frames? He must be a capitalist and he bought those glasses with the blood of the workers.'

Eleni tensed. 'You're wrong, my child,' she said quickly. 'My Christos is a cook in a restaurant owned by someone else.'

'I think he's a bloodsucker,' the man replied curtly. Then he turned the dime-store frame over and slid the photograph out the back. Behind the black-and-white image of Christos was another picture. Eleni saw to her horror that it was Queen Fredrika, wife of the newly crowned King Paul, who had assumed the throne when his brother George died on April 1, 1947. The young queen stared regally out of the frame, ropes of pearls around her white throat.

The guerrilla turned to Eleni with a triumphant grin. 'Look who's here, Amerikana! Who hid the German bitch for safekeeping? Your father?'

How did this child know about her father's royalist sympathies? Eleni wondered. 'I didn't even know it was there!' she said. 'When Christos sent the photo I gave it to someone who was going to Filiates, to buy a frame for it. You know they sell frames with pictures of kings, queens, war heroes already in them; it must have been there all this time without my knowing it!'

She dismissed the incident as an accident until several days later, when there was a battering on the gate. She opened it to find a tall, chestnut-haired, rather handsome young man in a lieutenant's uniform who looked at her as if she were an interesting specimen of insect.

He was a thirty-one-year-old former schoolteacher named

249

Sotiris Alexiou who had taken the *nom de guerre* of 'Sotiris Drapetis.' The villagers would soon come to know Sotiris as the sadistic intelligence officer for Lia.

Without a word, Sotiris pushed Eleni aside and began charging through the rooms, opening every box or drawer, tossing the contents on the floor, turning mattresses upside down. She realized that someone must have made some kind of report on her.

Eleni rushed ahead of Sotiris into the small pantry behind the kitchen, where Olga was sitting in her usual spot on top of the trunk that held her 'inside' dowry, which they had moved out of the good chamber after the arrival of the Gagas family. 'Quick, get out of here!' Eleni hissed at her. 'He's coming inside and he's going to open everything.'

Olga threw a terrified glance at the *velenzes* and blankets from Yannina which she had tied up in tight rolls, and then fled into the kitchen where Glykeria was hiding. Sotiris was right behind her mother. He pulled out a knife and cut the rope holding the *velenzes*, throwing them one by one on the floor and feeling between them.

Tossing the last blanket on the floor, Sotiris turned to Eleni and commanded, 'Open this trunk!' She searched frantically for the keys to the padlock – in her pockets; in the niches where she kept matches; in the box of letters from Christos, above the doorjamb; everywhere she kept keys – but she was shaking so much she couldn't think.

'Hurry up, woman!' Sotiris shouted as she rushed here and there. Disgusted at the delay, he strode into the good chamber and picked up the poker from the fireplace. He returned swinging it. As Eleni backed out, he began beating the padlock with the poker until it broke. In a frenzy now, Sotiris tore everything out of the trunk; dresses, slips, stockings, pillowcases, a crocheted tablecloth. He threw them on the dirt floor and pulled out more until the trunk was empty.

Breathing hard, he turned toward Eleni, who was huddled in the doorway separating the kitchen from the small room. 'I'm going to search your yard now, Amerikana,' he said, 'and if I find a gun anywhere, I'm going to kill you.'

The words 'gun' and 'Amerikana' shot through Eleni like

250

icicles. Someone must have told the security police, 'The Amerikana has a gun hidden on her property,' and she felt again the separateness that the word 'Amerikana' implied. Although she had never left the village, she was the foreigner, the one whose wealthy husband lived in a distant land where his money could never be confiscated. She wondered who had reported her, and how far the hatred reached.

'Have you found any weapons in our house, *effendi*?' she asked. 'We have no men, no soldiers here and no weapons. I can guarantee that you'll find nothing in the house, but I can't promise about the yard. What if someone has buried a gun there just to get me in trouble?'

Sotiris shrugged. 'You'd better pray I don't find anything. Get me a shovel.'

As soon as he was out the door, Eleni began pacing back and forth. 'They're going to kill us,' she said aloud several times. Then she called Glykeria out of the kitchen and spat on the floor. 'Before the spit dries I want you back here with Sioli Skevis! Tell him our lives depend on it. Thank God I've got some meat in the *gastra*! Where are the greens you picked this morning?'

By the time Glykeria returned, out of breath, nearly dragging the leathery old father of Spiro and Prokopi Skevis, the house was filled with the aroma of roasting goat, spiced with oregano and mint. Out in the yard Sotiris was digging holes, helped by two more *andartes*. As soon as Eleni saw Sioli, she began to cry. 'Please, *effendi*, look at those men outside! They're searching for guns. They found nothing in the house, but I'm afraid that someone may have hidden one in the yard.'

Sioli Skevis was a pious old man despite the trick he had played on the archbishop to get Spiro into the school in Vela, and he respected the Amerikana. He patted her shoulder, 'Don't worry,' he said. 'I'm here, and whatever they find, no one's going to touch you.' He settled himself into a comfortable corner. 'What's that I smell?' he asked.

By the time Sotiris threw down his shovel in disgust, Sioli had finished off most of the kid and, his belt loosened, was dozing happily by the fire. Sotiri had spent a wasted afternoon and found nothing, but Eleni had learned that someone in the village wished her ill. The familiar faces of her neighbors would never look the same again.

Perhaps Sioli Skevis told his son Spiro about the Amerikana's plight, or perhaps Spiro took a notion to strengthen his ties with a family that carried so much influence in the village. The commander of the battalion appeared at the Gatzoyiannis gate some days after the Sotiris incident, led on horseback up the steep path to the Perivoli by his orderly, who stood smartly at attention holding the reins as Spiro dismounted. Now his face was clean-shaven, his uniform pressed, his manner altogether different from the grim exaltation on the day Eleni heard him tell his men that they were going to squeeze his native village dry.

Kanta, working in the vegetable patch, stared in astonishment at the magnificent figure entering their gate. She recognized him at once, for he had been her substitute teacher in the second grade whenever Minas Stratis had to be away. Spiro remembered her too, even though she was now a young woman of fifteen. As she murmured 'Good day' and lowered her head, not looking at him directly, he said, 'You're Alexandra, aren't you? You were one of my best students.'

She looked down again.

'We need smart girls in the movement,' he went on with a teasing smile. 'I'm going to find you a captain to marry. How would you like that?'

'I'm too young to get married, *effendi*,' she said, looking at his boots.

'In a couple of years, then,' he replied. 'You'd like a handsome young captain, wouldn't you?'

Kanta's sense of irony got the better of her. 'Oh, it'd be fine if your army wins the war!' she said. 'But if you lose, the captain would probably end up herding sheep.'

'Don't worry, we're going to win,' he said cheerfully. 'Look out there.' He gestured, indicating the mountains rimming the bowl of the foothills below. 'You see Velouna, Plokista and Taverra?' he said, sweeping the horizon from east to west. 'Our men have taken all of them. The fascists are melting

252

away before us like spring ice. Soon we'll have the whole country. Your young captain might end up a minister in government instead of a shepherd.' He looked at her intently. 'I think you have an older sister, don't you?'

Kanta didn't answer. She knew Olga was hiding in the pantry with her kerchief over her face.

'You should tell your sister to marry,' Spiro said, not smiling now. 'With your father in America, she needs some kind of protection.'

Eleni had come out of the house to greet their noted visitor and heard the remark. She hurried forward, inviting Spiro into the house and summoning Olga from the pantry to prepare a cup of coffee, a glass of water, and some sweets for the major. When Olga brought the tray into the large chamber, she saw that Eleni had handed Spiro the last letter that Christos sent, the one that said she mustn't leave the house under any circumstances, and that the *andartes* were 'fellow villagers, fighting for their rights.' Olga saw that Spiro was chuckling. He muttered, 'Christos, you old rogue!' and then looked up at Eleni and said, 'I never realized he was with us.'

Eleni smiled and said nothing but motioned for Olga to bring the coffee over. The girl left the room as soon as she had served it. No one heard what Eleni and Spiro talked about after that, but Kanta noticed that when Skevis left the house and remounted his horse, he was whistling.

Several days after Skevis' visit, the village was electrified by the sight of a long ragged file of women guerrillas, perhaps a hundred in all, climbing down from the peak of the Prophet Elias, making their way through the Perivoli with *andartes* at their front and back, and two guarding the sides. The group of *andartinas* passed right outside the Gatzoyiannis gate, marching in step, guns on their backs, paying no attention to the excited buzz of the villagers who flocked to stare at them.

All the Gatzoyiannis children rushed to see them, even Olga, who hadn't left the house since the guerrillas arrived. The *andartinas* were peasant girls in their teens and twenties, with long, thick braids down their backs, but below the braids were khaki uniforms complete with – the villagers could

253

scarcely believe it – men's trousers! If they had been marching naked, it couldn't have caused more of a sensation. Nikola was mystified, thinking the soldiers were half man and half woman. None of the Gatzoyiannis children would ever forget their first sight of women in pants.

But Eleni scarcely noticed what the girls were wearing. She was searching their faces, thinking of the weeping villagers she had seen in Yannina.

Just below the Gatzoyiannis house the women were called to a halt by their male officers, who ordered them to fall out and rest in the yards of several houses, including that of Tassina Bartzokis. Eleni shooed her children back inside and hurried down to where her neighbors were drawing water for the *andartinas* to drink.

They lay on the ground with a lethargy that suggested deep exhaustion. Eleni sat down in the grass near a group who looked no older than Olga. She moved over next to a girl with the round face of a child and asked her name. The girl replied listlessly, adding that she was from the village of Vatsounia.

'You seem so young,' Eleni persisted. 'Aren't you afraid? I have two girls about your age. If they want to join the army, I don't think I could let them go. Your mother must be so worried!'

The girl turned black-rimmed eyes on her for the first time. 'Do you think my mother had a choice?' she said.

'They took you by force?' Eleni asked. 'All these girls?'

'All the girls over fifteen, the unmarried ones,' the girl whispered. 'Now go away! If they see us talking, they'll kill you and me both.'

As soon as the women soldiers were ordered to move on, Eleni ran back to her house. Now she understood what Spiro Skevis meant when he said that Olga should be married for her protection.

Eleni called Olga and Kanta into the kitchen and when she looked at their faces, she started to cry. 'They're going to take you! I knew it!' she wept. 'Why didn't you leave when I sent you to Babouri! What will happen to you now?'

The girls looked at her, bewildered. Soon Tassina Bartzokis burst in, also in tears. As soon as she saw Olga she cried, 'I'd

254

rather see you and Rano drown yourselves in the irrigation pool than have you taken like those poor girls!'

Eleni and her daughters sat up all night, trying to formulate a plan to save them from being conscripted. Eleni couldn't stop remembering the faces of the *andartinas* and imagining her two daughters, who had never spoken to a strange man, being forced to wear trousers, sleep side by side with the guerrillas and fight for their lives on the battlefield. By dawn she was pale but calm. 'Go get Rano,' she told them. 'We'll hide you where they'll never find you. Soon they'll leave and you'll be safe.'

The place she had decided on was the Kastro, crowning one of the two peaks above the village, where an ancient acropolis had stood three hundred years before Christ. It was built as a fortress by a race of blond-haired, blue-eyed, wide-browed Dorians as a sanctuary where the inhabitants of the settlements below could retreat when threatened by enemy attack. Here they slaughtered bulls and prayed to Zeus for protection, and here, a hundred years ago, archeologists thought they had found the ruins of the Oracle of Dodona before they settled on another site, sixty-three miles to the south.

It took little more than an hour, climbing straight up past the timberline, to reach the Kastro. The acropolis was originally surrounded by a high wall, and on the far side the precipice fell straight down, impossible for anyone to ascend. But if a climber lowered himself, hand over hand, fifty feet down, clinging to the rocks and shrubs, he would find a natural balcony which the ancients reinforced with a small wall, where lookouts could see for miles, making a surprise attack from the north impossible.

This tiny outcrop on the sheer northern face of the cliff had become so overgrown with scrub pine that no one would know it was there. Olga, Kanta and Rano slid over the top and let themselves down into it, rigid with fear, not looking down, knowing that a slip could send them hurtling into the depths below. Wedged into the little balcony, barely large enough for the three of them, they were invisible. Rano insisted that if the guerrillas came for them, she would throw herself over the side as the Souliote women had to escape the

Turks. Olga said Rano was crazy. Kanta said she was hungry and cold.

At night the wind screamed around their perch. The air was like ice water, and the rustlings and howlings from the ancient fortress walls over their heads reminded Kanta of the fearful ghosts she had been told lived in the ruins. Far below them, hawks and crows wheeled, watching the chasm where a stream glimmered like the scratch of a silver hairpin in the green.

They huddled together there for three days, sleeping sitting up, their backs against the cliff wall, their legs chafed by the underbrush. They couldn't get out, even to relieve themselves, for the rock balcony was their whole world.

Every day either Glykeria or Angeliki climbed up the height of the Kastro, and after a shout to make sure the fugitives were still there, tossed down bread and cheese wrapped in a cloth. The three girls had blankets to warm themselves, but their lips were blue, and the drifting snowflakes froze on their eyelashes. They cried and talked about what their families at home were probably eating and how warm it would be by the fire. Finally Kanta rebelled. 'Let them take me!' she exclaimed, her voice sailing into the great silence below. 'It's better than freezing to death!' And without another word she started climbing up, hand over hand, clinging to projecting rocks and shrubs. Even though she was the youngest, Kanta's defection drained Olga and Rano's courage, and they began to climb up after her.

When it was dark, Kanta crept back to her mother's house and knocked softly at the back door. As soon as Eleni saw her, she pulled her inside. 'They've come around asking for both of you,' she said. 'They have a list with names. I said you were away in the fields with the flocks. You can't come home now!'

She paced up and down the narrow hall, then she remembered another hiding place: the pit in Rano's backyard. It was a large hole that the family had dug during the occupation to hide trunks of valuables in case the Germans took the village. After the war the trunks had been dug up, but the pit remained and now was so overgrown that it was nearly invisible.

The three girls crawled into the hole, only a hundred yards from the Gatzoyiannis gate, and Eleni fortified them with more blankets and a pan of spicy boiled lentils. At first it seemed much better: they were protected from the wind, and the heat of their bodies would provide the warmth they needed.

They argued about who would sit in the middle and agreed to change places every few hours. They stayed awake telling ghost stories and gossiping about other girls in the village, but finally they fell asleep, and it began to rain. Even though the December drizzle did not form snow at this altitude, it seemed colder than on the peak of the Kastro. The hole smelled like a tomb, and in the night, slimy things crawled over their feet, leaving iridescent trails that shone in the light of dawn. They felt their resolution eroding. They were children, and all they wanted was home.

Two days were passed inside the pit, but on the second night when Glykeria came by with their evening meal, they begged her to ask Eleni for a better hiding place. Kanta complained that her feet had become like wood. She couldn't stand up if she tried. They were tired of being buried alive.

Soon Eleni appeared, standing over the hole, holding a pan that held the promise of meat. She told the girls she had found them a warm hiding place and took them to the cellar-stable of Vangeli Botsaris, two houses up from her own, inhabited by three gentle-eyed goats who stared at them quizzically as they burrowed their legs into the manure heap which radiated warmth. They didn't even notice the smell – they had been living too long with the odor of their own unwashed bodies.

It was far better than the Kastro and the pit, but the three girls spent only a day and a night there, their sleep punctuated by the coughing of the goats, until Eleni came running up, her hair flying loose from her kerchief, crying that the girls had to come at once or they'd all be shot. 'They said I had to produce you or I'd die.'

Olga and Kanta hurried home and scrubbed off the manure as best they could. Eleni washed, brushed and braided Olga's hair as she had when she was a little girl. Because Olga was the first-born, Eleni worried more about her than about the others. When Olga was a baby, Eleni used to get up and light a lamp and watch her lying in the wooden cradle, her tiny hands closed, her lips working, dreaming of the breast. Eleni had a horror of smothering the baby while she slept and would only nurse her sitting up. According to whispers she had heard, her own second sister, for whom Olga was named, died when Megali rolled over in her sleep on top of the infant.

Olga had always been spoiled and coddled, and now she was to be taken as a soldier. She had entered puberty at fourteen, and her body had the curves of a woman, while Kanta, now fifteen, still hadn't matured and was small for her years. Olga slept like the dead – who knows what the guerrillas might do to her in her sleep? But Kanta was a light sleeper and had a native shrewdness that Olga lacked entirely.

Eleni's mind raced like a mouse in a trap. While Megali and Nitsa wept over the two girls as if they were already dead, Eleni tried not to lose control. She thought about what would become of Olga if she was taken up into the mountains, to sleep beside the guerrillas and fight with a gun. She finally came to an agonizing decision. She would rather have her daughter mutilated and alive than dead or raped, she concluded. Once she had made up her mind, Eleni called the family together – including Nikola and Fotini, who listened to what she said, not yet understanding.

If Olga couldn't walk, the guerrillas couldn't take her, Eleni said. Olga nodded, frightened but proud of being the center of all eyes. They would pour boiling water over her foot, Eleni continued grimly, and tell the guerrillas it was an accident.

As they put a kettle on the fire, Olga tried to prepare herself. The only painful thing that had ever happened to her was when she fell out of the walnut tree and broke two fingers, but although she tried to remember how it felt, she couldn't.

When the water was boiling, Eleni handed Olga a cloth and told her to put it into her mouth so that she wouldn't scream and rouse the neighborhood. They propped her naked right foot on a stool and put a large pot underneath to catch the water. Olga had always taken pride in her small hands and feet, delicate as a child's. Eleni picked up the pot and shut her eyes. Everyone was watching.

The tense faces of my mother, sisters and grandmother seemed unfamiliar in the red glow of the fire. Unconsciously I had stuffed my fist into my mouth, in imitation of Olga with the cloth in hers. My mother took a deep breath and poured the water over the extended foot, while my aunt held the leg so that Olga couldn't draw back. For an instant there was silence and then, despite the cloth, Olga began to make high-pitched squeals that reminded me of the sound of a kid being slaughtered.

We all stood staring at the foot while Olga silently wiped her tears with the cloth. The skin on top immediately turned red and puffed up with blisters. After a while my mother and aunt exchanged looks as they realized the plan had failed. Olga's feet had become so hard from walking barefoot that it didn't look bad enough. The guerrillas would take her anyway.

My mother sat down heavily, looking sick. I saw her eyes stray to the fireplace where a poker was leaning against the wall. She went over, picked it up and held it in the flames. The others understood what she was doing before I did, and gasped. Olga began crying softly. When the end of the poker was glowing, I watched my mother walking toward Olga and I began to back away. Olga screwed her face up like a child waiting to be hit, her eyes squeezed shut. My mother leaned over the foot. There was a pulse beating just below the ankle. Her face seemed to age, and she turned away, dropping the poker. 'I can't do it,' she whispered. I realized I had been holding my breath and let it out explosively.

My grandmother spoke into the silence. 'I can,' she said, 'if it will save my granddaughter.' We all turned in amazement to look at the frail, birdlike old woman who had always seemed so helpless. She picked up the poker and reheated it in the fire. Then I saw my grandmother thrust it into the can of hydrochloric acid which was used for cleaning the inside of scorched pots. The poker was shaking violently as she turned toward Olga, who, forgetting about

259

the cloth, began to slide off the chair onto the floor. My aunt pinned her to the floor with both hands on her shoulders. My mother grabbed the ankle of the blistered foot and turned her face away. I felt I was in a bad dream; they couldn't be doing this! I closed my eyes to make the scene go away.

The sizzle of the poker hitting flesh filled the room. Then Olga shrieked and was cut off by my aunt clasping the cloth over her mouth. I heard an answering groan from my mother. I looked and saw my grandmother lifting the poker off Olga's foot with a gobbet of skin clinging to it, leaving visible raw meat below, white shiny tendons in the pale red flesh. There was a pungent odor in the room, which haunts me still. I bolted out the door and into the yard.

At the sight of her foot Olga screamed again, but Eleni gently turned the girl's face away and put a damp cloth to her cheeks, her own face wet with tears. Fotini could not stop looking at the foot. Megali hurried away and returned with a cabbage. She wrapped cabbage leaves around the raw wound to make it swell, and the prickly leaves were like alcohol on the flesh. Olga writhed and moaned while Eleni and Nitsa tried to hold her still. When she had finished her work, Megali wrapped the foot around with a white cloth.

For most of the night Olga lay sobbing in her mother's lap. Kanta couldn't sleep either. She couldn't get the sound of the poker and the smell of burning flesh out of her mind, and when she did doze off before dawn, she awoke with night-mares of huge, bearded soldiers chasing her. She knew that her mother had chosen Olga for salvation and decided on herself to go because she was younger and less likely to be raped. She felt terribly lonely.

The next morning Olga screamed again when they removed the bandages and the cabbage leaves. It was so swollen, it didn't even look like a foot. The ankle was gone. The wound was leaking pus, and angry red lines ran up the leg. Olga couldn't even sit up, much less stand. They gently re-wrapped the foot and left her lying on her pallet.

Later in the day Eleni walked over to Tassina's house,

which was being used by the guerrillas as a dispensary. She asked the guerrilla-doctor if he would be kind enough to look at her daughter's foot. It was just a kitchen accident, she explained, a coal rolled out of the fireplace and burned the top of the foot. 'We put mouse oil on it right away,' said Eleni, referring to the standard village burn remedy of oil in which a dead mouse has been suspended, 'but there seems to be something wrong – the foot is all swelled up.'

The doctor agreed to have a look, and when he unwrapped the bandages, the shock showed on his face. 'This is infected, she could lose the foot!' he exclaimed. 'I'll give you some ointment – none of that village nonsense! – and you must keep the wound clean and change the bandages every day. She isn't to walk on it for several weeks at least. I'll be back in a few days to see her.'

They all congratulated each other. Eleni had played her part so well that the doctor seemed to suspect nothing. But the next day two *andartes* came by with a list in their hands, containing the names of every unmarried girl in Lia over fifteen. They had heard from the doctor about Olga's 'accident' and demanded that the bandages be removed. When Eleni saw them wince at the sight, she knew that she had saved her daughter. But the soldiers seemed angry, and before they left, they commanded, 'Have your second daughter, Alexandra, ready to join the People's Democratic Army tomorrow morning.

CHAPTER NINE

By the end of December 1947 the Greek Communist Party
was ready to drive the linchpin of its new strategy and prove
to the world that it had the strength to seize power. Now
that key mountain strongholds were secure, the DAG would
announce the formation of a provisional government and
quickly capture a major population center to serve as its
capital.

The Communist guerrillas were in complete control of the
Mourgana massif, stretching for twenty miles along the
border between Greece and Albania, as well as the
Grammos mountains on the northern end of the Pindos
range, where the provinces of Epiros and Macedonia meet.
From these bases they could threaten the entire northwest
region of Greece including the capital of Epiros – Yannina.

On Christmas Eve the Democratic Army's radio station,
located in Albania, announced the formation of a
provisional Democratic Government of Free Greece under
the presidency of Markos Vafladis. The country tensed,
waiting for the other shoe to drop – the expected attack on a
town to serve as the new 'government's' capital. Yannina
seemed the likely target.

Within twenty-four hours, before dawn on Christmas
Day, the Communist guerrillas launched their attack not on
Yannina but on Konitsa, forty miles north of the provincial
capital. Konitsa had the virtues of lying between their major
strongholds in the Mourgana and Grammos mountains as
well as being just twelve miles from the Albanian border.

Only hours after the citizens had returned from midnight

262

mass, Markos threw his force of 10,000 guerrillas at the town of 5,000. The alarm was sounded and the defenders barricaded themselves in every house.

For the Communist guerrillas it was vital to win this battle. By establishing their capital in Konitsa, they hoped to earn recognition for their provisional government from socialist countries, and full material support from the one ally essential to their victory – the Soviet Union. An unconvinced Russia had, until now, provided only limited aid through the Communist countries bordering Greece – Albania, Yugoslavia and Bulgaria.

Markos concentrated all the manpower and heavy artillery he commanded on the Christmas Day attack. One of the first important positions captured was the bridge at Bourazani spanning the river Aoos, over which any reinforcements from Yannina would have to travel.

It seemed impossible that Konitsa could hold out against the vastly superior forces of the attackers, but the guerrillas had not counted on the desperation of the townspeople, surrounded and cut off from any escape route, who fought alongside the government troops, turning every house into a small fort. While the world watched, the battle of Konitsa stretched on from Christmas Day to New Year's Eve.

To support the attack, Markos pulled as many guerrillas as possible away from their positions in the Mourgana. The government troops, with superior manpower, tried to prevent the shift by attacking the guerrilla positions in the Mourgana. Suddenly the occupied villages like Lia found themselves engulfed in the maelstrom of war.

SEPARATING THE WHEAT FROM THE CHAFF

IT WAS ELEVEN days before Christmas, the night of December 14, 1947, when the guerrillas came to the Gatzoyiannis house and ordered Eleni to prepare her second daughter for the Democratic Army. Although she had managed to save Olga, she knew Kanta was lost. Eleni spent the hours until dawn mourning the loss of the daughter who was most like herself.

Olga and Glykeria had inherited the round contours and soft features of their father, but Kanta was angular and thin, with the same high cheekbones, sharply etched mouth and deep-set, intense eyes as her mother. She had passed her fifteenth birthday, only two days before the guerrillas occupied the village, but she still seemed a child, fragile and flat-chested as a boy.

Mother and daughter sat together, unable to sleep, and Eleni stroked Kanta's hair. 'If you faint and act like you're sick and pretend to be too stupid to learn, they may get disgusted and let you go,' she advised. 'Tell them you're afraid of the guns. How can they send a baby like you to the battlefield?' She paused to choose her words, then added, 'At night keep as far away from the guerrillas as you can. If you let down your guard and fall asleep at the wrong moment, you could be ruined forever.'

Eleni pushed back images of Kanta being raped or shot and consoled herself with the thought that although she was the frailest of the girls, she was also the smartest. Until she put on the kerchief, Kanta had been the best student in school. Like Eleni, she had always burned with the ambition to escape the village and discover the world beyond. The girl was also as fastidious as her mother. She complained that her sisters smelled bad, and refused to eat food cooked by Nitsa, making sarcastic remarks about her aunt's sloppy dress, greasy hair and dirty fingernails.

Although she was as thin as shepherd's crook, food was Kanta's obsession, just as fine clothes was Olga's. The only way Eleni could bribe her to spend a day in the high pastures with the flocks was to promise her a special dish for supper. Once, her patience stretched beyond its limits, Eleni half jokingly laid a curse on her two eldest daughters. 'You!' she said to Olga. 'May you grow up to have trunks of clothes and never find anything you like to wear! And you, black one,' she added, turning to Kanta, 'may you have a pantry full of food and never be satisfied with what you're eating.'

Eleni often indulged Kanta's moods because she knew the girl was more high-strung than the others, too sensitive to attend funerals, out the door at the first threat of tears or anger. Since she was a baby, Kanta had passed through phases of nightmares, sleepwalking, nervous stomach aches and fainting spells. Remembering all this, Eleni wondered how she could ever survive as an *andartina*. She could only pray that her intelligence and the stubbornness that lay at the core of that small body might save her.

When Kanta eventually fell asleep, Eleni covered her gently, then moved about the room, collecting things. She picked out two warm cardigan sweaters that she had made and a pair of heavy knitted stockings. When the eastern sky turned violet and Kanta awoke with a nightmare still in her eyes, Eleni crooned to her and dressed her as if she were a baby.

She wrapped the remains of a vegetable pie in a cloth bag and added pieces of cheese and some dried figs. Then she took a diamond-shaped, beaded pillow, about the size of a postage stamp and containing a paper image of St. Nicholas, and pinned it inside the girl's dress on her shift.

As Kanta sat holding an untouched cup of mountain tea, a shriek splintered the icy morning air, coming from a house high above them. The guerrillas had started collecting girls at the top of the Perivoli. Eleni ran outside to see them driving several young women down the path with blows from their rifle butts while the girls' mothers ran behind, lamenting as if for the dead. She rushed back into the house, where Kanta sat pale and quiet, her parcel in her lap.

'From the day you were born, I expected to see you leave this house to marry, not to learn war,' Eleni mourned.

The screams came closer. The guerrillas were next door, to seize Rano. They dragged her out, trailed by her sister Tassina Bartzokis, now eight months pregnant. The guerrillas turned their guns on Tassina and ordered her back inside, then they burst into the Gatzoyiannis yard, two men taking up positions on either side of the gate, two more pushing into the house.

Olga lay on a pallet with her bandaged foot propped on a stool, and Nikola and Fotini backed into corners. The rest of the family reached for Kanta, but the girl stood up and said calmly to the guerrilla in the lead, 'I'm ready to go. You don't have to hit me.'

Although her lower lip was trembling, Kanta shook loose the hands of her family and picked up her parcel. With guerrillas flanking her, each a head taller than herself, she walked out, her braids uncovered. She had left her kerchief behind.

The rest of the family followed, but at the gate, one of the two guards barred the way with the barrel of his rifle. Kanta looked back over her shoulder. 'Stop crying, *Mana*,' she said. 'I'll be all right.'

Eleni tried to push aside the gun barrel blocking her way while Nikola slipped underneath and turned to look up at the two guards. He noticed that although the one on the left, a teenager, stood stiffly erect, his rifle in parade position and his face an expressionless mask, he was crying.

In wailing knots, prodded by the guerrillas' guns, nearly forty unmarried women were herded toward the village square. They were pushed into a former coffeehouse and general store which the army had taken over, and sat there throughout the morning while other girls, strangers from distant villages, were crowded into the room beside them.

Still holding her parcel, Kanta sat next to her sister's best friend, Rano Athanassiou, a well-built woman of twenty-five with dark hair, and a clever face. Because her mother had died when she was a baby and her father was an invalid, life had made Rano strong and Kanta instinctively gravitated to her for protection.

By midday the large rooms were crowded with nearly eighty newly conscripted women sitting on the floor, guarded by a handful of guerrillas. A man with sandy hair, a small mustache and ironic brown eyes walked behind a wooden table and shouted for silence. The women would soon come to know him as Alekos, one of their three instructors.

'Quiet!' he ordered. 'Stop moaning and listen to me! From today you are soldiers of the Democratic Army. You will have the honor of participating in the struggle that will bring liberty to Greece!'

He spoke for several minutes about the cause and the party, traitors and monarcho-fascists and duty, but it meant nothing to Kanta. When he finished, she was startled to see Rano's hand shoot up. The lieutenant nodded and she stood, while Kanta slid a careful inch away.

'May I say a few words on behalf of all of us, Comrade?' Rano asked, as Kanta marveled at her audacity.

'Speak,' he replied with a tight smile.

'We want to assist in the struggle for our country,' Rano said. 'Let us be useful to you in a hundred ways. We'll sew and cook and wash your clothes and mend them. We'll be nurses and tend the wounded. But please, don't give us guns! What do women know of guns?'

The lieutenant's face flushed and he raised a clenched fist. 'We don't intend to see the women of Greece behind us, mending socks!' he bellowed. 'We want you fighting by our side!'

He pounded on the table and then jerked his hand back with an oath, staring at the blood trickling down onto his khaki sleeve. He had gashed himself on a nail protruding from the rough wooden table. The room fell silent and, against her side, Kanta could feel Rano begin to shake.

The silence thickened, then the sandy-haired guerrilla

pulled a handkerchief from his pocket and wrapped it around the wound. He made an abrupt gesture and the guards began herding the women out of the building and across the square to another former coffeehouse where they would have their barracks.

That night, while guerrillas stood guard in each room, the eighty young women slept on the floor, several bodies huddled under each sleeping blanket. Kanta wore both her sweaters over her wool dress against the bitter December chill and lay close to Rano, one of the few who didn't cry herself to sleep.

The blat of a bugle startled them awake the next morning before dawn and they were led in single file down the mountainside for two hours of calesthenics. Then they were given a breakfast of mountain tea in tin cups and corn-meal mush ladled out onto tin mess plates. When the short meal was over, the girls began gathering the dishes to wash them, but a sergeant, whom they would soon call Frixos ('the Mad One'), made them stop. 'You will clean your mess tins by taking off a stocking and using it to wipe them,' he announced. 'We do not wash dishes in the Democratic Army.'

He held up his hand at the chorus of protests. 'In battle you may have to eat off the ground – food with dirt in it, even blood,' he said. 'It's your own tin, your spoon, your stocking, your mouth. Get used to it!'

Kanta looked with loathing at the congealing remains of the mush in her plate. As she slowly removed one of her knitted stockings, she gagged. Her nausea increased five hours later when the noon meal was served – a huge pot of soup with lumps of ambiguous meat floating in a sea of shiny grease. Kanta hid in a corner chewing on the scraps her mother had given her.

The first days of military training blurred together in the pain of aching muscles, fits of dry retching from hunger, and fatigue that left Kanta numb and shaking. The recruits were allowed only six hours' sleep, from midnight until reveille, and then were hurled into the morning exercises. After breakfast they were set to cleaning and reassembling their empty rifles and machine guns until they could do it blindfolded. Kanta struggled with the malevolent pieces of metal and never finished in time.

They were taught to storm a height while guerrillas fired a hail of bullets over their heads to make them crouch low. And every morning there was target practice. The first time, the explosion of the rifle and the brutal kick of the recoil made Kanta drop the gun and burst into tears. 'Come on, *kouchiko!*' jeered Frixos, using the slang nickname the guerrillas had given her because she was the littlest. 'How can you hope to be an *andartina* if you're scared of your own gun?'

They learned to assemble and fire mortars and throw hand grenades, run obstacle courses and dig foxholes. To Kanta's surprise, Milia Drouboyiannis, the quiet, chubby, eighteen-year-old daughter of the tinker Nassios Drouboyiannis, became the star. She had always been a shy, sullen girl, not very clever in school, who held her round head cocked to one side on her short neck, suggesting someone with a hearing problem. Now, suddenly, she turned into a fierce little guerrilla, bellowing as she rushed the hill with her bayonet, eager to disembowel an enemy, winning all the target-practice competitions and loping three grenades dead onto a target in succession. Milia was the first to take their instructor's advice and chop off her long braids with scissors, while the other girls shuddered.

The women were never allowed to sit down between six in the morning and midnight except for the half-hour allowed for mealtime and the two indoctrination periods, morning and afternoon, when they were lectured to about the aims and philosophy of the DAG and the Communist Party. The lessons were given by Alekos and a pompous guerrilla called 'the Captain,' a lawyer in civilian life, both of whom had a weakness for metaphors. Before the grass could grow, the instructors intoned, it was necessary to cut down the nettles, which Kanta soon learned meant exterminating the Greek National Army, the bloodsucking capitalists, the degenerate Glücksburg royal family and anyone else who opposed the aims of the revolutionary fighters.

269

During Kanta's first days of training, Eleni moved around the village trying to learn what was happening to her daughter. She was hoping that the girl would be sent home as soon as the guerrillas saw how much smaller she was than the others, but she was waiting in vain. The following morning, when she heard from the direction of the village square the faint 'one-two, one-two' of the drill instructors, she hurried down toward the training field, but armed guards stopped her. 'No one is to have any contact with the recruits,' she was informed. During the succeeding days, every time she heard a distant burst of gunfire or the explosion of a grenade, Eleni saw a vivid image of Kanta blown apart in a training accident.

Several days after Kanta was taken, her family was surprised by the sudden departure of the teacher Elias Gagas and his family, and by the news that the Gatzoyiannis house had been chosen as Lia's guerrilla headquarters. It was to be the office and billet of Lieutenant Colonel Chronis Petritis, who ranked just below the leaders of the whole Epiros Command, stationed in Babouri.

Nikola and Fotini waited at the gate the next morning as Petritis, his aide and his orderly arrived, accompanied by half a dozen guerrillas carrying equipment, including the switchboard for their telephone.

Petritis was a short, stocky, sleek little man with curly dark hair and the smug expression of a well-fed spaniel, but he seemed magnificent to me as I followed him like a shadow into the good chamber, where the brass bed gleamed and the fire blazed. Petritis' first action upon entering filled me with admiration. He took a piece of cardboard and formed it into a cone which he fastened around the guttering kerosene lamp on the bare wooden table. Suddenly the lamplight was twice as bright, concentrated on the spot where he put down some files. I had never seen a lampshade before and couldn't wait to brag to my friends about the ingenuity of the officer who had come to live with us. In Communist school they taught us that DAG fighters were superior in every way to the enemy, and I felt proud and protected having Petritis in the house. It seemed to me that an army with officers as clever as this couldn't fail to win the war, but I would soon be shorn of both my admiration for Petritis and my faith in his army.

Eleni hardly noticed the lampshade as she hurried to bring the colonel firewood, blankets, walnuts in honey and some of her precious hoard of coffee. The moment Petritis walked in the door, a spark of hope ignited in Eleni's breast. This man had the power to release Kanta from the army and she was determined to win him over.

Petritis' arrival certainly seemed a stroke of luck. Eleni never suspected that he was the ELAS commander who had orchestrated the beatings of EDES sympathizers during the occupation, when her father Kitso was arrested, Vasili Stratis battered nearly to death, and a young man from Tsamanta murdered, his brain punctured by a nail at the end of a club. Petritis didn't look like a killer. His well-fed appearance and two shining gold teeth attested that he was an urbane, educated man, and the family was not surprised to learn from village gossip that he had once been a schoolteacher.

His aide, Antonis, spoke with an Anatolian accent, and was also a man of education. There was a sadness in his eyes when he looked at Nikola. Bit by bit, Eleni learned that Antonis was a schoolteacher from Constantinople who had returned to visit his parents in nearby Vishini and been conscripted into the DAG against his will. There were a wife and son exactly Nikola's age back in Constantinople whom he hadn't seen for almost a year. Eleni soon observed Antonis' protective attitude toward Nikola, scolding him when he climbed too high in the walnut tree or went out in the rain without shoes, and she knew that he was missing his own boy. She felt he was the most sensitive of the guerrillas and hoped to enlist him in her efforts to win Petritis' help.

As part of her campaign to win Petritis' help, Eleni showered the officer with small attentions. At the first opportunity she showed him the final letter from her husband, just as she had shown it to Spiro Skevis. Petritis read it and handed it back to her with an approving nod.

One day when Petritis came upon Eleni weeping over the

bread trough, she gathered the courage to tell him about Kanta being taken as an *andartina*. 'She's loyal to the cause, but she's so young – just fifteen – and so thin and sickly!' Eleni cried.

'Don't worry, she'll do fine,' Petritis said, and Eleni imagined a note of sympathy in his voice.

Kanta was not doing fine; she was starving because she couldn't force herself to eat out of the common pot. Rano knew how she was suffering and sometimes slipped her bits of food she managed to charm out of one of the guerrillas – an onion, a cucumber, an egg.

During one indoctrination period Kanta collapsed gratefully to the ground and rubbed her throbbing leg muscles.

'After the revolution, women will work side by side with men,' the captain was saying. 'Women can learn to fly airplanes, drive a car, even be lawyers. They'll get paid for the work they do, like a man. Women will have their own money!'

That novel idea appealed to Kanta, and, though in pain, she began to imagine what she would buy. She shut her eyes and drifted into a fantasy of short, silky American gowns, of tables groaning with rich *pitas*, stews of roast hare with onions like pearls and thick gravy that coated the spoon. How long had it been since she had tasted meat?

Her fantasy was interrupted by the turn in the lecture. It made her squirm.

'Why does the family of Minas Stratis eat meat, when all you have is corn mush?' Alekos thundered. 'Why does the Amerikana have a four-room villa, while the Yakou family lives in a one-room hovel? After the revolution, everyone will eat the same food, and if a family has three rooms, we'll give one of them to the poor.'

Kanta could feel the accusing eyes of the girls around her. She suspected that they were beginning to think of her family as part of the nettles that had to be cut before the grass could grow.

She protected herself by not listening. As soon as Alekos started pounding away with his favorite clichés, she wrapped herself back in her daydream. She closed her eyes and imagined herself in her mother's yeast-scented kitchen, working the churn, watching the golden crust of cream and globules of yellow butter rising to the surface of the milk.

Kanta didn't realize that she had fallen asleep sitting up until a stinging slap from Alekos knocked her sideways. 'Are we boring you, so that you take a nap during the lecture?' he inquired solicitously. 'If you find the goals of the Democratic Army so dull, perhaps you'd like to pass the time running up to the peak of Prophet Elias and back?' He pointed to the tiny chapel that crowned the mountaintop above them and shifted his gun. 'Get on with it!' he snapped. 'Run now, and don't slow down! We'll be watching you from here.'

Kanta saw the expectant eyes of the girls, some mocking, some sympathetic. No one believed she could make it so far up and back. She stood up and began to run, barefoot as she was. Soon she was scrabbling on her hands and knees up the sheer mountainside, clutching at bushes, her body shuddering with the hunger for oxygen, the edge of her mind conscious of the painful cuts on her knees and feet. She knew if she fell she would not get up again, and bit her lip until it bled to concentrate her energy and make herself keep moving. She had to show them that she couldn't be broken. When Kanta finally staggered back into the churchyard, some of the girls noticed a small triumphant smile on her face before she collapsed.

If Eleni had been outside in the yard that day and glanced toward the peak of the Prophet, she would have seen her daughter's punishment, but instead she was in the kitchen, brooding.

It had quickly become apparent that Petritis' presence was going to make life miserable for the Gatzoyiannis family. They were confined to the two small rooms – the kitchen and pantry – that composed the original section of the house. Every night their sleep was broken by Petritis' voice shouting over the telephone and by the heavy tread of couriers. When the war news was bad, Petritis made everyone around him pay. Eleni was constantly warned to keep the children quiet, or see them punished.

The worst part was the sight and smell of the food prepared by Petritis' orderly, a young man named Christos. The family was living on corn meal, beans and milk because the guerrillas had confiscated most of their winter supplies. One night the orderly prepared a huge pot of spaghetti for the officers while Fotini and Nikola hovered hungrily at the kitchen door, watching every move. First he boiled the spaghetti, then he fried it in a pan of sizzling butter and sprinkled it with a blizzard of cheese. Eleni looked in from the pantry and saw the expressions on the children's faces. 'Please, Comrade Christos,' she asked. 'Couldn't the young ones have a tiny bite? They haven't seen spaghetti since before the war.'

'Hush, woman, before Colonel Petritis hears!' hissed the young guerrilla, looking over his shoulder. 'I can't have a strand of it myself, much less give any to your children! Now, get them out of here before we all get in trouble!'

Nikola saw the anger and helplessness on his mother's face as she made a fierce gesture to the children, ordering them into the pantry. She warned them in a whisper never to set foot in the kitchen again when the orderly was there. Nikola felt her pain and wished he were a man so he could protect her from the cruelties of the tyrannical little colonel who had usurped his father's brass bed and ordered his mother about like a servant.

It was a day or so later that Eleni heard Petritis shouting and saw all the guards being summoned into his office before he stormed out the door. Soon, Eleni was called into the good chamber by Antonis.

Some of Colonel Petritis' belongings were missing, the aide told her; small things, but potentially dangerous in the hands of an enemy: bullets, a razor, even some tobacco. The colonel suspected there was a traitor among his men, not all of whom were volunteers. He was going to conduct an exhaustive inquiry.

Antonis waited for a moment, then added that it seemed odd for the thief to have taken the colonel's razor and tobacco. Perhaps it was only a child's prank. Eleni stiffened. 'My children wouldn't touch his things.' she said coldly. 'Colonel Petritis is a guest in our house.'

'Ask them, anyway,' Antonis persisted. 'It would be tragic if innocent men suffered as the result of a child's joke.'

Eleni could see that he was as frightened as she was. She went to the window and shouted for the children to come in. The note of panic in her voice brought them all at a run.

Gathering them in the kitchen, Eleni explained what had happened. She noticed that Nikola, unlike the girls, avoided her eyes and became very busy with the fireplace poker. She called him to her and took both his hands.

'You know that Colonel Petritis is a very powerful man, don't you?' she asked. He nodded, not meeting her gaze.

'You wouldn't want him to hurt Kanta, would you?'

Nikola looked at her, a spark of cunning in his eyes. 'If he got his things back,' he asked, 'would he let Kanta come home?'

Eleni hid her panic and kept her voice calm as she pleaded and coaxed. Though it took nearly a quarter of an hour, in the end he confessed.

As the neighbors returned home for the noon meal they saw a strange procession, led by Nikola and made up of his mother, Antonis and Petritis, and half a dozen guerrillas with shovels, all very solemn.

It took only a few minutes to unearth the plunder in the lower garden under Nikola's shamefaced instructions. One of the guerrillas reached into the hole and picked up a soggy brown sock bulging with lumps. Antonis shook it out on the ground and everyone turned to look at the boy.

Suddenly Eleni grabbed her son by the ear, twisted it and began shouting, 'You little beast! You black devil! Why would you touch the colonel's things? An honored guest in our house and you act like this!' She drew back her hand and slapped him across the face, her fingers leaving red welts.

It was the only time she ever hit me. The pain was eclipsed by the shock – the total incredibility – of the realization that she could turn on me. I wouldn't give her the satisfaction of seeing my tears. She had failed to understand that it was all done for her; my revenge on the man who had tyrannized and frightened her. She was blind to my devotion. She even slapped and humiliated me in front of the enemy. I went away to lick my wounds in my private hiding place, and not until years later did I come to the realization that she had attacked me first, hoping to defuse the punishment that Petritis was preparing for me.

It worked. Petritis confined himself to a warning: 'From now on, your family will stay on your side of the house and you'll keep your children in line, *Kyria*, or there will be very unpleasant consequences.' It was clear to Eleni that Nikola's prank had ruined her chances of ever convincing the colonel to have Kanta released. She walked wearily back to the house, through a bleak December landscape the color of a charcoal drawing that reflected her despair. By the time Eleni reached the door, a faint last hope had occurred to her.

The bearded young guerrilla, Nikola Paroussis, had stormed out the door when she reminded him how she hid him during the occupation. But that didn't alter the fact that he owed her a debt.

About a week after they were taken from their homes, the women recruits were submitted to one more indignity; the one they had been fearing from the start. They were each handed a khaki uniform, many of them bloodstained and worn, evidently taken from dead bodies. From now on, they were told, they would put aside women's clothes and dress like fighters of the Democratic Army – in pants. Some giggled but most blushed with embarrassment as they put on the baggy trousers. The smaller girls, like Kanta, had to roll up the legs several times before tucking them into the heavy, cleated boots.

Kanta would as readily have walked across the village square in her shift as in pants, but to her surprise a few of the girls seemed pleased by their new regalia, imitating the strut of the men, hefting their guns in a self-conscious mimicry of toughness. Girls like Rano and Milia Drouboyiannis seemed to put away their maidenly demeanor with the full-skirted wool dresses they had worn all their lives.

276

Their instructors informed them that the afternoon's indoctrination lesson would be replaced by a display of dancing in the village square. The *andartinas* would dance in their new uniforms, their guns over their shoulders. They were ordered to smile, to show how happy they were to be fighters in the Democratic Army.

As the church bells summoned everyone to the square, the *andartinas* huddled together for protection. When the villagers began to arrive, they stared at the spectacle of the local girls in their shameless apparel. Eleni came with her next-door neighbor, and searched frantically until she saw Kanta, trying to hide herself behind Rano. It was the nearest she had been to her daughter since the girl was taken.

Frixos arranged the nervous women in a line, putting Kanta, the smallest, at the end. When everyone was assembled, the male guerrillas began to sing, clapping their hands to the martial rhythm of the revolutionary songs. 'Today, today, today,' they shouted, 'the warriors stand like lions! Today, today, today, the women stand like cypresses . . .'

At a sign from Alekos, the girl in the lead, holding a white handkerchief, began the quick steps of the *kalamatianos;* three paces to the right, two to the left and then a dipping step back before the line snaked forward again. With her right hand on the shoulder of the girl ahead of her, Kanta was thrown off balance by the weight of the gun on her back. Her palms were wet and she couldn't keep up. Crimson-faced, she left the line and sidled over to Frixos. 'Please, Comrade Sergeant, can I dance without the gun?' she asked.

Angrily he motioned her back toward the line. 'You have to think of the gun as part of your body,' he ordered. 'Now get back there and don't forget to smile.'

Kanta did her best, her face frozen in a grimace, but she kept losing the step and scurrying to keep up. She saw her mother in front of the crowd, her face full of pain.

The line wound into a spiral and Kanta was pulled past the astonished faces of the villagers. When she came near her mother, Eleni's hands reached out, as if to help her. The expression on her mother's face told Kanta what she must look like in the obscene trousers. The girl dropped her head and Eleni saw her daughter's tears falling on the ground.

Several days before Christmas, the activity around Petritis became frenzied; grim, battle-soiled guerrillas arriving in the night, muffled arguments, much shouting. Eleni felt as if a thunderstorm was brewing. One night she heard Petritis bellowing into the field telephone, 'We'll send all we can, but we have to keep enough to protect our own positions.'

A few days later, several units of guerrillas collected in the village square, their equipment on their backs and on confiscated donkeys. Under the worried eyes of the villagers, they filed up the mountain to the northeast, passing out of sight over the peak of the Prophet Elias. It was clear that a major battle was looming, but where?

On Christmas Day the *andartinas* were put through their exercises as usual, but their instructors seemed distracted. The women heard enough to sense that something important was happening. No one told them that the guerrillas, under the eyes of General Markos, had launched the first major battle of the civil war that morning at Konitsa. Messengers from Petritis arrived at the training ground throughout the day, whispering in the ears of Alekos and Frixos, who seemed pleased with what they heard. The women went to sleep that night amid whispered rumors and speculation.

The next morning they awoke before dawn to hear the rumble of battle in the foothills below Lia and on the three heights that formed the opposite rim of the bowl, where the guerrillas had their forward lines. As the girls tumbled outside, they could see the smoke and fire of battles far to the south. Like spectators at the top of an amphitheater, they watched the red flare of mortars, the angry, erratic flash of machine guns, and the occasional, graceful arc of a blue flare. In order to divert the Mourgana guerrillas from sending reinforcements to Konitsa, the government troops had engaged the Communists in skirmishes in the foothills.

That night the *andartinas* were ordered to pack; they were moving out. The fighting was coming closer and they would be moved to the village of Vatsounia, five miles to the northeast over the top of their own mountains. The machine guns would have to be carried; each woman would take a turn. Kanta was among the first group to have one of the heavy guns strapped to her back.

The lack of sleep, the sound of battle, and the suspicion that they were being taken away to fight drained their strength. As Kanta struggled up the peak of the Prophet Elias, she bent low under the weight of the machine gun, the acid taste of fear in her mouth. She fought to keep up with the rest in the darkness, afraid of losing her foothold and falling under the gun.

It was Afrodite Fafoutis, a scrawny seventeen-year-old just ahead of her, who collapsed in a faint before they reached the flat threshing floor on the plateau below the chapel to the Prophet. The girl lay there motionless as the officers began to curse and nudge her with their boots. They discharged a rifle next to her ear to see if she was malingering, but when she didn't flinch, they angrily unstrapped the rifle from her back and ordered the rest to move on, leaving Afrodite lying where she had fallen. Kanta looked back once or twice until the pale figure faded into the darkness. A firm believer in ghosts, she felt the night was crowded with fleshless, grinning figures of death, waiting to seize her the moment she stepped off the path.

When they stopped for a five-minute rest to transfer the loads, Kanta heard the sound of a horse approaching. Someone lit a kerosene lantern and out of the darkness emerged a rider. It was Nikola Paroussis, the gaunt, fair-bearded young *andarte* whom her mother had hidden in the storeroom two years before. He dismounted and spoke to the officers, then walked down the line of women. As he came to Kanta he smiled in recognition and said, 'How goes it, little one? Have they made an *andartina* out of you?'

The kindness in his voice made her blurt out her fears. 'Oh, Nikola, I'm going to die! I can't carry the gun, I can't eat out of the common pot. I'm starving to death and I want to go home!'

He gave her a conspiratorial wink and made a 'chin up'

gesture. Then he vanished into the darkness, leaving Kanta staring after him.

When the villagers of Lia awoke on the morning of December 27, they realized that the battle to the south was coming closer, having moved down from the opposite hills into the foothills below. By midmorning Eleni made another discovery that left her pale and shaken. Glykeria came running into the house shouting, '*Mana!* The *andartinas* are nowhere in the village! They took Kanta away in the night!'

The mothers of the Perivoli gathered in worried knots to whisper, afraid that their daughters had been sent into the battles they could hear raging below. But toward noon, reassuring word reached them: the village girls had been seen marching in the opposite direction, toward the northeast.

It took all night for the group of *andartinas* to get to Vatsounia, where they were barracked in the school, set across a wide square from the small stone houses. Chilled and exhausted, they fell to the floor to sleep for the few hours that remained before reveille woke them at dawn.

After they were transferred to Vatsounia, away from their homes, a subtle transformation came over them. Kanta felt more miserable and lonely than ever, knowing that her mother had no idea where she was, but she noticed that the other girls were changing in puzzling ways. Some tried to outdo the others to impress their instructors with their marksmanship. Instead of gossiping and commiserating together, they divided into cliques, parroting the propaganda slogans of the indoctrination lectures and whispering about girls they suspected of disloyalty to the cause. Even Rano seemed different; harder, somehow, and freer in her conversation with the male guerrillas.

Some of the girls from the village, like Milia Drouboyiannis, who would have blushed if a passing shepherd bade them 'Good morning,' now openly flirted with the men. Kanta had never forgotten her mother's advice to keep as far away as possible from the guerrilla guards at night, and she often sat up in a corner, forcing herself to keep her eyes open until she was certain that the men in the same room were asleep.

One night she watched a pretty, blond girl of about twenty stretch herself out next to a young *andarte,* lying close enough to touch him. Kanta saw the man's face tense and he turned his back, pretending to be asleep.

The older girls in the group often whispered that the men were given a potion to suppress their sex drive, but Kanta suspected that their celibacy owed more to the fact that any *andarte* accused of tampering with one of the women could be tried, sentenced and executed before a firing squad on the spot. She had seen the dead body of a guerrilla accused of rape paraded on horseback from village to village to dramatize the fate of those who flaunted the DAG's rule of chastity.

Kanta sat up for many hours that night, watching the girl from her village and the young guerrilla sleeping side by side, and pondered the astonishing things she had seen and learned in the two weeks since she had been taken from her home.

While the unmarried women of Lia were being transformed into guerrillas, the married ones left behind were burdened with increasing duties as war approached the village. Because there were four adult women in the Gatzoyiannis house – Eleni, her mother Megali, her sister Nitsa and Olga – the guerrillas' representatives came nearly every day to demand one of them for a work detail. But Olga was still disabled by the burn on her foot, Megali wept and insisted that she was too old to go, and then, one day in late December, Nitsa delivered an announcement that she would no longer be able to participate in any heavy work either: she was pregnant.

The statement, delivered with satisfaction at the astonishment it provoked, stunned the family with the impact of a bomb. Everyone smiled uncertainly, convinced that she was joking. But the subject of pregnancy was no joke to Nitsa. She had prayed for a child every day for the past twenty-five years. She had swallowed holy candle wicks and bits of umbilical cords, stuffed her sleeping pallet with lumpy garlic bulbs, bought countless bits of malewort and bottles of magic water from the local witches. Last October, a month before her husband fled the village with the other men, she had launched her most ambitious charm.

She had made a flexible 'candle' a hundred yards long by applying soft wax to a great length of hemp rope, then placed it all the way around the outside of the burned Church of the Virgin. After lighting one end, she solemnly sat cross-legged in the middle of the rubble for an entire day and night until the flame traveled the circumference of the church. It was this spell, Nitsa told her amazed mother and sister, that had finally done the trick. 'The Virgin has made me a miracle, she has planted a child in my womb, and I refuse to risk my only chance at happiness by lifting or bending or doing anything that could cause a miscarriage,' she announced with great self-importance.

'God grant that it's so, sister,' Eleni said, 'but you're forty-four years old! How do you know that you're not having a change of life?'

'Nonsense!' Nitsa replied, unruffled. 'All the signs of pregnancy are there: my monthly bleeding has stopped, my breasts are swollen with milk, my stomach has already grown so that I can't fasten my skirts, and when a lead weight on a string is held over my belly, it swings straight back and forth. There's no possibility for doubt. So you see why I can't risk doing any heavy work.'

Nitsa's pregnancy became the talk of the Perivoli. All the women agreed that she indeed looked the part, and her belly grew so quickly that they began to talk of twins. She adopted the swaying gait that all proudly pregnant Greek women affect – back arched, stomach thrust forward – walking on her heels with the slow, side-to-side majesty of a rajah's elephant. The miraculous child would be born in August, she said.

Thus Eleni became the only female in the house still capable of fulfilling the family's obligations to the work details. Scarcely a day passed when she was not busy from morning to night working for the guerrillas, cooking, gathering firewood, carrying supplies and messages, mending uniforms and building fortifications. And ever since the fighting in the foothills began on Christmas Day, the women of Lia had been

282

assigned a new duty which Eleni found more disturbing than all the others: carrying the wounded.

From the foothills guerrillas came nearly every day carrying comrades bleeding from bullet and shrapnel wounds. The women had to transport the victims in relays to Babouri, where a new team would take over as far as Tsamanta, and still another group of women would carry them to Albania and medical help. After the government forces moved closer and entered Tsamanta on December 30, the westward route to Albania was cut off and the wounded had to be taken in the other direction; northeast toward Vatsounia.

The stretchers were made of canvas suspended between two long poles, and each one required four women. No matter how careful the carriers were, the wounded man would moan with each jolt. The women's palms became blistered; muscle cramps traveled across their shoulders and down into their legs.

Going uphill they struggled against the weight and often came to a full stop, swaying on their feet for a few seconds before they could get their legs moving again. On the down slopes their thigh muscles knotted with the effort not to run, to keep the stretcher level and moving slowly. If the man was heavy, the most the women could cover was several hundred yards before they had to stop and rest, breathing in gasps. They moved grimly in lock step, surrounded by the smell of blood and other fluids seeping from the wounded body. If the victim was conscious, he would often thrash and swear, mistaking them for the fascist soldiers. And every wounded man or woman repeated the same piteous refrain: 'For god's sake, water! Water!' The cry kept pace with their steps as they slogged on, a constant torment because no amount of water could ease such thirst. The pain of the body the women carried seemed to pass through the handles of the stretcher and up their arms. Often the cursing and weeping and cries of 'Water!' ended abruptly and they knew that the guerrilla's soul had left his body. Nevertheless, they didn't stop but staggered on toward their destination, crossing themselves with their free hand and uttering a silent prayer for his soul.

Eleni had done a great deal of praying since Kanta

disappeared from Lia on the day after Christmas. She stopped often at the Church of the Holy Trinity in the square to light a candle and ask the saints to protect her daughter and send news of where they had taken her.

One day Eleni and three other women were assigned to take a wounded guerrilla all the way to Vatsounia. There was an empty hole where his left eye had been, and the blood matted his curly black hair into a sticky mass. Eleni sighed as she lifted the back right-hand pole – after ten minutes they would change sides. She knew the journey to Vatsounia and back would take most of the day, so she had tucked a crust of bread, two hard-boiled eggs and a piece of cheese in her pocket for the return trek.

The guerrilla was still alive when they entered Vatsounia, coming over the mountain from the north. Far below, beyond the square, Eleni saw the schoolyard filled with two lines of figures marching in formation. She heard the sound of a shouted 'One-two! One-two!' and nearly dropped her corner of the stretcher. As soon as the women delivered their burden to the guerrilla doctor, Eleni hurried down toward the square. First she recognized the tall figure of Rano, then the smaller one of Kanta at the front of the line. She gasped at how thin her daughter had become and felt in her pocket for the food she had brought – at least she could give her that.

The *andartinas* were in the middle of rifle drill when Kanta heard her name called and looked up to see her mother standing on the mountainside, about a thousand feet away. At the vision Kanta bolted from the ranks of the other girls, running toward the figure in the brown dress and black kerchief. One of the guerrillas stepped in front of her and grabbed her by the shoulders, pushing her back until he shoved her against the wall of the school, knocking her head with a loud thud. 'Who do you think you are, *kouchiko*! Someone special?' he shouted. 'Get back to the drill!'

Eleni ran toward her daughter, but another guerrilla stopped her descent. 'What do you want?' he demanded.

'Only to give this bit of food to my daughter.'

'No one is allowed to speak to the recruits,' he snapped. 'They are being well fed. Go back where you came from.'

Eleni could see Kanta pushed against the schoolhouse wall, her head bouncing off the stone. Across the distance, their eyes embraced over the shoulders of the men who held them apart. Eleni wanted to fight the hands that held her, but it would only make trouble for Kanta. She stayed where she was until the girl rejoined the ranks of the marching women. When Eleni couldn't stand to watch any longer, she turned away.

With the weary tread of a beaten woman, she began to retrace her steps over the spine of the mountain range. When she reached the Chapel of St. Nicholas, high above Lia, Eleni went inside. Watched by the dim eyes of the saints on the ancient frescoed walls, she knelt before the altar and talked aloud to St. Nicholas, asking him to bring her daughter home safely, as he brought sailors back to port out of the storm. She promised him, in exchange for her daughter's return, a can of oil for the chapel's lamps. It was a solemn oath and one that she would carry to the grave, for she never had time to honor it.

Even after her death she returned in dreams to those who survived, reminding them of the unpaid debt, but by then the chapel lay in ruins, and there was no way her children could put her soul at peace by fulfilling the vow.

When Kanta saw her mother driven away, without even a word or touch exchanged, she felt her last tenuous hold on hope give way. The loneliness and exhaustion became worse, and her stomach was swollen with malnutrition. Kanta resigned herself to the fact that she was going to die.

For the next few days the temperature dropped close to zero and Kanta ached with the cold; one of her two sweaters had been taken from her by the guerrillas because it wasn't fair for the Amerikana's daughter to have two when others had none. One night, as she sat outside the schoolhouse with two other girls, huddled around a fire, trying to get some warmth out of one burning log, Kanta looked across the village square to see smoke rising from the chimney of a small stone house. There was warmth there, and perhaps food. The will to live dies hard at fifteen, and Kanta realized that she wanted to survive and that the only one who could save her was she herself.

She reached for her unloaded rifle and slung it over her shoulder. 'Bring your guns and come with me,' she said to the two other girls. 'And don't say anything. Let me do the talking.'

The two girls, who were both several years older than Kanta, looked at her in surprise, then obeyed. Silently, empty rifles on their shoulders, they crossed the square. Kanta beat on the door of the small house with her rifle butt. A quavering voice from within said, 'Who is it?'

'Open the door,' Kanta ordered.

'I can't,' the voice replied.

Kanta beat louder. 'Open the door in the name of the Democratic Army of Greece!' she demanded.

The door opened a few inches and two eyes peered out. 'What do you want, my child?' said the shaky voice, sounding surprised at the sight of the small, fierce girl.

Kanta put her foot on the door and shoved, holding her rifle in both hands. Inside, she saw to her satisfaction a roaring fire and two nearly identical old women, their white hair covered with black kerchiefs.

'Have you got any wood, grandmothers?' Kanta snapped, walking in. 'We need wood!'

'Yes, children, take some wood,' said the one who had opened the door. Her sister hurried to gather it from the neat pile by the hearth.

Kanta felt dizzy as hunger washed over her. 'You got bread? Bring us bread!' she ordered. The first old woman disappeared and returned with a round, crusty loaf.

Heartened by her success, Kanta plunged on. 'You got milk? You got potatoes? Bring the milk and throw the potatoes in the fire.'

'Yes, my girls,' quavered the crone. 'Whatever we have is yours.' She made a sign to the other, who tottered away, returning with three potatoes, and placed them on the burning coals. While the young *andartinas* waited for the potatoes to roast, they drained the bowl of milk. When she couldn't wait any longer, Kanta signaled for the potatoes to

286

be brought to her and gathered them in her handkerchief. Then, with a sign to her two comrades, she headed for the door. As soon as the *andartinas* were outside, they heard the bolt being shot into place. By the time they crossed the square, Kanta was doubled over with laughter, while the other two stared at her open-mouthed. 'If the guerrillas find out about this, they'll put us in front of a firing squad!' said one.

'They won't find out!' Kanta retorted, with more conviction than she felt.

They sat down around their fire, and Kanta tore open the handkerchief and stuffed one of the hot potatoes into her mouth. The oldest girl, who was Stavroula Yakou's sister, looked at her in horror. 'You must have gone crazy!' she whispered. 'Do you know what you just did? The same thing that the guerrillas did to our families!'

But Kanta wasn't listening, her whole being concentrated on the taste of the plump, charred, half-cooked potato in her hands.

On the eighth day of training in the village of Vatsounia, at the afternoon indoctrination session, all three instructors stood before the recruits and Kanta realized to her surprise that Nikola Paroussis was with them. She hadn't seen him since the night they walked to Vatsounia. Lieutenant Alekos began to address the women about the guerrilla offensive, which he had been reporting in edited form since their arrival in Vatsounia.

'You know of the glorious battle we have been waging on two fronts,' he said. 'Although General Markos did not take Konitsa, he inflicted great damage on the enemy there; they're counting their dead in the hundreds. At the same time, the attack of the monarcho-fascists on our own divisions in the foothills below the Mourgana has been totally repulsed, and they have fled back of the Great Ridge with their tails between their legs.' He paused momentously. 'Your training period is now nearly at an end,' he went on with pride, 'and within days you will be assigned to companies on both fronts. The time has come to separate the wheat from the chaff, to eliminate those among you who lack the strength and commitment to fight beside our brave warriors. The following women will step forward.'

He looked at a list in his hand and began to read: 'Athanassiou, Rano. Ziarras, Marianthe. Gatzoyiannis, Chryssoula.' Kanta flinched, but it was her cousin who was called. Eight more names. Kanta waited, her mouth dry. Alekos' eyes ranged over the silent women and stopped at her. 'Gatzoyiannis, Alexandra.'

Slowly Kanta stood up and joined the row of frightened girls. Alekos looked at them for a moment with distaste. 'Get your things, you're going now,' he ordered. Seeing their faces, he added, 'You're to leave. Go home!'

Kanta realized that her mouth was open and abruptly shut it. She tried to think what to do. This must be a new kind of test, and failing it could be fatal.

'We don't want to go!' she said quickly. 'We want to fight! We want to help liberate our country.' The other girls joined in, chorusing their devotion to the cause.

Alekos looked at Kanta accusingly. 'You're too young, too weak! You can't handle a gun properly. In a battle like Konitsa, your incompetence could cost a comrade's life.'

'I'll do better!' Kanta pleaded. Then she saw Nikola Paroussis standing directly behind Alekos. He caught her eye and moved his head sideways, pressing his lips together. He was telling her not to argue, but to shut up and go while she had the chance.

Kanta began to tremble. Was it possible that she was really being set free, just like that? Then she realized that Alekos was still talking to her. 'Maybe next year, when you're older,' he was saying, more kindly. 'From today, you'll be in the reserves, and if the army needs you, you'll be called back. But for now, you're too young to fight.'

'I don't want to go!' cried Chryssoula Gatzoyiannis suddenly. 'I want to fight with my comrades.' Kanta turned to stare at her cousin. She knew that Chryssoula, just seventeen and emaciated, was as miserable as she was. She tried to catch her eye, to tell her it wasn't a trap; she should go quickly. But Chryssoula was looking beseechingly at Alekos. 'I won't go home!' she insisted. 'Please give me another chance!'

288

He shrugged. 'As you wish.' Chryssoula returned to the ranks of the sitting women.

'*I'm* not too young,' Rano said with a challenge in her voice. 'Why are you sending me home?'

Alekos glared. 'We know where your family's sympathies lie!' he shouted. 'You pretend to be with us, but you're black inside. We don't want any fifth columnists in the Democratic Army. You're more dangerous than the ones who are weak and inexperienced.'

Rano bit her lip and said nothing. Frightened by his anger, still afraid it was a trap, the women who had been eliminated handed over their rifles to Frixos and headed back to the schoolhouse to change into the dresses they had arrived in. Before they set out for Lia, Kanta took her cousin Chryssoula aside. 'Why on earth aren't you going with us?' she whispered. 'This is your chance to save yourself!'

Chryssoula looked away. 'If I went home, I'd only be another mouth for my mother to feed,' she replied. 'But if I stay here and convince them I'm loyal, then my family may get better treatment from the *andartes* back in the village.'

Kanta stared at her, realizing that she was right, and her joy gave way to guilt. Perhaps it was her duty, too, to stay an *andartina,* to improve her family's poor standing with the Communists. But then she remembered the corn mush and the unwashed tin plate, the fear, exhaustion and humiliation, and she knew she couldn't do it. She wanted her mother too much. She gave her cousin a quick kiss and turned away. Chryssoula Gatzoyiannis was killed in battle six months later.

Eleni was kneeling on the bank of the washing pond, beating some wet clothes, when she heard a shout from below and saw her neighbor Marina Kolliou running toward her, waving her arms. 'Quick, Eleni!' she cried. 'Some of the *andartinas* are coming over the mountain!'

Eleni left the washing where it lay and ran up the ravine until she could see the path winding down between the peaks of the Prophet Elias and Kastro. She could make out about a dozen figures, too far away to identify. Pushing her way through the underbrush, she hurried up toward the plateau

289

where the village danced on the Prophet's feast day. As she entered one side of the flat area, the girls were just arriving at the opposite edge of the clearing. Splashing through the small, icy stream that divided them, Eleni ran, her kerchief flying off her hair, her arms reaching out until she held her daughter.

All the way down to the house, Eleni kept touching Kanta's face in disbelief, wiping away the girl's tears while her own flowed unnoticed.

Kanta emerged from her guerrilla training even more high-strung than she had been before. Despite her sisters' questions, she refused to tell what had happened to her during those weeks. But Olga noticed that some of the other returned *andartinas* had changed in a different way, including her best friend Rano. While Olga still hid in the house, emerging only with her kerchief wrapped around her face, Rano wore hers daringly back on her hair and moved about the neighborhood with a new assurance, even exchanging greetings with some of the guerrillas she passed on the road. If Olga didn't know Rano so well, she would suspect that she was flirting.

One day she saw Rano coming out of her gate, her red cheeks glowing, her hair carefully combed, wearing her best dress. She was off to the guerrilla's commissary, she said, with a bowl of eggs that her sister Tassina had given her, to see if she could coax the guerrillas into exchanging them for soap to bathe the babies.

Sometime later Olga was sitting in the Gatzoyiannis kitchen with her mother, Megali, Nitsa and the two closest neighbors – Anastasia Yakou and Marina Kolliou – gossiping over glasses of mountain tea, when Rano burst in, clearly upset. 'Aunt Eleni,' she whispered, 'could I have a word with you?' As the other women exchanged glances, Eleni followed her into the garden.

When they were out of earshot, Rano told Eleni what she had overheard just as she was about to knock on the door of the commissary: the voice of Hanjaras, the quartermaster, shouting over one of the field telephones. 'Yes, sir, I'll see to it right away,' she heard him say. 'Tonight, if you want. We'll turn the Amerikana's house inside out.'

'The minute I heard that, I started running,' said Rano, still holding the bowl of eggs. 'Before they come, you can hide whatever you want in our house. As soon as you have a chance, wrap everything up and throw it over the fence into our garden. I'll put it under my father's mattress, where they'll never think of looking for it, not with him lying on top of it.'

Immediately Eleni thought of Olga's dowry, the most valuable thing the family possessed. If the guerrillas took the rugs, blankets and linens she had bought with the last money Christos sent her, Olga would never find a groom. There were also some fine American suits and shirts Christos had left behind. Eleni hugged Rano and agreed to give her the things as soon as her visitors left. When she returned to the kitchen, her mother asked sharply, 'What did Rano tell you to make you turn so white?'

Eleni repeated what Rano had told her, and Marina Kolliou stood up nervously. 'If they're searching your house,' she said, 'they may search ours too. I'll warn my mother and hide some things.'

Anastasia Yakou took the news more calmly; she had nothing of value to tempt the guerrillas, anyway. But she left to go down to her house and found her daughter there, come to complain, as usual, about the tyranny of her mother-in-law. Anastasia swore Stavroula to secrecy, then told her what had just taken place in the Gatzoyiannis kitchen. Stavroula shrugged. 'If you ask me,' she said, 'the Amerikana has been the luckiest woman in the village. Her husband's not fighting, the way mine is. She managed to keep Olga out of the *andartinas* by a trick and got Kanta released while my sister's still in there – and now she's got the neighbors to hide Olga's dowry!'

'Bite your tongue,' Anastasia scolded. 'That's jealousy talking! Hasn't Eleni always been the kindest woman to us in the whole neighborhood? Didn't Olga embroider your wedding breads and Nikola sit on your dowry chest? Why are you begrudging them a little luck?'

Stavroula didn't answer. Since her marriage had proved a disappointment and her baby son died, the privileges of the Amerikana, denied to poor families like her own, had begun to rankle in her heart. With the Communists promising a new order that would eliminate privilege, Stavroula intended to make up for her bad luck in the past. Although her husband was fighting with the national forces, Stavroula believed the guerrilla propaganda. The old order was going to be overturned, and she was determined to be on the winning side. She had been the poorest girl in the village, but she had beauty and intelligence and intended to use them to become the most influential woman.

Stavroula looked at her mother's puzzled face and said nothing of her plans. All she said was, 'One of these days the Amerikana's luck will run out and she'll find that she's been too smart for her own good. You know what they say: "The clever fox gets caught by all four feet."'

CHAPTER TEN

The failure of the Democratic Army to take Konitsa proved
a devastating blow to the guerrillas. It bolstered the morale
of their enemies, discouraged their sympathizers in the cities
from joining their ranks, and raised enough doubts about
the future of their rebellion so that not a single country, even
in the Communist bloc, recognized their provisional
government, which remained rootless in the mountains.

On February 10, 1948, when a group of Yugoslav and
Bulgarian leaders visited Moscow, they found Joseph Stalin
ready to scuttle the Greek uprising altogether. As recalled
later by one of them, Milovan Djilas, Stalin turned to Edvard
Kardelj, vice premier of Yugoslavia, the country which was
the strongest supporter of the Greek guerrillas, and asked,
'Do you believe in the success of the uprising in Greece?'

'If foreign intervention does not grow and if serious
political errors are not made,' replied Kardelj.

'If, if!' Stalin interrupted. 'No, they have no prospect of
success at all. What do you think, that Great Britain and the
United States – the United States, the most powerful nation
in the world – will permit you to break their line of
communication in the Mediterranean Sea? Nonsense. And
we have no navy. The uprising in Greece must be stopped,
and as quickly as possible.'

But the writing on the wall was illegible to the obstinate
leader of the Greek Communist Party, Nikos Zachariadis.
He remained convinced that a string of victories by the
guerrillas would persuade Stalin to lend his full support to
the uprising.

To make up for the shrinking number of recruits joining the DAG, its leaders sent two brigades through Macedonia to seize as many young women and men as they could find. Both brigades met stiff opposition from government forces, and they not only failed to bring back many recruits but lost half of their 3,000 veteran fighters in skirmishes along the way.

Party leaders then decided to send another group of guerrillas south toward Athens to open a route to the capital over which urban Communists could march to join them in the mountains. A hand-picked band of 200 men was sent off on this impossible mission, and not one of them returned.

As the DAG's hope of finding recruits faded, so did its expectations of capturing major towns and cities. Zachariadis was forced to modify his strategy, but he refused to return to the hit-and-run guerrilla tactics favored by General Markos. The insurgents would not launch any more massive attacks on population centers, but they would hold on at all costs to the mountain strongholds they controlled, Zachariadis insisted, until the Greek National Army realized it could never defeat them, became totally demoralized and collapsed.

To make sure that everyone – guerrillas and civilians in the 'liberated' areas – remained loyal until that happened, the DAG's political commissars were reorganized and given authority to enforce discipline among all military units and cooperation from all civilians living in the occupied villages.

Meanwhile the National Army, assisted by American advisers under General James Van Fleet, began preparing a large-scale operation for the summer of 1948 to destroy the guerrilla army by capturing their main base in the Grammos mountain range. But such an offensive would expose the attacking army's western flank to assaults by the guerrillas in the Mourgana range. Before Grammos could be taken, it was necessary to clear out the guerrillas in the Mourgana mountains, whose center was the village of Lia.

OPERATION PERGAMOS

DURING JANUARY AND February of 1948, the muffled thunder of distant artillery became as much a part of life in Lia as the tintinnabulation of the goats' bells and the morning oratorio of the roosters. The constant rumble, like subterranean growls before an earthquake, grew in volume every night as hit-and-run patrols of guerrillas from the Mourgana crept across the valley below and up the distant hills of no man's land to harass the government troops.

After the defeat at Konitsa, the guerrillas in the Mourgana knew that a reciprocal attack was certain to come, so in the first months of 1948 they feverishly built fortifications to secure their positions in the 'guerrilla fortress,' as they called the Mourgana in their songs. In the mountains above and in Lia itself they built defense works everywhere, using teams of village women to carry the rocks and beams, mix the cement and dig ditches to serve as mortar pits and machine-gun nests.

Sinister pillboxes with one narrow slit facing south sprang up like scarecrows throughout the village at every spot with a view of the foothills. There were half a dozen in the Perivoli alone, where the guerrillas' base of operations was concentrated, and over 2,500 fortifications in the entire Mourgana range. It was clear to the Liotes that the guerrillas expected their fortress to be besieged.

Another harbinger of war entered the rhythm of village life. Every day about noon, a formation of four sleek Spitfires would appear in the distance from the east and split apart, one pair sweeping the Mourgana peaks north of Lia, bombing guerrilla artillery nests among the crags, and the other strafing the line of guerrilla positions in the foothills to the south, following the spine of the Great Ridge that loomed against the southern horizon.

The bellwether of the bombers was a single Harvard reconnaissance plane that passed directly over the village at dawn every morning, flown by a daring pilot who quickly became legendary among the village boys because of his skill. The guerrillas had christened the man 'Galatas,' which means 'milkman,' because of his regular early-morning rounds, but the villagers, knowing nothing of milkmen and their behavior, assumed that the pilot's name really was Galatas.

The milkman's job was to survey the mountain terrain below, pinpointing guerrilla fortifications and congregations which the bombers would attack later in the day. Preceded by the drone of his engine, Galatas would burst through the cleft between the peaks of the Prophet Elias and Kastro, flying only two hundred feet above ground, his camouflaged blue-bellied, single-engine craft skimming the rooftops, dodging anti-aircraft fire from the peaks, waggling his wings in mockery or greeting, so close that the children could see his face in its plastic bubble. They waved and shouted 'Galatas!,' watching with more admiration than fear until he was out of sight, swooping heavenward like an eagle.

As soon as Galatas began his dawn flights, Colonel Petritis called Eleni into his office and issued an order. Every morning, when the engine of the surveillance plane was heard, the guards outside the Gatzoyiannis gate would be withdrawn and she was to send the three youngest children – Nikola, Fotini and Glykeria – out into the yard to play. There was no danger, Petritis assured her; Galatas didn't carry bombs, only cameras, and if he saw women about and children playing in the yard, the fascists would avoid bombing the house. But if they suspected it was a guerrilla headquarters, it could become a target.

To the children it seemed a fine game. They waved enthusiastically at Galatas as soon as his plane burst between the mountain peaks, still shrouded in mist. But Eleni stood on the threshold and watched the great bird pass over, thinking dark thoughts of falling fire and death.

With the portent of impending battle hanging in the air, the children of Lia became obsessed with war games, happily mimicking the killing around them. In the neighborhood of the Perivoli the organizer of the battles was the son of the miller Tassi Mitros – a swarthy, powerfully built twelve-year-old named Niko who had physical daring and a gift for imaginative profanity that made the smaller boys worship him. Inevitably he was the one who would announce a mock battle and divide the rest of the neighborhood boys into two teams: the guerrillas and the fascists, with himself, naturally, the commander of the guerrillas.

Nikola Gatzoyiannis was in awe of the older boy and always hoped that Niko Mitros would choose him for the guerrilla side. But like his friend Lakis Bartzokis, Tassina's son, who was also only eight years old, and small at that, he always got assigned to the fascist team. Whether this was because he and Lakis were younger and weaker than the rest, or because their families were considered sympathetic to the nationalist side, Nikola wasn't sure, but he suspected it was a little of both.

Ever since a blizzard had left ample snow on the ground for ammunition, the battles had taken on a set ritual. The two teams would dig in on either side of a low stone wall and pile up a supply of icy missiles. The 'fascists,' as in real life, were always given the more vulnerable downhill position.

First came an exchange of curses imitating the taunts shouted across the foothills every night through bullhorns. 'Cuckolds! Cuntlappers!' Niko Mitros and his gang would bellow through rolled notebooks, and the 'fascists' would shout back, 'Gruel eaters! Masturbators! Dungkickers!' Eventually a sniper would poke his head over the wall, to be greeted with a barrage of snowballs. If he was hit, he was dead. When one team had whittled down the enemy to their satisfaction, they would launch a siege, storming over the wall in a hail of snowballs to annihilate the survivors.

Niko Mitros usually led the attack on the hapless 'fascists' while Nikola and Lakis forgot all about defensive fire and curled into balls, covering their faces with their arms. The game would end with bruises, cuts and black eyes for the

297

'fascists,' and with Lakis running home to his mother in tears. Nikola, pale and silent, refused to sympathize with his comrade at arms or even admit that Niko Mitros was singling them out for punishment. 'Lakis asks for it,' Nikola reasoned, 'because he's a crybaby.' He longed to be on the opposite team, the winning team, and see admiration instead of scorn in Niko Mitros' eyes.

Being the only male in a household of women, with no adult except his stern, tyrannical grandfather as a model, Nikola had learned to hide his feelings behind a protective shell of silence, and to keep his problems and fears to himself. He had absorbed the village conviction that a man must be strong, decisive and taciturn, while women were fragile reeds, bending with every breeze, victims of their emotions.

Nikola also realized at an early age that he would have to compensate for lack of brawn with shrewdness, and he vowed to become as wily as his grandfather. Now he set his mind to the problem of winning Niko Mitros' admiration.

Nikola knew that he had a double handicap: his size and the fact that his father lived in America. Secretly Nikola admired the father he had never seen, whose image sat in majesty atop the mantelpiece, and often he would search his own thin features in the small hand mirror for a resemblance to his father's rotund grandeur. Lately, however, he had begun to look at the photograph of Christos with reproach. If his father had only gone to Russia instead of America, he thought, then perhaps Niko Mitros would let him fight on the guerrilla side. But he couldn't repudiate his father or change the fact that his grandfather was a 'fascist.' He would have to win over Niko Mitros in spite of these disadvantages.

Nikola's part in the war games came to an abrupt end one day when a wayward bomb nearly hit a field above the Perivoli, where the mock guerrillas and fascists were battling. Grimly Eleni ordered Nikola not to play outside the family's yard, where she could keep an eye on him. That was the beginning of long, solitary hours spent pacing the boundaries of his prison as the snow melted, dreaming of unlikely exploits that would earn him a reputation as a fearless warrior. One day when he could almost feel the earth beneath his feet heaving with the approach of spring, he found a gray little thrush with one broken wing. He caught it, feeling the small heart beating against his palm like a pulse, and laughed at the way the bird opened its tiny beak to peck him, its whole body trembling with the effort. He designed a cage out of a discarded ammunition box and fed it with crumbs from his finger. The bird grew to trust him, and even after the wing healed and he released it, it would fly to him, studying him with one alert eye and then the other, waiting to be fed. Having always been the baby of the family, Nikola enjoyed nursing something weaker than himself, but he didn't mention the bird to the other children.

In previous years, the advent of spring had been heralded by the arrival of terrifying, scarecrowlike men called *kalogheroi* – in reality, village bachelors who dressed themselves in grotesque costumes made from the hide of a goat, pointed hoods over their heads with skull-like holes cut out for eyes, and strings of goats' bells across their chests. The *kalogheroi* would caper about the village frightening the children, pulling obscene stunts and enacting an ancient farce involving murder and a miraculous resurrection. The custom was rooted in the magical Dionysian rites of the ancients, intended to help the forces of nature fertilize the land, but with the coming of the guerrillas, such superstitions had been banned along with church ceremonies. In the children's imagination the guerrillas themselves took the place of the *kalogheroi:* sinister figures evoking fear and fascination.

One day in late February, Nikola accompanied his mother on a visit to Tassina Bartzokis' house across the path, where he witnessed a confrontation between two guerrillas that made a deep impression on him. Lakis was there too, but Nikola ignored him, not wanting to be seen associating with crybabies.

There was a guerrilla captain named Harisis Stravos billeted in the Bartzokis house, a man notorious throughout the Mourgana because, in front of his village church, he had once knifed a young woman to death because she refused to marry him. When the Germans occupied Greece, Stravos was released from prison and joined the ELAS. His penchant for stabbing those he captured became well known and his refusal to bring any back alive ultimately led to his demotion within the DAG.

While Tassina and Eleni sat gossiping in the Bartzokis kitchen, Nikola wandered out into the garden, where he found the infamous Stravos and another guerrilla captain engaged in target practice, shooting at a knot in a walnut tree fifty paces away. The dark, muscular Stravos reminded Nikola of Niko Mitros. His opponent was blond, thin and soft-spoken, but his first two shots hit the knot dead center, while Stravos fired twice and missed. 'It's not a fair match!' Stravos complained. 'You've got the better gun.' His face was flushed.

Coolly, with a hint of a bow, the blond captain handed Stravos his own pistol. Nikola made note of the gesture; the man's ironic self-control made Stravos' blustering seem ridiculous.

Muttering to himself, Stravos took careful aim and fired. And missed. His second bullet was inches wide of the mark. Then he went out of control. He stormed over to the side, and taking the pistol by the barrel, smashed it against the stone wall with such force that it broke in two. The other captain only watched with a thin smile.

Suddenly Nikola realized the solution to his problem. If he couldn't fight, he would become an expert marksman! Once he could hit a target better than Niko Mitros, the other boys would want him as a guerrilla.

Nikola spent hours every day by himself in the garden with his slingshot, shooting rocks at clods of dirt set atop the wall. The snow was gone, and carving slingshots from the resilient wood of the willow tree was as much a rite of spring for the boys as the Lenten fast. Nikola practiced with different-sized stones and measured until he knew exactly how far above the target he should aim to compensate for the fall of the rock in its descending curve. Finally he could hit the target four times out of five.

He was ready when Niko Mitros arrived one day with his mother. His slingshot in his belt, the boy ambled out to the yard, where Nikola was absorbed in shooting clumps of earth

300

off the garden wall, one by one. Niko Mitros watched for a while, then challenged him to a contest. This was the confrontation Nikola had imagined so often. He allowed the challenger to pick the target. The older boy pointed to the mulberry tree at the southern edge of the yard, which had several crows roosting in it. 'Think you can hit one of those?'

'Probably,' said Nikola, imitating the casual manner of the blond guerrilla captain. Both boys aimed and fired at the same time, but the blackbirds rose in a complaining cloud, untouched.

'Shit!' said Niko Mitros. 'The sun was in my eyes. Now what can we shoot at?'

Nikola looked around. He didn't want the other boy to become bored with the game before he had proved himself. He spied the small dun-colored thrush sitting on the wall near the gate.

'See that bird over there?' he said, tough and cool at the same time. 'Watch this!'

The bird wouldn't move, he knew. He selected a tiny pebble off the ground so that he wouldn't really hurt it. As he took careful aim, the bird watched him with one eye. The strap of the slingshot snapped and the missile sped with a whistling sound. Nikola was honestly surprised to see the bird topple off the wall. He ran over and picked it up. The moment he held it, incredibly light, like a handful of feathers, he knew it was dead, the tiny pulse still. Furious, he hurled the corpse away. Niko Mitros expressed his admiration with a whistle like the sound of a sky rocket. 'Great shot!' he exclaimed. Nikola waited for the sweet satisfaction he had imagined, but he only felt numb. Then he knew he was going to cry. He ran, rubbing his sleeve across his eyes, and as he disappeared behind the house, he heard a snort of laughter from the other boy.

Nikola didn't stop until he was covered by the rushes that grew beside the washing pond. He hid his face in his arms; after a while he turned over on his back to watch the weak rays of the winter sun filter through the rushes. Images of the bird dead and Lakis crying and himself cowering under the rain of snowballs were all mixed up in his mind. He tried to sort them out. To be tough like Niko Mitros and the guerrillas he impersonated meant taking pleasure in the sufferings of someone weaker, but Nikola could not make himself stop feeling the pain of the victim. One thing was clear – his chances of being chosen for the guerrilla team were ruined. He wasn't sure he was sorry.

While the signs of impending war fascinated the children and colored their games, the adults reacted with increasing fear. To Eleni it seemed that the government planes flew closer every day and that the whine and rumble of the artillery became louder every night, startling her out of her sleep. She would sit and study the faces of her sleeping children by the embers and imagine the fighting that was taking place on the distant mountains. All the villagers knew that it was just a matter of time until the pot boiled over and they were embroiled in the fighting; otherwise, why were the guerrillas so frantically fortifying the whole mountain range?

Eleni's waking fears crept into her sleep, and one night she had a dream that frightened her so, she told the family about it the next morning. As she slept, it seemed that she was awakened by the *brr* of the hand-turned bell on the gate. She saw herself get up in the darkness and go outside to undo the bolt. Standing there in the path, frosted with silver moonlight, was the round, smiling figure of her long-dead mother-in-law, Fotini.

The old woman reached out and touched Eleni's cheek with icicle fingers. 'Hello, my little bride,' she said fondly in a rustling voice like dry leaves. 'I've missed you! I was passing by up the path and knocked to tell you to prepare your things, because I'll be coming for you soon. But now, go back and finish sleeping. There's still time; I have to go and get Tsavena first.'

Eleni brooded over the dream all day. Tsavena, the old crone who had seen Nikola emerging from his homemade swimming pool, was the mother of their next-door neighbor Marina Kolliou. 'It means I'm going to die, and Tsavena before me,' Eleni said to Nitsa. 'Perhaps a bomb while I'm working on fortifications or a bullet while I'm carrying wounded. If I die, what will become of the children?'

'What do you know about dreams?' scoffed Nitsa. 'I should hope Tsavena's going to die before you; she's ninety years old! Her oil is nearly burned up. You were probably just sleeping on your left side again. How many times have I warned you it interferes with digestion? Your mother-in-law was probably just a fried onion that went down the wrong way.'

The code name that the government forces selected for their carefully planned attack on the 'impregnable' Mourgana was 'Pergamos,' an ancient Greek city in Asia Minor where the Greeks defeated the Turks in 1919 against crushing odds. Operation Pergamos was scheduled to begin on February 25, 1948.

Seven battalions of the government's Eighth Division – nearly 3,500 men – were assigned to Operation Pergamos to attack the four battalions – about 1,400 Communist guerrillas – entrenched in the Mourgana villages and the foothills below, one of them commanded by Major Spiro Skevis.

The government troops planned to attack the Mourgana in a pincer movement, three battalions and a squadron of mountain commandos striking from the north, and three battalions and a double company of irregulars coming up from the south and moving toward the large hills below Lia. The northern prong of the pincer would start moving down first, clearing out the guerrilla concentrations on the opposite side of the Mourgana peaks from Lia, while the southern prong would launch attacks to 'soften' the ground in the foot-hills below. The driving wedge of the attack from the north was to be an expert group of specially trained commandos called LOK, an acronym for the Greek words meaning 'Squadron of Mountain Commandos' – nearly 300 men trained in scaling mountain heights. Their assignment was to sneak through the enemy lines and secure a small but critical hill called Skitari within guerrilla territory, only two miles northeast of Lia but hidden from sight of the village by the peaks of the Prophet Elias and Kastro.

As soon as the commandos signaled their success in reaching the hill, the seventh battalion, moving in from the southeast, would rush to link up with them, and if the surprise worked, the guerrillas would be effectively sliced into two groups, forced to flee northwest into Albania or be crushed by the closing prongs of the pincer, which were to come together in the village of Lia.

On February 25 the three battalions of government soldiers in the north began to move down from the Pogoni area, pushing through the hills, sweeping the guerrillas they encountered either into Albania or toward Lia. The villagers could see nothing of this: the mountain peaks above them blocked their view, but they knew that an attack was under way because the government troops poised to the south, on the opposite edge of the valley that stretched below them, began the 'softening up' of the area they planned to take, bombarding the three high ridges forming the southern rim of the bowl of mountains and the foothills below. For three days the villagers watched as a constant rain of bombs, mortar fire and artillery in the distance pushed the guerrillas slowly back toward them.

On February 28 the massive force of government troops from the south began to move down into the foothills, while the guerrillas, vastly outnumbered, could only back up, trying to nip and snap at the enemy with ambushes and night attacks. 'Heavy and mechanical is the sound of the hard-headed moving enemy forces. They are the lifeless mass crawling along,' wrote Greek novelist Demitrios Hatzis, who was one of the Communist fighters in the Mourgana. For three days the guerrillas desperately fought to hold back the irresistible advance of the government fighting machine. But Operation Pergamos was proceeding exactly according to plan; the pincers slowly closed from both the north and the south. The commanders of the Communist forces, who had been stationed in Babouri, decided to move their headquarters to the mountain heights above Lia, where they would be better protected by large numbers of their men to the east and west, and the natural indentation of the mountain range into which Lia was nestled. In case the worst happened, they could retreat all the way up to the Albanian border.

*

Ever since February 25 when the heavy bombardment broke out in the foothills below, Eleni had kept the children in the house, watching from the windows as government planes strafed the guerrilla positions to the south, and mortar and artillery fire made a fireworks display in the night sky over the lowlands. But on the morning of March 1 a procession appeared, moving up the path outside the Gatzoyiannis gate, that brought the whole family out of the house to stare. The three leaders of the entire Epiros Command, flanked by their staff and equipment, were riding by on horseback, heading for the relative safety of the mountain cliffs above the Perivoli.

To my eight-year-old eyes they were the grandest men I had ever seen – the ultimate commanders of the whole guerrilla army; at least the half of it occupying Epiros. The horses they rode seemed to tower higher than elephants. The grim parade moved silently between the rows of our neighbors, who searched the faces of the three officers for a clue to the outcome of the battle. The one who resembled a bulldog, a square fortress of a man with curly hair and great bushes of eyebrows, was Yiorgos Kalianesis, the chief of staff. The sleek, fox-faced one with the small charcoal mustache, thick matted black hair and a dashing military coat thrown over his shoulders like a mantle was Kostas Koliyiannis, the political commissar. Riding next to him was the military commander, Vasilis Chimaros. I don't remember him very well, but I remember Kalianesis' gleaming pistol in his belt holster and the leather of his accouterments shining in the sun. Behind and in front of the three commanders came their retinue: mules loaded with arms and equipment, the headquarters staff, radios, provisions, and bodyguards surrounding their war lords. As I watched the procession pass, it seemed that there could be no greater embodiment of success than these three all-powerful men.

God is an ironist; the next time I saw Yiorgos Kalianesis, thirty-three years later, the magnificent martial presence had been reduced to a harassed night clerk behind the desk of a third-rate hotel in Yannina. The balding, heavy-jowled former major general was almost pitifully eager to describe his wartime exploits to the American reporter who seemed so interested, but his tales of glory were constantly interrupted by shabby tourists with backpacks demanding the keys to their rooms.

The appearance of the three commanders outside the Gatzoyiannis gate set off a flurry of activity inside. Lieutenant Colonel Petritis hurried to join his superiors in the mountain heights, and as soon as he, his aide and orderly were packed, they left, never to return to the house.

Eleni stood on the veranda watching the column of battle-weary guerrillas retreating up the path toward the heights, some carrying wounded comrades, and imagined that she could read defeat in their faces. Just a glance to the south made it clear that the government troops had already taken the distant height of the Great Ridge as well as its two neighbors: Plokista and Taverra. The line of battle had moved into the foothills, ever closer to the village. She knew that men from Lia would be approaching with the government troops, perhaps among them some of those who had fled to Filiates: her father and her brothers-in-law Foto Gatzoyiannis and Andreas Kyrkas.

The moment was approaching that would decide her family's fate, for if the soldiers reached this high, Eleni knew she could escape with the children behind their lines, down into the foothills, across the Great Ridge and on to Filiates, where relatives and help would be waiting. From Filiates she had only to telegraph Christos, who would send them the money to come to America. But first they had to cross the battle line.

As she watched the retreat of the guerrillas past her door, Eleni was working out a plan. As soon as it became clear that the government soldiers might reach the edge of Lia, she would take her family down to her mother's empty house in the lower village to be that much closer to the soldiers and farther away from the guerrilla headquarters. If anyone questioned them, they had a logical excuse for the move; the Haidis house, in a small hollow in the hillside, was much less exposed to the nationalist guns, which would be aiming at the guerrilla headquarters in the Perivoli and above.

The whole family lay awake that night, listening to the sounds of battle approaching from the south, not suspecting that the most critical phase of the battle was taking place silently just to the north of them, on the other side of their own mountain. There, as soon as darkness fell, the three hundred expert commandos of the LOK brigade crept through the guerrilla lines led by an elderly shepherd who knew every foothold on the almost sheer face of the cliff called Skitari. The commandos had been equipped by the Americans with fur-lined jackets, heavy sweaters and rubber-soled boots that clung to the rocks and made no sound. They were divided into four companies, one led by a lieutenant named George Vorias. Just before dawn on March 3, his company achieved the summit of Skitari, directly across from the tallest peak of the Mourgana range.

As the mountains' silhouettes began to take shape against the deep-purple sky north of Lia, the darkness was suddenly alight with swooping green flares, arching across the heavens, washing the startled faces of the guerrillas in the trenches and the sleepless villagers in their windows with a deathlike pallor. It was the signal to the nationalist reinforcements that Skitari had been taken. Now the link-up with the approaching 628th battalion had to be quickly made, and the back of the guerrilla forces would be broken. The battle was all but over.

The villagers stared at the green flares in confusion, but the guerrillas were galvanized into action. They realized that the nationalist forces had crossed their lines and come upon them from the north while they were concentrating on the south. A desperate race began; the guerrillas from all over the Mourgana dashed for Skitari, trying to surround and isolate the commandos on the height before reinforcements could reach them. Even the security guards protecting the three commanders were thrown into the race, sprinting over the top of the Prophet Elias toward Skitari.

When Eleni saw the green flares and the panic of the guerrillas she understood that the moment for escape had come. She shook the children awake and told them to get ready to move down to Megali's house in the lower village. She warned them to take nothing, only enough food for a day, so as not to arouse the guerrillas' suspicions. But when their mother wasn't looking, Olga tucked her favorite red kerchief in the bosom of her dress and Kanta put on two lace shifts under her clothes.

Just as they were ready to leave, there was a knock at the door. A guerrilla was standing there with a heavy bag of flour on his back. 'Where do you think you're going?' he demanded.

'We were moving down to my mother's house in the lower village, where we'll be safer from the mortars,' Eleni replied.

He made a sound of exasperation. 'We're fighting for our lives here! The men need food as much as ammunition and every house in the Perivoli has to provide bread today. Now get to work!'

As soon as he was gone, Eleni sent the rest of the family on ahead, with instructions to wait for her at the Haidis house. When she was finished baking, she would join them. They could escape that night after dark. With Megali and Nitsa in the lead, the children started down the path, drawing together every time a mortar from the distant ridge made its screaming arc over their heads, to explode in the cliffs above the Perivoli.

While Eleni and the other women of her neighborhood baked bread, the LOK commandos on top of Skitari fought for their lives. The Communists had arrived within an hour of the flares, surrounding the hill at dawn with several units. One unit climbed the peak directly across from Vorias' company, and so close they could shout across the void that separated them. Lieutenant George Vorias frantically telephoned for the reinforcements expected from the 628th battalion, but was told that it was pinned down three miles below in the foothills.

The guerrillas on the opposite peak included many *andartinas,* some from Lia. They found a ration tin on a dead commando with chocolate inside, and one of the young women guerrillas ate the candy and shouted, 'Hey, ass-kissers of Frederika! You fight on chocolate rations, I see! Tonight we'll have you all eating shit!'

As the day passed, the commandos stranded on top of

Skitari suffered heavy casualties, but the guerrillas, who had far more machine guns, could not cross the narrow incline that separated the two peaks. Vorias counted eight of his eighty-five men dead and twenty-four wounded, including a soldier from Skiathos named Katsibaris, who had a gaping wound in his chest and was bellowing with pain, the sound of his cries demoralizing the trapped commandos even more than the heavy fire. 'Don't yell so loud,' Vorias ordered the soldier. 'The guerrillas can hear you!' The prone figure fell silent, then gathered the last of his strength to channel his cries of pain into defiant singing. He shouted out a klephtic song. 'Somewhere a mother sighs,' he trumpeted, and kept singing until he died.

The commandos radioed for air support, but when their planes tried to drop ammunition, heavy winds carried the bundles northward, into the hands of the guerrillas. As the sun passed its meridian, they rationed the supply of ammunition. The guerrillas on the opposite peak began to plan a nighttime attack on Skitari.

In the cellar of the Haidis house while they waited for their mother to join them, the Gatzoyiannis children huddled together, separated from the skittish goats and sheep by a wooden divider. They tried to ignore the sibilant passage of the mortars overhead, rising from a distant low whine into an ear-shattering scream before the sudden detonation shook the ground beneath them. Kanta was clenching her hands in her lap to hide their trembling. All the terrors of her guerrilla training had returned with the artillery barrage. She kept imagining a mortar falling short of the target and landing on the roof. But she knew her mother was in far worse danger in the Perivoli. Olga tried to amuse the younger children with tales of what they would do once they got to America. Nitsa kept interrupting with groans that the trauma of battle would drive her to a miscarriage. Megali rocked back and forth in a corner, addressing her absent husband. 'Soul of the devil!' she wailed. 'How could you leave me to die like this?'

By late afternoon the mortar shells were pounding the Perivoli with unrelenting fury as a cover for the nationalists'

625th battalion, which had crossed the foothills, climbed the haunch of the Mourgana and was launching a direct attack on the village of Lia.

The government soldiers approached the village in two groups, one entering at the easternmost point, near the Church of Aghia Paraskevi (St. Friday), the other creeping up below the burned-out shell of the Church of the Virgin on the southern boundary, just above the house of Eleni's sister-in-law Alexo.

When the sunlight began to fade from the Haidis cellar, the wan glow of the one kerosene lamp gave a comforting intimacy to the faces grouped around it. Nikola thought it was a fine adventure. A war raged outside, where mighty deeds were being done; inside, he lay on a blanket spread over a compost heap of manure and straw which gave off a comforting warmth that made him drowsy. The heavy odor made him think of roasting chestnuts as he listened to the high-pitched singsong of his eldest sister's voice hymning the wonders of America. His only concern, teasing at the edge of his consciousness, was the absence of his mother. As soon as she arrived, his circle of security would be complete and he could fall asleep.

A great thump on the cellar door brought them all to their feet. Olga opened it to find two excited, dirt-stained guerrillas holding guns. 'We're evacuating the lower village!' they shouted. 'Everyone has to leave and move in with someone higher up. The fascists are nearly here! Get out now!'

The door slammed, leaving the family in a frenzy of indecision. If they climbed back up to their house, they'd lose their chance to escape; besides, no one wanted to hazard the mountain path in the dark under that blitz of artillery shells. Megali flatly refused to abandon her house, and Nitsa set up a keening wail. Olga suggested they make a run for their aunt Alexo's house, at the very bottom of the village, but Kanta insisted that it would be suicide trying to cross the battle lines. Finally someone thought of a solution that seemed safer. They would go to the Botsaris house and ask for sanctuary. It lay just above them and to the east, right across the path that divided the upper village from the lower.

Since Alexandra Botsaris had brought her starving children there, fleeing the 1941 famine in Athens, the hovel had been patched up. Angeliki had moved in to be with her widowed mother after her husband fled to join the nationalist forces. Angeliki still faced life with the same irrepressible spirit that had made her a favorite with the British commandos. She, too, would be hoping to escape to her husband on the other side, the Gatzoyiannis children knew, and would surely help them get away when the right moment came.

The children gathered up their things and prepared to dash the hundred yards to the Botsaris house, but Fotini hung back and began to cry. 'What about Mother?' she quavered. 'She'll come looking for us and we won't be here!'

'As soon as we get to Angeliki's, I'll go up to the house and tell her where we are,' Olga reassured her.

Holding hands, they emerged into a landscape out of hell. Artillery shells whispered and shrieked over their heads in red arcs; trees that had been hit by shells smoldered, the bitter smoke of battle burned their nostrils, and the distant rumble of the mortars shook the ground like the approach of a huge train. From the east, near the Church of St. Friday, where guerrillas and soldiers were mixed in hand-to-hand combat, machine guns crackled like a distant bonfire, punctuated by the occasional hollow pop of a grenade.

As they ran, there was the hard, slapping sound of mortar fire and the accelerating whine of a shell coming much too close. The scream grew, stopping them in their tracks. They looked around in confusion, then threw themselves on the earth. Kanta had been taught how to fall by the guerrillas. 'On your belly!' she shouted as the shell began its descending whine, but she saw Glykeria with her head down between her knees like an ostrich and her rear end sticking up in the air. 'Get your ass down, for Christ's sake!' Kanta screamed.

The explosion stunned them, as shrapnel and dirt clattered over their head. Then there was silence. They tensed for another blast, waited, then lifted their heads and looked around. Pell-mell they sprinted toward the pale light that glowed from the cellar window of the Botsaris house, hurling themselves in a crowd against the door.

Angeliki, swollen with pregnancy, was with her terrified mother and her screaming two-year-old daughter in the cellar. She pulled them inside, delighted to have their company during the hours ahead. She had a feeling that her husband was with the attackers, Angeliki said, and would come for her.

'We're going too!' Olga cried. 'But first we've got to find *Mana*. The guerrillas have her baking bread up in the Perivoli, but we've got to get ready to leave. They'll be here soon.'

The twilight was almost gone, and in the rank, steamy cellar, during lulls in the gunfire, they could hear the two armies taunting one another through their bull horns. 'Fascists! Cuckolds!' screamed the guerrillas, two words which rhyme in Greek. The nationalist soldiers' reply sounded just as close: 'We'll take your heads back to Yannina for souvenirs.'

Nikola shivered, knowing that the soldiers often collected enemy heads as war trophies.

'They're nearly in the ravine!' Olga cried. 'I've got to get *Mana*!'

'You can't go out in that!' Megali shrieked. 'You won't get ten feet from the door alive!'

'I'll just go as far as the Makos house and shout for her from there,' Olga said.

She slipped out of the door into the peak of the battle. The mortars and machine guns were concentrated on the Perivoli, and the racket of small-arms fire filled the village center. Bullets hissed by her head as she ran, hands pressed over her ears, praying to the saints for an invisible shield. She reached the edge of the Makos field, built on a projection of land over the ravine, where she could see her own house looming a hundred yards farther up, occasionally illuminated by the Stygian glow of a flare. There was no light inside. Cupping her hands over her mouth, Olga waited for a lull, then screamed, 'Ooohhh, *Mana*! Ooohhh, *Mana*!' There was no answer.

When the artillery shells began to rake the Perivoli, exploding all around her, Eleni had bolted from her door and run the fifty feet to the house just above, where she knew that

Marina Kolliou was also baking. The two women clutched each other, and leaving the bread to its fate, crowded into the storage hole under the trap door in the kitchen to wait out the bombardment. From their hiding place there was no way Eleni could hear her daughter calling.

Olga screamed for her mother until her throat was raw and tears streamed down her face. Giving up, she crouched under the swarm of bullets and scurried back down to the Botsaris house, where she collapsed in sobs, gasping that their mother was probably dead. Her announcement set off a general outburst of hysterics. Nikola retreated into the farthest corner, huddling with his hands pressed over his ears, trying to block out what his sisters were saying about his mother being shot.

By the time it was completely dark, the guerrillas and the nationalist soldiers in the eastern section of the village were fighting hand to hand, house to house, many *andartes* firing from the protection of the pillboxes. The guerrillas on the heights of the Perivoli were answering the nationalist artillery fire with such ferocity that the soldiers couldn't advance beyond the ravine that divided the eastern half of the village from the west.

Eleni stayed in the storage hole beneath Marina Kolliou's kitchen, waiting for a pause in the shooting, until it was an hour past sunset and she knew she couldn't wait any longer to join her children in the Haidis house if they were to escape. She ignored the warnings of her friend and wrapped her black kerchief around her face to make herself nearly invisible in the dark. She crept down to her house, jumped from her back garden down the terraced fields, circling west as she descended, away from the worst of the shooting, and then back east. She arrived at the Haidis house, only to find it locked and empty. In a panic she walked around it, pounding on the cellar windows, but the blows resounded in the tomblike darkness.

Her children had been swallowed up in this Armageddon! Eleni ran out the gate and over to the home of her friend Vasiliki Petsis, just to the east, but it was empty too. Then, on the other side of the path that divided the village, she glimpsed a faint light in the cellar window of the tinker Yiorgios

Mallios. She scrambled up to his cellar door and began pounding and shouting. When it opened, she saw that the tiny space was crowded with people who stared fearfully out of the darkness, lighted by one candle. Vasiliki Petsis was there, but as Eleni pushed into the crowd, she found no sign of her children's faces.

'The guerrillas came around evacuating everyone from the lower village,' said Vasiliki. 'That's why I'm here and the Haidis house is empty. But who knows where your family went? The guerrillas said the soldiers have already taken the Church of the Virgin. Your sister-in-law is below it, so perhaps they made a dash for her house.'

Eleni realized that she must be right; they had already moved down to the bottom of the village to wait for her on the very edge of freedom with her sister-in-law Alexo. But they were risking their lives crossing the ravine on the very edge of the battle zone. She took a deep breath and turned to go. If the children could do it, she could too. Perhaps she'd catch up with them on the way. Once they got to Alexo's alive, the road to freedom stretched easily in front of them.

Even in the dark Eleni knew the path through the Haidis bean field, down into the ravine and across the small wooden footbridge over the stream. She would have to climb up the other side of the crevasse, which would bring her dangerously close to the fighting, and angle off to the south, following the path that hung on the edge of the gorge until she came out at Alexo's house.

The lower she descended into the chasm toward the sound of running water, the safer she felt, for now the long-range artillery and mortar shells were arcing high over her head, still pounding away at the Perivoli, and to her ears it seemed that the hand fighting had come no farther westward than the village schoolhouse in the square. As she climbed the other side of the ravine, Eleni could see from that direction the flames of burning buildings and the firefly glimmers of bullets. She headed south on the narrow footpath that edged the top of the ravine, picking her way carefully, for one misstep would send her tumbling down into the chasm. Occasionally she dislodged a stone or clump of earth and heard it bouncing several times before splashing into the water below. She kept her left hand out, touching the hillside that rose beside the path, ready to grasp a branch if she started to slip.

Now and then a red tracer flare illuminated the landscape and she would shrink back into the shadows of the vegetation. Just as Eleni reached the last outward curve in the footpath before her sister-in-law's land, she drew back against the cliff, put her hand behind her to steady herself and touched someone's arm. She choked back a scream. The illumination of the flare was gone, but she could see a dark form, reclining in a half-sitting position against the hillside, loose-limbed, head lolling on its shoulder like a floppy rag doll. Eleni knew it was a corpse; she had felt the puttylike chill of the flesh beneath the fabric. Her teeth began to chatter and she turned and ran, afraid now to steady herself against the cliff, stumbling along the narrow footpath by instinct.

The light in the window of Alexo's house pulled her on with the promise of her children waiting for her. She could hardly shout her name as she leaned on the door. When it was opened, she saw her sister-in-law's kind, worried face peering out, wide-eyed. 'Eleni, how did you ever get here?' Alexo exclaimed. 'And where are the children?'

She almost fell before Alexo caught her and carried her to a chair. Eleni looked weakly around the room. There were half a dozen neighbors there, besides Alexo's eleven-year-old daughter, Niki. Finally she managed to say, 'I thought the children had come here so that we could all leave together. If they aren't here, then I've lost them!'

Alexo brought a tiny glass of *raki* and held it to her lips. 'The soldiers have been here, right in the house,' she said. 'I asked if we should leave and they said to wait until morning. By then they'll have the whole village, Eleni. Stay with us until dawn, and then the guerrillas will be gone and you can find the children.'

'You don't know what it's like up there,' Eleni cried. 'I can't leave them lost in the middle of all this!' Her mind flashed from one disjointed image to another: the corpse she had touched, her children lying in a gully, bleeding, calling out to her, Nikola frightened and alone.

Alexo held her tight as she shivered. Finally the fit of weakness left her and she willed herself to go back out into the darkness.

'You'll be killed – someone will take you for a soldier!' Alexo protested as she stood up. When she saw Eleni wasn't listening, she brought her a torch – a piece of kindling from the fireplace, smoldering at one end – and told her to wave it as a signal flare so that the soldiers would realize she wasn't one of the enemy. Eleni took it gladly. Even a burning stick seemed like some sort of protection against the horror waiting in the night.

As she retraced her steps along the precipitous footpath, holding the torch in front of her, the sounds of battle seemed to be nearer. She tried not to imagine what the corpse would look like in the light of the torch, but she never got that far. A dark silhoutte stepped into her path and demanded, 'Who are you? Where are you going?' Eleni held up her flare and saw more dark figures, ranged all the way up the hill.

'Eleni Gatzoyiannis, wife of Christos, from the neighborhood of the Perivoli,' she said, pointing across the ravine. 'I'm trying to find my children.'

The figure came closer and she could see the crown insignia on his two-pointed hat. 'You can't go any farther,' he said. 'The guerrilla lines are all across the upper half of the village. From here to there is a firing range.'

'But my children are over there!' Eleni exclaimed.

'We'll have the whole village by morning,' said the soldier. 'Wait till then.'

Eleni turned back, but as soon as she was out of sight of the soldier, she began to clamber straight down the steep side of the chasm, braking her descent by holding on to bushes and scrub pine, lowering herself a foot at a time down the sheer drop toward the stream that sang so far below. Somehow she held on to the torch. When she was finally at the streambed, she plunged into the icy water and began to walk upstream, wading across at a shallow point and passing by the wooden footbridge. She continued walking against the current, until she had to start climbing up the cliff beside the waterfall, pulling herself up by the underbrush. Finally she emerged at the point where a path passed just above the Haidis house, dividing the village horizontally. From there she could see the guerrillas just below her, aiming down toward the nationalist soldiers. They were nearly shoulder to shoulder, some firing rifles, others feeding belts of ammunition into machine guns. Eleni realized she could never get to the Haidis house, now in the middle of no man's land. She looked around helplessly and saw a glimmer of light from the cellar of the Botsaris house just above her.

Wiping tears of exhaustion from her eyes, Eleni scrambled up to the Botsaris cellar door and pounded on it. She heard footsteps, then it opened a crack. There was a scream and the door flew open. She saw Olga standing there, and her knees buckled.

Eleni sat and shuddered convulsively while Nikola crowded into the circle of her arms. Slowly her joy at finding her children turned to anger. 'Do you know what you've put me through tonight?' Eleni cried. 'If you'd been in the Haidis house, the way we planned, we could be safe now and on our way to Filiates!'

'But the guerrillas wouldn't let us stay!' Olga protested. 'They evacuated the lower village. That's why we came here.' She explained how she had tried to call to Eleni from the Makos house. When Eleni understood, she scolded her daughter for taking such a risk.

'But now that you've come and we're all together, we can leave!' Olga said.

Eleni shook her head. 'It's impossible! There's no way all of us could make it alive through the guerrilla lines. They're fighting shoulder to shoulder just below the house.' She stared into the shadows for a moment, thinking how close they had been to freedom, then she tightened her arms around Nikola. 'Never mind,' she said. 'We'll just have to wait and pray that the soldiers drive them up the mountain past us. Alexo said that by morning they'll have taken the whole village. We can leave then.'

The government soldiers never advanced beyond the lower boundary of the Haidis property. By 2 a.m. on March 3, the tide of battle had turned and the government troops were in retreat.

During the same night, the commandos lost the hill of Skitari. When darkness fell, Lieutenant Vorias discovered that he had only thirteen of his eighty-five men left; the rest had been killed, wounded or sent away carrying wounded comrades. When he asked for reinforcements from the LOK companies fighting lower down the hill, he learned that they had gone. After digging a trench in the snow to bury the dead, Vorias and his surviving men rolled down the steep face of the height until they reached a ravine and escaped to the southeast. Operation Pergamos had failed.

In the morning, as the villagers of Lia ventured out into the first daylight, the stink of gunpowder hung in the air and they saw the mountainside below their village littered with bodies and the refuse of battle. The soldiers had been driven all the way down to the rise of St. Marina in the foothills, where they were still being pounded by the guerrilla artillery.

The all-clear came at dawn as the guerrillas walked through the village shouting over bull horns that the fascists had been triumphantly driven back in retreat and that everyone could return to their homes. Exhausted, the Gatzoyiannis family retraced their steps to the Haidis house. The children still hoped that the soldiers might make another advance, but Eleni suspected that their last chance at escape had slipped through their grasp.

Nitsa, Megali and the children lay down on their pallets as soon as they entered the house, but Eleni was too troubled to sleep. She went next door to share her sorrow with Vasiliki Petsis. The two women sat on the steps, talking in low voices, wondering if the battle was truly over. From the corner of her eye Eleni saw a movement near the path and put a warning hand on Vasiliki's knee.

'Who's in there?' Vasiliki demanded. Out of the bush popped the frightened face of a young man, his brown hair matted with bits of leaves and twigs. When he stood up, the two women saw that he was wearing the khaki uniform of the nationalist army. 'Help me, ladies!' he pleaded. 'Tell me

318

which way the soldiers went. I've lost my company!'

Eleni and Vasiliki stared. The boy was swaying with fatigue and fear, but he didn't seem to be wounded.

'They've gone,' Vasiliki whispered. 'Go straight down the ravine. And be careful!'

The soldier stiffened as they heard footsteps approaching. Up the path came the figure of Spiros Christos, the village blacksmith, who was climbing from his home on the other side of the ravine toward the Perivoli. He stopped, examined the young man curiously and asked, 'What have we here?'

'A lost soldier,' Vasiliki replied.

The blacksmith blinked, then recovered his composure. 'Stay right where you are,' he said. 'I saw some soldiers going up the hill. I'll find them and bring them here.' He took one more look to make sure the boy was real, then hurried off.

The women glanced at each other, then Vasiliki burst out in an urgent whisper, 'Run, boy! He's gone to fetch the guerrillas! Run or you're dead!'

The soldier took off down the ravine like a startled quail. Minutes later, when half a dozen *andartes* led by the blacksmith crashed down the path into the yard, the two women spread their hands. 'We tried to keep him here,' said Vasiliki, 'but he went running off.'

She was pointing toward the spring above the ravine. Soon the women could hear the *andartes* calling to one another and beating the bushes with their rifles.

At guerrilla headquarters high above the Perivoli, the two commanders and Lieutenant Colonel Petritis had their heads bent over a map. Although they had successfully driven the enemy out of the Mourgana, there was still the danger of a counterattack. More than 3,000 soldiers, twice their own manpower, were reassembling in the foothills below. It was necessary to strike a decisive blow before the enemy could marshal their forces.

The guerrilla leaders decided on an offensive maneuver against the enemy's left flank which would be launched that night. The key element was surprise. They would send four companies, under the command of the fiery Major Spiro

319

Skevis, to attack Povla, the village on the southern rim of the bowl of mountains which the national forces had captured and secured several days before. Povla was occupied by the government's 611th battalion, and the slopes on the west of the village were in the hands of a detachment of seasoned irregulars under the command of a notorious Cretan with a bristling mustache named Mitsos Galanis.

Galanis had hand-picked the 250 men in his detachment, who wore distinctive green berets and shoulder patches with the special insignia of an attacking eagle. The Communists called Galanis 'the Butcher,' and the tales of his brutality were legion. Decades after the war Galanis himself insisted that the atrocities attributed to him, such as cutting off the genitals of prisoners and stuffing them into their mouths, were groundless. He admitted, however, that he never took prisoners alive. His victims were often decapitated and their heads sent by the sackful with couriers to Yannina, where they were displayed in rows in the courtyard of division headquarters.

To take Povla, Spiro Skevis would have less than half of the enemy's manpower – only 300 guerrillas against 700 soldiers – but he was eager to launch the attack and could hardly wait for nightfall. After dark he silently led his men through the bitter cold to the very edge of Povla, sending some behind the Albanian border where they circled around to seize the undefended hills south of the village.

The nationalist soldiers, having eaten and drunk well, were asleep at two-thirty when Skevis gave the command: 'On them!' The devil's own host seemed to have fallen out of the sky, guerrillas breaking down every door, fighting hand to hand with knives as well as guns. The soldiers, wrenched from sleep, were thrown into confusion and easily captured, but on the hills outside the village, Galanis and all but thirteen of his men managed to escape.

Several dozen soldiers inside Povla tried to take refuge in the village church and were caught by the company of Harisis Stravos, the convicted murderer who had broken his pistol in a rage. Like Galanis on the government side, Stravos did not believe in taking prisoners. He lined up the soldiers inside the church and stabbed each one in turn until the floor was awash with blood.

Other guerrilla captains took their prisoners alive. When Skevis' four companies marched away the next morning toward Tsamanta, leaving Povla's paths and doorways choked with corpses, they were herding 177 bound soldiers in front of them.

In Tsamanta four officers among the prisoners were tried and executed and the rest were given a choice: take up a rifle and join the guerrilla army, or turn in their uniforms for rags and return to their homes. Most of them took the latter course and were led away, but once out of sight, they disappeared and were never seen by their families again. Twenty-three years later a shepherd found a partially buried skeleton on a stream bank near an old lime pit outside of town. The lime pit gave up 120 skeletons, each one with its hands bound with wire and a bullet hole in the skull.

On the morning of March 5 the guerrillas of Lia announced the brilliant success of the attack on Povla with raucous exultation, filling the village with singing, shouting and announcements over the bull horns. But for the next few days, as the civilians moved about in a limbo of uncertainty and rumor, the most interesting news did not come from the bull horns, but from village gossip. It was learned that during the battle one man, a tinker named Elia Poulos, had crossed over from the government soldiers' side to join the guerrillas in Lia.

While Elia Poulos sneaked into the village, three women who lived in the easternmost part of Lia succeeded where the Gatzoyiannis family had failed and, one by one, crept out during the confusion of the battle and its aftermath. Although the guerrillas said nothing officially about the three women's escape, the villagers whispered about it for days, many jealous that they had not had the courage or opportunity to do the same. The guerrilla lookouts at observation points around the village were doubled to prevent any further defections, and Eleni knew that her best chance to get her family out of Lia had been lost.

About five days after the battle at Povla, the church bells

commanded the Liotes to a compulsory gathering unlike any they had seen before. Instead of dances, songs and skits, there was a real-life drama to entertain them. They assembled in the Alonia to find four men seated on chairs. The three on the left were strangers in fine civilian clothes. On a solitary chair on the right slumped a barefoot soldier, his feet swollen and discolored, his uniform torn, hands tied in front of him.

When all the villagers had gathered, staring in silence, one of the men stood up. Because of his theatrical gestures, neat appearance and stirring speaking voice, he would have been well cast as a cantor in the church. In fact, he was a former justice of the peace from Konitsa who now served the judiciary branch of the guerrillas' Epiros Command as an investigating magistrate and military judge. He had just come from trying and convicting the four nationalist officers captured at Povla. He was tall, with a pronounced Roman nose, abnormally small ears and receding salt-and-pepper hair. The moment he spoke, in a deep, sonorous voice that reached the farthest corners of the square, everyone fell silent. Even the shackled soldier looked up, startled. It was the first time any of them had heard the voice of 'Katis,' an Albanian word meaning 'judge.'

When Eleni saw the prisoner's face, a thrill of fear shot down her back. It was the same boy she had seen in Vasiliki Petsis' yard, the one who had been lost from his company. She caught Vasiliki's eye and bit her lower lip, meaning that they were in trouble.

The judge with the remarkable voice announced that the villagers of Lia were to witness the execution of people's justice. This traitor, apprehended within the boundaries of the village after the abortive attack by the fascists, was to be put to a people's trial.

No one knew what he was talking about. The Liotes had never seen a trial before and had no idea what role each of the men before them – except for the prisoner – was playing. The tall man who seemed to be in charge read off the defendant's crimes from a piece of paper. Then he turned to the bound soldier and began to ask questions, which the young man

322

answered hesitantly, like a student trying to pass an examination for which he has not prepared.

The soldier's first name was Evangelos, Eleni learned – she didn't catch the rest – and he was charged with betraying Greece and its people over the past five years, first as a member of the forces of the collaborationist Zervas during the occupation and now as a soldier in the monarcho-fascist army.

'Is it true that you fought with Zervas?' Katis asked.

The soldier nodded, staring at the speaker's lips, unconscious of the crowd around him.

'Did you go with Zervas willingly or by force?' demanded Katis.

'I volunteered,' replied the soldier uncertainly, 'but I have a wife and a little boy to support and I needed the money.'

After more questions Katis finally seemed satisfied. He put the paper down and signaled to the other two men, who got up from their chairs and went with him behind the huge plane tree at the edge of the square. While they whispered together, the congregation of villagers studied the prisoner, who was twisted around in his chair staring at the spot where the three men had disappeared. His face was pale as parchment and his hair stuck in clumps to his brow. His eyes had been blackened and there were livid red and purple marks on his face. His breath was coming in audible gasps.

After a few minutes the three men returned and took their seats. Katis stood up. 'It is the judgment of the people's court that this traitor is guilty,' he announced. 'The sentence is death.'

There was a crash as the soldier suddenly slid off his chair, knocking it over. Two guerrillas stepped forward and pulled him up, each with a hand under his armpit, while a third righted the chair. But they had to stand behind the prisoner and hold his shoulders to keep him from falling off again.

One of the guerrillas, trying to calm him, produced a cigarette and stuck it between the man's lips, then reached for a match, but the cigarette fell to the ground. The guerrilla put it to the prisoner's mouth again, but it fell once more and, disgusted, he wiped the saliva off and put it back in his own pocket.

Everyone watched silently, waiting to see what the next act in the drama would be. 'Haven't there been enough deaths?' said an old man's voice. It was the farmer Sioli Skevis, the father of Spiro and Prokopi Skevis.

Katis, the judge, turned on the grizzled old man. 'Just because you have a son in command doesn't mean you can meddle with justice,' he snapped. 'What we're carrying out here is the will of the people, who will not tolerate traitors. Ask your neighbors what they want. Their decision will be respected. Four men from Lia died during the occupation, killed by Zervas' bullets, perhaps from this man's gun. Should he be allowed to live?'

Katis searched the crowd, choosing his jury carefully. He found Calliope Bardaka, the plump, pretty young widow whose husband had disappeared carrying a message to ELAS troops during the occupation. 'Your husband died at the hands of Zervas' mercenaries,' Katis thundered, 'leaving you alone with starving babies. What do you say we should do to him?'

'Kill him!' Calliope replied without hesitation.

'And you?' Katis asked, turning to Elia Poulos, the tinker who had returned to Lia during the battle as the nationalist troops were retreating. 'What do you say?'

'Kill him!' exclaimed Elia Poulos.

Katis' eyes ranged around the crowd. Eleni shrank back, willing him not to look at her. His gaze came to rest on Spiro Michopoulos, the tubercular coffeehouse owner who had been appointed president of the village by the guerrillas. Michopoulos looked confused.

'You, Mr. President,' Katis persisted, 'what do you say is this man's proper fate?'

'Why, ah – whatever the people's court decides,' stammered Michopoulos, looking around for help.

'That's not good enough, Comrade!' snapped Katis. 'Should we execute him or not?'

There was a long pause, then the villagers heard Michopoulos answer faintly, 'Yes.'

324

Katis repeated his question several times more, selecting his witnesses. Each time he received the same answer.

As the polling went on, the prisoner searched the respondents' faces earnestly, as if he expected someone to speak for him, but his hopes faded with each reply. Eleni was perspiring, trying to think what she would say if the judge called on her.

Katis' small bright eyes came closer as he studied each face in turn. Then he stopped. He was pointing at Stavroula Yakou, who was standing only inches away from her. 'Your sister is fighting as an *andartina* for the Democratic Army,' Katis shouted at Stavroula, 'and this man was one of those who came here to kill her. What do you say his fate should be?'

Stavroula blushed, the sun reflecting on her wheat-colored hair, partly hidden by the cornflower-blue kerchief. She had never looked more beautiful, like an image of the Virgin on an icon. The soldier in the chair stared at the apparition, filled with sudden hope. Stavroula looked straight back at the judge and raised her chin.

'Kill him,' she said.

CHAPTER ELEVEN

Pedomasoma is a compound word that literally means 'the gathering up of children.' It entered the Greek vocabulary in March of 1948, when the Communist Provisional Government announced a new policy over its radio: all children between the ages of three and fourteen in the occupied regions of northern Greece would be collected and sent to 'people's democracies' behind the Iron Curtain that had offered to take them in. According to the announcement, this decision was made in order to protect the children in the war zones from cruelties perpetrated by the attacking fascist soldiers: hunger due to crop destruction, bombings and lootings.

This newest move of the 'government' of Markos Vafiadis was intended to be a brilliant propaganda coup. It would dramatize to the world the dangers imposed on civilians by the Greek armed forces and win international sympathy for the guerrillas. Furthermore, having their children held hostage in Communist bloc countries would ensure the loyalty of parents left behind in the mountain villages. And finally, the children would be indoctrinated in the party's philosophy and grow to provide future Greek Communist cadres of young militants.

It was a propaganda move that backfired prodigiously. At first the foreign correspondents of the international press, many of whom covered the war from the bar of the Grande-Bretagne Hotel in Athens, portrayed the *pedomasoma* as an authentically humanitarian move and dismissed reports that the children were being abducted. But as more and younger children were taken from their mothers, the United Nations condemned the *pedomasoma,* and the Athens government effectively used the program to help turn international opinion against the insurgents. Domestically, the abduction of the children to Eastern Europe added credibility to the government's charge that the guerrillas were betraying Greece to Slavic interests.

The abduction of their children was the final straw that turned the people of the occupied villages against the guerrillas and eroded the wide base of popular support that they had once enjoyed in northern Greece. Growing incidences of violence by the guerrillas added to the disenchantment of the civilians.

By the end of 1948 more than 28,000 Greek children had been taken away from their parents to camps throughout the Communist bloc. From the Mourgana villages, 300 children were sent to Albania, Bulgaria and Yugoslavia. Ten years would pass before the first children were allowed back into Greece. Many never returned. A dozen former children taken from Lia are still scattered in Communist countries from Poland to Rumania to Tashkent. Nevertheless, many Greek Communists insist today that there was never such a thing as the *pedomasoma,* and that no children were removed against their parents' will.

The program was, in fact, voluntary at first, but after a month, only 1,100 children from Greece were sent willingly by their parents to the Iron Curtain camps. The guerrillas hadn't reckoned on the deep-rooted Greek tradition of family solidarity. Even after eight years of war and famine the women of the mountain villages could not be induced to hand over their children to strangers in foreign lands. Finally the guerrillas decided that more stringent measures of collecting the children had to be initiated.

HOSTAGES TO FATE

IN LATE MARCH of 1948, as the villagers of Lia began planting the early beans, onions and corn, they saw the guerrillas at the village boundaries and down in the foothills planting another sort of crop: land mines, designed to blossom instantaneously under the weight of a human body into the red flower of death.

The nearly successful attack on the Mourgana earlier in the month and the escape of three village women had taught Lia's occupiers a lesson. They were determined to plug up the Mourgana villages like a corked wine jug so that no one could get in or out. It seemed certain that the attack of Operation Pergamos would be repeated, so all likely paths of approach throughout the foothills and up the ravines were heavily mined. The twenty-four-hour guards posted at lookout points throughout the village were strengthened to prevent any more embarrassments like the three escapes.

Eleni forbade her children to leave the yard for fear that a careless step would trigger a mine. Throughout the Mourgana the peasants became very careful where they put their feet down. But the inevitable happened in the neighboring village of Babouri. A group of local boys had been ordered to drive a herd of mules to Tsamanta for the guerrillas. Their leader, a slow-witted young man, stepped off the road to answer a call of nature and both his legs were blown off. The smaller boys managed to carry him back to the house of Eleni's cousin Antonova Paroussis, on the western edge of Babouri, but he died there, cursing and gushing his life's blood all over the floor while her small children watched.

328

The political commissar of the Mourgana, Kostas Koliyiannis, felt that land mines and more lookouts were not enough to guarantee the complete 'cooperation' of the villagers of Lia. He decided to establish a security police station in the village like the one that existed in Babouri. He needed to find a house large enough to contain the police office, interrogation rooms and a secure cellar for a jail. The only house in Lia of adequate size belonged to the Amerikana.

One morning in mid-March, Eleni opened her gate to find Sotiris Drapetis standing there. The sight of the reptilian eyes in the lean, handsome face made her throat tighten, remembering the day he had torn her home apart searching for guns.

Sotiris informed Eleni that the Democratic Army required her house for its new police station. For security reasons, no civilians could be allowed to remain living in it. She would have twenty-four hours to find another dwelling for her family.

She knew there was only one place left for them to go; the two-room house of her parents, which had been empty ever since Megali was beaten up by Sotiris' henchmen and came to live with her daughter.

Overnight the Gatzoyiannis family prepared to move out of the Perivoli into the lower village. Besides the fourteen goats, their sleeping blankets, clothes and some corn, there was not much to salvage. Sotiris ordered Eleni to leave the sewing machine and the gramophone behind; they were needed by the Democratic Army. She wrapped the photograph of Christos and the golden pitcher from Constantinople in some clothing, then silently began to take leave of the house where she had spent the twenty-two years of her marriage. She had given birth to her children and watched her mother-in-law die in these rooms. It was like leaving part of her body behind.

Eleni stood for a while before the corner iconostasis, where she crossed herself first thing every morning and last thing every night. She walked around, touching the luxuries which had made her house the finest in the village: the brass bed, the built-in shoe rack, the ingenious water supply of hanging barrels outside the kitchen, the huge gate with its brass handles and doorbell, the carved fireplace with her husband's name on it. She looked for the last time out the window at the view of the valleys and mountains to the south. She would never see the horizon from this perspective again. It was only a fifteen-minute walk down the mountain to where she was going, but it seemed half the world away.

Each of the daughters said goodbye in her own fashion to the house where she had been born. Olga collected her dowry from its hiding place in Rano and Tassina's house, lovingly wrapped it in a tarpaulin and carried it down to her grandmother's. Fotini clutched the small sack of baubles that she had been given by the commissary head, Hanjaras. Nikola silently walked around outside, paying a last visit to the places which were as familiar to him as his mother's face.

Leaving the house was the first major dislocation in my life. Invaders, battles, bombs, executions and famine had afflicted Lia in the eight years since I was born, but every day I had awakened to see the same view of the mountains below, with the mulberry tree in the foreground, and every night I had fallen asleep by the same hearth with my mother and sisters around me. I knew every inch of the Perivoli; where each chicken hid its eggs, when every tree would flower and bear fruit and where the crows would land to peck for food and perhaps blunder into one of my crude traps. I passed the spot in the garden where I had built my unsuccessful swimming pool and visited the hay shed up above the mill of the Mitros family where I once watched a newlywed couple, seeking privacy from their relatives, engaged in mysterious acrobatics which I described to my family with such vivid mimicry and sound effects that my recitation became an instant success throughout the Perivoli.

I took a last look at the hillocks and low walls where the boys of the neighborhood had played war. There were no boys my age living near my grandparents' house, and although I had never managed to win the admiration of Niko Mitros, I would miss the companionship of the neighborhood boys, even the crybaby Lakis, who was, in fact, my closest friend.

I knew my house and my yard as thoroughly as a prisoner knows his cell, and now that we were to leave, I felt the same foreboding a prisoner might have at suddenly finding his cell door open. My grandparents' house seemed a sinister place to me, because, even with my grandfather gone, his stern, threatening presence still filled every cranny.

The move from the security of the Perivoli to the Haidis house lower down was the first rent in the fabric of my life, more disturbing to me than the great move that would come later, from Greece to America. By then it didn't matter what place I left and where I went, because there was no longer a corner left in the world that could seem secure.

The next morning, three security officers arrived at the Gatzoyiannis house shortly after dawn. They were all large and muscular and had the cold eyes of police everywhere.

Worldlessly, the Gatzoyiannis family watched the men enter their house, accompanied by Sotiris Drapetis, who would be in charge of gathering intelligence in the village. Then, driving the animals ahead of them, they made the trip down from the Perivoli for the last time, never looking back.

The arrival of a security police station immediately made a subtle but pervasive change in the atmosphere of Lia. It brought the villagers heady new powers and a universal insecurity. Gossip had always been the spice that seasoned the drabness of village life and made it palatable. On a mountainside where each house overlooks the yard below, nothing can be hidden. If a woman fought with her husband or neglected to do her washing, if two men fell out over a backgammon game, everyone in the village would know it within twenty-four hours and argue the details for a week.

No one was immune to gossip. If a man was not ugly or short, a fool, a drunkard, a cheat, a miser or a cuckold – that is, if there was nothing reprehensible or in any way extraordinary about him – then he would be tarred with the brush of his clan. The grandfather of Lukas Ziaras, for example, had been a compulsive gambler, a slave to the dice, which is why his last name, Spiropoulos, was forgotten and replaced with *Ziaras*, meaning 'dice.' Forever afterward, the

331

Ziaras clan was suspected of having a weakness for gambling.

Village gossip had always been relatively harmless, but the police station suddenly gave it a new importance. Until the arrival of the police, no one really listened to the villagers' complaints against one another. Now a man could go to them and complain that his neighbor had chests full of corn while everyone else was going hungry, and the very next day a team of guerrillas would burst into the neighbors' house to confiscate all the corn. If a woman was tired of the constant work details and resenting the fact that her neighbor across the way was called less often, she might go to the security police and say that the other woman had put a stone in her mule's shoe to make it lame. The neighbor would promptly be arrested and led away. Neither of the informants was any better off than before, but it gave them a sense of power to see how easily their neighbors could be made to suffer. Every day the path to the Perivoli was busy with villagers who had some misbehavior to report, always with the insistence that their names be kept secret. The security police nodded and listened carefully, and after the informant left, they made notes and passed the information on to Sotiris, who wrote it all down in his notebook. Within weeks of the arrival of the security police, the village of Lia was engulfed in paranoia.

The police officers themselves encouraged this fear. They let it be known that favors would be granted to those who reported any words or actions that suggested lack of 'cooperation' with the guerrillas. Whenever two or more villagers were seen engaged in conversation, one of the officers would walk up and inquire what they were talking about. Furthermore, it was rumored that the police had Machiavellian machines that could hear the most intimate whispers right through the walls of houses. This was accepted as fact by the villagers, because visitors to the new police station had seen a heavy round machine with a hand crank sitting on the table emitting a sinister hum, no doubt storing up secrets and misdeeds in its insides. They didn't know that it was only a dry-cell battery to power the telephone.

Because the local men had fled in the wake of the guerrillas, Lia was primarily a village of women and children, so most of

332

the informers were female. Certain women were suspected of earning special favors not only by informing on their neighbors, but also by sharing the guerrillas' beds. Two women were most frequently accused of collaborating in this way. One was Calliope Bardaka, the pretty, round-faced young widow and devout Communist whose husband had disappeared in 1943, killed by EDES while delivering messages for ELAS, leaving her with two small children to feed. She was seen every day entering the security-police station and was often present as a witness when villagers were called in for questioning. The other was Stavroula Yakou Dangas, the village beauty whose husband Dimitri had returned to his bakery in Khalkis soon after the death of their baby son, abandoning her to the mercies of her mother-in-law. Although Dimitri Dangas was now fighting with the government forces, his wife was one of the strongest supporters of the guerrillas, who put her in charge of assigning village women and their mules to work details. Calliope Bardaka and Stavroula Yakou quickly became the most feared women in Lia.

The move to the Haidis house left the Gatzoyiannis family desperately short of food. In the Perivoli they had the produce from their garden and, surrounded as they had been by the army's slaughterhouse, bakery, commissary and warehouses, there were always ways to skim off a bit of the guerrillas' supplies now and then. Nearly every woman assigned to bake fourteen okas (about 40 pounds) of bread with a ten-oka sack of flour managed to hold back enough to make her own family one loaf, even though the guerrillas weighed the finished bread to prevent this. Hanjaras, the butcher, was not above slipping refuse meat – heads, tripe, brains and entrails – to children who begged winningly. A pretty young woman who was willing to flirt a little, like Rano Athanassiou, could convince the guerrillas to trade her a bit of flour, salt or soap in exchange for eggs.

One of Eleni's former neighbors was an expert at charming the guerrillas into giving her treats of food, until the presence of the security police dried up nearly all such under-the-table gifts. Kostina Thanassis was a plump, grandmotherly old woman with a jolly disposition whose house, just below the Gatzoyiannis home, was used to store supplies. Kostina fussed over the guerrillas as if they were her own sons, boiling their uniforms to kill the lice, darning their socks and playing on their homesickness. 'My golden boy, you're looking feverish!' she would croon. 'Let me brew you a cup of camomile tea. How your poor mother must be worrying about you!'

The guerrillas basked in Kostina's attentions, repaying her with gifts of unobtainable honey, marmalade and lard. Because the old woman had always made a special pet of Nikola Gatzoyiannis, she would occasionally walk down to the Haidis house with some of these precious items for the boy, which he would share with the whole family.

But without her garden and her proximity to the guerrillas' commissary, Eleni soon found herself with little corn flour and no salt at all. Kanta, still picky about food, stubbornly refused to eat the unsalted bread on the family's table. Her mother had exhausted her store of proverbs: 'Better today's bread than tomorrow's *pita*'; 'In a drought even a hailstorm is welcome.' Now, fixing the girl with a look that made her squirm, Eleni announced, 'Salt or no salt, you have to eat this bread to survive. And I'm going to see that you survive even if you have to eat roots and slugs!'

Nevertheless, her heart ached for the children as she watched them trying to choke down the tasteless bread. She confided her problem to Angeliki Botsaris Daikos, who lived just above the Haidis house.

'Come with me when I visit my Aunt Soula in the Perivoli,' said Angeliki, whispering in case any of the security police's listening devices were beamed her way. 'The guerrillas bake all their bread in her cooking shed, and I'm sure she could find you some salt.'

Eleni set out with Angeliki to climb the path to the Perivoli for the first time since the family was evicted. As she passed her own house she was shocked to see the pale faces of prisoners peering out of the small barred windows of her cellar, where the goats had been kept. Six guerrillas lounged about, standing guard. Eleni saw into the courtyard, where a woman in village dress, flanked by a girl of about thirteen, was talking earnestly to a group of guerrillas. The woman wore a long, red-bordered, sleeveless black tunic that showed she came from a village in the Pogoni region. The girl, with wavy russet hair, held her mother's hand. Eleni watched uneasily, assuming that they had come from a distant village to inquire about one of the prisoners. She moved closer, trying to eavesdrop, but one of the guards at the gate waved her away. 'Get along, there's nothing to look at here,' he ordered. As the two women quickened their pace, Eleni noticed that none of her former neighbors came out of their gates to greet her. A strange silence lay over her old neighborhood.

When they arrived at the house of Angeliki's aunt at the very top of the Perivoli, the comforting scent of baking bread and the warm welcome of Soula Botsaris lifted her uneasiness a little. Soula invited Angeliki and Eleni inside, and when she heard of Eleni's plight, disappeared, returning with a small cloth bag of salt. 'Don't talk about paying me!' she whispered. 'Neighbors have to help each other in difficult times. Just don't tell anyone where you got this.'

Suddenly a groan from the other room made the hairs on Eleni's arms rise. At first she thought it was a sick animal, but then the sound formed itself into a word: 'Water!'

Soula put her finger to her lips and motioned for them to peek through the keyhole into the other room. Eleni bent down to look and caught her breath. A man wearing the remains of a uniform lay on the floor inside, stretched out on a large wooden plank. His legs and arms were tied to the board with wire. He moved restlessly and Eleni saw that the wire had worked its way a half inch into the flesh of his ankles. His face was turned away but she could hear the nearly unintelligible moan: 'Water! Please, water!'

She turned to look at Soula and the woman whispered, 'It's one of the prisoners. They had too many to fit them all in your cellar.'

'For God's sake, can't you give him a little water?' Eleni demanded.

'Don't be stupid, child!' said the older woman in a suddenly

335

cold voice. 'If they caught me, I'd end up the same way he is.'

That night as the family crowded around to taste the fresh bread Eleni had baked with the salt, she watched them eat for a moment; then, in a voice that made them stop and look at her, she ordered the children never to climb the path to the Perivoli again. In answer to their questions she said only, 'Terrible things are happening up there. Everything's changed.'

Most of the children accepted Eleni's ultimatum without complaint. As respectable young women, Olga and Kanta were confined to the house anyway. Nikola and Fotini had become used to being allowed to play only within the boundaries of the Haidis land. Nikola had made the bean field below the house his private retreat and would often lie on his back there and watch the clouds scudding across the March sky. Because none of his friends came to visit, he had a lot of time to think.

But to fourteen-year-old Glykeria, who was incorrigibly curious, Eleni's warning was a challenge. One sunny afternoon when the rest were taking the siesta, she crept up the back gardens behind their old house to see what her mother meant. Climbing from one terraced field to another, she went as far as the retaining wall that bounded the lower edge of their property, and peered over, peeking at the side farthest from the path.

The air was sweet with the scent of the almond trees, and the breeze carried to her ears the rhythmic crunch of someone digging. As she poked her head higher over the wall, Glykeria saw a uniformed guerrilla standing in a deep hole shoveling dirt. On the far side of the hole stood two men, their hands behind them. In a flash the girl understood the tableau in front of her. The bound prisoners were going to be executed and the guerrilla was digging their grave before their eyes. She looked around and realized why the back garden seemed so different; it was studded with rectangles of newly turned soil – all graves.

Glykeria made a stifled sound; the guerrilla stopped digging and reached for the gun that lay on the ground. But she was already running as fast as her legs could carry her toward the

Haidis house. When she got inside, she guiltily picked up a broom and began sweeping the front steps, but her face and her unwonted industry gave her away. Eleni studied her, then said, 'All right, troublemaker! What have you been up to now?'

At first the girl protested weakly, then the whole story came out in a rush. Eleni pressed her lips together until there was a white rim around them, a habit she had when she was upset.

'I was lonesome for our house, so I went to visit it,' said Glykeria, near tears. 'But they're killing and burying people in our yard, *Mana*! I'll never go back there again!'

Eleni felt violated. The irony of it made her nauseated. She had forfeited her family's chances to leave the village ahead of the guerrillas in order to stay and protect that house, and now it had been turned into a prison, a killing ground. With the desecration of her home, she felt her last emotional tie to the village dissolve.

By the time spring set the Judas trees ablaze, executions were as much a part of village life as propaganda meetings had once been. The villagers plowed their fields and tended their crops and looked the other way. After all, only captured soldiers and strangers were being killed. In a civil war it was wisest not to inquire into such affairs, nor to tamper with the workings of the people's justice.

Only the children paid close attention to the executions, considering it a new form of entertainment. Nikola was not allowed to leave the yard, so he didn't understand where the bound, beaten prisoners that often passed by on the path were going, but other, less well supervised children quickly learned where they could hide to get a good view of the proceedings.

Only trials of important persons and those with propaganda value were held in the public square. Most executions were carried out in a much more summary way, with no witnesses other than the guerrillas involved and the children peeking from their hiding places. Many of the soldiers captured during the Pergamos campaign were executed in the cemetery behind the razed Church of the Virgin, at the southernmost boundary of the village, just before the mountain made a sharp drop toward the foothills below.

The children who lived in the few houses around the church would find vantage points high enough on the hillside so that the guerrillas couldn't drive them off by throwing stones. There they would cheer, hiss and boo like spectators at a football match as the condemned soldiers were forced to dig their own graves, then stand next to them to be shot. George Ziaras, the seven-year-old son of the tinker Lukas Ziaras, watched nearly every day with his six-year-old sister Olympia. George recalls that most of the prisoners died calling for their mother, but one imaginative soldier used his last second to scream: 'Uncle Leonidas!' In the stunned silence that followed, as the guerrillas looked at one another in surprise, the prisoner catapulted himself over the precipice in front of him and rolled out of sight to safety down the mountain. Of all the executions George Ziaras watched, that was his favorite.

Although Eleni tried to shield her children from knowledge of the killings going on around them, she didn't succeed. One day Kanta was sent out to graze the goats along with her friend Olympia Barkas and her family's flock. They took the path toward Babouri and let the animals wander down a ravine halfway between the two villages. Chattering away, the two girls walked with their eyes on the ground looking for the wild violet-blue tassel hyacinth and its white bulbous root, which they called 'turtledove's bread' because in the spring the birds pecked the tubers out of the ground. The villagers could wring nourishment out of dozens of wild plants: every part of the dandelion could be eaten; acorns and even pine cones were considered a delicacy. The white root called 'turtledove's bread' was one of Kanta's favorite treats, and she was hungry.

Walking with her eyes on the ground, the girl noticed a loose pile of rocks and stopped, paralyzed by what she saw. A human hand and arm projected from it. Kanta leaned down and frantically pulled up one flat rock and then another.

The woman in the red-bordered tunic was rigid in death, her arms spread open as if to embrace the sky, her eyes wide,

338

her lips drawn back into a grimace of terror. Kanta felt the thin saliva in her mouth that meant she was going to vomit. She turned to scream for Olympia, who was following the goats. Then she saw another body; a young girl lying with her head on one shoulder as if asleep, the aureole of her wavy hair glinting copper in the sunlight, her skin still pale-pink. She looked like a sleeping child, and Kanta involuntarily reached out and touched her cheek, then jerked her hand back. The body was warm. She found her voice. 'Olympia! Olympia!' she screamed. By the time her friend was close enough to see the two bodies she was screaming too, but Kanta had regained her senses. She crouched over the body of the girl. 'Hush!' she hissed at Olympia. 'That one's dead but this one is still alive! We've got to get help!'

A rustling in the bushes nearby made them both spin around with a shriek. Slowly two guerrillas who had been hiding there rose, their rifles pointed at Kanta and Olympia. Without a word they motioned with the gun barrels, signaling them to move on.

Kanta stood up, still feeling the warmth of the girl's cheek on her fingertips. She looked at Olympia, then both girls bolted toward home as if pursued, forgetting all about the animals grazing below. As soon as they were out of sight, they heard a shot.

When Kanta burst into the house and described what she had just seen, Eleni sat down on the floor and covered her face with her hands. The image flashed into her mind of the mother and daughter she had glimpsed in the yard of the police station talking to the guerrillas. She thought they were only inquiring about a prisoner, but they must have been prisoners themselves, and what she saw in the courtyard must have been their trial. Eleni remembered the way the girl had held her mother's hand so trustingly. Rage filled her, and a sick helplessness. She never thought it would go this far. She had believed what Christos wrote her, that the guerrillas were fellow Greeks fighting for their rights who would not harm her family. To appease them and protect her children she had given up her house, her belongings and food, she had sent her daughter to be an *andartina* and gone every day on the assigned work details, all the time being careful not to say anything that could be construed as criticism of the DAG. She had believed that submission, no matter how bitter, would protect her family from harm. But now they were killing women and children! No one in the village was safe.

The memory of the woman in the tunic and her red-headed daughter reproached her. 'Let's go back and find them,' Eleni said to Kanta, standing up. 'Perhaps they're still alive. We can't just leave them there!'

Kanta's eyes were hard, unsettling in a child's face. 'Even if they were alive then, they're dead now,' she said with heartbreaking logic. 'There's nothing we can do. I just wish I hadn't touched her.'

Ever since Pergainos, the guerrillas had been expecting another attack, and on March 30 it came. This time the nationalist troops called it Operation Falcon and again planned a pincer movement centering on Lia. As soon as the sound and smoke of the battle moved into the valley below her, Eleni allowed herself to hope; this time the family were all together in the Haidis house, and if the soldiers came anywhere near the village boundaries, they were ready to flee. But the guerrillas had planted their mine fields and fortifications well, and the attacking soldiers never advanced any farther than the foothills below the Mourgana. The battle lasted for seven days; the nationalist soldiers suffering three times as many casualties as the guerrillas. As they inched forward toward Lia, 267 soldiers were wounded or killed, and on April 5, Operation Falcon was abandoned in defeat.

Although the fighting never reached the village, one inhabitant of Lia died as a result of Operation Falcon. The victim was Tsavena, the aged mother of Eleni's former neighbor Marina Kolliou.

As the nationalist artillery battered the Perivoli from the Great Ridge in the distance, Tsavena, who was ill, fell into an exhausted sleep in the small room off her daughter's kitchen while Marina and Tsavena's granddaughter, Olga Venetis, tried to calm Olga's two little boys. After dark the women were startled by the sound of guerrillas pounding on their door. The *andartes* announced that they needed the house for the night to billet some of the reinforcements expected to arrive from Macedonia. Everyone had to clear out immediately.

'What am I supposed to do with my mother?' asked Marina Kolliou. 'Make her sleep on the ground? She's ninety years old and has a bad heart.'

'We don't care what you do. Take her by the leg and throw her into the ravine!' the guerrilla replied. 'Just get her out of here.'

Marina wanted to carry the old woman on her back down to a neighbor's house, but Olga insisted it would kill her grandmother if she was taken out into the hail of mortar shells and the cold night air. She suggested that they just lock the small room where Tsavena was sleeping and leave her there until morning, when they would come back for her. The guerrillas would never know she was there.

It might have worked, but when the guerrilla reinforcements arrived from Macedonia long after midnight, exhausted and impatient for rest, they began pounding on the windows as well as the door. The old woman woke up to see satanic, dirt-streaked, bearded faces peering through the glass, shouting and cursing, trying to break in. She screamed for her daughter but no one answered her cries. When Marina and Olga found her in the morning, Tsavena was lying on the floor paralyzed. She died before the day was over, while the guerrillas celebrated their victorious defeat of the fascists around her body.

With a heavy heart, Eleni climbed up to the Perivoli to attend her neighbor's funeral as the bull horns caroled the great victory. When the battle began Eleni had allowed herself to hope that the government soldiers might reach high enough for the family to flee. Now she was convinced there would never be another chance. The guerrillas seemed entrenched forever, too well fortified for the walls of their citadel to be breached.

Eleni listened to the funeral dirges lamenting Tsavena's death. It wasn't two months ago that Fotini had come to her in a dream and told her to get ready; she was taking Tsavena first, then returning for her. Now Tsavena had set out on the journey to Charon, and Eleni couldn't rid herself of the feeling that her own destiny was beginning to unwind, fulfilling her mother-in-law's words.

Suspicion and fear infected every home in the village, making next-door neighbors and even relatives wary of what they said to one another. Eleni was not immune to the general paranoia, and when she received an unexpected visit one morning in April from Spiro Michopoulos, fear made her hands tremble and her voice sound hollow as she greeted him.

Eleni had always sympathized with the young coffeehouse owner before the guerrillas made him village president, and she regretted the way the villagers ostracized him because of his brush with tuberculosis. To Eleni, Spiro Michopoulos had always been polite and soft-spoken, excessively eager to please. But she knew that such people often harbored hostility toward neighbors who had been treated better by life.

As he sat in the chair Eleni brought out on the veranda, his long, thin legs awkwardly akimbo, idly clicking his chain of worry beads, Michopoulos looked depressed. But then, thought Eleni, he always looked that way. There were permanent furrows between his eyes; his sallow face was a long, mournful inverted triangle with swept-back dark hair receding at the temples. Although his features were regular, Spiro's outsized ears and tiny toothbrush of a mustache gave him a slightly clownish look. But today he appeared far more sinister than comical to Eleni, and his visit seemed a bad omen.

She hid her nervousness in the bustle of bringing him some warm milk, then sat down opposite him. 'Are you all right, Spiro?' she ventured. 'You look like you lost a sovereign and found a drachma.'

His thin chest rose and fell with a deep sigh and he shook his head mournfully. 'The *andartes* keep asking me to give them more people for work details, more mules, more supplies, but the villagers want to stay home to protect their families and their fields,' he said. 'I understand how both sides feel, but I always get caught between the upper and the lower millstones.' He seemed to droop. 'I've tried to be fair.'

342

'I know, Spiro,' Eleni replied, wondering what he was leading up to.

'But people don't want me to be fair!' he burst out. 'They want their neighbor, who's disloyal to the cause, to be assigned more work than they have. And of course everyone is more dedicated to the cause than his neighbor.'

That must be it, Eleni thought. Because her father was a royalist and her husband an American, the villagers were complaining that she should be assigned more work as punishment. She tried to read Michopoulos' face, but he was staring out toward the horizon in a melancholy that reached to his fingertips. He turned the cup of milk around in his hands and began talking in a low voice, as if to himself. 'At the beginning, when we were fighting foreign invaders it was so simple, and so . . . right,' he said. 'Now it's all changed.'

He fell silent. Eleni was sure he was trying to trick her into saying something critical about the guerrillas, and didn't reply.

'It's going to get worse!' he shouted, abruptly turning on her. 'The village is not safe anymore! There'll be more attacks, more bloodshed. I don't want to see parents weeping for their children.'

Eleni couldn't understand why he sounded so urgent and excited. He took a deep breath, collected himself, then said, 'It was wise that you moved out of the Perivoli, Eleni. But even here it's not safe.' He searched her face. 'You should go farther down, Eleni! Go down as far as you can. Do you hear what I'm telling you?'

She stared at him, wondering why he was acting so strangely. Was he telling her to move down to the bottom of the village to live with her sister-in-law, farther away from the guerrilla emplacements which would receive the brunt of the enemy fire, or did he mean something else? As she was pondering how to ask him without saying something compromising, he wiped his mustache, leaped to his feet, nervously thanked her for the untouched cup of milk and left. After he was gone Eleni wondered fleetingly if he had been trying to tell her to flee the village altogether, but then she returned to her original conviction that his visit had been an

343

attempt to trap her into saying something against the guerrillas.

In early April the bull horn of the town crier broadcast a summons that spread excitement through the village: 'All mothers who have children between the ages of three and fourteen are to report to the Church of the Holy Trinity at once!'

The women hurried toward the town square, whispering questions about what it could mean. The rumor went around that there would be a distribution of food to families with small children. Nikola and Fotini were young enough to qualify, Eleni calculated. Any extra ration of sugar, lard or flour would be a godsend.

In contrast to the warmth of the bright spring day, the dark interior of the church was musty and cool. Ever since Father Theodoros fled the village, there had been no services. The icons and the bishop's seat were shrouded in dust, but the women entering the church, many carrying babies, automatically made their cross and stopped to kiss the image of the Virgin inside. By habit, they crowded into the women's section in the back, but a small dark woman, a young *andartina* in uniform with a bandolier of bullets across her chest, motioned the women to come forward. It seemed a good omen that they were to be addressed by a woman.

'Mothers of Lia,' she shouted. 'We've called you together because your children are in danger.'

The church became very quiet. Someone shushed a crying baby. 'The fascist attacks on this village will continue,' the *andartina* said. 'If your children are not hit by a bullet or a bomb, they will die slowly of starvation. You know that there's not even enough food left for our fighters. You've all heard your children crying with hunger.'

The women stared at her. They knew that it was true enough, but what did she expect them to do about it? When was she going to get to the part about more food?

'Your children are the reason for our struggle, to make a better Greece for them,' the woman soldier shrilled. 'You have to share our ordeal, but it's not fair to make *them* suffer

344

too. Because of the party's great concern and love for your children, our leaders have found a way to save them.'

She paused dramatically. 'We've called you here to announce that the people's democracies, including our neighbors Albania, Yugoslavia and Bulgaria have opened their arms to your children! They will take all children whose parents sign this piece of paper, care for them, feed them well, give them new clothes and educate them to become doctors, engineers, officers – whatever their abilities permit. And when the war is ended and the Red Flag flies over all of our country, they will return to you, tall, healthy and happy, ready to take their places in the new Greece.'

It took a moment or two for the village women to comprehend what the *andartina* was saying. They exchanged startled looks and unconsciously pulled toddlers closer to their sides. She was standing in front of them with a smile on her face and asking them to hand over their children to be taken away! The women stared at the piece of paper in her hand as if it were a snake.

The *andartina* didn't seem to notice the reaction. She plunged on enthusiastically. 'I want each one of you to step forward and give me your children's names and ages. In a month or so they'll be taken to their new life, free from danger, fear and hunger. Now, who will be first?'

The dark interior of the church, under the glowering eyes of Christ the All-Powerful on the dome, began to seem intolerably close. Eleni forced herself to stay calm. Her children were safe at home with Nitsa and Megali, and this young woman was only asking for volunteers. Being young and unmarried, she didn't know what it meant to have a child, didn't realize what she was asking. After a while, when none volunteered their children, she would see her mistake and let them go home. The main thing, Eleni told herself, was to remain quiet, not to anger the guerrillas or call attention to herself.

Tassina Bartzokis, next to her, learned over and whispered, 'If all of us say "No" with one voice, what can they do?'

Eleni gave a small shake of her head.

The young woman at the front of the church saw the

345

movement. 'Why are you hesitating?' she asked. 'Is there anyone or anything holding you back?'

Olga Venetis' voice answered her. 'Only our pain for our children,' she said. 'Nothing else.'

The *andartina* forced herself to be patient. 'You mustn't cling to your children and let them be killed out of selfish bourgeois sentiment!' she scolded. 'Would you rather see them die here or live happily in safety?' She arranged her face again into a smile. 'Now I'm going to ask each of you individually,' she said. 'Who will show the rest the right decision?'

Nearest her was Xantho Venetis, the wife of the cooper, who was holding her three-year-old son. 'Comrade Xantho, will you give your children the chance for a life without fear?'

The gaunt woman spoke without thinking. 'None of us will give up our children!' There was a gasp; Xantho had rashly presumed to speak for the whole group. The *andartina* studied her, then wrote something down on a piece of paper. Xantho swallowed, imagining it was her death sentence.

The women waited, hoping that Xantho's defiance would not unleash the guerrillas' wrath on all of them. A loud sob broke the silence and they turned to see Calliope Bardaka pushing forward through the crowd. The women exchanged knowing looks. As the security police's chief informant, Calliope was universally suspected of sleeping with the guerrillas.

'I'm the first!' Calliope wept. 'My husband was killed by fascists and I won't let the same thing happen to my children. I want to be the first mother to place them under the protection of our party.'

She came forward, wiping her eyes. The young *andartina* put an arm around her shoulders as she wrote down the names of Calliope's two children and showed her where to make her mark.

As Calliope returned to her place, another voice rang out, ragged with desperation: 'Take my children, all but the baby!' The women looked around and saw that the speaker was Nakova Daflaki, the last person they would have expected to step forward. Nakova's husband had been a member of the home guard, MAY, who fled at the approach of the guerrillas to escape certain execution. The DAG took revenge by throwing Nakova and her four small children out of their house and confiscating all their food. Since then, they had been sleeping in a hay shed. Nakova was often seen scavenging in the dirt of the guerrillas' stables for individual kernels of corn dropped from the horses' feed troughs. Now she was handing over her children to the very men who had been persecuting her.

After Nakova signed the paper, there was a strained silence, broken only by the sobs of the two women who had volunteered. 'These unselfish comrades have led the way,' said the *andartina*. 'Who will follow?'

The women shifted from one foot to the other, watching the speaker become more impatient. Finally she said, 'I want you all to go home and think hard about what is best for your children. If you truly love them, you'll let them go.'

Walking out of the church, the women pointedly avoided the two who had signed over their children. Nakova Daflaki was still weeping as she reached the door and blinked in the sunlight. She looked imploringly at the silent women and saw Eleni staring at her with mingled pity and horror.

'What else could I do?' she cried out in desperation. 'We sleep in a hay shed! I have nothing to feed them! I can't just watch them die, can I?'

Eleni didn't reply. Like the others, she turned away from Nakova and hurried home. That night she woke up several times and reached out in the darkness to make sure Nikola was still there on the pallet beside her.

My mother returned from the meeting in the church white-lipped with anger. She paced up and down, cursing the two women who had handed over their children, 'as if they were kittens,' she kept saying in wonder. I studied her, trying to read my own fate, and finally she saw my expression. She leaned over and took my face in her hands. 'Some women are sending their children away to Albania because they don't have enough food to give them,' she said to me, 'and because they are fools!'

347

My mother loved me, I knew, and she was no fool, but I also knew that there wasn't enough food in our house. The threat of being separated from her and my sisters frightened me so much that I resolved to minimize the danger by eating less, as little as I possibly could.

For as long as I could remember I had been hungry, but now my bones began to grow too fast for my skin, which would crack at the joints, bleeding. I woke at night feeling pains in my legs and the hollow ache of hunger, almost indistinguishable from fear, in my belly. When my mother put food on the table I tried not to look at it, to pretend it wasn't there, but even when I closed my eyes I could see it.

My clearest memory from that period is the day of the marmalade. Realizing that reasoning with the mothers wouldn't make them give up their children, the guerrillas decided to try a more primal appeal. We were called together – women and children – in the flat field near a mill on the eastern side of the ravine. I hid behind my mother, peeking out at the proceedings. A guerrilla and the tinker Elia Poulos stood in front of us. Next to them, in a row, were the dozen or so village children who had been volunteered for the *pedomasoma* by their parents. They were all dressed in clean new clothes and, I noticed with surprise, they were all wearing shoes.

There was a table in front of the guerrilla, with a great crusty loaf of bread that seemed as big as a mill wheel, and a two-liter can. The guerrilla opened the lid and air whooshed out with a delicious odor like an orchard of pomegranate trees. He dipped in with a large spoon and brought out a scoop of marmalade, gleaming golden brown in the sun, the color of the finest honey.

What we called 'marmalade' was a rich, viscous sweet made of wild fruits or berries cooked with sugar until it was so thick it could be cut like butter. I watched him scooping out great hunks of the stuff and spreading it on slabs of the bread – white bread – nearly an inch thick with marmalade. I had never seen so much marmalade. Before the revolution, we sometimes bought tiny cans of it from the general store, but since the guerrillas came, none of us had tasted any sweet, not even sugar or honey.

When the guerrilla dipped down for a fat scoop of marmalade and let it ooze back, my mouth flooded with saliva and I unconsciously stepped from behind my mother to get a closer look. With the ceremonious gestures of a priest, the guerrilla cut large wedges of the bread and slathered them so generously with the marmalade that some dripped onto the ground, bringing tears to my eyes. He presented each of the well-dressed children in front of him with a piece of bread, which they devoured like animals, spreading marmalade all over their faces up to their ears and soiling their fine new clothes.

'You see, mothers of Lia!' the guerrilla shouted. 'If you send your children to the people's democracies, they will eat like this every day! And any child who steps forward at this moment to join the rest will be given as much bread and marmalade as he or she can eat. Here it is for the taking!'

Mesmerized, I took another step forward, filling my eyes with the sight of the snowy bread dripping with the glossy, seed-speckled marmalade, so thick that it dripped over the side of each slice onto the deep golden crust. I took one more step and was brought up short by my mother's hands gripping my shoulders and jerking me sharply back against her. When I realized what I had almost done, I was frightened and mortified. The hollow pain under my ribs, where the hunger was, began to spread through my body to my arms, legs and heart.

More than thirty years later I had dinner with an Athenian couple, two former children from Lia about the same age as myself, who were taken that summer in the *pedomasoma*, first into Albania, then to Rumania, where they grew up, married, then returned to Greece ten years after they left.

They never saw marmalade like that again, they told me, as they began reminiscing. In the barracks in Albania, they survived mostly on soup made of leeks and on raw dandelion greens, which they scavenged from nearby fields. Their 'play' was devising races with their body lice on the barracks floor. But things improved when they were moved on to Rumania a year later, they said, for it was there, in their dormitory, that the matrons set up the first Christmas tree they had ever seen. Their faces, now middle-aged and well-fed, lit up at the memory of that vision. On the wonderful tree were hung bright, paper-wrapped candies, one for each child.

As the guerrillas increased pressure on the women of the Mourgana to give up their children, Eleni decided to go to Babouri to find out how the women there were reacting to the *pedomasoma*. She set out alone to visit Antonova Paroussis, the wife of her husband's cousin, who was known to be a strong supporter of the Communists.

Although the two women were almost opposites in temperament, Eleni had always liked the outspoken young woman. It was her affection for Antonova that had made Eleni consent to her pleas to hide Nikola Paroussis and the other ELAS guerrilla in her house just after the occupation.

Despite their different personalities, Eleni and Antonova had much in common. They were both married to men considerably older than themselves who had made their money in America. Antonova's husband spent more than a decade working in the factories of Worcester, Massachusetts, before he came back to Babouri in 1932 and married the high-spirited sixteen-year-old girl who was famous for her sharp tongue, fine complexion and the kind of large-boned, buxom figure that was considered the epitome of feminine beauty.

Paroussis was one of the wealthiest men in Babouri, having converted most of his American savings into gold sovereigns and real estate, and like Eleni in Lia, his wife found herself the mistress of the largest house in the village, envied by all her friends. But unlike Eleni, Antonova was able to take advantage of her husband's indulgent nature and weak health to do exactly as she pleased, and she soon gained a reputation as a firebrand. During the occupation Antonova was so moved by the ELAS speeches that she took up a gun and joined the guerrillas in the battle of Lista, an adventure that scandalized the villagers of Babouri. 'Imagine a married woman with three small children going off to fight with men while her husband sits home!' the women whispered.

Antonova took no notice of what anyone said about her and no one dared criticize her to her face, including her husband.

Eleni knew that Antonova was sympathetic to the guerrillas, so she was surprised to hear her friend nearly stuttering with indignation about the *pedomasoma*. 'It's unbelievable, asking us to give up our children!' the young woman fumed. 'When I heard that, I tell you, Eleni, I parted company with them. I'm turning from red to black!'

Antonova was not shy about using her influence to sway village opinion. She told Eleni that she had warned the women of Babouri, ' "The first mother who hands over her children will have to deal with me personally." ' She added, 'We have to present a united front. We have to tell them with one voice to go to hell!'

Eleni looked around nervously to see if anyone had heard this outburst. She admired her friend for her defiance, but she knew that Antonova's outspokenness was likely to get her into trouble. She thought again of the woman and girl Kanta had found lying in the ravine.

'Hush, cousin, someone will hear you!' Eleni whispered. 'You mustn't go around the village talking this way.' She looked at Antonova's flushed face and wondered how she could make her understand. 'Think what pheasants do if a fox approaches their nest,' Eleni said. 'The male puffs up his bright feathers until he looks twice his size, and screams at the fox. The female, the color of dried grass, gathers her chicks and slips away. Which one is more likely to survive?'

Antonova looked at her without comprehension.

'God gave us brains to measure danger and choose the best way of surviving,' Eleni elaborated. 'If we're cornered, there's no choice but to give in, but the guerrillas say their program is voluntary. Let each mother make her own choice! Your first responsibility is to your own children. If you stand up and speak against the program, the guerrillas can say you're betraying the cause, and make an example of you. That would leave your children helpless and frighten the other mothers into submitting.'

Antonova tossed her black braids. 'The guerrillas know I'm

351

not a fascist,' she insisted. 'Didn't I fight like a man at Lista? Haven't I turned over half my house to them? I've been as loyal to the cause as any woman in Babouri, but this is an insane idea and somebody's got to tell them!'

Eleni left Babouri disturbed by her cousin's words. She hoped that Antonova's protest would have an impact on the guerrillas, but she was afraid it would only harden them. For herself, she would not risk speaking out publicly against the *pedomasoma*. There were too many people in Lia who would use her words as a weapon against her. But Eleni knew she could no more give up any of her children than cut out her own heart. She prayed the guerrillas would be satisfied with the number who had been proffered for the *pedomasoma* so far and leave the rest alone.

Despite house-to-house visits by the propaganda representatives of the guerrillas, only a dozen children from Lia had been volunteered for the relocation program by the end of April. This was an embarrassment to the political officers of the DAG, and when the central committee looked at the number of children signed up from the Mourgana villages, it would be even more embarrassing to Kostas Koliyiannis, the political commissar for the Epiros Command, who had the ultimate responsibility for ensuring the cooperation of the civilians.

One day while the rest of the family was in the house for the afternoon siesta, Nikola went out to his secret sanctuary, the bean field below the Haidis house. He loved to lie on his back on the warm red earth, alone among the even rows of broad beans spiraling up the poles toward the sky, imagining himself in a silent forest. All around he could hear the tranquil sounds of the village, the braying of a donkey, the complaints of his grandmother's rooster, the hollow music of the goats' bells high above on the mountainside. The yellow-green walls of the bean rows seemed to set him apart as he drowsily gazed up at the sky, watching a hawk soaring, clouds melting from one shape to another. Since the coming of the guerrillas ended his two years of schooling, Nikola found himself brimming with questions, but whenever he asked adults, they became

352

impatient and shooed him away. How did God tell a bean to grow into a bean plant and not a squash vine? How did the plant know when to stop reaching toward the sun and sprout beans? Why were the cocky blue-and-yellow wagtails too clever to enter his traps, while the crows were not? Nikola lay very still, imagining that if he was quiet enough, he could hear the beans growing.

He was beginning to doze off under the caress of the sun when he heard the sound of horses. He could tell the difference between a horse and a mule by the hoofbeats, and horses were rare in the village. Nikola peered between the bean rows and saw two shapes approaching from the direction of the square, following the path that ran across the bottom of the bean field, only yards from where he lay.

As the riders came closer, he recognized one as Sotiris Drapetis, the cold-eyed intelligence officer who had evicted them from their house. The other man was a stranger, but Nikola could tell by the deferential way Sotiris was listening that it must be an officer of importance, probably from the guerrillas' headquarters in Babouri.

The boy rose to his knees to follow the progress of the two men as they passed just below him, only yards away but shielded by the bean rows. The officer seemed to be scolding Sotiris. 'A dozen children from Lia is simply not acceptable,' he was saying. 'The success of this program is of the highest priority! Not only are the party leaders fully committed to it, but the prestige of all the countries in the Eastern bloc is at stake.'

Nikola began creeping along his bean row, keeping his head down, hurrying. It seemed vital to hear what they were saying.

'We've tried everything, even holding food under their noses as an incentive,' Sotiris replied. 'But these are ignorant peasant woman. They won't listen to reason. Even if they were drowning, they wouldn't let go of their children.'

'Whether they want to give up their children or not is irrelevant,' snapped the officer. 'They're *going* to give them. And it's up to you to make them, no matter what you have to do.'

Nikola stopped before the end of the bean field and threw himself down on the musky earth. The officer's words were the confirmation of the nightmare that had been haunting him. They were going to take him away by force.

When the sound of the horses' hoofs faded away, Nikola began running toward the house, the dirt rising in puffs under his feet. Even before he was inside he was crying: '*Mana! Mana!*' Eleni sat up from her pallet, startled.

'They're going to take me, *Mana*,' he cried, throwing himself into her arms. 'I heard them! They're going to take me whether you give me or not!'

It took her a while to calm him down enough so that she could understand what he was telling her. He was clutching her, his head burrowed against her breast, repeating the same words over and over. When Eleni finally understood what Nikola had overheard from the two men on horseback, she knew her prayers had failed. It was what she had dreaded from the moment of the gathering in the church. She had tried every way she knew to appease the guerrillas and keep her family intact, but now she understood that they were going to be destroyed. She could no longer yield, but had to defy them.

Eleni put her cheek on the boy's head as she held him to her and there was resolution in her eyes.

'Quiet, my soul,' she said. 'Forget about what you heard. You mustn't be afraid; no one's ever going to take you away from me.'

She pulled him deeper into her embrace and spread the fingers of her hands, covering his shoulders and the back of his head as if trying to shield him from invisible blows.

354

CHAPTER TWELVE

Although the guerrillas had managed to repell two major attacks on the Mourgana, they were vastly outnumbered by the nationalist troops in both men and arms, and their success couldn't continue much longer.

After failing twice to take the 'citadel' of the Mourgana, the Greek army turned its attention to the guerrillas in the mountains of central Greece, who had no Communist country at their rear to supply them. On April 15, 1948, the government forces launched Operation Dawn on the spine of mountains dividing the trunk of mainland Greece. Aided by a freak snowstorm, three successive waves of soldiers battered the insurgents. Government squadrons of LOK mountain commandos were reinforced by regular units who traveled at night to launch surprise assaults at sunrise, catching the guerrillas off guard.

The 2,500 rebels in the mountains of central Greece were outnumbered five to one. After a month Operation Dawn ended in defeat for the DAG, with 1,300 insurgents captured, another 650 killed, and the rest retreating toward the main guerrilla base in the Grammos mountains.

Operation Dawn was a turning point in the war. The battered Communist leadership began to consider a negotiated settlement. On May 31, the provisional government of Markos Vafiadis broadcast a call for a cease-fire through the rebel radio in Belgrade. While still denouncing 'foreign imperialists and Greek traitors,' the Communists declared themselves ready 'to accept and encourage any initiative which would help Greece return to a state of peace.'

But Nikos Zachariadis, the volcanic secretary general of the Greek Communist Party, did not appear to agree with his commander in chief. When an emissary from Athens arrived in the Grammos mountains, Zachariadis announced, 'We will not entertain discussions until the members of the Athens government are put on trial as war criminals.'

The Greek prime minister, eighty-eight-year-old Themistocles Sofoulis, wanted to know who was speaking the true feelings of the rebels – Zachariadis or General Markos – and decided to use the explosive issue of the *pedomasoma* as a test. He sent a telegram to the governments of Albania, Bulgaria, Czechoslovakia, Hungary, Poland and Yugoslavia, demanding the repatriation of all Greek children taken so far from the occupied villages.

'This is . . . . a certain way of learning the intentions of the Soviet Union's satellites, as well as testing the sincerity of Markos' proposals,' Sofoulis said. 'If the various governments reject the Greek demand or, indeed, do not reply at all, that will mean that they did not intend to restore relations with Greece, and that Markos' proposals are nothing more than propaganda tricks without any meaning.'

Within a week, both Poland and Hungary turned down his request. The gathering of children, which had begun as a propaganda ploy, had become a political hot potato, and in order to save face and prove to the world that the people of Greek mountain villages were, in fact, eager to send their children behind the Iron Curtain, the guerrillas set about with new urgency to collect greater numbers of children for the *pedomasoma*.

CAST A BLACK STONE

THE CONVERSATION OVERHEARD by an eight-year-old boy hidden in a bean field on an April afternoon in 1948 would change the lives of everyone in the Gatzoyiannis family forever. As Eleni tried to calm her son with soothing words, she realized she was at the crossroads she had been trying to avoid for so long.

However grim the circumstances, it is a reflex of human nature to believe in one's own survival no matter how many others die. 'If I just keep quiet, do what they say and don't make myself conspicuous, then they'll let me live another day,' thinks the inmate of the ghetto, concentration camp or occupied village. 'This can't last forever.'

The people of Lia were no different. 'Take the wind as it comes,' they said. If the DAG demanded children for the *pedomasoma,* mothers rationalized, they would give up one or two so that the rest could survive.

But as much as Eleni tried to appease the guerrillas, she could not compromise when it came to her children. Keeping her family alive and together was the purpose that had filled her life for twenty years. Now she knew that they were going to take the two youngest away from her; eventually the two eldest girls would certainly be conscripted into the besieged rebel army. Submitting to the will of the guerrillas had accomplished nothing. In order to save her children, she had to defy them.

Eleni decided to gamble all their lives on the chance that she could get the family out of the occupied zone before the guerrillas separated them. She began to plan something that no one else in the half-dozen Mourgana villages ever dared: a mass escape.

She spoke to Nikola quietly, repeating words that sounded hollow to her ears but seemed to soothe him: they would never be separated, she would never allow anyone to take him. He lifted his eyes and she saw faith in her ability to protect him.

Eleni knew she couldn't lead her family out of the village without being seen by the guerrilla lookouts, stumbling into a minefield, unless she had help. She needed to bring into her plot a man who could learn the movement of the guerrilla patrols without raising their suspicions; someone who was familiar with the paths through the foothills connecting Lia and the Great Ridge; someone who had an idea of the placement of the minefields. But it had to be a man Eleni could trust not to betray her to the security police's informers.

There were few men left in the village, and those who remained were either very loyal to the guerrillas or old and frail. Spiro Michopoulos would have been ideal to lead the escape, Eleni reflected, if only she could be sure his visit to her had been a warning to flee. But she had no way of knowing if that was what he meant or if he had been sent to trick her.

After much thought Eleni reluctantly came to the conclusion that the only man left in the village who had the qualifications she needed was the tinker Lukas Ziaras. Lukas was considered a ne'er-do-well who tried to make up for his small stature and meager earnings with coffeehouse bravado. But he was married to one of Eleni's first cousins, Soula Haidis, who had grown up under the same roof and was like a younger sister to her. That made Lukas a relative. Despite his garrulity, she felt sure he would not betray her plans to the security police.

Eleni knew that Lukas' low standing in the village had always rankled him. She suspected that the idea of leading the escape might appeal to his ego, for if they succeeded, the exploit would make him famous throughout the Mourgana. She knew, too, that despite his weaknesses Lukas was devoted to his five children and wouldn't want to lose them to the *pedomasoma*. He spent hours whittling wooden toys for the little ones, returning home every night to make the sign of the cross over each of his sleeping children with a paternal solicitude, rare in a Greek village.

Lukas had one outstanding qualification to recommend him as a leader of their escape: he and his family lived in one of the southernmost houses in the village, just next to the ruins of the Church of the Virgin, where the guerrilla lookouts were posted, and the night raiding parties dispatched. Because of the location of his property, he would know the paths leading from his fields down the mountain and through the foothills and would have seen where the mines were planted. And without exciting suspicion, he could stroll over to the church at twilight to smoke a cigarette and engage the guerrillas in conversation, learning where they were sending the raiding parties that night.

These patrols were made up of the most fanatically loyal young guerrillas and *andartinas:* those willing to risk their lives on the four-hour walk across the foothills after dark to harass the soldiers on the slopes of the Great Ridge. Eleni had seen one of the young raiders, a boy nicknamed 'Mermingas' ('the ant') at the house of Angeliki Botsaris, where he brought his lice-infested uniforms to be boiled. Mermingas strutted before the women with a bazooka on his back and bragged, 'With this I'm going to blow away every fascist on the Ridge.' Eleni knew the night raiders would pose the greatest danger to her family's surviving the escape, and only Lukas was in a position to see which routes they took.

As for Lukas' wife, Eleni had no reservations about trusting her. Soula Haidis Ziaras was a good-natured, uncomplaining woman totally dedicated to the welfare of her children. When a bearded guerrilla came to her house and demanded three of the youngest for the *pedomasoma,* the normally gentle Soula shouted, 'I'll see them eating dirt from my garden before I give them to you!' The *andarte* hit her so hard that one eye filled up with blood and was swollen for weeks afterward. Eleni knew that Soula would be as eager as she was to escape when she learned what the guerrillas intended to do with their children.

Before her resolve could waver, Eleni set out toward the Ziaras house, praying that Lukas would agree to lead them. Even if his thirst for glory and his love for his children didn't sway him, she suspected that he would agree to do it for the amount of money she planned to offer him.

Eleni found Lukas listlessly mending a pot in his yard, wearing the white towel around his neck that had become his trademark, to the amusement of the rest of the village. Lukas was terrified of being conscripted by the guerrillas or sent on daily work details, so he had developed a clever ruse to convince them he was an invalid. Nearly everyone suspected he was malingering, but only his family knew how he did it so convincingly. He packed a roll of pounded nettles around his neck to make it red and swollen. Then he painted the inside of his throat with a solution of diluted hydrochloric acid, which every tinker used to scour pots. This gave Lukas his chronic cough and hoarse, wheezing voice, widely mimicked by village wags. He went everywhere with a towel soaked in camomile tea wrapped around his neck – the sign of an invalid. The trick succeeded in convincing the guerrillas that he was unfit to work, but twenty-five years later, Lukas would die of cancer of the throat.

The tinker was surprised to see Eleni and jumped up to greet her. Lukas always reminded her of a bantam rooster with his strutting walk, small squinty eyes and long nose reaching toward a sharp chin. When Eleni told him that she wanted to speak to him and his wife in private, suspicion, fear and curiosity mingled on his face.

In the kitchen, Soula and her daughter Marianthe were preparing boiled greens while the youngest Ziaras child, Alexi, two, slept in the wooden cradle. Lukas ordered Marianthe to leave them alone and she shot him a black look. Marianthe, who had been conscripted as an *andartina* along with Kanta and released with her, was a cunning girl. Guessing from Eleni's face that something important was in the wind, she positioned herself under the kitchen window to eavesdrop on the adults inside.

'I'm going to open my heart to you, because we are blood,' Eleni said in a low voice. 'But however you feel about what

I'm going to say, you must kiss the cross and never repeat it, because it could mean death to me and my children.'

Soula glanced at her husband, then took off her apron and sat down near the cradle. The couple listened in silence as Eleni repeated the conversation that Nikola had overheard, Lukas occasionally interrupting with soft puffs of astonishment: 'Po! po! po!'

'They're going to take our children at gunpoint, whether we volunteer them or not,' Eleni concluded. She looked around and lowered her voice. 'I've decided to take my family out, but I can't do it alone. I need a man to lead us, someone clever who knows the guerrillas' movements and the paths through the minefields.' She turned to Lukas, who was nervously shifting the towel around his neck. 'That's why I've come to you.'

'We've been talking about the same thing, Eleni,' whispered Soula, as if it was a relief to speak the words aloud, but Lukas gave her a withering look that stopped her in mid-sentence. The little man paced silently up and down, making a great show of thinking and rolling a cigarette. It was true that his wife had been begging him to lead them out ever since the guerrillas came for their children and blackened her eye. But Lukas had vacillated, knowing he would have a hard time crossing to the other side even if they did survive all the way to the Great Ridge. Because he had stayed behind in the village, the government troops might think he was a Communist plant, a spy. But if the Amerikana and her family came with him, he wouldn't be suspected of treachery – her father's royalist sympathies and her American husband were well known.

Eleni watched Lukas pacing and thinking, then she added, 'If you succeed in getting all of us out, together and alive, as soon as we get to Filiates I'll telegraph Christos to send you one thousand dollars.'

The tinker's small eyes widened at the sum. He stopped pacing and extended his hand to Eleni. 'Our children are the only thing that count,' he wheezed.

Soula rocked miserably back and forth in her chair 'And if we're leading them right to their deaths?' she cried. At the sight of the grim resolve on the face of her older cousin, Soula bowed her head. 'If what Nikola heard is true, then I suppose we have no other choice,' she said. 'May the Holy Virgin protect us!'

Lukas was already carried away with enthusiasm, dragging on his cigarette as he worked out a plan. It occurred to him that God's hand was in the arrival of Eleni Gatzoyiannis at his door. Lukas had always felt life didn't deal him a full deck. He was a second son, cheated of his father's attention and the patriarchal house in the center of the village. He felt that if his parents were better off, like Minas Stratis' family, or had tried harder on his behalf, as Spiro Skevis' father did, then he, too, could have been an educated man, a leader. Mending pots was a waste of his talents; he was meant to be a schoolteacher or a military officer, of that he was convinced. Now destiny had handed him the opportunity to prove his cleverness by defying the whole guerrilla army and making Spiro Skevis and his fellow officers look like fools. He would lead a mass exodus of women and children to safety right under the noses of their persecutors, like Moses leading the chosen people out of the wilderness.

In his excitement, Lukas unwrapped his towel from around his neck and began issuing orders like a general. Some preparations would have to be made, he said; he would take care of everything. They had to select a night when the moon was waning and the weather, winds and omens were right. In the meantime the main thing was for the two families to carry on their daily routine without doing anything to arouse suspicion. Eleni must not be seen visiting his house again. She was to work in her bean field every morning, and Soula would come to her there on the day he chose. Then, on the chosen night, as soon as darkness fell, Eleni must send her family in pairs, by different routes, down to the now abandoned Haidis mill in the ravine, where they would all gather in the cellar. When they were assembled, they would slip down the ravine, walking from the spot where it dispersed in the foothills straight across to the Great Ridge.

Lukas was talking excitedly, interrupted only by the coughing fits which got worse when he was agitated. Eleni

362

watched and listened to him with growing trepidation. Finally she said in a stern voice, 'Remember, Lukas, this is just between our two families. You mustn't tell anyone else – your brother, your parents, your sister-in-law. Just a careless word could destroy us.'

Lukas gave her a look of reproof. He was a man, wasn't he, and the leader of this mission? Who understood the risks better than he did?

As she returned home from the Ziaras house, Eleni tried to calm the misgivings that were growing in her. She called the family together and told them what she was planning. She had no fears about Nikola and Fotini betraying the plot; Greek village children understood from an early age that life pitted the family against the rest of the world and they protected family secrets as zealously as their parents did.

No one objected to Eleni's announcement, least of all Nikola. If the idea of trying to slip out of the village at night under the guns of the guerrillas frightened him, it was less terrifying than being abducted into Albania and separated forever from his mother and sisters. Even his grandmother Megali agreed that they had no other choice, although she began to weep at the thought of leaving her house. Nitsa moaned about the trauma of the escape bringing on a miscarriage, but she quickly rejected Eleni's suggestion that she stay behind. Olga said nothing. Secretly she mourned the loss of her chances to become the wealthiest and most envied bride in Lia. Kanta had always longed to escape the lusterless life of the village, but her mother's announcement brought back all the terrors of her weeks with the guerrillas. Now the men who had trained her to kill would be hunting her family.

During the days that followed, the pressure of waiting made everyone irritable. It seemed pointless to plant and tend crops they would never harvest. Eleni went every morning to the bean field but there was no sign of Soula Ziaras. As she worked, she rehearsed the escape over and over in her mind, trying to anticipate the dangers. She knew that Nitsa and Megali would be so frightened that they'd create more of a risk than the children. She wished there was someone calm and reliable to share the burden with her. Inevitably, Eleni thought of her sister-in-law Alexo. Ever since Alexo's husband, Foto, had fled to Filiates ahead of the guerrillas, she had been living in her house alone, except for her eleven-year-old daughter Niki. Two of Alexo's married daughters, Athena and Arete, lived elsewhere in the village, and the other six grown children were living in areas of Greece not occupied by guerrillas.

Eleni made up her mind to invite Alexo along on the escape. Despite what she had said to Lukas, she knew that her sister-in-law could be trusted not to betray them and her presence in the group could help keep everyone calm. At the end of the long walk to her house, when Eleni saw Alexo's smile of welcome and felt her strong arms embracing her, she knew she had made the right decision. But Alexo listened to her and then shook her head. 'I can't leave Athena alone here in the village, eight months pregnant,' she said, 'and she could never survive the walk in her condition.'

Alexo lapsed into a depressed silence for a moment, then turned and seized both Eleni's hands in hers. 'Take Arete with you instead of me!' she whispered, naming her eldest daughter, who was barren. 'They're sure to conscript her as an *andartina* if she doesn't get out, and if they do that, her husband will never take her back. Ever since he learned she can't have children, he's been looking for an excuse to divorce her, and if she was drafted, that's all he'd need. I'll stay to help Athena through her delivery – they won't hurt an old woman like me – but you must save Arete!'

Arete was the daughter Alexo loved best. Eleni hesitated. Ever since Arete had been sent to Yannina for the operation that removed her womb, she had been excitable and nervous, and she was not the smartest of Alexo's children, but, Eleni reflected, she was young and strong and could help Megali or one of the children on the walk. Besides, she couldn't refuse Alexo a favor after the woman had helped her through so many crises, becoming dearer to her than any sister. Eleni nodded and told her to warn Arete; they would send word somehow on the day of the escape. 'But what if the guerrillas punish you for her leaving?' Eleni worried.

'How can they blame me for what my married daughter

does?' scoffed Alexo. 'Ach, Eleni, I wish I could go with you!'

'You'll come soon,' Eleni reassured her. 'When this is over, we'll meet in Filiates and take the bus to Igoumenitsa, where we can sit all afternoon at a restaurant by the pier, eating fish and watching the dolphins play in the harbor.'

'From your lips to the ears of God!' exclaimed Alexo.

The two friends sat and whispered together all morning, making plans for after the war, but they both knew they were lying. Once Eleni set out from the village, whether the escape succeeded or failed, their lives were unlikely to cross again. Both women struggled to hide their tears as they embraced for what was probably the last time.

For several days it rained and the sound of the water dripping off the eaves eroded Eleni's patience. On the first sunny day, Eleni, Olga and Nitsa carried three giant copper washing kettles of clothing down to the Haidis bean field below the house near a small ditch which collected water from the nearby spring for irrigating the crops. Under the clothes, Eleni had hidden some of the family's valuables – pieces of Olga's dowry, some of Christos' best suits, the golden pitcher and the iridescent taffeta pillow from Constantinople.

Eleni removed the old clothes she had piled on top of the kettles and carried them to the irrigation ditch. Olga and Nitsa took a hoe and shovel and went into the bean rows nearby, pretending to turn over the soil but really digging holes big enough to conceal the kettles, while Eleni went through the motions of doing the laundry. When all was ready, the three women lifted the kettles into the cavities, put waterproof tarpaulins on top and quickly buried them, replanting the beans on top of the spot. As Eleni patted the earth firm, she wondered when she would look on her treasures again.

In the distant neighborhood of the Church of the Virgin, Soula Ziaras was also busy. She cut up a blanket to make a pouch that would hold the baby on her back, leaving her hands free. She made holes for the child's legs and put a piece of board covered with padding inside for support. One evening at twilight she risked the ten-minute walk to the

Haidis mill. There Soula hid some clothes in a nettle patch below the mill so the fugitives could collect them on their way down the mountain.

About a week after her original visit to the Ziaras house, Eleni was working in the bean field when she saw Soula coming up the path. Eleni's mouth grew dry.

From a distance Soula called, 'Did you cut all the beans, cousin? Are there any left? I haven't a thing to feed the children.'

'There's plenty here!' Eleni shouted back. 'Come pick a potful.' As the women bent together over a row of beans, Soula whispered, 'It's tonight, as soon as it gets dark! Be sure no one sees you going down to the mill.'

After the agony of waiting, it suddenly seemed there wasn't time to get ready. Eleni sent Glykeria to tell Arete, who lived halfway up the Perivoli. Although Eleni had warned the children to take nothing, Olga began to put on layers of clothes: two slips, her best dress, an embroidered apron, another dress on top of that and her long embroidered sleeve-less tunic. She stuffed her good red kerchief into her bosom and filled her sleeves with lace-edged handkerchiefs and underwear. 'You look like a stuffed doll,' Kanta jeered. 'How do you expect to walk like that?' But Olga was pulling on a second pair of knitted stockings. Nitsa rummaged through the kitchen, eating everything she could find. 'No point in leaving good food behind,' she muttered now and then, with her mouth full. 'After all, I have to eat for the baby too!' Fotini had all her plastic baubles spread out on the floor and examined them as she put them in a small sack, like a miser counting his gold. Megali huddled in a corner, moaning repeatedly that they should leave her behind; her old legs would never carry her. Nikola followed his mother around like a shadow, so close that he kept bumping into her.

Eleni watched her family's growing hysteria with irritation. They were about to set out on a journey that would require all their cunning just to stay alive, and they were acting like half-wits! The waiting, the inactivity, made her want to scream or shake someone, but she knew she had to remain calm as an example to the rest. She put out a pot of bread soaked in milk. No one wanted to eat it, but Eleni insisted; how did they expect to walk all night on an empty stomach? She dipped a large metal spoon into the pot to dish up the first portion and then jumped as the bowl of the spoon broke off, falling with a plop. The room grew silent, all eyes focused on her holding the spoon's handle. Megali's voice was like the squawk of a bird: 'It's a bad sign! A warning!'

Megali and Nitsa both made spitting noises as Eleni glared. 'Nonsense!' she snapped, reaching for another spoon. 'Now eat!' She saw Kanta push back her plate untouched.

Before the last light left the west, Eleni sent Olga to feed tender branches to the animals in the cellar, so they'd stay quiet all night. A few minutes later a great outburst of bleating assailed her ears and Olga reappeared, her forehead gleaming with perspiration. 'It's the goats, *Mana*!' she exclaimed. 'The sheep took the food but the goats are trying to climb the gate. They're crying as if they know we're going!'

Eleni rapidly discarded several desperate thoughts and decided they would just have to leave at once and hope that the goats would quiet down when they were out of sight. Hurriedly she sent Nitsa, Megali and Glykeria on ahead, to take the route through the bean field and down the ravine. As they disappeared into the chill, starlit night, Eleni could hear Megali's soft moaning with every step. She silently counted to a hundred, then motioned for Kanta to start with Fotini. Eleni reached for Nikola's hand and was surprised at how cold and small it felt. She glanced at him and he returned her look, calm but pale. Ignoring the braying animals, Eleni locked the door and set out toward the Petsis house, where they would follow the ravine from the opposite side.

Her eyes quickly became accustomed to the darkness. On her left was the impenetrable black-green of the ravine; in front of her were patches of wan silver between the shadows of the trees, large enough to hide a man. Eleni had never realized how full of noises the night was. The mournful sound of the goats pursued her, the crackling and rustling of Kanta and Fotini in front sounded like a huge animal crashing through the underbrush. All her energy was concentrated in her eyes and her ears.

367

When Eleni was nearly certain that they had lost their way, the huge square hulk of the Haidis mill loomed suddenly before them, rising out of the darkness. From the deepest part of the shadows Eleni heard a sound and gasped, then realized it was Arete, already there, waiting. The sound of Megali, Nitsa and Glykeria approaching from the other side was clearly audible. There was no way a guerrilla in the vicinity could help hearing them. Eleni sighed. It was in the hands of God.

She pulled a large rusty key from her pocket and opened the door to the cellar of her father's mill, herding her family inside. They huddled together in the darkness until there was a knock at the door – two loud and two soft. Soula came in first, the baby's carrying pouch on her back, followed by the rest of her family. Lukas arrived last, still wearing his towel, fairly vibrating with nervous excitement.

Eleni lighted a single kerosene lantern in the huge windowless space, revealing the frightened faces of the fugitives. The women and children gathered close together as Lukas lectured in a hoarse stage whisper about the importance of keeping silent once they went out the door. The first lap of the journey was the riskiest, he warned, because they were still in sight and hearing of the guerrilla lookout posts. Once down in the foothills, they had only the roving guerrilla patrols and the mines to worry about. At this Nitsa and Megali set up a duet of moans and Lukas glared at them. Running out of instructions, Lukas came to a halt and then glanced at Eleni, his uncertainty showing. She said nothing, only crossed herself, and the rest followed suit. They were ready.

Lukas told Kanta and Marianthe Ziaras to go first, as far as the fields of Foto Gatoyiannis below, and then wait for the others. Because the two teenaged girls had been trained as *andartinas*, he was sending them on ahead as scouts.

The others waited a few minutes, then left the mill all together following in single file behind Lukas. The small sliver of moon had been wiped out by a cloud, and the night was dark and cold. As they descended the ravine from the mill, a gust of wind struck them, waking the baby Alexi. He let out a wail like a wounded cat.

Eleni hurried forward and lifted the baby from the pouch. She tried to muffle his cries against her shoulder, feeling the soft warmth of him as he struggled, but he only screwed up his face and cried louder, pummeling her with his small fists. Soula took him from Eleni and tore at the buttons on her dress, trying to quiet him by offering him her breast, but he refused to be distracted, screaming louder with each breath. As the women and children stood around helplessly, Lukas rushed up to them, wheezing, his face a caricature of terror. 'Shut his damn mouth, woman!' he sputtered.

'I can't!' Soula cried.

'Put your hand over his mouth,' Lukas hissed. Soula did as she was told and there was sudden silence. They all expelled their breath and looked around, expecting to see guerrillas crashing through the trees. Soula was having trouble holding the baby; he writhed frantically. Gradually, his struggles became weaker as his face took on a blue tinge.

'I can't do it, he's dying!' Soula sobbed, letting go. There was a moment of suspense before the baby got his wind back and let out a scream twice as loud as before, fear now replaced by outrage.

'Back into the mill, quick!' gasped Lukas.

They scampered up the ravine, expecting the guerrillas at their heels. When they re-entered the cellar, they lit the lantern and stood staring at the tiny piece of humanity who was destroying them. His face was purple with rage, tears coursed down his cheeks, mixing with the snot from his nose, and his fists and feet pumped furiously as he let out an ascending series of screams.

'Give him to me, I'll strangle him!' It was Lukas' raspy voice. Everyone turned to look at him, thinking it was a bad joke, but they saw he was serious. Lukas had anticipated every mishap but this, and now his own son was going to rob him of everything: freedom, money and fame. He reached for the baby but Soula backed away, shielding Alexi, terrified by the distorted face of the man who had always been such a gentle father.

Eleni grabbed his arm. 'What are you saying?' she whispered.

369

'We have to think of the rest!' Lukas muttered, close to tears. 'What's one life measured against fifteen?'

'How could we go on living if we had the baby's death on our souls?' Eleni asked. Then she spoke loud enough to be heard over his cries. 'We'll just have to go back,' she said firmly. 'He'll never stop crying now. Nothing's lost as long as we can get home without anyone realizing we've been gone. We'll leave again in a day or two, and next time we'll give him something beforehand to make him sleep.'

Her words broke the spell of fear that had paralyzed everyone. 'Of course!' they all exclaimed, smiling. They'd go home and try again later. Lukas frowned like a ship's captain who smells mutiny, but secretly he was as relieved as the rest to put the ordeal off until another day.

For Nikola, the second escape attempt two weeks later was infinitely more frightening than the first. The terrors of that first time – the bad omen of the spoon, his grandmother's moans, the cries of the goats, the screams of the baby and the contorted face of Lukas Ziaras reaching to strangle his own son – had all taken root in his soul and incubated there, growing into a nameless fear that now followed him around, lurking in corners and showing its face as he fell asleep. The threat of the guerrillas surprising them in the darkness had been frightening enough, but the panic of the adults and their helplessness infected him with a far greater sense of dread.

The moment Nikola and his family slipped out of the house the second time, they realized the weather had turned. The air was chill and clammy, and a fog was rolling in from the foothills. Again the animals set up a terrific bleating as the family picked their way down the ravine, leaving from different spots. Just as they came together above the Haidis mill, they were stopped by what seemed the hand of God Himself. Nikola felt the hair on the back of his neck rise. Half of a huge plane tree had fallen, blocking the path, evidently struck by lightning. In the rising mist it loomed like a wall, the stump of the branch still smoldering sulfurously. Nitsa and Megali began to mewl in fright: 'Another bad omen!'

As they circled around the fallen tree, the mist lapped at

370

their feet, curling up around their legs until it enveloped them completely, closing off all senses but touch. To Nikola the fog was the incarnation of the horror that was stalking him. It was worse than the sound of approaching footsteps, for it blanked out all sound; the world seemed wrapped in cotton. He clutched his mother's hand as they stumbled down the ravine, blindly following the slope of the land. Eleni resembled a ghost, cloaked in white vapor, her hand extended in front of her. Finally they walked directly into the stone wall of the mill and felt their way gingerly around its circumference until they found the door.

They were the first ones inside. There was a soft knock and swirling shapes appeared in the doorway, plumes of white vapor steaming from their clothing and hair. Lukas crept in, trailed by his wife and children. Arete was next. Nikola felt his mother tense and reach for him as still more figures materialized in the doorway; strangers who were not a part of their group. They braced themselves for the sight of guerrillas, but the newcomers were a middle-aged woman and two young girls who were both wailing with fear: 'I'm frightened, *Mana*!' they whispered. 'I want to go home! We're going to die!' Their fears infected Nikola, who began to tremble as if he had a fever.

'Plug up your traps or I'll take a stick to you,' snarled the woman, whom Eleni recognized as Alexandra, the short-tempered wife of the tinker Nassios Drouboyiannis. Nikola saw the fury on his mother's face as she snapped, 'Lukas, I want a word with you outside!'

They disappeared into the suffocating blanket of mist which filled their nostrils and lungs and Nikola followed. Lukas was a faceless silhouette as Eleni turned on him. 'What are Alexandra and her daughters doing here?' she asked in a tight voice. 'Didn't you promise you would tell no one?' Nikola was more frightened by her anger than by the fog.

Lukas wheezed with guilt. 'Nassos is my best friend!' he whined. 'We grew up on two sides of the same house; we shared one door. They've already taken his oldest daughter for an *andartina* and they want the other two for the *pedomasoma*. How could I face him if I left his family behind?'

371

Eleni was silent for several beats, then she said in a voice that came disembodied out of the air, 'You may have put us all in the grave. There's no way we can go tonight in this fog. We've got to postpone it again. Alexandra's got a daughter with the guerrillas; the other two are hysterical. Do you really think they can be trusted, knowing what they do?'

To Nikola, Lukas' form in the mist seemed to shrink. The defeat in his voice was like a death knell. 'Perhaps we're not meant to get away, Eleni,' he said. 'Everything has gone wrong. All my life it's been the same. It's my damnable luck!'

Nikola felt his throat closing. If the only man in the group was giving up, he thought, then they were lost. He began to tremble and Eleni felt his fear and pulled him closer.

'You can stay or go as you wish,' she said, 'but I'm going to keep trying until we're either free or dead.'

There was a long silence from Lukas, then a chastened voice said, 'I agreed to lead you, Eleni, and I will.'

'As you wish,' replied Eleni. 'We have to set out again soon, before it's too late. Next time don't bring the Drouboyiannis women or even tell them that we're going. You can see for yourself they'd ruin us before we got started.'

Out of the white mist came Lukas' reply: 'I won't tell them.'

He went back into the mill to send the others home and Nikola and Eleni waited outside, wrapped in the fog. Eleni bent down and whispered to the boy, 'We'll make it next time, I promise!'

He believed her. The phantoms in the mist couldn't touch her, he had seen that. As he walked back up the ravine toward the house, his hand in hers, Nikola realized that the thing that had been stalking him for so many days was no longer beside him.

Angeliki Botsaris came by the house early the next morning with the news that the young guerrilla they called Mermingas had been killed in the night. The guerrillas had taken advantage of the fog cover, Angeliki said, to send out half a dozen raiding parties to harass the nationalist soldiers. Eleni raised her eyes to the corner iconostasis. If they hadn't turned back, she realized, they would surely have been intercepted.

372

This must be a sign that God was protecting them. The third time would be the charm.

A second visitor arrived at the gate about noon, the elderly, simple-minded town crier, Petros Papanikolas. With two guerrillas at his side, he cheerfully informed Eleni that the People's Army required a woman from her household for a work detail. The village president, Spiro Micholpoulos, had called for forty women to go to Vatsounia to cut hay and wheat in the surrounding villages. The women were to report to the commissary within three hours.

Eleni held on to the doorframe for support, fighting to hide her panic. 'Why so quickly?' she asked. 'We're ready to harvest our own wheat, and whoever goes will need time to make ready. Isn't tomorrow soon enough?'

'Today,' said one of the guerrillas and watched her a moment before they turned to go.

She fought down the wave of hysteria that was fogging her mind. There must be a solution, if she could just think fast enough.

She called the family together and explained what had happened, looking from one grave face to the next. Her gaze stopped at the swollen figure of her sister. 'If you go,' she said to Nitsa. 'They'll send you back as soon as they see your condition and we can still all leave together.'

'Hah!' exploded Nitsa. 'I've prayed twenty-five years for a child and in the autumn of my life God has granted me a miracle. I should risk my baby so you can save your children?' Overwhelmed by self-pity, Nitsa began weeping, her arms clutching her belly protectively.

Eleni sighed and looked at her mother, who spread her hands in apology. 'I'd go if I could,' Megali quavered, 'but I'm too old to walk that far or swing the scythe, and if they got angry and beat me, I'd spit out the whole plan for the escape.'

Eleni patted her arm wearily. 'That's all right, *Mana.*'

'I'll go!' It was Olga, who looked nearly as frightened as Megali. 'My foot's well now and I could escape alone from over there.'

'Absolutely not!' Eleni snapped. 'If you or Kanta go, they'll never release you. They'll make you into *andartinas* as soon as the harvest's over. Think what the guerrillas would do to you if we escaped!'

Olga bowed her head under her mother's logic. They all sat in silence, staring at Eleni, then a small voice piped up: 'Send me, mother.'

They turned to see fourteen-year-old Glykeria, her round cheeks nearly as red as the scarlet wool dress she was wearing. She returned their stares bravely.

'I'm too young to be an *andartina* and too old for the *pedomasoma*,' Glykeria plunged on. 'No guerrilla would want to rape me, and I can escape from over there alone, like Olga said.' She swallowed, remembering how she always fussed about helping with the threshing, complaining that the scythe gave her blisters. She felt tears gathering at the back of her throat and savored the delicious agony of martyrdom and self-pity.

The rest were looking at the girl in astonishment, but Eleni realized it was true. Glykeria, scarcely five feet tall, was too young to tempt the guerrillas. She was so hopeless at manual labor that they would surely send her back as useless. Then they could all escape together. Eleni held out her arms to the daughter who had always caused her the most worry. 'My child!' she cried. 'It's the best thing. You're a brave girl! Don't worry, we won't go without you. We'll wait until you come back.'

Eleni immediately began to prepare her third daughter for the long journey. She combed her hair, braiding it into two golden plaits, and brushed the red homespun dress. The wool was too heavy for summer, she knew, but it was the only presentable dress Glykeria owned. Then Eleni gathered some food into a cloth bag, and, standing the girl in front of the iconostasis, sprinkled holy water on her. She prayed to St. Athanassios to bring her back quickly.

Before the rest could adjust to Glykeria's new status as a heroine rather than the family troublemaker, she was gone.

During the first weeks of June, the threat of the *pedomasoma* became a reality to the people of Lia as the first group of children were taken away. One day when the mountainsides were gilded with crocuses, those who had been volunteered by their parents were led from the village in a colorful parade. It passed right above the door of the Haidis house as Eleni and her children watched in horror from the windows.

The twenty-odd children ranged in age from three to fourteen. The two 'escorts' who would accompany them into Albania from Tsamanta were slightly older village children, self-consciously wearing guerrilla uniforms. As they marched along, singing Communist songs, someone played a clarinet. Spiro Skevis, Lia's most famous guerrilla, strode at the head of the procession. A flock of weeping women followed behind, one or another occasionally trying to embrace a lagging child. Eleni wept too as the procession of children filed by and Nikola stared, imagining himself among them. The rumor spread that another group would be collected and sent away within days. Everyone began to understand that whether they volunteered or not, Lia would soon be a village without children.

Among the parents who rebelled at the thought were Calliope and Tassi Mitros. Old Tassi's mill, at the top of the Perivoli, was the only one still operating. The guerrillas kept his family working long hours every day to grind the flour needed for their forces. Tassi's seventeen-year-old son Gakis had been conscripted as an *andarte*, but had managed to obtain a temporary release because of a back injury. Now the miller learned that the boy was to be the escort for the next group of children, and would probably be conscripted again once he reached Albania. Furthermore, Tassi's younger son Niko, twelve, the former hero and tormentor of Nikola Gatzoyiannis, was scheduled to be taken with the next group.

The husky, balding, sun-grizzled miller had always considered life a bad joke to be endured with cynical humor, but when it became clear that he was going to lose both his sons, Tassi stopped joking about his miseries and hunted for a way to save his boys. He confided in his brother-in-law Lukas Ziaras, who, when he heard that Tassi was searching for a way to get his children out of Lia, spilled out all the details of his two failed escape attempts.

375

'You're lucky they failed!' Tassi exploded. 'You're an idiot to lead them down the ravine! Where it levels out, you would have to cross fields that have just been harvested, and the lookouts would be sure to see you.'

Lukas bristled. 'Where do you suggest we leave from, the town square?' he retorted. 'Tell me, so that in my ignorance I may learn.'

'From your own house!' the miller replied.

'But we're fifty yards from the main lookout post. Two dozen people walking out under their noses? Be serious!'

'I was hunting those foothills with Foto Gatzoyiannis before you were born,' Tassi countered. 'Directly below your house is a patch of underbrush with gullies in it. And below that is a wheat field that hasn't been cut yet. Once you're past that, you're practically in the forest. And then you're out of sight and rifle range. I'll bring my family with you the next time and show you exactly how to do it.'

Lukas had an uneasy feeling that the reins were being wrested from his grip, but he had to admit that Tassi's plan sounded better than his own.

While the two men worked out the details of the new strategy, Soula Ziaras was sent to inform Eleni that they could wait no longer for Glykeria's return. They had to leave in three days. Next Sunday, June 20, there would be a waning moon and the weather would no longer be a problem. The wheat was high and golden in the summer sun and it hadn't rained since the end of May.

When Soula found her in the bean field and whispered the date for the new escape, Eleni turned to stare at her. 'We can't leave without Glykeria!' she whispered.

'Do you want to lose all of the children?' Soula replied. 'Lukas heard they're going to take them within the week.'

Eleni's hands shook so that she dropped the beans she was picking. Like every mother, she had a special love for the child who was the most troublesome. She couldn't bear to leave her behind, to be beaten, imprisoned or sent to fight in the front lines in retaliation for their act. Glykeria lacked the strength or endurance to be a guerrilla, Eleni thought. She had been spoiled all her life.

'Are you coming or not?' Soula demanded. 'We've got to leave on Sunday!'

Eleni didn't trust herself to speak, but nodded her head.

'Good!' Soula breathed. 'There's a new plan. We're leaving from our house instead of going down the ravine. Send your family two at a time as soon as it gets dark.'

'That's too risky!' Eleni said, surprised.

'Don't worry,' Soula said, turning away. 'Lukas has everything worked out.'

During the next two days, while Eleni desperately searched the mountain peaks for a sign of her daughter returning, the Ziaras and Mitros families made preparations. Gakis Mitros was a close schoolfriend of the young guerrilla Andreas Michopoulos and he paid a visit to the lookout post at the Church of the Virgin one evening to see him. 'It must be tough,' Gakis said to Andreas, 'spending all night combing the foothills for fascists.'

'Oh, it's not so bad,' Andreas replied, shifting his rifle importantly. 'Most nights we just send one patrol down the ravine and another down from Parayianni, and as far as the area in between, it's so steep we could hear and see the bastards coming from miles away. Anyway, the mines would probably get them first. So we usually just sit here and keep our eyes open.'

Soula Ziaras, too, paid a visit to the guerrilla lookout post, carrying the baby Alexi in her arms. She told the commanding sergeant that she was worried about mines. 'Have you put any near my fields?' she asked. 'You know that my babies play all around there.'

'Don't be afraid, *Kyria* Soula,' the man said. 'It's clean all the way down to the wheatfields.'

Early on Saturday morning, the day before the escape, Soula and her daughter Marianthe went carefully along the path the group would follow down through their fields. They cleared away every stone or branch that might cause someone to trip or make a noise. When they returned to the house, jittery at the thought of what tomorrow held, they found two guerrillas waiting for them.

*

That same morning, as Eleni was despairing of ever seeing Glykeria again, there was a knock on the door, filling her with hope. But she opened it to find the town crier back again, grinning vacantly. 'I'm sorry to tell you, *Kyria* Eleni, that we need another woman from your household,' he said. The guerrillas were demanding forty more women for the threshing fields, half from Lia, half from Babouri. 'The Liotes have to go today,' he concluded.

Fear shot through Eleni to her fingertips. Her mind began to spin. If she could stall him, they could move the departure up to tonight. 'Please, Petros,' she said, 'I'm not feeling well; I have a fever. But I could go with the Babouriotes tomorrow. I'm certain I could be ready.'

'It has to be today, whomever you send,' he said, and then, smiling, he repeated his familiar rhyme: 'Put a loaf in your pack and to Venetis' house make track!'

Eleni closed the door and collapsed in a chair. She tried to clear away the mist of fear that blurred her thoughts. Another person had to be sacrificed. If she chose carefully, perhaps it might improve Glykeria's chances of fleeing. She called the family together, and as soon as the children saw their mother's face they knew something had gone very wrong.

Eleni told them about the new order from the guerrillas and turned to Nitsa. 'You'll have to go this time, sister,' she said. 'If I send Olga or Kanta they'll make her an *andartina*, but in your condition they won't touch you. And you can find Glykeria and escape from the threshing fields.'

Nitsa began to screech. 'You have five children! If you lose one or two, what does it matter? You want to sacrifice me and the child in my womb to save your own family! You've always had it easier than me.'

Anger washed over Eleni like a convulsion, making the squat figure in front of her seem out of focus. She had bottled up her resentment of her lazy, selfish older sister for too long and now it burst out. 'Easier!' she screamed. 'I refused to go to America with my husband in order to stay here with you and our parents! My children and I have suffered for the last ten years because I made that choice, and now you want me to sacrifice another child so that you won't be inconvenienced!'

'Eleni, your sister's right,' Megali scolded in her quavering voice. 'Nitsa doesn't have your strength or your cleverness. She'd never have the courage to take Glykeria and escape.'

Eleni bowed her head. All her life she had been expected to be the strong one, and she was tired of it. Her greatest mistake had been her loyalty to her sister and her parents. The ties that had bound her to them, bonds of love, weakness and need, had become chains that were going to destroy her and her children. After a long silence Eleni turned to Olga. 'I'll go to Glykeria,' she said dully. 'You take Nikola and your sisters and go with Lukas Ziaras.' She did not look at Nitsa.

All the children began crying. 'We won't go without you!' Olga protested. 'We'll stay here and wait until you get back.'

'Then this family won't survive,' Eleni retorted. 'They'll take Nikola and Fotini for the *pedomasoma* and conscript you and Kanta.'

'We'll face those risks like everyone else in the village,' Kanta insisted.

'I won't see my family destroyed!' Eleni said very slowly and firmly. 'If you won't go, I'll tell them what we've been planning and they'll kill me right before your eyes.'

No one could meet her gaze. Nikola saw his mother's face contorted with agony, pale as a bone except for two circles of red burning on her cheeks.

'Now go away,' she said. 'I want to be alone to think.'

Once the decision was made, Eleni felt an unexpected peace come over her. She no longer had to torture herself, wondering what to do. Like a stream flowing down the mountain, she had no control over her path. But her last responsibility, before she surrendered herself to fate, was to advise the children as best she could in the minutes she had left.

Eleni was icily calm now. She had to think of all the eventualities. First she took Olga aside, into the good chamber. As the eldest, now nearly twenty-one, she would have the responsibility for the other four children. Eleni looked into the girl's large brown eyes, wide with fear, and wished that she were a bit more serious, a shade cleverer and less innocent in the ways of the world. But she knew Olga would protect the younger ones like a mother hen.

'Before you leave tomorrow night,' Eleni told her, 'You must write me a letter and leave it in the niche by the fireplace, where the *andartes* will be sure to find it. Write that Lukas and Megali forced you to go, that they did it to get money from your father, that you didn't want to leave and I mustn't worry about you but you had no choice. Write anything that you can think of to make them believe you've left without me knowing.'

She paused and thought for a moment, then added, 'Tomorrow, when you're certain that you're going, find one of the women they're bringing through here from Babouri, someone you can trust, and send word to me with her. If you say, "The wheat is ready to cut," then I'll know you're going that night and I'll try to escape with Glykeria. If you say,' "The wheat is not ready," then I'll know you've postponed it and I'll wait.'

'I can't go without you, *Mana*!' Olga cried. 'How will we ever find you again?'

'Don't be foolish,' Eleni said. 'Glykeria and I will get out easily. The Kalamas is much shallower there and we can wade across. We'll find you in Filiates. As a sign that you've reached the soldiers, when you get to the Great Ridge, light a big fire and I'll be able to see the smoke from Vatsounia. Then I'll know that you've made it to the other side.'

She looked away. 'But if we don't come to Filiates after a few days, I want you to telegraph your father and tell him to get you out to America as soon as possible. Don't say anything to anyone on the other side about the guerrillas or what's going on here that could leak back and get us into worse trouble. You must go on to Igoumenitsa or Yannina to wait for your papers, because the guerrillas may attack Filiates, and I want you to be safe.'

She reached out and turned Olga's face toward her, willing her own common sense to flow into the girl. 'Your grandfather will try to talk you into staying behind,' she said. 'Don't let him trick you or Kanta into marrying someone from Filiates or Igoumenitsa. All the men will be after you because you have a father in America; don't let them use you by appealing to your vanity. My parents only want someone to stay in Greece and care for them in their old age. But whether I'm living or dead, I won't rest until you're all in America and safe.'

Olga nodded, frightened by her mother's intensity.

Eleni fell silent, thinking. Had she forgotten anything? 'Tomorrow, while you're waiting for the sun to set,' she added, 'go to your grandfather's fields by the mill. Cut some of the wheat, because it's ready and if you don't tend to it, someone might become suspicious.'

She couldn't think of anything else. She searched Olga's face, trying to find reassurance there. 'The other children are now your responsibility until you hand them over to your father,' she said. 'I'm hanging them around your neck.'

Olga began to cry.

While Eleni was saying farewell to her children, a similar scene was going on in the Ziaras house at the bottom of the village. The two guerrillas had arrived at the door to announce that a woman was required at once for the threshing field.

Soula began trembling so at the sight of the uniformed men that she could hardly stand. As soon as the door closed behind them, she turned and looked at Lukas, who was pacing like a caged animal. Things had been going too well, he told himself. Now this! Truly God had stacked the deck against him.

Soula forced herself to speak calmly. 'It's all right,' she said. 'I'll go to the harvest and you take the children tomorrow as we planned.'

Lukas exploded. He would never admit it, even to himself, but it was inconceivable to him to risk the escape without the quiet, solid presence of his wife beside him.

'Yes, that's right, you go!' he sputtered. 'And when we get to the other side, who's going to look after all these mewling children? You want to make me a wet nurse, don't you? I won't stand for it! Marianthe will go to the threshing fields. She's young and strong and smart enough to escape on her own.'

Marianthe stiffened angrily. She had spent her life caring for the endless parade of babies, working as hard as her mother, and now her father was discarding her as if she was worthless. But she knew it would be fruitless to argue. He would only lash out at her because he felt guilty. Sullenly she began to gather up some things for the journey to the harvest.

Lukas decided to escort his daughter to the guerrillas' commissary. As they passed by the Haidis house he stopped and knocked at the gate. Eleni hurried out distractedly to meet him. Looking at Lukas' and Marianthe's stricken faces, Eleni said, 'They came to your house too?'

He nodded. 'Marianthe's going,' he said. 'God protect her!'

'So am I!' said Eleni. 'My worthless sister has refused to go. But Glykeria and I hope to escape on our own from there. Of course, I'll take Marianthe too. If we can't get away, I'll look after her, Lukas. But you must take the rest as we planned.'

Eleni looked at the small, nervous man who would have to lead her children through a hundred dangers, and her heart faltered. She tried to think of something to say that would lend him wisdom and courage, but all she said, in a voice so low he had to lean forward to hear, was, 'I'm turning my children over to you, Lukas, and I'll ask you for an accounting, if not in this life, then in the next.'

Eleni realized that she had only a few minutes left with her children. She used a few of them to braid Fotini's honey-brown hair for the last time. Nitsa was seated cross-legged in a corner, watching her, but Eleni would not acknowledge her presence.

When she had finished both braids, Eleni hugged Fotini fiercely, making the girl squirm. 'Don't worry, sweetheart,' she said. 'Glykeria and I will get out and soon we'll all be together in Filiates, on our way to America.'

'No, you won't, Mother,' the ten-year-old replied without emotion. 'We're all going to leave, but you'll always be here.'

Megali gasped and spoke for the first time since the argument between Eleni and Nitsa. 'Bite your tongue, you wicked child!' she said. The old woman put her apron over her head and began to keen a lament.

Eleni told Kanta and Nikola to come up to the commissary

382

with her, to stay with her until the last moment. Olga and Fotini were to remain in the house and act as if nothing was wrong. 'We can't all go up there in a parade,' she said. 'It would make everyone suspicious. We'll say goodbye here.'

Suddenly there was no more time. With numb fingers Eleni removed her apron and took down her long black sleeveless tunic with two red vertical stripes. She put it on over her brown wool dress, faded from washing. Not looking into their eyes, she gave Fotini, Olga and Megali a last kiss, then quickly wound her black kerchief around her face.

Eleni left her sister without a farewell, just as her father had done to her. Megali's keening increased in volume as Nitsa turned toward the wall. Fotini and Olga trailed their mother outside, reaching out to touch her. As Eleni started out the gate, Olga grabbed her arm, crying 'Wait, *Mana*! I want to kiss you again!' Eleni pulled away and averted her face, hidden in the folds of her kerchief. Olga reached up and pulled down the kerchief, seeing the tears that she had tried to hide. Neither spoke as Olga rose on tiptoe and kissed her mother for the last time.

As Eleni and the two children continued on up the path toward the Perivoli, Olga's sobbing brought their curious neighbor, Vasilena Karapano, out of her house. She trotted up to take a close look at Olga. 'Why on earth are you carrying on like that, child?' she asked. 'Your mother's only going to the wheat fields! What's the matter with you?'

Megali came out the door and led Olga back into the house.

Eleni, Kanta and Nikola climbed silently up the path toward the Venetis house, now the commissary, which lay next to the old Church of St. Demetrios. The other women, some leading donkeys, were slowly gathering in the yard. Eleni was shocked to see that her sister-in-law Alexo was in the group. The two women exchanged frightened looks but did not speak to each other for fear the guerrillas would notice and remember it when their children escaped.

Eleni settled down on the steps of the house and took the boy in her lap, where he sat quietly. She put her cheek against Nikola's, breathing in the familiar smell of him, feeling his warmth against her cold skin. Since the day this son was born, his warmth had been there, next to her, his small body like an extension of her own.

A guerrilla came around, taking down the names of the women and giving each one a piece of bread with a slice of thick marmalade. Eleni carefully broke the marmalade in two, handed a piece to Nikola and the other one to Kanta. She put the bread in her pocket.

She moved Nikola back next to her so that she could look at him. He was wearing striped, homemade knee pants with suspenders over a white knitted long shirt. He was barefoot. His hair was clipped short in the village style, golden brown in the sun and uneven where it made a widow's peak on his wide forehead. Eleni longed to touch him, but she simply looked, trying to burn his features one by one into her memory: the pale scar on his forehead where he had fallen from the mulberry tree, the square hands and thin dusty legs.

She tried to imagine what he would look like as a man, but she couldn't. His face now was as open as a flower, his eyebrows drawing together over the deep-set brown eyes. They were rimmed with red, the sign that always told her he was upset or about to come down with something. The corners of his mouth were turned down as if he was going to cry. She thought of all the times she had shrugged off his incessant questions. Who would answer them now?

Eleni turned to Kanta and took a breath. 'Tomorrow night, from the moment you leave the house, Nikola will be your responsibility.' she said. 'Olga has enough to worry about, so I'm putting him in your care. Protect him like your own eyes.'

Kanta's face was as pale as her mother's. 'I promise, *Mana*,' she said. 'Just come back to us!'

'If I don't,' Eleni said harshly, 'remember this: Anyone who stays in Greece, who doesn't go to America, will have my curse. When you leave the house, I want you to throw a black stone behind you so you'll never come back!'

Kanta nodded and swallowed. Eleni turned back to the boy, pulling him against her, trying not to frighten him with the intensity of her embrace. He came obediently into her arms and they sat a moment that way, as she felt his head under her chin and gazed up the hill at the house where he had

384

been born. When he was only days old she had thought he was dying and had him baptized in haste. How much more it hurt to lose him now. They had been everything to each other for too long. No one else knew his fears and hopes or the way he hugged a problem to himself, growing quiet and distracted, until he arrived at a solution. He was always bringing her gifts, producing them out of his pocket like a sacred talisman: an iridescent beetle, speckled plover's egg, an odd-shaped stone. He would hand it to her, his eyes bright with suspense, waiting for her reaction. What could she give him now to protect him from what lay ahead? She remembered how frightened he had been in the fog. 'Tomorrow night,' she whispered, 'you must hold Kanta's hand and be very brave for me.' She felt him nod his head against her breast.

'Everybody up!' shouted a guerrilla, making the three of them jump nervously. 'We're leaving from the Makos house.'

The whole group set out up the hillside. Eleni held Nikola's hand. When they arrived at the house of Athena Makos, the world fell away below their feet and they could see far to the east, where the women would disappear around the mountain. She turned to look at Nikola and realized he was trying unsuccessfully to smile. 'I'll be brave, *Mana*,' he said.

Eleni looked from Kanta to Nikola, of all her children the two who were most the flesh of her flesh. Then she embraced Kanta.

She felt Nikola's hand slip back into hers and closed her eyes, praying for the strength to do what she had to. Then she remembered. She reached up and lifted a large chain from around her neck. It held her most magical possession – a cross-shaped box with a crude figure of Christ inscribed on the front, which held a splinter of bone from a saint. She lifted the chain over the boy's head, then smoothed his hair with a quick gesture. He frowned in embarrassment.

'Kiss me. This one time,' she said and he moved into her arms. 'My blood and heart!' she whispered.

Then she put his hand in Kanta's and turned away.

It was the look in her eyes as she put the chain around my neck that filled me with the awful knowledge of what she was doing. She was giving me this charm, which felt so heavy on my chest, as a consolation for losing her. I didn't want the silver cross, I wanted the warmth of her body, the comfort of her face, which was now so white that it seemed I could see through to the bones which pulled the skin taut. She had made me promise to be brave, and I resolved to keep that vow, to be as stalwart as the Spartan boy while the fox gnawed at his bowels, so that she would come back to me.

Kanta was crying, but I stood silent, frowning in the sunlight, as my mother set off down into the ravine, the last woman in line. Every few steps she would turn around as if to reassure herself that we were still there.

Standing on the edge of the great chasm, we watched the dark line of women descend into the depths until they were hidden by the green foliage along the stream flowing through the bottom of the ravine. After about five minutes the serpentine line reappeared on the other side, crawling like a column of ants up to the base of the hill of the Prophet. If I hadn't known that she was last in line, I never could have recognized her as the small brown-and-black figure that stopped every now and then to look back.

The line of women continued on into the distance, around the base of the hill. There was a spot where the path curved around a myrtle tree and out of sight. I concentrated all my energy on holding my mother in my sight. When she reached the spot where she would disappear from view, she stopped and turned around again. As she looked toward the cliff where she knew we were watching, she raised her hand above her head.

Years later I would have moments, even days, when my mother's features would blur and grow dim in my memory's eye, but I never lost the clear image of her gesture and the way she looked on that green and gold summer day when she turned around to wave to me for the last time.

386

PART FOUR

RETRIBUTION

Behold me, what I suffer and
from whom . . .

– SOPHOCLES, *Antigone*

CHAPTER THIRTEEN

On June 14, 1948, five days before Eleni and the other women from Lia were dispatched to the threshing fields of the Mourgana, the government forces launched the first major attack on the guerrilla headquarters in the Grammos mountains, eighty miles to the northeast of Lia on the Albanian border. The offensive, code-named Operation Coronis, was supposed to capture the insurgent stronghold within two weeks, but the battle would stretch on for seventy-four days, taking an appalling toll in lives, and would ultimately decide the outcome of the civil war.

The guerrillas had chosen a forbidding natural fortress as their refuge. The Grammos range is a series of steep ridges stretching south of the Albanian border, ranging in height from 5,000 to 8,000 feet. There was not even a dirt road around the mountains that the Greek army could use in their attack, but on Grammos' northern tier in Albania an old road, built by the Italians, ran along its entire thirty-mile length, making it easy for the guerrillas on the summits to be supplied by the Albanians.

General Markos had long been expecting an attack on Grammos, and he had gathered 12,500 of his best fighters there, leaving light forces in other parts of occupied territory. He positioned his men along two lines of defense, two circles of walls that had to be breached before Grammos could be taken. The outer line blocked the passes leading up to the heights, and the inner line, formed by strong, well-camouflaged fortifications, encircled the center of the mountain fortress. The approaches to both rings of defense were lined with dense carpets of mines.

The Greek army sent more than four times the manpower of the guerrillas to attack Grammos: five entire divisions – 40,000 men – supported by air force, artillery and commando squadrons. They also had a new weapon, being used in battle for the first time – napalm.

'May the Grammos range become Slavo-Communism's gravestone,' was the battle cry of the government forces. They planned to surround the guerrillas with two divisions, cutting them off from their supply base in Albania, while three more divisions moved in from the perimeter. But they failed to complete the circle along the Albanian border or to breach the guerrillas' outer defense wall. The Greek army's general staff then tried a new strategy: direct frontal attacks by all five divisions. Finally a fifteen-mile hole was broken through the outer defense line, and the attackers moved toward the inner wall around the main guerrilla base. By that time the slopes around it looked, according to one observer, as if they had been 'fried in napalm.'

The critical battle raging at Grammos created frenetic activity among the guerrillas stationed in the Mourgana villages. They had to provide sanctuary for raiding parties sent to strike at the enemy communications deep inside nationalist territory; they engaged the soldiers on the rim of ridges to the south to keep them from being sent to reinforce the army's divisions on Grantmos, and every night raiding parties crept across the foothills to harass and snipe at the soldiers. It was also the Mourgana guerrillas' responsibility to mobilize civilians to harvest the wheat, beans and other grains critical for the survival of the beleaguered fighters to the northeast. The Grammos range was the vital core of the DAG, and to protect it, every able-bodied person in the occupied villages had to be thrown into the effort.

WAITING FOR THE SUN

AS THE FILE OF women struggled over the mountaintops toward the threshing fields to the northeast, Eleni tried to concentrate on her approaching reunion with Glykeria, but she was remembering the image of her son standing on the edge of the cliff, thinking how vulnerable he looked to the dangers he had to survive if she would ever see him again.

By the time the group reached Vatsounia, it was clear that their destination lay farther on. All around them the fields of hay and wheat had been cut and the stubble burned, leaving ugly, black scars on the red earth. They spent the rest of the night sleeping in the deserted houses of the village, then moved on at dawn, the temperature rising with the sun in the sky until the dust of the road clogged their lungs and their clothes stuck to their backs.

About noon they came to a halt in Granitsopoula, a town of ancient two-story stone buildings around a square shaded with spreading plane trees. Nearby flowed a wide, shallow stream, a tributary of the Kalamas River, which was faintly visible in the foothills below. The Kalamas marked the boundary of the guerrilla-occupied territory.

As they stood marveling at the beauty of the place, the still air carried to them the sound of women chatting on the bank of the stream. They had caught up with the first group of workers taken from Lia. Eleni broke out of the line, calling Glykeria's name as she ran; a figure in a red dress detached itself from the crowd on the grass. Eleni stared at her daughter. Glykeria's baby fat had melted away, replaced by hollows on her sunburned cheeks and under her eyes. Her face and arms were scratched and bleeding, and her hair and dress were matted with the prickly chaff from the wheat. One side of her jaw was swollen, but she was smiling.

'My poor child, you've been suffering!' Eleni exclaimed, reaching for her.

'I'm fine, *Mana*, now that you're here!' Glykeria cried. 'I was afraid I'd lost you.' She caught sight of her aunt Alexo, and ran to hug her, too.

It was the midday break for the harvesters and Eleni sat down with her daughter in the shade out of earshot of the others. She whispered that the family was preparing to escape, and that the two of them would have to flee separately. Glykeria seized her hands in excitement. She was fed up with the backbreaking work of threshing and ready to leave immediately. 'I know all the paths around here!' she whispered. 'We'll make it to the Kalamas easily. Let's go tonight!'

'Tomorrow night,' her mother replied. 'First we have to be sure the others are really going. If we leave before them, they'll be caught and maybe even killed. Olga's going to send a message with one of the women from Babouri that they're setting out, and I told them to light a signal fire from the Great Ridge to let us know they reached it.'

That night the women stretched out on the polished wood floors of the empty houses to sleep. Eleni and Alexo put Glykeria between them, all under one blanket, and they spent most of the night whispering. Glykeria told them of her misadventures while she was moving with the harvesters from one abandoned village to another. 'Three weeks in this wool dress! I thought I'd die!' she grumbled. 'I got my period and had nothing else to wear, so I had to wash my clothes and put them on wet. That gave me a fever and then I got a toothache. I cried for you every day, *Mana*, and the other girls picked on me for being lazy and slow, but now that you're here, we'll escape and I'll never pick up a scythe again!'

After Glykeria fell asleep, Eleni went outside in the darkness and spent the rest of the night staring in the direction of the Great Ridge, waiting for the sign of a fire and repeating a wordless prayer for the deliverance of her children.

At sunup, weak with fatigue and worry, she returned to the room where Glykeria slept. Eleni had a feeling that the children had set out as planned at sunset, but there was no sign that they ever reached the Great Ridge. She tried to avoid the obvious explanation: that they were intercepted on the way.

That morning the women set about threshing under the incandescent disc of the sun, Glykeria and Eleni working side by side. Each time they came to the end of a row, mother and daughter would straighten up, rubbing their backs, and gaze at the Kalamas, beckoning them from the distance with the promise of freedom.

Eleni kept scanning the top of the hill, waiting for the group to arrive from Babouri, one of them carrying a message from Olga. Just before noon, twenty women entered the village, and Eleni anxiously searched the faces of the new arrivals. Finally one of them, Mitsena Migdales, walked up to her and said, 'Olga came up to me yesterday morning as we passed through Lia, and told me to tell you that she was going to cut the wheat.'

The woman was startled when Eleni seized her hands gratefully, then ran off to speak to Glykeria. They took up their scythes with new energy. The waiting was over; the family had gone. They could leave that night to cross the Kalamas and, God willing, find the children on the other side. Eleni tried to stay calm by imagining the family together again and free.

She had only a few hours to savor her dream. The harvesters were sitting in the shade of a grove of trees, devouring the noon meal of cheese and bread, when two guerrillas arrived on horseback from the nearby threshing ground. Eleni was astonished to see Rano Athanassiou, Olga's best friend, riding behind one of them. Rano had been sent to the harvest in the first group, along with Glykeria, but Eleni looked in vain for her among the women cutting wheat. Glykeria said enviously that Rano had been chosen to supervise the women at the threshing floor, a much easier job. Now the Gatzoyiannis women stared as Rano neared them.

The two guerrillas dismounted, and one of them called for

the group's attention. 'Half of you are needed to go to Vistrovo, where there are more fields to harvest,' he shouted. 'The rest will stay here until we're finished.'

Eleni watched in an agony of suspense as the guerrilla went about arbitrarily choosing the women who would go to Vistrovo. When he came up to her and Glykeria, his eyes rested on them for a moment too long, then he said, 'The girl goes.'

'Please, Comrade!' Eleni begged, trying to keep the desperation out of her voice. 'Let my daughter stay here. I haven't seen her for three weeks. Let me have just one more night with her.'

'No, she's going,' he replied sharply and moved on. Eleni noticed that Rano was watching them. Eleni got up and went over to the young woman, who had always been like one of her family. It was Rano who had come to warn them when she overheard the guerrillas planning to search their house, and she had hidden with Olga and Kanta when they began conscripting women.

'Please, Rano!' Eleni begged. 'They'll listen to you! Tell him how important it is for me to have a little more time with Glykeria. The girl's sick; she's just a baby! She's been working all these weeks. You could take her place in Vistrovo. Do it for me!'

Rano said she'd do what she could. Eleni watched as the young woman went over to the guerrilla and whispered in his ear. He turned to look toward Eleni and Glykeria, who stared back imploringly. But when they ordered the women for Vistrovo to line up, Rano didn't move. The guerrilla walked over to Glykeria. 'I told you, you're going with them,' he snapped. Eleni could see Rano lift her shoulders in a shrug of helplessness.

Mother and daughter looked at each other in despair, their hope of freedom slipping from them. They barely had time for a last kiss before the guerrilla pulled Glykeria away and the group set out toward Vistrovo. Rano stood nearby, watching impassively.

All that afternoon Eleni worked mechanically. As the sun began to set and the women filed back from the fields, Alexo ran to catch up with her. 'You have a clear night for it,' she whispered. 'As soon as everyone's asleep, you can slip down into the foothills.'

Eleni turned and looked at her. 'I can't go now!' she said, as if explaining to a child. 'Think what they'd do to Glykeria if I escaped. I can't go to the others and leave this one to die!'

Alexo argued with her in whispers, but she refused to answer. That night Eleni passed her untouched dinner ration to her sister-in-law and then went outside to sit on the steps of the house, facing south toward the shadow of the Great Ridge. One of the guerrillas guarding the women noticed her all-night vigil. It seemed to him that she was watching for something.

With Eleni gone, the Gatzoyiannis children scurried about like a flock of chicks without the hen, trying to prepare for the escape. Following their mother's directions, Olga and Kanta set out early in the day to make a show of cutting the wheat in the family's field, but they did more whispering than harvesting, and returned home early so that Olga could compose the letter she was supposed to leave behind. As neighbor women passed them on the path, the girls imagined suspicious looks and sinister undertones in every greeting. All day long they vacillated between fear that the escape would be canceled and hope that it would. Then Olga wrote with a pencil stub in her childish scrawl:

> *Mana*, we're leaving. Lukas Ziaras and Grandmother are taking us to Filiates to send us on to Father in America. Don't be upset – we didn't want to leave you, but Lukas said we had to or he would write Father that we didn't want to go to him. Forgive us.

She studied the letter, weighing each word to see if it rang false. Then she hid the paper in the wall niche beside the fireplace, and worried aloud that the guerrillas wouldn't find it.

Eleni had explained the new procedure to them. In order for the whole family to assemble at Lukas Ziaras' house without arousing suspicion, they would go at different times. Well before the sun set, Kanta would take Nikola and Fotini with her and lead the two milk goats to graze in the fields of their uncle Foto at the bottom of the village. After sundown they would abandon the goats and slip into the Ziaras house nearby, while Megali and Nitsa would start out from the Haidis house. Olga would come last because she had to wait until the family's flock of sheep had been brought back from the pasture by the half-witted shepherdess, Vasilo Barka, who had been paid to take them for the day. Once the animals were securely locked in the cellar, Olga had to hurry to the Ziaras house and the exodus would begin.

Distraught by the responsibility that rested on her shoulders, Olga hovered in the window, watching the sun, until she decided it was time to send off Kanta, Nikola and Fotini. Suddenly Fotini plunged the household into a crisis. The ten-year-old couldn't find the precious sack that held her collection of hair bows, charms, tin rings, and baubles handed out by the guerrillas' commissary head. When life seemed unjust to Fotini, as it did nearly every day, she displayed the histrionic range of a tragedienne. 'That child started crying with her first breath and hasn't stopped since,' Eleni often complained, clapping her hands over her ears. Now Fotini was screaming that without her treasures she wouldn't set foot out the door. She was interrupted by a sharp knock that stunned everyone into silence.

Olga hesitated, but the knocking became more insistent. She peeked out and saw Kostina Thanassis, their plump, grandmotherly neighbor from the Perivoli, whose home was a warehouse for guerrilla supplies.

Kostina chirped that she had brought some marmalade as a treat for her favorite little boy. Nikola obediently let the old woman kiss and cuddle him while the rest watched tensely. 'Poor child, with your mother off at the harvesting,' she crooned. 'You must come up to Grandma Kostina's house tomorrow. I'll see if I can't find you a chocolate somewhere.' The girls sucked in their breath, afraid Nikola would reply that tomorrow was too late, but he only nodded and stared at the floor.

It was past the hour for Kanta and the youngest children to

leave, but Kostina rattled on about the terrible things happening in their old neighborhood. While the girls gave each other desperate looks, Megali crept behind her and sprinkled a few precious grains of salt – the charm to make unwanted company leave. Finally Kostina stood up. As Olga held the door open, the old woman suddenly embraced Nikola and whispered, 'My golden boy, may God protect you!' Then she was gone, leaving the rest to wonder how much she knew.

The departure of Kostina Thanassis plunged the Gatzoyiannis family into frantic activity. Kanta ran to the cellar and tied the two milk goats on ropes, then went back for Fotini and Nikola. Fotini had renewed her wails over the lost sack of keepsakes, and Nikola stood inside the doorway, frowning with worry, holding his school bag – the brown-and-tan leather satchel that his father had sent from America. In it was a rusty Byzantine sword blade that the boy had unearthed at the spring outside his grandmother's gate, along with the carefully ruled notebooks he had used in his two years at the village school. 'What are you doing with that?' Kanta demanded.

'If I don't show them my lessons, they may make me take first and second grades over again when we get to America,' Nikola explained.

'Nonsense!' Olga shrieked, her voice rising. 'You can't take that with you! They have better notebooks and school bags where we're going.' She snatched the valise out of his hand and threw it behind the door, then shoved him out into the path, where Kanta handed him the lead of one of the goats.

As Kanta dragged the two children down the path, Fotini uttered a shuddering sob and Nikola turned around for a last glimpse of the house. Although Olga, Nitsa and Megali were still inside, the place seemed sad and deserted to him in the vivid late-afternoon light, and he felt a pang of sympathy for the house and animals, abandoned so suddenly. They had left everything behind: his sword blade, two years of schoolwork. Even his mother's good brown dress still hung on a hanger in the good chamber, like an echo of her presence.

When the sun was balancing on the crest of the Great

Ridge, Olga ordered Megali and Nitsa to set out, heading for the Ziaras house by a roundabout route, taking care not to arouse anyone's suspicions. She could see that was a wasted warning; Megali was already sobbing and Nitsa's last dramatic cry before she waddled out the door was, 'This is the night I'm going to die! I can feel it!'

Olga stared out the southern window at the setting sun, watching small pink-tinted clouds chasing one another across the sky. When twilight fell, Kanta would enter the Ziaras door with Nikola and Fotini, but Olga had to wait until Crazy Vasilo brought back the family's flock, and she was afraid that the others would get impatient and leave without her. She couldn't start before the animals came, because Vasilo would find the house empty and raise the alarm.

The family of the miller Tassi Mitros also spent the day making preparations for their escape. They had to be especially careful because one of the guerrillas' cooks, a crochety old man named Kyriakos, lived in their house.

Tassi's wife Calliope had been telling her neighbors for days that her sister Soula's baby was gravely ill. She left early in the morning for the Ziaras house, saying to Kyriakos that the baby was dying. Her husband Tassi and her two sons, Niko, twelve, and Gakis, seventeen, planned to join her at dusk, using the same excuse. In the meantime the younger boy was sent with the family's flock up to the pasture at the top of the Perivoli.

Late in the afternoon a messenger from the guerrillas arrived at the Mitros house and told the shaken miller that he was summoned to appear before the village council to face charges that he had refused to go to Tsamanta to repair a mill. Out of earshot of the nosy guerrilla cook, Tassi told his elder son that he would try to get away from the hearing in time, but if he didn't, Gakis should pick up Niko from the pasture and head for the Ziaras house without him.

When the sun was low in the sky, Gakis climbed up to the pasture where Niko was grazing the sheep. There were two other children there with their families' flocks, a girl of about nine and a boy even younger.

'Come on, we're going!' Gakis hissed to Niko. 'Father's not coming back in time.'

'But what do I do with the animals?' Niko asked.

'Leave them here!' Gakis ordered. As he pulled his brother down the path, they didn't hear the other two children calling after them, 'Where are you going? You forgot the animals!'

The Gatzoyiannis family had worried that they might be betrayed by nosy neighbors, sharp-eyed guerrillas or even the bleating of their own sheep and goats, but nothing like that raised the alarm and set the Communists in pursuit; it was these two small children. Jealous of the way Niko walked off, leaving his animals behind, the little girl and boy did the same and returned home empty-handed, making their astonished mothers so angry that one of the guerrillas came over to see what the commotion was about. When he learned of the odd behavior of the Mitros boys, he set out for the miller's house, where he found no one but the perplexed guerrilla cook.

Kanta, Nikola and Fotini arrived at the Ziaras house even before the sun set. In their eagerness they had turned the two goats loose to forage in Foto Gatzoyiannis' precious fig tree and slipped away early.

Kanta was startled to find Calliope Mitros there, bending with Soula Ziaras over the cradle of the baby. While Soula watched in alarm, Calliope was spooning *tsipouro,* the clear, fiery moonshine, into Alexi's mouth. There was a wad of cotton soaked in the same spirits taped to his navel. The burning taste made the baby scream, and he spit out the liquor as fast as his aunt poured it in him while Soula cried, 'Enough! You're killing him!' Eventually Alexi stopped screaming and his eyelids began to close. Finally he fell silent and Calliope straightened up, her face gleaming with perspiration.

Lukas was smoking nervously in a corner. Kanta went over to him and asked in an angry whisper what Calliope Mitros was doing there. Had he told her about the escape? The tinker stamped out his cigarette, avoiding her eyes, and shrugged. After all, he said, Calliope was his own wife's sister and the guerrillas were threatening to take both her sons. Besides, he added, it was safer to have another man along, and Tassi Mitros – he cleared his throat self-consciously – knew the foothills nearly as well as he did himself.

'You promised *Mana* not to tell anyone!' Kanta reproached him, wishing her mother were there to handle this new threat. But there was a soft knock at the door, and Lukas turned away. Angrily Kanta led Nikola and Fotini over to a corner to await the arrival of the others.

Gakis and Niko Mitros came in out of breath and when they told their mother that Tassi hadn't returned from the village council yet, Calliope wailed like a lost bird, 'We can't leave without him; they'll hang him tomorrow!' Niko Mitros watched his mother's outburst wide-eyed and pale. Nikola saw how frightened he was and wondered at the transformation of the tough 'guerrilla captain' who had terrorized him and the other younger boys of the neighborhood.

Shortly after sunset Megali and Nitsa arrived, preceded by the sound of their frightened moans. Their fear infected the others, and Kanta nearly shrieked when the door opened to admit three unexpected figures: a woman and two girls who crowded into the smoky room carrying sacks of belongings. Everyone recognized the tall, gray-haired amazon who towered a head above Lukas Ziaras as Chrysoula Drouboyiannis, forty-one, a sister-in-law of the woman whom Lukas had invited on the second attempt. Kanta's nerves snapped and she turned on Lukas, accusing him of spilling the plot to half the village, now that her mother was not around to make him keep his promise. But her cousin Arete, who had come behind the new arrivals, stepped forward and admitted that she was the one who had invited Chrysoula to join them.

Arete and Chrysoula had been childhood friends. Both shared the stigma of being barren and knew they were in danger of being conscripted as *andartinas* because their husbands were living far away in Crete. Chrysoula had brought along her two teenaged nieces, who had been left in her care by their mother, Constantina, when she was forced to go to the threshing fields in the same group as Eleni. Chrysoula was usually a sensible, cool-headed woman, but now she was trembling after the ordeal of walking from the eastern edge of the village past two guerrilla outposts. She reported that in the distant one, at the Church of St. Friday, a noisy party was going on, celebrating the birth of a son to the notorious guerrilla Stravos.

Lukas began to pace. 'Where the hell is Tassi?' he muttered. 'This is the time to leave!'

'Olga isn't here yet either,' Kanta reminded him.

Lukas cursed under his breath. He raised a corner of a lace curtain to peer out the window, then abruptly dropped it and reached for his white towel, wrapping it around his neck. 'There's someone coming this way from the church!' he exclaimed. 'And he's got a gun. Everyone into the stable, and for God's sake plug up your noise! I'll stand on the trap door.'

Lukas and Gakis Mitros herded the Gatzoyiannis family, the Drouboyiannis women and Arete into the small dirt-floored cellar where the animals were kept, then closed the hatch over their heads. Kanta crowded against the others, cobwebs brushing her face, and took Nikola into her lap.

The Ziaras and Mitros families stayed upstairs to carry on the charade of attending to the baby Alexi, who now was wheezing in his alcoholic stupor and looked convincingly ill.

From the cellar the hidden fugitives could hear everything: Lukas coughing nervously, his wife Soula sobbing. She was so frightened that it was easy to produce tears for her 'sick' child. 'Oh, my poor little boy! Sweet Virgin, save him!' she cried as the guerrilla rapped on the door. Kanta could hear Lukas' footsteps overhead, on his way to open it.

At the door was a young man from the nearby lookout post, carrying a handful of dried tobacco leaves. The fugitives learned to their relief that he had come to the Ziaras house, the nearest one to the church, simply because he wanted to use a knife and a cutting board to shred the tobacco.

Seeing the weeping women, the guerrilla inquired solicitously about the baby. Lukas shook his head and said his son might not survive the night. Studying the child, who was flushed and evidently unconscious, the *andarte* offered his sympathy and suggested they apply upturned glasses with candles burning inside to his chest to draw out the evil vapors.

While the guerrilla set about chopping the tobacco leaves, Lukas made a strained effort at conversation. 'How goes the struggle, Comrade?' he asked. 'What do you hear from Grammos?'

'It's still holding,' the young man replied, 'but it won't last much longer. We've lost too many men. Every day there seems to be more of them and less of us. Next place they'll attack is here. If you ask me, we'll be pulling back into Albania soon. But don't worry, we won't leave you to the fascists. We'll take everyone and everything that can walk. Within a month, mark my words, there won't be a rooster crowing in this village.'

Hearing this from the cellar, Kanta shivered. Their mother had been right; they couldn't have waited any longer. She heard Lukas say meekly, 'Do what you can, Comrade! That's all the people can ask of you boys. Whatever happens, we're with you.' Then she heard his rasping cough and the sound of a match being struck.

Kanta's trembling infected Nikola. They were both praying that the guerrilla would leave before Olga walked in.

Finally the visitor finished his cigarette and left with wishes for the baby's recovery. As they climbed out of the cellar, Kanta began to fret that Olga had been captured on the way; it was now long past sundown. But within minutes there was a timid knock at the door. Olga hurried in and nearly screamed at the sight of all the strange faces in the room.

'Damn your husband!' Lukas said to Calliope Mitros, growing increasingly frightened at the realization he would have to lead the group without Tassi's help. 'We can't wait any longer. We've got to start.'

'But you can't just leave him behind to be killed!' Calliope cried. 'And he's bringing all our sovereigns.'

'It's time for the children to get started,' Lukas said. 'If we wait any longer, the lookouts will get suspicious at seeing them up so late.' He explained the plan: the children were to pretend they were playing hide and seek, and gather in the gullies below the house, making plenty of noise. One by one they would creep together beneath the underbrush in the gullies. The mothers would set out next, calling for their children to

402

come home, and when they reached them, they would crawl into hiding beside the children and wait for Lukas to come last and lead them through the wheat field just below.

Lukas surveyed the frightened faces gathered around him and wondered how he had ever agreed to this harebrained enterprise. There were nineteen people crowded into the small room, eight adults and eleven children. He had counted on the presence of Tassi Mitros, who worked out this plan. Now he would have to lead these terrified women and children out alone. Lukas squared his shoulders and mustered his courage. Why should he share the glory with his arrogant brother-in-law?

In his croaking voice, Lukas reminded the group that the first leg of the journey was the most dangerous. After they left the gullies, they had to pass through a field of tall ripe wheat that was within sight and hearing of the lookout post. They must crouch down below the top of the wheat and walk very quietly, moving slowly. Once they were out of the wheat field there was a patch of open hillside, then they would be in a thick, dark grove of trees which would shield them from the sentinel's eyes.

Lukas examined the women and children to see if they had understood and was struck by what an unpromising group they were for such a risky undertaking. He tried to conceal the desperation welling up in him by assuming the demeanor of a military officer. 'If anyone makes a sound, I'm sending them back!' he snapped, glaring at Nitsa, who was emitting a constant, wordless moan to herself. 'And if anyone – woman or child – gets lost or separated from the rest, we leave them. We can't sacrifice the whole group to save one life.'

Everyone jumped as a tattoo of knocks assaulted the door. Lukas opened it a crack and then nearly staggered with relief at the sight of the miller standing there, his fringe of gray hair disheveled and his face pale. 'We've got to go now!' Tassi gasped. 'I went back to the house to get the sovereigns I had there and that bastard Kyriakos was standing in the door wanting to know where everybody was. He was so suspicious I told him I'd bring Calliope and the boys back right away. It won't be long until he starts raising a hue and cry.'

Lukas shooed the children out the door, his own offspring leading the way to the gullies. Nikola tried to shout with the rest, 'Here I come, ready or not!' but his voice stuck in his throat. As the children approached the hiding place and crept together into one of the hollows, they fell silent and huddled together, shivering in the damp night air, heavy with the scent of gorse and heather.

A few minutes later Soula Ziaras stood on her front steps with the baby's pouch on her back and shouted in a shrill voice: 'George, you wicked boy! Where have you got to now? Devil take those children!'

One by one the women appeared in the gully, crowding in on top of one another until Fotini giggled that it was just like a game of 'sardines.' Kanta put a hand over her mouth.

Tassi and Lukas came last, tense and silent. When they were all together, they sat for a moment, listening to the discordant singing and the melancholy lament of a harmonica, faintly audible from the lookout post on the far eastern edge of the village, below the Church of St. Friday.

Lukas passed the word along that they must take off their shoes to lessen the noise of their steps through the brittle straw and follow him in single file. 'Keep low,' he hissed. 'If they see a head popping up, we're done for.'

Lukas crept off first, choosing a path he had stamped out earlier that day. He put down each foot heel first, bringing the toe down gently, as he did when stalking game. He slipped into the wheat field holding his breath, walking crouched over, almost on all fours, and disappeared into the sea of wheat, weaving through the crackling straw to diminish the rustling.

Kanta came next, walking ahead of Nikola and Fotini in case she stepped on a land mine. Soula Ziaras, with the baby on her back, held Olympia and George by the hand while her daughter Eftychia, ten, crowded behind. Megali leaned hard on Arete, who whispered to her, trying to make her hurry.

Behind them came Nitsa, sighing loudly and clutching Olga. Last of all, at the rear of his family, came the miller Tassi Mitros, who kept looking over his shoulder, expecting to see the guerrillas in pursuit. His ears ached with listening, his nerve ends were raw, his muscles clenched to run.

While the twenty fugitives were navigating the wheat field just below the Church of the Virgin, a group of three guerrillas from the security police station, led by the snake-eyed intelligence officer Sotiris Drapetis, were hurrying across the ravine from the direction of the Perivoli, headed for the Ziaras house. When they reached it, the windows were dark and no one answered their knock. 'Break it down,' Sotiris ordered, already knowing what they would find. Under their cleated boots, the door flew open and the three stood silently, staring into the emptiness.

'Mother of God, they've done it!' Sotiris muttered.

Within minutes the police were at the nearby lookout post; Sotiris was shouting into the field telephone and cursing the guerrillas around him at the same time. He discovered that most of the sentries had gone to join the party at St. Friday, leaving a skeleton crew. Among those left behind were Andreas Michopoulos and a young guerrilla who swore that he had seen the Mitros and Ziaras families not half an hour before, weeping over the dying baby. 'Maybe they've taken him to find the doctor,' the boy said, but Sotiris could feel in his guts that it was an escape – a premeditated mass breakout – the very thing he had been sent to Lia to prevent. Koliyiannis would castrate him, he thought as he shouted into the field telephone, 'I want two patrols of five men each – immediately – one down the ravine on the west, the other going from St. Friday. Look under every bush and rock, but make sure you get to the place where the paths cross at the Great Ridge before the traitors do!'

Hanging up the phone, his face pasty beneath the stubble, Sotiris muttered, 'And I thought Mitros was with us!'

He turned around to face the frightened guerrillas behind him. 'Tomorrow the plane tree in the square is going to be hanging with corpses,' he said. 'Either the traitors or you.'

Just below the bottom of the wheat field there was a small naked incline leading to a thick grove whose impenetrable black-green shadow would shelter them from the eyes of the lookouts. But first they had to cross a hundred feet of bare dirt, wanly silver in the light of the newborn moon. The fugitives tiptoed out of the wheat, still crouching, their shoes in their hands. At the rear Nitsa tripped over a large stone and tumbled down the steep hill, rolling like a barrel. The stone was knocked loose, and as it fell, dislodged a shower of pebbles that tumbled and clattered ahead of her. Tassi Mitros, several dozen feet to her right, heard the sudden burst of noise, the thing he had been fearing ever since they left the house.

'Run!' he croaked in a strangled voice. 'It's the guerrillas!' They all plunged toward the safety of the woods ahead, scampering in every direction, dropping their shoes and their belongings, even their children, in the desperate sprint to save themselves.

Olga and Calliope Mitros were at the back of the line near Nitsa, and they saw what had caused the sound. Curled up in a fetal ball, Nitsa lay on the ground, her hands over her ears, convinced that the guerrillas were upon her. Olga and Calliope turned back as the others disappeared into the woods below. They grabbed Nitsa under her arms and lifted the moaning, pear-shaped figure, dragging her with them down the hill. Nitsa's shoes were gone and she groaned louder with every limping step she took. The three women plunged into the underbrush and didn't stop until they were deep in the shadows under a thick, spreading oak tree. They leaned against the trunk and listened, panting hard. Calliope Mitros, who had become rather deaf from a childhood illness, watched Olga and Nitsa for a clue as to what they heard. But there was nothing: only the sound of their own labored breathing and the rustling and murmuring of the trees. No shouts, no pursuing footsteps. They looked at one another in sudden fear. They couldn't even hear the sound of their own people. They had veered to the right when they entered the forest, instinctively heading downhill and west, toward the ravine. Lukas Ziaras had led the others in a different direction. Now they were lost.

Several hundred yards to the east, the rest of the party came to an exhausted halt in a grove of beech trees. They all stared at Tassi Mitros, who had sounded the alarm. He shrugged, then said, 'I didn't see them, but I could hear them, right behind us.'

'You're sure it was the guerrillas?' Lukas whispered, his thin body shuddering with the aftermath of his terror. He covered his mouth with the towel to stifle his cough.

'Who else could it be?' countered Tassi.

Suddenly there was a small cry, ragged with fright. 'My mother's not here!' It was Niko Mitros, on the edge of tears. Everyone looked around, trying to make out the faces of the dark shapes nearby. 'Where's Nitsa?' Kanta whispered. 'Don't tell me they got Nitsa!'

'And Olga!' cried Fotini. 'Olga's gone too! She's dead!' The girl began to sob.

The sound of Fotini's grief set off Niko Mitros. 'We can't go on without *Mana*!' he cried. 'Please, Father! We have to go back and find her!'

'Shut up! Damn that woman!' said Tassi Mitros. 'Forget your mother! We're better off without her. There's no turning back now. We've got to save ourselves.'

There was a stunned silence, broken only by the quiet sobs of Fotini and Niko Mitros. Nikola Gatzoyiannis listened, amazed, as his hero wept against his brother's shoulder. Nikola had lost his mother too, and now his eldest sister. The ache in his stomach that had begun two days before was rising toward his throat, but he clenched his teeth, determined not to let anyone see his weakness. He had promised his mother that he'd be brave, and no matter what happened to them that night, he wouldn't cry. Kanta took Nikola's hand, and then Tassi Mitros began cursing, quietly but audibly, as the group started to move slowly downhill through the trees. 'May the devil fuck her mother and her mother's mother!' he was saying. 'May she rot in hell for what she's done to me!'

While one patrol of guerrillas went crashing down the ravine, following the route Lukas Ziaras had originally planned to take, the three women who were lost strayed aimlessly through the woods, headed in the same direction. Because

Calliope Mitros was hard of hearing and Nitsa was hysterical, Olga realized she would have to lead them or they'd surely be caught. She was terrified of stepping on a mine and tried to figure out where they were, but in the dark there were no familiar landmarks. She could only follow the slope of the ground. Finally, through a clearing in the trees, Olga spied the Southern Cross in the sky and realized they had gone much too far west to come out at the right point, the crossroads on the Great Ridge. She took the older women's hands and began to lead them back toward the east. Suddenly Nitsa sat down with a groan. 'I think the baby's going to come now!' she cried, clutching her belly. 'Christ and the Virgin Mary, don't leave me to die! I can't walk anymore! I lost my shoes when we ran and my feet are in shreds.'

Olga took out of her pocket some iodine and a roll of bandages her mother had told her to bring along. She began painting the cuts on Nitsa's feet, bandaged them, then tore off her aunt's kerchief and her own and wrapped them around the bandages. 'You walk or you die alone!' she whispered. 'Now get up!'

Olga led them farther back toward the east and downhill until the land began to slope more gradually. Finally they were stopped by a wide, shallow stream. Nitsa was still moaning that she couldn't go on. There was a cluster of low, spreading plane trees dipping their branches into the fast-flowing water, so Olga decided to stop there, to figure out what to do next. Pushing and pulling, she got her aunt up into the crotch of the branches of one of the trees, then signaled to Calliope to climb up beside them.

While the women were sitting there exhausted and in despair, some distance to the west a guerrilla patrol searching down the ravine stumbled upon the white roll of bandages that Olga had accidentally left behind. The five men were led by Vasili Bokas, a guerrilla chosen for the assignment because he came from Lia. 'They must be just ahead of us,' Bokas whispered to the others.

Olga, Nitsa and Calliope Mitros huddled shivering in the branches, chilled by the cool breeze, when there was a sound of footsteps creeping through the underbrush and coming toward them. Then they heard a man's voice. 'Fuck their god!' it muttered. 'Fuck the mother of their god!'

Olga and Nitsa clutched at each other, but Calliope Mitros heard nothing. 'What is it? What's wrong?' she whispered. Olga clapped a hand over the woman's mouth and Nitsa began to moan, 'They've found us!'

The footsteps came closer while Olga sat paralyzed, not breathing. Then she saw something white approaching on the path that passed by the trees. It was a flour bag on someone's shoulder. She leaned forward, holding on to a branch for support, and saw several smaller figures emerging from the shadows. 'It's Tassi Mitros swearing!' Olga whispered. 'I can see his bald head!'

Tassi yelped when a figure came crashing out of a tree directly into his path, and he put up his arms to ward off the bullet he expected to shatter his skull. By the time he heard his son cry '*Mana!*' and understood that it was the missing women, he realized to his deep embarrassment that he had wet himself in fear. Luckily it was too dark for anyone to notice his loss of nerve. 'Useless woman!' he muttered at his wife, who couldn't make out what he was saying. 'I'd have been better off if you'd stayed lost!' But Calliope was caught in a bear hug by her two sons as Olga was surrounded by her sisters. 'I was so scared,' Olga whispered to Kanta, 'that if you cut me, I wouldn't bleed.'

Nikola watched the reunions silently, not admitting even to himself that he was jealous of Niko Mitros for having his mother back. Standing there, Nikola shivered and swayed against Kanta with fatigue. He had lost his shoes near the wheat field and his feet were badly cut by thistles and sharp stones, but he wouldn't tell anyone. It was part of the test of his courage.

While the others rejoiced in their luck at stumbling upon the lost women, Lukas Ziaras surveyed the wide stream they would have to ford. It was the last obstacle before they reached the gently rolling foothills and the final lap of their journey to the Great Ridge. He knew that the stream was no more than waist-deep, but the current was tricky. In a whisper he ordered each adult to take a child by the hand

and to hold on tight. He would go first and Tassi would bring up the rear.

It was much harder than they had expected, keeping a foothold on the slippery rocks as the current tugged at their legs. Soula Ziaras had seven-year-old George by one hand and the baby on her back, still unconscious. The children whimpered as the icy water enveloped them. Lukas stood on the opposite bank, pulling each pair out of the stream.

Megali was one of the last to cross. Her legs slipped out from under her and with a great squawk she was carried away, but her voluminous clothes kept her afloat and she drifted like a black ship down the stream, shrieking for help. 'Let her go!' Olga heard herself exclaim, but Chrysoula Drouboyiannis, who was just behind, let go the hands of her two nieces and plunged after the old woman, a resolute giantess cleaving the water. She finally caught up with Megali and managed to drag her back to the point where Lukas Ziaras could help lift her out.

After the excitement of Megali's rescue the group had walked several hundred yards into the foothills before Soula Ziaras realized that her six-year-old daughter Olympia was no longer hanging on to her hand. The little girl had been staggering with fatigue the whole way, whimpering to be carried. Soula hurried to catch up with Lukas. 'Where's Olympia?' she demanded. 'Didn't you carry her across?'

'I thought *you* did!' he answered.

'I had George and the baby!'

'Well, there's no going back for her now,' Lukas said. 'You'll never find her, anyway. We have to think of the others.'

But Soula refused to listen, and handing the baby and his pouch to Calliope, she plunged back across the stream while Lukas added his curses to Tassi's. She searched frantically along the stream bank, then stopped and listened. She could hear a quiet sobbing. Finally she found her daughter huddled under a bush near the edge of the stream, trembling like a shorn sheep.

When Soula returned, carrying the little girl, Lukas was so upset by the several near-disasters that he and Tassi sat down against a tree trunk and lit cigarettes, cupping the match in their hands. 'Are you insane?' Olga hissed. 'You might as well light a signal fire for the guerrillas!' But the two men ignored her and she could see the embers of their cigarettes shaking in the darkness.

The sodden, exhausted company staggered on through the no man's land of the foothills like automatons, no longer thinking about the noise their footsteps made or the danger of mines. They blundered into clumps of nettles and thorns, and the children begged to be carried. Their wet clothes clung to them, the underbrush whipped their bare legs and feet. They lost track of how far they had come and how long they had been walking when suddenly Lukas stumbled and fell into a shallow hole.

Everyone stopped as they realized that the ground ahead of them was pitted with the strange craters. 'It's mines!' trilled Olga, her voice tight with fear.

'No, it's not. They're from grenades and artillery shells.' said Lukas. 'This is where the soldiers shoot, trying to flush out the guerrilla night patrols. Look!'

They raised their eyes, and squinting into the darkness, made out the immense bulk of the Great Ridge looming above them, almost invisible against the night sky.

'We have to stay here and wait for the sun,' Lukas whispered. 'If we come out of the trees, the soldiers will fire on us, taking us for guerrillas.'

'And if we stay here, they may start strafing the trees with grenades and machine guns,' fretted Soula.

'You choose,' said Tassi dryly. 'We can turn back into the guerrillas' arms, walk out into the open and be killed by the soldiers or stay here and take our chances.'

They all sank to the ground amid the thick bushes, huddling close together for warmth. The only one who still had a dry blanket was Arete, and at Nitsa's insistence she shared it with her. Kanta hugged Fotini and Nikola against her for warmth, and Soula gathered her brood around her. The baby was beginning to stir as the effects of the alcohol wore off.

Shuddering in the chill wind, they all sat and contemplated

the monumental shape of the Great Ridge. The children fell asleep on the adults' laps, but for the rest the waiting was worse than the walking had been. They were on the very edge of salvation, but they felt more vulnerable now than at any time since they emerged from the wheat field. Their eyes burning with fatigue and the effort of staring into the darkness, they sat in silence, wrapping themselves in their prayers, waiting for the sun.

The guerrilla patrol led by Vasili Bokas followed the ravine to its end and hurried straight on until they, too, reached the edge of the Great Ridge at the place called 'The Apple Trees.' From the shadows of the forest they peered out onto the slope leading up the height.

'We can't go any farther without being seen,' said one of the guerrillas. 'The traitors must have made it over to the other side.'

'No, they're somewhere in the forest doing the same thing we're doing: waiting,' replied Bokas. 'They can't risk going out there and getting shot any more than we can. I want three men to search all along the edge of the trees. We have until dawn to find them.'

Nikola woke, his head in Kanta's lap. He had been dreaming that his mother was calling to him. The sound of her voice speaking his name still echoed in his ears. She had been trying to tell him something, and he knew it was vital to understand what it was. But she faded before he could make out her words.

He sat up and heard voices – men's voices – and the sound of twigs snapping in the forest to their right. Everyone heard it and they sat frozen, listening. Then the voices began to fade and the sound of footsteps became more distant. Tassi Mitros spoke with quiet fatalism. 'There's nothing we can do now,' he whispered; 'what is written will happen.' After that, no one dozed and they all watched as the silhouette of the Great Ridge slowly took shape against the pre-dawn sky.

First the heavens were inky purple, then slowly they paled to lavender, the colors unfolding like a peacock's tail, and

412

from the east a pink finger of light touched the summit of the ridge, dappling the rocks and knolls with the shades of burnished copper. The warm colors of the dawn only emphasized the cold that gripped them. The slope of the ridge appeared lifeless. As the light grew stronger, they could make out great, gnarled tangles of barbed wire barring them from the heights which Lukas had told them were mined. They had come out exactly where he intended, Lukas noted proudly.

Lukas began to bustle about, making plans for their triumphal exodus from the periphery of the forest into the clearing. They had to attract the attention of the soldiers and convince them it was not a guerrilla ambush. The soldiers were justifiably suspicious, he knew. Although an occasional escaping peasant or defector from the DAG managed to reach them, it was a common trick to send *andartinas* dressed as peasant girls to beg for sanctuary and then, when the soldiers came out of their foxholes, the *andartinas*' hidden comrades would open fire while the women themselves hurled grenades.

Lukas selected the two oldest women in the group, Megali Haidis and Calliope Mitros, to go forward waving the white flag of surrender. The nationalist troops could hardly suspect two women well past middle age to be *andartinas*. But both firmly refused to leave the shelter of the forest. 'We'll step on a mine! They'll shoot us down before we can open our mouths!' Calliope wailed while Megali just sat and rocked and moaned. Next Lukas pleaded with Nitsa and Arete, but they were equally unwilling. 'I'm all alone; my husband has no one else!' cried Arete. 'Take a woman from a large family.'

Nitsa used the excuse of her pregnancy once again, and added that after the traumas of the night she was too ill to walk, much less risk the mine fields.

Finally Chrysoula Drouboyiannis stood up, a figure of impressive height and stature, and volunteered to go first. 'I have no children,' she said. 'As long as you save my nieces, I'm willing to risk it.' She begged Olga to come along with her. 'Your voice will carry all the way up the ridge.' Olga looked around, blushing, then reluctantly agreed.

Both women went behind a bush and removed their slips, tearing them into rags and attaching them to branches to make white flags. Olga mournfully fingered the fine lace of the best slip from her trousseau before she ripped it apart.

As the rest of the group watched tensely from their hiding places, Olga and Chrysoula emerged from the woods, waving their makeshift flags and shouting at the top of their voices, 'Soldiers! Brothers! Save us! We've escaped from Lia! Please come and help us!' The silent, barren hulk of the ridge yielded no answer.

They walked forward gingerly, Olga carefully placing her feet where Chrysoula had stepped. After a few paces they came to a halt and redoubled their screams. They stared upward and finally saw a small figure appear on a shelf partway up the height. 'Stop right there!' he shouted. 'Don't come any farther! Who are you?'

'We're women and children from Lia!' Olga shrieked, her knees visibly starting to shake. 'We escaped from the guerrillas!'

She squinted, not certain from this distance whether she was talking to a soldier or to a guerrilla who was trying to trick her.

'No one's coming down. You come up here!' shouted the man.

'But we're afraid of the mines,' cried Chrysoula.

'Just come straight ahead, through the gap in the barbed wire, straight toward me, and you'll be all right,' he called.

Chrysoula and Olga took a few faltering steps forward. Behind them from out of the trees emerged Lukas Ziaras, followed by his wife with the baby on her back; three small children behind her. Next came Kanta leading two more children; Megali tottering behind, Arete leading the Drouboyiannis girls; Nitsa, with her two kerchiefs wrapped around her feet, crawling up the slope on all fours; Gakis and Niko Mitros on either side of their mother. Finally Tassi Mitros appeared, a gnarled giant nervously bringing up the rear. It was an astonishing sight. From behind every rock on the Great Ridge, soldiers' heads popped up, gaping in amazement. Olga could see as she came closer that they really were soldiers, not guerrillas; they all wore the two-cornered khaki cap with the crown on it.

414

The sun had already heated the naked limestone of the Great Ridge until it burned their feet, and as Nikola stepped on a rock he heard a sizzling sound. He looked around and whimpered when he realized that it was his own blood from the cuts on his bare feet bubbling on the hot surface. A trail of bloody footprints stretched behind him.

The bizarre parade straggling out of the trees drew the astonished soldiers from their foxholes on the Great Ridge, but there was another hidden audience: the five guerrillas concealed in the place called The Apple Trees. The leader of the patrol, Vasili Bokas, watched in growing disbelief. His frantic commanding officer had told him that the Mitros and Ziaras families had escaped, but he had never expected to see a crowd like this. He recognized Lukas Ziaras at the head, then focused on the children and young women behind and emitted a low whistle. First he recognized Chrysoula Drouboyiannis by her unusual height, then he took a good look at the rest. The family of the Amerikana was with them! Bokas winced as he imagined the reaction of his officers to the news that the children of the most respected family in Lia were among the defectors.

'They're right out in the open,' said the man beside him, raising his machine gun. Bokas shook his head. 'It's too far, and the fascists will have a dozen bazookas on us in a second,' he whispered. Silently he watched the long string of figures stumbling higher up the ridge.

He felt a secret relief that he hadn't caught the fugitives, Bokas confided to a friend thirty years later, shortly before his death. Although he was loyal to the cause, he had no stomach for killing women and children from his own village. As he watched the soldiers come down to meet them, the guerrilla shook his head in wonder. 'Imagine Lukas Ziaras leading out such a crowd and getting away with it!' he muttered to himself.

The small, sallow tinker approached the government soldiers, then he stopped for a moment, and removing the white towel wrapped around his neck, threw it away with a sweeping gesture of triumph.

The first soldier to reach them seized Lukas' arm. He couldn't believe that such a crowd could have slipped away unseen. 'Did the Communists let you leave?' he demanded. 'Are they evacuating the villages?'

It was the proudest moment of Lukas Ziaras' life. He described to the growing assemblage of soldiers how he had personally led the refugees to freedom through the guerrilla patrols, thanks to his knowledge of the terrain and his carefully plotted escape plan. The grizzled miller stood by listening cynically and spat on the ground.

By the time the group reached the top of the Great Ridge, a major and all the officers of the battalion were waiting for them, their faces dark with suspicion. They wrote down the names of all the fugitives, then they took aside the three men – Lukas Ziaras, Tassi and Gakis Mitros – to interrogate them. A few minutes later they also sent for Kanta, having learned from the men that she had once been an *andartina*.

While those four were being questioned, the soldiers stood around the rest of the group, examining them like creatures in a zoo. Seeing the hunger and fatigue on the faces of the children, some of the soldiers brewed mountain tea for them over small cooking fires. As Nikola held a heavy tin cup of tea in his hands and drank, a soldier offered him a piece of the soft white bread called *kouramada,* a delicacy he could hardly remember. The boy gobbled half of it and tucked the rest in his pocket, thinking he would share it with his mother when she reached Filiates. He imagined describing to her the adventures of the past night and how pleased she would be at his bravery.

The sight of the cooking fires reminded Olga of her promise to her mother and she walked over to the major. 'Please, sir,' she said, 'We have people back there who are waiting for a signal that we're safe so they can escape too. We have to light a large smoky fire so that they'll know we've made it.'

'Impossible!' snapped the major. 'A signal fire would be an open invitation to the Communists to hit us with every mortar they have.'

'But we have to!' Olga pleaded. 'How will my mother and sister know we've escaped?'

'No signal fires,' repeated the officer and turned his back. The subject was closed.

The twenty fugitives spent the whole day in the nationalist encampment at the top of the Great Ridge, and that night they slept in the soldiers' tents. 'You'll have to be patient; we have to run a check on all of you through Alpha Two,' one of the soldiers told Olga, referring to the intelligence branch of the Greek army.

Early the next morning word came back from army headquarters. The refugees from Lia were to be escorted to the village of Aghies Pantes (All Saints) where the road began. From there army trucks would transport them to refugee facilities in Filiates. The fugitives climbed to their feet, energized by the thought of being reunited with relatives on the other side. Only Nitsa refused to get up, insisting she could not walk another step. She sat there adamant as a mule until the soldiers relented and provided a large black horse for her. Then the barefoot parade set out on their hour-long walk down from the Great Ridge, with Nitsa riding at the head like an empress, her stocky body rocking from side to side, her kerchief-bound feet protruding at a sharp angle from her ballooning abdomen.

The sun came out from behind a cloud and its warmth revived them. The mist rose from the valley below like incense, and the heavy fragrance of late pears, laurel and osiers affected their senses like wine. Suddenly it struck all of the fugitives that they were really free. The nightmare was over and they had survived. Like a silken ribbon, Arete's voice rose into the air. 'When shall we go to the city,' she sang, the words of an ancient lullaby, 'to buy golden rings and pearls for my lady's dowry, silver bangles for her ears and perfumes for her hands?' One by one the voices of the other women joined in. At last they really were going to the city to see the wonders there.

The children began to laugh and walk hand in hand in time to the music. Soon they were all singing, swinging their hands and smiling as if it were Easter Sunday. Then the cry of Soula Ziaras rose like a malediction over the music. 'It's not right!' she shouted. 'How can we sing when my girl and my cousin Eleni are still trapped back there? We're free, but what's going to happen to them?'

At her words Nikola turned and looked back toward Lia, but the Great Ridge blocked the view of his mountains. He saw that the universe had been turned upside down: all his life he had stood at the top of the world, the valleys and foothills spread out far below. Now he was walking in an abyss between two rows of strange mountains which seemed about to fall in on him. Soula's words chilled his heart; for the first time he understood that his mother might never get away. The bulwark of stoicism which he had constructed suddenly crumpled and the tears that he had held back since his mother left him overflowed.

'Mother, Glykeria and Marianthe will be fine!' Kanta said soothingly. 'They'll turn up in Filiates, you'll see.' But the euphoria of the fugitives was gone, and they walked on in silence, following the soldiers until they reached Aghies Pantes shortly before noon.

The people of that village crowded around shouting questions about relatives and friends trapped in the occupied territory. The commotion frightened the children, who shrank against their parents. The little town, where the road began, seemed huge to them, and the soldiers herded their frightened charges over to a large, mud-colored army truck. The Liotes stared at it curiously. The children had never seen a vehicle with wheels and they had no idea what it was for. The back of the truck had metal arches with canvas stretched over them to form a tent, but the canvas flaps were rolled up and tied. They walked around the truck, touching its metal hide with tentative fingers. The headlights looked to Nikola like eyes, but the creature seemed to be dead or sleeping.

The soldiers told the refugees to climb into the open back of the truck and sit on the two benches which ran along the sides. Nikola held tight to Kanta's hand. When the truck suddenly came alive with an angry growl, pulsating beneath him, he clutched one of the metal thwarts with the other hand. The sound reminded him of the approach of the bomber planes and he was terrified of the thing that had him in its belly.

With a gut-wrenching lurch, the truck flung itself into motion. To the children and to many of the adults as well, it seemed that the earth had begun to move, an apocalyptic upheaval as everything fell away. Despite the slow speed of the lumbering vehicle, the grass, trees, sky and staring towns-people of Aghies Pantes seemed to be whizzing into a chasm.

Everyone in the truck screamed when it began to move, but Fotini became hysterical and tried to leap out to save her life. Olga had to hold her to keep her from throwing herself off. 'The trees are moving, the earth is moving!' cried Fotini in a voice that carried far beyond the village. 'Please, God, somebody make it stop! Let me out!'

Olga held on tight and tried to calm her, but once Fotini began, her cries rose and fell like a siren and by the time they reached the town of Filiates, a half hour later, all that was left of her voice was a ragged sound like something not human.

The sound of my sister's scream, caught in her throat as if choking her, trailed behind us all the way to Filiates like a streamer in the wind. It was the music that accompanied me on my journey into the future as we hurtled between two immense walls of limestone that funneled us toward the unknown with the swiftness of an arrow. I looked back and saw the tunnel closing on the circle of mountains that had been my universe. As the truck rattled our teeth, I imagined my mother trapped inside that great bowl like a fly struggling to get out. I was overwhelmed by the immensity of the journey we had already made and the impossibility of her finding us under a new sky with only the thread of Fotini's cry to guide her.

On Tuesday, June 22, Rano Athanassiou worked on the flat threshing floor at Granitsopoula as the other women, including Eleni, cut the wheat in the fields up on the hillsides. A guerrilla led a team of horses in blinders around in endless circles, trampling the wheat, while Rano and several other women tossed great armloads of it in huge round sieves of tin, punctured by metal nailholes to separate the grains from the chaff. As they bent and scooped and tossed and bent again until their arms ached from the neck to the fingertips, Rano heard the guerrillas around her talking excitedly. She moved closer and managed to overhear enough to understand what had disturbed them so: a group of twenty villagers from Lia had disappeared, including the family of the Amerikana.

As soon as a break was called, Rano put on her cape, for the wind had turned chill, and began to walk up the slope to the wheat fields, searching among the bent figures of the threshers for Eleni. She found her at the end of a row. 'Aunt Eleni,' she whispered urgently, 'your family has fled the village! I heard the guerrillas talking.'

Eleni put down the scythe and stood up, crossing herself as she looked toward the southeast where the Kalamas glimmered. 'Thanks to Christ and His Holy Mother, my family got away!' she exclaimed.

Rano stared at her. 'As soon as you get the chance, when the guerrillas aren't looking and you're at the end of a row, you've got to run,' she hissed. 'If you don't, they may kill you.'

Seeing the guard's eyes on them, Eleni picked up her scythe and began to swing it in a smooth rhythm. 'I can't run away and leave Glykeria,' she said. 'Now go on back to the threshing floor before they wonder what you're talking to me about.'

That night as the women prepared to sleep on the floor of the largest house in Granitsopoula, a guerrilla came in and said, 'You, you, and you! You're not to go to the fields tomorrow with the others.' He was pointing to Eleni, Marianthe Ziaras and Alexo Gatzoyiannis. They looked at each other, knowing that they were going to pay for the freedom of their loved ones. They didn't speak to each other that night about what awaited them, but none of them slept.

Early the next morning Eleni, Marianthe and Alexo left Granitsopoula under the guard of three guerrillas and quickly covered the five miles to the mountain village of Lista, which lay halfway between the threshing fields and Lia. On the two-hour walk the guards said nothing about why they were being taken and the women pretended ignorance, asking if they were going to harvest somewhere else. But when they were thrust into the main room of the police station and found themselves confronted by two scowling officers seated behind a desk, it was hard to hide their fear.

420

One of the men stood up and shouted, 'Why didn't you leave with the others?'

'What others?' the women chorused.

'You know very well!' he snapped. He pointed at Eleni. 'Sunday night your mother, your sister and your children left the village without permission.' He turned swiftly on Marianthe. 'And your father led them, with all your family.' Then he looked at Alexo. 'And your daughter!'

The women had been holding in their panic since the night before. Now it was easy to let it spill over into tears. They began to weep, as if horrified at what he had told them. 'What right did Lukas Ziaras have to take my children?' Eleni cried.

The sounds of the women's sobbing irritated the officer. 'You knew that they were leaving, Amerikana,' he said. 'You told them to go.'

Eleni wiped her eyes. 'How could I know? Haven't we all been at the harvest for days, doing your work? If I had been home with my children, that fool Lukas Ziaras would never have been able to take them from me.'

'He certainly *was* foolish,' smiled the guerrilla, 'but he's paid for his stupidity. We intercepted them in the foothills. They've all been shot. You'll see their bodies as soon as you get to Lia.'

The guerrilla's bearded face began to swim before Eleni's eyes and she felt her knees give way, but she was unconscious by the time her head hit the wooden floor.

CHAPTER FOURTEEN

On the day the twenty fugitives set out from Lia,
representatives of every Communist Party in the world were
convening in Bucharest, Rumania, to consider the growing
feud between Soviet dictator Joseph Stalin and Yugoslav
leader Josip Broz Tito. This feud would shake the
Communist world to its foundations and ultimately have a
critical impact on the rebellion in Greece.

Irked by the independent course Marshal Tito was setting
for Yugoslavia, and jealous of his international fame, Stalin
had begun trying early in 1948 to bend Tito to his will. He
brought economic pressure on Yugoslavia, used Soviet
agents to undermine Tito's power at home and even
delivered an implied threat to the resistance hero's life. 'We
consider that the political career of Trotsky is a good
enough lesson,' he wrote Tito, referring to the Soviet rival
whom Stalin first had expelled from the party, then exiled
and finally ordered assassinated. Tito refused to yield, and,
realizing that Stalin might try to topple him, he isolated
Russian advisers in Yugoslavia and jailed die-hard Moscow
supporters in his own party.

Stalin then called on the Cominform, the international
organization of Communist parties, to judge Tito. Aware
that the body was the tool of the Soviet dictator, Tito
refused to participate. The Cominform met in Bucharest on
June 20, and eight days later its delegates passed a
unanimous resolution condemning Titoism.

The Yugoslav leader and his top aides were accused of
every crime in the Communist calendar: abandoning

422

Marxism-Leninism, slandering the Soviet Union, persecuting good Communists, making concessions to the imperialists. The resolution called upon loyal Yugoslav Communists to pressure their leaders to correct their errors, and if they refused, to replace them.

The Tito-Stalin split put the Greek Communists in an awkward position. They knew they could not risk Moscow's displeasure because only Russia could give them the massive support they needed to win the war. At the moment, however, Yugoslavia was giving the insurgents the most help of any Communist country, and the Greeks couldn't afford to anger Belgrade, either.

A few days after the Cominform decision, Greek Communists held their fourth plenum on Grammos while the losing battle for the mountain range seethed around them. They decided to take a middle road in the dispute, secretly supporting the Cominform decision but not criticizing Yugoslavia publicly. This attempt at fence-sitting satisfied neither Moscow nor Belgrade, and in time Yugoslavia would deal a mortal blow to the guerrillas by cutting off all aid to them and sealing their border with Greece.

The growing Stalin-Tito split was just one of several ominous clouds gathering over the embattled insurgents, who were fighting desperately to protect their shrinking mountain stronghold. Guerrillas in the front lines and the civilians in the occupied territories could read the omens as well as the military leadership, and there were increasing calls for a negotiated settlement.

Hearing such pleas sent the obstinate Zachariadis into a fury. 'Such fighters show that they have been broken,' he wrote to one of his commissars, Nikos Belloyiannis. 'Those who are guilty of such treachery must be arrested, condemned by public outcry, and executed in the presence of their comrades.'

WANDERERS

LUKAS ZIARAS GOT his wish; his name became a part of the folklore of the Mourgana villages. Even the outwitted guerrillas eventually composed a mocking ditty about the great escape, which came to enjoy considerable local popularity:

> He came to the Great Ridge
> To take a little air.
> He looked toward Taverra Hill
> Took off his towel and left it there.
> 'Won't you tell us, friend Luka,
> How did you find things in Lia?'
> 'Fellows, boys, what can I say?
> Work and more work, night and day!
> And they've got comrades, warrior women
> To terrify the fascist vermin.'

But on the morning of June 21, when twenty civilians were discovered missing from the village, none of the guerrillas was smiling. The news of the escape exploded throughout the Mourgana, reverberations reaching all the way to the pinnacle of the Democratic Army's Epiros Command. It was inconceivable that so many men, women and children could walk out in a group under the very noses of the guerrilla lookouts. Even worse, these were some of the most influential families of Lia. Tassi Mitros and Lukas Ziaras were among the few men who had stayed to welcome the guerrillas on their arrival; they had in turn been rewarded with places on

424

civilian committees set up by the occupiers to give the impression of local participation in the running of the village. Lukas, living just below the lookout station, was considered not only a sympathizer by the guerrillas, but a sort of fellow sentry as well. And with them had gone the family – the children, sister and mother – of the Amerikana, the most respected woman in the village. It was impossible that the crowd of fugitives could have blundered safely through the guerrilla patrols and minefields on their own, the DAG officers reasoned. They must have had help – from the inside, perhaps among the guerrillas themselves, or from the outside – some fascist who had come to the edge of the village to lead them out.

The escape dramatized not only the widespread discontent in the occupied villages, but also the failure of the security police, who had been brought to Lia to prevent just such an act of apostasy. All the secret information Sotiris Drapetis and the police had been collecting had given them no warning. On the morning the disappearance was confirmed, Sotiris and the three police officers hysterically issued and countermanded orders. First they let it be known that the twenty fugitives had been captured, were being interrogated and would soon be brought to public trial. Then they pulled in every guerrilla who had been on duty that night and began interrogating them. Among those under suspicion was Andreas Michopoulos, who had been on duty at the Church of the Virgin on the evening of the escape.

While insisting that the fugitives had been apprehended, the guerrillas ran frantically through the village trying to unearth clues as to how they had gotten away. The Mitros house, the Ziaras house and the Haidis house, where the Gatzoyiannis family had lived, were searched with such ferocity that built-in wooden alcoves were ripped out of the walls and sleeping pallets were slashed to shreds. The guerrillas found the letter that Olga had left for her mother in the wall niche, and at the Mitros house they discovered the twenty-four gold sovereigns that Tassi Mitros had been forced to abandon.

Fearing that more villagers would be tempted to follow the fugitives' example, the guerrillas issued a proclamation: from

425

that day on, everyone living in the southernmost section of the village would be forbidden to stay at home after dark. If they could not find a relative's house higher up the mountain to sleep in, they would have to spend the nights in the caves above the Perivoli.

While guerrillas were dispatched to the distant threshing fields to bring back Eleni, Alexo and Marianthe, all other relatives of the escapees were called in for questioning. Giorgina Bardaka, daughter of the miller Tassi Mitros, was breast-feeding her six-month-old baby girl when the guerrillas came up the path toward her door. They were seen by Giorgina's sister-in-law, Calliope Bardaka, the best-known collaborator of the guerrillas and the first mother to give her children to the *pedomasoma*. Although most of the village women regarded Calliope with a mixture of hatred and fear, she was loyal to her relatives and friends, often intervening with the guerrillas on their behalf. This morning, sensing trouble for Giorgina, she asked the men why they were headed for her sister-in-law's house. As soon as she heard their reply Calliope told them that she would bring Giorgina in herself, and rushed ahead into the house, where she whispered to the young woman, 'They're coming to get you because your parents and brothers escaped yesterday! Whether you knew they were going or not, tell them you didn't or they'll kill you! Tell them if you knew about the escape, you would have gone with them because you want to be with your husband on the other side.'

Shakily, Giorgina walked out the door beside Calliope toward the security station, carrying the baby in her arms.

As soon as the army truck filled with fugitives entered the town of Filiates, it was surrounded by an excited crowd. News of the incredible escape had preceded the refugees, and dozens of men who had fled ahead of the guerrillas crowded around, shouting questions about their families still trapped in Lia.

As the truck moved slowly over the cobbled streets, Nikola's eyes widened in astonishment. He had never seen a real town before, and he gaped at the trucks and army vehicles, the great Turkish-style villas hidden behind vine-covered walls. There was a whole street of shops, all with large windows that displayed a dizzying variety of goods. The boy was embarrassed at all the attention they were receiving, but he was also excited to find himself in such a grand place.

When the truck stopped in front of army headquarters, Nikola got a better look at the crowd around them. Someone ran off to find his grandfather and Nitsa's husband Andreas. People were asking where his mother was, and the question brought back the ache of her loss. He ducked the arms of those who tried to embrace him and took shelter behind Kanta, staring down at his bare feet which the soldiers had bound in torn strips of cloth to cover the cuts and blisters.

One by one the adults among the group were led inside to be questioned while the rest tried to satisfy the curiosity of the crowd. Now that they had made it out safely, their adventures took on epic proportions. Each detail was enlarged and embroidered – whoever was speaking cast himself in the starring role. Lukas was basking in the admiration of the crowd, but Olga and Kanta exchanged nervous glances, worried that someone would let slip a detail that could be used against their mother. They tried to silence Nitsa when she launched into her recitation of how, seven months pregnant, she had fearlessly battled her way through hostile guerrilla patrols, but the more she talked, the more fantastic her story became.

Because Kanta had been an *andartina* with the guerrillas, she was one of the first called inside. She was taken to a room where two soldiers had a map of Lia and the surrounding area. They asked her to point out the exact locations of the guerrilla headquarters, major storehouses and fortifications, but Kanta shook her head. 'The *andartes* are animals and they're doing terrible things to the people there,' she said. 'I hope you'll be able to liberate the village. But I've left my mother and sister behind, and I promised them not to say anything that could harm them until they get out too.'

Next the soldiers brought in Olga, who repeated the same sentiments. The other adult women in the group were back out on the street within minutes after being questioned, but when Lukas Ziaras went inside, preening under the admiring gaze of the crowd, he was gone for over an hour. When he returned, Olga whispered, 'What did you tell them?'

'What should I tell them?' he answered. 'The truth! How everyone in the village is fed up, even the president, Spiro Michopoulos. How despite the first two setbacks, my final plan for the escape worked perfectly.' He was flushed and wheezing with excitement. Nothing he had attempted in his life had succeeded so well, and he was anticipating the free drinks he would collect in the coffeehouses of Filiates in exchange for the tale of his exodus.

Olga shook her head disapprovingly. 'What did Mother tell you about careless words harming the ones we've left behind?'

Lukas turned on her. 'Don't be a stupid girl!' he snapped. 'This is the intelligence branch of the army. Do you think its officers trade secrets with the guerrillas? Everything I've told them can only help drive the Communists out.'

Upset by the whispered argument and the threat of danger to his mother, Nikola leaned against Kanta, exhausted from the long journey. His wounded feet hurt, and the hot sun and noise of the crowd was suffocating him. He searched the onlookers for the faces of his uncle Andreas and his grandfather – a link with the familiar scenes he had left behind in the village.

Seeing the boy's unhappiness, one of the men in the throng stepped forward and handed him a flat-bottomed waferlike cone topped with a scoop of white stuff. It reminded Nikola of the thick vanilla cream they used to drop into glasses of water, then eat with a spoon on summer days when he was little, a treat that Greeks call a 'submarine.' The boy looked at the man, who nodded encouragingly, and then took a big bite, filling his mouth.

He had never tasted anything frozen before and at the first instant, the icy cold seemed a scalding heat. He doubled over and spat the mouthful on the ground. 'It burned me!' he cried while the crowd exploded with laughter. Tears of mortification were threatening to overflow when Nikola saw his gaunt uncle Andreas pushing toward him through the crowd.

As usual, great emotion made Andreas almost speechless. He put a hand awkwardly on the boy's shoulder, looked at his rotund wife and muttered, 'You're here.' Olga and Kanta began to cry.

Nikola eagerly hugged his uncle. Nitsa, blushing, pulled her black dress tight against her great belly. 'God has granted us a miracle, husband!' she announced. 'We're going to have a child. I'm seven months pregnant!'

Andreas turned pale and swayed so that Nitsa had to reach out to steady him. Then there was a shout and Nikola saw his grandfather shoving his way through the crowd. The craggy face under the white hair was as fierce as he remembered. Kitso did not embrace his wife, Nitsa or his grandchildren. He stood and glared at them, looking from one to another. Then he said two words: 'Where's Eleni?'

At once they all started explaining how Eleni and Glykeria had been forced to stay behind to harvest crops in the villages near the Kalamas. 'But *Mana* and Glykeria are going to escape together from there, grandfather,' Olga cried, 'as soon as they get our message that we've left.'

A light went out of Kitso's eyes. He had fled the village without speaking to Eleni, leaving her behind in anger. His desertion of his daughter had been festering inside him ever since, as reports of suffering and brutality filtered out of the Mourgana. When he heard of the miraculous escape of his family, a weight had lifted from his heart, but now it descended again, along with the ancient fear that his children had not finished paying for his murder of the Turkish brigand.

Kitso turned away from his grandchildren and uttered two more words: 'Eleni's lost.'

It was not until two days after the escape – when the villagers of Lia saw Eleni, Alexo and Marianthe brought shackled into the village on foot, led by armed guerrillas – that they knew the fugitives had truly gotten away. The silent procession passed through the village center and up the path to the Perivoli, where the gate of the security-police station closed behind the three women.

During the next days the guerrillas interviewed them

individually in the small room next to the main office. While two guerrillas stood by, Sotiris Drapetis conducted the interrogations, his eyes watching each captive like a snake contemplating a frog. The women were asked the same things over and over, to make them admit they knew about the escape plot. Sometimes they were threatened with a gun held to their temple; sometimes they were slapped or their ears twisted when they were slow in answering a question. There were no systematic beatings or torture at first.

Eleni told her friend Olga Venetis some weeks later that the worst moments were when Sotiris said, 'We've caught all your children and killed them.' She thought it was probably a bluff to break down her defenses, or else Sotiris wouldn't be so insistent about trying to learn what she knew of the plot.

But each time he said it her tears began, despite her resolution to remain calm. As she wept, Eleni would blame Lukas Ziaras for kidnapping her children.

'Why would he take them away?' she cried. 'How could my mother and my sister let him do it?'

She suggested that Ziaras had taken the children for the money he knew he could collect from their father. 'My husband was preparing the final papers for us to go to America,' she said. 'Lukas must have convinced them to leave because the papers would lapse if they waited too long, and they'd lose the chance to go.' She spread her hands helplessly. 'How do I know what he told them; how he convinced them to desert me? I was working for you, threshing the wheat. I knew nothing of the plot.'

'That's not what your daughter Olga says,' Sotiris replied.
'I thought you said she was dead.'

Sotiris held up a piece of paper. 'She wrote you this letter. We found it in your house. Isn't this her handwriting?'

'It looks like it,' Eleni admitted. 'I'd have to see it closer to be sure.'

'I'll read it to you,' Sotiris answered smoothly. He read, inserting phrases that Eleni knew Olga would never have written: ' "*Mana*, we're leaving with Lukas Ziaras and Megali, just as we planned, to go find Father." '

430

Eleni shrugged. 'If she wrote that, it makes no sense. I knew nothing about any plan to escape.'

Each prisoner was questioned several times a day. Eleni was forced to go over and over such details as how long her husband had been in America, how much money he made, what kind of work he did. Every day she repeated her ignorance of the escape plan. 'That devil Lukas Ziaras had no right to take my children,' she would cry. 'They were everything I had in the world! Now all I have is Glykeria.'

Marianthe Ziaras insisted that her family had abandoned her. 'If my father loved me, he would have taken me with them,' she repeated, wiping her eyes. 'But my parents always liked me the least, that's why they left me behind.'

Alexo stolidly maintained that her daughter Arete never confided in her. 'She was a married woman, married fifteen years! She didn't tell me her secrets; she hardly ever spoke to me, living halfway across the village.'

One of the guards who led the captives back and forth to the interrogation room, a young man with a kind face, whispered to them, 'Whatever story you've told, stick to it. Be sure not to change a single detail. That way, perhaps you'll have a chance.'

Eleni, Alexo and Marianthe saw that despite the constant inquisitions, threats and occasional slaps, they were being treated far better than the other prisoners in the police station. The three women, along with Tassi Mitros' daughter Giorgina and her tiny baby, were kept in the upstairs rooms of the house. They were allowed to walk out in the courtyard and to go to the outhouse at will as long as they didn't approach the gate.

The women from Lia recoiled from the sight and stink of the prisoners in the basement, whose ghostly faces peered out at them from the small barred windows. They could hear them weeping and moaning, and the screaming when they were beaten. They saw the collected shoes and some clothing, from the dead, covered with lice, stacked in the pantry behind the kitchen. At night they often heard prisoners led outside to be executed behind the houses. When the women walked to the outhouse, they picked their way between dozens of

431

shallow graves in the yard. The odor of rotting flesh permeated the whole neighborhood.

Eleni and the other three from Lia were occasionally sent, under guard, to collect water from the spring near the mill of Tassi Mitros. On one of these trips, while an *andarte* watched from a distance, Eleni was approached by Vasili Bokas, the guerrilla captain who had pursued the fugitives on the night of the escape. Many years later, after he returned from exile in Poland, Bokas described how he leaned over to drink from the spring and whispered to Eleni that her family had indeed reached the other side safely; he had seen them himself as they climbed the Great Ridge to be greeted by government soldiers. Eleni straightened up, struggling to keep her face under control, and turned eyes full of gratitude on the guerrilla.

Free of the gnawing fear that her children had been captured, she returned to the prison with new strength to withstand Sotiris' inquisition. She calmly replied to all his questions: No, she knew nothing of the plot, nor of any UNRRA supplies that her father was rumored to have hoarded on his property. The guerrillas were welcome to take everything they could find, she added. She had no more use for possessions, now that Lukas Ziaras had broken her heart by taking her children. All she had to live for was the hope of seeing her daughter Glykeria come back from the threshing fields.

One day the guerrillas brought Alexo's eleven-year-old daughter Niki, a thin, solemn-eyed child, up to the police station and questioned her in the garden. Eleni peered from the window of the small pantry behind the kitchen; Niki remembers seeing her bite her lip and shake her head as if warning the girl to say nothing.

The youngest of Foto Gatzoyiannis' nine children, Niki was questioned from ten in the morning until late in the afternoon by Sotiris. Niki had known all about the planned escape. She had even watched her sister Arete and her mother bury a fifteen-pound spool of solder – the principal wealth of Arete's tinker husband – in an isolated field below Alexo's house.

Niki expected Sotiris to grill her about her sister's escape, but then he threw her off guard by demanding to know where Arete had hidden the solder. Niki realized that someone must have seen them hiding it, but she shook her head dumbly. Then Sotiris asked her how many times her father had sneaked back into the village to collect secrets about the guerrilla movements. 'Never!' the girl replied, and backed up as Sotiris came toward her.

'Everyone knows your father acts as a guide for the fascists,' the intelligence officer shouted. 'He's been spying for them too, and your mother has been helping him.'

In a thin, reedlike voice Niki denied knowing anything about solder, escape plots or visits from her father. Sotiris' eyes flickered and he slapped her so hard that her ears roared.

'All you can say is "No"!' he shouted. 'We'll put you in there' – pointing to the cellar – 'and soon you'll have plenty to tell us!' But after several hours of inquisition, Sotiris released the girl with the warning: 'Think about our questions. We're going to bring you back again and the next time we want the truth.'

The first moment they could talk to each other, Eleni whispered to Alexo that Niki had been brought in and questioned. The girl had suffered no more than a few slaps, she reassured her sister-in-law, but the older woman turned the color of candle wax. The next morning Sotiris called Alexo in and announced, 'Your daughter Niki told us all about the solder that you hid on your property. Like all possessions of traitors, it belongs rightfully to the Democratic Army. Are you going to show us where it's hidden or shall we beat the information out of your daughter?'

Alexo nodded, in defeat. She knew that by pointing out the solder, she was weakening her claim to ignorance of the plot, but she had to do it to save the child. 'I'll take you there,' she said, and Sotiris smiled for the first time since the escape.

As head of intelligence gathering in Lia, Sotiris Drapetis knew that the mass defection was not only an indelible blot on his record but a possible threat to his survival. After the disaster, the Epiros Command had sent the man called Katis, who served in the judicial branch both as judge and investigating officer, to find out what had happened.

433

It was Katis who had made such a strong impression on the villagers with his spellbinding voice and urbane manner when he conducted the trial of the soldier captured during Pergamos. He was also the judge who sentenced the four officers captured in Povla to be executed. Now Katis was in Lia to unearth the reasons for the escape, and his breath was hot on Sotiris' neck. Sotiris interrogated the relatives of the fugitives with the desperation of a drowning man. After a week of this, Katis called the intelligence officer into his office and demanded to know what he had learned. Sotiris came up with an answer which he hoped would make him look less culpable. 'I'm convinced that it was organized on the outside by the fascists who came from Filiates and led their relatives out,' Sotiris told him. He paused momentously and added, 'And they're going to try again.'

Katis leaned forward, frowning under his heavy brows. 'Is this what you've learned from the women you've been interrogating?'

Sotiris lowered his eyes to the pile of papers in front of Katis, the summary of the interrogations. 'Well, so far the suspects persist in saying they knew nothing,' he began nervously. 'But Alexo Gatzoyiannis has admitted hiding solder for her daughter Arete before the escape, which seems to prove that she was in on the plot.'

'Seems!' Katis shouted in a voice that made Sotiris jump. 'Koliyiannis personally sent me here to find out how this fiasco happened – who was responsible – and to make such examples of the traitors that no one else will ever again think of defecting. I need evidence; I don't want to know about how things *seem* to you.'

'Of course, we *could* get confessions from the women under detention if we increase the pressure on them,' Sotiris said quickly. 'But they're only the tip of the iceberg. That wouldn't get us the fascists who came and took the others out.'

'You're sure the twenty were led out?' Katis asked, lifting a skeptical eyebrow as he took a noisy sip from a small cup of coffee.

'All my informants in the village are convinced of it,' Sotiris replied. 'They say it was Kitso Haidis, father of the

Amerikana, and Foto Gatzoyiannis, her husband's brother. Both men are notorious fascists, sir. If we captured them, the two biggest fish from this village, it would demonstrate our reach and squelch any more thoughts of crossing over.'

'Are you volunteering to go to Filiates and bring them back?' Katis asked dryly.

'We can lure them back,' Sotiris said, trying his best to sound convincing. 'The two people they wanted most, the Gatzoyiannis women, are still in our hands because they were in the threshing fields on the night of the escape. If we release the women as bait and watch them closely, we'll wind up getting everyone with one stroke: the fascists, the women and the others in the village who are preparing to go with them!'

'Others are planning to escape?' Katis asked, his cup clattering into its saucer.

'My informants suspect as many as thirty,' Sotiris replied knowingly.

'All right, let them go,' Katis conceded. 'If it's an outside conspiracy, and more are joining it, then they've all got to be crushed. But if you manage to lose either of those women or any other traitors, you'll end up wishing your father had masturbated on the night he conceived you.'

The shine of perspiration was visible on Sotiris' upper lip as he saluted and turned to go.

On the eighth day of their captivity, Eleni, Alexo and Marianthe were called by Sotiris into the good chamber. He handed them each a document summarizing the testimony they had given – that they were ignorant of any escape plot – and they signed it. Then he informed them that they were being released. Guards would escort each of them home, he said. From now on they must not be seen talking to one another or communicating in any way. They were not to go near the boundaries of the village. And every personal possession of their relatives who had fled must be handed over.

As she was led down the path, Eleni steeled herself for the sight of the house: the hearth, the niches and corners, all silent and empty of her children's presence. But she wasn't prepared for what she saw inside the broken door: clothes on the floor, pallets slashed, even the icon tossed in a corner. She stood in the doorway and stared at the chaos as the guerrillas began collecting things. They had been ordered to leave a minimum amount of clothing and food for Eleni to survive. They took all the supplies except for a few pounds of flour, all the clothes except for Eleni's brown dress, and most of the animals, leaving her two goats and four sheep.

Watching the guerrillas packing up her belongings, Eleni consoled herself that she still had the fields – the beans and corn that had not been harvested. As she waited for them to finish, she pushed the door open all the way and felt something blocking it. She peered around behind it to find Nikola's beige-and-brown book bag, the one he had carried to school so proudly in the days before the guerrillas came. It held his scrawled and smudged notebooks and his cherished Byzantine sword blade. The sight of his satchel made Eleni realize he was really gone. She could imagine him carefully packing his treasures and then at the last moment leaving them behind because someone told him the bag was too heavy to carry such a long way. The notebooks were all she had left of him.

She bit her lip, determined to stay in control until the guerrillas were gone. As soon as they led away the protesting goats and kids, she slumped to the floor and gathered the book bag into her arms, letting the tears come.

Eleven-year-old Niki Gatzoyiannis was at home when she saw her mother approaching, trailed by two guerrillas and a mule. She ran out and embraced her, but Alexo silently continued on past the house to the field below and pointed to a spot where the guerrillas began to dig. They quickly uncovered the spool of solder that Arete had hidden before her escape. Niki's heart was racing. She knew that her mother was implicating herself. Alexo stood silently, her hands on her daughter's shoulders, as the guerrillas loaded things on the mule and went away. When they were out of earshot, Niki whispered, 'Mother, why on earth did you show them the solder?'

Alexo looked at her. 'Didn't you tell them about it? They said you did.'

Niki grew indignant. 'I didn't tell them a thing, even when they hit me!'

Alexo realized that she had been tricked: she had played into Sotiris' hands, trying to protect her daughter. She put one arm around the girl, leading her back into the house. 'What does it matter?' Alexo said. 'Let them have the solder. At least they let me go.'

Giorgina Bardaka was not released with the other three women. She was the only one who had been in the village on the night of the escape, and Sotiris suspected that she knew all about the conspiracy, despite her claim that her family had abandoned her.

On the twelfth day of her captivity, Giorgina was taken out of the security prison, still carrying her tiny daughter, who was wrapped in the traditional swaddling clothes. Two other women – strangers to her – were brought out of the cellar to join them. Three guerrillas carrying shovels led the prisoners down the path, past the Haidis gate, on down and across the ravine to the churchyard behind the rubble of the Church of the Virgin.

One of the women with Giorgina was in her early forties and wore a large key tied to her belt. The other was older, perhaps fifty, and she was the first to be ordered to dig her own grave. She worked doggedly, in silence, her callused hands trembling. When she had dug a narrow channel only about a foot deep and long enough to contain her body, the guerrillas made her sit in it. One of them shot her with his rifle from a few yards away, blowing off the entire back of her skull.

Then it was the turn of the younger woman with the key on her belt. The whole time she was digging, she wept and screamed, 'Michalaki! My son, where are you?' They had to force her to sit in the grave, and she was still crying out 'Michalaki!' when the bullet opened her skull and she died, flapping like a gutted fish.

The guerrillas turned to Giorgina Bardaka and told her to

437

put down her baby in the shade of a nearby tree. They handed her a shovel and one of them said, 'You can still save yourself by naming those who organized the escape.' Her mind numb with terror, Giorgina took the handle of the shovel and began to make a few scratches in the earth. Everything seemed warped, as if she was seeing through a pane of flawed glass. She began to tremble uncontrollably. A terrible pain shot across her chest and she fainted. 'I don't know how long I was unconscious,' she recalls, 'but when I came to, they picked me up and said, "You're lucky you have a baby." They carried me back to where she was lying and let me go. But I couldn't walk; they had to help me back to my house.'

For a long time after that, Giorgina couldn't speak about the aborted execution without fainting. Today she's a good-natured woman of fifty-eight with salt-and-pepper hair who lives in an Athens suburb with her husband, a baker. But several times a year Giorgina starts to tremble, the pain rips through her chest and she faints, although doctors can find nothing physically wrong with her.

The morning after Eleni was released from the jail, she awoke in the empty house and went out to the yard to stare at the great mauve and gray-green bowl of the foothills spread below her, the cloudless sky arching over it like a dome. She watched a hawk lazily circling in the heavens and fiercely envied it its freedom. Later that morning, when she went out the gate to draw water from the spring, Eleni discovered a small pile of cigarette butts. Someone had crouched there all night, watching her.

There were no walls, no chains limiting her movement, but amid the infinite vastness of her familiar mountains, Eleni was as much a prisoner as the captives in the cellar of her house. Her feelings of claustrophobia became stronger every day. As she moved about the fields and ravines, the invisible fetters that trapped her there became heavier. Like a zoo animal compulsively exploring the boundaries of its cage, Eleni wandered about the periphery of the village, often going far down to the southern fields and staring toward the distant mountains which hid her children.

One day Olga Venetis, her neighbor in the Perivoli, was climbing down past the Haidis house to irrigate one of her family's fields on the southern boundary. She saw a small brown figure far below, climbing the path, and recognized Eleni, who carried a load of kindling on her back, stopping now and then to add to the burden. Olga shouted and signaled and Eleni approached slowly, walking like a woman much older than her forty-one years. When they were close enough to speak, Eleni said, 'Come by my house in a little while so that we can talk. But don't come by the path, stick to the back gardens so no one will see us together.'

Olga nodded and continued on. When she made her round-about way back to the Haidis garden, Eleni quickly opened the door and pulled her inside. The two embraced and Eleni told Olga about her wanderings. 'I've been as far down as the monastery of St. Athanassios, pretending to gather wood,' she said. 'They watch me at night but today I didn't see anyone. I could just have kept going and reached the other side.'

'Why didn't you?' Olga asked.

'I can't leave with Glykeria still in their hands,' Eleni replied. 'They'd kill her! I don't think they're going to kill me – otherwise they would have done it already, but if I leave, it would be her death.'

Olga looked at her friend's drawn, sallow face and felt her despair; she had two little boys herself – Dimitri, five, and Yiorgo, three. 'Let's go together,' she said impulsively. 'Let's go now. I'll get my boys. You can carry one on your back and I'll carry the other.'

Eleni shook her head with a look of gratitude. Then she turned imploring eyes on Olga. 'Please do something for me – bring Dimitri down to see me one day. He has the same kind of hair as Nikola, the same way about him. Bring him down for a little while so that I can hold him.'

Olga Venetis did bring Dimitri down to see her. For a few minutes Eleni filled the void in her arms with another woman's child and it numbed the ache of Nikola's absence.

After the tumultuous arrival in Filiates, the Gatzoyiannis family spent two nights at the house of a relative there, hoping for word from Eleni and Glykeria, but they knew they couldn't stay long. Eleni had warned them that Filiates was too close to the battle zone and had insisted that they wait for her in a safer place: the seaport town of Igoumenitsa or even the island of Corfu. Camps were already being set up in Igoumenitsa for homeless refugees from the occupied territory, and the Gatzoyiannis family resolved to move there as soon as they had bought a few essentials.

Christos Gatzoyiannis had sent $500 to his brother Foto in Filiates on the chance that he could get it to Eleni. The children and their uncle used some of it to buy food, new clothes and shoes. To distract Nikola from his worry about losing his notebooks, his grandfather bought him new ones, along with some bright-yellow pencils.

Before moving on, the family had a photograph taken to send to Christos; concrete proof of their escape. In the fading sepia print they are posed stiffly in front of a stone building with a padlocked wooden door, frowning into the camera. The grandfather, Kitso, is seated next to his black-cowled wife Megali in the front row, the old woman with a comforting arm around Nikola's shoulders. The boy, clutching his new pencils and wearing his fine new shoes, short pants, pullover and coat, is staring dubiously into the camera, imagining his unknown father peering back at him. Fotini stands at stiff attention in a new school dress, her chin raised, looking very much as her mother must have at the age of ten. In the back row Olga, Nitsa and Kanta, in shapeless village dresses and braided hair, seem transfixed by the camera while Andreas towers above them, worried as always, his baldness covered by a cap.

Accompanied by Kitso and Andreas, the family left Filiates behind, traveling by bus to Igoumenitsa, on the west coast, just across from Corfu. They were luckier than most refugee families; because of the number of people in the group, they were lodged on the top floor of an unfinished house that was being built for civil servants. The rooms were bare, the walls unplastered. A spiral metal outside staircase led precariously up from the ground floor, where another family of refugees was living.

In their new quarters there was a small room which the

children were told would be a bathroom. They surveyed the mysterious pipes and the hole in the floor for an indoor toilet, exclaiming at the thought of having such an unsanitary fixture right inside the house. They were glad that it had not yet been installed and made do with a small drainage ditch outside the house that filtered down toward the sea.

The children felt more at home in Igoumenitsa than they had in the winding cobbled streets of Filiates. The town was built on a steeply rising cove of land cupped around a natural harbor, and their house was high on the hill. It was like being back in the Perivoli, with the world falling away below them, only now their vista stretched down not to the valleys and foothills far below but toward a shining immensity which was the sea.

As soon as they were settled, Nitsa went, at the insistence of her mother, to visit the doctor who was treating the refugees. Nitsa was now huge with child and she had never been examined during her pregnancy. The pinch-faced medical student had seen many ailments among the refugees – malnutrition, goiter, rickets and tuberculosis were the most common – but when he examined Nitsa he was nonplused. He had read about hysterical pregnancies in women who wanted a baby so much that their bodies imitated every symptom right down to the labor pains in the ninth month. Patiently he tried to explain to Nitsa that she wasn't pregnant at all; there was nothing in her stomach. Once she accepted that fact, the swelling would disappear. But Nitsa looked at him as if he were speaking Chinese. Finally, rolling his eyes in exasperation, he shouted, 'There's nothing in there but wind! It's a wind pregnancy!'

Nitsa's face lit up with comprehension and she crossed herself. 'The wind!' she said. 'And me a decent, God-fearing woman!' The doctor shook his head as she hurried off.

Nitsa returned to the house in great excitement, saying that the children must go search in the woods and fields at once and find her a tortoise. Bewildered, they did as she told them, and Fotini soon returned with a large hissing specimen that peered balefully from its tessellated mud-colored shell. Nitsa mercilessly threw the tortoise into a pot of water boiling on

441

the kerosene stove, and when it was cooked, wrenched open
the shell and began to devour the meat.

'It's the only counterspell to the *daouti*,' she explained to
the wide-eyed children. 'The doctor said it was the wind that
got me with child, but I know it was the Shadowy One. I must
have fallen asleep when I waited for the candle to burn all the
way around the church, and the monster saw me and was
aroused by my beauty. Thank God I found out in time!
Imagine giving birth to a child with cleft hoofs and the horns
of a ram!' She sliced the slippery flesh into pieces as the
children watched queasily. 'Not a word of this to Andreas!'
she whispered. 'He'd say I did something to encourage the
Evil One, but no one is safe from him. I've seen it happen to
sheep and goats, and the poor animals swell up within days.'
She finished the tortoise meat and waddled off to a local witch
to buy a charm containing dog's droppings and a dried
snake's head. That night Nitsa went to sleep early, and the
next morning her abdomen had already begun to deflate, like
a balloon punctured by a pin. When, within a day or two,
Andreas asked in bewilderment what had happened to the
miraculous pregnancy, Nitsa blushed and said it had been no
more than the result of having nothing to eat in the village but
beans. 'You know what they say,' she told him. 'He who eats
beans bears witness to beans!'

On one of the first days after the family was settled in
Igoumenitsa, Nikola decided to explore. He wandered down
below the house where soldiers were putting up corrugated-
iron Quonset huts to house the increasing number of refugees.
Then he followed the path past the small wooded area which
he had chosen as his new 'thinking place.' Continuing down
the hill, the boy found himself at the harborside, which was
bustling with the arrival and departure of small motor-driven
caiques and flat, bargelike ferryboats plying the route from
Igoumenitsa to Corfu and Brindisi, Italy. The vastness of the
sea left him silent with awe; he had never imagined such an
infinity of water. He walked to the edge of the dock and
looked down into the dirty green depths where schools of
small silvery fish flickered.

Nikola fingered the 10-drachma coin in his pocket that his grandfather had given him and began to walk west along the harborside. He crossed the road to the shops that lined it and stood mesmerized in front of one which bore the legend 'Patisserie.' In the window were huge trays of pastries cut into neat squares and diamonds; one tray was enough to feed the entire population of Lia. They were the traditional honey-drenched sweets made of hundreds of leaves of crisp golden fyllo pastry layered with ground nuts, thick sweet cream and custard, sprinkled with cinnamon, bristling with shredded coconut. The tray that caught the boy's eye held *reveni*, a heavy confection like a pound cake, doused in honey. He felt for the silver coin in his pocket, then went in and managed to negotiate the purchase of one square of *reveni*, wrapped in a piece of greased paper.

Stuffing the cake into his mouth, Nikola walked along the harborside toward the west, enjoying the sense of being a city dweller. He left the commercial area as the road turned into a shady avenue bordered by spreading plane trees which came together over his head like the roof of a cathedral.

Proud of his success in navigating the metropolis, Nikola continued along the road. The sea, now lapping against a sandy beach, winked at him between the trees. He saw people playing on the beach and went closer to investigate. A number of teenaged boys, wearing colored shorts which Nikola imagined to be the underwear of city dwellers, were splashing in the waves, throwing rubber balls to one another. He crept down onto the warm sand and saw people moving through the water by churning their arms. He remembered his attempts to build a swimming pool. If only his mother were here now to see that the reports his father had given were true! These people were swimming and Nikola decided to do the same. He shed his muslin shirt and his short trousers with the suspenders, standing in the undershorts that his mother had knitted for him. The older boys laughed at the figure he made, but he ignored them and plunged into the water.

It was a cool, sensuous embrace, cleansing him of the dirt and heat. Nikola pushed on until the water was up to his chin. He saw a boy near him dive into an oncoming wave and begin swimming. It looked easy – the water must buoy him up like a rubber ball, he reasoned. Nikola imitated the older boy and threw himself headfirst into the green, glassy sheet. Suddenly he was sinking to the bottom, fighting the heaviness that dragged his limbs down. Burning water filled his nose and throat. He couldn't find the surface and flailed about, knowing he was lost. As he opened his mouth to cry out, the vile liquid poured into his stomach and lungs and he began to lose consciousness. Suddenly his head popped above water and before the next wave slapped him under, he managed to scream: '*Mana!*'

Eleni started out of her dream, finding herself sitting up on the pallet, drenched with sweat. She had heard Nikola calling her and knew he was in danger. Sometime later that afternoon Athena Haramopoulos, a neighbor from the Perivoli, passed by the Haidis gate and found her sitting on the threshold, weeping.

'Come now,' said Athena kindly. 'All that time you were in the jail you didn't cry, and now that they've let you go you're carrying on like this!'

'I dozed off,' Eleni murmured, 'and my little Fotini came to me with her hair all tangled and unbraided. Then I saw Nikolaki calling to me in fear. And just now I realized that today is his birthday. He's nine years old!'

'Aren't you ashamed of yourself!' Athena scolded. 'Go and find him! Just follow that path and go.'

Eleni shook her head and explained that she had to wait for Glykeria. Athena leaned forward and put her hand on Eleni's knee. 'You can't wait, Eleni,' she whispered. 'They're killing our own people now, like Easter lambs! Last night they killed Antonova Paroussis from Babouri behind your house. Everyone in the Perivoli heard her screaming.'

Eleni's face turned ashen as Athena told her what nearly everyone else in Lia already knew. Nine days before, Eleni's fiery young cousin had been sentenced at a public trial in the churchyard of Babouri, watched by the whole village, including Antonova's husband and young children. She was accused of spreading defiance among the mothers of

Babouri, convincing them not to send their children with the *pedomasoma*.

Antonova's wealth and position, her Communist sympathies and sharp tongue were no longer enough to protect her from the consequences of her defiance. She was sentenced to death and told that she would be held in Lia's prison for three weeks to await a decision on an appeal to General Markos for clemency. Her grieving husband had to sign a paper acknowledging her guilt and begging for mercy. She was dragged forcibly up to the cellar of the Gatzoyiannis house, her best blue American-made suit filthy with mud, her fine chestnut hair in disarray as she fought her captors and screamed with every step, 'People! My people! What have I ever done to you? Why are you killing me? Have pity on my children!'

After only nine days, long before her family could have received Markos' reply, Antonova was taken out of the cellar at night and made to stand in a grave dug in back of the Gatzoyiannis house. Marina Kolliou had seen many such nighttime executions. Her eyes had become accustomed to deciphering the shadows below, and she would stand at the window watching, memorizing everything she saw. Marina Kolliou appointed herself the sexton of the unmarked graveyard around the prison. Many years later, the aged grandmother with a face like a skull would direct strangers and villagers to the exact spot where they would find the bones they were hunting.

Ten years after her death, Antonova's husband and children identified the buttons of her suit and her gold teeth. Marina said she saw many executions, but she never again heard screams like those of Antonova Paroussis on the night she realized that the guerrillas who had been her comrades really were going to kill her.

For hours after Athena Haramopoulos left her, Eleni sat on her step pondering Antonova's death. Her warning to her cousin had come true: Antonova had made herself too conspicuous and the guerrillas were forced to make her a scapegoat. Now the children she had refused to give up would be sent away to Albania, carrying the memory of their mother's face at her trial as her own townspeople testified against her and her husband stood by in silence. Eleni mourned her friend's bravery and her futile death. Antonova had lost her life and her children's freedom as well, but, Eleni consoled herself, four of her own children were safely out of reach. And unlike Antonova, she could not be charged with ever speaking a word in public against the guerrillas.

After Antonova's execution, the number of villagers willing to greet Eleni on the path dwindled rapidly, especially when word got around that the security police were following her to find co-conspirators.

Soula Botsaris, whose house was used as a bakery by the guerrillas, was warned one day by Christos Zeltas, the burly head of the secret police, 'Be careful of the Amerikana. Observe her carefully. Tell us where she goes and whom she talks to. There's an organized conspiracy in the village and more are going to try to leave. They're watching her to see who else is in it.'

Soula nervously thought of the time she had lent Eleni some salt. She hurried down to see Tassina Bartzokis, who had been Eleni's next-door neighbor and close friend. 'If you should see Eleni coming up here, tell her to turn back,' Soula implored her. 'Even though she means no harm, they'll use her visit against us.'

Eleni also remembered the favor of the salt, and one day in late July, having picked more beans than she could possibly use for herself, she set out for her old neighborhood to take some to Soula Botsaris in return for her charity. As Eleni passed the old washing pond above her house, Tassina saw her and began walking along beside her, speaking under her breath. 'How are you?' she asked uneasily.

'As you would expect,' Eleni replied. 'I'm taking Soula some beans for her children.'

Tassina looked nervously about and whispered what Soula had said. 'It's better for you to go back home, Eleni, and not to visit her,' she urged.

'Thank God you told me,' Eleni said sadly. 'I didn't mean to do her harm. Here, you take the beans for your children. I won't come up again.'

446

Tassina hesitated, torn between her fear of being implicated and her need for food to give her family. She was silent for a moment, then said, looking rather shamefaced, 'Perhaps you'd better walk by the other side of the house and throw the bag into the courtyard as you pass. I'd rather not be seen taking anything from you.'

Tassina remembers that Eleni turned away without a word. When Tassina returned home she found the sack of beans lying in her yard. She picked it up with a mixture of relief and guilt and never spoke to Eleni again.

As Eleni walked about the village, avoiding former friends and neighbors for fear that she might do them harm, watching women she had known all her life turn away from her, she was struck by the irony of her position. She had always scrupulously obeyed the rules of village behavior while secretly feeling like an outsider. Now she couldn't leave, and she was stunned by the hostility that surrounded her. Perhaps she really was an alien and everyone had realized it at last. She was reminded of the baby chicks, dyed a brilliant scarlet, which were sometimes sold by traveling peddlers during the Easter season to amuse children. They rarely survived for more than a few days unless they were kept isolated in a cage, because the ordinary fowl, outraged at their unconventional plumage, would peck the bewildered fledglings to death.

Nikola was pulled out of the sea by one of the boys who had laughed at his hand-knit underwear. They held him upside down and shook him, then kneaded his stomach. When he finished retching and lay embarrassed on the sand, he looked up at his rescuers, and for lack of anything else to say, murmured, 'Why does the water taste so bad?' They shouted with laughter. 'Because it's salt, bumpkin!' one of the boys exclaimed. 'Hasn't anyone ever told you the sea is salt?'

Chastened, Nikola got dressed and headed back up the hill toward the unfinished house, determined not to tell anyone about his near-drowning. He had imagined that swimming would be as natural and pleasant as flying is to a bird, but now he had acquired a fear of the ocean that he would never quite conquer.

He returned to find the family in great excitement. 'Where have you been?' Olga scolded. 'We have to go at once to the refugee office! They're going to give us a relief payment.'

The bureaucrat who handed each member of the family 150 drachmas picked his ears with the clawlike nail of his little finger and delivered a lecture as he put the paper money in Nikola's hand. 'This is yours, and you can spend it any way you want,' he announced, 'but you must buy something sensible that you need – food or clothing.'

Nikola nodded solemnly. He was quickly calculating in his head: with 150 drachmas he could buy fifteen pieces of *reveni* or several of the rubber balls the boys had been playing with, or some more school books or several pairs of stockings. But what he really wanted was something to take the taste of the sea water out of his mouth. As soon as he could, he returned to the waterfront, clutching the fortune in his hand. He stood for a long time in front of the shop window full of pastries before finally moving on to a candy store nearby where a huge box of white, sugary cubes of *loukoumi* – Turkish delight – caught his eye. The box cost nearly 100 drachmas.

Nikola bought the whole box and carried it to the tree stump in his secret thinking place. One cube at a time, he ate the *loukoumi*: the sweetest of all confections, the synonym for feminine beauty; a gelatinous, chewy candy, crunchy with chopped almonds, covered in thick snowdrifts of confectioners' sugar. Each melting bite seemed to mask the bitter salt-bile taste of the sea and lessen the emptiness inside him. But then he stopped and the acrid taste of salt and the hollow ache of loneliness returned. He wished he were back in his house in the Perivoli with his mother. But no one had *loukoumi* in Lia. He reached for another piece.

Eventually, as the sun was beginning to set, his uncle Andreas found Nikola sitting on the ground, leaning against the stump, clutching his stomach. The empty *loukoumi* box told its own story. Gently Andreas carried the boy back to the house. After Nikola was repeatedly dosed with camomile tea and began to think he might survive, his sisters scolded him for squandering his relief money on a box of candy. Then they laughed at his prank and wrote about it to his father, who sent back a letter of stern reproach to his son for his irresponsibility. The boy was abject; he desperately wanted to please the father he had never seen, and now he had made him angry. Nikola spent more and more time down by the tree stump brooding and nursing his loneliness.

By the end of July, Eleni, Alexo and Marianthe had been free for nearly a month, but the guerrillas shadowing them had not found a shred of evidence that they were conspiring with one another or meeting with fascists from the other side. Sotiris could feel the noose tightening around his neck and redoubled his efforts to justify his conspiracy theory by calling in more informants from the village. There was no lack of women willing to give testimony against the Amerikana. They resented seeing Eleni walking about the village alive and well after her whole family had succeeded in slipping through the guerrillas' fingers. She had always had privileges and an easy life, the village women muttered, and it was time she was toppled from her high horse.

The road up to the security-police station was busy with women who came to whisper about the Amerikana: that she had ordered her daughters to wear kerchiefs around their faces to hide them from the eyes of the guerrillas; that she had hidden her husband's fine American clothes and her daughter's dowry from the fighters of the Democratic Army. Who knows how much wealth in food and sovereigns she had cached away somewhere? they would ask with knowing expressions.

Sotiris doggedly recorded each innuendo, but he knew he didn't have enough to convict the Amerikana or to retrieve his reputation with his superior officers. You couldn't kill a woman for wearing a kerchief or hiding a jacket. What he needed was proof of a village-wide conspiracy tied to the fascists on the other side.

Then one day Sotiris received a piece of information that seemed to be the break he had been waiting for.

It came indirectly from Andreas Michopoulos, who had been on duty at the Church of the Virgin on the night of the

449

escape. Although Andreas was badly frightened by the grillings he received immediately after the flight, he had by now recovered his cockiness and continued to exploit his uniform to impress his friends in the village. He had a crush on a sixteen-year-old village girl named Magda Kyrkas, and one day when he was visiting her house, the subject of the escape came up. 'Oh, there are plenty of others who would like to follow in their footsteps!' Andreas said airily. 'Just the other day Dina Venetis came up to me and said, "Andreas, if someone was to leave the village, what would be the safest route to take?"'

This remark was overheard by an *andartina* from the village of Parakalomo who was billeted in the Kyrkas house, and she dutifully went to the security police to report it. Sotiris gripped the desk in excitement. He was certain that Andreas knew more than he had admitted. Sotiris ordered the boy brought back to the police station, and this time made sure that he was beaten thoroughly. Like most bullies, Andreas could not tolerate pain; the blows and kicks of the security police soon had him babbling the names of fellow villagers who he claimed were preparing to leave. Sotiris was jubilant. One by one he arrested the people named and interrogated them, locking them up in the cellar along with the terrified Andreas.

Under the flexible rods and cleated boots of the security police, each villager swore complete loyalty to the cause and tried to stop the beating by suggesting other villagers who they were certain were harboring thoughts of escape. But after a week had passed, with the number of arrests snowballing, Sotiris despondently admitted to himself that he would have to discard the hope of trapping fascists from the outside. Although the villagers were eager enough to implicate one another, none of them had seen anyone from nationalist territory sneaking into the village to organize subversion. The scapegoats would have to be found among those still in Lia.

When Sotiris delivered his files on the new arrests and interrogations to Katis, he knew he was in for a painful scene, and the investigating magistrate showed no mercy. He castigated Sotiris for failing to prove anything about a conspiracy

450

or even to come up with any solid evidence. He acidly pointed out that headquarters' patience had been stretched beyond its limits. Ringleaders and traitors had to be named; a concrete case had to be built against them, and quickly. The Gatzoyiannis women had been walking about the village at liberty for weeks, and instead of serving as bait to trap other traitors, they were only flaunting their treachery, giving the village the impression that the DAG could be defied with impunity.

Sotiris sat up late that night poring over his files. He had heard whispers that the Drouboyiannis women knew something. The three sisters-in-law all lived in the section of the village near St. Friday, and one of them, Chrysoula, had been part of the escape, taking her two nieces, the daughters of Constantina Drouboyiannis, with her while their mother was at the threshing field. Sotiris ordered both Constantina and Alexandra Drouboyiannis brought in for questioning.

Ever since the day of the escape, they had been living in terror of being arrested. Alexandra was the dark, irascible woman who came with two of her daughters on the second escape attempt and grew hysterical when the fog spoiled their plans.

When Constantina, a dull-witted, gregarious woman, was ordered to go to the threshing fields, she had turned her own two daughters over to her other sister-in-law, the childless Chrysoula, saying, 'If you can find any way to escape while I'm gone, take the girls with you.' She had heard from Alexandra about the two failed escape attempts. Now Constantina burst into tears at the sight of the guerrillas at her door and wished she had never given her daughters to their aunt. They were free and she would have to pay for their deliverance.

Disgusted at Sotiris' failure to produce anything concrete, Katis decided to conduct the interrogation of the Drouboyiannis women himself. The investigating magistrate had set up his office just below the security headquarters in the home of Kostina Thanassis, the grandmotherly old woman who had brought Nikola a treat of marmalade on the eve of the escape. An incorrigible busybody, Kostina liked to

451

eavesdrop near Katis' door while he questioned prisoners, and she reported many details of what went on there to her neighbors. Now, when she saw Constantina Drouboyiannis being led in weeping, she patted the woman's arm sympathetically and whispered, 'Whatever you know, dear, for God's sake tell them and it may save you!' Constantina nodded tearfully. She realized she was not very clever and she was terrified of being caught in a web of lies. She decided to cooperate with the guerrillas and reveal whatever she knew, leaving out, of course, the fact that she had begged Chrysoula to take her daughters to the other side. After all, she had been in the threshing field on the day of the escape and no one could repeat what she had said except for Chrysoula, who was now far beyond the guerrillas' reach.

A few hours later Katis sent an urgent summons to Sotiris, and the intelligence officer nearly ran down the path to the office of the investigating magistrate. On the way he passed the two Drouboyiannis women, bruised and weeping, being led up toward the jail. The guards told him that Katis wanted them confined in the upstairs rooms, isolated from the other prisoners. Sotiris swore under his breath. If Katis had managed to unearth something that had escaped his own informants, he was in serious trouble. He brushed past the hovering figure of Kostina Thanassis and into the office of the hawk-faced Katis, who sat twiddling a string of onyx worry beads behind his desk, evidently lost in thought. Then the eyes of the magistrate focused on Sotiris with a small gleam of satisfaction and his melodious voice said, 'I want you to get the daughter of Alexandra Drouboyiannis, who's with our company up at Skitari, back here as fast as you can.'

'You mean Milia?' Sotiris replied, mystified. 'But what could she know about the escape? She's only eighteen and one of the most dedicated guerrillas we have. She was at Skitari on the day they left.'

Katis produced a smile that made Sotiris' skin crawl. 'It seems that there were two previous escape attempts, before the traitors succeeded in leaving,' he announced. 'They started out two times under your noses and turned back, and you never knew it!' He paused momentously. 'And the Amerikana was with them! She organized it all. If we can get convincing witnesses to testify to this in public, we have enough evidence to hang her and everyone associated with her!'

It was at the beginning of August, during the two-week Lent that precedes the feast of the Assumption of the Virgin, when a neighbor, Eugenia Petsis, called Eleni down from her bean field to the deserted mill where Eugenia lived with her daughter. 'I've just made a *skotaria* from goat's intestines,' she said, trying to cheer up Eleni, who had become thin as a rail, with purple hollows under her eyes. 'Come, sit down, have some with us.'

Eleni thanked her and shook her head. 'I'm observing the fast,' she said, 'hoping that the Virgin will help me.'

Eugenia, a motherly woman with a face like a russet apple, began to scold her. 'Forget about fasting!' she said. 'You have to live. You owe it to Glykeria to survive until she gets back from the harvest.'

Eleni sat down weakly and nodded. 'Perhaps I'll go back to the house and drink a little milk,' she conceded. 'The Virgin will forgive me that much, but I won't eat meat.'

Before the sun had set, Eleni was back at Eugenia Petsis' door, her face the color of sulfur.

'There are three guerrillas at my house, waiting to take me to the police station,' she said, out of breath. She looked at the older woman beseechingly. 'If I don't come back, look after the animals and send me a little milk now and then with your daughter,' she pleaded. She paused for a moment, then seized Eugenia's hands. 'If Glykeria comes back and I'm not here, please take care of her!'

Before the astonished woman could reply, Eleni was gone.

CHAPTER FIFTEEN

Throughout the long summer of 1948, guerrillas and government forces were locked in battle for control of the Grammos mountain range, the main stronghold of the insurgents. By the end of July, the nationalist troops were beating at the central gate of Grammos, the towering mountain called 'Kleftis' ('the Thief'), a natural obstacle, over 6,000 feet high, which blocked the western approach to Grammos. As long as the guerrillas held Kleftis, their stronghold could not fall.

The government forces threw everything they had at the exposed slopes of Kleftis, fighting with guns, hand grenades and bayonets for every rock. At dawn on July 26 they managed to take the summit, only to be driven two hundred yards back down by a daring counterattack from the guerrillas two hours later. Both sides displayed desperate courage. The partisans, including many young women and adolescent boys, fought with heroic determination, believing they were giving up their lives as the final sacrifice before victory. There was no opportunity to bury the dead on the exposed cliffs, and soon the stench of rotting bodies under the scorching sun was unbearable. The Greek generals were determined to take Kleftis at any cost. 'Don't withdraw even half a meter!' General Thrasyvoulos Tsakalotos, commander of the government offensive, ordered his field commanders when they suggested a temporary retreat. 'Kleftis will be captured even if it takes the whole First Army Corps.'

On the last day of July the government forces bombarded

the summit of the mountain with 20,000 shells in preparation for a final assault and in the rear positions, King Paul, Queen Frederika, and the chief of the American mission, General James Van Fleet, visited the troops to raise morale.

At 4:30 a.m. on August 1, Battalion 583 managed to take the summit of Kleftis with a sudden assault. The battalion's first squads leaped into the trenches of the guerrillas and defeated them in hand-to-hand combat. The gate to Grammos had fallen.

Within a week, government forces had captured most of the guerrillas' positions on Grammos. But the rebels continued to resist ferociously, dying to defend every yard.

Such a determined defense was costly to both sides, but the guerrillas could least afford it because they had no way of replenishing their losses. Nevertheless, the Greek Communist Party leader, Nikos Zachariadis, insisted they fight to the death despite strong criticism from his commander in chief, General Markos Vafiadis. Why were the guerrillas forced to stand and die in droves to hold on to untenable positions? Markos asked. Why weren't they returning to the tactic that brought them such success at the start of the revolution – hit-and-run attacks? But Zachariadis was inflexible. If his strategy was failing to hold Grammos and drive back the enemy, he charged, 'it is because bad Communists have failed in their duty.' Hearing his words, the Communist leadership in the occupied territories began to search in their midst for scapegoats on whom the failure could be blamed.'

REAPING THE HARVEST

THE MONTH OF August ushers in the harvest season and the Feast of the Virgin on the fifteenth. The overflowing abundance of grapes, figs, melons, tomatoes, corn and walnuts makes it relatively easy for the pious to renounce meat and dairy products during the two-week fast which precedes the holiday of the Holy Virgin. 'August, my good month, if only you could come twice a year!' the peasants say as they gather in the bounty of the fields and vines.

The Feast of the Virgin is a day for miracles. From all over Greece the lame, blind and dying converge on the small island of Tinos in the Aegean hoping to be cured by the famous Icon, which is carried from the church over the prone bodies of thousands of invalids who lie on the streets. Pilgrims who have made vows to the Virgin throughout the year fulfill them on Her day; on Tinos hundreds of women can be seen every August 15 walking barefoot the long distance from the harbor up the steps of the great church, their hair unbound and uncovered, their hands crossed over their breasts. Some of them make the journey crawling on their knees.

In Lia, Eleni was determined to observe the fast, hoping for a miracle from the Virgin: her salvation. But when she saw the three guerrillas arriving at her gate to take her back to the jail, she was not surprised. For weeks she had felt that the invisible bars holding her prisoner in the village would eventually be replaced by real ones.

News of Eleni's arrest spread through the village like a summer grass fire and eventually reached Alexo on the far southern perimeter, casting her into a profound depression.

456

Her daughter, Niki, remembers how, early the following afternoon, Alexo went to the spring to fill a large barrel of water, a heavy load for a woman of fifty-six, and when she brought it back, she sat in silence by the door for the remainder of the daylight, so low in spirits that nothing the girl said could rouse her. Just before dark a guerrilla came to their gate to take Alexo to police headquarters. He was young and he felt sorry when he saw how Niki clutched her mother and wept. 'Don't be afraid,' he said. 'They only want to talk to her for a few hours.' But both mother and daughter knew he was lying. As the guerrilla led her away, Alexo turned to look back at her daughter standing in the doorway and sighed, 'I'm never going to see my house again.'

For the past days the security police had been filling the jail with new prisoners from Lia, beginning with those implicated by Andreas Michopoulos. The first to be brought in was Dina Venetis. Dina was only twenty-eight, a slender woman with high cheekbones and arched black eyebrows – a face of such dark, exotic beauty that one would have expected to find it in an Athenian actress rather than in a black-kerchiefed peasant woman. Dina was grazing her family's flock under the midsummer sun when the guerrillas came for her on a still afternoon, heavy with the scent of fruit and broken boughs. 'What are you going to do with me?' she asked as they led her toward the police station. 'We're going to slaughter you so it'll rain,' one of them chuckled. But of all those held in the Gatzoyiannis cellar, Dina Venetis is one of the few who survived to describe the treatment of the prisoners during the summer of 1948.

Each villager brought in to the security-police station was kept isolated at first in one of the upstairs rooms, left to wonder what crimes he or she was suspected of committing. After a few days of suspense, the prisoner was taken outside to the back of the house to be beaten and interrogated in the garden. Finally, the prisoner was thrown into the filthy subterranean jail, which was becoming more crowded every day.

Dina Venetis, whose three small children were left alone to

wander around the neighborhood begging for food like stray puppies, was kept in solitary confinement for two days before she was led out behind the house to a patch of holm oak, stepping on soft ground pitted with graves, choking at the stench of rotting bodies.

The young woman was accused of planning to escape in order to join her soldier husband on the government side. While Sotiris interrogated her, several of the security police held her and beat her with the flexible branches of the cornel tree. The first blow cut her hand and split one of her fingernails. Every blow of the switch broke the skin, leaving a ribbon of blood.

Dina Venetis showed an unexpected defiance for such a fragile-looking woman. Instead of denying that she wanted to escape, she said, 'What woman wouldn't want to be with her husband? But I never made plans to leave – how could I, with three small children?' As they continued to flail her with the rods, she cried, 'That's right, hit me! I deserve it because I could have escaped and I didn't! I thought you were human beings!'

Sotiris ordered the guards to bring Andreas Michopoulos out of the cellar to confront her. He had been beaten much worse than Dina and his head lolled as he tonelessly repeated his statement that Dina had asked him what path would be the safest to follow out of the village.

'Whom do you expect us to believe,' Sotiris challenged her, with the police standing by, rods in their hands, 'you, whose husband is a fascist officer, or this guerrilla who is one of us?'

Dina looked at Andreas, her face contorted with contempt. 'That is a piece of shit!' she said. 'And everyone in this village knows it. I don't even say good morning to that scum, let alone ask his advice! If I wanted to leave, I know the paths out of this village better than anyone else, living where I do.'

They took Andreas away and continued beating Dina until her body was covered with welts, then they dragged her across the yard. Christos Zeltas, the head of the security police, gave her a kick that sent her flying into the cellar.

Every day more beaten prisoners were booted into the jail while Andreas Michopoulos crouched behind the door, avoiding the eyes of those he had implicated. Not long after the young guerrilla's uncle, Spiro Michopoulos, and the cooper Vasili Nikou were brought in, Alexo Gatzoyiannis was thrown through the cellar doorway. The prisoners learned that the Amerikana was in the house, but that she was being kept upstairs, isolated from the others. One young village woman who was brought in several times for questioning, Athena Daflakis, remembers seeing her sitting cross-legged on the threshold of the kitchen.

Like the others, Eleni was taken outside and beaten with cornel rods while Sotiris shouted that she had organized her children's escape and was a ringleader in the conspiracy. Despite the kicks and blows and the stinging lashes of the rods on her flesh, Eleni stuck to her story: that Lukas Ziaras and her mother had stolen the children while she was working at the harvest, unaware of the plot. Sotiris was unperturbed by her denials; he knew that Katis had a surprise in store for her.

A few days after her incarceration Eleni was taken down the path to the home of Kostina Thanassis just below, now being used by Katis as his office. Tassina Bartzokis, her old friend and next-door neighbor, watched from her window; not much that happened around security headquarters escaped Tassina's sharp eyes. And Kostina Thanassis was startled to see her former neighbor being led, bound and bruised, into her house. Inveterately curious, she made sure to overhear what went on between the magistrate and Eleni, and later described the confrontation to other neighbors.

Katis studied Eleni like a collector contemplating his prize specimen and then, with exaggerated courtesy, gestured for her to sit down. Eleni was expecting another beating. She looked at this urbane man with the large nose and small neat ears, and terror crept over her. She remembered him orchestrating the trial of the captured soldier after Operation Pergamos.

'Amerikana,' Katis intoned in his sonorous voice, 'you planned your children's escape from this village.'

'That is not true, as I've said over and over again,' Eleni replied. 'I knew nothing of the escape. I was working in the threshing fields.'

Katis went on smoothly, 'You planned this whole thing in league with the traitor Lukas Ziaras, and you talked other women in the village into joining the escape. What do you say to that?'

Eleni raised her chin defiantly. Now she was on solid ground. She had been scrupulous not to drop the slightest hint, much less tell anyone to join them. The only person she had confided in was Alexo, and Alexo would never betray her.

'That is a complete lie,' she said.

Katis raised one eyebrow. 'What if I told you that among the women you induced to send her children away was Constantina Drouboyiannis?'

Eleni blinked in surprise. She had learned long after the escape that Constantina's two daughters and their aunt Chrysoula were with those who fled while Constantina was working with Eleni at the harvest. The news had astonished her after the tongue-lashing she had given Lukas for including Alexandra Drouboyiannis and her two daughters on the earlier attempt. How the three new Drouboyiannis women and the Mitros family had come to be on the successful third try was a mystery to her. Her mind raced. If only Lukas had done as she told him and kept the escape a secret between their two families!

Katis brought her out of her thoughts. 'Well, answer me! Did you convince Constantina Drouboyiannis to send away her daughters or not?'

'Of course not! It's totally false.'

'Would you swear to that?'

Eleni stared straight into his mocking eyes. 'Yes.'

Katis got up and opened the door. He spoke to a guerrilla standing outside. 'Go up to the Amerikana's house and bring me the icon that hangs in the good chamber at once.'

Tassina Bartzokis, who was still watching the path from her kitchen window, was astonished to see the guerrilla coming by with the Gatzoyiannis' icon under his arm.

Katis stood before Eleni like a priest, holding the wooden icon of the Virgin and her Child, their heads encircled in hammered gold. It was the image before which Eleni had crossed herself every day of her married life until she had been evicted from her house. Now she stared at the sweet face of the Madonna, praying for guidance.

'Do you swear that you never told Constantina Drouboyiannis to send her daughters along with your family to the fascists?'

Eieni put her hand on the Virgin's image and felt a shock of fear shoot through her. 'I swear it on my life.'

'Swear it on the life of your son,' Katis ordered.

Eleni turned to meet his eyes, not removing her hand from the icon. 'I swear it on the life of my boy, Nikola.' Speaking his name made her tears start to flow and she sat down abruptly, huddled in the chair, aware of the cold hollow in her chest and the ache of the welts from the beatings.

Katis put the icon down on his desk and walked to the other door of the small room. He opened it and snapped, 'All right, come here.'

Eleni stared as Constantine Drouboyiannis stepped hesitantly into the room. Constantine was a small woman some years older than Eleni, her simple, round face creased with smile lines, but she wasn't smiling now. She glanced at Eleni nervously, then looked away.

Eleni continued to stare at her curiously. She and Constantina had been working together at the threshing fields on the day of the escape, but they hadn't exchanged a word. Eleni had never suspected that the woman knew about the escape or that her daughters would be part of it.

She looked hard to see if Constantina had been beaten. There were no signs of cuts from the cornel rods, but her face was bruised, her hair unkempt under her kerchief. Katis pointed to a chair, which Constantina took, turning away from Eleni.

'Look at the Amerikana,' Katis ordered. Constantina did so reluctantly.

Katis addressed Eleni. 'I ask you for the last time: Did you know about the escape of your children and did you discuss it with other women in the village?'

Eleni sat with her hands in her lap. The Virgin's icon was on the desk in front of Katis. She remembered the young

461

guard's warning that she had to stick to her story if she hoped to save herself.

'I knew nothing about my children's escape,' she said, looking Katis in the eye. 'I've told no one in this village to send their children away.'

She heard a choking sound from Constantina and turned to her. For the first time the older woman returned her gaze. 'Ach, Eleni,' she sighed. 'Now you've done it!'

Katis stood up and walked toward Eleni. 'You might as well stop lying, Amerikana,' he said in a voice that would have filled a cathedral. 'We know everything, and the more you lie, the deeper you dig your grave.'

He turned to Constantina and began snapping out questions: 'Didn't the Amerikana and her family try to leave twice before they finally got away?'

'Yes,' Constantina mumbled, looking at the floor.

'Didn't they turn back the first time because the Ziaras baby cried?'

'Yes.'

'And didn't they turn back the second time because of a heavy mist?'

Constantina said nothing but inclined her head. Eleni was staring at her, rigid with shock. They knew about the first two tries! If they had proof, she was finished. But how could Constantina Drouboyiannis have told him? She hadn't been along either time. She could only have learned the details through village gossip. If she claimed she was with them, she would only incriminate herself. Eleni straightened up in her chair. It would be her word against Constantina's, and Constantina was only repeating hearsay.

She stared directly at the woman, who seemed to have shrunk in her chair. 'Why are you trying to bury me?' Eleni asked her, every word clear as the strokes of a bell.

'I didn't tell them, Eleni!' Constantina burst out, her eyes overflowing. 'They knew everything already, every detail!' Catching hold of herself, she lowered her voice. 'Someone else told them, Eleni. It wasn't my fault!'

Eleni turned to Katis, her cheeks burning. 'I never talked to this woman about any escape at any time,' she said. 'If she

462

says I did, she's lying to save herself. I swore on the Virgin's icon and on my son's life.'

Katis smiled, evidently pleased at the way things were preceding. Constantina wiped her eyes with the hem of her skirt. Katis stood up and opened the door. 'Take the Amerikana back to the security police,' he said to the guards waiting outside. 'I think she's ready to tell us the truth.'

As Eleni was led back up toward her house, her head was throbbing with the effort of trying to work out how she had been betrayed. She could feel the village gossip closing in on her like a net, its menace lurking near her like a shadow clinging to the walls. Who could have told them about the first two escape attempts? Certainly not Alexo or Marianthe, who would be destroying their own defense if they admitted they knew about them. Constantina must have learned about the two abortive attempts from her sister-in-law Alexandra, who had come along on the second effort, but Alexandra would never cut her own throat by confirming the story to the guerrillas. And as long as they had no eyewitness to testify, Eleni told herself, they couldn't prove she had been there. She struggled up the path, oblivious to the clouds of white cabbage butterflies busy among the patches of yellow broom. She silently prayed to the Virgin that the young guard had been right; if she stuck to her story, she might still save herself.

As she entered the brass-handled gate of the Gatzoyiannis house, Eleni looked up. A woman in a guerrilla uniform was coming out of the door. Her body was stocky, her dark hair cropped into a black frizz. It was Milia Drouboyiannis, one of the most vocal converts to the cause. Eleni remembered Milia shouting over the bull horns before she left for the battlefields, 'People of Lia, the Democratic Army has given purpose to my life! I no longer have mother, father and sisters; my family is the Democratic Army!'

But in fact Milia did have a mother: Alexandra Drouboyiannis, who was at that moment being held prisoner in the jail. Suddenly Eleni realized who would know about the first two escape attempts and would be willing – even eager – to report them to the security police. As the small simian figure of Milia strode by, her rifle slung over her shoulder, their eyes met, and in that instant Eleni realized that she was a dead woman.

Eleni was locked back in the small, dirt-floored pantry behind the kitchen, separated from the others, including Alexo and Marianthe, so that she could not tell them what Katis already knew. Then the systematic torture began, designed to strip her of every ounce of resistance she had left. Katis directed Sotiris to use whatever physical punishment was necessary to get a confession out of the Amerikana.

Among the men standing guard around the security prison was a twenty-one-year-old guerrilla named Taki Cotees, a small, prematurely balding youth with the pointed face of a malevolent elf. He remembers seeing a woman in her early forties with light-brown hair being interrogated. 'They took her out in the backyard and they beat her,' he recalls, 'and finally she confessed to everything.'

While Sotiris fired questions at her, Eleni was tortured by rotating teams of guerrillas. One of the men would stand behind her, place his knee in the small of her back and hook one arm around her throat, pressing forward with his knee while wrenching her body backward until the spine threatened to snap. If the grip of the pulling arm was too tight around the throat, the prisoner would pass out and they would have to wait until she came to before they could start again. The pain traveled up and down Eleni's spine, and the arm across her throat cut off the air supply, giving her the constant feeling of suffocating. With her body contorted backward at an impossible angle, she gasped for air like a fish and sometimes vomited from the pain. She longed for unconsciousness, but the guerrillas were careful to allow just enough air to prevent that relief.

The beatings took place on the southeast side of the house, where Eleni was surrounded by what had been her own fields and gardens, within sight of the mulberry tree which had been the family's pride and the gullies where her children had played. She was aware of none of this, only the insistent voices of her torturers above the rising and falling fever of pain that consumed her and the constant silent scream: 'When

464

will it stop; when will I die and be finished with it?'

When the beatings were over for the day, they threw her back in the dirt-floored pantry behind the kitchen. There was no light, but Eleni, crouched in a corner, didn't notice the darkness and the sound of the rats. She became oblivious to her surroundings, her perceptions blurred by the throbbing ache of her body. Sometimes her children's faces swam before her and she felt a lessening of her pain.

It probably took only a few beatings before Eleni broke. The glimpse of Milia Drouboyiannis had shown her her fate. She was lost, but her children were safe. There was little point in continuing to protest her ignorance of the plot if agreeing to their accusation would stop the torture. Finally she admitted to everything that was true: Yes, she had planned the escape with Lukas Ziaras. Yes, they had set out two times and turned back. But she would not admit to falsehoods: she had never tried to talk anyone else into escaping. The only reason she had sent her children away, she gasped between blows, was that there wasn't enough food to keep them alive. The guerrillas had taken her house, her gardens and most of her provisions. On the other side of the battle line, the children would be able to receive enough money from their father to survive.

Sotiris seemed satisfied with her statement. He prepared a document enumerating the points Eleni had confessed to and held the pen in her palsied hand as she signed it. After that they left her in peace on the floor of the small storeroom as the rats rustled in the corner.

Besides Dina Venetis, Marianthe Ziaras is the only surviving witness to what went on inside the security police headquarters and the cellar prison in those first days of August. Like the rest, she was kept isolated for a time after she was rearrested, locked in the small storage room next to the good chamber, which now served as an office. The storage room was directly above the entrance to the cellar and Marianthe found a knothole in the floor through which she could peek at the prisoners in the crowded basement below. Marianthe could see Dina Venetis just beneath her, wedged

465

among other seated prisoners, all with their hands tied in front of them.

Marianthe hissed at Dina Venetis through the hole in the floor until the dark-eyed young woman looked up.

'It's me, Marianthe Ziaras!' the girl whispered. 'They've just brought me in.'

Dina and Marianthe were neighbors on the southern edge of the village. Dina asked tensely, 'Have you seen my children?'

Marianthe replied that she had seen Dina's son Vangeli on the path and that he had said, 'My mommy's in jail.' The words made Dina start to cry.

'What are you here for?' Marianthe whispered.

Dina pointed to Andreas Michopoulos, who was cowering, half hidden by the cellar door.

'I'm here because of that miserable boy,' Dina hissed. 'He said I asked him how I could escape from the village.' She turned on Andreas. 'How could you tell those lies about me and destroy me, leaving my children alone on the road?' she cried, her voice rising.

Andreas huddled farther into the corner and muttered, 'Oh, leave me alone, will you! Can't you see what they've done to me?'

Dina turned her attention back to Marianthe. 'I'm in here because of my babies,' she said. 'If they weren't so small, I might have done what this vermin accuses me of and tried to leave, but I didn't.'

At that point she began to sob louder, and Vasili Nikou, the sunburned cooper who was sitting near her, made a sign to Marianthe to be quiet and go away from the peephole. Dina Venetis believes that the guerrillas overheard the conversation between herself and Marianthe and that it made them realize that Andreas' charges against her were false. 'They were always eavesdropping on us – from the doorway, from the windows, from the trap door that led down from the office to the cellar,' she says.

The same day that Marianthe spoke to her, Dina Venetis was called upstairs and interrogated once again by Zeltas, the head of the security police. She sensed a change in his manner toward her.

466

'From the time I spoke to Marianthe, they knew that I was telling the truth,' Dina Venetis insists. 'That's what saved me.' Others in the village disagree, saying that Dina saved herself by giving secret testimony against some of the others imprisoned with her in the cellar.

Although she was only eighteen years old, Marianthe Ziaras, the small stocky eldest daughter of Lukas Ziaras, had a stronger will than most grown women. Even though she had been taken by force to be an *andartina* and later was released for suspected disloyalty to the cause, she had become an expert fighter, to the surprise of her instructors. Marianthe had also inherited her father's quick, devious mind, along with his dark coloring.

When Marianthe was beaten and interrogated outside the prison by the holm-oak trees, she stuck doggedly to her story that her family had left her behind because they didn't love her. They were traitors, she said, and if the guerrillas had really captured them and killed them, then they had received their just punishment. She didn't flinch or cry when her captors threatened to show her the bodies of her family, although inside she was sick with fear.

There was a deeply religious side to Marianthe that seemed incongruous with her ferocity as a guerrilla. She had always spent more time at prayers than the most devout village crone, and she is convinced that she is still alive only through the miraculous intervention of the Virgin. 'I was saved,' she says, 'because even after the Germans burned the Church of the Virgin I used to take oil and go to light Her lamps in the rubble in front of the altar. My mother would ask me what I'd done with the olive oil and I'd say that I used it to cook for the children, but I stole it for the Virgin's lamps. That's why She saved me.'

Several days after her arrest, Marianthe was thrown into the cellar with the other prisoners, except for Eleni Gatzoyiannis. Her description of the conditions there correspond with Dina Venetis' accounts.

There were between twenty-five and thirty prisoners in the tiny cellar by this time, so crowded together that they had to sleep sitting up, leaning against one another. During that

467

period, all of them had their hands tied except for Alexo Gatzoyiannis, perhaps because the guerrillas felt she was too old to try to escape. 'What a wonderful woman she was!' Dina Venetis exclaims. 'Alexo would come around to each of us and massage our hands and rock our bodies so that we wouldn't go numb. While she was tending to us, she'd be crying for her eldest daughter, Arete, the one who had escaped. "She was the child who loved me the most," she would say. "And now she's brought my destruction."'

The prisoners were filthy and covered with lice. They were led in a group to the outhouse once or twice a day, but not frequently enough to control their bladders, so the stench in the cellar was suffocating. Once a day, tin plates of a thin soup were passed through the small barred windows by neighborhood women who had been ordered to prepare it. Olga Venetis recalls handing forty-five portions of soup into the cellar one day, but the number of prisoners varied drastically as some were taken out to be executed and others were brought in from distant villages.

Almost every evening Sotiris, Zeltas and other security police would come into the basement and choose a prisoner to kick and beat in front of the rest. Spiro Michopoulos and Vasili Nikou were often the ones they chose, though all the while they were being thrashed the men cried that they were innocent, completely loyal to the guerrillas.

When the day arrived for a prisoner to be executed, he would be called out of the basement in the evening, led upstairs and never be seen again. The sound of machine-gun fire regularly shattered the sleep of the Perivoli as Marina Kolliou peered from her window into the languorous summer night, memorizing the location of another grave plot.

A few of their fellow prisoners remain vivid in the memories of Dina Venetis and Marianthe. One of them was a madman, a half-witted shepherd who had been arrested for allegedly carrying messages to the government soldiers, even though he could not even speak intelligibly. When the guerrillas beat and kicked him, he would babble frantically in an incomprehensible gibberish, bubbles of spit forming at the edges of his mouth and running onto his filthy clothes.

There were bearded priests in the cellar, and an old whiskered patriarch who had been arrested when the guerrillas came searching for his soldier son in a village near the Kalamas River. Although the prisoners were not permitted to talk to each other, watched constantly by guards peering from the trap door in the ceiling and outside the cellar door and windows, they managed to exchange whispers with those sitting next to them. Dina Venetis remembers a slight young woman from the village of Gribovo, 'a mere wisp of a girl,' named Sofia Mitrou. She was teased constantly by the guards because she wound her kerchief around her face in the old-fashioned way, like Eleni's daughters.

Sofia had been arrested when the guerrillas came to her house searching for her father, a priest whom she loved with the filial devotion of an Electra. Dina felt a special pity for the girl, whom the security police decided to beat one night in front of the others, throwing her down and kicking her with cleated boots until the rest thought she was dead. Later Sofia huddled against Dina and consoled herself, 'At least my father got away.'

One night both Dina and Sofia had strange dreams; in the morning they told them to each other in whispers. Dina had imagined herself weaving at a loom, sending the shuttle back and forth. Sofia's dream was of rolling up string into a ball but she ran out of string when the ball was still tiny. No matter how she searched, she couldn't find any more. Like most village women, Sofia was expert at drawing omens from dreams. 'Yours means that you're going to be set free,' Sofia told Dina with a sad smile. 'My dream means that my life is over.' That night they took Sofia out of the cellar and she did not return.

Both Marianthe Ziaras and Dina Venetis have indelible memories of a prisoner named Despo, a tall, striking young woman of thirty with curly black hair who had been arrested near her evacuated village of Mavronoron when she tried to sneak back into her house to get some food. In the cellar prison Despo kept crying for her two baby sons. The beatings had begun to affect her mind and she lived in a delirium of fear, unable to bear the thought of the bullet that would kill

469

her. She talked to herself all night long, weeping and bargaining with death. One night Despo's hand came in contact with a long nail stuck into one of the rough beams of the cellar. She managed to work it loose, a rusty skewer nearly six inches long. With a convulsive movement she grasped it between her bound hands and plunged it deep into her belly, just below the rib cage.

Despo's suicide attempt was a failure. Despite the deep puncture wound, she couldn't die but remained conscious, begging the guards for help – a bandage, something to kill the pain – but they mocked her. The sound of her moans kept the other prisoners awake and it was almost a relief when Despo was taken upstairs one evening, along with the white-bearded old man. As she realized that her ultimate fear was coming true, Despo filled the building with screams, clearly audible in the cellar below: 'You're going to kill me! I know it!' Then they could hear the sardonic voice of Katis replying, 'Would we kill Despo, our pampered one, our favorite?' Over the sound of her sobbing they heard him add, 'You must write to General Markos tomorrow for clemency. He may give you a reprieve.'

Then the scornful voice of the bearded old man was heard. 'Clemency!' he snorted. 'Clemency! You're going to kill me, but you're not going to make a fool of me!'

Later that night the prisoners heard the shots that ended Despo's agony.

When a guerrilla would come into the cellar in the evening and call a prisoner's name to take him upstairs, the others heaved an involuntary sigh of relief. They might be beaten, lice-infested, starving, covered in their own filth, unable to speak aloud or to move their hands, but they were to be spared for one more day. Except for Alexo Gatzoyiannis, they clung to hope, waiting for a reprieve, a rescue or some kind of miracle.

Eighteen-year-old Marianthe Ziaras had her unwavering religious faith to sustain her. She was beaten often, once thrown against a wooden chest in the upstairs room so hard that several ribs cracked. Her feet and legs swelled from the

470

beatings until her shoes no longer fit, but her belief in a miracle never waned. And one evening, some days before the Virgin's feast day, she had a dream.

Every Greek village has several women who are considered particularly holy, endowed with the ability to exorcise the evil eye, read omens and detect signs of impending doom in the face of the household icon. Marianthe was one of these favored women, and no one, least of all herself, thought it extraordinary for the Virgin to appear to her.

Marianthe dreamed that she was weeping, her head on her knee, repeating over and over, 'Mother of God, save me!' when, as she tells it, 'I felt a tear fall on my arm. As I looked at it, it shimmered and turned white. Then I heard a voice say, "Enough now! You've cracked my heart with your prayers." I raised my head and there by the door was the Virgin, all alive, glowing with light. "Don't be afraid," She said. And from that moment I knew I was going to be saved.'

That evening Marianthe's name was called and she was led upstairs under the pitying eyes of the other prisoners. When the guards brought her to the first floor, they tightened the rope around her hands so that it cut off the circulation and the girl cried, 'If you were Germans, you wouldn't hurt me so much! Can't you loosen it?' One of the guards took pity on her and did as she asked. Then she was pushed into the small, dark, dirt-floored pantry behind the kitchen where Eleni had been kept, but Eleni was no longer there.

Marianthe fell into the room amid a clatter of pots and pans, and as soon as her eyes became accustomed to the darkness she realized that Andreas Michopoulos was huddled in a corner, also with his hands bound. He had been beaten badly; his eyes were dark and swollen, his face bloody and terrible.

Marianthe sat in silence, taking in her surroundings. There was one small window, about two feet square, with two vertical iron bars embedded in the wooden window frame. The bars were old; every window in Lia was fortified in this way, a practice dating back to the days of the brigands.

The tiny room contained a large pile of shoes which Marianthe realized must have belonged to prisoners who had been killed. After *falanga* – the widespread torture of beating on the soles of the feet – shoes could no longer be worn. Marianthe's beatings had caused her feet to swell, but she still had her shoes with her, tucked under her arm. She was determined not to lose them, even in her last extremity, because they were fine black leather ones, almost new, that her father had bought for her.

Marianthe and Andreas regarded each other in silence, both certain that they had been brought upstairs to be executed. They could hear the guards breathing just outside the door. There were other sounds – the snorting of the horses tied below the window, the laughter of guerrillas playing cards in a nearby room, and a constant clatter among the pots and pans within the small pantry. 'I don't know if it was mice or the spirits of those who had been killed,' Marianthe says now, 'but the pots and pans never stopped rattling. That helped us a lot because the guards couldn't hear what we said.'

Marianthe twisted at the ropes on her hands until the skin of her wrists was blistered, but she eventually got one hand free, then the other. She went over to Andreas and untied his hands as well. 'They're going to kill us,' she whispered. 'We've got to get out of here!'

'And go where?' he answered incredulously. 'Through the ceiling? If they catch us, they'll do worse than kill us!'

Marianthe had never liked Andreas, who had been in her grade in the village school. She considered him a braggart and a coward for implicating so many other villagers. His doglike acceptance of his fate irked her. She was convinced that her dream meant she was to escape.

'We're dead anyway!' she hissed. 'Give me your belt.'

Andreas painfully loosened the webbed canvas belt from his bloodied uniform and handed it to her. Marianthe looped the end of it around one of the bars, embedded in the old window frame, and commanded Andreas to help her pull. With a crunch of breaking wood the bar came loose, leaving a gap of more than twelve inches. Andreas and Marianthe stood stunned for a moment, then the boy, despite his wounds, slithered through the hole. He was thin and he pushed through easily, tumbling out of sight. It was a steep drop to the ground, and Andreas landed in a pile of garbage. Marianthe winced at the sound of the fall and the moan that escaped Andreas as he landed, but nothing happened. She pushed a box under the window and tried to climb through, but she was much stouter than Andreas and became wedged in. Breathing hard, she planted her feet on the box beneath her, braced her hands on either side of the window and gave a great push, which dislodged the whole window casement with Marianthe still stuck in it. With a cry she fell into the garbage. Painfully, she stood up and freed herself from the window frame.

Andreas stood dazed as if waiting for directions. Marianthe held her breath, but no one came after them. Suddenly she remembered her shoes, which she had left behind. For reasons Marianthe still can't explain, she went back for them, making Andreas boost her up until she could climb into the empty window hole. After she re-emerged with the shoes under her arm, they crouched in the shadows for a few moments, listening to the voices of the guerrillas inside. Then Marianthe grasped Andreas' hand and they began to run through the shadows across the fields. It was almost dawn. As the sky began to lighten in the east, the two took refuge in a tiny storage shack in a field near the southeast corner of the village, where they burrowed under a pile of newly harvested ears of corn.

The disappearance of the pair was discovered near dawn by the astounded guerrillas, setting off much shouting and running about, all audible to the prisoners below. The head of the security police, Christos Zeltas, frantically ordered every villager able to walk to join in the search for the teenagers. By 6 a.m. the whole village was outside beating the bushes in frightened groups while the guerrillas fired shots into dense trees and haystacks trying to flush out the fugitives. Hearing the commotion all around them, Andreas and Marianthe spent the entire day hiding under the dusty, sweltering pile of corn, nearly delirious from thirst and heat. After darkness fell that night they crept out of their hiding place and parted company, Andreas heading toward his parents' house below the Alonia, and Marianthe going toward the house of her grandmother near the Church of St. Friday.

Marianthe knocked at her grandmother's door, hoping to get a change of clothes, for her red wool skirt would attract the searchers' eyes like a signal flare, but the old woman peered out the door and hissed, 'Run, child, quickly! They're everywhere around looking for you!'

'At least give me some bread!' Marianthe pleaded, but her grandmother snapped, 'I won't give you anything. Get out of here!'

Weeping, Marianthe ran back to the shack full of corn for lack of anywhere else to go, but someone must have seen her, for within minutes after she burrowed back to the very bottom of the pile she heard guerrillas firing their guns in the darkness and shouting, 'Marianthe, come out! We know you're here! If you come out nothing will happen to you, but if we have to find you, you'll wish you'd never been born!'

A pair of guerrillas even opened the door of the tiny shed in which she was hiding and looked in, but as Marianthe braced herself for a bullet, they closed the door and sat down outside, leaning against it. They stayed there for the rest of the night while Marianthe listened to every word they said and prayed to the Virgin that the dust of the corn wouldn't make her sneeze. Curled into a ball deep under the corn, she had no idea when it became light, but after many hours she heard church bells. 'Let's go,' she heard one of the guerrillas say. 'Either she's gotten away or one of the bullets has found her.'

When they were gone, Marianthe crept out of the shed. She hadn't eaten or slept for forty-eight hours. She saw a path and prayed: 'Mother of God, let this lead me to the Great Ridge.'

She walked for six hours without being seen, and passed two rotting corpses among the roots of trees – whether the bodies of guerrillas or soldiers she couldn't tell as she turned away from their eyeless faces grinning at her. When she finally emerged at the Great Ridge and hailed the nationalist soldiers camped on its summit, they refused to believe that the girl wasn't an *andartina*. They made her advance with her arms over her head, still clutching her shoes.

The first three soldiers she reached stared at her in

474

astonishment. 'Why are you carrying your shoes instead of wearing them?' they asked.

Marianthe couldn't find her voice to answer and stood there dumb, tears pouring down her cheeks. She finally managed to say that she was the daughter of Lukas Ziaras and had escaped from the guerrillas' jail in Lia. The soldiers found it incredible that anyone, and a girl to boot, could do such a thing. Marianthe held out her arms, showing the burns and blisters of the ropes that had bound her for so many days that the flesh was gray. 'My hands are my witnesses,' she said.

They finally believed her, and one of the soldiers reached out to take the shoes clutched in her hand. She had been holding them for so long that she couldn't let go and they had to pry her fingers open.

A search party of village women found Andreas Michopoulos crouching in a field near his house, devouring a cucumber that he had stolen, nearly mad from hunger and thirst. Xantho Stamou, the first woman to see him hiding behind a bush, hesitated for a moment under his pleading gaze. But several months before, Xantho had been arrested, beaten and interrogated herself on charges of encouraging young women in her husband's nearby village to escape; and as she stood there, uncertain about what to do, she thought that it could mean her own death if she didn't sound the alarm. She stared back at Andreas' swollen red eyes in his gray face, the sagging jaw, the half-eaten cucumber frozen halfway to his mouth. The ragged boy trembled as if he had a fever and shook his head beseechingly. Xantho raised her hand and pointed. 'It's Andreas Michopoulos!' she screamed to the other women. 'Come quick! I've found him!'

Eleni, now being held in the kitchen, heard the outburst of activity among the guerrillas when the escape was discovered. Like the prisoners in the basement she listened to the shouts and gunfire that rang through the village for the next day and night, torn between hope that the fugitives would get away and terror that the remaining captives would be made to pay for their flight.

On the second morning after their disappearance, Eleni watched from the kitchen window as Andreas Michopoulos was dragged between several guerrillas back through the gates of the security headquarters, his feet trailing in the dust.

The guerrillas made sure that all the prisoners witnessed Andreas' punishment. In the front yard, in clear view of the cellar and kitchen windows, they stripped him naked and tied him to a log, the way a sheep or goat would be trussed for roasting. They suspended the log between two notched supports so that they could turn the boy's body around, as a goat is turned to be basted. Then his former comrades took turns beating Andreas with wooden sticks, turning him this way and that to find spots which were not already livid with bruises. When their arms tired, they left him there in the August sun, and soon his body was black. His tongue was protruding from his mouth, but he was still making sounds. He moaned like an ox, covered with blood which clotted his hair and mixed with the mucus running from his nose and mouth.

Eleni tried not to look or listen to the young guerrilla's punishment, but she was constantly drawn to the window with a perverse fascination. She could feel the impact of the wooden rods on his bare flesh and could see the skin puffing. She prayed that he would die.

She lingered at the window when the sun began to set, shadows mercifully creeping over the shape suspended in her yard. In the distance the mountains shone as a soft yellow cloud spread its wings above the sunset until it blazed up into the color of autumn leaves.

She continued to stand there as the light ebbed and died and a full August moon slowly rose above the cypress trees around the churchyard of St. Demetrios. The azure sky paled and the purple shadows of the trees crept like fingers over the immobile body on the spit while the foothills in the distance were bathed with a cold luminousness. Between the slender forms of the cypresses, an infinity of stars winked at her like jasmine blossoms. A heavy silence hung over the world.

It was while watching Andreas' punishment that Eleni first came to the realization that death could be a solace, to be

476

embraced like a lover. At the beginning, she had passed every hour starved for the love of her children, a love which had unceasingly nourished her soul. For days now she had forced herself to put the thought of the children away from her and to prepare for the journey into the other world. She felt the presence of her long-dead mother-in-law, Fotini, drawing near to her, brushing her eyelids as she slept, and tried to draw comfort from that. But now a new fear seized her, creeping out of the shadows below. Eleni whispered a prayer that her own death would be swift. She had always been so careful to conduct her life with decorum and self-control, and she prayed to die the same way, like a human being, not an animal.

The prisoners in the cellar expected their treatment to deteriorate in retaliation for the escape of Marianthe and Andreas, but to their surprise, in the days that followed it became marginally better than it had been before. The change was infinitesimal, but to captives with nothing to do but analyze every gesture and word of their jailers, it seemed profoundly significant.

After twenty-four hours Andreas was taken down from the spit. A few days later he was returned to the cellar, and the other prisoners saw that he had been dressed in fresh clothing and his wounds had been tended. He slumped in a corner, silent and in a stupor, but he was alive.

The regular beatings of prisoners stopped except for an occasional kick or blow from a guard. Relatives were permitted to bring food to the captives. Although no adults were allowed inside the cellar to see them, some days after the escape Niki Gatzoyiannis, Alexo's young daughter, was allowed to speak to her mother.

Niki had come to the prison many times with food for Alexo and each time the guards had taken the plate away from her, torn any bread into small pieces to make sure nothing was concealed inside, and told her to come back for the empty dish the next morning. But one day in mid-August the guards told Niki she could see her mother. They led Alexo out the cellar door into the yard, where she blinked in the sunlight. Niki ran forward to embrace her, but Alexo made a sign for her to stay some distance away. 'Don't come near me, sweetheart!' she said. 'I'm covered with lice.' Niki stopped, suspecting that her mother didn't want her to see how badly she had been beaten. Under the eyes of the guards they exchanged a few lame words about the house and the flocks, trying to stay calm, then Alexo tearfully thanked her daughter for the food and was led back into the darkness of the cellar. Niki saw no sign of her aunt Eleni.

From her vantage point in the kitchen window, Eleni watched the encounter between Niki and Alexo, and it set her to worrying about what had happened to Glykeria. She began to wonder if the girl had been arrested in the threshing fields, and beaten to elicit information about her mother's complicity in the mass escape.

The food fed to the prisoners began to improve and they were permitted to receive changes of clothing brought by relatives. For several nights after the punishment of Andreas, no one was taken out to the garden to be executed. The captives' hands were inexplicably untied.

On the fourth day after Marianthe's disappearance, Sotiris appeared in the cellar early in the morning and called the names of the prisoners from Lia: Dina Venetis, Alexo Gatzoyiannis, Andreas Michopoulos, Spiro Michopoulos and Vasili Nikou. As they stared at each other in terror, he ordered them brought upstairs. No prisoners had ever been taken up for execution in the morning, they thought. If they were to be interrogated and beaten again, surely they wouldn't all be taken together.

Sotiris and the guards led the five up the stairs into the police office. The brass bed gleamed, the icon hung in the eastern corner and the gramophone was in its accustomed place. Waiting for them in the room were two more fellow villagers: Eleni Gatzoyiannis and Constantina Drouboyiannis. Relieved at seeing that Eleni was all right, Alexo ran to embrace her.

At an order from Sotiris, the guerrillas began to tie the prisoners together in pairs. Eleni and Alexo were bound hand to hand. Spiro Michopoulos was tied to his nephew Andreas, who could barely stand up. Vasili Nikou was tied to Dina

Venetis. The only prisoner left unfettered was Constantina Drouboyiannis.

When all the prisoners were tied together, Sotiris cleared his throat. 'Today your fate will be put in the hands of the people's justice,' he said. 'You will have the benefit of a public trial before all your fellow villagers. Evidence will be given against you, witnesses will be called, and you will be allowed to defend yourselves against the charges. You will see that the Democratic Army does not punish the innocent, only the guilty.'

He signaled to the guards, then said tensely, 'Come along now, the judges have arrived.'

CHAPTER SIXTEEN

By mid-August it was clear even to Communist Party leader Nikos Zachariadis that Grammos was lost. The guerrilla fighters had tried everything: rolling improvised mines down the slopes onto the enemy, leaving booby-trapped mules to wander the hillsides, starting landslides of rocks, but by August 17, the 9,000 surviving guerrillas were trapped on the very top of Grammos with 90,000 government soldiers surrounding them. After eight weeks of savage fighting, with a loss of life on both sides that horrified the foreign correspondents covering the battle, the guerrillas had no choice but to retreat.

At the headquarters of the exhausted survivors, Nikos Zachariadis and Markos Vafiadis were once again at loggerheads, arguing over the method of retreat. General Markos urged that they break through the enemy encirclement to the north and disperse their units to harass government forces throughout the region. Zachariadis was advocating a push eastward to the Vitsi range, where the guerrillas could entrench themselves along the Yugoslav border. If they did so, he knew, and were ultimately defeated, he could always blame the loss of the war on lack of support from Tito.

Zachariadis got his way as usual. Before dawn on August 21, the guerrillas managed to break through the enemy lines and slip off, carrying their wounded, toward Vitsi.

Zachariadis refused to admit that the loss of Grammos was the result of his misguided strategy. Instead, he laid the blame on the performance of Markos' officers, who, he said, had been derelict in their duty. Among the most tempting scapegoats for Zachariadis to name was Colonel Yiorgios Yannoulis, a tall, ascetic-looking young lawyer who had fought bravely throughout the German occupation, with a skill that made him rise swiftly in the Communist ranks. When the attack on Grammos was begun, he led his men to infiltrate the enemy lines with exceptional mobility and daring, and cut the government troops' supply and communication arteries. Later Yannoulis was given the heights of Batras to defend on the western slope of Grammos and was ordered to hold it to the death. He complied until his brigade had been whittled down to only fifty survivors, then he led them in an expert withdrawal.

But Zachariadis badly needed villains on whom to blame the Grammos defeat, and Yannoulis served his purpose well. He was closely associated with Markos, having worked with him from the outbreak of the civil war, organizing units in Macedonia. If the young colonel was labeled a traitor, it would impugn Markos and his supporters as well.

Yannoulis was arrested, charged with treason and even accused of harboring rightist sympathies because he had briefly joined a resistance movement at the beginning of the occupation that was not Communist-controlled. After a parody of a trial, the officer's execution was personally ordered by Lieutenant General Yiorgos Goussias, a former cobbler and a lackey of Zachariadis.

'Confirmation of the sentence is on the way from headquarters,' Goussias announced shortly after the trial. 'No point in waiting; shoot him now.'

When the attack on . . . . , he led his men to
infiltrate the enemy lines with exceptional mobility and

JUDGEMENT

AS THE SEVEN defendants from the village of Lia were led,
tied together in pairs, down the path from the Perivoli, across
the ravine and into the town square, they were wrapped in
their own thoughts. At Sotiris' statement that they were going
to have a trial, hope, mankind's last solace in misfortune, had
been rekindled in each prisoner.

Dina Venetis walked toward the square, her dark, heavy-
lashed eyes lowered, tied hand to hand with Vasili Nikou. She
searched her mind for some promising sign, some indication
that the guerrillas did not intend to kill her. The fact that her
husband was a lieutenant fighting on the nationalist side
would certainly be held against her, she knew, but her main
accuser, Andreas Michopoulos, had completely discredited
himself by trying to escape, so how could they condemn her
on his testimony?

Vasili Nikou stumbled along at Dina's side. Nikou was the
father of four grown daughters – three of them would be
watching the trial. Aged by tragedy beyond his fifty-seven
years, Vasili Nikou had seen more of war and killing than any
of the guerrillas who now held him prisoner. He had fought
in the Greek army for nine years, beginning with the Balkan
wars in 1912 and ending with the Greek campaign in Asia
Minor in 1921. After that he returned to his family in Lia and
traveled from village to village eight months of the year – from
March to October – working as a cooper.

Nikou had just returned from his annual rounds in the fall
of 1947 when he heard that the guerrillas were approaching
Lia. He had been a sympathizer of the EDES forces of

482

Napoleon Zervas during the German occupation and he knew that the guerrillas would hold his rightist leanings against him. He fled south to Kostana, but when he woke up the next morning he discovered that the guerrillas had entered the town; he was trapped. He told the guerrillas he had come to join them and asked to be taken to Spiro Skevis, whose eldest brother, Yiorgos, was married to Nikou's sister Calliope. Skevis gave him a pass to return to Lia, where Nikou, one of the few men left in the village, was put on the committee which administered civilian work details.

As he walked now down the path toward the village square, Vasili Nikou consoled himself with the thought that he had consistently claimed loyalty to the cause since the guerrillas arrived. If worst came to worst and he was convicted, he did not believe that Spiro Skevis would let his own sister-in-law's brother be shot.

Spiro Michopoulos, the sickly village president, and his nephew Andreas made an odd, silent couple as they walked slowly down the path, the boy staggering because of his recent torture, the older man, a tall, gangly figure, all elbows and knees. Spiro wondered if his nephew had given false testimony against him, as he had incriminated so many others. Spiro was determined to cheat death again, as he had conquered the tuberculosis that left him wasted and a village pariah. Perhaps it had been a mistake to try to distribute work assignments fairly, arousing the hostility of the fanatic Communists in the village, he reflected. But after all, hadn't he stayed behind to welcome the guerrillas when all the other men had left, and expertly administered the village for them?

Andreas could hardly keep up with his uncle. He ached to the very marrow of his bones from the beatings he had received after his escape and his broken skin burned under the sun as if he had a fever. Nevertheless, he too was nursing hope. He knew the escape attempt would weigh the scales against him, but he had willingly enlisted in the guerrillas' ranks and then, when they brought him in for interrogation, he had given them all the information they asked for and more. He ran his free hand through his dark, matted hair and thought that it would reflect badly on the guerrillas if they killed one of their own, and an eighteen-year-old boy at that.

Of the seven defendants wending their way toward the village square, the most optimistic was Constantina Drouboyiannis, the round-faced, slow-witted woman who had denounced Eleni in Katis' office. Constantina was delighted to see she was the only prisoner who had not been tied for the walk. Her hands swung free as she reflected that of all the defendants, they had the least evidence against her. Even though her daughters had been taken to freedom by Lukas Ziaras, she had not come along on either of the earlier tries, and no one could prove that she had told her sister-in-law to flee with the girls. Besides, she had been more than cooperative with her captors, telling them everything they wanted to hear.

Eleni and Alexo were bound hand to hand – the first time the two sisters-in-law had seen each other since they were rearrested ten days before. Although they didn't speak, Eleni drew solace from the nearness of Alexo, who had always her comforter in times of crisis.

Eleni concentrated all her energy on having to meet the eyes of the curious with composure. She knew that she was not going to be acquitted – she had already admitted going on the early escape attempts and helping to organize the plot. She also knew that she was the one woman in the village the guerrillas most resented because of her position and her American husband. But she could not stop the tiny voice of hope inside her which repeated, 'I never tried to convince anyone else to escape or spoke against the guerrillas. Perhaps I'll receive a prison sentence instead. As long as I'm alive, there's a chance I may see my children again.'

It was ten o'clock on the morning of Thursday, August 19, a brilliant late-summer day, when the villagers were summoned to the town square by the church bells and bull horns of the guerrillas. No one lagged, because they anticipated the drama they were about to witness: the first public trial of civilians from their own village.

The stage was the area under the huge plane tree at the southeast corner of the square; a small table waited with three chairs in a row behind it. The defendants were told to sit on a platform created by the gnarled roots of the huge tree, while the three judges took their places in the chairs facing the audience. As they filed past, the three magistrates, all in civilian clothes, impressed the watching crowd by their physical stature alone. They were all considerably above average height, and the giant who brought up the rear, a man named Grigori Pappas, but called by the villagers 'the tall one,' towered half a head above the other two.

The crowd filled the square and stretched up the slopes above it. Children scrambled into the branches of nearby trees to get a better view. The villagers seated themselves on the ground under the sunlight, which flowed like molten lava. The whitewashed walls of the church threw off a dazzling glare, and black-and-yellow hornets attacked the heavy grapes hanging on nearby trellises.

The watching peasants had no idea how the ritual of justice was carried out, but they understood that the three imposing men seated solemnly at the table held the power of life and death over the seven prisoners, and they leaned forward, the better to hear what was to be said.

The silence deepened as a tall, balding, gray-haired man of middle age with a chiseled oval face, large nose, jutting chin, and intense eyes, stood up. He wore a dark-blue suit, which pronounced him a man of education and urbanity, and his long, delicate fingers rested lightly on the table before him. The villagers stirred expectantly. They recognized this man with the mesmerizing eyes as the person they called Katis ('the Judge') and they sensed that he was in charge of this drama, as he had been at the trial of the soldier captured during the battle of Pergamos.

Katis' face showed no strain nor did his sonorous voice betray a quaver, but his nerves were coiled. He was the author, director and stage manager of what was to take place, and he felt the combination of exaltation and fear that fills every performer on opening night. As the man personally appointed by Koliyiannis to handle this case, he had a difficult task. It was essential to repair the loyalty of the civilians, which had eroded during the past months. The villagers had at first been overwhelmingly behind the Democratic Army, but they were now tired of work details and of having their food and possessions confiscated. They had grown weary of battles and artillery fire and the increasing brutality of the beleaguered guerrillas. They objected to giving up their daughters to be *andartinas* and almost unanimously balked at abandoning their children to the *pedomasoma*. Twenty of the leading citizens had boldly fled, damaging the authority of the guerrillas even more.

Katis knew that it was his duty in the orchestration of this trial to intimidate the watching Liotes to the point where no more of them would consider such treachery. Moreover, by marshaling evidence against the defendants, he had to make the villagers despise the accused and rally in support of the guerrillas.

Katis was acutely aware of the eyes of one of the judges sitting behind him, a tall, handsome, mournful-looking man of forty named Yiorgos Anagnostakis. Katis had been appointed president of the court for this particular trial by Kostas Koliyiannis, the political commissar of all Epiros, but Anagnostakis, who was also serving as a judge, was Katis' superior officer, the chief of the judicial branch of the Epiros Command. Katis resented Anagnostakis. Not only was Anagnostakis three years younger and his superior, with the rank of colonel in the DAG, but he had no judicial experience in civilian life, while Katis had been a justice of the peace in the town of Konitsa. He also knew that Anagnostakis enjoyed the respect and friendship of the third judge, Grigori Pappas, both men coming from the same area in southern Epiros, and Katis was determined to impress his colleagues with the amount of evidence he had amassed and the thoroughness of his prosecution.

Anagnostakis had entered the Communist-led resistance early, after joining the party in law school, and had swiftly become the chief of the judicial branch of ELAS during the occupation with a reputation as an efficient judge who meted out swift justice to the opponents of ELAS in many important trials. Katis came into the DAG after the resistance and he knew he didn't have the credentials that the younger man did. Katis' most important case had been the trial of four nationalist officers captured during the battle of Pergamos. Before that trial Anagnostakis suggested freeing one of the officers, a doctor, noting that the guerrillas had greater need of his medical skills than of another execution. But Katis stood firm: no matter how desperately doctors were needed to treat wounded guerrillas, the man had served as an officer with the enemy and must die. In the end Koliyiannis backed him up, Katis was vindicated and the doctor was killed.

Perhaps Anagnostakis was growing soft, Katis reflected. He was proud that Koliyiannis had taken his side against his chief of the judicial branch, and now had appointed him to run this trial in Lia. He was determined to twist the knife blade in Anagnostakis' pride by demonstrating that he was just as good a lawyer as his superior, and he was aware that Koliyiannis would have several informers on hand to report back to the committee on the handling of the trial.

He paused to choose his opening words. It was essential that the events about to take place be presented to the ignorant peasants before him in just the right way; they had to leave the trial convinced that the People's Army was just, and at the same time aware that even thinking about escaping the village would bring deadly consequences.

Katis spoke to the assemblage in simple phrases. He did not need to shout through a bull horn; his voice carried to the farthest edges of the silent crowd. The villagers watched him with expressions of fear and awe, and the prisoners leaned forward in the intensity of their listening.

Katis said that the people of Lia were about to witness a trial of seven defendants from their own village. He announced with a trace of pride that guerrilla intelligence had uncovered the existence of an organization among fascist sympathizers within the village that had been transmitting vital information to the enemy about the guerrillas' defenses. Furthermore, the organization provided the means for fascist supporters to escape to the enemy. A group of twenty traitors had already left, and more were organizing themselves to follow. The defendants would be tried before the eyes of their neighbors, he said, because the guerrillas knew that every true patriot in the village abhorred this treachery that endangered

487

the brave men who were risking their lives to liberate Greece. This was clear, he added, raising one eyebrow significantly, 'because all the evidence about the crimes of these defendants has come from their fellow villagers who are loyal to the revolution.' There was an uneasy stir among the audience and everyone avoided his neighbor's eyes.

The prisoners would first stand to hear the charges read against them, Katis went on, then witnesses would be called to confirm those charges. Turning to face the defendants, he thundered, 'We are not here today to condemn you. It is your fellow villagers who are your accusers. When their testimony is heard, we will render our judgment based on their evidence.'

'Vasili Nikou,' Katis began, and the gray-haired cooper slowly stood up, hindered by the fact that his arm was still tied to the wrist of Dina Venetis. 'This man is a long-time fascist,' said Katis, each word sounding like a drop of rain falling on still water. 'He stayed behind in the village in order to send information to the enemy and to promote hostility against the cause among his neighbors. He was a leading organizer of the escape of the twenty traitors and was planning more escapes until the day he was arrested.

'Spiro Michopoulos,' he shouted next, and the fidgeting, scarecrow figure unfolded itself like a jackknife. 'This man pretended to be a supporter of our struggle. He was even appointed president of the village,' Katis intoned. 'But he was in fact a fifth columnist in our midst who distributed work assignments unfairly to protect the supporters of the fascists and to promote hostility toward us from our loyal followers. While our fighters suffered and his neighbors went hungry, Spiro Michopoulos hoarded food and supplies for himself.' The expression of wronged innocence on Michopoulos' gaunt face deepened and he began to deny the charges, but Katis cut him short and motioned him to sit down.

'Andreas Michopoulos,' he called out. The young guerrilla tried to stand up but could not succeed until his uncle pulled him up by the rope tied to both their wrists. 'This traitor joined the Democratic Army so that he could betray us by giving information to those who wanted to escape,' Katis

488

said. 'Without his aid, they would not have succeeded in fleeing and taking information about our defenses and movements to the fascists.

'Constantina Drouboyiannis.' The round-faced little woman with small brown eyes and tomato-red cheeks stood up, trying to arrange her expression into something between penitence and obedience. 'This woman is charged with sending her two daughters to escape from the village in the company of the other fascists while she was working in the threshing fields,' Katis said, glancing at some notes on the table.

'Dina Venetis,' he continued, and Dina stood up, her hands still tied to Vasili Nikou. 'This woman, whose husband is an officer in the monarcho-fascist army, is charged with planning to escape from the village.

'Alexo Gatzoyiannis,' he shouted in a louder voice. Eleni had to nudge her sister-in-law to make her stand. 'This woman not only arranged for her eldest daughter to escape with the traitors, but she has also betrayed our cause by providing secrets to her husband who visited her clandestinely on at least three occasions to collect information about the movements and activities of the People's Army.' Alexo gave him a look of graphic contempt but said nothing.

Katis paused and surveyed the attentive faces before him. 'Eleni Gatzoyiannis,' he announced in a softer voice, so that his listeners leaned forward. Eleni stood up and stared at the back of his balding head as he turned to the audience. 'This woman is the daughter of a known fascist and the wife of an American capitalist,' he said. 'Her husband's country sends the bombs and planes to kill our men. She is charged with planning the escape from the village of four of her children as well as her mother and sister, her niece, and thirteen other fascist sympathizers who fled to take our secrets to the enemy.'

Eleni stood impassive as a statue until he motioned for her to sit down. 'We will call fifteen witnesses against the accused,' Katis announced in a voice that sent an apprehensive shiver through the crowd. 'These are your own neighbors, who will reveal how the defendants betrayed the revolution. We will also read corroborating testimony from

489

other villagers about the treasonous activities of the accused. The defendants will then be allowed to speak on their own behalf, and any of you here who have information to add will be permitted to address the court.'

He paused and then said louder, 'The justice of the Democratic Army, even in the midst of battle and revolution, is even-handed! It will separate the guilty from the innocent as clearly as oil from vinegar.'

Katis involuntarily glanced back at the defendants, then sideways at his fellow judges, pleased with the way he'd expressed himself. He turned back to the audience. 'We will now call the witnesses. Each person summoned will step forward and sit over there, to the right of the prisoners, until his turn comes to speak.'

As Katis began to call witnesses from a list in his hand, the crowd was distracted by a noise like thunder and a puff of smoke from the crest of the Great Ridge in the distance. Seeing the large crowd gathered in the square, the Greek National Army had chosen that moment to bomb the village. The first mortar shell raised a crater halfway up the peak of the Prophet Elias and the second crashed down to the east of the square, near the Church of St. Friday. As heads swiveled and mothers reached for their children, the third mortar landed only a hundred yards east of the square. With one movement the throng rose to its feet and began to shout. Katis stood stunned. The guerrillas in the crowd raised their rifles and everyone looked at them nervously, torn between their desire to flee and their fear of the guns. Katis began to perspire. Suddenly a mortar shell landed just on the edge of the square, in the space between the Church of the Holy Trinity and the great plane tree. The impact of the explosion sent everyone – judges, witnesses, prisoners and villagers – scrambling for safety, stripped of all concerns except the primal instinct of survival. Leaves, branches, stones, dirt and shrapnel sprayed everyone within yards of the tree; the prisoners were battered with a hail of branches. Still tied in pairs, they crowded and pushed, screaming, as was everyone else, to the nearest shelter.

When the shelling stopped there was silence, broken only

490

by the sound of falling roof tiles and tree branches. As soon as the cloud of dust began to disperse, Katis stepped out from where he had huddled in a doorway and called the guerrillas together. 'The trial is being suspended for this morning!' he shouted in a tight voice. 'This spot is too exposed! We will reconvene this afternoon at five-thirty in the ravine below the Spring of Siouli. Everyone in the village must be present.'

Lowering his voice, Katis said to the guerrillas around him, 'Gather the prisoners and take them back to police head-quarters.'

After a few minutes as the square rapidly emptied, panic broke out among the guards. 'The prisoner Constantina Drouboyiannis has disappeared!' someone shouted. Katis blanched. She was the only one who had not been tied, and now he realized that had been a mistake.

They found Constantina in a corner of the Kokkinos cellar, crouched behind a sack of flour. 'I wasn't trying to get away!' she wailed, covering her head with her hands against the anticipated blows. 'I was just trying to save myself from the mortars like everybody else!' Weak with relief, Katis ordered her tied up at once for the remainder of the trial.

At the top of the Perivoli, just below the flat spot called the Vrisi where the villagers danced on the feast day of the Prophet Elias, the cliff fell straight down into a green, leafy ravine. On the side of the ravine, centuries of dripping water had carved a sort of grotto, a green, ferny alcove as big as a large room. It was here that the judges' table and chairs were set up, so that even if a mortar shell fell directly on them, they would be protected by the roof of stone. The streambed in front of the grotto was damp and swampy most of the year, but by August it had dried up, and the prisoners were seated on the flat polished stones directly before the judges. Rising from the streambed, the earth sloped gently upward into a concave bowl, and the villagers were told to arrange them-selves on this grassy incline with the oldest men, the patriarchs of the village, in the front row.

The large ravine thus formed a perfect semicircular amphi-theater, with the grotto as a natural stage. A magical place, it is usually carpeted by ferns uncurling delicate tendrils, dappled by ever-changing patterns of sun and shade, butterflies fragile as a thought fluttering through the cathedral-like hush of the hollow. But on that day, the butterflies were gone, and the ravine was filled with the uneasy murmur of several hundred voices, for the villagers on the ascending slopes knew they were more exposed to the danger of mortar shells than the guerrillas.

Katis finished calling the names of the fifteen villagers to be questioned as witnesses. He made them sit facing the judges and the prisoners, off to one side on the floor of the natural bowl. Among the group called forward were Stavroula Yakou, the blond favorite of the guerrillas; Alexandra Drouboyiannis, the swarthy, sharp-tongued sister-in-law of Constantina, who had gone on the second escape attempt; and her eldest daughter, Milia, who was wearing her uniform and carrying her rifle.

When the witnesses were assembled, Katis raised a hand for silence and began to read off the testimony he had collected against the first defendant, Vasili Nikou. Katis read the statements of twenty-two villagers to substantiate details of the old cooper's treachery and disloyalty to the revolutionary struggle, to show that he was a fascist, organizing escapes from the village, sending information to the enemy. As Katis read their names, villagers who had whispered statements to the security police under the impression that they were speaking in confidence, paled and ducked their heads, trying to disappear among the crowd. Despite the dank coolness of the glen, cloying with the odor of laurel berries, many of the listeners began to perspire. Among those named as giving evidence against Nikou were Stavroula Yakou and Marianthe Ziaras, whose statements had been taken before the latter's escape.

The two eldest daughters of Vasili Nikou sat near the top of the ravine, and they remember the testimony well. The first and most damaging witness called against their father was Foto Bollis, a hook-nosed little tinker who lived in a house near the Gatzoyiannis property with his wife and five children.

492

Foto Bollis had been caught out of the village in the midst of his tinker's rounds when the guerrillas occupied Lia in November. But he was a fervent Communist, and on May 30, 1948, he had managed, along with Christos Skevis, a cousin of Spiro Skevis, to sneak through the government lines from Filiates back into the village.

'What do you know of the defendant, Vasili Nikou?' Katis demanded, like a prompter giving an actor his cues. Bollis drew himself up to his full height. Now he had a chance to make his fellow villagers pay for all the years they had ignored him.

'He's black, black as midnight, poisoned with fascism to his fingernails!' he shouted. He plunged on, telling that when he had been stuck in Filiates behind the government lines, he often saw the fascists receiving intelligence reports sent from Vasili Nikou, detailing guerrilla activities in the Mourgana villages.

The second witness called was Stavroula Yakou, who defiantly returned the cold stares of the village women. As she stood proudly before the judges, the play of sunlight and shadow in the ravine emphasized the smoothness of her golden skin and the mane of honey-colored hair.

'He's my mother-in-law's brother, but the truth can't be hidden,' she announced, casting a look of triumph toward her hated mother-in-law. Eleni saw Stavroula's mother, her old friend Anastasia, turn her face away. 'When Vasili Nikou was assigning work details, he sent weak old women to carry the wounded,' Stavroula continued, unabashed, 'so that the wounded fighters would be dropped or die before they got medical help. And once, when his own mule was wanted for a work detail, Nikou put a nail in its hoof so that it couldn't walk.'

The next witness called against Nikou was one of his fellow prisoners, Constantina Drouboyiannis, who now had her hands prominently bound together to foil another disappearance like the one that morning. Katis read a statement Constantina had made about an incident that occurred when she once called Vasili Nikou to fix a lock on a door of her house. As he worked, according to Constantina, he told her,

'You're a lucky woman! You've managed to send your daughters away and saved them. But what about my daughters? What am I going to do?'

'Did the defendant Nikou say this to you?' Katis prompted. The woman glanced at him nervously, then lowered her eyes, as if examining the ropes that bound her hands, and nodded faintly.

Suddenly Anagnostakis stood up, a movement that startled Katis. He knew that all the judges had the right to question the witnesses, but he had orchestrated this trial so carefully in his mind that he hadn't expected any of them to intervene. Anagnostakis was the last person he wanted tampering with his carefully prepared witnesses.

'Were any other people in the room when the defendant said this to you?' Anagnostakis asked in a soft voice.

Constantina looked at him in confusion, wondering if she had somehow missed her cue. 'No,' she replied. 'He wouldn't have said it if there was anyone around,' she added, as if explaining to a child.

'So he told you this in confidence because he trusted you?' Anagnostakis asked.

Constantina's already ruddy cheeks took on a deeper hue. She nodded.

'Then why are you betraying his trust now?' he persisted.

Constantina looked from one judge to another, completely at sea. She turned from Katis' frowning face back to the younger man, who seemed kindly. 'Because I'm afraid!' she blurted out. A murmur ruffled the silence of the crowd.

This was the last thing Katis wanted to hear because it gave the transfixed audience the clear impression that the witnesses were being terrorized into making their statements. He made an impatient gesture at the bewildered Constantina. 'But tell the truth, woman, did Vasili Nikou in fact make this statement to you or not? Is your testimony a lie?'

She studied him for a minute, then answered, in a nearly inaudible voice. 'He said it.'

As Katis surveyed the audience, with a sideways glance at Anagnostakis, trying to gauge how much damage Constantina Drouboyiannis' testimony had done, Eleni remembered the

494

woman's tearful face on the day she was brought into Katis' office to confront her. Clearly she was trying to save herself by testifying against the others.

In an effort to remedy the impression Constantina was making, Katis told her sharply to sit down. He took a paper from the table in front of him. 'As is known to the court,' he said, 'there was one other defendant who would have been on trial here, but due to the negligence of the security police, she has fled the village. But before she did, she made a long statement and I will now read from it the part regarding Vasili Nikou. The prisoner Marianthe Ziaras was asked, "Did Vasili Nikou know about the escape of the twenty before it happened?" and she replied, "Yes, he frequently talked with my father about taking their families out."'

Katis motioned for Vasili Nikou to stand up. He snapped at him, 'Isn't it true that you want to leave here and betray us, that you've made plans to flee several times?'

Vasili Nikou regarded him levelly and replied, 'No, Comrade Katis, it is not. My relative, Spiro Skevis, is one of your glorious commanders. Why should I want to betray the cause we're all fighting for? I was on my way to Filiates when I heard that you had arrived and I turned around and came back. And last March, when the enemy was at the edge of this village, Spiro Michopoulos told me, "Let's leave now. We'll never get a better chance." But I didn't go.'

All eyes suddenly swiveled to the thin, pale former village president who was nervously using his free hand to pick his teeth with a tiny twig he had found. He froze as Katis shouted at him, 'Is all this true, Michopoulos? Did you say that to him?'

Michopoulos made a pathetic effort to arrange his face into a crafty smile. 'Yes, I did,' he replied. 'But only to test him! He never supported our side during the occupation and I couldn't believe that he was really with us now, so I said it in order to make him reveal himself. If he had agreed with my suggestion, I would have brought him to you immediately.'

The two prisoners locked eyes and glared at each other with naked hatred. Each was now trying to save himself by sacrificing the other, but Michopoulos' ploy didn't work.

495

'Why didn't you tell us your doubts, Comrade?' Katis shouted. 'Why didn't you tell us what you suspected?'

Spiro Michopoulos' face collapsed and he whispered, 'I thought it best to test him first.'

'You didn't tell us because the fact is that you wanted to leave yourself!' Katis exploded.

Michopoulos began protesting so frantically that he wrenched Andreas' wrist with his convulsive movements.

'I've been with you from the start!' he cried. 'I supported ELAS when Vasili Nikou was with EDES! I supported the Democratic Army and have worked tirelessly for you since the day you arrived. May I swim in God's blood if I ever betrayed our cause!'

Katis cut him off. 'Sit down, Michopoulos,' he said. 'We'll soon find out how much support you have given the cause.'

He turned to the other judges. 'We have a number of witnesses who will show that the statements of loyalty made by Spiro Michopoulos are all lies.'

He called forward Chrisoula Kouka, an old crone all in black, whose house and property bordered that of Spiro Michopoulos. Chrisoula, sixty-five, was notoriously crochety, given to arguments with other villagers over boundary lines and water rights. As she stood trembling, suddenly over-whelmed by finding the entire village hanging on her words, Katis read out a statement made by Chrisoula, charging that Spiro Michopoulos was an enemy of the cause, who favored the fascist sympathizers when passing out work details in order to curry favor with the enemy in case the nationalist forces ever retook the village. Her most damaging evidence against her neighbor was that she had seen him burying a large stock of foodstuffs from his now closed general store in his basement – boxes of soap, cans of oil, which should have been shared with the fighters of the Democratic Army. Katis announced triumphantly that the goods had indeed been found under Michopoulos' cellar floor: 'A king's ransom of provisions, while our fighters and loyal supporters were suffering from hunger and cold.'

After reading every few lines, Katis would stop and ask, 'Isn't this true, Comrade Kouka?' but the crone, terrified at

496

hearing her words read in public, began to equivocate. 'That's the way it seemed to me,' she muttered. 'That's what I heard. Yes, you're probably right.'

Katis flushed with anger at her temporizing. Finally he threw down the paper and thrust his hand at her, twisting it like the movement of a snake. 'Eh, Comrade Kouka!' he spat. 'Not like the eel that slithers away from the knife! Tell it now as you told it to us before.'

The old woman stared at his hand as if it were a live thing, then began to nod her head. 'Yes, what you have read is true,' she said, and turned to look at the neighbor whom she had finally humbled. Spiro Michopoulos could no longer contain himself. He could see that the eccentric old woman was venting all her rancor against him and was killing him in the process. He clambered to his feet, elbows and knees jabbing every which way. 'Not only have I supported the cause since the occupation, I was severely beaten by the fascist police for it!' he cried.

The old woman uttered an explosive laugh, and forgetting her timidity before the crowd, she shook a knobby finger at him. 'They beat you because you stole one of their sheep!' she crowed.

Feeling better, Katis read testimony from nearly two dozen villagers against the unhappy former president: that he had unfairly chosen loyal supporters of the guerrillas for work duties, that he had favored the fascist sympathizers, that he had hinted to many individuals that they would be wise to escape the village. As each statement was read Michopoulos' face grew paler; his long body seemed to fold in on itself, shrinking before the spectacle of death.

The last witness called by Katis against Spiro was Dina Venetis. She stood up, her oval face so pale that the high cheekbones seemed about to break through the skin. Years later Dina Venetis insisted she couldn't remember anything about what she said at the trial; she was too frightened. But other villagers recall her testimony well.

'Did you pay a visit to the village president, Spiro Michopoulos, a few days after the twenty left?' Katis asked, leading her carefully.

'Yes,' Dina replied in a nearly inaudible voice. 'I went to ask him for some corn from the village stores because I had nothing to feed my three small children.'

'And what did he reply?' Katis encouraged her.

No one could hear her answer. 'Speak up!' Katis ordered.

Dina raised her voice. 'He said to me, "I have no corn left. You should have gone with the others."'

'That will be all,' Katis told her, and she sat down in relief.

When all the testimony against Spiro Michopoulos had been read, the ravine was filled with shadows and the setting sun was sending up fingers of fire on the crest of the hills to the west. Katis announced that the trial would be halted to resume the following morning in the same spot.

The first defendant called forward to be charged the next day was Andreas Michopoulos. The boy stood shakily, still weak from the torture after his attempted escape, as Katis addressed the crowd.

'Two months ago, twenty civilians fled this village. For so many to escape without being observed, and to reach the fascist forces on the Great Ridge, it was necessary for them to know where our patrols were moving and where land mines were planted. All that information was given to them by Andreas Michopoulos, a traitor to the uniform we gave him when we came to this village.

'If there remained any doubt about his complicity in the escape,' Katis went on, 'it was erased by the attempt he made to flee the justice of the people. Realizing his guilt, Andreas Michopoulos is now prepared to admit to his crimes.'

Katis turned toward Andreas, who licked his lips nervously. 'Did the traitor Lukas Ziaras come to you as you stood look-out at the Church of the Virgin and on several occasions before the escape ask you about the movements of the patrols and the location of the minefields?'

'He did,' Andreas answered.

'And what did you tell him?'

'We were just chatting, sir,' Andreas began haltingly. 'I thought he was with us. I talked about patrol duty and where

498

the patrols usually went. I had no idea that he wanted to leave.'

'If you had known he was going to flee, would you have informed us?' asked Katis, warming to his task.

'Yes, Comrade, of course!'

'Did Dina Venetis ever tell you that she intended to leave the village?' Katis continued.

The boy's face fell, realizing where he was leading. 'Yes,' he muttered.

'What did she say, exactly?'

'She came to me while I was on lookout duty and asked me which was the safest path to take to leave the village.'

'And did you go immediately to your officers to report this conversation?'

Andreas paused, trying to collect his thoughts. 'No, not right away,' he said unhappily. 'But later, when you asked me, I told you.'

Katis smiled. 'Yes, later, after you told others in the village about the conversation and we learned it from them,' he exclaimed. 'You shame the uniform you wear!'

He turned to the prisoners. 'Dina Venetis will stand up.'

Dina stood, a tiny figure facing the might of the court.

'Is it true that you came to Andreas Michopoulos and asked him how to escape from the village?' Katis demanded.

Dina's black eyes flashed. 'It's a complete lie!' she retorted, turning to glare at Andreas. 'I live at the bottom of the village and know the paths out of it better than anyone! I would never ask this man for advice!'

'Then you deny that you wanted to escape, to join your husband who is fighting with the monarcho-fascist forces?'

'I don't deny that I would have liked to leave, to take my children and join my husband,' Dina replied, meeting Katis' eyes. 'But I do deny planning to escape. It would have been impossible for me to leave safely with three babies. Andreas Michopoulos is a liar, and he has shown how much you can trust his word by trying to flee.'

Addressing the judges, Katis said a bit proudly that Andreas had named twenty-three more Liotes whom he suspected of planning to leave. This confirmed the suspicions of the security police that there was a village-wide conspiracy.

The next witness to be called was Constantina Drouboyiannis, accused of sending her two teenaged daughters on the escape with her sister-in-law. She rose, still trembling from the ordeal of testifying against Vasili Nikou, afraid that she would anger Katis even more.

'Did you know that your daughters were going to leave?' he asked.

'No, I didn't,' she replied miserably. 'I was threshing grain for the Democratic Army when they left.' She went on to say that her sister-in-law had taken the girls without her permission and against her will. Katis did not probe, fearing that the dull-witted woman would make another gaffe in front of Anagnostakis. He moved quickly on to the charges against Alexo Gatzoyiannis, who, he said, had sent her eldest daughter on the escape.

Alexo rose and faced him, full of fire. 'My daughter Arete has been a married woman for fifteen years and was not under my control,' she said. 'The daughter who lives with me is still here. That should be ample proof that I had no knowledge of what the others were planning. If I knew, wouldn't I have sent my youngest girl along?'

'And if you had no idea that Arete was leaving, why did you allow her to bury five okas of solder in the field behind your house and then show us where it was hidden?' Katis rejoined.

'That solder has been there for months, ever since Arete's husband left, long before the guerrillas came to this village,' Alexo replied.

'You answer glibly to our accusations,' Katis said, 'but we have proof that you are guilty of something much more damaging to the Democratic Army. Your husband has repeatedly sneaked through our lines to visit you and collect information about our defenses. But you are such a loyal and secretive wife that you won't admit it.'

Alexo lost her temper entirely and began to shout. 'Even during peacetime my worthless husband was never around the house. Would he come now? How could he do it without someone seeing him?'

'But he *was* seen,' Katis said triumphantly. He called forward Olga Noussi, a thirty-year-old woman who was thin and yellow from the cancer that was spreading through her body and would kill her a few years later. She, too, had been accused of passing on guerrilla secrets and had been imprisoned for many days in the security-police station while her three children, all under seven years old, begged for food from their neighbors and dug potatoes out of the ground to eat. After she was released, Olga Noussi told several other women that the guerrillas had hung her upside down by the ankles and beaten her with rods. Now, as Katis put questions to her, she hesitantly testified that her neighbor, Alexo, had received a visit from her husband.

'Is it true that Foto Gatzoyiannis paid secret visits to his wife at night?' Katis asked.

'I heard Foto Gatzoyiannis come to meet his wife in the field below their house,' Olga Noussi replied. 'I saw her standing by the edge of the cornfield and I saw the cornstalks in front of her moving. Then I saw her talking to him.'

Anagnostakis was suddenly on his feet again. Katis felt a stab of apprehension. 'Did you see his face?' Anagnostakis asked the sallow-faced woman. 'Did you actually see Foto Gatzoyiannis speaking to his wife?'

There was a long pause as she glanced at Katis. Then she looked down, twisting the fabric of her apron, and muttered, 'I didn't see his face, but I know it was her husband hiding in the corn. Who else could it be?'

Katis quickly dismissed Olga Noussi, covertly watching Anagnostakis' expression. He called for Foto Bollis to come forward.

'When you were on the other side, on the Great Ridge, before you were able to return to this village, whom did you see helping the monarcho-fascists?' Katis demanded.

'Foto Gatzoyiannis,' Bollis replied in a ringing voice.

'How was he helping them?'

'He was telling the soldiers about the lay of the land, the footpaths, the guerrilla fortifications in and around the village.'

'And how would Foto Gatzoyiannis possess such knowledge?'

'He came to his home secretly.'

'How do you know that?' Katis persisted.

Foto Bollis turned to grin at Alexo. 'He said so, boasted about it to everyone.'

Katis faced her. 'Having heard this testimony, do you still deny that your husband visited you?'

Alexo raised her chin. 'I told you; I haven't seen that soul of a devil since last November. If he had come, why would I keep it a secret? To tell in the next world? I know what's in store for me!'

Somewhat discomfited by her defiance, Katis ordered her to sit down.

The testimony of Alexo Gatzoyiannis ended the second day of the trial. There remained only one more defendant to examine – Eleni Gatzoyiannis – and for the testimony against her, Katis wanted to interrogate a special witness who was not yet in the village.

While Eleni was standing trial in Lia, her daughter Glykeria was working with the other women sent to the harvest, threshing grain and building pillboxes near the village of Vatsounia. It was now sixty days since she had been separated from her mother.

A few days after she arrived at Vatsounia, Glykeria was joined by Rano Athanassiou, who had also been sent from Granitsopoula. Rano told her that Eleni had been taken from the fields with some other women back to Lia, but Glykeria did not realize she was under arrest. She simply felt relief that her mother had been released from the heavy labor of threshing.

In the two months that ensued, Glykeria became more and more worried about what had happened to her family. She knew nothing about the success of the escape or her mother's imprisonment. She was wrapped up in her own problems; still suffering from the heat, struggling to keep up with the older women in the fields. Sometimes the girls from Lia taunted and hit her for her slowness. 'Why did your mother send you, when you can't do any work?' they complained. 'She should have sent your sisters instead!'

It was natural that Glykeria should turn for help to Rano Athanassiou, her sister Olga's best friend, just as Kanta had taken comfort in her strength when they were both conscripted as *andartinas*. Rano encouraged Glykeria to keep up with the other girls, and she slept next to her on the wooden floors of the village houses at night.

One morning in mid-August, just as the women were awakening, a guerrilla arrived on horseback and called the name of Rano Athanassiou, saying that she was to return with him to the village. Rano's first thought was that something had happened to her married sister Tassina or that their invalid father had died. She tried to hide her apprehensions as she kissed Glykeria goodbye.

'If you see my mother and sisters in the village, tell them I miss them!' Glykeria called after her.

All the way back to Lia, Rano bit her lip to keep from asking questions. There was no way she could have guessed that she had been named by Stavroula Yakou as someone who knew details of the Amerikana's treachery, and that she was being called back to testify against Eleni at her trial.

On August 21, the third day of the trial, the slopes of the ravine were crowded long before the prisoners arrived, and the place was filled with a buzz like a million bees. Everyone knew that the testimony would end today and the sentences would be decided. The only defendant remaining to be tried was the Amerikana.

Eleni stood still as a figure on an icon as the charges were read against her. The foliage of the plane trees sifted sunshine on her pale, immobile face and dark-blue dress.

The main thrust of Katis' case against her was that Eleni had organized and led two previous unsuccessful escape attempts, that she had sent away her children and that she had tried to convince other women in the village to do the same. Her actions had seriously undermined the efforts of the Democratic Army in her village.

Katis paused, scanning the faces before him to judge the reaction to what he had said. Then he added that the

503

Amerikana had stayed behind to organize more escapes, that she had sabotaged the program to relocate village children, that she had slandered guerrilla fighters and hidden clothing and food needed by the army.

As he spoke, Eleni turned to look at the group of witnesses gathered at one side. She gasped as she realized there was a new face among them: Rano Athanassiou. She turned and searched the audience; if Rano had returned from the threshing field, then perhaps Glykeria had too. But nowhere could she see her daughter's face or her red dress.

Katis planned to lay the ground for his condemnation of Eleni by establishing her fascist leanings and disloyalty to the cause. He had not previously interrogated Rano, but Stavroula Yakou had told him what questions to put to her. He felt his hands perspiring as the bewildered girl was called to testify. This was the climactic day of the trial and the most important prosecution and Katis was determined to conclude his case with an overwhelming barrage of testimony against the Amerikana.

Rano stood petrified. She had no idea what she would be asked or how she should answer to protect herself from punishment.

'You lived next to Eleni Gatzoyiannis for many years and you spent much time in her house,' Katis began. 'Answer the following questions: Why did the Amerikana make her daughter Olga Gatzoyiannis wear her kerchief tied around her face? Doesn't this imply a distrust of our *andartes*, who have respected the honor of every woman in this village?'

Rano stared at him, blinking. 'Many of us wear our kerchiefs that way, especially in winter!' she replied. 'But Olga has an additional reason; she has a goiter on her neck. She was hiding the goiter because we are young girls and it doesn't take much to be left a spinster.' Rano jumped at the sudden outburst of laughter from the villagers.

Katis frowned. This girl was clearly not smart enough to understand how she was supposed to answer, but he would show her the risks of protecting the Amerikana. 'We know, Comrade, that one day you went to the defendant and told her that our men were going to search her house,' he said, 'and that you took clothing and valuables of hers to hide in your own house. Why would you do that?'

While Eleni was remembering that Stavroula Yakou had been sitting in her kitchen on that day, Rano swallowed and looked about as if for help. Then she shrugged unhappily. 'I don't know. Call it a stupid mistake . . . call it friendship . . .'

'But isn't it true that at a time when all of her neighbors were sharing their goods with the Democratic Army, Eleni Gatzoyiannis was hoarding luxuries that no one else in this village could ever hope to own?'

Rano cleared her throat. 'She hid the clothes, yes.'

'That will be enough,' snapped Katis, tossing down his papers with a satisfied air. Two guerrillas stepped forward and led Rano away. She was given just enough time to kiss her invalid father as they passed her house in the Perivoli, and then she was taken to Tsamanta, where she was assigned to Spiro Skevis' batallion as an *andartina*.

Eleni struggled to keep her face impassive as she watched Rano being led away. They were using the people closest to her to put the last nails in her coffin. She ached to know what they had done with Glykeria.

'Stavroula Yakou,' rang out the voice of Katis. Eleni turned around to see the tall blond girl stand up and approach the judges' table. Stavroula's mother, Eleni's friend Anastasia, uttered a heartbroken moan. The sound seemed to jar the girl, and when she met Eleni's unnaturally wide eyes, she blushed to the roots of her hair.

Katis looked at her and in a resonant voice began to read a long statement from Stavroula testifying that Eleni was a known fascist, that she had burned her eldest daughter's foot to keep her from being drafted as an *andartina* and that she had stubbornly refused to send her children to the people's democracies. After he read a few sentences, Katis stopped and asked Stavroula, who was listening with her head bowed, 'Is this not true, Comrade?' But Stavroula only stood like a statue of a saint in meditation and did not answer.

Katis read a bit more and repeated his query; then, seeing that she was determined not to reply, he lost his temper. When he had interrogated her in private, Stavroula overflowed with

505

accusations against her neighbor, but now, before the united gaze of the village, she was tongue-tied. 'Don't be afraid of Eleni Gatzoyiannis, woman!' Katis thundered at the mute figure. 'She has no power here any longer! Where is the strength you showed when you gave this statement?'

But still Stavroula would not speak and stared at the ground as Katis' voice read on, piling up the allegations she had made against Eleni. The audience sat transfixed, watching the most feared woman in the village tremble. Katis reached the end of his patience. He gestured violently with the sheaf of papers in his hand, and a vein rose on his neck just where his collar pressed it. 'Speak, damn it!' he shouted. 'Did you say these things about the prisoner or not?'

The tension mounted until Stavroula's mother Anastasia could bear it no longer. She had suffered in silence for years as this headstrong girl had done exactly as she pleased, flaunting the village traditions by arranging her own marriage, dishonoring her husband by becoming a collaborator of the guerrillas; a woman whose name was always spoken with a leer. It had been wormwood and gall to watch Stavroula stand up before the assembled village at the trial and denounce Vasili Nikou, but now her testimony was being used to condemn the woman who had been the kindest of their neighbors during the years of poverty. Something in Anastasia snapped and she rose to her feet, shrieking at her frightened daughter, 'That's right, Stavroula! Tell it! Say it out loud! Let us hear everything you've whispered to them about Eleni, just as you said it on that paper!'

Stavroula looked up with wet eyes and shook her head. Then she sat down without having said a word.

Stavroula Yakou's unexpected refusal to testify threw Katis off balance. He hurriedly continued before the embarrassing scene made too great an impression on the other judges and the onlookers. He turned fiercely to Eleni.

'Amerikana,' he said, giving the word a sarcastic emphasis, 'did any of our fighters ever annoy your daughters or make the slightest suggestive remark to them?'

'No,' Eleni replied, 'I never said they did.'

'Then why did you hide your daughters inside the house,

506

try to prevent them from going on work details, which is the responsibility of every strong young woman in the village, and make them cover their faces with kerchiefs?'

'I always told my daughters to avoid becoming the subject of gossip in the village,' Eleni replied calmly. 'That is the responsibility of a mother, especially when her husband is not present to help protect his daughters' reputation. As for the kerchiefs, look around you; almost every woman here is wearing one.'

There was a stir among the crowd and Katis realized he had stepped on marshy ground. He returned to the main point of his condemnation. 'Your actions hardly support your words,' he snapped. 'You showed your contempt for the revolution by organizing the defection of your family and thirteen other civilians from this village. Listen to what the escaped prisoner, Marianthe Ziaras, had to say about your role in that betrayal:

'"I was in the house cooking when Eleni Gatzoyiannis came. My father asked me to leave the room, but I went outside and listened under the window. I heard the Amerikana tell my father that she would give him one thousand dollars if he would take her family to the other side. When the first two attempts were not successful and it became necessary for her to go to the threshing fields, she told my father, 'I'm going to where Glykeria is and if we can find a way to leave too, we will. But you must take my family and don't think about us.'"'

He put down the papers and looked at Eleni. 'What do you say to that?' he asked.

Eleni sighed. 'It's too bad that Marianthe isn't here to speak for herself,' she said.

Katis' brows drew together. 'We have a witness who is present and is more than willing to say these things to your face,' he said. 'I call Milia Drouboyiannis.'

The stocky young *andartina* with the masculine frizz of black hair came forward, holding her rifle at her side. She eagerly answered the questions Katis put to her, testifying that the Amerikana had organized the escape attempts and that Lukas Ziaras had tried to convince her mother, Alexandra Drouboyiannis, to take two of her daughters and come along.

She described the first two attempts in convincing detail: how the group had turned back once because of a baby's crying and again because of a heavy fog. 'My mother and sisters were persuaded by the fascist Lukas Ziaras to consider leaving,' Milia declared, 'but then I found out what they were planning and I told them that wherever they went, the Democratic Army would come. Soon all Greece will fly the Red Flag.'

The stocky girl, her face contorted with the intensity of her emotion, pulled herself up to her full height and thumped the butt of her rifle on the ground, a bit of theatrics that made an indelible impression on the watching villagers. 'I swear by the gun I'm holding that my mother and my sisters abandoned all thought of leaving with the Amerikana's family after I spoke to them!' she cried. As she testified, her mother sat on the sidelines, nodding her head at everything the girl said.

Heartened by the impression Milia Drouboyiannis had made, Katis turned suddenly on Eleni. 'You organized the escape of your family and your friends because, like your father and your husband, your heart is with the fascists!' he charged. 'You have tried from the beginning to turn the people of this village against us!'

Her face was ashen, but Eleni was calm. Unlike her cousin Antonova Paroussis, she had been careful not to speak out against the guerrillas and she would not admit to what she had not done.

'That is untrue,' she answered. 'Show me a single mother who will say that I told her not to give up her children.'

Katis looked around. 'Who will answer her? Stand up and speak!'

The silence was complete, except for the mechanical whine of the cicadas. After several moments Katis turned on Eleni angrily. 'You didn't have to use words to influence the women of this village,' he said. 'By refusing to volunteer your daughters and by holding on to your son, you were defying and sabotaging the goals of the revolution. By sending them to the fascists, you betrayed us all.'

Eleni regarded him in silence for a moment, then she said, quietly but clearly, 'I had one daughter conscripted but she was sent back. Another daughter is now threshing wheat for the Democratic Army. But what could I say to my husband if I gave up his only son? I sent my children to where their father could support them because I could no longer feed them here. I have done no harm and wished no harm to anyone. I only wanted my children to be safe.'

There was a murmur in the audience and the face of the judge Anagnostakis furrowed in a frown. Even the swarthy, high-cheekboned face of the third judge, Grigori Pappas, who had until now kept himself carefully impassive, showed concern. Katis spoke quickly. 'This woman, like all the seven civilians on trial today, has betrayed our struggle to bring freedom and independence to Greece.' As he took another breath, he was interrupted by a young guerrilla who whispered in his ear. Katis looked up and announced, 'There will be a short recess to permit the parents of children who are leaving for the people's democracies to say goodbye.' He pointed to a throng coming into view along the path that wound past the ravine, up toward the peak of the Prophet Elias. 'The parents of these children, who are setting out on a new and better life, have demonstrated their love for them without betraying our cause.'

The heavy shelling on the village two days before had convinced the guerrilla command that it was time to send the second group gathered for the *pedomasoma* out of harm's way. The twenty-year-old daughter of the newly prominent Communist, Foto Bollis, had been chosen as a senior guide of the group, and his nine-year-old son Sotiris was among the twenty children who were being led up the mountains toward Albania, where they would be put into camps.

Everyone turned around to look at the parade passing by on the road overhead. Relatives of the children suddenly pushed toward them. Before the eyes of the assemblage, mothers began to cry as they took their children in their arms. Eleni watched the scene and her own eyes filled with tears. She realized from the testimony against her that she would probably be judged guilty, but she knew that even if she lost her own life, she had won: Nikola was safe.

As Eleni stood there, the small blond son of Foto Bollis

came down into the ravine to say goodbye to his father. Although the Bollis family had lived near her in the Perivoli, Eleni had never been close friends with Agathe Bollis. But there was a bond between them: both women had suffered the misfortune of giving birth to four girls before both had finally managed to produce a boy; Sotiris was born only forty days before Nikola.

The Bollis girl, Olga, who was guiding the group of children, recalled thirty-three years later, when she was found living in a village of Greek Communist refugees in Hungary, that Eleni embraced the tow-headed little boy with her free arm and kissed him. Sotiris, who had no idea that Eleni was a prisoner on trial, looked at her and asked eagerly, 'Where's Nikola? Why isn't he going with us?'

Eleni smoothed his hair and smiled. 'Nikola's gone to his father,' she replied.

It took some time to bring the throng back to order after the children passed out of sight. Muffled sobbing could still be heard as Katis said, 'You have listened to the testimony of your neighbors verifying the charges against these defendants. Before the court withdraws to consider its verdict, is there anyone who wishes to speak on the charges?'

Everyone in the audience involuntarily drew back. They had been spectators at this life-and-death drama, and now they were being asked to become participants. There were sidelong looks and nervous coughs, but no one spoke. Then one of the old men in the first row climbed with difficulty to his feet. It was sixty-five-year-old Gregory Tsavos, who, before his retirement, had been a cooper and a field warden in the village, mediating disputes over boundaries and water rights. He lived above the Gatzoyiannis house in the Perivoli.

Now he stood resolutely before Katis, a bearlike, awkward figure, his cheeks and nose red from drink, his jowls trembling over his scrawny neck. He raised his chin and spoke firmly. 'I have known Eleni Gatzoyiannis all her life,' he said. 'She lived nearly on my doorstep. And I know that she has done no injury to anyone in the village. On the contrary, she always shared whatever she had. And she has a letter from her husband that clearly shows –' But Katis cut him off. 'Enough!'

510

he shouted in exasperation. Then he examined Tsavos suspiciously. 'What work do you do in this village, old man?' he asked.

'I was a field warden.'

Katis brought down his fist on the table in front of him. 'Sit down, platelicker of the police!' he exploded.

As Tsavos obeyed, another of the old men in the first row got to his feet. His name was Kosta Poulos. He was thin and white-haired, and unlike Gregory Tsavos, he was a well-known Communist, highly respected by the guerrillas because his son had died fighting with them.

'Speak, Comrade!' said Katis in an encouraging voice, far different from the tone he used with Tsavos.

The former coffeehouse owner surveyed the prisoners, the judges and the witnesses. Everyone waited to hear what one of the Communist pillars of the community would say about this trial of his own villagers. Poulos' gaze came to rest on Katis and he drew himself up. 'What Tsavos said was true,' he growled. 'I had only one son and he died fighting for the cause, and I'm speaking the truth. Eleni Gatzoyiannis has done nothing wrong. None of them has done anything to be killed for.'

Katis could hardly believe that the old man was defying him so blatantly. 'Sit down!' he shouted.

With increasing irritation Katis called on three more villagers, who rose in turn. They all spoke for the defendants. Two of them were elders of the village: a woman named Yianova Pantos and a man named Vangeli Sioulis. The third was a young woman, Sofia Depi, who lived at the edge of Lia near Alexo's house and came from a well-known Communist family. No one spoke against any of the defendants. None of the prisoners' close friends or relatives said a word.

Katis could see that calling upon the villagers to speak had been a mistake. Each voice that described the innocence of the defendants eroded the impact his prosecution was making on the other judges and on the wide-eyed peasants. He raised his hand and shouted, 'If you have evidence to add, then speak up, but otherwise, keep silent!'

There were no more volunteers. After a few moments of

silence, Katis nodded. 'The court will now retire to consider its verdict,' he said.

An excited buzz rose toward the branches of the plane trees as the three judges stood up from their chairs and filed behind a large tree at the edge of the ravine. For what was only a few minutes but seemed much longer, the villagers looked from the spot where the judges were whispering to the faces of the prisoners, who sat rigid with suspense. Spiro Michopoulos still picked his teeth with a twig. The women prisoners showed no emotion, except for Constantina Drouboyiannis, who crossed herself several times. Andreas Michopoulos had his head resting on his knees. Vasili Nikou gazed dully into the distance. Eleni studied the tense faces of the villagers seated before her. The prisoners stiffened to attention as the three judges filed back and took their places behind the table. Katis stood in the middle, facing the wall of expectant faces. He waited, impressing his presence upon them.

'After carefully considering the evidence,' he announced, 'the court has rendered the following verdicts: In the case of two defendants, Dina Venetis and Constantina Drouboyiannis, the evidence was not conclusive and they are found not guilty. The evidence against the other five – Spiro Michopoulos, Andreas Michopoulos, Vasili Nikou, Alexo Gatzoyiannis and Eleni Gatzoyiannis – was overwhelming. They have been judged guilty on all charges and are sentenced to death.'

A sound like a gust of wind roared through the ravine. There were no cries, only a few stifled moans from relatives of the condemned, a flutter of hands making the four taps of the Cross. The prisoners themselves sat stunned. Only Spiro Michopoulos buried his face in his arms.

Katis raised his hand for silence. 'Today we do not condemn, we do not sentence!' he shouted. 'The loyal people of this village provided all the evidence against the prisoners. You have told us where the last hen lays its eggs, and this is your judgment.'

His small black eyes gleaming with excitement, Katis studied the audience, brown faces mottled by the sunlight, black kerchiefs ruffled by the breeze, but in the eyes turned toward him he read only shock and fear, not the approval he had expected. He paused, then moved his hands benevolently like a priest. 'But the People's Army is not vindictive,' he added. 'The condemned may yet be saved.'

The prisoners leaned forward in sudden hope. 'They will be given the opportunity to send appeals for clemency to the president of the provincial government, Markos Vafiadis,' he went on. 'We will await his decision on their petitions before carrying out the sentences.'

The drama that the village had watched for three days was in fact not a trial at all, but a carefully staged propaganda play in which all the sentences had been decided long beforehand. In such civilian trials in the Mourgana villages, which became more numerous in August and September of 1948 as the guerrillas were losing the war, the facts of each case were sent to Kostas Koliyiannis, the political commissar of the Epiros Command who ruled the Mourgana. From his headquarters in Babouri he sent back to the security police in each village the sentences which the judges would then pretend to reach after hearing the evidence.

During my investigation of my mother's trial, this fact was confirmed by several people, including Christos Zeltas, the head of the security police in Lia, and Yiorgos Kalianesis, chief of staff in the Epiros Command. They all said that the decisions of life or death on those brought to trial were made beforehand by Koliyiannis, who sent judges to carry on a mockery of a trial.

'Headquarters controlled everything,' Zeltas told me. 'Nobody could be arrested, beaten or executed without authorization from the political commissar, Koliyiannis. . . . The judicial service sent him the reports and then they talked to him by phone as to what was to be done, execution or release. Then the trial was held to give a legal appearance to the process. At division headquarters, you must understand, Koliyiannis was the final word. If he said burn, we burned; if he said kill, we killed. No one else had the authority to do that.'

As the Greek Communist Party's principal agent in the Mourgana, Kostas Koliyiannis was clearly carrying out the party's will in ordering the civilian executions. He was rapidly promoted for his performance as leader of the Epiros Command and he ultimately replaced Nikos Zachariadis as party leader.

During his ten-month rule of the Mourgana range, Koliyiannis sent more than three hundred men and women before firing squads, including at least five civilians from every guerrilla-occupied village in the region.

CHAPTER SEVENTEEN

On the same day that Katis was telling the condemned prisoners that they could petition General Markos Vafiadis for clemency, the guerrilla commander in chief had abandoned his army and was fleeing for his life toward Albania to escape the assassins sent after him by Greek Communist Party leader Nikos Zachariadis.

Their irreconcilable differences over war strategy, aggravated by the loss of Grammos and the summary execution of Yannoulis, boiled over during the retreat from Grammos. According to an account pieced together by French author Dominique Eudes from interviews with guerrilla leaders, Zachariadis decided that Markos must be eliminated, and ordered him north to Albania while the rest of the guerrillas retreated northeast to the Vitsi range along the Yugoslav border. Aware that his life was in danger, Markos selected ten of his most trusted men to accompany him and plunged immediately into inaccessible mountain terrain.

As soon as Markos had gone, Zachariadis summoned a guerrilla named Polydoras, an assassin he had often used in the past. He was to pursue Markos and kill him, Zachariadis explained, making it look as if he had died in an unfortunate border incident while headed toward Albania. Polydoras and his men were used to such missions, but when their quarry was their own commander in chief, it gave them pause, and they lagged a bit, not catching up with Markos and his men until they had already entered Albanian territory. The first shots fired by Polydoras' men drew the attention of an Albanian detachment patrolling nearby and they provided covering fire which enabled Markos and his men to escape. Markos went straight to the Soviet mission in Albania and asked for protection.

Zachariadis, at Vitsi, tried to cover up Markos' absence by issuing orders in his name while telling Markos' loyal officers that the commander was sick. Markos' second-in-command, Lieutenant General Kikitsas, felt a shudder of fear when he was called to Vitsi headquarters on August 25 and told by Zachariadis, 'Markos is gravely ill. We think he's going to die.' Kikitsas refused to accept Zachariadis' request to take over Markos' command, and three days later he was sent away to travel the people's democracies as a roving ambassador, ostensibly to sell the Communist countries on supporting the revolution. Most of Markos' loyal *kapetani* soon were sent into exile on similar pretexts.

Meanwhile, the battle-weary guerrilla forces dug into the Vitsi range. Although their orders still bore Markos' name, they were issued by a supreme war council totally obedient to Zachariadis. That council included Kostas Koliyiannis, head of the Epiros Command.

Out of optimism, desperation or madness, Zachariadis continued to tell his exhausted troops that victory had never been closer; at any minute, brigades of international Communists would come rushing over the border to their assistance. But the officers in the trenches knew better. Zachariadis' own aide, Yiorgos Goussias, was overheard saying, 'It's all over already, but we've got to hang on a while longer.'

Like a bulldog who refuses to loosen his grip even when mortally wounded, Zachariadis would hold on for another year. In that time a great many more Greek men, women and children would die.

THE LAST SEVEN DAYS

THE DRAMA HAD reached its conclusion and the seven protagonists were led through the silent throng of villagers, feeling the eyes of their neighbors and families searing their faces. They were numb; the condemned had not yet been able to register the totality of their disaster, and the exonerated still did not believe in their deliverance.

In the yard outside the security prison the two women who had been acquitted – Dina Venetis and Constantina Drouboyiannis – were separated from the rest. In a bizarre gesture of restitution, the head of the security police ceremoniously handed each of them a package containing pieces of dried bread, announcing in ringing tones, 'You see, Comrades, the Democratic Army punishes only those who deserve it.' Then the dumfounded women were told they were free to go home.

The five who had been condemned were herded into the jail, the first time Eleni had been incarcerated in the filthy cellar along with the rest. There were about a dozen prisoners already in the room, strangers from other villages.

The knots of people wending their way home from the trial walked in silence, their heads down, avoiding one another's eyes. As one candle lights another, shame had spread through the village. Not even the most fervent Communists among the Liotes had believed that five of their most prominent neighbors would be sentenced to death.

The judges who carried out the orders of Koliyiannis and condemned the five had been startled at the reaction of the audience during the trial and the unexpectedly unanimous

517

defense of the prisoners offered by the villagers who stood up to speak. They realized that the trial had not been the propaganda success that was intended, despite Katis' careful planning and the number of accusers. The attitude of the villagers worried them.

Yiorgos Anagnostakis was especially disturbed by the trial. When the other judges signed their names to the execution order he hesitated. Instead of signing it, he took the paper in his hand and set off for the headquarters in Babouri to discuss his reservations with Kostas Koliyiannis. Many years later Anagnostakis told a guerrilla from Babouri named Mihali Bouris what happened that day.

Koliyiannis, forty-two, was a slow-moving, ursine figure with eyes of glowering hostility behind his dark-rimmed glasses. He had a lush crop of white hair and a sparse mustache sprouted beneath his bulbous nose. A zealous Communist since he left his village outside Thebes to study law in Athens, Koliyiannis had spent the last dozen years of his life either on the mountain or in prison. The commissar was notorious for his lack of humor and his hair-trigger temper, and on that day, August 21, he was in a particularly foul mood.

When Anagnostakis arrived in Babouri and was told to sit in the busy waiting room outside Koliyiannis' office, he nervously rehearsed the words he would use to explain his reservations about the trial. After some time he was ushered into the great man's presence, and Koliyiannis glared at him with obvious impatience.

Anagnostakis cleared his throat and began, 'We've held the trial in Lia, Comrade, and we've condemned the five to be executed.' He was rewarded with a curt nod and plunged on, 'But the reaction of the villagers was very negative. All those who rose to speak testified in favor of the defendants. Two local women are among those to be killed. I haven't added my signature to the execution order yet because I believe that a lot of harm might be done to our cause by these executions.'

The commissar's heavy brows drew together and he contemplated the nervous judge as if he were a pesky mosquito buzzing around his head. Koliyiannis had just been through a

518

very trying week, perhaps the worst since the civil war began. Three days before, Grammos had fallen and it was clear that the guerrillas would ultimately be defeated; it was only a matter of time. Koliyiannis also knew something that few other men on the Mourgana did: the feud between Zachariadis and his commander in chief Markos had finally erupted, spouting disaster. Zachariadis had taken complete charge of the war and was sure to continue his misguided policies.

Koliyiannis knew that soon the guerrilla army in the Mourgana would be forced to retreat into Albania. Already morale was so low that the commanders were having trouble controlling the epidemic of desertions. But there was one small bit of solace in the general debacle. With Zachariadis and Markos at each other's throat and the army in disorder, the Greek Communist Party would be reduced to chaos. If he played his cards right, Koliyiannis knew, the tidal wave of defeat might cast him up on the heights of the party hierarchy. But he had to use all his cunning to avoid being sucked under with the rest by the disaster.

When the time came to retreat into Albania, it would be up to Koliyiannis to see that all the civilians in the occupied villages went docilely with the guerrillas, along with their animals and provisions. They would be essential for feeding and supplying the army in exile; and from the ranks of these peasants would come the Communist cadres of the future. Like all good Greek Communists, Koliyiannis was convinced that the Democratic Army would eventually launch another round in their rebellion against the fascists.

But he knew it was not easy to convince peasants to leave their homes and fields behind. The only way he could ensure complete cooperation from the civilians when the day came to retreat was to terrify them into compliance. That was why, in the late summer of 1948, there were public show trials in nearly every Mourgana village of civilians who were charged with disloyalty to the cause. To Koliyiannis, it seemed an effective way to cow the remaining villagers into obedience on that approaching day when retreat into Albania would be inevitable.

There were dozens of occupied villages under Koliyiannis' command, and it was not surprising, on August 21, 1948, with the war, the fate of the DAG and his very career hanging by a thread, that Koliyiannis was not in the mood to hear quibbles from one of his judges about the condemnation of five peasants in Lia. The village had been a thorn in his side ever since the mass escape there created such an embarrassment for his command. The commissar's frown deepened. 'Twenty people were allowed to walk out of that village under our very noses,' he snapped. 'If no one is punished for this crime and we ultimately have to abandon the Mourgana, do you think the villagers are going to follow us meekly or rush over to join the fascists?'

'But if we execute these people, the village will turn against us!' replied Anagnostakis. 'They seem to feel these five have done no harm.'

'Whether the villagers follow us out of loyalty or fear doesn't matter, as long as they understand the consequences of defying us!' Koliyiannis thundered. 'I'm busy now. Wait outside in the other room and I'll discuss this matter with you later.'

Anagnostakis went into the outer room, the execution order still in his hands, and started to worry. He was afraid that Koliyiannis might begin to doubt his own loyalty to the cause; after all, he had been appointed head of the judicial branch by Koliyiannis and had been ordered by him to attend the trial and sign the execution order. He thought about the kangaroo court and snap execution that had snuffed out Colonel Yiorgos Yannoulis only days before.

As grim-faced guerrillas bustled in and out with messages for Koliyiannis, Anagnostakis considered the possible results of his reluctance to sign and became more and more frightened for his own life, which he began to weigh against his scruples. Impulsively he scribbled his name below the other two on the execution order, handed the paper to the guerrilla who was serving as Koliyiannis' chief aide, and said, 'Give this to the Comrade General.' Quickly Anagnostakis disappeared out the door in the direction of Lia before Koliyiannis could call him back into his office.

Anagnostakis never forgot his lapse of courage: twenty years later the former judge confided the incident to another exiled guerrilla in Tashkent, Russia, and told him that the sudden failure of nerve was 'a burden that I have carried through the years. I signed the execution order so that they wouldn't use it against me.'

Living among refugees in the unfinished house in Igoumenitsa, the Gatzoyiannis family had no idea that there had been a trial. While they waited for news of Eleni to leak from the other side of the battle lines, life took on a kind of normalcy. Even though it was summer, a school was set up for the refugee children. Fotini and Nikola, who had not entered a classroom since before the guerrillas occupied their village, attended it every day, Nikola carrying his new notebooks and pencils. Olga and Kanta found themselves to be the belles of Igoumenitsa, besieged by women acting as go-betweens who wanted to cement a marriage proposal between some male relative and one of the Gatzoyiannis girls. Marrying one of them would be a wonderful opportunity for an ambitious young man, enabling him to receive papers eventually to emigrate from bankrupt, war-ravaged Greece and make his fortune in America. The girls' grandfather encouraged these suits, but they remembered their mother's warning: 'You're all to go to your father in America, and if you don't, my curse will be on you! The things we've been suffering here don't happen in America. In Greece you wouldn't be safe anywhere.'

Even though the family didn't have to pay rent, there were expenses in setting up housekeeping in Igoumenitsa. They had to buy plates, pans and wood for the fireplace as well as food, and they soon ran short of money. Olga decided to travel by bus to Filiates to ask for more of the money her father had sent her uncle Foto. When she got there she was surprised to find the small Turkish-style town crawling with government soldiers, military equipment and tanks, which looked to her like large slow-moving swamp animals.

When Olga tracked down her uncle and asked for some more money, Foto rolled his eyes heavenward. 'Didn't I buy all of you new shoes and clothes and pencils and notebooks and pans and I don't know what all?' he exclaimed. 'The money's gone, used up! What do you think I am, a bank?'

Olga's cheeks flushed and she told her uncle that she'd write her father what he had said, but Foto, who was as wily as Olga was naive, managed to talk her out of it. 'Any day now your mother will be out of the village and I'll discuss it with her,' he temporized. 'Can't you see what's going on here? They're preparing an attack on the Mourgana with so many men and so much equipment that it can't possibly fail. The guerrillas won't stop running until they reach Tirana! Then your mother will be free and we'll settle these petty matters between us.'

Excited by what she had seen and heard, Olga went back to Igoumenitsa with a light heart and told the others all about the huge military operation that was being readied to liberate their village and free their mother.

The well-intentioned objections about the trial expressed by Judge Anagnostakis to Commissar Koliyiannis at the headquarters of the Epiros Command boomeranged in an unexpected way. While Koliyiannis was pleased when he learned that the judge had regained his senses and quietly signed the execution order, he remembered what Anagnostakis had said about the negative reaction of the villagers to the trial. If the decision to execute the five Liotes was an unpopular one, then it was necessary to discredit the condemned in the eyes of their neighbors; to convince the village that these five deserved to die for their treachery to the rest of the community. The Amerikana, especially, must be stripped of the position of respect that she held in the village. Proof had to be found that she was a traitor and not just a mother trying to save her own children. Koliyiannis scribbled off a message and ordered it sent to Katis in Lia.

Katis had been relieved that the case against the Liotes was completed, but when he received Koliyiannis' directive, his face clouded. He sat down at his desk with the thick files of statements his intelligence sources had collected and thought hard. The best way to besmirch the reputation of the

Amerikana, he decided, was to convince the villagers that she had been living luxuriously on gold sent by her capitalist husband as well as on goods hoarded and kept back from the poor of Lia by her fascist father Kitso Haidis. Katis was aware of the widely held opinion in Lia that the shrewd old miller had squirreled away a fortune in relief supplies during his stint as distributor of UNRRA goods.

Katis called in his interrogators in the security police. He ordered them to concentrate on the Amerikana, using whatever forms of torture were necessary to make her admit to hiding possessions and money. She must be broken, publically humiliated and made to confess to those crimes. The same methods were to be used on the other condemned Liotes, especially the former village president Spiro Michopoulos, to wring out of them every detail of the treason they had committed against the Democratic Army and their fellow villagers.

No one survived to describe the exact methods of torture used against the condemned villagers, but it is known that they were all submitted to *falanga*, and Eleni suffered it more severely than the others. She was taken out of the cellar and tortured, perhaps in a room upstairs, perhaps in the hidden part of the garden behind the house.

It takes three men to administer *falanga*. The victim is stripped of shoes and stockings and made to lie on the ground or a table. Two men slip the bare feet between the barrel of a rifle and its strap, twisting the gun until the strap presses the balls of the feet tightly back, exposing the soles. While two men hold the rifle rigid, a third applies the blows to the soles of the feet with a metal or wooden rod.

As a method of punishment, *falanga* has many advantages, which accounts for its popularity in every country where organized political torture is the norm. Each blow of the rod is felt not just on the soles of the feet, painfully flexed upward as the club smashes the delicate nerves between the heel and balls of the foot; the pain shoots up the stretched muscles of the leg and explodes in the back of the skull. The whole body is in agony and the victim writhes like a worm, soon losing all control, although never passing out. The primary virtue *of falanga* is that it does not leave the kind of marks that other tortures do, like burning cigarettes. But in Eleni's case it must have been mismanaged, because the next time any of the villagers saw her, her legs were swollen to twice their normal size and entirely black from the beatings. She was unable to walk and could speak only with difficulty.

It probably took a few days of concentrated torture before Eleni was completely broken to the point where she not only confessed to hiding Olga's dowry and other valuables in the bean field but agreed with every accusation Katis made against her. The first time the village saw her again was several days after the trial. What emerged from the cellar prison was a far different figure from the self-contained woman, her features composed beneath the dark kerchief, who had parried Katis' questions.

Tassina Bartzokis was at her kitchen window when she saw Eleni being led out of the prison gate on a mule, leaning heavily against the back of the wooden saddle. Tassina's eyes widened in horror at the sight of her closest friend, whom she could scarcely recognize. Eleni's hair was no longer covered with a kerchief, but hung loose and unkempt, like that of women performing penance on the Virgin's feast day. Her dress, which had always been modestly buttoned up to her neck, was open, exposing a V of white flesh mottled with bruises. Her legs, swollen to freakish dimensions, were naked and wrapped in rags. She could barely sit erect on the wooden saddle, but when Tassina came out into the yard to look closer, Eleni met her eyes with a flicker of recognition. Three guerrillas preceded the mule, one carrying a shovel, another a pick; and two riderless packhorses followed behind. At this sight Tassina felt fear wash through her stomach and into her bowels.

Farther down the path at the bottom of the Perivoli another close friend, Angeliki Botsaris Daikos, saw the procession passing by. Consumed with curiosity about what was being done to her neighbor, she took an empty barrel as if to gather water from the spring below, and circling around, came toward the Haidis house from the back.

A third woman who remembers the event was Ourania

Haidis. She was married to one of Eleni's cousins, but when she saw her kinswoman passing by, Ourania and her mother-in-law hid, watching the proceedings from behind their shutters, too frightened to show themselves.

The only neighbor who had the courage to come over and ask what was happening was Vasiliki Petsis. She came out of her yard and over to the Haidis gate, where the procession had come to a halt. Eleni never got down from the saddle – her legs were far too swollen for her to walk. She only sat there and pointed toward the Haidis bean field. 'It's there, under the patch of dry beans,' she said to the guerrillas in an unnatural voice. Vasiliki recalled the day, during the time Eleni was released from the prison and living alone, that she had asked her why she neglected to irrigate that particular patch of beans. 'Why bother?' was Eleni's laconic reply. 'Who's going to live to eat them?'

Now, while the guerrillas dug at the spot with their shovel and pick, ripping up the parched bean plants, Vasiliki crept close to where Eleni was sitting on the mule, her chin on her chest, her back propped against the backrest of the saddle.

'Eleni, child!' Vasiliki whispered. The prisoner raised her head and her eyes focused on her neighbor with difficulty. Slowly she lifted a trembling hand and gestured for her to leave. It was difficult to understand the words that issued from the swollen, cracked lips. 'Go,' Vasiliki heard her say, 'or they'll do the same to you.' But the older woman hung around long enough to see what the guerrillas unearthed: several large copper pots full of clothing, linens and *velenzes* – Olga's cherished dowry.

The guerrillas fell to their knees and scrabbled among the contents of the pots, pulling everything out on the ground. Their faces fell as they realized that the clothing and linens were all rotten, covered with a gray-green mold, the fabrics falling apart in their hands. Somehow, water had seeped through and as they pulled each object out, they threw it away in disgust.

The guerrillas fumbled through the mess and shouted as they found solid objects; perhaps the treasure Sotiris had told them about. But it was only some copper pots and pans, a corroded pitcher and a framed photograph that was no longer recognizable. They cheered as they unearthed some tins of canned meat and powdered milk. Angeliki Botsaris, hiding nearby with her empty water barrel, crept closer to see what Eleni had hidden. She remembers the guerrillas spreading on the ground some 'American towels, like nothing we had ever seen, thick, with flowers on them. And there was even a jar of honey.'

'You can see what the fascist traitor has hidden away, what wealth!' the head of the guerrillas shouted to the silent, watching windows of the nearby houses. They made a great show of gathering up the things, but clearly they were disappointed; they had hoped to find a treasure and had come up with only some mildewed blankets and linens. Angrily they packed all the goods on the backs of two horses, to take them up to the commissary, where they were carefully spread out in the yard so that everyone in the village could see what the Amerikana had buried in her garden. The mule with the prisoner on it was led at the head of the parade of plunder in a slow procession back up the path to the Perivoli.

Eleni Gatzoyiannis, expressionless and slumped in the saddle, passed before the horrified and fascinated eyes of her neighbors as she was led back into the cellar of her house.

During the last seven days, the anchor that Eleni used to keep her tenuous grip on sanity was her thoughts of her children. Shortly after the trial, probably when she was brought up to the good chamber in preparation for the first round of torture, she found a way to leave a message that would reach them after she was dead, her only written testament.

Eleni was left alone for a brief time in the good chamber, which had been the show place of her home before it was made into an office for the security police. Her eyes automatically sought the iconostasis, which hung in the eastern corner. It was a glass-fronted triangular wooden box holding the family's icons. Eleni had never permitted any of the children to touch it; attending to the iconostasis was her personal duty. She walked up to look at the familiar framed image of the Virgin and Child – the centerpiece of the

526

iconostasis. Inside the small cabinet, before the Virgin, there still sat a red Easter egg, a sprig of laurel from the Palm Sunday mass, and a small bottle of water blessed by the priest on Epiphany. Around the edge were tucked a half-dozen small cardboard images of saints and holy figures, each one purchased many years ago in Filiates or Yannina to commemorate some special blessing or feast day.

Eleni stared into the Virgin's face, her heart tight with worry about her children. She knew she was to die, probably to be buried in some obscure ravine or in her own yard, and she imagined her children returning after the war, searching for her throughout northern Greece and perhaps in the Communist countries. She wanted to tell them her fate and at the same time console them that she was at peace under the protection of the Holy Virgin.

Suddenly Eleni reached up and pulled out one of the small cardboard icons tucked into the rim of the cabinet. Then she went to the desk used by the police and snatched up a fountain pen. She tried to think what she could write that would tell them she was to be killed and yet not be so incriminating that she would be further punished by the guerrillas if they found it.

Eleni was holding a small paper icon of a brown-eyed Madonna in scarlet robes, smaller than a playing card; about three inches high and two wide. She turned it over and hurriedly scrawled on the back:

> Sweet Virgin
> protect my moth-
> er there where
> you are together
>
> Eleni Ch Gat

She wrote in bold, firm black strokes, the lines slanting upward in her haste. The letters show that her hand was not yet palsied with the effects of the torture. But because she was hurrying so, she made several mistakes in forming letters, which she swiftly crossed out and wrote over. Those few words took up five lines on the back of the narrow card and she centered her name on a line by itself, the way it would appear on a tombstone.

Eleni studied what she had written. If they found it, the guerrillas would not realize she had written it about herself, but her children would know her handwriting and understand she was dead. She imagined their tears when they returned to the house for the first time in search of her and discovered her message in the iconostasis. Then she took the pen and scribbled in ever smaller letters to make it fit:

Don't be upset
I am all right

In tiny letters below it she signed 'Mana.'

As she began to put the card back in the iconostasis, Eleni thought of Alexo, whose children would also be hunting for their mother, not knowing what had become of her. She scribbled a last line, fitting it in with difficulty around the bottom of what she had already written: 'God have mercy also on the soul of Alexandra.'

Hearing the sound of approaching footsteps, Eleni threw down the pen and ran to the iconostasis, where she opened the glass door and shoved the tiny card behind the large framed icon of the Virgin and Child. She had barely closed it and turned around when the door opened to admit the guerrillas who would administer her torture.

Pain beyond the limits of endurance destroys the mind as well as the body, driving it to take refuge in madness. Spiro Michopoulos had always been weak, a result of his near-death from tuberculosis, and by the time he died, the torture had reduced him to a slavering, trembling creature, unable to walk or speak. But to his last intelligible breath Michopoulos cried that he had always been loyal to the Democratic Army. Despite the torture, the guerrillas never managed to wring out of the former village president the location of any more hoards of goods besides the chests that had been dug up from the cellar of his house.

Andreas Michopoulos was more or less left alone, for Katis knew that Andreas' execution would create no propaganda problem in the village. Ever since his childhood as the village troublemaker, the boy had been unpopular in Lia.

Alexo Gatzoyiannis, who was at first a source of comfort to the other prisoners in the cellar prison, had long ago given up any hope of survival. To Eleni, her sister-in-law always seemed one of the strongest women in the village, uncomplaining despite her difficult life and many children. During her testimony at the trial, Alexo blazed with defiance and cynicism, but the pain of torture eventually destroyed her mind. Those who saw her during the last days of her life say she seemed oblivious of her surroundings, her eyes blank, recognizing no one.

The gray-haired cooper Vasili Nikou, a veteran of nine years as a soldier in the Balkan wars, had drunk his life as a cup of gall. The horrors of his military service and the death of his only son had hardened him like a tree on a cliff, constantly battered by the elements. The torture did not destroy Nikou's sanity nor shake his cynical despair. His daughter Chrysoula, who was twenty-eight at the time, saw him shortly after the trial. Although no other prisoner was permitted visits from their family, Chrysoula was allowed to bring him food, which she had to taste first to prove that it hadn't been poisoned in order to end her father's pain. At her request, the cooper was brought to the door of the cellar.

'His face was swollen and black around the eyes,' Chrysoula remembers, 'and on one side his upper lip was puffed up. It must have hurt him to talk, because he spoke so slowly. We embraced, despite the lice crawling all over him, and he tried to put up a brave front. "Don't worry about me," he said. "Jails are for men. Go home and look after your mother." '

After this visit, Chrysoula and her younger sister Olga, accompanied by their aunt Fotina Makou, made a pilgrimage to the hills below Tsamanta where Major Spiro Skevis was based as commander of a battalion. They were hoping that they could convince Skevis to intercede with his superior officers on behalf of their father. Nikou's other sister, who had been sent into Albania with the entire Skevis clan two months earlier, was married to Skevis' eldest brother, Yiorgos, a tie of kinship that was not taken lightly in a village like Lia.

When the group reached the shed in the mountains which Spiro Skevis was using as his headquarters, they encountered one of his nieces who was serving as his telephone operator and assistant. The women from Lia demanded to see Skevis, but the girl insisted that the major wasn't in. 'We're not leaving here until we see him,' Chrysoula insisted.

The nervous young assistant told her kinswoman to go farther up the hill and she would try to find Skevis. Soon they saw him come out of the shed and climb up toward them.

As a schoolteacher in Lia, Spiro Skevis had been a tense, emaciated figure, vibrating with fanatic devotion for the resistance movement, but now he was even thinner and paler, and his ill-tended beard and burning eyes gave him the appearance of a maddened scarecrow. As soon as he was within hearing distance of the women, Fotina Makou shouted to Skevis, 'Is it true, Spiro, that you're going to kill my brother?'

Skevis stared at the three women from his village, two of them his nieces, and grew red with anger and shame. He and his brother Prokopi had begun their resistance organization in Lia during the occupation afire with humanitarian ideals and the longing to bring about equality of all men. They had wanted to eliminate the tyranny of the bloodsucking ruling classes. Now it had degenerated into this: the killing of his own relatives.

The knowledge was eating at his heart. Skevis had already gone to Koliyiannis to protest the condemnation of the five Liotes and had discovered that his rank of major, despite his brilliant record, carried no power to sway the political commissar. Skevis was sent away in humiliation with the warning to tend to his own business and not to meddle in civilian affairs. Now his feelings of frustration erupted into anger at the petitioners. 'We're going to kill Spiro Michopoulos, who was one of us!' he shouted 'Do you think we can spare Vasili Nikou, who has always been a fascist?'

530

The older woman began swearing at Skevis, once the pride of the village, universally admired for his learning and his revolutionary ideas. But Skevis swore and shouted even louder than she did. 'Leave me alone, for God's sake!' he cried. 'Go away, all of you!' He turned on his heel and strode back to his headquarters while his niece barred the door to her cousins. Silent with despair, the three women set out on the long walk back to Lia.

The desire of the political commissar to improve the image of the guerrillas and smooth over the bad feelings caused by the trial led to a grotesque incident that occurred a day or so after Eleni was led down to show where she had hidden the 'treasures' in the bean field.

Since their arrival in the village, the guerrillas had forbidden any religious services. But as Angeliki Botsaris Daikos was caring for her baby boy, born four days before the mass escape, there was a great clanging of church bells. The guerrillas announced through their bull horns that there was to be a mass baptism of all newborn babies immediately in the Church of the Holy Trinity on the village square. 'All mothers of unbaptized babies, prepare your children at once!'

About fifteen babies had been born in the village since the guerrillas closed the churches, and their mothers, like Angeliki, were stunned at the announcement. She wondered if it was a new trick of the guerrillas as she searched for something to put on her tiny son. All the baby clothes were in rags, so she took a slip of her own that was still in good condition, left over from her dowry, swiftly cut armholes in the sides and wrapped it around him.

The fifteen mothers and their crying infants assembled in the village square to see the guerrillas leading toward them an archimandrite, the highest rank a married priest can attain in the church hierarchy. He was a gray-bearded man of about sixty-five whom the guerrillas had been holding prisoner in the same cellar as Eleni. 'He was either from the village of Moshini or Parakalamo,' Angeliki recalls, 'and he looked very solemn.'

The guerrillas provided a small cupful of oil to pour into

the water of the tarnished baptismal font, and the archimandrite set about intoning the familiar ritual. Confused, every woman quickly turned to ask another to serve as godmother for her child. The second baby to be baptized was Angeliki's son, and she whispered the name she had chosen for him – Constantine – as the priest took him from her arms. One woman handed over her tiny daughter and announced that the child's name was to be Laocratia, which means 'the people's rule.' The old priest frowned; the Greek church requires that every infant must bear the name of a recognized saint, but he said nothing and lifted the squalling, naked infant three times into the air, then submerged her in the font, chanting, 'In the name of the Father and of the Son and of the Holy Spirit, I baptize thee Laocratia.'

When the archimandrite finished with the last of the babies, he called all the mothers together and admonished them sternly, 'I charge all of you with the solemn responsibility to take care that none of these fifteen infants ever marry one another, because they have all been baptized in the same oil and they are now spiritual brothers and sisters. For any of them to be married would be incest.'

The women were frightened by this unorthodox ceremony led by a prisoner priest, their babies in rags, with none of the usual joy and dancing, tossing of coins and Jordan almonds for luck. They nodded obediently as the priest spoke. Then the old man in his black gown and stovepipe hat was led back toward the prison by his captors. The next day he was executed.

Katis was extremely disappointed with the mildewed linens and few cans of food that had been dug up in the Haidis garden. He had to prove that the Amerikana had hidden enough riches to provoke the envy and resentment of the villagers. After all, many of his informants reported that she had a considerable cache of gold sovereigns concealed somewhere. He ordered that she be put to the torture again.

On the sixth day after Eleni had been sentenced to death, Angeliki Botsaris Daikos was feeding her newly baptized son when the assistant to the head of the security police, a man named Mihalis Hassiotis, appeared at her door. 'What a fearsome man he was!' Angeliki says. 'Whenever we saw him walk by we made our cross that he didn't stop for us. But this day he came right to my door and said, "They want to question you."'

Angeliki picked up the baby, hoping that the guerrillas would be more gentle with a mother holding an infant in her arms, and Hassiotis led her up the path toward the Gatzoyiannis house. On the way, Angeliki saw the head of intelligence, Sotiris Drapetis, leading Ourania Haidis in the same direction. Ourania was married to a cousin of Eleni's who had made a comfortable fortune in the black market during and after the occupation. Angeliki and Ourania exchanged frightened glances. They had both been hidden witnesses to Eleni's ordeal a few days before when she was forced to show where her daughter's dowry was hidden.

The two women were led into the security police station. Ourania Haidis was put in the small dirt-floored pantry behind the kitchen where the window had been securely repaired since Marianthe Ziaras' escape. Angeliki and her baby were led directly into the good chamber – the office – where she came face to face with Katis.

The balding judge with the doomsday voice began by asking Angeliki her parents' names, her husband's family's names, and then he said, 'Are you related to the Amerikana?'

'No, just fellow villagers,' Angeliki replied.

'Then why did she and her family visit your house so often?'

Angeliki felt her throat closing. 'It's the custom here, whether related or not,' she quavered. 'We were neighbors.'

Katis leaned forward, fixing her with the eyes of a predator.

'Now I'm going to ask you some questions and I want precise answers,' he snapped. 'What day, what hour, did the Amerikana give you three gold sovereigns and what did you do with them? Who did you give them to?'

Angeliki looked stunned. She didn't know what was happening or what she should answer. 'Comrade Katis!' she pleaded. 'I never got three sovereigns from the Amerikana!'

'If you lie,' replied Katis, 'you will receive the same fate she does.'

Angeliki told him that she did in fact have six sovereigns, which she wore constantly in a leather pouch tied around her neck under her clothing, and that she had six more sovereigns which she had given to her mother to wear in a similar pouch in case one of them was killed. But, she insisted, they had been given to her by her husband, not the Amerikana.

Katis pressed his lips into a thin line which had the hint of a smile. He called in Hassiotis and ordered him to take Angeliki down to the cellar prison, where she could speak directly to the Amerikana.

Angeliki found Eleni sitting on the threshold of the door that led to the cellar. Her legs, black and swollen, were stretched out in front of her, and her blue dress with the three black stripes was open at the throat and filthy. Eleni was blinking in the sunlight and seemed at first not to recognize Angeliki. Hassiotis prompted the prisoner like a director. 'Tell us again, Comrade Eleni, how you gave three sovereigns to this woman.'

Eleni's eyes focused on Angeliki and she made a gesture of recognition. 'Yes, that's right, child. Give the man three sovereigns.'

Panic washed over Angeliki and she began to tremble with anger. She put the baby on the ground and, leaning forward, seized Eleni by the shoulders, and shook her fiercely. 'You never gave me any sovereigns, Eleni!' she shouted into her friend's face. 'What do you want to do, take me to the grave with you?'

Eleni made no more response than a rag doll. When Angeliki released her she sat there, her swollen legs extended before her, and her vacant gaze fell on the swaddled baby lying on the ground, reaching with his plump hands for a mote of dust floating in the sunlight. 'Oh, if I could only touch them one more time!' Eleni said, as if to herself.

Angeliki was startled. 'What did you say?'

'If only I could feel my arms around them one more time before I die!' Tears were spilling silently down Eleni's cheeks.

Angeliki looked at the wreckage of her friend and fear for her own safety gave way to compassion. She reached out and

534

touched Eleni's hand. 'All right, Aunt,' she said. 'I'll give them the sovereigns they want.'

Eleni did not reply. She just nodded vaguely in Angeliki's direction.

Hassiotis and the other guerrillas led Angeliki back to the presence of Katis. Still carrying the baby, she took off the pouch of sovereigns from around her neck and dropped it on the desk in front of him. 'Take them!' she said.

Katis seized the pouch and threw it across the room at her. 'These are not the Amerikana's sovereigns; these are yours and we know how you got them!' he said, in a tone implying that Angeliki had been rewarded with gold for her services to the British. 'A million such sovereigns couldn't buy the Amerikana's life,' Katis shouted. 'Traitors must be executed! Now tell us what you know of the Amerikana's sovereigns.'

Katis got up from his chair and walked around the desk to where Angeliki was standing, the baby in her arms. He drew back his hand and slapped her hard across the face. 'I must have lost my senses when he did that,' Angeliki says, 'because when I opened my eyes, the baby was not in my arms but was being held by a guerrilla. He never stopped crying.'

Katis continued to grill her. 'Who did you give the Amerikana's sovereigns to? What was she paying them for?' But Angeliki kept insisting that she had no sovereigns but her own. Finally they handed the baby back to her and told her to go. Shakily she walked out the door. When she neared the gate, she turned around to see Eleni still sitting in the same spot on the threshold of the cellar.

Angeliki started toward her to explain what had happened upstairs: she had tried to give up her own sovereigns to save Eleni's life but the guerrillas realized that whatever Eleni had told them about handing over sovereigns of her own – words wrung out of her by torture – was not true. The two guerrilla guards outside the cellar door stepped forward, barring her way, and motioned for her to leave. As Angeliki paused, Eleni raised a hand in farewell and spoke, the clearest words Angeliki had heard from her that afternoon.

'Don't forget me!' Eleni called after her.

Angeliki raised her hand in response, and stood a moment

trying to think of something to say, then she turned silently and went out the gate.

While Angeliki was being questioned, Ourania Haidis, a stocky, high-strung young woman, was kept waiting in the small pantry, surrounded by piles of shoes taken from prisoners who had been subjected to *falanga* and then killed. When Angeliki had gone, Katis ordered Ourania brought in and asked her the same questions: Where were the three sovereigns the Amerikana had given her? She made the same response – the only sovereigns she had were those her husband had left her.

Ourania and Angeliki were the only women in the village who had gold sovereigns. Eleni must have known it and under the insistence of her torturers, given their names in hope they would come to her aid. But Ourania, like Angeliki, protested that the Amerikana had given her no sovereigns. When Katis slapped her, she became hysterical. They told her they were taking her down to face Eleni. Ourania claims that she and her cousin never exchanged a word. 'She seemed to be in a daze and didn't look at me,' Ourania says, beginning to stammer at the memory and avoiding the eyes of her questioner. 'When I saw her like that, I fainted, and when I came to, they sent me home. We never spoke to each other.'

During the final week of Eleni's life, Glykeria still worked the fields of Macrohori and Vatsounia. She sweltered in the same red wool dress she had worn for nearly three months; her fourteen-year-old body could not keep up with the demands of cutting wheat from dawn to dusk and carrying large stones to build pillboxes for the *andartes*. Because the women from Lia picked on her, hitting her and complaining of her laziness, Glykeria had begun working with the more sympathetic group from Babouri.

Early on the morning of August 28 the women from Babouri, working near the village of Macrohori, had just started the day's threshing when they were visited by an imposing figure, Lieutenant Alekos, who had been one of the instructors of the *andartinas* taken from Lia. He arrived on a

536

fine white horse and informed the threshers, 'You young girls, all those who are unmarried, get ready to leave! You're finished with the harvest, you're all being inducted into the Democratic Army today.'

The girls from Babouri began screaming and crying while the nearby group from Lia, working on an adjacent hillside, jeered. There was such a rivalry between the two neighboring villages that the Babouriote women had always bragged they were spared from being guerrillas because they could cook, clean and care for the troops so much better than the useless Liote women, who were good for nothing but cannon fodder. Now as the women of Babouri wept, Glykeria sat in silent bewilderment. She didn't know if she was to be inducted with them or not. She stood up and asked the lieutenant and he looked at her strangely. 'No, you're not to go with them,' he said. 'You're going back to your village along with the unmarried girls of Lia.'

Glykeria knew she should have felt relieved – her summer-long ordeal was over – but she was filled with a vague anxiety. There were tears in her eyes as she kissed her friends among the Barbouriotes goodbye. She would never see most of them again. The young girls were so inadequately trained before they were thrown into the last doomed battles of the war that many died quickly.

The journey back to Lia took over two hours, and Glykeria walked under the scorching sun with some of the other unmarried girls from her village, including Xanthi Nikou, the sixteen-year-old daughter of the condemned Vasili Nikou. Their route led over the mountain peaks, southwest toward Lia, past the hills of Tserovetsi and Skitari. The girls passed the Chapel of St. Nicholas, tucked in the hidden green valley amid prehistoric grave tumuli. Glykeria made her cross and said a silent prayer as they moved on. Just beyond the chapel they came upon a group of guerrillas, some of the dozens who were camped on the peak of the Prophet Elias just above their heads on the strategic height which overlooked the country for miles. They were hard at work digging a large square hole at the lowest point in a field that belonged to Tassi Mitros, just above a small brook. The girls hurried on past them, not

537

stopping to speak to the guerrillas or to wonder what the ditch was intended for.

They quickened their pace as they passed over the flat, verdant nose of the triangle, the Agora, and then stood looking down on their village from the top of the man-made series of terraced stone steps which the villagers called Laspoura, meaning 'muddy.' From that point Glykeria could make out her own house in the Perivoli, and the sight of it filled her with an inexplicable fear. She could see half a dozen guerrillas outside the gate.

Glykeria and the rest nearly ran down the path toward the Perivoli. Just above the spring, by the mill of Tassi Mitros, they encountered Tassina Bartzokis. At the sight of the bedraggled girls, Tassina began to cry and threw her arms around Glykeria. It was from Tassina that Glykeria and Xanthi learned their mother and father had been condemned to death and were being held prisoner in the Gatzoyiannis house, pending their execution.

The two girls, fourteen and sixteen years old, ran to the gate of the security police station and learned from the two guards stationed outside that it was true. They began to cry at the top of their voices. 'Shush, quiet!' the nervous guards told them. 'We're not going to kill them! They'll probably get a reprieve from Markos any day now.'

Still weeping, Glykeria and Xanthi sat down in the dust outside the gate and refused to move until they were allowed to see their parents. Soon they were joined by the two elder Nikou girls, Chrysoula and Olga, who had heard the commotion and learned that their sister and Glykeria had come back from the harvesting. They added their pleas to those of the two teenagers: 'We won't go home until we see them! You have to let us in!'

It was about eleven o'clock and the uproar caused by the four girls drew nearly everyone in the Perivoli to their windows. Inside the police station's office Katis heard the shouts and cries. He thought in disgust what kind of impression the commotion must be making on the neighborhood. Finally he sent word out to the guards at the gate: Bring in the women; they would be allowed to see the two

538

prisoners. Anything to shut up their caterwauling!

The four frightened girls were led into the good chamber, where Katis stood, his face like a thundercloud. He made a signal to the guards, and soon Eleni and Vasili Nikou were led into the room, both supported by a guerrilla on each side. The two prisoners were dazed and frightened, nearly unconscious of their surroundings. All they knew was that they had been led out of the cellar and they were certain the time for their execution had come. Even when their daughters began to scream at the sight of them, they didn't recognize the children. Both prisoners slumped down on the floor, leaning against a wall. Eleni, catching sight of the familiar iconostasis in the corner, murmured, 'My poor house! What have you come to?'

Both Vasili Nikou and Eleni were bruised about the face, their lips swollen, their eyes livid from blows. They were infested with lice, and Eleni, in far worse condition than the man, sat with her grotesquely swollen legs in front of her. Wailing, the girls threw themselves on their parents and the commotion in the police station became even worse than before. Katis angrily ordered one of the guerrillas to crank up the gramophone and put on a record full blast to drown out the sounds of their laments. The incongruous melody, a raucous *rebetiko* from the sailors' bars in Piraeus, blared out in the breathless noonday hush while the guerrillas and Katis moved closer to hear what the prisoners and their daughters were saying to one another.

Glykeria knelt on the floor in front of Eleni and reached for her. '*Mana*, what have they done to you?' she cried. There was no answer and the girl stared in growing horror at her mother's unkempt hair, unbuttoned dress and ghastly, misshapen legs and feet.

The touch of Glykeria's hand and the sound of her voice brought Eleni out of her daze and she recognized the daughter she had been praying for every day. 'My child!' she said, repeating it several times. Then, speaking slowly to make herself understood, she said, 'Don't worry about me, my soul. Look at you! You're worn to a husk!'

Glykeria pressed her face against her mother's breast and

cried, 'I missed you so! What have they done with the others?'

'The children left,' Eleni replied, stroking her hair. 'They're safe and I don't care what happens to me now. You mustn't cry. I just want you to be well. I don't want to think of you crying like this.'

While Glykeria and Eleni whispered together, the guards taunted Vasili Nikou, who had also recognized and embraced his daughters. He was embarrassed at their tears and at being seen in his wretched condition. 'Go home now, girls,' he said quietly. 'For God's sake, go home!'

'Don't despair, Uncle Vasili,' said one of the guards with a smile. 'Now is the moment to tell your daughters anything you have to say to them. If you have any sovereigns hidden somewhere, tell them now.'

The leathery old cooper turned a look on the man which cowed him into silence, despite the prisoner's black and distorted face.

'Everything I have, my children have,' Nikou said. 'If you've carried the gun for two years, I carried it for nine. I know about war and I know what you're going to do to me. I know it all.' Then he turned back to his daughters and said sternly, 'Leave now. Go back to your mother.' They did as they were told, but on the threshold Chrysoula turned to Katis and spoke one word: 'Vulture!'

'Hold your tongue, Comrade,' said the judge, flushing, 'or you won't leave here.'

Eleni and Glykeria were sitting together holding hands, each trying to stay calm so as not to frighten the other. Eleni told Glykeria she should go home and rest; she looked sick and exhausted. The girl kept asking her mother what she could do for her.

'Rest first,' Eleni told her, 'then look to see if there are any tomatoes in the field and bring me one. Go to Eugenia Petsis – she has our animals – and see if she can send me any milk or *shilira* with you.' She touched the girl's cheek and added, 'If anything happens, I've left several okas of corn and wheat in the house for you, and there's the fields and the animals.'

Glykeria started to protest, but Eleni silenced her. 'You

must save yourself,' she insisted, then she sighed. 'Lucky Constantina Drouboyiannis,' she added.

'What do you mean, Mother?' Glykeria asked, bewildered.

'She's a lucky woman. She saved her daughters and she saved herself.'

Eleni paused and looked at the girl as if struck by an idea. Then she motioned to Katis, who was standing nearby. He came closer in order to hear what she was saying over the blare of the gramophone.

'Comrade Katis,' Eleni said politely, as if speaking to a social acquaintance. 'Could I have a word with you in private?'

'Of course,' he said amiably.

Bracing herself on her daughter's shoulder, Eleni struggled to her feet. She walked with Katis the few steps to the hall that divided the good chamber from the pantry. Glykeria stared after them, but she could hear nothing that Eleni was saying. She saw her whisper to Katis and make a gesture in her direction. Glykeria got the impression that Eleni was begging or bargaining with Katis to spare her daughter from torture or death. The magistrate listened and nodded, then the pair returned to the good chamber.

'Go now, child,' Eleni said unsteadily. 'Go and rest and then come back. I want to see you again.' She stood there, looking at Glykeria. Then she touched her cheek again. 'My daughter, may you live for me as long as the mountains.'

Glykeria gazed at her mother's thin face, sorrowful as that of the Madonna on the family's icon, her eyes filled with hard light, the fine skin of her forehead etched with tiny wrinkles like silk cloth. The dark circles around her eyes made them seem unnaturally large and luminous. She seized Eleni's hand and pressed it to her cheek, feeling the rough fingers against her flesh, wet with her tears. They kissed, and then Glykeria turned and went out the door. When she turned around, she saw her mother standing, framed by the front door of her house, staring after the girl as if to fix her image in her mind, holding tight to the doorjamb for support. Eleni raised her hand in farewell. Glykeria shouted, 'Don't worry! I'll be back!' and then she walked toward the

541

gate. Before it closed behind her, she turned again and saw the face of her aunt peering from the cellar window, her hands clutching the bars. The girl made a sign to her but Alexo seemed not to know her. She was silently shaking her head from side to side.

Glykeria found the Haidis house closed and dark, bare of anything edible. She ran down to where Eugenia Petsis lived in the bottom of the wrecked mill and the kindly old woman insisted that she sit down and eat some *shilira* while she also prepared a plate for Eleni. Eugenia tried to reassure the shaken girl; her own daughter Coula had been taking food to Eleni nearly every day in the prison, she said. Now that Glykeria was back, Eleni's prayers had been answered. All she wanted was for her children to be well. 'Before you go back up to your mother, you must sleep a little,' Eugenia told her. 'You can't let her see you looking like this!'

Glykeria rubbed her eyes, thanked the woman and took the plate of *shilira* back to the Haidis house. On the way she found two ripe tomatoes in the family garden. In the cool darkness of the house, a relief from the blazing noontime heat outside, she lay down on the single pallet where her mother had slept. Eleni's best dark-brown wool dress hung on a wall peg. Seeing it there gave the girl a comforting sense of her mother's nearness. She would just close her eyes for half an hour, she thought, and then she would take the food back up the mountainside to the prison. She was still trembling from the strain of her long walk and the shock of seeing her mother so changed by the torture. She fell immediately into a troubled sleep.

It was about two in the afternoon when Glykeria reappeared at the prison, carrying the *shilira* and the tomatoes. As soon as she approached the gate, she knew something was wrong; all the doors, including the one to the cellar prison, were wide open. The guards outside were sitting casually on the ground, chatting. 'Where's my mother?' Glykeria cried in alarm. 'Where are the prisoners?'

'They're fine, they've taken them to another prison, a bigger one at Mikralexi, over the mountains,' replied one of the guards. He saw the doubt on the girl's face.

542

'I was supposed to bring this food to her and now she's gone,' Glykeria said, as if talking to herself.

'Don't worry, she'll be better off now,' the guard replied, trying to soothe her. 'They just took them. Look, if you don't believe me. Up there.' He pointed. Glykeria followed his arm and saw a procession of tiny dark figures wending its way up Laspoura toward the pass which separated the Prophet Elias from Kastro – the same route she had descended earlier that day. She could see that most of the figures were walking, a few were on horseback. They were too tiny and far off to identify.

'Are you sure she'll be better off there?' Glykeria asked uncertainly. She didn't know what to do. They were so far up the mountain, she could never catch up with them now.

'Of course she will,' responded the guard. 'Go on home now and don't worry.'

But Glykeria went a little higher up, to the cool, green place by Tassi Mitros' mill where her mother and sisters had so often washed clothes, and she sat there in the shade all afternoon, holding the untouched food. Sometime later Giorgina Venetis, descending the path from the heights, found the girl sitting there crying. Giorgina herself was pale and shaking. 'What's the matter, child?' she said.

'They've taken my mother and the others up to Mikralexi and I didn't get to say goodbye to her,' Glykeria answered. 'Who knows how long they'll keep her there?'

Giorgina Venetis looked away, mumbled a few comforting words to the girl and hurried on. She knew where the prisoners had been taken, news that had already begun to spread through most of the village. But Glykeria, feeling better, went slowly back to the Haidis house by herself, ate the food that she had not been able to give her mother, and spent the night lying on the pallet hugging her mother's brown dress in her arms for comfort, alternately praying to God, St. Nicholas and St. Demetrios. 'Whatever I have, I'll give it to you if you bring her back,' she murmured to her familiar litany of saints, her cheek against the rough brown fabric. She repeated the promise over and over until she fell asleep.

*

543

Shortly after noon on Saturday, August 28, thirteen prisoners including the five from Lia were taken out of the cellar of the Gatzoyiannis house and told that they were being moved to a prison in Mikralexi, a three-hour walk over the tops of the mountains to the northeast. It was an exhausting climb, but all the prisoners set out on foot except one, Spiro Michopoulos, who was entirely out of his senses and could only tremble like a man with the palsy. He was put on a mule and a board was tied upright to the raised back of the wooden saddle, then Michopoulos was bound with rope to the plank so that he would not fall off. Except for the trembling of his limbs, he seemed to be unconscious, his head rolling lifelessly from side to side.

The other barefoot prisoners, their legs black and swollen, walked painfully behind, escorted by several armed guerrillas. One of them was twenty-year-old, gnome-faced Taki Cotees. He knew where the prisoners were actually being taken, and it disturbed him that Andreas Michopoulos, only eighteen years old, who had fought as a guerrilla at his side, was about to die.

As the slow procession set out up the path from the Gatzoyiannis house toward the cleft in the mountaintops, they soon approached the Spring of Siouli near the mill of Tassi Mitros, where Eleni had gone daily to draw water. Coming down from the spring was eleven-year-old Kanta Bollis. She carried a pitcher of water in her hands and a small barrel of water on her back. Frightened, the child stepped aside to let the guerrillas and their prisoners pass. As she did, Eleni recognized her smallest daughter's friend. Kanta Bollis remembers that Alexo Gatzoyiannis walked by in a daze, appearing to see nothing, but that Eleni spoke. 'A little water, Kanta,' she pleaded. One of the guards nodded and the procession stopped. The child came forward and held out the pitcher toward Eleni.

'I didn't say a word to her, I was too afraid,' Kanta Bollis recalls. 'Her hands were black and blue and they were trembling as she bent down to take the pitcher. She was so thin and pale, like something that came out of a cemetery! After she took a few swallows, she looked at me with terrible

eyes and said, "Oh, my child, my little Fotini, where is she?"
Then she started crying. When she did that, one of the guards
grabbed the pitcher from her hand and shoved it back into
mine. "Go! Go!" he said.'

At the spring itself, thirteen-year-old Antoni Makos had
stopped to drink. He remembers Spiro Michopoulos tied to a
horse, his shirt bloodied in stripes where he had been beaten,
a cloud of flies following him. One of the guerrillas came over
to the boy, demanded his water flask and drank from it. Then
another guerrilla snapped, 'Hurry up! Let's go before the
planes see us!' Antoni Makos stared hard. He would remember and recognize the caved-in elfin face of the guerrilla Taki
thirty years later.

Above the spring, as the procession struggled up toward the
terraced steps called Laspoura just at the entrance to the pass
between the two mountain peaks, it encountered a group of
village women, brown faces burned the color of a copper
skillet under their dark kerchiefs, bent double under the loads
of wood they had been gathering for the guerrillas. As the
women moved aside for the prisoners to pass, one of them,
Fotina Makou, burst into tears at the sight of her brother
Vasili among the prisoners. The cooper did not look at his
sister.

Once the captives were led over Laspoura – the ancient
stone steps made slippery by mud and trickling water – they
moved into the narrow pass between the twin peaks, out of
sight of the villagers as suddenly as if they had fallen off the
earth. They entered an idyllic green, flat area, an Eden no one
would expect to find cradled among mountain peaks. It was
like the palm of a cupped hand; the fingers were the peaks:
Kontra, Skitari, where so many had died during the battle of
Pergamos, and Tserovetsi. Rising sharply on their right was
the Prophet Elias, the small chapel riding the height like a
ship's figurehead.

After struggling up the slippery steps of Laspoura, it must
have been a relief for the prisoners to enter the Agora – the
marketplace of the Hellenistic community that lived among
the peaks three hundred years before Christ. Just beyond the
Agora, the fields in the palm of the hand became slightly more

uneven and were gently terraced in three steps, leading down to a musical brook shadowed by spreading plane trees. On the far side of the fields lay the Chapel of St. Nicholas, where, three centuries before, itinerant monks painted glowing frescoes on its walls. Just beside the chapel stood three large grave tumuli studded with anonymous upright boulders sunk deep into the ground. Spirits of the dead have peopled this silent place since long before recorded history.

As the prisoners entered the Agora, they encountered a second group of women from Lia returning from a work detail. Among them was Giorgina Venetis, a garrulous village woman who had once found Eleni weeping while she grazed her flock and invited her in for a cup of tea. As they watched the prisoners pass, then resumed their walk toward Laspoura, the women began to argue about whether the prisoners were being taken to another village or were about to be killed. Giorgina was more curious and daring than the rest. She decided to double back and covertly follow the group to find out their fate. Once the prisoners passed out of sight over a small rise in the distance, she left the other women and began shadowing the procession.

The prisoners walked on, the rustling of naked feet treading over dry leaves of the plane tree, until they passed the rise. They looked down upon the rolling pasture studded with autumn crocuses and saw the mass grave, several meters square, waiting at the bottom of the terraced field next to the brook. The march of the condemned came to a halt as they realized their journey was to end not in Mikralexi but in this ravine, filled with the calls of wild birds and the crystal sound of running water. At the same moment, nearly thirty guerrillas began to descend the side of the hill of the Prophet Elias toward them.

According to the guard, Taki, the members of the execution squad were selected from guerrillas stationed atop the Prophet Elias who came from distant villages and would have no emotional ties to the victims. The lieutenant who was in charge was from Macedonia.

The prisoners were lined up in a row on the edge of the second-lowest step of the terraced field, just above the bottom level where the grave pit had been dug. They were stood at the edge of the field so that when they fell, it would be easy to roll the bodies over the terraced edge of the step into the grave below. Spiro Michopoulos couldn't stand, so he was propped in a sitting position.

At the back of the line of prisoners rose the height of Prophet Elias topped by its small chapel. To their right a huge plane tree, roots bared by the erosion of the stream, stood like a sentinel. In front of them towered the connected summits of Kontra, Skitari and Tserovetsi, where Eleni had walked on the day she was sent with a message for Spiro Skevis, telling him it was safe to move his guerrillas into the village. This was the last thing she would ever see.

Twenty-six guerrillas were assigned to shoot the thirteen prisoners, two to each one. There was grumbling among those assigned to kill the women. Despite the number of deaths they already had on their souls, it was a task they found distasteful. The lieutenant made it clear that they had no choice. The executioners and the condemned stood a few yards apart. The officer in charge was in a hurry to get the job over with. He wanted his men to return to their sentinel duties atop the Prophet Elias as soon as possible.

Giorgina Venetis tracked the prisoners back across the Agora and was just climbing the small rise that cut off her view of the terraced fields when she was frozen in her tracks by a scream, a woman's voice, the most terrible sound she had ever heard. The harsh cry contained all the sorrow and pain of the universe and it formed itself into words: 'My children!' Then there was a volley of shots.

The sound paralyzed Giorgina. Suddenly she felt a warm sensation along her legs: in her fear, she had lost control of her bladder. From somewhere she summoned the strength to begin running, and she didn't stop, sliding and stumbling down the muddy steps of Laspoura, until just above the Perivoli, out of breath, and still shuddering from the terror of that cry, she found Glykeria Gatzoyiannis sitting by Tassi Mitros' mill in tears. Giorgina spoke a few words to the girl, then hurried on, saying nothing of what she had seen and heard.

547

Taki, the only person who admits to being an eyewitness to the killings, says that one of the women, the one with the chestnut hair, screamed and fell to the ground in the instant before the guns opened fire. He says that when the lieutenant went from one body to another, administering the *coup de grâce* to the skull, her wound did not bleed.

The execution was over in minutes, the bodies thrown together, face down, into the grave, where they were covered with enough rocks to be hidden from view. Then the guerrillas of the execution party filed back toward the Prophet Elias, leaving the verdant ravine near the Chapel of St. Nicholas to the silence that had reigned there for centuries.

CHAPTER EIGHTEEN

On August 29, 1948, the day after the executions in Lia, Nikos Zachariadis still insisted that with the people of Greece behind them, the Communist guerrillas would soon achieve victory. 'Our strength is the people's trust,' he announced. 'And until the rights of the people finally prevail, our slogan will remain: "Everyone to arms, all for victory."'

But that victory was a fantasy to be nourished in blood for another year before it was finally abandoned. By the end of August, after the fall of Grammos, guerrilla bands operating in central and southern Greece were finding it difficult to get arms and supplies. The strongest concentrations of guerrillas were based on two mountain strongholds with their backs to Communist countries – Mourgana in western Epiros and Vitsi in western Macedonia, where the borders of Yugoslavia, Albania and Greece converge.

The main body was on Vitsi, and since it was so dug in that it was clear the nationalist army could not dislodge it before winter, the Greek generals turned their attention to the Epiros Command in the Mourgana mountains. They assigned the whole Eighth Division plus a brigade to the assault and code-named it Operation Taurus to show their determination to capture Mourgana despite two previous failures.

The offensive began on September 10, with five brigades attacking the guerrillas on all fronts. The insurgents held on to their positions with fierce desperation for several days, but a daring maneuver on September 16 put nationalist forces on Mourgana's summit and forced the guerrillas to abandon their fortress at last. As they retreated, one group moving northwest into Albania and another eastward through enemy lines toward Grammos, they took all the civilians from the occupied villages with them at gunpoint.

After the fall of the Mourgana, the surviving guerrillas scored a few temporary successes during the autumn and winter, retaking some sections of Grammos and launching surprise raids on important towns in northern Greece which they held for several days before being forced to withdraw. These victories were fleeting, however, and by late spring of 1949 the government troops were ready to deal the death blow to the Communists.

They began by clearing the Peloponnesos, the hand-shaped peninsula in the south, of all guerrilla bands. Then they moved against the insurgents in the mountains of central Greece, forcing them to withdraw northward toward the final showdown on Vitsi and Grammos in the summer of 1949.

The Greek generals prepared carefully for the confrontation, conscripting 30,000 new recruits and bringing in the latest weapons from the United States, including fifty-one Curtiss Helldivers, the most effective ground-support aircraft in operation. They code-named the final campaign Operation Torch and assigned eight divisions, more than 50,000 men, to the assault.

The guerrillas, too, tried to prepare themselves. They had only 5,000 men on Grammos and 8,000 on Vitsi, but they controlled the high ground and were dug into strong defenses. To make up for the losses they had suffered through the winter and spring, they conscripted everyone they could find, including boys and girls as young as fourteen. Among the adolescent conscripts sent to defend Vitsi to the death was the fifteen-year-old daughter of Eleni Gatzoyiannis – Glykeria.

DIASPORA

AS THE FIRST daylight pierced the darkness of the ravine below the Chapel of St. Nicholas and illuminated trails of dried blood leading to a pile of rocks by the stream, Glykeria was still lying on the pallet in the Haidis house, holding her mother's brown dress in her arms. She was awakened by a knock on the door and opened it to see a middle-aged guerrilla with a dirt-stained beard and eyes narrow with apprehension.

'You mustn't blame me for bringing you this news,' he said, glancing nervously around the empty house and then back at the small blond girl in the red dress. 'Yesterday afternoon we executed your mother. I fired one of the shots myself.' Taking a breath, he hurried on, 'It wasn't right to kill her, but we had no choice! We were under orders. It was your own villagers who betrayed her.'

Glykeria put her hands over her ears, trying to block out his words. Then she fell to her knees, reaching for the brown dress. She began to scream '*Mana! Mana!*,' a sound so full of pain that the neighbors closed their shutters and avoided one another's eyes. The guerrilla moved a step closer. 'Now you have to come up to the security police station to answer questions,' he said. 'They sent me to bring you.'

Choking on her sobs, Glykeria pleaded that she couldn't walk, but the guerrilla took her by the arm and pulled her up. Eleni's dress fell from her lap to the floor.

The girl cried aloud all the way up to the Perivoli, and the few village women they passed averted their faces and scurried out of her way. She was led into the small tin-roofed

551

storage room, where Sotiris Drapetis was waiting for her. He asked where her mother and grandfather had hidden valuables, but she cried that she didn't know; how could she? She had been away at the harvest for the past three months. Sotiris frowned but he didn't hit her, only warned her to think carefully; he would call her back until she was ready to cooperate. When she was dismissed, Glykeria hurried out the front door and saw a grotesque face peering at her from the kitchen window, swollen and black from blows. It was Spiros Migdalis, a tinker from Babouri who had been caught when he sneaked back from Filiates, hoping to lead his wife and children to the nationalist side. Glykeria saw his tall wife standing behind him, also badly beaten.

The girl hurried out the gate and down the familiar path as the reality of her mother's death pressed in on her like a suffocating weight. When she reached the Church of St. Demetrios, now being used as the stable, she looked up at the brightly painted icon of the saint on horseback set in a niche beside the door. She stared at the saint, as real to her as any neighbor in the Perivoli, and anger bubbled up in her chest. Raising a small fist, she began to scream, 'Damn you, St. Demetrios! Don't you see what they've done? Why don't you strike them down? Why don't you blind them, tear out their eyes?'

She heard a stirring behind her and spun around to see a man in guerrilla uniform who had been feeding his horse in the churchyard. It was Antonis, the aide of Colonel Petritis who had lived in their house and worried over Nikola because the boy reminded him of his own son. He came toward her, his head bent to hide the tears in his eyes. 'I know what's happened, child,' he said quietly, 'but I couldn't do anything to stop it. Your mother was a good woman who never harmed anyone.' Then he walked away, leading the horse.

When she entered the Haidis gate, Glykeria was approached by two of the family's small goats who had been left free and were scavenging in the bean field below. One had been nicknamed 'Orphana' by the children because it was an orphan, and the other was called 'Skoulerikia' because the two dewlaps of flesh hanging from its ears looked like

552

earrings. The kids nuzzled her, crying plaintively for her to feed them; the sight of their mournful gold-irised eyes fed her anger. She shoved them away, crying, 'We're all orphans now and you can die for all I care! We're all going to die!'

The only woman in the village brave enough to speak to Glykeria was the feeble-minded shepherdess, Vasilo Barka, who had long been the butt of Glykeria's cruel teasing. Drawn by the bleating of the hungry kids, she came to Glykeria's door and offered with tears in her eyes to care for the animals for free. 'It's the only thing I can do,' she cried, hugging the girl. 'Your mother was like one of my family.' Remembering the many times her mother had scolded her for baiting the unfortunate woman, Glykeria hung her head as she mumbled a few words of thanks.

Later that day, as Glykeria wandered the fields, looking for something to eat, neighbors like Tassina Bartzokis and even relatives like Kitchina Stratis, her mother's first cousin, turned away without a word when she wished them 'Good day.' There seemed to be no one left on earth who would share her grief.

The carrion birds of the guerrillas arrived at her door the next morning in the persons of Foto Bollis, Christos Skevis and Elia Poulos, the die-hard Communists who had returned to the village after Operation Pergamos and been rewarded with administrative positions. 'Give us everything, whatever you have,' Foto Bollis demanded. He opened a wooden chest and found a few pounds of flour and some ears of corn that Eleni had left. The men loaded everything in cloth sacks. 'Leave me enough to bake a loaf of bread,' Glykeria pleaded. 'We've been authorized to confiscate everything,' Bollis replied. To the others he said, 'I saw some ripe corn in the fields. Get it.' As he turned away, the girl took off one of the slippers she was wearing and threw it at him, bouncing it off the back of his head. When the door slammed, she curled up in a ball, still clutching her mother's dress, and prepared to die.

Later that day Eugenia Petsis came up from the ruined mill nearby where she lived. 'Come to my house, child,' she whispered. 'Your mother asked me to look after you, and I

553

will. But you have to promise not to try to escape or they'll kill us all.' Glykeria nodded obediently. Before she walked out the door, she took off the red dress she had been wearing for three months and put on her mother's brown dress, the only garment left in the house.

The next morning Stavroula Yakou tracked the girl down in the Petsis mill and ordered her back to the security police for more questioning. Stavroula took pleasure in persecuting the daughter of the Amerikana, one of the girls she had envied when her own family was living off the scraps from the Gatzoyiannis table. She made Glykeria her special victim during the next two weeks, arriving every morning to lead her up to the security-police station for questioning, assigning her every afternoon to work details: carrying wounded guerrillas and supplies to Tsamanta. It was a dangerous journey, leading an overburdened mule over the mountain paths through heavy shelling. Glykeria moved like an automaton, deaf to the cannon fire and the cries of the wounded. She often returned from Tsamanta on the back of a mule, so tired that she would doze off and fall from the saddle. At the end of each day's journey, Stavroula Yakou would be waiting for her with the words 'Now you're going again, this time for Olga and next for Kanta's turn.'

One morning after the daily interrogation session, Stavroula was leading Glykeria back down the path when she stopped at the door of her mother, Anastasia Yakou. As they were talking, a procession on horseback passed by. It was Sotiris Drapetis leading the Migdalis couple and another prisoner back to Babouri. All three had been savagely beaten and had their hands tied behind their backs. Sotiris preened under Stavroula's admiring gaze. 'Hey, girl,' he shouted to her as she smiled at him, her teeth gleaming like bleached almonds. 'After we go round that bend down there, listen and you'll hear three bullets. I'm going to kill them and dump them in the ravine.'

Within minutes, just as Sotiris had promised, they heard three shots and Stavroula's mother crossed herself. 'The poor souls are gone,' she sighed. But later they learned that Sotiris had only been amusing himself by frightening the prisoners. They were put to death the next day in a public execution in

Babouri's churchyard before the eyes of the entire village, including their elderly parents and small children, who were warned that if they made a sound, they, too, would die. Koula Migdalis was a strong woman and it took several rounds to kill her. Afterward the guerrillas left the bodies in the churchyard for several days as an example to the villagers.

The guerrilla command decided to send a last group of children for the *pedomasoma* to Albania. They would have to go over the mountaintops to the northeast, because the roads toward Tsamanta were under heavy shelling.

Dina Venetis, who had been released after the trial, was approached by a woman guerrilla who told her to prepare her nine-year-old son, Vangeli: 'He's leaving today.' Dina ran down to her house. 'I found him some clothes,' she says, 'a little jacket. Some shoes he never liked. They were too tight but I made him put them on.'

The mothers and children were gathered in the village square. 'There were about a dozen of us from Lia,' Dina recalls. 'Other groups of mothers and children came up the mountain from other villages. One boy had been bitten on the way by a rabid dog. "Don't worry, he'll be fine once he's inside," the guerrillas told us. "Our doctors will take care of him." When they got to Albania he went crazy. They shut him up in a room and tied him because he was biting his own hands. He died in terrible pain.'

The mothers were told they could accompany the children as far as the Chapel of St. Nicholas. 'When we got to the place,' Dina says, 'I kissed Vangeli and turned away. I was afraid to cry in front of him. As soon as he took a few steps, the heel came off one of his shoes and I watched him limping all the way up the mountain.' When she mentions the shoes she always starts to cry. 'He was nine when he left, and when he came back, he was sixteen years old,' she adds, recovering her composure, 'but he looked twelve, no more, thin as an ax handle, his bones pushing through his skin.'

As news of the planned attack on the Mourgana filtered back to the refugee community in Igoumenitsa, the Gatzoyiannis family passed each day in increasing suspense. Marianthe Ziaras, who had joined her family in Filiates after her escape, said that Eleni and Alexo were in jail but had not been tried. Then word reached them that a young *andartina* from Lia named Xantho Michopoulos had been found gravely wounded on a battlefield near Vrosina and was carried by soldiers to a hospital in Filiates. The girl had been conscripted into the same group as Kanta and was a cousin of Spiro Michopoulos. She would surely know what was happening in Lia. Kitso Haidis decided to go to Filiates to learn what he could. Nitsa said she would go with him. The children were left in the care of their grandmother, Megali, and their uncle Andreas.

Xantho Michopoulos did not live long enough to reach Filiates, but before she died she told the soldiers the names of the five civilians executed in Lia. When Kitso arrived at the army hospital in Filiates, he learned of his daughter's death. Crazed with sorrow, he lunged for a wounded guerrilla nearby and tried to strangle him in revenge. Soldiers pulled him away.

Nitsa heard whispers as she shopped in the open market of the town. When she went to the house of Lukas Ziaras, one look at the faces of the tinker's family confirmed her worst fears and she collapsed on the floor, screaming. She continued to keen for her sister all night until her voice was completely gone and she could only croak. In the morning Nitsa boarded an army truck back to Igoumenitsa, but her courage failed her and she told the children in a whisper that she had caught a cold which had developed into laryngitis. She added that the soldiers were about to attack the Mourgana villages and their grandfather had stayed behind to follow the army into Lia and learn the fate of their mother. 'She knew about the executions all along and never said a word,' Olga exclaimed later, 'even though I was going around Igoumenitsa in a red kerchief, like a bride.'

Kitso stayed behind in Filiates to nurse his grief alone and wait for the liberation of Lia. He walked about the old town, his features blurred by a stubble of beard, his erect posture replaced by the shuffle of an old man. He was a true peasant, loath to bare his feelings, suspicious of everyone. He became obsessed with the idea of returning to Lia to see the truth with his own eyes. The soldiers said it was only a matter of days before the attack on the Mourgana would begin.

The plan of Operation Taurus called for two brigades of government troops to advance toward the Mourgana villages from the south in a diversionary action and to unleash a downpour of bombs and heavy artillery on the guerrilla fortress until the morale of the 1,500 men barricaded there was shattered. Then two other brigades, creeping along the peaks of the Albanian border down from the northeast, would launch the main thrust of the attack, a surprise assault on the highest peak of the Mourgana. If it fell, the guerrillas would be cut off from their escape route to Albania and the pipeline through which they had been receiving reinforcements and supplies.

The assault, bombing and artillery fire from the south began on September 10, two weeks after Eleni's execution. The rain of death was heavier than the village had ever seen. Several houses were hit by bomber planes. One village woman was struck by a piece of shrapnel which entered her mouth and projected from the side of her head, but she would not die for several days.

The guerrillas ordered the Liotes to gather in caves high above the Perivoli. Most of the people spent the night of September 11 huddled in the same caves where they had hidden from the Italians and where their ancestors had taken refuge for centuries. Glykeria was crowded in with her second cousin, Vangelina Gatzoyiannis, and her five children. Before dark, a bomber swooped low over the clearing, disgorging a blizzard of paper leaflets. Gregory Tsavos, the elderly field warden who had spoken up for Eleni at the trial, picked up one of the leaflets and read it aloud to the crowd that gathered. It was signed by General Thrasyvoulos Tsakalotos, the commander of the First Army Corps, whose Eighth Division was leading the assault, and it told the villagers to take courage and stand firm: 'We are coming to liberate you. We will soon be in your village.' Their eyes swollen from lack

557

of sleep, the Liotes exchanged nervous whispers as they crawled back into the caves; the soldiers were on their way but they knew the guerrillas would never leave them behind to welcome them.

On the morning of September 12, tense, battle-weary *andartes* roused the village, ordering all civilians to prepare to evacuate. 'Just take what you can grab,' they shouted. 'Don't talk and don't delay. They're going to blow up every house!' The guerrillas were in a murderous rage. Villagers remember that a young man, a stranger from another village, balked at being evacuated and when he asked a question, they shot him on the spot.

The man put in charge of the evacuation in Lia was Elia Poulos. All during the day of September 12, as the bombs and artillery pounded the mountainside, he ran to every house and hiding place ordering the people to make ready to leave for Albania. Wherever he went he repeated the same refrain: 'Don't take anything. You'll get plenty of food in Albania. The pots are boiling just over the border.'

As Glykeria sat near the mouth of a cave, Stavroula Yakou pushed through the milling crowd and ordered the girl down to her house, where she began loading all her possessions on Glykeria's back: blankets, rugs and her best dresses. Bent double under the weight, Glykeria cried, 'Please, Stavroula, I can't carry any more!'

'You have to!' the woman retorted, then began to wheedle, 'You don't have a blanket of your own to carry, and when we get to Albania, I'll let you share mine.'

By dusk the villagers were gathered by the caves. Vangelina Gatzoyiannis had her sixteen-month-old son tied to her back and her three-year-old daughter on her shoulders. The wounded and elderly who couldn't walk were packed into large wicker baskets on muleback, balanced by baskets weighted with pots, clothing or children. Dogs and goats followed their owners, barking and bleating. Live chickens were suspended from scythe handles, saddles and packs.

In the bedlam, Elia Poulos frantically tried to make certain that everyone had been accounted for. He realized that Constantina Drouboyiannis, who had been exonerated at the

558

trial, and her friend Sofia Papanikolas were missing. Turning on Sofia's mother-in-law, he shouted, 'If those women don't appear in five minutes, I'm having you shot!' The throng fell silent, but as the last light faded, the two missing villagers were seen approaching, struggling under heavy loads of possessions.

One old woman remained behind when the village was evacuated – the ancient, blind crone Sophia Karapanou. As the artillery exploded all around her, Sophia lay down on her pallet to sleep. She had survived the arrival of the Germans when they threw her neighbor Anastasia Haidis into the flames, and if this time her lamp had burned all its oil, she was resigned. Her roots were too deep in the earth of Lia to leave it now. She did not intend to die on the road to a foreign land.

It was midnight of September 12 when the great throng of villagers lurched slowly into motion, driven by the mounted guerrillas and Elia Poulos. A chorus of wails rose toward the heavens as the multitude set out toward the west. They were leaving the fields they had scraped out of the rocky hillsides, the homes they had built stone by stone, the bones of their ancestors. Many of the women and children had never been outside the Mourgana mountains; now they were headed for a future they couldn't imagine. They staggered forward, the thud of feet on the red earth, carrying their children and invalid parents. 'Move along, gypsies!' shouted Elia Poulos, drunk with the importance of his task.

Glykeria walked like a beast of burden beside Stavroula Yakou. She left Lia with nothing but the brown dress she was wearing; no blanket, not even stockings or shoes. She remembers the sound of hundreds of feet shuffling along beside her, the moans of the wounded, the sleepy protests of the children, the frantic cries of the abandoned dogs and goats. She turned around to see the shadows of the village, eerily dead, not a candle shining in a window. Her mother's body was back there, her sisters and brother were far away and now she was being taken by her mother's killers into the Communist world.

The guerrillas tried to keep the procession off the road,

moving through ravines in order to avoid the government bombers. The Liotes passed through Babouri and found it as desolate under the cold moonlight as their own village. The inhabitants had already been evacuated and were somewhere ahead of them on the way to Tsamanta. They stepped around corpses, including one which Glykeria recognized as the farmer Elia Gatos, who had been shot days before. Made careless by his reputation as a loyal Communist, Gatos had refused to answer Nikos Vetsis, head of the intelligence division under Koliyiannis, when he was asked which village houses contained large beams that could be used for fortifications. 'I'm not going to become an informer on my own neighbors,' he said. 'Find out yourself.' His impudence was punished instantly with a bullet and his body was left unburied.

Soon after she passed the corpse of Elia Gatos, Glykeria nearly stepped on an eyeless, bearded head grinning up at her, projecting from the earth. A woman nearby heard her yelp of fear and whispered, 'That's a priest who was executed. They like to bury the priests with their heads above ground.'

Tsamanta was three miles to the west of Lia, a mile below the Albanian border in a natural cleft between the mountains. The Liotes arrived there just before dawn and found that many streams of peasants from other villages had come together into a wide river of refugees, their eyes reflecting the flames of battle, their faces grimy and tight with fear. As dawn broke, baring them to the sight of the bomber planes, they were told to hide in a ravine shaded by plane trees. Later in the morning a mist obscured them from the attackers, and Elia Poulos and the guerrillas drove the Liotes up the slopes leading to Albania. At the border itself, they passed before the astonished eyes of Greek-speaking Albanians, gathered to watch the exodus. They hissed at the refugees, 'What are you doing here? Why have you left your homes to come here?' But the Greeks only shook their heads and pressed their lips together. Life as they had known it ended that day in September 1948, and none of them would see Greece again for years.

Elia Poulos escorted them a mile over the border to the

Albanian town of Leshinitsa, where they were handed over to other guerrillas. There was a distribution of food: small round pellets of bread made from the hard hulls left after wheat had been ground into flour. The rough bread cut their lips and was impossible to chew. There were some water-boiled squash, and as one woman, Athena Haramopoulos, remembers, every family was given one leek. 'One leek to a family!' she exclaims. 'I asked Elia Poulos, "Where are the boiling pots of food you promised us? What am I going to feed my babies?" As he walked away, Poulos replied, "You're lucky you're alive, woman!" I cursed him, "May a black bullet find you!" and it did before another year was out.'

The evacuation of the Mourgana villages left the mountains solely in the hands of the guerrillas, who braced themselves for the main assault, which they expected to come from the south. They thought they could still hold on to the Mourgana heights, turning them into a 'Greek Stalingrad' that would be invulnerable. They were counting on the fortifications they had dug on the southern and eastern sides, and on the steady flow of arms they would receive from Albania to the north.

The two brigades of nationalist forces made their way down from the northeast along the frontier and managed to take some outposts. But as they approached the highest peaks, they were stopped by strong fire from the guerrillas as well as from Albanian long-range artillery shooting over the border. General Tsakalotos then decided to take a bold initiative. Ignoring possible international repercussions, he ordered Greek artillery to fire on the Albanian guns. He also sent a crack infantry company inside Albania to approach the key Mourgana height from the rear. At the same time other units crept along on the Greek side of the border over slopes so steep that the guerrillas had left them thinly protected, thinking them impassable. On Thursday, September 16, the critical highest peak of the Mourgana was seized by nationalist forces. They sent a white flare arcing into the sky between the ghost towns of Lia and Babouri. It was a signal to the two government brigades on the south to press forward and connect with those on the north, cutting off all paths of retreat. It was also notice to the guerrillas that their citadel had fallen.

Guerrilla leader Kostas Koliyiannis ordered an immediate retreat, but because the escape route through Tsamanta was already closing, he pushed his men eastward toward Granitsopoula and the Kalamas River, crossing it and running for the Zagoria mountains.

At the vanguard of the retreat was the battalion of Spiro Skevis, including Rano Athanassiou, the friend and neighbor of the Gatzoyiannis girls who had been taken only three weeks before from testifying at Eleni's trial and conscripted into Skevis' fighters. Without learning the outcome of the trial, Rano was plunged into training; the Taurus assault on the Mourgana was her baptism of fire. Eventually she became a seasoned guerrilla, even giving propaganda speeches in occupied villages of northern Greece, but her first encounter with battle terrified her. 'As we retreated, we passed through Lia just as the mountains to the north were overflowing with government soldiers,' she says. 'We went down to Kostana, and as we pushed eastward, there were dead bodies everywhere – horses, men, young girls. I saw the dead body of an *andartina* I knew from Tsamanta, a beautiful girl named Eleni, her long blond hair all matted with blood.'

Rano and the rest of the Skevis battalion continued to push on toward Zagoria, treading gingerly through the hills above government-held Yannina, close enough to see the lights of the city below. They finally reached the mountains of Zagoria and found remnants of the guerrilla forces who had been driven from Grammos. There the exhausted, starving survivors of the DAG would spend a bitter winter before making the last stand of the war the following year.

The government soldiers entered Lia on the heels of the retreating guerrillas, reaching it on September 18, but there was no one left to be liberated. With the soldiers came some of the men who had fled Lia nearly a year before in the wake of the guerrillas. One of the first to arrive was Foto Gatzoyiannis, who had acted as a guide for nationalist troops approaching from the south. He rang the church bells of Holy

Trinity to see if he could coax any villagers out of hiding, but the only answer to his summons was the slow tapping of Sophia Karapanou's cane as she emerged from her hut. Foto seized her by the shoulders, demanding to know where the villagers had gone. 'I don't know, my boy,' the old woman croaked, turning her sightless eyes to the heavens. 'For days now I haven't heard a human voice, only the sound of the crows.' Foto looked up and saw that she was right; clouds of black birds were circling over the village.

Soon he heard someone else approaching. It was another village woman, Mihova Christou. Mihova had hidden in a cornfield on the night of the evacuation. She told Foto that she was among the women returning from a work detail on the day of the executions and had seen the condemned being led to the killing ground. Mihova agreed to show him the area where he would find the bodies of his wife, Alexo, and his sister-in-law Eleni.

Foto slept in his empty house that night and the next day was joined by several more village men who had approached slowly behind the soldiers, taking a roundabout route, stepping carefully from stone to stone to avoid the land mines, which were everywhere. The newcomers included Kitso Haidis and young Dimitri Stratis, a son-in-law of Foto and Alexo. Within hours they were joined by Costas Gatzoyiannis, Foto's seventeen-year-old son, who had also come from Filiates, searching for news of his mother. Foto, his son Costas, Kitso Haidis and Dimitri Stratis decided to set off at once, with Mihova Christou as a guide, to find the mass grave.

As they climbed the path through the Perivoli, they walked through a landscape that seemed to have been stripped of its inhabitants with the suddenness of a thunderclap. Every small cave and ravine was full of pots, blankets, rotting food and piles of clothing. The bloated bodies of dead mules, goats and sheep lay in their path, and packs of stray dogs watched them with yellow eyes.

When they reached the Vrisi, surrounded by caves, they found an open mess hall left by the guerrillas: dozens of pots of coagulated food hanging over burned-out fire pits, carcasses of slaughtered lambs and goats suspended from plane trees and covered with shiny, quivering black coats of flies. Several tables for officers were set with fine china dishes that must have been taken from homes in wealthier towns. Infuriated at the sight, Costas Gatzoyiannis began smashing the fragile plates in a frenzy of anger and grief until his father pulled him away.

Mihova Christou led them up Laspoura and through the Agora. When they reached a spot overlooking the fields below St. Nicholas, they found a pair of leather sandals placed side by side on a rock. Foto Gatzoyiannis identified them as ones he had made for Alexo. There was a choked sound from Costas as the men silently wondered whether Alexo herself had kicked them off and left them there, a sign to those who would come looking for her, or whether someone, guerrilla or passer-by, had placed them there to mark the grave site.

Mihova Christou pointed to the field below and said, 'I'm not going any farther. You'll find them somewhere there at the bottom of the ravine.'

They didn't have to search. There had been no rain since the execution and trails of dried blood led the way to the grave. They found shell casings at the execution spot and when they came closer to the pile of rocks, the stench brought them to a halt. The boy Costas turned away. Foto began pulling up the boulders. The first came loose, releasing a cloud of flies which rose like furies from hell. They looked upon the body of the gray-haired cooper, Vasili Nikou, lying face down in his familiar tan jacket. A wire was bound around each wrist. Foto Gatzoyiannis had seen many bodies in his life; he hadn't even balked at cutting two fingers off a dead Italian soldier to get his gold rings. Now, holding a handkerchief to his nose, he reached down to feel in the pocket of the cooper. He found a pouch still containing some tobacco and an official order for Nikou's execution, signed by Kostas Koliyiannis.

As Costas Gatzoyiannis watched from a distance, Foto and Kitso pulled away more boulders. Next to Nikou lay Spiro Michopoulos, then his nephew Andreas; finally they found Eleni and Alexo Gatzoyiannis. The bodies were all face down, bound together with wire. The men recognized Eleni by her light-chestnut hair, which still shone with glints of red and gold in the sunlight. Foto identified Alexo by the black home-spun skirt and a small patch she had sewn to cover a hole in the back of her black sweater. Foto's cheeks were wet with tears, but he had lost another wife in his youth and had learned to keep tragedy at arm's length. His son Costas lacked his objectivity. At the sight of his mother's body the boy began to scream that he would put on a uniform and pay for her death with the blood of every Communist guerrilla. His lust for vengeance ultimately cost him his life. Costas enlisted in the army as soon as he left the village and fought with suicidal recklessness. Five months after his mother's death, as he stood in an exposed spot shouting curses at the guerrillas, he was killed by a bullet fired by a young *andartina*.

Kitso Haidis was shaken by racking sobs as he stood over the corpse of his daughter. The sight of the broken body beneath the mass of burnished hair released all the tears he had never shed for his other four daughters, dead in their doll-sized coffins. He grieved for them and for this favorite child, whom he had abandoned in anger without ever saying goodbye.

There was no way the dead could be moved. The men built a small retaining wall of stones and mud below the grave site so that the stream would not wash away the ground; then they removed the boulders and covered the bodies with dirt.

The sun warmed the newly turned earth, and insects and birds filled the ravine with sound as the men shouldered their tools and set out back toward the village. Kitso dreaded the ordeal ahead of him – telling his grandchildren what had happened to their mother.

Two days after the liberation of Lia, a refugee arrived in Igoumenitsa with a message for the Gatzoyiannis children that their grandfather would be returning that afternoon from the village. Olga and Kanta anxiously put chairs out on the small cement balcony so that they could see him the moment he stepped off the army truck.

Nikola paced nervously. To distract him, his uncle Andreas

took the boy out to the wooded spot, his 'thinking place,' and drew a chalk checkerboard on a flat tree stump there. Using black and white pebbles, Andreas set about teaching him to play checkers. But Nikola could not concentrate on the game, and as the shadows lengthened, he made excuses and left. He went to sit in the dust beside the road on the edge of town waiting for the first glimpse of his grandfather. His chest hurt and there was a tightness, like unswallowed food in his throat.

It was late afternoon when one of the canvas-topped army trucks roared past me, stirring up clouds of dust, and I glimpsed my grandfather's shock of white hair in the back. I shouted and began to run after the lumbering vehicle, nearly catching up, when I saw my grandfather turn his face away from me, a week's growth of beard making him look old and ill. '*Papou!*' I called as the truck picked up speed, entering the long shady avenue roofed with plane trees. The dust and exhaust stung my lungs as I hurtled into the tunnel of shade, tears of frustration dimming my sight. As I emerged into the sunlight where passengers were climbing out of the parked truck, I spied my grandfather walking away from me. Staggering, trying to catch my breath, I reached him and seized his arm. 'What is it, *Papou?*' I asked. 'Where's *Mana?*'

He looked away, new furrows of pain inscribed on his forehead. He gazed up at the unfinished house on the hillside, then reached into his pocket and pulled out two 100 drachma notes. 'Take this, go down to the harbor and buy sweets,' he said in a choked voice. 'Buy *reveni,* enough for many people.' Then he walked off, leaving me standing in the dust, clutching the money, staring after him.

The sun impaled me to the spot as a hollow ballooned inside me. He had told me in the only way he could. I had never seen my grandfather part with money for a frivolous reason. Those two wilted 100 drachma notes were to buy sweets to serve the mourners who would come to our door with condolences. I tried to believe that I was mistaken; perhaps the sweets were for a celebration. But his face had told me otherwise.

I ran at top speed to the pastry shop and my hands trembled as I waited for the huge white cardboard box to be filled and elaborately tied with a golden ribbon. I grasped it by the knot and sprinted toward our house. As I came near, a wave of sound rushed out, draining the last strength from my legs. It was a cry of despair, a sinuous, rising and falling chorus of pain, the funeral laments of my sisters. The box became too heavy and fell from my hand into the dirt. I couldn't deceive myself any longer. The sound of their grief knotted my stomach and I ran, not knowing where I was going, until I hurled myself on the cool grass near the tree stump with the checkerboard. I pressed my face into the musk-smelling earth and clapped my hands over my ears, trying to shut out the awful screams that were the death knell of my mother.

Olga and Kanta were standing on the balcony watching the stooped figure of their grandfather climb the hill. They both realized at the same moment that he had grown a stubble of beard, the sign of mourning for a death in the family. They reached for each other's hands and Olga said in a tight voice, 'Perhaps he didn't have a razor in the village.' When he entered the door, they both ran toward him shouting, 'What happened to *Mana*?'

Kitso looked at them wearily. 'They've taken Glykeria into Albania,' he said in a toneless voice. 'But she's all right.'

'Never mind Glykeria!' snapped Kanta. 'What about *Mana*?'

The old man looked out toward the sea, which shone like a sheet of hammered gold under the setting sun. He couldn't say the words. 'Glykeria's alive. They didn't hurt her,' he said. Then they understood.

Olga rushed out on the shaky spiral staircase and vomited over the railing. Kanta seized an icon of the Virgin framed in glass from the mantelpiece and smashed it on the floor, stamping on it with her feet and screaming, 'You could have saved her but you didn't!'

At the sound of the uproar, two refugee women who lived on the other side of the house hurried in. They understood at

567

once what had happened. One saw Fotini, pale and wide-eyed, backed in a corner. She picked up the girl, crooning, 'My poor child!' But Fotini turned into a fury, kicked and bit the woman, who dropped her, startled. Then Fotini ran out of the room, down the staircase and into the shadows, taking refuge in the foul-smelling ditch that served as a latrine. After a while, when the stench became unbearable, she crept back into the house, now crowded with what seemed to be the whole population of Igoumenitsa. Many of the refugee women, long prepared for this moment, had already baked cakes and sweets as condolence gifts. One of them offered a piece of baklava to the little girl. She dried her tears on her sleeve and with the first bite, the awful pain of her mother's death began to lift.

Nitsa's voice still hadn't returned to normal, but she added her hoarse wails to the general confusion. Andreas didn't say a word through it all, but as the twilight faded, he looked around the room and asked, 'Where's the boy?' No one replied.

I had been lying in the grass for a long time when I realized that someone else was there. I looked up and saw my uncle seated on the edge of the large stump with the checkerboard. He beckoned and said softly, 'We never finished our game.' I nodded and came to sit opposite him, but the checkerboard swam in front of me. Wordlessly I shook my head. Then he gathered me in his wiry arms and carried me as if I were a baby back up to the house. The room was suffocatingly close with crowded bodies, sympathetic murmuring, wails and sobs and the odor of cooked food. As Andreas carried me into the room, everyone fell silent, looking at me. Out of the corner of my eye I could see a neighbor woman at the fireplace leaning over a bubbling vat of black dye and carefully dropping in my sisters' bright-colored clothes.

Christos Gatzoyiannis received the news of his wife's death in a letter sent to the room he rented on Front Street in Worcester for $8 a week. When he saw the name 'Gatzoyiannis' on the back he thought for a moment that,

568

after two years of silence, Eleni had somehow managed to get a letter out to him. A closer look showed that the envelope had been mailed from Athens by Yianni Gatzoyiannis, the eldest son of Alexo. When Christos opened it, a tiny newspaper clipping fell out. It was from the Greek paper *Kathimerini,* dated September 5, 1948:

CHILDREN AGES 5–14 YEARS
From the Area of the Mourgana Transported by the Guerrillas into Albania

YANNINA, 4 SEPT. – A guerrilla who surrendered in the Mourgana area described the abduction of children ages 5–14 whom their mothers, beaten and at gun point, escorted to Koshovitsa inside Albanian territory where they were forced to abandon them and brought back under guard to their occupied villages. The dramatic march of mothers and children into Albania took two days amid lamentation and mourning.

The same guerrilla disclosed that an improvised guerrilla court in the Mourgana villages sentenced to be executed the sixtyish Alexandra Katsoyiannis and Vasilis Nikou, Spiro and Andreas Michopoulos, and Eleni Katsoyiannis, wife of an American citizen.

The bit of newsprint fell to the floor as Christos unfolded the letter from his nephew. It stated in a few words that the condemned had been executed. 'I was all alone and when I read that I got crazy,' Christos recalled twenty-six years later. ' "Killed my wife?" I cried. "For what? Why?"

'The people from the restaurant came around to see me and I said I wasn't going to work for a week. I stayed home, mourning my wife, writing letters everywhere, trying to find out the details, but there were no answers. I had no one.'

In Leshinitsa, just over the Albanian border, Glykeria was still struggling under the weight of Stavroula Yakou's possessions. When she pleaded exhaustion, Stavroula pointedly reminded her that she was in a Communist country now, and without a powerful friend to protect her, her chances of survival were small.

The Greek exiles at Leshinitsa were divided into groups of ten and sent on foot to Delvino, fifteen miles away, where they were met by a lumbering convoy of battered army vehicles which stretched for miles into the distance, ferrying the refugees to Aghies Sarantes, twenty miles farther west on the coast. The port was choked with displaced families from all over northern Greece who were to be sent by ship to northern Albania, far from the reach of the Greek army. The Liotes waited for two days, sleeping in a mosque, until room was found for them on one of the flat-bottomed barges. It was in Aghies Sarantes that women from Lia happened on a group of children headed for Rumania with the *pedomasoma*. Among them were some of those who had been taken from Lia only days before.

Dina Venetis began frantically searching for her son Vangeli. She found him in a large barnlike structure where Albanian women were stripping the children and boiling their clothes to kill the lice. Vangeli blushed at having his mother and other women see him naked. He hung his head and Dina saw that it, too, was covered with lice. She borrowed a pair of scissors from another woman and began to clip the boy's hair down to the scalp, but she cropped only half of it before he was summoned by one of the guards and pulled out of her grasp to collect his wet clothing. She would not see Vangeli again for seven years.

After two days the villagers were driven onto barges for the two-day trip up the Adriatic coast to the port of St. John (or 'Shengjin' in Albanian) and then inland to Shkodra. They were crammed together, 250 to a boat, unable to move. For peasants who had never seen the sea, the journey seemed like the ride to Hades on Charon's raft. The overladen barge yawed and rocked on the stony surface of the water as women and children screamed and became seasick. Soon the deck was awash with urine and vomit. Glykeria squawked in protest as one neighbor threw up right in her lap. Vangelina Gatzoyiannis recalls that an old woman urinated on a small sack of dry porridge that she had managed to carry with her.

Later, when her children began to starve in Shkodra, Vangelina cooked it and fed it to them anyway.

Athena Stratis, the third daughter of Alexo Gatzoyiannis, was sitting near Glykeria trying to hold on to her four small children. Certain that they would tumble over the low sides, she cried, 'Help me, Glykeria! Take one of the children! They're going to die!'

'I'm dying myself!' Glykeria moaned, holding her stomach. But that night, when Alexo's daughter Niki pushed her way to the side to vomit, the little girl fainted and nearly slipped into the black water. Glykeria reached out and caught her by the back of her dress, saving her life.

When they disembarked at St. John, trucks took the refugees twenty miles north, to the city of Shkodra on the bank of Lake Skutari, which extends into Yugoslavia. The exhausted peasants were deposited before a two-story dilapidated barracks which had been used as stables. 'This is where you're going to live,' they were told by guerrillas. 'You'd better start cleaning it out, because you're sleeping here tonight.'

Glykeria gagged as they began shoveling out the manure that had accumulated on the two floors of tiny cubicles around a large central hall. That night she slept in one of the stalls along with fifteen other people from her village, including her cousin Athena and Tassina Bartzokis and their six children. She had nothing to sleep on; Stavroula had disappeared with her blankets, but Tassina put the girl under a rug with her three babies.

Glykeria lived in the barracks in Shkodra for six months. The daily ration of food was one scoop of beans and a piece of rock-hard bread for each person. The refugees spent the daylight hours searching the surrounding area for pieces of firewood and wild greens that they might eat, and washing their lice-infested clothing in the lake. Glykeria had never been so hungry in her life. There was an old woman named Nikolena Fanayea in the same cubicle who was dying of a cancer that blocked her throat. She couldn't swallow the crusts of bread, only the center, so Glykeria would beg from her the soggy, chewed remnants, and if any of Tassina's

571

babies didn't finish its bread, she would snatch the crust out of the child's hand before its mother noticed.

In March of 1949, as an icy wind whistled through the barracks, a rumor spread among the hundreds of refugees that all unmarried women were going to be sent back to Greece to the battlefields of Macedonia as *andartinas*. The frightened girls, including Glykeria, fled the barracks and hid in a deserted mosque, but Stavroula Yakou found them there and told Glykeria, 'Don't bother trying to hide, I'm making sure they send you.'

Glykeria turned for help to an old woman who was the mother of her godfather, Nassios Economou, and therefore shared a responsibility for her welfare. Together they searched out the central office of the guerrillas and petitioned a bored official. 'This girl doesn't belong in the army; she's only fifteen,' the old woman quavered. 'I was at her baptism and can testify to her age.'

The man searched through some files and slapped a folder on the desk with an air of finality. 'Her name is written here by officials from her village. She has to go,' he announced.

They returned to find the barracks in an uproar as screaming girls were being dragged into two army trucks parked outside the door. There was a guerrilla from Lia named Yianni Kepas identifying the ones to be taken; the same young man who had played the tragic heroine in the Skevis brothers' skit, 'Homes in Ruins.' He pointed to Glykeria, and two men came toward her while one of her girl friends clung to her and wept.

As parents watched their daughters led away to fight for a doomed cause, knowing that they had little chance of survival, their voices rose in a great outpouring of grief. The sound was suddenly punctuated by hysterical screams, like the cries of a wounded animal, startling the crowd into silence.

They looked around to see Stavroula Yakou being dragged toward the truck by guerrillas, kicking and scratching.

'You've made a mistake! I'm a married woman! You need me here!' she was screeching as she writhed in their hands. Although Stavroula had won a position of influence with the guerrillas through her beauty and cleverness, she was terrified of gunfire and had never expected to be conscripted as an *andartina*. She fought with the strength of blind panic and managed to break free, but the guerrillas caught her by the back of her dress, ripping it open.

As they carried Stavroula back toward the truck her dress was open to the waist, exposing her breasts as she struggled and bit her captors. The villagers watched slack-jawed with astonishment. In a society where even a woman's hair must be hidden, Stavroula should have been shamed for life, but she seemed oblivious to her condition as she let loose a stream of curses. The guerrillas threw her into the truck while the other girls drew aside; the thud of her body was audible in the hush. Instantly Stavroula scrambled out, still screaming. As the guerrillas tossed her ignominiously back in, Yianni Kepas signaled for the driver to start and the truck roared away until Stavroula's cries were lost in the distance. The Liotes took a grim satisfaction in seeing the despised collaborator humbled, but no one was as pleased as Glykeria, the only one who rode off toward the battlefields with a smile on her face.

While Glykeria was headed for Macedonia, the other four Gatzoyiannis children, dressed in black mourning, waited in Igoumenitsa for the papers that would take them to America. They had been moved out of the relative luxury of the unfinished house into one of the corrugated-tin Quonset huts which the soldiers were building in the fields below to accommodate the flood of refugees. The eight members of their family lived in one room and did their cooking at outdoor fires, drew water from a nearby stream and used the fields for a toilet.

Christos had written the children asking if they wanted to live with their grandparents in the village, make a home in Athens, or join him in America. Their grandfather, Kitso, tried to frighten them into staying in Greece. 'You'll never see the sky for all the smoke from the factories,' he predicted gloomily. 'You'll never eat olive oil, feta cheese or lamb again. It's an evil country filled with foreigners. You girls will marry Italians or worse!'

573

But the children were adamant in their determination to sail to America, as their mother had commanded. Kanta wrote a letter to her father saying, 'We're strong. We'll work in the factories and keep house for you.' At the age of fifty-six, Christos realized that his days of married bachelorhood were over; he would finally have to face the responsibilities of raising four children, including the son he had never seen.

Because their father had been a United States citizen since before 1920, their papers were cleared quickly despite Greece's wartime status. Shortly after New Year's Day, 1949, the children were notified by the American embassy in Athens that they had only to appear at the consulate to collect their passport.

Olga announced to her grandfather that before she left Greece, she was determined to go back to the village and transfer her mother's body from the unmarked ravine to a church. Reluctantly, Kitso agreed. The two of them set out for Lia along with the fourth daughter of Alexo, Stavroula Vrakas, who would join her father, Foto, to disinter her mother's body at the same time. They found the village desolate, inhabited only by a half-dozen men living like squatters, waiting for their families to return.

Olga and Kitso slept in the Haidis house that night, but in the morning the girl awoke to find her grandfather gone. After waiting several hours, she walked down to Foto Gatzoyiannis' house, where she asked her cousin Stavroula, 'Have you seen my *papoul* He's been gone all morning.'

'So has my father!' Stavroula exclaimed. 'They must have sneaked off to dig up the bodies without us so we wouldn't see them!'

The girls hurried up toward the Chapel of St. Nicholas, but when they reached the spot, the two men had already finished depositing Eleni's and Alexo's remains together in a small box which Kitso had fashioned of rough wooden planks. It was about three feet long and lettered on the front in crude, angry splashes of white paint were the words: 'Eleni C. Gatzoyiannis, 41, and Alexandra F. Gatzoyiannis, 56, murdered by Communist gangsters.' Olga ran to open the box, screaming, 'I want to see my mother!' but her grandfather held her back.

574

The two old men, followed by the two weeping girls, carried the box down toward the village. When they reached the Spring of Siouli they set it down to rest. Waiting until the men had turned their backs, Stavroula Vrakas darted up and opened the cover. Both girls peered inside to see only one skull, the head of Alexo, with bits of flesh and hair still clinging to it. Olga began to shriek: 'There's only one head in there! Where's my mother?'

Her uncle Foto glowered. 'What do you want to see your mother's head for?' he snapped. 'It's in there, but in pieces!'

Kitso grasped Olga's arm and spoke more kindly, 'Your mother's hair is just the same, shining like silk, but her skull is broken – perhaps when they piled the boulders on the bodies . . .'

Olga couldn't stop the hysterical cries which poured out of her all the way down to the Church of St. Demetrios. As the box was deposited without ceremony in the church ossuary, she was seized with the idea that the Communists had killed Eleni by stoning her – a form of execution that was not unheard of in the villages. She wept for her mother all that night until she fell asleep exhausted. Then, she says, Eleni appeared to her in a dream, her face wet with tears, and said, 'No, my child! They didn't kill me with rocks. They shot me here,' indicating her heart.

The dream startled Olga awake, and as she sat watching the sun come up over her familiar mountaintops, she was relieved to think that her mother had died swiftly. As they set out on foot back to Igoumenitsa, she felt a kind of peace. Her mother lay in the neighborhood Church of St. Demetrios beside the bones of her beloved mother-in-law, Fotini, and now Olga could turn with a clear conscience to the journey that lay ahead of the children, fulfilling the destiny that Eleni had wanted for them.

The departure from Igoumenitsa was a tearful one, for when the four children sailed on the ferryboat that would take them to Corfu, to board a larger ship for the port of Athens, they left their grandmother and Nitsa and Andreas behind, perhaps forever. Their grandfather was escorting them to the capital to put them on the ocean liner that would take them to New York.

Megali and Nitsa wailed that they would never see the children again while Andreas grimaced with the effort of hiding his emotion. But just as the warning whistle signaled that it was time to board, Fotini ran up to him with a parting gift, a coin she had been hoarding, worth less than a penny, and Andreas began to cry.

Kitso Haidis set off on the journey in a foul humor, still trying to convince the girls not to leave Greece. They spent the night in Corfu in a hotel room on the harborside and the children gawked at the arcaded streets and the huge public squares. The next morning they boarded a ship headed for Athens' port of Piraeus. Nikola watched the island slip behind the horizon without emotion. Since the night they left the village he had been careful not to let himself become attached to any one person or place. Only the farewell to his grand-mother and his uncle Andreas hurt a little, but he frowned and scuffed the toes of his new oxfords and managed to look unconcerned.

Yianni Gatzoyiannis, the handsome twenty-nine-year-old son of Alexo and Foto, was on hand to meet them in Piraeus and take them by bus into the city of Athens, which was beyond anything the children had imagined, even though it still bore the marks of war and the collapsing Greek economy. Yianni worked as a waiter in an Athens restaurant and the children couldn't get over his fine clothes and city manners. He led them to the Hotel Cyprus, where they gaped at the high ceilings and huge doors. They were all put in one room and their grandfather showed them the greatest wonder of all: a toilet in a cubicle down the hall, where he demonstrated how to pull the chain so that it flushed. Fotini and Nikola were fascinated by the exciting sound of running water. As soon as they could evade their grandfather's eyes, they scurried down the hall to pull the chain and watch the waterfall over and over again.

They were invited to Yianni's small house in Kolonaki for dinner, where the children shot sidelong glances at his beauti-ful nineteen-year-old wife Katie, with her short curly hair, blue polka-dot dress and lipstick. They all whispered that she must be an immoral woman to be painted that way.

On February 19, 1949, shortly after their arrival, Kitso herded the family to the American embassy, where they were given a passport in the name of Olga, who had just passed her twenty-first birthday. On the way out they rushed up to examine the American guard standing outside a sentry box, the first black man they had ever seen. They stared and poked at the discomfited Marine until their grandfather dragged them away muttering, 'It's a human being, idiots! What do you think it is?'

There were many mysteries to ponder during the two weeks in Athens. Olga grappled with the intricacies of a telephone, holding the receiver at arm's length. Her grandfather took her to see one of the great department stores, Diamantopoulos, where she walked straight into a mirrored wall, then became insulted when she addressed the smartly dressed mannequins with a polite 'Good day' as her mother had taught her and did not receive an answer. 'They're statues!' sputtered her exasperated grandfather. 'Do you want the whole world to know you're an ignorant peasant?'

On the last day of February, Kitso led the children back to the port of Piraeus, trying all the way to talk them out of leaving, but when the launch came to take them out to the converted troop carrier, the *Marine Carp*, Kitso's lower lip began to tremble beneath his white mustache. 'Take a good look at that sky; you'll never see it again!' he growled, wiping a sleeve across his eyes. Nikola watched his grandfather impassively. He felt nothing at leaving Greece, only trepidation over what lay ahead. He followed his sisters into the launch; when they reached the ship they climbed the shaky ladder up to the deck, crowded with passengers in strange, foreign-looking clothes. As the ship began to pull out, he looked back and saw the shrunken figure of his grandfather frantically waving the walking stick he had carved from the branch of a cornel tree, polished to a dark sheen by the touch of his hands over the years.

The journey of the *Marine Carp* took twenty-one days. The

ship first went east to Haifa, Israel, and then turned back, stopping at Palermo, Sicily, before heading west toward New York. When it pulled into the Italian port, Nikola watched a flock of ragged beggar children no older than himself who crowded the dock begging the passengers to throw them food and cigarettes, which they puffed with practiced aplomb. He realized that if it weren't for a parent in America, he would be a beggar too. Because Olga and Kanta were confined to their hammocks with seasickness in the crowded dormitory, he was left to his own devices. He spent the journey trying to teach himself the English alphabet and numbers in order to impress the father who would be waiting in New York.

On the morning of March 21, 1949, the *Marine Carp* steamed into New York harbor. Most of the immigrants rushed to marvel at the Statue of Liberty, the 'Saint Freedom' Christos had written about, but Nikola looked with dismay at the land, where dingy gray snow lay in the hollows. He realized that he had left a country where oranges and lemons were now ripening under a brilliant blue sky for this dismal, unwelcoming place.

A muscular seventeen-year-old boy from the village of Babouri, Prokopi Koulisis, stood near him at the rail. As the ship pulled closer to the dock, Nikola noticed the swarm of automobiles filling the streets. 'Is America at war?' he asked the older boy in alarm. 'Why are there so many vehicles rushing around?'

'In America, ordinary people have cars just like diplomats and ministers in Greece,' Prokopi explained. Nikola silently digested this fact. He had never known anyone who owned an automobile.

At the dock, the excited passengers could make out a throng of people waiting to welcome them. In the very front was a small, portly man with a smart felt hat and a three-piece suit visible under his overcoat. Prokopi Koulisis knew Christos Gatzoyiannis, and while Nikola searched the waiting faces without recognition he felt the other boy's strong arms lifting him off his feet.

Christos Gatzoyiannis described the scene in English twenty-five years later, when he was eighty-one years old: 'I was on the dock watching the boat. Olga recognize me. And I waved to them. Prokopi Koulisis, he picked Nikola up and showed him to me from the deck. First time I see my son. Oh my tears! My heart broke that minute.'

The old man paused, trying to collect himself while two small grandchildren played around his feet. 'They start to come out,' he went on doggedly. 'I hugged him, his little arms. They was so cold! My own childrens!' He turned apologetically toward the machine that was recording his words. 'I think I have to stop now, because I'm going to cry.'

Nikola was less moved by his first sight of his father, who was smaller than the patriarch he had always imagined. The boy stood awkwardly apart from the tearful reunion of Christos with his daughters, then he wandered over to the side of the pier, examining the steely depths of the water far below. He heard someone snap at him: 'Get away from there! What do you think you're doing?' Nikola reflected that he didn't even know this man and he was already ordering him around in a threatening voice.

But when he saw the rented automobile that would drive them to their new home in Massachusetts, Nikola began to be impressed by the wealth and importance of his father. And when they stopped somewhere along the way to buy gasoline and he heard Christos speak to the attendant, he decided his father must be a man of exceptional intelligence to have mastered this harsh-sounding foreign tongue.

A tentative spring was pushing buds up through the snow of the Vitsi mountains when Glykeria reached the front lines. The guerrillas had taken away her mother's brown dress and given her a baggy uniform along with cleated boots to cover her bare feet. She was assigned guard duty shortly after her arrival and remembers hearing the unexpected notes of a hymn wafting through the air from the direction of the government emplacements to the south. It was the triumphal Easter psalm, 'Christ Is Risen.' She peered through her field glasses and saw the soldiers in their foxholes cracking red eggs together to celebrate the resurrection of Christ. Although she prided herself on her toughness, her eyes filled at the thought that somewhere her sisters were enjoying the familiar rituals of the Easter season without her.

Glykeria quickly demonstrated that she was hopeless as a fighter. She fell asleep on guard duty, handed over her gun to a fellow guerrilla even though it was a capital offense, and ran screaming for cover every time the soldiers began to strafe their positions. When a friend of hers from Babouri, a girl named Athena Langa, was cut in half by machine-gun fire, Glykeria cried for days and refused to take up her gun. It was finally decided to make her a telephone operator so she could work at the switchboard in the relative safety of an underground bunker. She soon became adept at handling the calls from the field, working with three other *andartinas* in the subterranean room. By night they laid the telephone cables in the ground, deep enough so that the bombs would not sever them, and fortified them with land mines.

The sight of the government soldiers so near inspired Glykeria with the ambition to cross over to the other side. She knew, however, that she would be in mortal danger from both armies, for many *andartinas* had tried to infiltrate the government lines and the soldiers were deeply suspicious.

The Gatzoyiannis family in Massachusetts learned that the villagers evacuated from Lia were taken to Shkodra. One day Glykeria received a letter that had been sent to the barracks there and forwarded to her after being opened by the guerrilla censors. It was from Olga and inside was a photograph of her family standing in front of their new house in Worcester. Olga wrote that they were praying every day for Glykeria to escape and join them in America. After studying the photograph, she carefully folded the letter around it and put it in the pocket of her uniform.

A few days later Glykeria was called to guerrilla headquarters and confronted by a short, swarthy lieutenant who informed her that an examination of her records showed she was below the age to be conscripted and that she was free to return to the barracks in Albania at once. She stood there blinking, thinking that if she left, she would be losing her only chance to escape. Trying to sound convincing, she protested that she was determined to fight for the revolution. The lieutenant eyed her suspiciously. 'Your mother was executed and you say you're loyal to us?' he asked. Glykeria retorted that she was a true Communist and that was why her family had abandoned her. The officer listened skeptically. 'I'll look into your background and decide what to do,' he said.

Glykeria lay awake that night certain that her only hope of escaping was about to be snatched away. The next morning she and another girl were ordered to prepare graves for two guerrillas who had stepped on a mine and died in the night. They reached the spot where the mangled bodies lay, and Glykeria almost cried out in relief when she recognized one of them as the dark lieutenant who had called her in the day before. She gave the corpse a sharp kick with her cleated boots and spat into the powder-blackened face, 'You piece of shit!' Then the girl, not five feet tall, began dragging the heavy body toward the grave.

Glykeria quickly became hardened to sights that would have sent Kanta into a nervous faint. During the times she left the bunker to drink water from a nearby spring, Glykeria only stared curiously when she passed a severed leg, blackish-yellow and hairy, crawling with fat white worms; she closely examined a decapitated head, its swollen tongue protruding from the gaping mouth. During the height of a battle she once found a stream running red with blood from the bodies clogging it higher up the mountain. 'But I was so thirsty, I drank the water, blood and all,' she says now, laughing at her callousness.

Vitsi, where Glykeria was based, was the best fortified of the two remaining DAG strongholds, with 8,000 guerrillas. Grammos, to the west, had only 5,000. On August 2 the Greek army began a diversionary attack on Grammos with heavy artillery shelling and aerial bombardment. As expected, the guerrilla command rushed all reserves to the battlefront. Eight days later the nationalist artillery suddenly turned around and attacked Vitsi to the east, hitting the unprepared insurgents from five different points. The guerrillas fought with the strength of desperation, knowing that after three years of struggle everything depended on the outcome of this battle, but the government soldiers, particularly the expert

LOK commandos, made deep penetrations into their lines. By the time the DAG gave up and ran in confusion toward Albania, there were 997 guerrilla corpses rotting on the mountainsides of Vitsi.

Glykeria was working in the underground bunker with one other telephone operator on August 10 when the nationalist forces turned their attention from Grammos toward Vitsi. Over the static of her earphones she heard the downpour of artillery shells and bombs outside and knew that the soldiers were approaching. Suddenly the telephones in the guerrillas' front lines, which had fallen silent more than an hour before, crackled into life. A strange male voice asked, 'Who is this?'

'What is the password?' Glykeria replied automatically as she had been taught.

There was a pause. 'I don't know,' said the voice.

Glykeria held her breath and glanced around, but the girl working with her, Marika, was busy speaking into her mouthpiece. Glykeria thought for a moment. She was almost certain that the voice on the other end was a soldier, not a guerrilla trying to trick her. She could visualize exactly where he was standing; she had placed the cables there herself.

'Listen carefully,' she whispered, keeping one eye on Marika. She described where the guerrilla officers were based and where the underground pillboxes were concealed, directing the enemy fire against her own comrades. As soon as the mortars began to hit home, ever closer to her own position, an *andarte* rushed into the bunker and told the operators to retreat. He handed Glykeria two of the heavy yellow suitcaselike telephones to carry.

The two girls emerged into a night illuminated by the red glow of bullets whizzing past their heads. They tried to dodge and run uphill in the direction the guerrillas had gone, Glykeria staggering under the weight of the telephones. She had been told that in battle, combatants may not realize they've been hit by a bullet even as their life's blood flows out, and she kept setting down the phones and running her hands over her body to check for wounds.

When the two girls reached a spot where they could look back, they saw that the government troops were almost upon

582

them. Glykeria seized Marika's arm. 'Let's give ourselves up!' she whispered.

The older girl stared at her in the flickering light, then reached for the rifle slung over her shoulder. 'Are you suggesting that we betray our comrades?' she exclaimed, leveling the gun at Glykeria's chest. The two girls stood, frozen in indecision as Glykeria waited for the bullet to tear into her. Then an artillery shell screamed close over their heads and Marika turned and disappeared into the shadows.

Glykeria left the telephones and ran, tumbling into a deep ravine nearby. She curled up behind a rock, making her body as small as possible. Shivering in the darkness, she thought she could hear the harsh breathing of others around her, but there was no movement.

Glykeria cowered behind the rock for a long time, not daring to look up, when she heard the sound of running feet. Then she heard a voice saying, 'This way, lieutenant, sir.' She knew that if it had been a Communist, he would have said 'Comrade Lieutenant' instead of 'sir.' Cautiously she peered over her rock and saw the silhouette of a man wearing a round, flat cap with a feather on it – the uniform of a nationalist commando. He flinched as she jumped into his path, waving the photograph of her family in one hand and screaming, 'Mr. Lieutenant, I give up! The Communists killed my mother! My father's in America! I'm with you!'

As the soldiers came forward to take a close look at her, Glykeria suddenly heard cries from all over the ravine: 'I surrender!' – the voices of her fellow *andartinas* who had fallen behind in the retreat.

The soldiers roughly herded the prisoners back toward their camp, where they were collected into a barbed-wire enclosure. Glykeria sat near a Macedonian peasant woman with a cradle strapped to her back. The *andartinas* watched nervously as a wounded soldier lying nearby, blood pouring from his mouth and nose, struggled to reach his rifle, shouting, 'Let me shoot them all! I'm dying and these are the women who killed me!'

By the light of dawn the guarded prisoners could see a spectacular view of the battle above them as the soldiers drove the guerrillas up the corpse-littered peaks. The number of prisoners in the compound grew and Glykeria trembled as she saw soldiers beat captured *andartinas* with their gun butts because the women would not speak Greek, only their Macedonian dialect.

Their captors took this as proof that they were loyal to the Communists, who had promised to create a separate Macedonian state in northern Greece.

Glykeria saw a mounted figure of terrifying splendor plowing through the crowd of prisoners toward her, a Greek officer in the uniform of a colonel, a gaunt, sunburned man in his mid-fifties with a brush mustache and glasses. He pulled up his white horse directly in front of the girl, probably singling her out because her fair hair, ruddy skin and wide forehead among the darker faces around her reminded him of his home province.

He examined the child in the guerrilla uniform and said, 'Hello, little one. Are you from Epiros?' He introduced himself as Colonel Constantinides from Vrosina, a village only fifteen miles from Lia on the Kalamas River. When he learned that Glykeria was from Lia, the colonel asked her if she knew Kitso Haidis. 'He's my grandfather!' she exclaimed.

The officer smiled. 'I've slept in his house,' he said. After asking her more about her family he said, 'Wait here until I come back. I'm going to get you out of this place.' He returned within the hour and took her to the headquarters tent, where she was told to sign some papers and was questioned about the positions and fortifications of the guerrillas. A soldier with a small camera snapped a picture of the uniformed girl, solemnly pointing out to the colonel and other soldiers the mountains from which she had come.

Colonel Constantinides told her that he had arranged for her to go to the detention center in Kastoria where she'd be treated more humanely than the prisoners suspected of Communist loyalties, who would be sent to Kozani. 'I know a man from your village who owns several stores in Kastoria,' he said. 'He's a pillar of the town and can arrange things that others can't. I'll have him get you out of the detention camp

584

and look after you. His name's Christos Tatsis. Do you know him?'

Glykeria eagerly lied to the colonel, saying that she did, and he succeeded in having her sent to the prison camp near Kastoria. Christos Tatsis, a tall, graying man with a large nose and a good-natured grin, came to visit the girl several times, but it took two weeks before he could convince the military authorities to release her into his custody.

On the rainy day she emerged from the iron gates of the camp, Glykeria was driven to the police station in town to sign more papers denying any Communist affiliation. Then the shopowner gallantly held out his umbrella to shelter the girl for the short walk to his home, but Glykeria, painfully aware of the figure she made in her filthy uniform and oversized boots, her hair matted and tangled, her whole body covered with red welts from her infestation of lice, refused. 'Please, Mr. Tatsis, let me walk behind you,' she begged, 'so that nobody will guess that you know me.'

The shopowner set about transforming the ragged little guerrilla with the help of his elderly mother and his sister. They burned her uniform, bought her new dresses and cut off her long braids, which were too tangled to comb. Every day the sister bathed her in a large wooden trough and applied a homemade ointment to the red welts. They fed her until her face resumed its former roundness. Finally Christos Tatsis sent a telegram to his cousin Leo Tatsis, who owned a wholesale grocery business in Worcester, Massachusetts, and would know how to get in touch with Christos Gatzoyiannis.

On the night of August 24, 1949, in the cabbage-rose-papered bedroom she shared with Kanta and Fotini in the first-floor tenement her father had rented for his new family on Greendale Avenue, Olga Gatzoyiannis had a dream about her mother. It was four days before the anniversary of her death. In the dream, Eleni told her eldest daughter that she should instruct the other children to take off the black of mourning and allow themselves to sing and dance again, because Glykeria was alive and would soon find them.

The next morning Olga went into the bathroom where her

father was shaving and told him about her dream. Christos stared gloomily into the mirror and said, 'It probably means that Glykeria was killed last night, wherever she is.'

He sounded so certain and resigned that Olga began to cry. When the telephone rang, she was sobbing too hard to answer it, so her father threw down his razor and picked up the receiver. The caller was Chrysoula Tatsis, the young wife of Leo Tatsis, who had been one of the first women from Lia to immigrate to the United States before the war. She began to break the news gently. 'Christos, have you had any news of Glykeria?' she asked.

His face fell. 'No, I think she must have been killed by now,' he replied. 'Olga had a dream about her last night and I'm afraid it's a bad sign.'

Olga stifled her sobs to hear what her father was saying. She was electrified by a whoop of joy and the sound of her father shouting, 'Chrysoula, you bring that telegram over here and I'm going to kiss you, married woman or not!'

The remnants of the guerrilla forces who had been driven out of the mountains of Vitsi in mid-August regrouped with the last of their surviving comrades on Grammos for a final desperate stand. On August 28, 1949, the highest peak of Grammos was taken by the nationalist forces and the guerrillas were routed. It was exactly one year to the day since Eleni Gatzoyiannis had been executed. Two days later, all hostilities between the guerrillas and the nationalist army ceased. The war was over.

On February 10, 1950, the steamship *LaGuardia* pulled into New York harbor, where Christos Gatzoyiannis waited to meet the last of his children. He took Glykeria directly back to the house on Greendale Avenue, which had been readied for her arrival with new furniture of dazzling maroon velvet. The children had changed from black to new clothes in bright colors. Over the protests of her father, Kanta had even bobbed her hair.

A dozen Greek immigrants from Lia crowded into the small living room. Reporters from the local Worcester paper waited to record Glykeria's arrival in her new country. The girl was photographed smiling, holding a doll in Greek costume. Her father told the reporters that now she would have to learn all over again how to be young and happy.

That night the five children sat up talking excitedly, laughing and crying as they recounted the adventures of the twenty-one months since they were separated. They avoided the subject of their mother's death because the wound was still too fresh.

Although their father had provided three beds for them, they all fell asleep huddled together in one, just as they had slept on the floor of the kitchen before the hearth in the Perivoli next to their mother. Eleni was not with them but she had accomplished the goal for which she struggled through a decade of war and revolution and for which she ultimately died.

Her children were together and safe in the land she never lived to see.

PART FIVE

DISCOVERY

But from each crime are born bullets
that will one day seek out in you
where the heart lies.

— PABLO NERUDA

THE PAIN THAT NEVER SLEEPS

WHEN FATE PRESENTED five children to my father, who had lived all his fifty-six years as a bachelor, he assumed the role of a Greek paterfamilias, shouldering the burden of our upbringing, which had always been our mother's responsibility.

Shortly after our arrival the diner where he had been working as a short-order cook closed down, but he donned his best three-piece suit and dove-gray felt hat, and with me at his heels, walked the streets of Worcester until he found another job in a restaurant which paid $50 a week.

There was no way we could survive on his salary, so my three eldest sisters were sent to work in a Greek-owned factory that produced baked goods, where a knowledge of English wasn't essential.

My sister Fotini and I, eleven and ten years old, were sent to the local public school, which had no provisions for non-English-speaking students. On the first day we found ourselves in an ungraded class filled with children of every shape and size, who we quickly realized were all retarded. Soon I managed to learn enough English to be promoted to a regular grade. To my surprise, the teacher didn't beat her students but draped a comforting arm around me when I struggled to recite aloud, a maternal gesture that touched a well of loneliness within me.

Although Fotini had earned good marks in Greece, she never quite adjusted to school in America and dropped out as soon as she reached the legal leaving age of sixteen.

My father turned his attention at once to the matter which had been my mother's greatest concern: finding suitable husbands for her four daughters. Within ten years of our arrival in America, each girl was provided with a groom, beginning with the eldest and moving down.

Although Olga had lost her cherished dowry, her American citizenship was dowry enough. Within months of our arrival, a letter came postmarked 'Kastoria, Greece,' from a young tinker named Constantine Bartzokis whose family originally lived in Lia. So revered was the Gatzoyiannis name, the young man wrote, that he would deem it an honor if my father would consider him as a potential husband for any of his daughters. Christos replied that he would accept him as a groom for his eldest, and would put through papers for him to immigrate.

Olga had given up her dream of marrying nothing less than a professional and she vaguely remembered the tall, dark-eyed Constantine visiting relatives in Lia when she was a girl. When the groom arrived, my father got him a place as salad chef in the restaurant where he worked, and we were even allowed to use one of the private dining rooms for the dinner and dance that followed the wedding ceremony.

By 1954 my father had saved enough money to send Kanta back to Greece, ostensibly to sell the half of the store in Yannina which he still owned but also to use the proceeds to outfit herself for a wedding, after she found a suitable groom under the surveillance of my grandfather.

From the moment she was met by Kitso at the boat in Athens, Kanta was deluged with a blizzard of invitations from the relatives of eligible young men, but not until she reached Lia and met a thin, mustached young man named Evangelos Stratis did she make up her mind. The couple's formal engagement was sealed within days of their meeting, and after the wedding, Kanta returned to her job on the line at Table Talk Bakeries in Worcester until her husband was permitted to immigrate and found work with a Greek produce seller.

One floor was no longer enough to house our growing family, so my father bought a three-story wooden tenement in Worcester for $13,000. Olga and Constantine and their new baby lived on the top floor, Kanta and her husband on the middle floor, and the rest of us on the ground floor.

Glykeria was a veteran at Table Talk by the time our family went to a relative's house in Worcester to welcome a new arrival from Babouri, twenty-eight-year-old Prokopi Economou, who had found a job in a shoe factory in Worcester. Glykeria was impressed by the innocence and openness of his round face. When, at a Greek picnic, Prokopi began singing old love songs and looking at her meaningfully, she knew he returned her admiration. Although Glykeria was not permitted to have dates, the two talked on the phone. Prokopi explained that he was not free to marry until his sister back in Greece had been satisfactorily wed. But Glykeria hadn't lost her willfulness and she set the young man a deadline for him to declare his intentions or never speak to her again. Finally Prokopi defied his parents and married Glykeria in 1956.

Fotini was the only one to select her husband entirely on her own. She went with our father to a name-day party of a relative in Philadelphia where she met a handsome young cabinet maker from Fatiri, Greece, named Minas Bottos. On her return, Fotini announced to her sisters that she was in love. They warned her against making such a decision on her own, at the age of nineteen, but Fotini was adamant. The only love match among the four girls was the only marriage that eventually ended in divorce.

Eleni Gatzoyiannis had suffered the births of four daughters before finally bearing a son, but her daughters produced a total of eight boys and only two girls. Olga, who never quite conquered the English language or the complexities of American life, gave birth to three boys and one girl. Her children all began first grade speaking only Greek but graduated from top colleges to become either lawyers or doctors.

Under the burden of family responsibilities, my father blossomed into a worthy patriarch, not only to his new family but to a growing community of refugees from Lia. One by one, he sponsored relatives who followed us to Worcester, until Christos Gatzoyiannis became the godfather of the large community of immigrants from Lia and Babouri who settled there.

In his seventies and eighties, my father would sit with the dignity of a king on the chair of honor at the annual summer picnic of Liotes in Worcester. A serpentine line of dancers spiraled around him under the shade of the oak trees, and the hundreds of immigrants who owed their new lives to him paid homage. Although many women set their caps for the prominent widower, he never considered remarrying after my mother's death and I never heard him speak of any other woman.

If my father was the godfather of the immigrant community, I grew to be the *consigliere* after I entered college on a scholarship. As the only Greek with an education, I was in charge of doing all the immigration papers, citizenship applications, tax returns and medical forms for the burgeoning Greek populace. I helped to enroll their children in school and to interpret when necessary between my fellow villagers and the American doctors, teachers and judges.

When I returned to Lia for the first time in 1963, I carried a wallet stuffed with gifts of cash from Worcester immigrants to their relatives back home. The Greeks seemed to absorb the Calvinist work ethic with their first step on American soil. They abandoned afternoon siestas and long, lazy hours in the coffee shops to work fourteen-hour days – husbands, wives and children side by side. They paid for their homes and automobiles in cash. Many of the Mourgana Greeks in Worcester, including all four of my brothers-in-law, saved enough eventually to open pizza parlors throughout New England.

It was on that first trip back home in 1963 that I became close to my maternal grandfather. He had been such a distant figure in my youth but, as adults, we became friends after he shared with me, as a kind of peace offering, the secret of the Turk he killed when my mother was a child.

In 1967 my grandmother, Megali, died at eighty-five. My grandparents had been married for seventy-one years, ever since they were both in their early teens. Although Kitso had fought with his wife every day, he couldn't live without her. He fell ill and died a month later. As his life ebbed, he placed three long-hoarded gold sovereigns on a table near his bed and said he would give them to the first person who told him Nikola was coming up the mountain. But I was delayed by a crisis in my job as a reporter and he died before anyone could collect the reward.

My grandfather had a long-standing rivalry with my uncle Foto as to which one would bury the other. My grandfather was eighty-seven when he died, and Foto was eighty-five then. Today Foto is a hundred years old, the Methuselah of the Mourgana. He still hunts and climbs the steep mountainside from his house to the *cafenion* in the village square every day, raising his first glass of *tsipouro* before noon. His mind and his ascerbic tongue are as sharp as ever as he spins tales of his long life: how he killed the Turk who insulted his first wife in 1909; uncovered the body of his second wife, Alexo, executed by the Communists; saw his son Costas throw his life away in a futile search for revenge on his mother's killers.

After Alexo's execution, my uncle took a third wife, forty years his junior, who cares for his house, animals and garden, leaving him free to enjoy his longevity. It bothers Foto not at all to drink at the same table as villagers who testified against Alexo at her trial.

My father, Christos, remarkably like his brother in appearance but entirely different in character, seemed to share Foto's vitality, but as he approached his nineties, his health began to fail. He can no longer drive his Oldsmobile around Worcester to pay calls on his vast circle of relatives and admirers. While Foto seems destined to live forever, my father is now frail, his mind wandering among the tragedies of the old years, unable to walk, his heart and lungs failing.

My uncle often brags that he has lived so long by tossing the tragedies of his life behind him, but my father gradually became increasingly obsessed with the unfairness of my mother's death. In that way, I resemble him.

During the years I lived in Greece as a journalist, I was constantly drawn back to Lia. The village was slowly dying; only a few hundred old people were left behind as their children moved to the metropolitan centers in search of a better life. I began to undertake projects to revitalize the village: finding government money for a new water system, setting up a development company that would use donations from American Liotes to rebuild village landmarks, and raising the funds to construct a ten-room inn with a restaurant and a shop to sell the local crafts of tinworking and wood carving, which were in danger of dying out.

At first I didn't stop to think about why I was undertaking these projects until one day I was told a remark my uncle Andreas had made. Someone said to him, 'It's a wonderful thing that Nikola is doing for the people of the village,' and he replied with heavy sarcasm, 'Well, of course, he owes it to them! After all, they killed his mother!'

When I stopped to examine my motives, I realized that I was unconsciously trying to build a monument to my mother that would reflect the charitable acts she had done in the village – a monument that could not be torn down or defaced like a gravestone or shrine. These projects would be a visible daily reminder of her existence, but they would also be an enduring rebuke to those who had betrayed her, proof of their failure to destroy Eleni Gatzoyiannis and her children.

My sisters did not share my interest in the village or my attachment to Greece. Like my uncle and aunt, they held the villagers responsible for my mother's fate and they turned their backs on the land where they had suffered so much. They embraced all the luxuries, conveniences and opportunities of America, and obedient to my mother's warnings, insisted they had no nostalgia for the old country.

The question of avenging our mother's death also divided my sisters and myself. They were certain that in time, God would punish the guilty. 'Though the mills of God grind slowly, yet they grind exceeding small' is an article of faith rooted in the earliest Hellenistic thought. 'Wicked men who congratulate themselves on escaping immediate trouble receive a longer and not a slower punishment,' Plutarch affirmed in his essay on 'the tardiness of God's punishments.'

From childhood I could not share my sisters' complacent belief that revenge was best left to God, although I understood why they embraced it. They had spent more years than I had in the cauldron of wartime Greece where tragedy rained on every head, and what they had seen had made them fatalists.

In the decade of war from 1939 to 1949, one out of every ten Greeks was killed – 450,000 during World War II and 150,000 during the civil war. Of the survivors, nearly 100,000 had been exiled behind the Iron Curtain, some by choice, many by force. Families were rent apart, not to be reunited for many years, often forever. The children taken in the *pedomasoma* from the Mourgana villages were sent to Rumania, while their parents found themselves in Hungary or Poland; the girls conscripted as *andartinas* wound up in Russia or Czechoslovakia. No wonder simple village women like my sisters considered themselves helpless pawns of destiny.

Greek women through the centuries have had little choice but to accept tragedy with resignation and try to survive. Only men were expected to grapple with the Fates, no matter how unequal the contest. It was also a man's responsibility to seek revenge for the sufferings of weaker members of his family.

Although I was only a nine-year-old boy when I arrived in the United States, I knew even then that the day would come when I had to take some sort of vengeance against my mother's killers. It was the only balm for what Aeschylus' Clytemnestra, speaking of the long-ago murder of her daughter, called 'that pain which never sleeps.'

During my years of growing up in America, my sisters bolstered their argument that God would punish the guilty by citing the fate of those who had contributed to our mother's death. As news filtered back to us from Greece, it seemed at first that divine retribution was working with merciless efficiency.

Prokopi and Spiro Skevis, the two brothers who sowed the seeds of Communism in Lia, both died before the war was over. Prokopi, the intellectual one, famed as an orator, was killed by a stray bullet in the mouth during his first battle after he came out of Yugoslavia in the summer of 1949. His brother, the fiery major who led a battalion in the Mourgana, was promoted to colonel, a reward for the skill with which he led his men on the retreat to the Zagoria mountains. In the

597

last days of the civil war, shortly after he learned of his brother's death, Spiro stepped on a land mine which had been set by his own men. The shrapnel tore away part of one leg and he bled to death over the next two days.

Spiro Skevis' success in bringing Communism to the Mourgana villages had turned to ashes in his mouth. The execution in Lia of his five fellow villagers tormented him. A captain in his battalion later told me how, shortly after the retreat from the Mourgana, Spiro went out of control and tried to kill one of the chief aides of Kostas Koliyiannis, drawing a gun on him and screaming that the man was a criminal, a murderer of women. Other guerrillas jumped Spiro before he could pull the trigger. He went to the grave tormented by the perversion of the movement that he and Prokopi had begun with such high intentions. After his death he was promoted by the Communists to brigadier general.

The tentacles of the village grapevine, reaching all the way to Worcester, also brought news that two of the women from Lia who betrayed our mother had suffered tragic setbacks.

The blond village beauty, Stavroula Yakou, feared as a collaborator of the guerrillas, had given evidence against my mother and tyrannized Glykeria after the executions. When Stavroula was taken by force to be an *andartina,* Glykeria had the satisfaction of seeing her reduced to groveling hysteria by shell shock in the last months of the war. Stavroula's sufferings multiplied after she returned from exile in Tashkent to Lia in the late 1950s. A wasting cancer eroded her beauty and killed her slowly.

Her words on her deathbed seemed proof of Plutarch's contention that 'there is no need for either God or man to punish evildoers but that their lives are sufficient, all distraught and ruined as they are by their own villainy.' During her last hours, Stavroula's mind was obsessed with Eleni Gatzoyiannis. From her deathbed she said to Olga Venetis, our neighbor who had been one of my mother's closest friends, 'Tell the Gatzoyiannis girls that I wasn't the reason their mother died. What I said was nothing compared to what others said against her. How could I speak against her? We survived on the bread she gave us.' The worm of guilt had

598

been gnawing at Stavroula all those years.

On the last day of my mother's life, she had referred wistfully to Constantina Drouboyiannis. 'She's lucky,' my mother said to Glykeria. 'She managed to save her daughters and herself.' What she didn't say, but everyone knew, was that by testifying against her, Constantina had destroyed my mother's defense that she didn't know about the escape plan. Constantina Drouboyiannis succeeded in having herself exonerated but ultimately she was not the lucky woman my mother had supposed.

After Constantina returned from exile in Hungary and rejoined her husband and children in Crete, she saw her son die, another victim of cancer. A woman who was related to both Constantina's family and our own later told us that after the boy's death, one of Constantina's daughters turned on her mother and exclaimed, 'You've always said that you were blameless in Eleni Gatzoyiannis' fate. Now you see the harvest of what you did!' Like most Greeks, the girl shared Euripides' conviction that 'The gods visit the sins of the fathers upon the children.'

Through the decades after the war, I followed the fate of the Greek Communist leaders with dogged interest. From books and articles, some written by the guerrillas themselves, I learned that the leading Communist officers of the war years also seemed pursued by an avenging Nemesis.

After the last mountain stronghold of the DAG fell in August of 1949, Communist Party leader Nikos Zachariadis led his men into exile behind the Iron Curtain and announced on October 16 that he was ending hostilities 'to prevent the total destruction of Greece.'

Zachariadis at first managed to retain control of the party despite his disastrous leadership of the insurrection. With the efficiency of a Stalin, he quickly eliminated those who tried to topple him and even caged one of his most vocal critics, a former physician and guerrilla general, in a specially built cell in the basement of Zachariadis' own dwelling until the prisoner died.

But Zachariadis was a staunch Stalinist, and following the denunciation of the Soviet dictator by Nikita Khrushchev in

1956, the party leadership was wrested from him. Battles broke out between supporters and opponents of Zachariadis in Greek exile communities throughout Eastern Europe. In Tashkent, a skirmish among the Greek Communist exiles involving clubs and knives was so vicious that Russian police had to be called in to break it up, and more than a hundred Greeks were hospitalized. In the end, Zachariadis was toppled. He ended his days in 1973 as a clerk in the Department of Waters and Forests for a village lost in the Urals.

While Zachariadis' ignominious end gave me gratification, as I began probing the fate of other Communist leaders after the war, I learned that two of the men most responsible for my mother's death had not suffered for their crimes. Kostas Koliyiannis, the individual who held the single greatest responsibility for the executions in the Mourgana villages, had floated to the top of the party leadership after Zachariadis' downfall, winning his crown as leader of all Greek Communists. The glowering, bear-like political commissar of the Epiros Command had played his cards well.

Koliyiannis proved to be every bit as dictatorial as Zachariadis had been. In 1968 there was a revolt as dissidents seized the party's radio station and denounced Koliyiannis' methods. His winning streak finally came to an end and Moscow removed him from power. Spurned by the party he had devoted his life to, Koliyiannis died in Hungary a bitter old man in 1979. He returned in a casket to the country from which he had been exiled for thirty years.

When I learned of Koliyiannis' death, I had been living in Greece for two years. I could take some satisfaction from his fate, but it angered me that after all his crimes, Koliyiannis had risen to the top of his world and been allowed to die in bed. When I came to Greece in 1977 as foreign correspondent for the *New York Times*, I intended to track down my mother's killers, but political upheavals throughout the Middle East kept me out of the country almost continuously. The news that death had cheated me of confronting Koliyiannis convinced me that if I was ever going to find her killers I had to do it at once.

The final catalyst that made me leave my job to devote

myself completely to the search was my discovery that the other primary actor in my mother's fate, Koliyiannis' agent Katis, was still alive and living comfortably in Greece. Katis was the man who had assembled the case against my mother, prosecuted her and ordered her torture. If Koliyiannis was my Himmler, Katis was his Eichmann, and I couldn't postpone my need to confront him any longer.

It was at this point that I obtained an unmarked, unregistered hand gun, a Walther PPK, which I brought to Greece in a shipment of personal belongings, concealed inside the canister of an Electrolux vacuum cleaner. I had no clear idea what I intended to do with the gun, but I didn't want to face Katis without it.

The move to Greece in 1977 had been a rude awakening for me, shattering any belief I might have had in my sisters' view of divine retribution. From overseas I had found solace in the Communist Party leaders' fate – outlawed, imprisoned and torn by internecine battles. But I arrived in Athens to be confronted with a resurgence of Communist power in the country.

Immediately after the end of hostilities in 1949, the Communists who had not fled behind the Iron Curtain were persecuted and imprisoned with all the rancor that had taken root during the war years. But slowly the pressures on them relaxed. In 1954 the first exiles were allowed to return from Hungary: carefully screened Greeks who could prove that they were taken by force and harbored no sympathy for the party. Among them came many of the villagers abducted from Lia. After that, refugees began to return in increasing numbers, and the screening process that allowed them back in the country was made more liberal.

After the Communist Party was legalized in Greece in 1974 and the thirty-year statute of limitations on all crimes committed during the war years passed, the Greek Communists in exile came flooding back and began to propagate their own version of the war, making the Communist guerrilla leaders into popular heros. When I moved to Greece, I was confronted daily with the party's success in winning the loyalties of Greeks who had been born since the war. Fresh-faced

601

college students knocked at my door every weekend, handing me propaganda leaflets and inviting me to the ubiquitous Communist youth festivals. If they were asked about the *pedomasoma*, civilian executions and guerrilla brutalities, they smiled and shook their heads at my ignorance: those things had never happened, they explained patiently.

There was no escaping the Communists' success in glamorizing the guerrillas in the eyes of modern Greek youth and rewriting the history of the war, even in the minds of children born to those from my own village. Once, at a name-day party full of Liotes, I overheard a friend about my age arguing with his nephew, a twenty-two-year-old university student. The uncle was saying to the boy, 'Didn't they break up our family, drag your grandmother, your mother and me out of our village and put us in camps in Hungary for six years?'

'They did it for humanitarian reasons,' the boy replied levelly, 'to save you from the fascist bombs.'

'And what about the thousands of civilians they executed in the occupied villages? Was that humanitarian?' his uncle persisted in a louder voice. 'What about the five they killed in Lia?'

The boy's eyes narrowed. 'They wouldn't have killed them without a reason,' he said. 'They probably had a very good reason.'

To erase these atrocities from the Greek consciousness, the Communists, as soon as they were legalized, launched a widespread movement to stop all official memorial services for those killed during the civil war, victims who included my mother. They succeeded in persuading the new socialist government, which came to power in 1981, to abolish such services.

By then I had left my job with the *New York Times* and was spending all my time investigating my mother's death. My years in Greece had convinced me that it was important to write about her fate not only for my sisters and myself, but also for my fellow Greeks, especially the postwar generation, who would perhaps learn something they didn't know about the civil war.

By the time my investigation was complete, I would have interviewed more than 400 individuals: former villagers and soldiers who fought on both sides, British commandos, nationalist and Communist officers, murderers and the survivors of their victims. I traveled throughout Greece as well as to the United States, England, Canada, Poland, Hungary and Czechoslovakia. Many of the accounts I recorded were contradictory or incomplete, but piece by piece the puzzle began to take shape.

The original clue given me by the baker Makos, who happened to recognize the guerrilla Taki twenty years after my mother's execution, had set me on my way. Each fact I learned led me to another witness. At first all my efforts to find the judge Katis ended in frustration. The former guerrillas who had been exiled with him seemed to think that he had died in Czechoslovakia.

Eventually, an urbane judge, Demitris Gastis, and a former guerrilla general turned hotel clerk, Yiorgos Kalianesis, gave me the information I needed to track Katis to his home. But before I confronted him face to face, I knew I had to exhaust every last witness to his crimes.

There were still two major holes in the web of evidence I was assembling against the man who had been my mother's judge and torturer. I had learned that the guerrilla we called 'Zeltas,' the head of the security police in Lia, lived somewhere in Greece, but I needed his real name and his location in order to interview him. It was also essential that I travel behind the Iron Curtain to find a handful of former Liotes still in exile – some of whom were personally involved in betraying my mother, others well-known collaborators of the guerrillas in Lia who would have essential information about what went on there.

When I had put together the necessary visas to travel to Eastern Europe, I flew on November 28, 1981, from Athens to Budapest, Hungary, then drove through a snowstorm to the refugee village of Belloyiannis, forty miles to the west. It rose like a mirage from the snow-covered farmlands: a bleak series of barracklike buildings, dingy brown, gray and yellow. Belloyiannis looked like an army camp despite pathetic efforts

603

to make it seem a Greek town by giving the streets Greek names. This forlorn place was where most of the villagers evacuated from Lia eventually ended up after a year spent in Shkodra, Albania. They built the long rows of barracks with their own hands. Most of the refugees who could get permission returned to Greece in the 1950s. Those still living in Belloyiannis either were refused repatriation because of their Communist ties or stayed behind in fear of retribution from relatives of their victims.

I had come to Belloyiannis to confront Foto Bollis. He was the main prosecution witness against my aunt Alexo and came to the Haidis house two days after the executions to steal the last bits of food that my mother had left behind for Glykeria.

I found Bollis to be a thin old man, shuffling about with a coat thrown over his pajamas in the small apartment he shared with his wife and grown son. He walked with precarious balance, and his sallow skin revealed sharp bones underneath. A drop of moisture hung from his beaked nose. When I confronted Bollis with his role in the trial and asked him why he had sworn falsely against my aunt, saliva sprayed from his mouth in his eagerness to protest his innocence. He insisted that he had said nothing against the two women on trial, and also denied taking Glykeria's food.

I quickly grew tired of his lies. An insignificant man of poor repute in Lia, he had betrayed all his moral scruples for the chance to be the center of attention, rewarded by the guerrillas for his cooperation, but now he was as powerless as he had been before his moment in the limelight. I said to him that he alone knew why he acted as he did in 1948, but it was too bad that his wife and children had to suffer for it ever since, living in this wretched place. The rodentlike old man seemed to shrink under my words and avoided the eyes of his family.

Bollis' daughter, Olga, had been the twenty-year-old guide for the group of children taken from the village on the day of my mother's trial. As we sat in Belloyiannis, Olga told me how the trial was halted long enough for the children to say goodbye to their parents and how my mother had embraced Foto's son Sotiris, who was just my age.

I looked at Sotiris, who was listening; a plump, balding man with a puffy face and several missing teeth, sitting in baggy brown pants with no stockings to protect his slippered feet from the cold. He appeared years older than I did, and as I studied him I realized that I was looking at what my fate would have been if my mother hadn't saved us from the *pedomasoma*.

My visit to Belloyiannis convinced me that Foto Bollis did not deserve any further punishment for his treachery to his neighbors. He was a gutless, mean little man who had been manipulated by the guerrillas through his desire for power, eager to lie on the witness stand in exchange for crumbs of glory. Now he was reduced to his original insignificance, and I could only feel contempt for him, not hatred.

My next stop was Zgorzelec, Poland, where I hoped to find Calliope Bardaka, the widow who had been considered by the Liotes the most wanton of the village collaborators, informing on her neighbors and eagerly giving her children to the *pedomasoma*. She had sat in on many of the guerrillas' interrogations of villagers, and if anyone could give me details about the workings of the security police, she could.

Zgorzelec, the former German city of Gorlitz, was given to Poland after the war, and it was nearly empty until Greek exiles were brought there to revive its factories. When I found the address I had been given in a housing project and climbed the dingy staircase to knock on the door, it was hard to reconcile the gray-haired, pasty old woman who opened it, bundled in a house dress, a threadbare flannel robe and a jacket, with the pretty young widow who scandalized the village. But when she led me into the one room of the unheated apartment to sit under a naked light bulb, I saw on the wall a picture of Calliope as she had been then: a full-figured, pretty woman with a sensuous mouth. When she learned who I was, she welcomed me effusively and began a long tale of woe: how the guerrillas had brought the Greek exiles to Zgorzelec to work in the idled factories, where she labored on a production line making handbags. She said that the Communist Party took half their meager salaries, ostensibly to aid jailed comrades in Greece but really to permit the

Greek party leaders in Poland to live in luxury. She quickly became disenchanted with Communism, she added, and left the party.

When I asked Calliope about her wartime cooperation with the guerrillas, she glibly produced excuses and rationalizations. 'I had little choice after my husband was killed,' she said. 'I didn't have food for my children. The Germans had burned my house. I was caught between a chasm in front and a precipice in back. We may have made mistakes, some of us, but we got carried away because we had never known such barbarians before, and when we realized what they were really like, we were linked to them, stuck with them.' As she talked, she kept straightening the doilies and shawls that covered the worn furniture. 'They had our children. We could only say and do what they wanted us to.' She dabbed a handkerchief to her eyes as she described how she fainted on the day she was separated from her seven-year-old son and six-year-old daughter, whom she didn't see again for seven years.

I mentioned several instances in which Calliope had accused fellow villagers of disloyalty just to ingratiate herself with the guerrillas, and I asked her if she realized that her testimony might have cost them their lives.

'Oh yes, you're quite right,' she agreed. 'One wrong word could kill in those days. But in such times you just don't *think* about it. You think of yourself.'

Calliope insisted that she had no part in my mother's condemnation and death. 'If it is found out that I said a word against your mother,' she declared melodramatically, 'may all my children burn in the same oven! Your house was the first house in the village. Everyone looked up to your mother. I could never have said anything against her!'

It was true that none of the villagers I interviewed named Calliope as one of my mother's accusers. I had come to Poland because I wanted information from her, especially the name and address of the head of the security police, 'Zeltas,' with whom she had been on close terms. When I asked Calliope about him, a spark of the old cunning ignited in her eyes. She whispered, 'He has a sister living here. Don't you worry! I'll pay her a visit and find out where he is. Before you leave, come back here and I'll have the information you want.'

As I left Calliope's apartment for the one hotel in town, I was thinking how little she had changed. She was obviously hoping that I might help her in getting out of Poland and was eager to betray one of her former comrades if it would be to her advantage. I could see what a dangerous woman she must have been.

The next day I returned to Calliope's apartment, where she wished me a safe journey and insisted on giving me a bag of food for the trip. I asked her in Greek if she had obtained the information I wanted, but she looked around as if the walls had ears and said only that she would see me to my car. On the way down the stairs she slipped a piece of paper in my hand. 'It's all there,' she whispered, 'but you must never tell anyone where you got it!'

I unfolded the paper and read: 'Zeltas – Christos Nanopoulos – Alkiminis 24, Salonika, Greece.' I glanced back at Calliope's puffy, smiling face. Feeling vaguely embarrassed, I put a $20 bill in her hand and hurried off. On the road leading out of Zgorzelec I admitted to myself the reason for my discomfort: I had used the same informant and the same tactics as the guerrillas in order to get the information I wanted. I tried to comfort myself with the thought that while the guerrillas exploited morally weak villagers to give false testimony in order to achieve a predetermined political goal, I was interviewing them to find out the truth, without knowing in advance who were the prime movers in my mother's death.

My last stop in Eastern Europe was the small town of Znojmo, Czechoslovakia, where Milia Drouboyiannis was living under a Czech version of her maiden name: Mila Drabkova. She had been the fanatically loyal young *andartina* who testified against my mother in order to protect her own mother, swearing as she stood with her gun beside her that she had convinced her family not to join the Amerikana in the escape because 'soon all Greece will fly the Red Flag.'

I flew from Warsaw to Vienna, rented a car at the airport and drove the fifty miles to the border of Czechoslovakia. It was dark when I reached the border, which proved the most difficult I had yet to cross. I was interrogated at length as to whom I was visiting and gave the border guards Milia's name and address with no regrets for any difficulties it might cause her. They began pulling out the contents of my suitcase, but when they found a copy of one of my books on organized crime which had been translated into Hungarian, they apparently felt I must be sympathetic to Communism to be so honored. They let me through.

I drove a few more miles to the small city of Znojmo and began to circle around aimlessly until I found someone who recognized the name and address written on the paper I had with me. When I knocked on the door of Milia's apartment, it was opened by a man in his thirties, a large husky Czech with a red beard. When he was told there was a foreigner asking for Mila Drabkova, a middle-aged woman appeared, peeking out fearfully from behind his body. I told her who I was and she began speaking in a falsely accented, broken Greek, protesting that she had left the country so long ago she didn't remember the language.

Milia was a small chunky woman in her early fifties with jet-black hair framing a round face. She kept cocking her head to one side in an odd movement, suggesting someone who either has difficulty understanding or is mentally deranged. I said that while I was only nine when I left Greece and she was at least eight years older, she must surely remember enough Greek for us to communicate. Reluctantly she let me in and led me to a tiny kitchen where we sat at an aluminum table. There was a room off the kitchen where I saw her tall, redheaded daughter and two small boys – her grandchildren. She demanded to know what I wanted of her.

'I have come a long way,' I said, 'to find out why you betrayed my mother.'

Milia's Greek quickly lost its awkwardness as she denied she had ever betrayed anyone, all the while bobbing her head excitedly like a bird.

I named the many villagers who described how she gave the most damaging testimony against my mother at the trial, thumping her rifle on the ground and shouting, 'I swear by the gun I hold that everything I have said is true!'

Milia protested that she couldn't remember anything about a trial. 'I was a young girl when they made me fight in the mountains in the cold and snow,' she whimpered. 'I left the village very young and remember almost nothing. My first husband left me. My nerves were shattered and I had to be put in a hospital. Now I have that man you saw. I'm forced to work as a cleaning woman to survive. And only twelve days ago my mother died.' She jumped up and removed a bottle of pills from a shelf, popping one into her mouth.

I persisted in my questions and Milia began to speak disjointedly, skipping from one subject to another, from the present to the past: 'My mother talked about leaving with my younger sisters. I remember being up in the mountains as an *andartina*. They came and took me down to see my mother, who was in the jail, and she started to cry. I tried to look, but they turned my head away. More I don't remember. They asked me questions. They said my mother and sisters wanted to escape. I said I told them not to go, and they didn't. I told them that other people suggested to my mother to go; it wasn't her idea, but I talked her out of it. I was afraid.' She paused, at a loss for words, then asked me imploringly, 'What would you have done?'

Her disjointed monologue began again, a litany of the sufferings of her life. I began to feel suffocated by the small airless room and her self-pitying recital. I stood up to leave but she grabbed my arm. She hadn't wanted to let me in, but now she didn't want me to go. 'Stay a little,' she pleaded, her eyes wet. She began to repeat the same details and I headed resolutely for the door, but she held me back. I sensed that there was something she wanted to communicate but didn't know how.

She touched the sleeve of the leather coat I was wearing, admiring it like a child, asking where I got it and how much it cost. She asked how I had arrived at her door and if I owned an automobile. I told her I had come in a rented car but owned one in Greece and one in America. She stared wide-eyed, imagining the cars, the clothes. Then she fixed me with an expression that I couldn't decipher. It might have been envy or regret or even relief. She took her hand from my sleeve and said with a sigh, 'The years have been good to you.'

As I drove back from Znojmo to Vienna, I was so physically and emotionally drained that I felt ill. I couldn't shake off Milia's desperate question: What would I have done in her place? I reassured myself that I would not have acted as she did, but I knew that she had been a young girl, frightened and convinced that to save her mother she had to lie and betray my mother. I no longer could muster the desire to see Milia punished any more than life had already made her suffer.

My sisters had always believed that our fellow villagers caused my mother's death, but my encounters in Eastern Europe and my interviews in Greece had convinced me that the villagers were not the instigators of her suffering. The guerrillas had selected civilians who would betray their neighbors out of fear, moral weakness, envy or a desire for influence, but it was the villagers who were the puppets and the guerrillas who pulled the strings.

Before my search was complete, there was one more visit I had to make. In my pocket was the name and address of Zeltas, the head of the security police in Lia. None of the scores of people I talked to described any instance when Zeltas interrogated or tortured my mother, but I wanted to see him face to face to satisfy myself that he had not been one of her tormentors. I also wanted to learn more about the role of his guerrilla superiors and to verify from someone on the inside what I had already learned about Katis' culpability in her death. The investigative reporter's primary tenet is to confirm every piece of information with several independent sources. I had always been scrupulous about cross-checking, and this time I wanted to be irrefutably sure of my facts.

In Vienna I boarded an Austrian Airlines plane that flew directly to Salonika. It was raining when I reached the street, lined with concrete slabs of apartment buildings, where Zeltas lived under his real name of Christos Nanopoulos. The main entrance was open. According to the cards posted beside the bells, Zeltas lived in the basement flat, so I walked down the stairs and knocked at his door. There was no answer, but

610

when I turned away I heard a sound and looked back to see a pair of faded gray eyes peering out.

I introduced myself, asking for Nanopoulos, and he reluctantly opened the door wider, revealing a dark narrow hallway that ended in a room barely large enough to hold two single beds with a wooden table wedged between them.

Zeltas was taller than I, and despite his seventy years he had the muscular body of a man who had spent the last three decades working on a construction site in Russia. He studied me suspiciously before relenting, leading me toward the single room.

We sat facing each other on the two beds with the table between us. There was also a wood-burning stove in the room with a metal poker beside it. Zeltas studied me with the cold eyes of the military police officer he had once been. As we talked, I couldn't help remembering how the former guerrilla, Taki, described my mother being tortured by one of the police outside the prison, her body twisted backward, his knee threatening to snap her spine. At the memory, the same pulsing anger began to rise in me. If Zeltas let slip any clue that he had been the one who tortured her, I knew I couldn't stop myself from attacking him, making him feel as much pain as she had. I glanced toward the poker beside the stove, mentally measuring how far I would have to reach to seize it and use it on him. It seemed fortunate that there was no one around to stop me.

Perhaps Zeltas glimpsed my intentions in my eyes; he began to fidget uneasily. But when I identified myself and asked about his responsibilities as head of the security police in Lia, his answers had the ring of truth. I had learned, in interviewing guerrillas and villagers alike, that those most culpable in my mother's fate always were the most voluble in affirming their innocence, insisting that they not only didn't betray my mother but had done everything possible to help her. But Zeltas listened to my questions passively, searched his memory and said only that he didn't remember my mother specifically, but he did remember that there was one woman detained for a time in the jail whose husband was in America. 'I remember her because my own father spent many years in

Bristol, Connecticut,' he said. 'I remember telling that to this woman, but I don't remember what happened to her.'

He added, 'You have to understand that while one of my responsibilities was the security militia in Lia, I was also a captain in a battalion based there. I spent most of the time away from the village on missions. I went out and inspected the guard posts. I spent very little time at the jail.'

His memory of the prisoner Andreas Michopoulos was much more vivid. Zeltas said that he roused the whole village to search for the two missing prisoners because their escape would be blamed on him. He said that the boy was tied to a board and beaten, 'but not on my orders. It was others in the judicial branch who had the power to order interrogations.'

I pressed him for the names of those in charge of the beatings and executions in Lia and he replied, 'Headquarters controlled everything. Nobody could be arrested, beaten or executed without authorization from the political commissar, Koliyiannis. Beatings might be done with the authorization of Koliyiannis' agents, but not a single execution was carried out unless he authorized it personally. Reports and accusations would go to Koliyiannis and he would decide to execute or not. Before the trial came Koliyiannis' judgment. Then the trial was held to give a legal appearance to the process. For me this didn't seem right. We harmed our own cause.'

I leaned forward, watching his eyes. 'You say that Koliyiannis based his decisions to kill or set free on the basis of intelligence reports prepared for him by his agents in Lia. Exactly who were those agents?'

Zeltas replied without hesitation, 'There were several; but the head man in Lia – the investigating magistrate – was a man we called Katis.'

I had the final confirmation I needed.

I flew from Salonika to my home in Athens on December 6, the feast day of St. Nicholas, knowing that I had exhausted every avenue and that my investigation was over. Now I had to decide what to do about Katis.

It was clear beyond doubt that Katis was the primary living instigator of my mother's death. It was Kostas Koliyiannis, at the pinnacle of Communist guerrilla leadership in Epiros, who had made the policy, deciding to prosecute and execute civilians in each village to terrify the populace into submission. But it was Katis and the men at his level – the intelligence gatherers and investigating magistrates – who decided which individuals in each village were to be singled out for this purpose and sacrificed to the commissar's political ends.

Because December 6 was my name day, the telephone rang incessantly with relatives and friends calling to wish me the traditional 'many years,' but my replies were perfunctory. While my wife and children were busy with Christmas preparations, I could think of nothing but my mother and the judge Katis. I had assembled all the pieces of the jigsaw puzzle that had occupied me for so many years, but I still had to put them together in a meaningful pattern to answer the question that was tormenting me: what to do about Katis? I knew that whatever I did when I confronted him, I had to be free to act without worrying that my family would suffer repercussions for it. I decided it was time to move them back to the United States. I didn't tell them the real reason for the move, only that my work in Greece had come to an end.

When the moving van came to collect our household belongings, the Walther PPK pistol was not among them. I left it in the safekeeping of a friend in Athens who I knew could be trusted. We flew back to the States on New Year's Day of 1982 to settle in a house we owned in Massachusetts.

Soon, I knew, I had to go back to Greece to deal with Katis, but first I buried myself in the writing of the final chapters of my mother's story – her trial, torture and execution. I was hoping as I put these events on paper that it would become clear what I must do next. It was a lonely and painful few months in the worst of the New England winter, while I relived the agonies of her last days.

By the time I had finished, I knew I had accomplished one of my goals: I had come to know my mother truly, in full dimension, not from the limited perspective of childhood memories.

Until the war threatened the one thing that she held most dear – her children – she was an ordinary peasant woman, subject to all the doubts, fears and prejudices planted by her upbringing and her primitive world. But when she was caught in a vise and saw her family faced with destruction, she discovered the clarity of vision to know what she must do and the strength to do it.

That was her *kairos,* her decisive moment, and I knew my own was approaching. As my jigsaw puzzle began to take shape, it seemed that Katis had been left behind specifically to test me. All the others responsible for my mother's death were now either dead and beyond my reach or, as I learned in tracking down the villagers who betrayed her, not prime actors in her fate but weak individuals who had been manipulated by the guerrillas, not deserving of punishment, only contempt.

But Katis stood apart like a beacon, drawing me toward him. He had been convincingly proved the most responsible individual for her suffering still left alive. As far as I knew, he had not suffered, nor was he likely to suffer for his crimes unless I took some action against him. I had to test myself by returning to Greece and facing him.

Circumstances forced me to make that trip before I was ready. In March I received a midnight telephone call telling me that my aunt Nitsa had suddenly died in Lia, after gloomily predicting her own death for so many years that we had all stopped listening. I took the first plane I could for Athens, but she was buried within hours of her death and I arrived too late for the funeral.

Although I had always harbored a deep resentment against Nitsa – I knew she could have saved my mother by going in her place to the threshing fields – for years she was the only remaining link I had with my mother's family and our life in the village. It was painful to return to Lia and find my grandfather's house empty of her comical, outspoken presence.

During the years I lived in Athens I had visited Nitsa nearly every month and she came to think of me as the son she never had. Now there was only my eighty-three-year-old uncle Andreas, bereft and lost after fifty-nine years of marriage. I stayed with him for the nine days until my aunt's memorial service, trying to comfort him as he comforted me on the day

I learned my mother was dead. On the tenth day I drove down the mountain to Yannina to pick up a headstone I had ordered for Nitsa's grave.

When the stonecutter proudly unveiled the cross of gray marble, I stared at it in astonishment. Although it bore the correct date of Nitsa's death, instead of her birth date, he had engraved the birth date of my mother: 1907. He insisted he had carried out my instructions exactly.

Shaken by my mistake, I left the stonecutter's shop in the center of Yannina and began to walk aimlessly. I came to a stop outside 46 Napoleon Zervas Street, Katis' apartment building. There was a scrap of paper taped over the spot where his name had been. I went closer and read: 'Kotrotsis, Ioannis.'

A band of fear tightened around my chest at the thought that Katis had escaped me while I was delaying our confrontation. Panicky, I didn't wait for the elevator but bolted up the four flights to his door and leaned on the bell. When no one answered, I frantically rang the bells on either side. Breathing hard, I raced back down the stairs and accosted a young woman in the lobby who was talking to a delivery man. 'What happened to the Lykas who lived on the fourth floor?' I panted.

She looked at me curiously, then decided I was harmless; just an eccentric foreigner.

'He's moved back to Konitsa, where he came from,' she replied. 'He's built a retirement home there.'

Luckily, I had an acquaintance living in Konitsa. I telephoned him to ask if he knew Achilleas Lykas. Like most towns in northern Greece, Konitsa is small enough for everyone to know everyone else's business. My friend informed me that Lykas and his wife were indeed living there in a new house, along with their daughter and her husband, a career army officer stationed in Konitsa. 'But if you want to find Lykas,' he added, 'he's not here now. He's just gone to Athens on business.'

Having Katis in Athens, away from his family, suited my purposes well. I needed to find where he was staying, so I called a relative who, like Katis' son-in-law, was an officer in northern Greece. I prevailed on my relative to call the young man and tell him that an American friend, writing a book about the civil war, was in Athens and wanted to interview his father-in-law. I told him to mention the names of other prominent guerrillas I had interviewed to calm any suspicions Katis might have and to say that I would be at the Caravel Hotel. Soon my relative phoned back. The son-in-law didn't know where Katis was staying, but he promised that when his father-in-law called home, he would pass on my message.

Back in Athens I took a room at the Caravel and recovered the pistol I had left behind. Then there was nothing to do but sit in the room and wait for Katis' call.

From time to time I checked and cleaned the pistol, testing the spring in the cartridge to make sure it was working smoothly. I tried not to leave the room except during the hours of two-thirty and five-thirty in the afternoon – the siesta – when Greeks don't make telephone calls or pay social visits. There was no way I could sleep, so I got in my rented car at two-thirty every day and began to drive. I headed north toward the gently rising slopes of Mount Hymettos, a green, wooded retreat not far from the door of my hotel.

On the first afternoon of my vigil, I drove up the road that winds around the mountain, past the twelfth-century monastery of Kaisariani, surrounded by cypresses, built on the site of an ancient temple to Aphrodite. I pulled up at a curve in the road which suddenly revealed a sweeping view of the city below.

As I studied the prospect, the slopes around me wore the Easter colors of lilacs, red poppies and yellow daisies. The air was heavy with the odor of thyme, lavender and clover. Above on the mountain's peak was a radar station, where a statue of Zeus once stood. I knew that the secluded ravines of Hymettos had been used during the occupation by the Germans for the execution and burial of hostages. As I sat there, I admitted to myself for the first time what had brought me to Hymettos: I was looking for a place to dispose of Katis' body.

As Friday and Saturday passed and Palm Sunday began Holy Week, I found myself on the mountain every afternoon.

Gradually my plan took shape, almost without my volition. When Katis called me I would invite him to come by the hotel at the usual visiting hour of six-thirty, right after the siesta. I would ask him questions about the civil war and the trial of the four officers captured at Povla, his most important trial. I would phrase the questions in such a way as to inflate his ego and quash any suspicions he might have. Then I would offer to drive him back to where he was staying in Athens.

Once Katis was in my car, I would be on the slopes of Hymettos within minutes. When he asked where we were going, I would reply that I was not quite finished asking him everything I wanted to know. We should reach Hymettos just about sunset. I knew that the drive up the mountain was closed to the public after dark, but I had often driven around the sign standing in the middle of the roadway and up the mountain to admire the view of the city at night. I never encountered a police car to stop my ascent.

In the solitude of Hymettos after dark, I would question Katis about his role in my mother's execution. Then I would kill him, leaving his body in a ravine, covered with branches and rocks, just as my mother's had been. I would drive straight to the airport, taking the first plane leaving for anywhere. By the time the body was found, I would be far from Greece.

With my plan fixed in my mind, it became harder every day to wait. My relative in the military called Katis' son-in-law again and was told that the young man had passed on the message for his father-in-law to contact me at the Caravel. My impatience grew while I wondered if Katis suspected something. As Holy Week crept by, my hopes dwindled. I knew that by Good Friday every Greek would have returned to his home and family to celebrate the most solemn days of the Easter holiday. On Holy Wednesday I called my friend who lived in Konitsa. He casually said in answer to my questions that Katis had already come back from Athens. I hung up the receiver in despair. My preparations had been useless. Katis had ignored my message and now I would have to confront him on his home ground.

The next day, Holy Thursday, when in every Greek

household eggs are dyed the color of Christ's blood, I took the first plane to Yannina, arriving at about ten in the morning. I immediately began to drive toward Konitsa. For months I had been growing a beard, shot with gray at the jaw line, and I was wearing my most formal blue suit and tie. I looked older than my forty-two years and knew that as soon as I shaved and put on blue jeans, my appearance would be completely transformed.

Outside Konjtsa I stopped the car and put the pistol inside my belt in the small of my back, covered by my suit coat. I also slipped a Pearlcorder tape recorder, no larger than a pack of cigarettes, in the top of my right stocking. As an investigative reporter I had used this mini-recorder many times when interviewing criminals and informants. It was a sensitive machine, which would tape up to an hour of conversation. By crossing one leg on the knee of the other I could manipulate the off-on control through the fabric of my clothing without anyone noticing. I wanted a record of what Katis and I said to each other, no matter how the conversation ended.

A single highway leads from Yannina to Konitsa and then on eastward toward Kastoria. Konitsa is built on the curved slope of hills rising in stages above the road, the houses looking down on the Aoos River Valley. To reach the home of Achilleas Lykas – Katis – one had to follow a winding, narrow road that left the main highway and snaked lip the hill.

Lykas' house was almost at the top of the village, a gleaming new two-story residence designed with stone walls and an arched wooden door for the main entrance. I rang the doorbell and heard a voice from overhead saying, 'Who is it?' Looking up, I saw a handsome, dark-haired young woman in her thirties leaning from a second-story window. When I said my name she replied, 'Oh yes, you want my father. My mother will come down and let you in.'

The door was opened by a plumper and older version of the daughter; a woman in her late fifties with dyed auburn hair and olive complexion, in a somber but smart brown dress. She received me hospitably and led me up marble stairs to the main living room on the second floor. To the right I saw a

618

long hall leading to what were clearly bedrooms. The spacious living room was decorated with carved wooden furniture, Greek rugs in bright colors, and touches of local handicrafts. The wood floor shone as if it had just been waxed. Everything was new but harmonious with the traditional architecture of the town. I wondered how Katis, an unemployed former Communist justice of the peace, managed to live in such luxurious style.

The woman apologized for her husband's tardiness – he had been napping and was now getting dressed. While we waited she served me ouzo and a cup of Greek coffee and questioned me politely but persistently about my origins. I told her that I had been born in the United States and that my parents came from the Greek town of Finiki.

From somewhere I could hear the sounds of food frying and a small child talking. I cursed my bad luck in finding Lykas surrounded by his wife, daughter and grandchildren. The craving to hurt Katis was eating at me like a tumor, but I had no appetite for harming women and children as well.

Lykas made a rather theatrical entrance. He was taller than I had expected, and despite the heat, wore a heavy gray suit. The vest was unbuttoned over a small paunch and the coat was thrown over his shoulders cape style, giving him a jaunty, military bearing. He walked with his shoulders back and his stomach projecting, his long legs slightly bent at the knees. Although he was seventy-eight years old, his arms were well-muscled and his eyes were sharp, but his gait was that of an old man. His white hair was cropped close all over his head into a military brush. Because the villagers had described Katis as gray-haired during the war, although he could have been only in his early forties at the time, I had expected him to look older than he did now. His beak of a nose had become his dominant feature, and I could see muscles and tendons working beneath the skin and the skull. Several teeth were missing on the left side, which caused his face to have a lopsided, comical air, an air that disappeared as soon as he began to speak. The voice was mellifluous, with a slight nasal quality, but the missing teeth blurred his enunciation as if he had a mouthful of something.

He introduced himself with studied dignity and shook my hand. He sat down on a chair opposite and began to quiz me about Gastis, the former guerrilla judge from Dilofo, and Kalianesis, the hotel clerk who had been the chief of staff of the Epiros Command, as if testing to see whether I really knew them. When I told him about my interviews with Gastis in his village and Kalianesis at the hotel where he worked, he seemed satisfied. I noticed that Katis' wife ignored him, as if he wasn't in the room, and I sensed tension between them.

'What can I do for you?' Katis asked. I began by telling him that I needed his insights for a book I was writing, especially on the subject of military justice in the DAG. I asked about the trial of the four officers, including a doctor, captured at Povla after the battle of Pergamos and tried at Tsamanta. He conceded that he had been president of the court that tried them. 'Listen, Niko,' he said, assuming an earnest expression. 'You did say that your name was Nicholas? Whomever we tried, we sent their cases to headquarters with the hope that their sentences would be commuted. From that point on we had no responsibility. In the case you mention, there were five judges and a prosecutor – Yiorgos Anagnostakis, who died of cancer. There was Grigori Pappas, who was the examining magistrate,' he added, naming the man who had been the third judge at my mother's trial. 'He died in Tashkent.'

His wife raised her head. 'Where was he from?' she asked belligerently. 'He must have been a smart one, like you!'

'Let us talk, will you?' Lykas snapped. Turning to me he said, 'She's a nervous woman. We were separated for so long. Twelve years.'

'Twelve!' his wife exploded. 'It was seventeen! Seventeen years! My daughter was one month old. He was going to free the world, my hero there,' she added contemptuously.

'Will you stop?' Katis said in a louder voice. 'Will you let me speak to this man? Or shall we get up and leave? We know all about your ordeals! You don't have to keep telling us.'

Katis began to explain how he had gone to the mountains to join the guerrillas in 1945. He had been a justice of the peace in Konitsa, and after the war, informers identified him as a sympathizer of ELAS. Afraid that he would be imprisoned or worse, he joined the DAG. I brought him back to the subject of the four executed officers and he repeated that as president of the court, he had sentenced them with the hope that they would be pardoned. 'We rendered the verdict that we were called on to give,' he added. 'The responsibility for the fate of the four men rested with Koliyiannis.'

I asked if the accused had anyone to represent them at the trial, a defense attorney or counsel. 'Counsel?' Katis uttered a short laugh. 'Where do you think we were? These were military trials in the mountains!'

There was another incident I wanted to ask him about, I said, and I noticed that my words became slower as I got nearer the point. 'There was a trial of civilians in Lia in which you took part.'

'No, no!' he interjected before I finished the sentence. 'I tried no civilians.'

'But there were three hundred villagers present,' I said. 'They all remember you.'

He was becoming uneasy and kept uttering denials before I could complete my questions. 'They are wrong!' he said. 'They made a mistake. I tried no civilians.'

'The villagers all remember Katis,' I said. 'Didn't they call you Katis?'

'No, I had no pseudonym.'

'All the guerrillas I interviewed told me you were called Katis. Your friends Kalianesis and Gastis both told me that "Katis" was the name of Achilleas Lykas from Konitsa. Now you tell me you never used the name.'

He sat up straighter. 'I have no connection with any Katis,' he said, waving the question away with his hand. 'The important thing is that all those matters were settled at headquarters by Koliyiannis. No one else was responsible. Not Kalianesis, the chief of staff. Not Chimaros, the military commander. Not the military courts. We did our duty, and we sentenced everyone with the wish that they would be pardoned.'

He stood up abruptly. 'That's it,' he said, his manner a model of magisterial hauteur. 'Do we have anything else to discuss?'

621

His arrogance infuriated me. 'Aren't you ever going to admit the truth?' I snapped.

'That is the truth,' he said, and shrugged. 'What am I telling you – lies?'

I began to speak very slowly and clearly, trying to organize my thoughts. My hatred for the man began to blur my planned series of questions. 'Listen, Lykas,' I said. 'I have come a long way to see you, and as you can surmise, I have talked to a lot of people already. I know everything that happened, so I don't want to hear lies from you—'

Unexpectedly, his wife broke in. 'Listen to him,' she admonished.

Katis glanced at her and sat down with a harassed expression. 'I'm listening.'

'In the village of Lia,' I began, finding my breath with difficulty, 'there was a trial of five people. The president of the village. His nephew, eighteen years old. Another man, fifty-seven years old—'

'I told you—'

'Wait, wait . . .'

'Don't tell me anything!' he exclaimed. 'You can tell me we tried fifty. I'll let you, if that's what you want . . .'

'Are you going to let me finish?'

'No!' he shouted, still trying to dismiss me. 'I won't let you because you're saying things that are not supportable! The only persons I tried are the officers and the doctor I told you about.'

'There were five people executed in Lia,' I continued doggedly. I was determined to get it all out no matter how many times he tried to stop me. 'Three men and two women. The trial began in the village square and then because of artillery fire from the Great Ridge it was transferred to a ravine at the top of the village covered by trees—'

'I don't know anything about any Great Ridge or any military trial taken from one place to another,' he exploded.

'I know you're lying because—'

'You won't tell me any more because our conversation is over!'

'You're covering up!' I shouted.

622

His voice rose in pitch. 'Do you hear me? What I have told you is it! I have nothing more to say. It's past. It's over!'

'It's not over for me,' I said.

He had me figured out by now. 'I don't know. For you it may not be over, of course,' he said without concern, 'because I don't know who you are and what you're harboring or if you had some relative who was a victim.'

His wife's eyes were going from my face to his, registering astonishment at what was happening in her living room.

'I have,' I nodded. 'And you were the cause. I was nine years old and they took my mother and they tried her on August twenty-first in front of the entire village. Everyone was there. And they took her on August twenty-eighth above the village and they shot her—'

'Listen, Nikola,' Katis broke in.

'—and now you pretend you know nothing!' I finished. 'Why don't you tell the truth? Why do you lie even now?'

Katis was trying to calm me. 'Why don't you go to the courts?' he asked. 'Why don't you follow a judicial—'

'You know the law,' I broke in. 'You know that the statute of limitations lapses after thirty years, even for murder!'

Katis pulled himself up coldly. 'That is your own affair,' he said. 'The only trial I presided over was for the officers and the doctor. I told you about that.'

I was beginning to stammer in my anger. 'I want to ask you one thing.'

'Yes,' he replied.

'The last day of my mother's life, August twenty-eighth, they let one of my sisters see her one last time.' I was trying to remind him of the moment my mother had asked him something on behalf of her daughter, but I was having trouble getting it out.

'Yes,' he encouraged.

'Eleni Gatzoyiannis. Her name was Eleni Gatzoyiannis.'

'Eleni Gatzoyiannis,' he repeated, wrinkling his brow. 'I never heard of her. If others tried her, I don't know.'

'You presided,' I said.

'I never tried any woman,' he intoned. 'I am being serious now. This is not a matter for—'

His wife broke in, her face twisted with uncertainty. 'Maybe you made a mistake,' she said to me.

'There were three hundred people at the trial,' I replied. 'Are all of them lying?'

Katis shook his head. 'I don't remember more than fifty people at any trial. I remember once there was a woman in Presba . . .'

He proceeded to tell me about a trial that took place on Vitsi, where he claimed to have saved a woman from being sentenced to death, but I wouldn't let him finish, or even stop to point out that he was contradicting what he had just said about having presided at only one trial. I was determined to get to the last act in my mother's life, in which he was a participant.

'And on the day my mother died . . .' I said.

'Don't blame me for any woman's death!' Katis shouted. 'I'm offended!'

'You're offended? You killed my mother!'

'I am not involved.' He was speaking now with his former magisterial loftiness.

'You are responsible!'

'If you please! I was not involved in the trial of any woman.'

'I can bring you dozens of witnesses,' I insisted.

'I was involved in the trial of those officers, yes, but Eleni Gatzoyiannis I never tried,' he repeated. 'You have to find out who did.'

'I've found him,' I shouted. My hand had retreated behind my back to the gun, hard and cold under my palm. 'Three hundred people aren't all lying.'

'You have been given wrong information, my friend,' Katis insisted. 'I wasn't in the Mourgana long. I left there when Mourgana fell, I went to Grammos and Vitsi.'

'That was on September sixteenth,' I said.

'Exactly,' he nodded.

'My mother was tried on August twenty-first and executed on August twenty-eighth.'

Katis laughed harshly, the sound echoing in the silent room. 'Impossible!' he exclaimed. 'We were preparing the evacuation then.'

624

'Then you're telling me my mother wasn't shot?' I asked, my voice rising. 'She's still alive?' I turned toward his wife, whose face showed that she was beginning to absorb what I was saying with a horrified conviction that it was true. 'They took them up to the ravine, *Kyria*,' I said, speaking to her now, trying not to look at his face, contorted and staring in hatred. 'And they shot them and threw them into a gully without even burying them.' I turned back to Katis, who kept saying, 'Listen! . . . Listen!'

'And when my grandfather went to find her body . . .'

At that point my voice failed me completely and I couldn't say another word. I had my hand on the gun and while I was talking, thoughts were passing through my mind; images really, flashing by like a slide show run at a manic pace. My mother's body. My son's face – the same age now that I was when my mother died.

I knew now absolutely that I wanted to kill Katis. But the logical part of my mind was telling me there was only one road out of town. To have any chance of escaping, I would have to kill Katis' wife as well, who had been listening to me with compassion and belief, and his daughter, too, who was somewhere inside with her child. Or I would kill only him, and the women would call the police and have me arrested before I was out of Konitsa.

While we were arguing, I had time to wonder what would become of my children. The thought was holding me back. I wanted to goad him until he came at me. The touch of his hand would drive out reason, propelling me into action. I needed to be pushed beyond logic to forget everything but my hatred. If he attacked me, I knew I would be able to shoot him without reflecting on the consequences, and I desperately wanted to see his blood spilling out, staining the rugs at our feet.

The thought of my grandfather uncovering my mother's body drove me over the edge, and words gave way to action. I stood up and spat on him. There was enough saliva to cover his twitching face and drip down his neat shirt and vest. In Greece, to spit on someone is the worst possible insult, worse than the most terrible verbal abuse, a slap or a blow. Katis leaped to his feet, and for an instant he was the guerrilla judge in the prime of his strength and power. 'You spit on me? On me! Do you know who I am?' he bellowed. I waited for his blow to fall, wishing for it, to be answered by the sound of my gun. But his wife jumped up. Perhaps she saw my hand behind me, perhaps not. Her shrill voice shattered the moment of frozen silence as we faced each other.

'Achilleas! Stop! Don't you move!' she screamed.

Slowly his hands opened, no longer fists, and he slumped back into his chair, his face dripping with my spittle.

The moment was gone. He had collapsed into an old man as his wife stood, waving her hands excitedly. Drawn by the commotion, his daughter appeared at the door. 'What's happened?' she cried. 'What's going on here?'

I turned to her. 'My mother was murdered,' I told her, 'and your father was responsible.'

She looked at me as if suddenly understanding everything. 'Ah, that's why you came here,' she said.

'That's why,' I replied and started for the door. I could still hear Katis' wife exclaiming as I slammed the door with a report like the pistol shot I had been waiting for. The moment had slipped past and I hadn't done it.

There's no other sound on the tape but the quick rhythm of my footsteps on the gravel, going on and on.

As I drove back toward Yannina, everything around me in the sunlit landscape seemed changed, warped, as if seen under water. I was sick with frustration. I had looked on the face of Katis and he was still alive. I had acted in the heat of my emotions, but at the critical moment, something stopped me. If only he had come at me, I knew I would have shot him. Now I was cheated of the satisfaction I had been pursuing for so long. The pain that had brought me to his door was stronger than ever.

There was no doubt in my mind that Katis deserved to die. I was convinced he hadn't changed in the years since he sent my mother to her death. I had seen the arrogance and the killer's cold indifference in his eyes when he came toward me. I vowed that I would confront him again, when I could act

626

without emotion and without fear of interference from his family, and I did.

It was four months later, in the port of Igoumenitsa on the Ionian Sea, where I learned Katis and his family had taken an apartment for the summer. I waited outside the building until I saw his wife, daughter, son-in-law and two grandsons leave the apartment and head toward the beach for a swim. I had shaved off my beard, and his wife walked by me without recognition.

Knowing that Katis was alone, I let myself into his apartment by forcing the lock with a plastic card. I opened the door slowly and saw him in front of me, asleep in a chair pulled up to the picture window of the living room. In the merciless sunlight, his gap-toothed mouth hung open, his head resting on one shoulder. The pajama top he was wearing over his trousers was open to reveal the caved-in chest and wrinkled potbelly. His flesh was gray.

He didn't stir as I examined him from a few yards away. I felt no pity for him, his age and his helplessness, only hatred and revulsion. He looked like a cadaver. I had the gun in the small of my back but I realized I could simply smother him with a pillow and leave. His family would return to discover that Katis had died in his sleep. No one would suspect I had ever been there.

I stood staring at the man who had killed my mother for a few minutes, perhaps more. Then I turned around and walked out, closing the door softly behind me. This time I knew it was truly finished. I had found the perfect opportunity for killing him and I couldn't do it. At the end of my long journey I learned that I didn't have the will.

This ending is not the one I had expected when I began to write. There is no satisfaction in it. The pain of my mother's murder is still as sharp, and the anger that her killer lives increases every day.

I have done nothing since leaving Igoumenitsa but ask myself why I didn't kill him. I know it was fear that stopped me: partly the fear of being separated from my children and of setting in motion events that would continue the killing and the suffering into future generations. It was also something

627

else: the understanding of my mother that I had gained in my examination of her life.

During my search I had learned some of her last words, clues to her thoughts as she prepared to die. To Glykeria, our mother remarked on the good fortune of Constantina Drouboyiannis in saving both her daughters and her own life, but she said nothing of hatred or revenge. When Angeliki Botsaris was brought to face her on the day before the execution, my mother did not speak of the pain of her torture, but only of her longing to embrace her children one last time. And her final cry, before the bullets of the firing squad tore into her, was not a curse on her killers but an invocation of what she died for, a declaration of love: 'My children!'

Unlike Hecuba, my mother did not spend the last of her strength cursing her tormentors, but, like Antigone, she found the courage to face death because she had done her duty to those she loved. Sophocles' Antigone tells the man who has condemned her to death, her uncle and king, 'It's not my nature to join in hating, but in loving.'

That was Eleni Gatzoyiannis' nature as well, and Katis had not been able to destroy it by killing her. Like the mulberry tree in our yard, which still stands after the house has fallen into ruins, that love has taken root in us, her children, and spread to her grandchildren as well.

If I killed Katis, I would have to uproot that love in myself and become like him, purging myself as he did of all humanity or compassion. Just as he had abandoned his baby daughter and wife to become a killer for the guerrillas, I would have to put aside thoughts of what I was doing to my children's lives. My mother had done everything out of love for her own children.

Killing Katis would give me relief from the pain that had filled me for so many years. But as much as I want that satisfaction, I've learned that I can't do it. My mother's love, the primary impulse of her life, still binds us together, often surrounding me like a tangible presence. Summoning the hate necessary to kill Katis would sever that bridge connecting us and destroy the part of me that is most like Eleni.

628

A NOTE FROM THE AUTHOR

THE WORLD IN which Eleni lived and died has been reconstructed in this book not only from the memories of myself and my sisters but also from the recollections of scores of people who are now scattered in more than a dozen countries. All the names, places and dates are real. Every incident described in the book that I did not witness personally was described to me by at least two people who were interviewed independently of each other. All the interviews were recorded – secretly in the case of uncooperative witnesses – and translated into English by me. The transcribed interviews and the documents I collected – journals, letters, military reports, photographs, battle maps – fill a wall of files in my home.

Some of those interviewed possess a remarkable memory and were able to describe not only incidents but also how the people involved dressed, moved and spoke in precise detail. In other instances, however, I was given only the rudiments of a conversation, and following the example of Thucydides, 'I put into the mouth of each speaker the sentiments proper to the occasion, expressed as I thought he would be likely to express them.'

To bring characters in the book to life, I have sometimes described their thoughts and feelings as well as their actions. Most of the thoughts of Eleni and others who are dead were deduced from things they said to surviving relatives and friends, who passed them on to me. In a very few instances when no information was available – such as the last images Eleni saw before being executed – I went to the actual sites and tried to imagine myself in her place.

All the skills learned and sharpened during my two decades as an investigative reporter were put to use in this most difficult and important investigation of my life; the reason I became a journalist in the first place. From the testimony of aging peasant men and women; former Communist, nationalist and British army officers; relatives, friends and enemies – from the endless single-spaced transcripts of interviews and the yellowing documents stored in my files – I have gained to my own satisfaction, a true vision of the person who was Eleni Gatzoyiannis and of the world that created her life and death.